Charles Olson

Also by Tom Clark

'Charles Olson,

The Allegory of a Poet's Life

TOM CLARK

W · W · NORTON & COMPANY
New York   London

The text of this book is composed in Galliard.
Composition and manufacturing by The Maple-Vail Book Manufacturing Group.
Book design by Jacques Chazaud

First Edition.

Excerpts from previously unpublished Charles Olson manuscripts and letters, copyrighted 1991 by the University of Connecticut Library and the Estate of Charles Olson, are quoted with permission of the Library and the Estate.
    Excerpts from *The Maximus Poems* by Charles Olson, edited by George F. Butterick, published by the University of California Press and copyrighted 1983 by the Regents of the University of California, are quoted with permission of the publisher.
    Excerpts from *The Collected Poems of Charles Olson,* edited by George F. Butterick, published by the University of California Press and copyrighted 1987 by the Estate of Charles Olson and the University of Connecticut Library, are quoted with permission of the publisher.

Library of Congress Cataloging-in-Publication Data

Clark, Tom, 1941–
    Charles Olson : the allegory of a poet's life / Tom Clark.
        p. cm.
    Includes bibliographical references and index.
    1. Olson, Charles, 1910–1970—Biography.   2. Poets, American—20th
    century—Biography.   I. Title.
    PS3529.L655Z62   1991
    [B]   90–43054

ISBN 0-393-02958-1

W.W. Norton & Company, Inc., 500 Fifth Avenue, New York, N.Y. 10110
W.W. Norton & Company, Ltd., 10 Coptic Street, London WCIA 1PU

1 2 3 4 5 6 7 8 9 0

They are very shallow people who take every thing literally. A Man's life of any worth is a continual allegory—and very few eyes can see the Mystery of his life—a life like the scriptures, figurative—which such people can no more make out than they can the hebrew Bible. Lord Byron cuts a figure—but he is not figurative—Shakespeare led a life of Allegory: his works are the comments on it—

—John Keats to George and Georgiana Keats,
February 14, 1819

These places & persons as things & spots are all inside any one of us. . . . the whole world & all experience is, no matter how real, only a system of metaphor for the allegory (Keats called it) a man's life is.

—Charles Olson to Robert Duncan,
August 24, 1955

One does have a life to live, exactly that much. And . . . because it is that much, and it is one's own, it has a scale. That is, it isn't more of the same, or so much "humanity" and all that, any of the counters now offered. . . .

How to say it, so that it is abundantly clear. It isn't at all unlike Keats' proposition that a man's life (he was speaking of Shakespeare and his plays) is an allegory.

—Charles Olson, *The Special View of History*

Contents

Acknowledgments

For everything I know of Charles Olson's story beyond what could be learned of it from the words he left behind and from those late, isolated moments in which as a young writer and *Paris Review* poetry editor I was privileged to share (we began corresponding in 1965 and met up a few times in England during his transatlantic travels of 1966–1967), I am beholden to the memories and observations of those persons among whom, at whatever complicated and secretive distances, he made his life.

Frances Boldereff Phipps, first of all, opened the way for me into that brief but intense season Olson later described as "riot in my soul," the creative and emotional explosion from which he would date his true beginnings in poetry. On all that came later, not surprisingly, my best witnesses were those closest to him in that calling. Robert Duncan, first of his important friends in the vocation and his final consultant on the "holy things" that bound them, spoke compellingly of the Olson story in terms of poetic archetypes, encouraging me in my early hunch that this conundrum of a life was one that could make sense only as the parable or allegory Olson himself projected it to be. Two equally intriguing and perhaps complementary angles of approach were suggested by Olson's elective "running mate" Robert Creeley, who early on proposed as hypothetical models for Olson biography the Freud / Bullitt life of Woodrow Wilson, a highly speculative study of the Oedipean formations of the Great Man character type, and Hugh Trevor-Roper's classic account of brilliant intellectual bluffing *The Hermit of Peking*. Stressing the latter line of interpretation, Olson's student and good friend Ed Dorn gave me a perceptive account of him as creative gambler, a "great intellectual punter constantly at the gaming tables of thought and literature."

Invaluable family background as well as revealing testimony on the poet's personal life were provided by Olson's daughter Kate Bunker Olson and by Jane Atherton and Jean Radoslovich, the sisters of his two common-law wives, Constance Wilcock Olson and Elizabeth Kaiser Olson.

Faye Rosenblum gave me a vivid picture of adolescent overachiever Charlie Olson at Worcester Classical High School, Fred Buck of Charlie Olson at the Gloucester Post Office, Paul Metcalf of Charlie Olson at Harvard. John Finch and Harry Levin were especially helpful on the poet's academic years, Ephraim Doner and Rosa Shuser on the remarkable Olson / Dahlberg relationship. Frank Moore was a key source on Olson's Washington years, as were Elizabeth Frawley, Senator Alan Cranston, Lee Falk and Sally Almquist. For the foundations of my treatment of the Black Mountain chapters of the story I'm indebted to three sensitive witnesses in particular, Fielding Dawson, Mary Fitton Fiore and Wes Huss. And the poet's Buffalo "company" days and final years—as well as many of the larger analogical aspects of the life as a whole—were greatly illuminated by the generous testimony of his friends Jack Clarke and Harvey Brown.

Richard Wilbur, Gladys Hindmarch, Philip Whalen, Warren Tallman, Joanne Kyger, Albert and Carol Cook, Ed Sanders, Joyce Benson, Albert Glover, Laurence Michel and Drummond Hadley supplied detailed evidence that enlightened important periods of the story. Also deserving of thanks for their response to my queries and for other favors are John Wieners, Donald Hall, Ellen Tallman, Bill Berkson, Phil Green, Thomas Parkinson, Clark Coolidge, James Laughlin, Bobbie Louise Hawkins, Jennifer Dunbar Dorn, Helene Dorn, Tom Raworth, Anselm Hollo, Anne Waldman, Robert Grenier, Larry Eigner, Fred Wah, Pauline Wah, Robert Hawley, Duncan McNaughton, Charles Stein, Charles Doria, Vincent Ferrini, Andrew Crozier, John Huston, Richard Wirtz Emerson, Michael Wolfe, Stephen Rodefer, Henry May, Monroe Engel, Barbara Joseph, Saul Touster, Richard Grossinger, Lindy Hough, Linda Parker, Kevin Opstedal, Eric Purchase, Mary Shore, Gerrit Lansing, Bob Callahan, Michael McClure, Jack Levenson, Norman Solomon, Ralph Maud, Zoe Brown, John Martin and Jay Leyda.

Glen Hartley and Lynn Chu, my agents, and Amy Cherry and Don Lamm of Norton were instrumental in the literal, nonallegorical, business end of this project.

I am grateful to several librarians. Holly Hall, curator of Special Collections at Washington University in St. Louis, and Anne Hyde, curator of Special Collections at the Kenneth Spencer Research Library of the University of Kansas, made their collections available to me. Mike Boughn of the Poetry Collection at the State University of New York at Buffalo provided tapes of several Olson Memorial Lectures. And special acknowledgment is owed the Olson Archive of the University of Connecticut, curator George Butterick and director for Special Collections Richard Schimmelpfeng. It is through the unique coloration of his own words that Olson's soul ultimately seems best revealed; for the preservation of the vast corpus of them as well as for the permission to use those which have been culled for inclusion here, the Olson Archive is hereby thanked.

Finally, I am grateful for family support above and beyond the call of love or duty over nearly five years of a biographical project whose multiple trials, frustrations and delays no doubt owed as much to authorial irresolution and infirmity as to the notorious difficulty of its subject. Angelica Heinegg Clark, my wife and writing partner, made essential contributions to the research and conception of the book (not to mention her seemingly endless toils in typing it over and over).

Tom Clark
Berkeley
Midsummer Day 1990

Charles Olson

1

Trinity
(1910–1928)

> I was born
> 1 hr and 4 minutes after sunrise on the day of the year
> when the sun returns again from its farthest point. . . .

Throughout his adult life, but especially in his final years, Charles Olson placed great importance on the *timing* of his birth—December 27, 1910. To the poet who believed that "love makes the sun inside us," and that "the state of the body—the beauty of it—shall depend upon the potency of the source of its light and heat," the fact that he came into this world just after the winter solstice held special significance. It was always a challenge for him to get past the cold, dark month of his birth, a time of year linked in his mind with fears of mortality. Jean Radoslovich, his sister-in-law and close companion during his last years, recalls that every winter solstice she and Charles would have dinner together, and he would ask her to summon what he believed to be her psychic powers to help him predict his own death:"Well, Jean, is it going to be this year?"

It was Olson's habit in the 1960s to write an annual letter around Christmastime to his fellow poet and Capricorn Robert Duncan, sharing a sense of renewal that grew increasingly mystical over the years. "Eternity is more interesting than infinity," he told his friend. In that final season of his life he found not only some defense against his instinctive dread of death but other kinds of spiritual consolation as well in a concept of cyclic time borrowed from medieval Ismailism. In personal terms "the End of the World / is the Turn-About" was a formula of great promise, allowing Olson the lapsed

Catholic to think of time not as a straight line inevitably exhausted in death's finitude, but as a looping rubber band that never lost its elasticity. The poet's chronic, compulsive work drives, his lifelong stretching and pushing of himself in defiance of other men's schedules and calendars, were expressions of an instinctive search for release from time's fatal dominion into the broad spaces of eternal return. To this being of huge appetites and energies, who in his poetry ranged freely "Across Space and Time," no space-time coordinates were more important than those that marked his personal entry into this world, the beginning of his own part of the great cycle.

It began modestly enough, in a little white house on Middle River Road (later Mitchell Street) in the industrial city of Worcester, Massachusetts. The house had long been the home of his maternal grandparents, Jack and Susan Hines. "Black Jack" Hines was an Irishman born in Cork, brought up in Galway, who worked as a furnace stoker and later as a night watchman for the U.S. Steel Company. Jack's daughter, Mary Theresa, stayed at her now-widowed father's place for her lying-in. It was a suspenseful occasion, because just a year earlier Mary had delivered a son who had died at birth. When she bore a big, healthy second son that cold December dawn, it was a moment of great relief for the sickly mother, who had suffered from anemia during her pregnancy, and great joy for her husband, Karl, who had ardently hoped for a son. Charles John Olson was baptized a Catholic, in accordance with his mother's faith.

The proud father, Karl Joseph Olson, was, like Jack Hines, an immigrant. Born the son of Elof and Ida Olson of Örebro, Sweden, in 1882, he had been carried by his mother to America when less than a year old, and became a U.S. citizen in 1890, the year of his mother's naturalization. (The immigrant son would one day anglicize his own name to Charles.) Like his Swedish ancestors, hard-toiling gardeners and iron-factory hands, Karl learned early to be a diligent worker. At age fourteen he took a milk route to help his mother support him and his two sisters. After high school he was employed by the Stewart Boiler Works in Worcester. He became the leader of a crew of "master builders" who went all over New England replacing old brick factory stacks with new iron chimneys. This hazardous profession was later regarded with awe by Karl's son. "My father . . . had to go up on stagings, and that meant danger. He was high steel."

The brave smokestack-raiser had also impressed Mary Hines of Worcester, wooing her with postcards sent from what his young son would imagine as the "unknown lands and continents in Rhode Island, Massachusetts, New Hampshire and Maine." It was a cautious courtship, Mary giving Karl plenty of time to demonstrate the seriousness of his intentions. In 1906, he proposed to her by mail from Calais, Maine, "the farthest outpost" on his New England circuit. Soon afterwards, to provide security for the family he planned, he gave up his itinerant steelworking job and took a position with the Worcester Post Office. The period of engagement lasted another year. On January 23, 1908, Karl and Mary Hines were wed. Mary was thereby saved from a spinster's fate. At the time of their marriage, she was almost thirty-six, ten years older than her husband. Because Karl was not a Catholic, the ceremony had to take place in the parish rectory instead of the church proper. It was a bitter cold day, and leaving, they were met by not only a rice shower but driving snow. The gallant groom shielded his bride with an umbrella.

Physically, the lanky (six foot three), big-boned, square-jawed Swede towered over the diminutive, plump, moon-faced Irish-American woman. Their hazel-eyed, auburn-haired son took after both parents—inheriting Mary's rounded features and weak eyes, but growing up at great leaps into a beanpole of a lad who by the age of twelve could look down on his mother. The temperamental differences between Karl and Mary would also soon manifest themselves in the boy: his own ingrained "laziness" and "vacillation," Olson once claimed, had come from his mother, his "physical and mental energy" from his father.

A clear preference for that father soon developed in young Charlie Olson. Karl was a gregarious man, a much more attractive figure, in the boy's eyes, than the aging and anxiety-prone Mary. But Karl also had a difficult side, a streak of stubborn pride and stern self-demand not always immediately evident to casual acquaintances, yet in time to have a great impact on his son, who inherited these same character traits. In both father and son, between the outer "incredible showman" and the moody, variable inner person there was a considerable gap. The showman could tower above the world, but the introvert was often wounded into grudges and resentments by its blows. "He had a way of being liked, for his energy," Olson said in a sketch of his father written as he himself approached middle life.

> He'd sing and dance and play tricks, get up fishing parties or walks. There was a bravura about it, a hectic tone which I could only put up with because I had seen the other thing, the sudden distaste, or sombreness, the sense of effort wasted. For he was awkward, unable to cope with the failings of life except by himself, in his early morning walks, fishing, painting, or carpentry, when he could bear down and get his restless flying off from the nubs of life concentrated.

Though in such published writings and interviews Olson presented an idealized portrait of Karl, from his private letters and journal entries a somewhat more complicated picture emerges. Two personalities so alike were bound to clash or compete at times. Both father and son were powerful talkers. Olson once recalled the competition at home for talking rights: "My old man used to say to me (who was so like hisself) 'what you need is a jaw-tackle'!" Both were also intelligent, sensitive, and hesitant about expressing private emotions. Inevitably there were occasional tense moments between them. During his college years, his father's lack of education and worldly polish would become an embarrassment to a suddenly class-conscious Charlie. Although he never ceased to admire Karl's "old fashioned" working man's integrity ("notions having to do with courtesy, modesty, care, proportion, respect") he also never overcame a certain vague shame and anger regarding his father's waste of natural gifts. Karl, he wrote in a 1939 journal, "had an intellect and nothing but newspapers to use it on. That was his fault." And an early draft of his 1950 poem "ABCs: For Arthur Rimbaud" contains a revealing line he later deleted from the published version: "oh my washer-woman mother, oh my alcoholic dad."

This ambivalent attitude towards his parents carried over into Olson's adult relations with others. He took great ostentatious delight in the company of down-to-earth working people, waitresses, fishermen, truck drivers, and cooks, yet actually spent far more time cultivating the rich and powerful, persons of worldly influence and success in art, politics, business and public life. An unconscious snobbery, whether bred of class insecurity or a natural aristocracy of taste, showed itself in both the earnest climbing and the democratic stooping. One of the favorite books of Olson's early manhood was Dreiser's *An American Tragedy,* the story of a boy from the wrong side of the tracks trying to make it up the social ladder. It was a theme with which the ambitious Worcester youth could easily identify.

He grew up in a rented third-floor tenement flat at 4 Norman Avenue. The run-down building was one of a row of unremarkable and identical three-decker structures jammed into a cul-de-sac. The immediate neighbors were blue-collar workers from the local textile factories. There were occasional hard times in the Olson household. The flat's main heat source was a coal stove, and sometimes toward the end of the month Charlie was taken along on a work detail he would not soon forget, walking the Boston & Maine tracks with Karl to pick up the coke chunks scattered by the passing tenders. But the boy did not have to look far for evidence of a better life. Only a short walk away from the shabby cul-de-sac was "the best part of town, where the money and authority was." Charlie's double sense of his family's poverty and of the marvelous rewards just a few rungs up was dramatized by visits to Karl's older sister Vandla Hedges. Aunt Vandla had married well, and now lived in a comfortable Wellesley Hills home considered stately and grand by the boy, who daydreamed such glorified circumstances might be within his reach one day.

His own tenement home meanwhile provided a much more prosaic setting for the growth of his imagination.

> *. . . a five-petaled flower*
> *restores the fringed gentians I used so to love*
> *I'd lie amongst them in the meadow near the house*
> *which was later covered by a dump to make an athletic field*
> *and the brook was gone to which we tried to speed our sleds*
> *from the hill the house stood on and which the dump*
> *was meant to join, the loss punctuated by the shooting*
> *my father taught me with the rifle he gave me from the back porch*
> *of the three-decker, the rats living among the cans and peat*
> *as the dump came closer, and I hated*
> *all of it . . .*

The squalid small world of this junk-littered meadow-dump, where wild irises
bloomed sparsely on the banks of a narrow trickle called Beaver Brook, was
the site of Charlie's early boyhood shadow-games with a fantasy companion
named Cabbage. Their imaginary adventures included baking potatoes by a
campfire like hoboes on the road out West. Later, inspired by reading turn-
of-the-century American author Joseph Altsheler's juvenile wilderness-adven-
ture novels, Charlie enacted Indian wars there with real-life playmates.

Mary Olson would summon her son from play with a whistle she kept on
the back porch. She was overprotective of her only child, showing a motherly
solicitude which sometimes made the boy uncomfortable. She "pushed" him,
with a "tough emotional insistence" which he began to resent as a teenager
and eventually felt driven to resist, developing a strong emotional block against
her. Yet through his adult life he was drawn to a series of female "protectors,"
her incarnations. "What did my mother do," he once asked the most protective of them all, his first wife, "or not do, that left her such a fixed image of
woman in me? My hunch is that she didn't give me enough love to slake the
appetite of a son, especially an only son. Or was it too much—too close, that
Trinity!—and so smothering . . . and why I fight any attachment?"

Mary was rather superstitious, believing unquestioningly in leprechauns
and other "little people." Her favorite pastime was sitting in her rocking
chair, crocheting as she gossiped with neighbor ladies of the parish. A devout
Catholic, she went to Mass every Sunday with young Charlie dutifully in
tow. This was a custom that continued into his adolescence. Later, when he
left home to attend college and stopped going to church, he was bothered by
guilt feelings. Guilt also accompanied childhood curiosity about sex. It was
hard for him to separate the curiosity from fears of his mother somehow
finding out: when as a five-year-old, egged on by another boy, he exposed

himself to an older girl in a neighbor's barn, the reward was "no sexual feeling at all—only guilt at being discovered or guilt at my mother knowing I had undressed."

Not until the age of seven did Charlie get a bedroom of his own, and then only under traumatic circumstances, inheriting the deathbed of his Hines grandfather, who'd been staying with the Olsons, and whose body—with "liver spots, and cold the lovely flesh"—the small boy discovered one morning in going to wake him. Prior to that he slept on a small couch bed in an alcove in his parents' bedroom. Lying in it, he spent long hours furtively fantasizing about being a doctor who held men and women captive in order to perform sex-change operations on them. He later speculated that he had been sexually deformed by environmental factors in his childhood, foremost being the inhibitions of his parents, who were "tidy people . . . she sentimental & Catholic, he very modest, and gentle, not an experienced man." No more than Mary could Karl help with the growing boy's questions about his maturing body.

Charlie's confused feelings about the opposite sex, fear battling with fascination, drove him to identify with the less threatening image of maleness represented by his father. The bond with Karl was his strongest emotional link. Most afternoons he held an impatient vigil, waiting at the head of Norman Avenue for his father to come home. That first sight of the returning postman was the day's high point. If Charlie and his pals were busy playing ball in the field behind the house, Karl was hailed by his son as he came down the street, and stopped to knock out a few fly balls to the boys. On weekends father and son went off together on purposeful little trips, scavenging for coal in the railyards and for scrap iron in the city dump, or rambling the countryside at the end of the urban trolley line, gathering berries or wild grapes for Karl's homemade wine.

Powerful as it was, the relationship with his father was not without hints of competitive challenge. On those weekend treks, the long-striding postman was hard to keep up with, and the lagging youth became the target of much paternal needling. He found at an early age that he did not like losing to his father in anything. Once, when Karl defeated him at Parcheesi, he threw the dice in his father's face. As punishment, he was threatened with his first paternal beating, but Mary intervened. Karl settled for giving his hair a stern yank. Charlie did his best to keep back tears. He was determined not to be a sissy in his father's eyes.

In the summer of 1915 Karl took the family off on the first of many holidays at the Cape Ann fishing and resort town of Gloucester. Situated on the Atlantic shore thirty miles northeast of Boston, separated from the mainland by the Annisquam River (a tidal estuary connecting Gloucester Harbor with Ipswich Bay to the north), the boy's adopted part-time "island"-hometown would become the adult poet's creative precinct, "my front yard," as he called the place in later years. He would not be the first artist to appreciate the imaginative ambience of Gloucester's maritime setting, its piers and fishing boats, beaches and rocky coves. T. S. Eliot, who spent school vacations at his family's house there, evoked the wild Cape Ann coast in "The Dry Salvages," and painters like FitzHugh Lane, Winslow Homer, Edward Hopper and Marsden Hartley recreated its unique light and spaces on canvas. By the time the Olsons became regular summer residents, the town was already well known not only for its long seafaring tradition, attested to by such landmarks as the Fisherman's Monument on Western Avenue and the statue of the Virgin cradling a ship atop Our Lady of Good Voyage Church on Prospect Street, but for its growing art colony and summer tourist industry.

During the Olsons' first local stay, Homer Barrett, the mayor of Gloucester, had construction underway on some holiday camps at Stage Fort Park. Karl rented one of Barrett's camp cottages, a tiny "henhouse" of a place where Mary and Charlie spent that summer. Karl himself commuted from Worcester by interurban trolley, rejoining them at the shore on weekends and during his annual two-week vacation. For the next few summers the Olsons moved from cottage to cottage, finally taking out an extended lease on a two-story frame place with screened-in porches, located in Barrett's main camp on Stage Fort Avenue behind the park. The cottage featured a rather chintzy nautical decor and was called Oceanwood, a name spelled out atop a skipper's wheel mounted on the roof. Just across the road, a dirt path led straight down to the beach.

Oceanwood was soon a home away from home. The Olsons made many friends. One was camp developer "Homey" Barrett, their landlord and neighbor. A nervous, cigar-chewing little man "with fingers as fine as a woman's" who spent much of his time tending his garden, Barrett was the veteran of many a City Hall kickback deal. Later, when Charlie himself went into politics, he thought often of Barrett, a sort of old-time, small-town template of the profession. Homer Barrett embodied the traditional democratic "form of power," a more or less upstanding local bigwig who "took his take, from the West End of Main Street, and put it / back, in entertainment, over the Park."

Karl, an avid amateur angler, also soon befriended some of the veteran Gloucester fishermen, including a pair of brother-in-laws, Lou Douglas and Frank Miles, who made a big impression on Charlie. In long summer twilights the two fishermen, great storytellers, smoked and talked till dark on the big rocks by the Barrett camp's "piazza." Behind those rocks Charlie hid out, taking careful mental notes, his imagination captured by the high romance of oceangoing. With a chum from the camp, Gordon Boone, as partner, and some makeshift fishing tackle, he set out to become a fisherman himself, but the experiment proved premature. The proud catch of a day's angling off one of the piers was a can of sculpins, "bloated, freckled bags of wind" which the grown-ups laughed at. Novice fisherman Charlie couldn't help bursting into tears over having his triumphant moment treated as a joke. It would take him some years to learn his fate was to mythologize the sea's heroes, not imitate them.

This sensitive, dreamy boy started school in September 1917, at the Abbott Street Grammar School in Worcester. Early motivation in his studies was contributed largely by his father. Never comfortable with books himself, and slowly proceeding with his own education by mail order, Karl was bent on compensating for this deficiency by way of his son. He was fascinated by history, particularly that of America and Gloucester. At Worcester holiday parades he turned out in full Revolutionary War regalia along with his fellow members of the Continentals, a local social club and marching band. Among his gifts to Charlie were a five-volume edition of *Everybody's Cyclopedia,* a sort of omnibus historical encyclopedia, and a set of Mathew Brady's Civil War photographs. The Brady photos came in large blue folios the youngster lay spread-eagled on the floor to read, as other boys would the Sunday funny papers. They gave him a look at the real images behind "the painted surfaces of war," scenes of horror and violence he found compelling. Pleased by these evidences of a serious scholar in the bud, Karl went out of his way to nurture his son's historical interest.

Every year he took Charlie to a local performance of the stirring Civil War play *The Drummer Boy of Shiloh.* In 1920, on the three hundredth anniversary of the Pilgrim landing at Plymouth, there was a special father-and-son trip to the tricentennial pageant. They camped at the home of the North Plymouth postmaster, spent their days inspecting a model of the *Mayflower* and visiting the graves of Miles Standish and Priscilla Alden, and at night attended the open-air pageant. Its broadly played dramatic reenactments of early settlement made history come alive for the impressionable boy, endowing it with a lingering magic.

Other long-term consequences of the Plymouth junket proved less positive, however. Karl had been granted a week's leave from the post office to make the trip, and when this was rescinded at the last minute, he had stubbornly defied his supervisor's orders. For this act of insubordination he was "busted," suffering a pay cut and transfer from his route. Later, hounded on the job by inspectors, he became certain he was being made an example, not only for the unauthorized holiday but for his organizing efforts in the postal

workers' union. He kept up the union work doggedly, but the strain took its
toll; as the years went by he seemed more and more a bitter, defeated man.
He developed high blood pressure and other physical complaints. By the
time his adoring son was ready for high school, the look on the returning
postman's face, as he turned that last corner every evening, was "more often
grim than gay."

Though Karl's troubles with the postal authorities shook his faith in his
adopted country, causing him to turn for support to his fellow immigrants
in the Swedish American Federation, the passion for America's history and
fascination with its founders which he had inculcated in his son did not flag.
To Charlie there now seemed no idea more noble, no act more heroic than
"to 'plant' a plantation, found a country." One who had attempted that feat
in the Olsons' own neighborhood was Captain John Smith, seventeenth-century explorer of the New England coast. Smith, not only a man of action but
a scholar, had written impressive verse and prose about his wide travels. (The
adult Olson would incorporate an entire Smith poem into his *Maximus*.)
Charlie's earliest encounter with the locally famed English adventurer came
in Gloucester during the summer of 1923. In the course of a game of Indian
tracking with some other boys, he was surprised by an elaborately costumed
figure jumping out of a bush and shouting "Tragabigzanda! Tragabigzanda!"
It was "John Smith all got up in ruff and armor, supporting some swooning
Turkish Princess on his arm . . . a moth-eaten Elizabeth from a bad movie."
Charlie and his companions "dropped to the ground like the trained Indians
we were," and spied on the strange apparitions, who turned out to be actors
rehearsing for Cape Ann's tricentennial pageant. He had soon forsaken the
Old West for hanging around the show grounds, and before long won himself a part as one of the "towns-people, with square shoes, and that damned
collar."

In the fall of 1924, the inquisitive thirteen-year-old enrolled at Worcester
Classical High School, "a great old Victorian humanistic base of education
for the poor" located just a few blocks from the Olson home. One of New
England's finest traditional classical schools, comparable in many respects to
Boston Latin, Worcester Classical was, in the words of one student of the
time, "a no-nonsense school," whose main business was preparing the bright-
est students of the industrial city's lower and middle classes for college, pref-
erably the Ivy League. The gifted Olson boy seemed headed in that direction;
his father had long dreamed of seeing him a college man someday, while
Mary envisaged him as a lawyer, professor, or—in sanguine moments—a
scholarly priest. Charlie had already begun to appear the part of the book-

worm, his neatly combed hair parted down the middle choirboy-fashion, his owlish eyes encircled by steel-rimmed spectacles acquired to correct near-sightedness and contributing no little to his perpetual round-eyed look of astonishment.

At Worcester Classical, though "definitely not a social lion," the energetic, gangling adolescent—"too long-armed for his jacket, always in a hurry"—soon made his mark, qualifying for the honor roll in each of his four years. Languages were his strong suit academically. In advanced Latin classes that were Classical's most demanding, he was a standout. Adept at sight-reading, he was capable of breezing through daily homework exercises in a few minutes, regularly teaming up for this purpose with an equally talented female classmate: they met up at seven forty-five each school morning in a hallway outside his first-period classroom, and raced through the day's assigned passage of Cicero's *Orations,* Virgil's *Aeneid* or Ovid's *Metamorphoses.* (Ovid, the poet of love and transformation, was Charlie's favorite among the ancient writers.) In English class with instructor Percy Howe, the future poet developed a strong interest in the Romantics. Howe taught verse by the old recitation method, with great stretches of declamation. Classmates could see that for Charlie these poetry sessions were an "inspiration." Before arriving at Classical High his attempts at writing had been limited to some doodling with stories based on the news (the most ambitious concerned the 1923 Tokyo earthquake); now he became conscious of literary form, tried his hand at a few secret verses, and also, in his first fling at writing for publication, penned articles for the school paper, the *Argus.*

His true forte in classmates' eyes, however, was his exceptional ability to express himself not on paper but out loud. At Classical High, Olson showed a native gift of gab, and along with it the quick wit necessary for elevating mere talk into powerful persuasion. This talent gave promise of big things ahead for him. He became the school's premier public speaker, star and captain of the debate squad. As a junior and senior he ran for student office and was elected both times, first as president of the student council, then as president of his graduating class. There were those at Classical who foresaw a political career for him, as perhaps "a Senate majority leader or Whip." In his senior yearbook, he was lauded for his debating triumphs and for "a charming personality, a sterling character and a keen mind."

The climax of his high school public-speaking career came just before graduation, at the 1928 national oratory championships. Victorious in the Northeastern regional finals, he advanced to the national championship competition in Washington. The pressure of the upcoming event exacerbated his natural tendency to demand too much of himself. After exhausting himself on anxious practice speeches delivered before his debate coach Howe and at home in his room, he fell ill on the brink of the contest and had to deliver his decisive speech through the effects of a bad sinus cold. Still he finished third, good enough to win him a whirlwind visit to Europe that summer.

The brief trip yielded two memorable incidents. One was a meeting in Ireland with the poet W. B. Yeats, whose polite remarks about the lineage of the Hines clan were sufficient to convince Charlie that his own mother's aunt must have been the same Mary Hines who had, according to Yeats, been "the beloved of the blind poet Raftery and the most beautiful woman in all Western Ireland." The other big moment came during a stop in Cologne, when, on a dark rainy night near the cathedral, the young traveler received an offer from a street whore. He was sorely tempted. At seventeen, he still had no real knowledge of "the act" beyond what he'd gained from some graphic illustrations found in a library book. The library discovery, occurring during a period of desperate sexual curiosity in his sixteenth year, had caused a certain crisis in his religious and family life; afterwards he'd experienced a wave of violent fantasies that so troubled his conscience he'd stopped going to Mass and Confession, thereby provoking great battles with Mary. Instilling in him a fear of women and of his own body had been the priests' work, he was starting to believe, with his mother acting as their accomplice. ("Fear of my mother turned into fear of god and sin and the church got all mixed up with sex," he would one day conclude.) On that rainy night in the shadow of the Cologne cathedral, his fear overwhelmed his curiosity, and he turned down the whore's offer. His sexual initiation would have to await his fuller emergence from the Trinity's "amniotic cocoon."

2

Show 'Em
(1928–1932)

That September of 1928 Charlie repacked his European-trip suitcase, now proudly papered-over with exotic railway and steamship company labels, and headed off for Wesleyan University in the small manufacturing city of Middletown, Connecticut. He was entering as a scholarship student, recommended by Percy Howe, a Wesleyan alumnus. The Wesleyan of that time has been described by one of Olson's teachers as "a small college with an excellent reputation in the academic world. The faculty of forty-nine men were for the most part serious, dedicated teachers. The student body, numbering about 550, was made up largely of businessmen's sons who believed that C was a gentleman's grade. They wanted to have a good time, make friendly contacts, and delightfully prolong the days of their 'infancy.' A few, sons of ministers, teachers, and missionaries, had academic aspirations. These were a distinct minority. Now and then there was a boy who wanted to become a writer. They were a still smaller minority."

The immigrant postman's son was immediately distinguished from the Wesleyan majority by his size—his 210 pounds stretched out over an elongated frame now approaching six foot eight—and by a lower-class background easy to deduce from his modest dress, his lack of pocket cash and his broad South Worcester accent. He took much ribbing from his Phi Nu Theta fraternity brothers at Eclectic House, who appear to have had little idea just how sensitive he actually was. Their thoughtless attempts at collegiate humor could seem to him cruel taunts, making him feel "left out and laughed at." Leaving the ego-bolstering protective security of family and home ("the womb of 4 Norman Avenue") proved a real jolt, one whose effects were carefully concealed from those around him but set down in painfully self-conscious journals. These became the testament of a suddenly discovered subjectivity, documenting his adaptive donning of a "coat of cynicism and 'smart aleck-ness' " as shield against "the teasing and pestering of fellows." But if a bluff social demeanor allowed him to brush off the needling, especially the constant stream of comments about his gigantism, the damage was internalized. In low moments he feared that he "was, somehow, not 'human.' " His only way to conquer such awful self-doubts was to turn the tables—to accept and make an asset of that in him which was different. By setting his own sights beyond ordinary men's estimates and standards, he could perhaps convert his uniqueness to his advantage. "It is the bigness of the Prometheus of Shelley that I want—and need."

The foremost problem facing him, he believed, was learning to "deal with others." Notebook declarations of independence notwithstanding, he remained in fact all too reliant on others' esteem. In a social environment governed by appearances, he could impress only by competing furiously for external rewards that would vindicate, if not erase, his physical strangeness. He determined "to 'show 'em,' by prizes, positions, etc." In all his classes, not only those in his major field of English but in such humanities electives as history, government, American literature, and philosophy, he strove to attain not gentleman's C's, but A's; the A-plus he recieved from his American literature professor, Alec Cowie, for an essay on the poetry of Emerson, was said to be the only such grade Cowie had ever awarded. And the push to "show 'em" was not limited to academics. As goalie on the college soccer team, he earned a varsity letter sported with pride on campus. He wrote editorials for the college newspaper, and for a while nursed vague· ambitions of becoming a journalist. As at Worcester Classical, however, his best thinking was done not for print but on his feet. His tryout session for the debating team made an instant Olson fan of the coach, professor of English Wilbert Snow. Charlie became Wesleyan's lead debater in his sophomore year. He lost very few debates thereafter. The heat of intercollegiate competition brought his "show 'em" energies to fever pitch. "With his height of six feet eight inches and his booming voice," according to Snow, "he was so overpowering on the platform that the judges didn't dare give the decision to anyone else!"

Snow would remain a friendly influence throughout Olson's undergraduate years and beyond. The sympathy between them was bred of kindred interests. A serious literary man, "Wild Bill" Snow had published two volumes of verse and was a good friend of Robert Frost's. As a down-east Maine native, furthermore, he knew the Northeast backwoods as thoroughly as an Iroquois scout, and had once even worked as a reindeer agent in Alaska. Charlie revered him as an "Irish Indian," as well as a "father." Snow's course on modern poetry fired a new Olson passion for the work of W. B. Yeats, of which the professor was a great admirer. Pupil and teacher shared many out-of-class hours arguing the relative merits of Yeats' youthful lyrics, favored by Snow, and the more complex later verse, preferred by Olson. With his remarkable memory, Charlie was soon able to declaim by rote extended passages of the Irish bard's work. Snow awarded him an A and high praise ("thorough enough for a university thesis") for his term paper on Yeats. Still, it was not until the end of his senior year that Charlie got up the nerve to approach the professor with some of his own poems. The results were not encouraging for the hopeful versifier. Snow, a lifelong Democrat who had once been a candidate for the Connecticut state senate, advised him to put his brains to better use by pursuing a career in politics.

At this point Charlie himself felt a more direct route to self-development lay in prose, with its greater intellectual rigors: "I love the swing of poetry and its beautiful wording. I like to listen to it when I don't have to bother to think what it means. But when it comes to getting an intellectual conception, to gleaning pure thought, I want prose." Hungry for "intellectual food," he haunted bookshops and libraries, keeping up with the latest in American fiction. New works by major writers were assessed in notebook reviews that reflected a certain tension between his catholic tastes and budding critical faculty. He savored Willa Cather's "true genius," Pearl S. Buck's "earthiness," and Somerset Maugham's "final wisdom," but took exception to the overly "conventional" characterizations of Ellen Glasgow, faulted William Faulkner's *Sanctuary* for cheap "sensationalism," and dismissed Hemingway's *Winner Take Nothing* as the depreciated product of a "castrated ex-winner." His omnivorous eclecticism, in fact his very bookishness itself, sometimes troubled him. Did he "lean too heavily" on books? Were they providing him real inspiration, or just an intellectual crutch? "Occasionally they set me off on an individual thought and I 'run along the line of that ray' and do something creative, but it is infrequent," he worried late one night. "That is my tragedy." He traced the "tragedy" of a sluggish imagination, apparent cause of his inability to launch forthwith into great literature, all the way back to early childhood. The Norman Avenue cocoon had failed to equip him with the basic cultural tools requisite for self-invention. "My imagination is earthborn and the god-awful thing is that my youth pegged it down. Mother. Religion. Poverty of art. Environment. This terrific energy that burns within me must be (or might have been?) turned into artistic creation if taste and joy and beauty had been mine. I guess it is that vacuum of background has me licked. I think that is why I have the omnivorous thirst to read and to learn now, rather than to express."

At college he worked hard to revise his fate, to fill up the "tragic vacuum" of his background by immersing himself in art and culture. This took no little dedication, as attested by his painstaking journal accounts of earnest attendance at campus cultural events, from harp recitals to lectures on modern painting. "To be really cultured is to be really great," he declared roundly in the draft of a speech composed in his capacity as senior class historian for the 1932 Wesleyan commencement. His speech on the "American Scholar" commemorated the famous address of that title delivered ninety-five years earlier as a Phi Beta Kappa oration at Harvard by Ralph Waldo Emerson, a grand culture-synthesizer whose lofty amplitude of mind, insecure beginner Olson modestly acknowledged, made him feel dwarfed, an "intellectual pygmy" in comparison. For all their inequalities of achievement, the nineteenth-century Yankee thinker's call for American independence from European cultural leadership struck a chord with which the young man could readily identify. The role of latter-day "American Scholar" as wide-roving intellect was one the mature Olson would later strive to fill. By then, however, he would dismiss Emerson as a mere "mechanical summarizer"—and this whole phase of his own intellectual development as one of shameful "whoring after culture," in which he'd been the victim of a slavish worship of the false idols of academia.

In his struggle to acquire culture during his college years, Charlie found a companion and accomplice in a new girlfriend, Barbara Denny. Babs, as he called her, was his first big flame. He met her at a party while at home in Worcester over Christmas vacation of his freshman year. Socially, she was of a totally different world, with a bloodline extending back to one of New England's oldest families, the Connecticut Griswolds (another member of the family owned an expensive Worcester jewelry shop). The dissimilarity in their backgrounds was mediated by a common passion for the arts. Babs was soon accompanying Charlie to exhibitions of painting, plays and foreign-language films. They began exchanging literary gifts: he gave her modern novels and Shelley's *Adonais,* she presented him with Emily Dickinson's poems and books on his beloved Gloucester. A lovestruck Charlie had fantasies of Babs and himself appearing together as paramours in popular plays (like Barrie's *The Admirable Crichton*), and, in notebook moonings inspired by Keats' letters to Fanny Brawne, expressed a romantic longing to be "preparing one home with her."

The transcendent yearnings in which he sublimated the periodic intensities of his seven-year relationship with Barbara Denny would be attributed by an older and harder-eyed Olson to a retardation of normal adolescent sexual development; it had all been, he later thought, merely a long-drawn-out exercise in "ridiculous middle class nonsense" from which he could have saved himself simply by accepting the solicitation of that streetwalker in Cologne. His closest actual physical contact with Babs was the kind of breathless kissing one saw in films. A more specifically sexual interest, meanwhile, involved him in a simultaneous crush on a common working girl in Middletown. One day while sitting in a barbershop waiting to have his hair cut, he saw this town girl pass by on the street outside, and experienced a violent "convulsion" that shook him to his vitals. Unable to interpret this troubling episode because hopelessly "green" in sexual matters, he reacted, in characteristic self-dramatizing reflex, by making up his mind he was destined to remain forever "instinctively a solitary."

The new dilettante Charlie who came back from Wesleyan to join the family at Oceanwood Cottage in Gloucester during the summers was increasingly a challenge to the patience of his serious, hardworking father. Karl had begun to question the wisdom of having guided the boy toward college; the results were making his son seem at times a stranger to him. There was now a perceptible tension between them, exacerbated by economics. In his first summer back from school, instead of picking up a part-time job—as he had done on high school holidays, when he had worked as a cement carrier on the Gloucester wharf, or as an icehouse loader or print salesman in Worcester—Charlie maintained himself in a cavalier state of unemployment, spending much of his time following the pleasures of the shore resort's idle *hoi polloi,* and frequenting those "havens of gossip" the rented villas populated by the summer art colony. Ignoring his father's hints about the availability of remunerative day labor on the wharves, he chose to indulge his artistic nature by enrolling in a drama workshop at the Gloucester School of the Little Theatre. Classes, conducted by Mrs. Constance Taylor, were held in an old sail loft on Rocky Neck, and Charlie came to them by sea, rowing a dory across Gloucester Harbor. Mrs. Taylor's school brought out a natural capacity for the dramatic in the young giant. His energetic execution of posture exercises could make the hardwood floor tremble, and in elocution drills his booming voice shook the loft's high rafters. Practicing on passages from Shakespeare, he was taught to refine a little of the Worcester broadness out of his vowels. Though dramatic training did nothing to enhance his economic self-sufficiency, his cultural self-invention proceeded apace.

His new theatrical expertise was put to use directly upon his return to Wesleyan. He joined the college drama society, and was soon being featured as a comic actor in a series of farces that included *Ten Nights in a Barroom, Gammer Gurton's Needle, Merton of the Movies* and—his most memorable performance—Molière's *Doctor in Spite of Himself.* In the college newspaper review of the Molière production, penned by his philosophy teacher Cornelius Krusé, Charlie's "ability and charm of acting" in the role of Sganarelle were singled out for praise. (It was the example of Krusé's "thin dry high" intellect that was responsible for his own abstract, cerebral approach to poetry, Olson later claimed only partly in jest, adding that the Wesleyan philosophy professor had "ruined" him with Schopenhauer.) Collegiate dramatic triumphs, modest though they may have been, gave rise to brief visions of a career in the theatre. "The ham was certainly there," a friend from these early years observes.

The "endless dreamer," as one teacher called the Olson of this period, was brought back abruptly to earth by Depression reality in the middle of his sophomore year. At last acceding to his father's urgings, he took the first preparatory steps toward obtaining employment, sitting for the civil service letter carrier's examination in February 1930. He passed, though to his chagrin with a lower score than his father had received. When there was no immediate opening for him as a postman that summer, he hired on as a brush-clearer at the Babson Reservoir construction site in Gloucester, a job from which, to his secret relief, he was discharged after just twelve hours. The following summer, however, he was hired as a carrier by the Gloucester Post Office. The *Gloucester Times* reported the hiring as a curiosity item: "Carrier Force Adds College 'Giant' to Fernwood Route." At his swearing-in the rookie mailman "was so high up in the air he was forced to get down on his knees to place his fingers on the fingerprint paper that lay on the table." Big "Chaalie Olt-sen, the boy from Woos-tah," soon became a legend in the Gloucester Post Office, his great head looming up over the dusty tops of the sorting racks, talking nonstop as he sorted the incoming mail. Once, he became so absorbed in discussion with a fellow postman that when he went to load his truck, he forgot to duck for the roof as he threw in a sack of letters, and knocked himself out cold.

The mail had to go through, which meant a rude termination to dreaming every morning at the crack of dawn. But the unpleasantness of pulling himself out of a warm bed—for Charlie the hardest part of the job—had its rewards. At that hour it was a pleasure to walk the "Cut"—the Blynman Canal connecting the Annisquam River with Gloucester Harbor. The harbor air fresh and clear, "gulls / already bummaging"—to Olson this was a form of atmospheric poetry. In his first summer of duty, rambling a daily fifteen-mile route, he swelled his pocket notebook with high metaphysical speculation ranging freely over the world and his place in it. He called this "walking myself down," and on a given day it could delay the completion of his route by as much as two hours. By his second summer an impatient foreman of carriers had switched him to a truck. Undaunted, Charlie kept up his errant rovings and scribblings, frequently parking his postal vehicle to jot down literary reflections. He was moreover not impervious to offers of "coffee & gab" from friends he encountered on the course of his route. Eventually these habits brought him official censure. One of his customary stops was a painter's studio on Rocky Neck. A pair of elderly sisters spied on him and called the post office to report a mail truck left unguarded on the corner of Rocky Neck Avenue. The following day Charlie's foreman walked in on him in the middle of an unauthorized coffee break and insisted on accompanying him on his truck for the rest of the route, a stern, silent presence at his side. Despite this episode, the undependable postman managed to hold on to the precious civil service job for the next several summers.

His collegiate career was meanwhile progressing at full steam. The former fraternity butt had developed, within a few years, into an assertive, outgoing overachiever, with a friendly nose in everybody's business. His ability to manipulate others had, in fact, earned him a nickname: "Stage Manager Olson." Enormously competitive, he pushed himself to excel in everything he did. That furious driving hunger to succeed was no secret. Friends had him "pegged": "the Politician—the Pusher-of-other-people Around." His public-speaking career reached a climax in his senior year in a debate at Brown University pitting him against the Ivy League's champion debater, a young man who had been his chief rival for three years. In the actual event, however, his most serious adversary proved to be not the opposing speaker but the pressure of his own excessive self-demand. Uneasy for days beforehand, he lost his nerve—and his train of thought—in the middle of his concluding remarks, faltered, and was defeated. Immediately afterwards he was overcome by feelings of humiliation, disappointment and anger far out of proportion to the actual importance of the match. Instead of returning to Wesleyan with the team, he jumped into a taxi in Providence and ordered the driver to take him all the way back to his parents' home in Worcester, charging the $60 ride to his university. Though dumbfounded by this episode, the endlessly supportive Wilbert Snow prevailed upon Wesleyan president James L. McConaughy to pick up the star debater's huge cab bill. In his journal Charlie fretted at length over the Brown defeat and its causes. "It is at once an aid and handicap that my style of debating depends on my mental exhilaration," he wrote. "I hate to prepare formal arguments. . . ."

Despite such strains, however, in the long run his "show 'em" campaign had worked: he was now a campus force to be contended with. When he graduated in June of 1932, it was as a star of his class. He had vindicated

himself in the eyes of his parents, also. The symptoms of frivolity and irre-
sponsibility which had disturbed his father were shown to have been but a
passing phase. He had established his credentials for greatness, his outstanding promise. He presented his Phi Beta Kappa key to his mother, who would
carry it proudly in her purse for the rest of her life. To the ambitious young
man, however, his academic triumph seemed incomplete. In a final decisive
contest, the regional competition for a Rhodes scholarship, he was beaten
out by the senior class president and captain of the basketball team, John A.
Wells. Later, Wells became a prominent lawyer, active in Republican party
politics. Still dwelling on that early loss, in the 1940s Democrat Olson would
follow with jealous interest the career of this symbolic rival; even at a subsequent time when he'd long since left both politics and academia behind, the
mere mention of the name Jack Wells, reminder of his desperate struggle to
impress during his undergraduate years at Wesleyan, could pitch him into
momentary "sickness."

3

To Tell of Ishmael's Father
(1932–1936)

That fall the twenty-one-year-old Olson entered Wesleyan's graduate school
as a master's candidate in English. His year of study toward the degree
would include some course work at Yale, supported by an Olin fellowship
and accomplished by commuting from Middletown to nearby New Haven.
At Wesleyan the focus of the year's efforts was his M.A. thesis. Wilbert Snow
suggested a long paper on a subject of mutual interest, Herman Melville, and
agreed to serve as his adviser. Snow imposed one condition: the candidate
must guarantee the originality of his judgment by promising not to read
what past critics had said about Melville (a stipulation indeed made almost
unnecessary by the prevailing academic neglect of that author in 1932). Charlie consented, and they set out together on what the teacher considered a
"monumental task," exploring in detail the nineteenth-century writer's complete prose works.

A copy of the Modern Library edition of *Moby-Dick,* presented him by
his father on his nineteenth birthday, had been the young man's introduction
to Melville. The gift had come with a "bad pun" of Karl's as dedication:
"When o'er this book, you cast your eyes, / Forget your studies and Moby-
lize." Combining those two pursuits, studies and *Moby*-lizing, would be the
principal endeavor of an epoch in Charlie's life now opening with characteristic enthusiasm and flourish. His new roommate at Eclectic House, an aspiring dramatist, poetaster and "debonair aesthete" named John Finch, recalls

young Olson as Melville's faithful "clerk," reciting the canon "at midnight, in Paul Bunyan's bathrobe, his great eyes gleaming, his hair crazy like a fright wig, pacing the room in a rapt adagio, Melville in his hand, Melville on his lips. The Melville in his hand was his first and favorite *Moby Dick,* the little, green, back-broken, dog-eared, all-underlined Modern Library edition. . . . And the words? Almost anything out of the Pequod's long voyage. . . . Charlie would holler, 'That's prose, Finch! Prose is the stuff! Match that in poetry. See, you can't do it! Yah, yah, you can't do it!' "

But as its due date of May 1, 1933, drew nearer, the master's thesis precipitated a major personal upheaval of the kind often to attend Olson writing ordeals to come. The longer he put off beginning the big job he'd committed himself to, the more he suffered from internal stress of self-demand. He worried, lost sleep, fell ill and underwent minor sinus surgery early in the year; then in the spring, still struggling to get the thesis underway, he collapsed with exhaustion and a bad case of flu. A week's rest in the college infirmary provided a necessary restorative and turning point. Upon his emergence, feeling mentally and spiritually "starved," he went back to his room and threw himself down on his cot to read Melville's tale "Benito Cereno." From this "vivid entry," the thesis began to develop. He had soon gotten through all of the writer's work, scratched up what he could of the life, and even traveled to the New York Public Library to pursue a biographical lead in Melville's letters to Evert Duyckinck. A month before his deadline there was a minor emergency brought on by a term paper on "Whitman and the Orient" due for a graduate seminar, but once it was over the writing of the thesis began in earnest. Wilbert Snow was kept in a state of suspense right down to the wire. In mid-April Charlie phoned his adviser at two in the morning requesting an immediate meeting at the professor's campus office. A sleepy-eyed Snow found the excited "stutterer to the stars" holding up a typed manuscript, which, he announced momentously, had just reached chapter eighteen. He proceeded to read that out loud. Two weeks later, Snow got another middle-of-the-night phone call, this time at three o'clock in the morning. Charlie aired his crowning chapter, linking *Moby Dick,* Shakespearan tragedy and the Greek conception of fate. His patient academic friend listened attentively. "Professors wouldn't do that for many people," Snow commented years afterward, "but you would do it for Charlie."

It was a proud moment. The ambitious book-length treatise, "The Growth of Herman Melville, Prose Writer and Poetic Thinker," was finished. It contained, as preface, "the first complete bibliography of Herman Melville ever attempted." Wilbert Snow's impassioned advocacy won over certain recalcitrant members of the thesis committee, and for his "original estimate" of Melville, Charles J. Olson, Jr., was awarded his M.A.

Driving a mail truck back in Gloucester that summer, Charlie decided there was more of a future in further research on Melville than in confronting the harsh realities of the Depression job market. The thesis work had whetted his curiosity about possible literary sources underlying *Moby-Dick,* sources which, Wilbert Snow had agreed, so far remained but a tantalizing mystery. Olson already sensed Melville had been the kind of writer he himself fancied one day becoming, an artist who "read to write," whose ability "to appropriate the work of others" was the key to a complex process of original creation. Hoping to unravel that process, he now resolved to track down Melville's personal library, an undertaking no previous researcher had attempted. He disclosed the plan to Snow, who went again on his behalf to Wesleyan president McConaughy. The only university research funds available at the moment were earmarked for work in economics, but Snow again prevailed, and those funds—a total of $900—were written over to his protégé in the form of an Olin fellowship.

With Wesleyan as home base, Charlie set forth that autumn on a quest through the Northeast for books once owned by Melville. Much of the early going took place in Cambridge, Massachusetts, where he stumbled onto his first lucky break, gaining the trust of Melville's granddaughter Eleanor Metcalf. After a few visits, his obvious love of her ancestor's books, along with his natural charm, had won him unqualified acceptance into this good woman's Grey Gardens East household, where he was welcomed as a sort of surrogate family member by her husband, Harry, and their sons, David and Paul, given a standing dinner invitation, a bed to sleep in whenever he was in Cambridge, and, most usefully of all, a direct pipeline to the Melville family papers. Among Eleanor's keepsakes was a file of ancient reviews of her grandfather's many books. One afternoon, sitting in the Metcalfs' parlor idly leafing through the tattered, yellow-edged old clippings, Charlie came across an item that caught his eye, a few lines in a nineteenth-century French review of one of Melville's novels. Slowly piecing together the meaning with his imperfect French, he saw that the reviewer was reporting a personal encounter with Melville's brother-in-law, a man named Lemuel Shaw. Shaw, according to the article, had revealed an intimate knowledge of the writer and his work. Charlie went into the kitchen and asked Eleanor about Lemuel Shaw, and whether he'd left any papers. She made a phone call. Within an hour he was witnessing the opening of some dusty cartons at the Massachusetts Historical Society. The Shaw archive contained personal testimony of a close confidant who therein "confirmed all Melville's experiences in the Pacific, 1847," as Olson noted. This find was his real baptism in Melville research, and in original scholarship.

Eleanor Metcalf's help had soon led him to his project's decisive contact, her sister, Mrs. A. D. Osborne of East Orange, New Jersey. Charlie and a friend made the drive to East Orange over slick, icy back roads one freezing Sunday in December. The hair-raising ride was forgotten as soon as he had laid eyes on ninty-five volumes once personally owned by Melville. Mrs. Osborne allowed him to carry them off. Many of the books, he soon found, contained marginal annotations in a strange, barely legible pencil script— Melville's private shorthand. These annotations, once deciphered, would shed essential light on Melville's use of other writers, from immediate contemporaries to classics. Some would be shared by Olson with fellow scholars. Melville's notes on works by Hawthorne and Emerson, for example, would prove of substantial value to Harvard professor F. O. Matthiessen, who would employ them in his book *American Renaissance.* The real treasure, however, Charlie reserved for himself: Melville's Shakespeare, a seven-volume edition set in the "glorious great type" that had allowed the weak-eyed author to read the plays for the first time in 1849, at a crucial point in his development, only months before starting *Moby-Dick.* The annotations of the tragedies, especially *King Lear,* provided clinching evidence for his view of Melville as creatively engaged with a "usable past." They documented, furthermore, a process of imaginative conversion, a pivotal shift from a naturalistic narrative approach to the larger symbolic dimensions of tragedy and myth. Melville had produced his own Lear in Ahab. *Moby Dick,* concluded Olson with no little excitement, had been "precipitated by Shakespeare."

He resumed the hunt in New York in the spring of 1934, sleeping in YMCAs and plodding from bookshop to bookshop in a persistent search he later compared to a pig's rooting for truffles. After running into many blind alleys, he turned up a helpful ally in John Anderson, a 23rd Street dealer who had handled some of Melville's books after the writer's death in 1891. Anderson directed him to A. F. Farnell, another dealer. Farnell, who had taken off a large cartload of those books, reported he'd sold some to the Brooklyn Public Library, others to a family named Hennessey who lived—as the humble researcher noted—in "some pretentious part of Brooklyn." At the Public Library Charlie identified Melville's copy of Thomas Wharton's *History of English Literature,* at the Hennesseys' his copy of Bishop Thomas Fuller's *The Holy State and the Profane State.* Later the trail took him back north to Massachusetts, where further volumes appeared in Melville's hometown of Pittsfield. Another tip led him to South Yarmouth, where he found somebody who knew how to lay hands on Melville's set of Lord Byron. Though his meager resources kept him from following out every last lead, by June 1934 he had managed to locate 124 books, the heart of Melville's library.

While all this dogged bibliographic tracking kept the scholar occupied, the frustrated artist in Olson began to show signs of rebellion. One cold

January evening after a sleepy research session with Melville papers in "cas-trated Cambridge," he ducked out to a greasy spoon for a midnight ham-burger and sat on at the counter afterwards to complain in his journal of a "constipation" of expression he felt was stifling him. Assailed by similar anx-ieties back in Middletown a few weeks later, he fretted that his current lack of "creative flair" would doom him forever to the secondary role of mere critic and footnoter. That May, following more worrying over the creativity question, he made a pilgrimage to Melville's last resting place at Woodlawn Cemetery in the Bronx, hoping for a sudden infusion of inspiration. He planned to fling himself down on the hallowed grass over Melville's remains, but, approaching the grave, noticed it was cloaked in a daunting tangle of ivy, and held back.

> Even nature seemed ready to challenge my presumption in hoping to come close to Herman Melville. It was chastening to be so near his bones and the dust of his bones and be no closer. . . . I proposed to uncover his mind and soul quite as ruthlessly from the grave of his books and letters as though I had struck a spade into the soft turf there this afternoon. I had hoped to be like Ishmael—
> "And I only am escaped to tell thee,"
> to tell of Ishmael's father. God, how I was humbled.

By this time the earnest pilgrim had come to view his existence within the confines of academia as but a cloistered shadow-reality. Writing at least offered a "road into life." He continued to daydream about doing a big book on Melville, something free-ranging, sweeping and original. By summer, however, the 'Olin money had evaporated. The writing would have to be delayed. He accepted a modest $1,000-a-year teaching position at Clark Uni-versity, a respectable liberal arts school in his hometown Worcester.

In his new post he soon found himself more than ever dulled by the humdrum grind of academia. Serving at once as freshman English instructor, debate coach and assistant dramatic instructor left him little time for getting on with the Melville work that lay dormant in his research files. In truth the research files had become a burden to him also. "The task I've set myself—the reconstruction of Melville's library—is one for the pale usher," he admit-ted in an after-dinner speech to a Melvilleans' gathering at Pittsfield that October. His two years of treading water at Clark were a time of growing uneasiness. Sporadic attempts at political involvement—leading discussion groups on socially conscious plays (like *Waiting for Lefty* and *Awake and Sing*), delivering occasional speeches at campus rallies—did little to relieve his dis-content. He lamented the bloodlessness of the university environment, its "terrible plague . . . the Fifth Horseman, pernicious anemia of the mind." Clark's English faculty seemed as "bodyless and dead as French aristocrats on the pikes of revolutionists." In notebook confessions, however, he himself appeared in a not much better light. Having exhausted his former "show 'em" drive, he was now suffering from the damaging effects of a "loose backbone."

At Oceanwood Cottage in the summer of 1935, he relinquished his post office duties in favor of the rhythms of the great biological up-and-down. For three long, idle vacation months at the shore, he was reduced to a passive "lie-abed, feather-flounder, mattress-mauler, pillow-lover, sleep-squeezer, day-killer." He decided there were only four things in life he still "loved completely to do: read, cinematego, theatrigo, eat." Beguiled by "do-nothingness," he wondered if all his busy pushing for worldly success and recognition had been but so much futile gnawing toward the grave. "To be, only to be, to pluck the petals of a lotus flower from red dawn to red dawn by a blue sky forever," seemed to make more immediate sense.

Among the casualties of this do-nothing phase was his connection with Barbara Denny. Having latterly arrived at the conclusion Babs was too "middle class" for him, he'd allowed the romance to lag, and during that slow summer they officially split up. In the aftermath of the break, Barbara charged him with coldness, with hiding inside himself and retreating from feeling behind a mask of self-sufficiency. For once he found himself hard put to come up with a good answer. Placing the blame for the failure of the relationship on the young woman, for being too narrow and conventional, and smugly congratulating himself for having "finally rid myself of her sterility," was not quite enough to dispel his "shame at the years wasted." It would take him years to admit to himself that there had been unacknowledged emotional conflicts on his part that had impeded the romance with Barbara all along. Primary among these was the resistance of Karl, whose instinctive distrust of her had been a constant strain on Charlie's relations with the girl.

The disagreement over Barbara was but one aspect of worsening father / son relations. Karl's trouble at work and decline in morale following the 1920 Plymouth trip continued to cast a pall over the whole household, and Charlie's own increasing immersion in a far-off world of books and ideas further widened the distance between them. The final breakup with Babs, however, helped bring about a temporary thaw between father and son. During the short-lived reconciliation they spent a day together at Karl's favorite fishing spot outside the Gloucester Harbor breakwater. On the morning of the outing, Charlie woke up suffering from an outbreak of nasty skin sores that had turned his face into a "well-diseased biscuit." Karl, meanwhile, appeared haggard and worn, older-looking than his son had ever seen him. Charlie was moved, and though little was actually said that day in the boat, he sensed Karl was trying to communicate with him somehow—if only through the motions of his familiar, "incoherent" yet expressive hands, fumbling with the tackle box. He himself experienced a sudden upwelling of "innocent," "stupid" childish love, that all-encompassing "Black sea" in which he had once been able to drown his fears.

But the brief rapprochement was followed a month later by a much less happy episode between father and son. Karl was to attend a national convention of mail carriers in Cleveland. On the Monday morning of his departure from Oceanwood, he woke his son at dawn to ask for the loan of a suitcase. It was Charlie's pride-and-joy European-trip bag, with the cosmopolitan steamship labels. He declined curtly, saying he had plans to use it himself, then turned over and went back to sleep. Karl left in an angry mood. He had to stop off in Worcester to catch up with his postal-union paperwork before heading on to the convention. While at home he became unwell. On Thursday a stroke paralyzed his right side. Charlie and Mary rushed to his hospital bedside. Still conscious, a stunned, embittered Karl communicated by signs with Mary, but refused to acknowledge his son's presence. On Saturday, August 31, a second stroke caused heart failure. Karl went into the ground of Worcester's Swedish cemetery without having yielded his son a last paternal blessing. The denial of the suitcase, imaginatively transformed into a symbolic act of parricide, was still haunting Charlie years later.

Karl was gone at fifty-three, far "too soon," as his son would one day say in a poem. After clearing out the Norman Avenue flat, Charlie returned to his drone duties in the academic assembly line at Clark, feeling more stagnant and restive than ever. A $90-a-month raise left him still unable to contribute more than a few dollars to the upkeep of his widowed mother, now nearing her mid-sixties and barely getting by on Karl's post office pension, supplemented by a small income from summer boarders at Oceanwood. The uninsulated cottage had never been suitable for winter occupation, and now a new cold-weather home for her had to be found. That October she moved in with a Worcester spinster lady named Nora Reidy, Charlie's baptismal godmother.

Following Karl's death, the bereaved son went through a period of guilty depression and introspection. He brooded over his loneliness and failure, conscious of a "pathological disappointment" with himself. Eventually, however, there appeared surprising signs of change. At twenty-four, he belatedly discovered the secret pleasures of masturbation, and "came through sexually" with a woman for the first time. He was dating several local Worcester girls, one of whom, a poor Catholic girl named Ann, administered his actual sexual initiation after only a brief display of resistance. The conquest itself brought unexpected sensations of disgust. He momentarily concluded Ann must be a "nympho," and experienced a strong impulse to get away from her. But his "first woman" was less easily dispelled from his dreams, where the pale, consumptive girl became a White Queen whose very fragility lent her a strange, luminous sexual desirability. He went on seeing her now and then, convinced the source of her attraction for him came from her seeming a "soft & white" reincarnation of the young Mary Hines.

By the spring of 1936, nearing the end of his second long, unproductive year at Clark, Olson had decided it was high time to pull together his "unorganized life" and begin his big Melville book in the only way available to him, as a Ph.D. thesis. He applied to Harvard graduate school, was admitted as a doctoral candidate, and with F. O. Matthiessen's help secured a teaching assistantship. While waiting at Oceanwood for the fall term to start, he attempted another step toward self-improvement, fulfilling a lifelong ambition by going to sea.

"A Man's life of any worth is a continual allegory." The mature Olson liked to quote that Keats line, and to view his own life from the same kind of parabolic vantage. In his personal allegory, the spur-of-the-moment gesture of hiring himself out as a sailor was both a "keeping the faith with Melville" and an act of appeasement directed toward the restless ghost of Karl Olson. In his boyhood, Karl's influence had caused him to keep scrapbooks of famous maritime exploits, great races, catches and rescues at sea. It was therefore only natural that "true sailors" had become the heroes of his first collegiate creative-writing efforts, imitations of the storytellers of the Gloucester wharves, with anecdotal content taken from local sources like James B. Connolly's *The Book of the Gloucester Fishermen*. Death at sea had long seemed to Charlie a particularly powerful theme. His early one-act play *The Fish Weir*, published in the Wesleyan literary magazine, concerned a young fisherman's drowning, with heavy sentimental weight put on a family tragedy theme borrowed from his favorite dramatist of the moment, Eugene O'Neill. *The Fish Weir* was more revealing as psychological document than as literary work, clearly betraying the neophyte author's dread of sailing on the open ocean.

Before entering Harvard, he had something to prove to himself. On the first Tuesday after Independence Day holiday he went down to the waterfront to look for a job on one of the local commercial vessels. His hope was to find a place aboard Captain Jimmie "Gracious" Abbott's historic *Ruth and Margaret,* built for sail just after the turn of the century and still the pride of the Gloucester fleet. But Abbott's boat was still out at sea, so he tried the Atlantic Supply Company wharf on Harbor Cove, where wharf manager Ben Pine, a hero to him ever since the thrilling week in 1923 when Pine's *Columbia* had bested a Canadian boat to take the International Fisherman's Cup, was able to help him out. Pine provided an introduction to Captain Cecil Moulton of the swordfishing schooner *Doris M. Hawes,* who signed him on as a deckhand for a three-week voyage to begin early the next morning. Charlie couldn't believe his good luck. Swordfishing, with pulpit on bowsprit, harpooner, masthead sights and the timeless excitement of the chase, was, he felt sure, "as close as you can come to old American whaling."

When he returned to the harbor late that night shouldering his sea kit, he found the *Hawes* resting serenely at anchor in the moonlight with all hands benignly drunk below deck. Within hours the schooner was under way, moving over a soft southwest swell toward "the Banks," rich fishing shoals of the northwestern Atlantic from which Gloucester drew its livelihood—Brown's Bank, due east of Cape Ann, and the larger Georges Bank, 190 miles off Cape Cod. "Brown's" and "Georges," later sacred precincts of his *Maximus,* would be visited by Olson just this once. Clearly aware of the uniqueness of the opportunity, he was ready to make the most of it, setting out armed with a fresh journal, pens, pencils, and even a camera.

After an impatient week of learning the ropes, the eager but inexperienced "college feller" got his first real taste of action when appointed to stand a watch at the wheel in the midst of a heavy easterly blow. He survived it, and by the end of the watch was getting around deck on newfound sea legs that allowed him to "piss to the wind-ard so that never a drop spatters the taffrail." Mounting a lookout's watch aloft two days later, he spied his "first fish" and yelled a warning to the harpooner. Moments later, he saw the catch "ironed and bleeding the blue depths red." Before long, squinting flat into the low late-afternoon sun, he called out a second strike. After this catch there was a flurry of comment from his seemingly appreciative crewmates. The greenhorn's blood "ran with joy." (He would later be embarrassed to learn that there had been a condescending element in the fishermen's show of approval: by looking directly into the sun's glare he had violated a cardinal rule of the swordfish watchman, and only luck had saved him from damaging his eyes.) He watched proudly, and took pictures, as his fish were stripped of their swords and lashed to the stern of the *Hawes,* to be "borne home like scalps or like the nuts of a bull, to be eaten, to be drunk, to be divided" (in his journal he solemnly echoed Eliot's "Gerontion"), and as the sun went down lingered on the still-bloody deck to commemorate the closing of this epic day with florid Miltonic similes calculated to rival Melville's grand style and "character heroic."

When foggy weather idled the fishing fleet, Charlie had a chance to row over to Captain Abbott's fabled *Ruth and Margaret* for an inspection tour. Newman Shea, the *Hawes'* pipe-smoking elder and one of Charlie's favorite characters on board, accompanied him as guide. Shea was a former president of the Gloucester Fishermen's Union. According to waterfront legend, he had once been charged with stealing a crew's pay. But he now kept the *Hawes'* books, and was known to be one of the ship's most able men, sharp-eyed, sure-handed and reliable under pressure. Because Shea had once "talked Cunrudd" with him during a dawn watch, the literary-minded Charlie couldn't help studying the veteran seaman for traces of some Conradesque tragic flaw. As they rowed back and forth between the becalmed boats in a dory, the young man tried to sneak a glance into Shea's eyes, searching for "the shape [of the] man's fault." At sea, human behavior had a way of seeming to him starkly etched; men of the *Hawes* like Shea would one day become clear moral emblems in his poetry.

During the weather-induced lull, Olson was also elected to employ his long arms in rowing the captain around the fleet on traditional social rounds. The welcome chore brought him his first awed look at another legend, skipper Carl Olsen of the *Raymonde*. Olsen epitomized Gloucester's indigenous strain of fearless, hard-drinking sea captains; in a celebrated episode, he had once rescued a half-drowned dory-mate, after their boat had capsized in a blizzard, by heaving him in a fireman's lift over one shoulder and making a three-mile swim through heavy seas. The fifty-year-old captain was also famed for his acute vision—"the sort of eye" Olson would one day write, "which . . . knew the Peak of Brown's / as though it were his own garden." While later to be celebrated in the *Maximus* as "a giant / of the experience of being / a man," in person this legendary "Hyperion" now seemed to Charlie less hero than hulk, a "brutish creature of 6' 3 and heavy in muscle and fat," with eyes that appeared not so much acute as "animal and stupid." Still Carl Olsen's mythic aura was not diminished by such human flaws. The idealization of Gloucester's sea heroes long ago inculcated by Karl was not easily dispelled; well into the poet's maturity, they would remain for him major landmarks in "the geography of our being," in whose company he became again a tongue-tied child. "You're in the presence of the fathers, and you dwindle . . . you can only hide your eyes in the face of God."

It was to be a man among such men that he had gone to sea, as he confided in his *Hawes* journal.

Melville, I think, saw to it I went swordfishing; but I do not think he stirred me to the eastward. I suppose it was Gloucester and her people around me as a boy that, when I became a man, caused me to respect their way of life—or rather, become aware of my respect. Fishermen are like gulls, tough ones. There's a muscularity about them, not of the biceps, but of the whole stuff of man, the gut . . . a command and thus a dignity . . . over this thing we introverts grapple for and

miss and call life; they don't bother to name it but they've got it. . . . Death alone
defines life. . . . These men meet it every day, in a snapped piece of riggin', in sun
or storm, fog or moon. . . . When you come to grips with death you've got more
of a hold. . . . I guess I came to sea to live with men who unawares do that every
day even though I know myself I will continue to live landed and civilized.

If he was fated to live a landed life, he could at least gain vitality in his
writing by paying close attention to the "Elizabethan vigor" of such men's
talk. In bunk and galley he scribbled "nervous notes," smuggling choice snip-
pets of "the sea's vocabulary": "mug up," "shag-locker," "deadeye," "marlin'
spike," "gooseneck," "hook block." Translating the natural metaphors of his
shipmates' Cape Breton down-east dialect took up whole pages of his journal.
"Bone in her teeth," for instance, meant "the vessel is breaking a foam under
her bow on both sides," and "put a jib on the blood" was Newman Shea's
colorful way of saying "pass the catsup." (The Shea phrase would one day
make it into Olson's "Projective Verse" as elemental illustration of the poetic
principle of "syntax as passage of force.")

In quieter shipboard moments Charlie kept busy copying out the *Hawes'*
purchase accounts and compiling lists of nautical knowledge, loading up his
journal with potentially useful data about seabirds' habits and the price of
coffee, tidal patterns and engine horsepower. By the third week of the voyage, however, there came a certain ebbing in the power of the lore and lingo
of the sea to occupy him. This was in some part due to a declining variety in
the topics under discussion belowdecks. The fishermen's talk narrowed down
to one recurring subject, the whores of Boston and Ipswich, "cunts and clap,
crabs and syphilis." Tired of recording such stuff, Charlie lapsed back into his
chronic landlubber's angst. He was, he decided, a hopeless misfit in this floating club of the fathers. "The more I read & write, the less I'm liked by these
men, men who respect the hand more than the mind, so that a boy of 14
who whittles out the model of a vessel is more to be liked than a boy of 24
who listens & is sometimes seen writing in a notebook suspiciously, quietly."
Above all else, in his mind, it was his furtive journal-keeping, symbol of a
guilty introversion, that set him apart. In point of fact he more than measured
up physically to the "true sailors" of the *Hawes,* being the biggest man in a
crew of bruisers. But that great raw size, he now feared, did not conceal an
inner inferiority, the relative deficiency of his maleness in psychic terms. The
real "hell of a tall man's life" was internal.

His brave show of manhood, put on to impress his more seasoned cohorts,
was nonetheless maintained to the end. In Boston, while Captain Moulton
sold the swordfish catch, Charlie joined his crewmates in an elbow-bending
session at the Bucket of Blood, a dive at the end of Fish Pier. And once back
in Gloucester, he tagged along to the informal final stop on the cruise, Bill

Callahan's tavern, for an extended last round. In his pocket was his cut of the trip's take, $50.78. His seabag, though, held the real treasures of his trip, three rolls of film and some seventy pages of journal notes. Recuperating at Oceanwood, he wrote former Wesleyan roommate John Finch to boast of his adventures at sea. He had sprouted an impressive beard, he told Finch, eaten with "the belly of a Falstaff," and tasted the joys "of a physical, simple world of men without women."

4

Killer-Place
(1936–1939)

The cloudy, introspective side of Charlie's nature, the bothersome discordant element that had made him feel "out of joint" even at sea, closed in more and more upon resumption of his sedentary scholar's life. Back in Gloucester that August he continued to be haunted by old specters—his loneliness, the loss of his father—as well as by new fears and self-doubts generated by thoughts of Harvard and the accelerated "intellectual war" that lay ahead. Still unsettled, and now dominating his thoughts, was the central career dilemma of recent years. Academia and writing loomed as diverging and apparently irreconcilable paths. Already he sensed he would have to opt decisively for one or the other if he was ever to move forward, but the backboneless state of "vitiated will" in which Karl's death had left him made all large choices problematic. At this crossroads, a new forceful guide entered his life, supplying the instigation, direction and support once provided by his lost father. The fateful stranger was Edward Dahlberg, whose ultimate role in his life allegory, as Olson would one day come to acknowledge, was nothing less than to have "sprung me from the educators" and "taught me how to write."

Although only ten years his senior, in terms of writing and world experience Dahlberg had already advanced light-years beyond Charlie, the uncertain beginner. His grimly autobiographical social realist novels told the story of an unusually traumatic childhood. Illegitimate son of an itinerant lady

barber, he had spent much of his youth in a squalid neo-Dickensian orphanage. The accumulated scars and bruises of these early years still showed in a
sensitive, touchy and bitter temperament regarded even by friends as somewhere between difficult and impossible. Largely self-educated and convinced
by a brief encounter with "canonized illiteracy" at Berkeley and Columbia
that "anybody who had read twelve good books knew more than a doctor of
philosophy," Dahlberg had set out to fortify himself against further hard
knocks by saturating himself thoroughly in the ancient classics, a process that
was now facilitating his transformation as a writer, from the tin-can realist
style and "repulsive consciousness" of works like *Bottom Dogs* (1930) and
From Flushing to Calvary (1932)—prime specimens of a new "literary Marx
Brothers" proletarianism to which Olson had devoted a studious college essay—
to a uniquely parabolic, Biblical, recondite prose of mythic paradigm and
fable which he was at this point still laboring to perfect. He had a reputation
as a political gadfly, his recent exit from the Communist Party having cost
him his former favorable standing with the critical sages of the left; perhaps
as a consequence, his latest novel, *Those Who Perish,* had gone virtually ignored,
and sold only two hundred copies. His current undertaking was a book one
day to be titled *Do These Bones Live,* a series of essays on the social and spiritual isolation of American writers, from Thoreau, Hawthorne, Melville and
Poe to the short-lived libertarian philosopher and hunchbacked genius Randolph Bourne. Bourne's deformity was the focus of Dahlberg's interest, source
of a perceived affinity; he himself was marked by a noticeable physical defect,
a blind eye, remnant of a condition left untreated during his orphanage years
and now a constant reminder of his victimization by fate. A "city-nomad,
hunter Jew, Ishmael" (as Olson would call him), he identified strongly with
all exiles, losers, underdogs and scapegoats. Don Quixote, that "victim of
Nature" doomed to battle the "windmills in his head," was his metaphorical
emblem of the American writer's struggle. In the "obscure youth" and mon-
ster-giant Olson, he believed he had found not only a partner in that endless
struggle against society's and nature's obstacles, but, as the early course of
their friendship indicates, a symbolic substitute for the son he lacked and had
long desired.

That August, Dahlberg had fled the dog days in Greenwich Village to
pursue his prose oracle amid Cape Ann's fresh ocean breezes. Olson was
tipped off to the visiting writer's presence in Gloucester by an academic
acquaintance who also reported on Dahlberg's recent negative review of a
popular Melville biography by Lewis Mumford, a book Olson himself disliked. Eager for some creative spark to bring him out of his doldrums, Charlie
took the initiative and went calling at the boardinghouse where Dahlberg
was holed up. To avoid a houseful of noisy holiday painters, the New York

writer had barricaded himself in his upstairs room, and Olson had to cool his heels for several hours until the ruckus in the parlor ended. When slightly after midnight Dahlberg finally descended he found himself confronted by an unlikely Gulliver "near seven foot high" with "noble brows" and "a nose finely molded by Euclid," peering down at him through large round "pedantic spectacles." Charlie, too, was faced with a startling prospect—an angular, striking wilderness prophet in mustache and sideburns, with that dead-looking eye staring out as if in baleful judgment of all the evils looked upon in a long, painful exodus from the promised land.

The exile's hardened heart proved no match for the patented Olson charm. Charlie put on his best show, demonstrating that he "knew pages of Shakespeare's *Measure for Measure, Lear, Troilus and Cressida, Timon of Athens* by rote ... had devoured *Moby Dick, Mardi,* 'The Encantadas,' 'Bartleby the Scrivener,' 'Benito Cereno,'" and even venerated that "small spermal candle in American literature" held sacred by Dahlberg, Melville's "Hawthorne and His Mosses." "Soon I gave him my complete devotion," the older man would one day ruefully recall, "immolating my own interests to his advantage."

Confident that he had discovered "a demi-god of our literature," Dahlberg began issuing proud announcements in letters to New York friends like the photographer Alfred Stieglitz, portraying young Olson as a "porous personality" sure to "do something with his life." When in subsequent talks Charlie revealed his anxieties about going up to Harvard, Dahlberg was quick to exhibit paternal apprehensions, telling Stieglitz, "I should hate to see him get in difficulties and not know where to turn for his bread and butter." If the older man appeared to be looking for a demigod to adopt, Olson himself was not without unconscious motive. A misdirected and overactive "love of father," one day to seem to him "sexual at base" and an ominous sign of "psyche unresolved," now inclined him to surrender with little resistance to his solicitous, insistent new friend's powerful intellectual sway.

A journal he inaugurated on September 1, three weeks into their budding relationship, provides a graphic record of "Dahlberg nudges." Its first entry lists readings on politics and history prescribed by the more experienced writer to cure Olson's "socio-politico-economico naivete": Bourne's *Untimely Papers* and *History of a Literary Radical,* works on or by Marx, Lenin and Hitler, and two books on the history of the Americas by Dahlberg's friend Waldo Frank, a radical cultural critic and editor of the *New Republic.* Charlie was also prescribed a cram course on myth, starting with Frazer's *Golden Bough* and Jane Harrison's *Ancient Art and Ritual.* During this initial impressionable phase, even his prose style took on a mimetic coloration. In a letter written to Dahlberg upon the latter's return to New York in early September, he adopted the caustic tone of Dahlberg's own prose jeremiads, professing a "Timon-like hate" for the vulgar cosmetic modernity of an America corrupted by empty Hollywood visions and "Max Factor faces." Dahlberg responded warmly, encouraging him to get on with the Melville book he wanted to write. "Inaction spawns inferiority. . . . Remember, start work. . . . I believe in you." Confidence, it already appeared to his concerned mentor, was going to be a critical commodity for Olson as a writer; for all his bluff and brilliance, he did not yet seem to have found it in himself.

Advances would not come easy to Charlie in Cambridge. Exchanging the comfortable security of Oceanwood Cottage for Harvard's coldly imposing red brick and hoary gray stone, he needed every shred of self-belief he could summon. He took up digs with a trusted friend, John Finch, in a small apartment not far from Memorial Hall. Finch was now a Harvard graduate student in English. Charlie himself was entering as a Ph.D. candidate in the university's new American Civilization program. The program's promising blueprint for a convergence of three interrelated disciplines, literature, history and sociology, was in fact the main thing that had drawn him to Harvard at this time. It offered, in his rather hopeful envisaging, a place outside the traditional English-oriented academic stronghold, where that perennial neglect of American studies which he had once decried in a Wesleyan commencement speech as a "thorn in our educational flesh" could finally be removed, allowing his idol Melville equal footing with the classics.

Unlike most Harvard men, Olson would have no family financial cushion to fall back on; his own upkeep, such as it was, would have to come solely from his piecemeal wages as a teaching assistant. He was assigned to read and grade class essays and exam papers for English 7, the American literature survey presented jointly to students at Harvard and Radcliffe. Instead of receiving a base salary as he had at Clark, he was now to be paid a set fee for each blue book graded, an arrangement that placed great importance on organizing time and accomplishing dull routine tasks—never his forte. With up to 250 students per term crowding the survey sections, there was more than enough of the grading piecework to go around; Charlie's difficulty lay not in finding work, but keeping up with his allotted share. Old problems of oversleeping and procrastinating returned to haunt him. His inability to face the growing pile of blue books became a matter of amusement to roommate Finch, a reader in the same course. Olson's chronic "slight hypochondria," Finch recalls, had a way of intensifying dramatically as end-of-term due dates loomed and the stack of ungraded blue books on his desk mounted. It was then his bad teeth and sinuses always seemed to act up, driving him to his bed in apparent misery but also creating a convenient pretext for further work avoidance. Finally, late on the eve of the last deferred deadline, able to escape the grim chore no longer, he would install himself in the flat's warmest room, the bathroom. Bundled in heavy sweater and shawl to ward off dangerous drafts, the heat turned all the way up, he would stay there until sometime around daylight he'd finished off the last blue book.

Such eccentric work habits, reflective of Olson's unique physical and emotional makeup, with its peculiar cyclic rhythms, were not at all tailored to the achievement of ultimate success in academia. Moreover, they could hardly be blamed on the influence of his most significant Harvard role models, his four survey directors, Professors F. O. Matthiessen, Ellery Sedgwick, Jr., Kenneth Murdock and Perry Miller. All possessed impeccable academic credentials as well as considerable eminence in the emerging field of American studies.

Matthiessen, soon to earn recognition as a master of that field with his grand work *American Renaissance*—and acknowledged by Olson as the top Melville man on campus—was a complex and divided man, leading a precarious triple life as High Church Anglican scholar-academic, radical political activist and private homosexual. A founding member of the Harvard Teachers' Union, he carried over his political convictions into the classroom. In his American literature courses, he proposed a version of the nation's literary history that weighed the hopeful democratic assertiveness of Whitman and Emerson against the tragic insight and vision of Melville, Hawthorne and T. S. Eliot (on whom he had just published an appreciative critical study). Olson signed up for a Matthiessen seminar in the spring of his first Harvard year. In his term paper for the course, he adopted his teacher's counterbalanced principles, the democratic and the tragic, to shape his own definition of Melville's "democratic prose tragedy."

Though in a poem he would one day acknowledge Matthiessen as an early motivating figure ("the cause, the cause"), Olson appears to have harbored some reservations about his academic mentor from early on. To start with, the popular professor—"Matty," to students and friends—was surrounded by an inner circle of disciples whose effete sophistication made Olson uneasy, causing him to keep his distance. Perhaps equally a factor was an unstated, subtle but real territorial rivalry over Melville, a predictable result of the unusual reversal of roles that had taken place when Olson became Matthiessen's student after earlier providing him original research materials. (The acknowledgment of his work on Melville's reading in a respectful footnote in *American Renaissance* would do little to slake his unrealistic expectations of a more extensive credit.) He sometimes found it difficult to restrain himself from publicly challenging Matty on the subject of Melville—and actually did so on at least one memorable occasion. Inspired by beer and the heat of the conversational moment, he stunned the soft-spoken professor of English by boldly declaring across the bar at Clancy's, a faculty watering hole, that he intended nothing less than to "re-write *Moby-Dick*."

Later to be associated with Matthiessen in Olson's memories of Harvard was a second survey director toward whom he felt a less qualified sympathy, W. Ellery Sedgwick, Jr. Sedgwick and Matthiessen had much in common: both were delicate, troubled, brilliant men, both were dedicated Melvilleans, and both ended up, in Olson's mind, as long-term symbols of the damage done sensitive souls by the academic and institutional life, especially as lived in New England. A particularly disturbing personal parallel for Olson in Sedgwick's case was their shared Catholic background. But Sedgwick's own family pedigree was otherwise considerably more distinguished: he was the scion of a prominent New England literary family and son of a former editor of the *Atlantic Monthly*. As his teaching assistant in the Radcliffe section of the American literature survey during the 1936 fall term, Olson came to know "Young El" quite well. A shy and retiring man, Sedgwick was content to remain in Matthiessen's shadow as a Melville expert even though occupied with developing his own view of Melville's "tragedy of the mind" in an original critical study (it would not appear until after his premature demise). In Olson's eyes, the actual tragedy seemed Sedgwick's own, in being the victim of a desperate Harvard intellectual "rat race" that drove him into psychoanalysis, drinking problems, and eventually suicide. As early as his first fall term, the pressure of the competitive struggle was affecting Olson as well, allowing him real insight into his friend and teacher's plight. (They were eventually to leave Harvard in distress at around the same time.)

The fledgling Ph.D. program in American Civilization had actually been the brainchild not of Matthiessen or Sedgwick but of two other colleagues, program chairman Kenneth Murdock, senior professor of English, respected literary historian and seventeenth-century scholar, and Perry Miller, brash, brilliant young revisionist historian of Puritanism. While the curriculum of the program bore equally the imprint of both men, it was Miller, an atheist and existentialist, "romantic tough guy" and "learned Hemingway," who had the greater personal impact on its general style and direction. Henry Nash Smith, a young Texan joining Olson in the program in 1937, would later describe Miller as "a much more important influence" than even Matthiessen on Harvard's graduate Americanists of the period. His survey lectures and popular seminar were a forum for historical ideas advanced in his *Establishment of Orthodoxy in Massachusetts* (1934). Miller's fresh perspective on the early New England fathers was strongly affected by his existentialist leanings. Beneath the iron determinism of Jonathan Edwards he made out a philosopher's imaginative depth, a heroic stoicism behind the Puritan rigidity. Olson, by now highly doubtful about the cultural heritage of the Puritan ethic, was distrustful of Miller and his views, which he regarded as little more than an intellectual apologia for the cruel, repressive "new englandism" he was already beginning to hold responsible for the slowness of his own emotional and creative development. Once, during an informal coffee-break debate, he tangled with Miller over the prose style of Whitman, whose *Specimen Days* he held up as a salutary corrective to the Puritans' agonies of conscience. The episode confirmed Olson's status as oddball of the American Civilization group.

By the end of his first fall term he was complaining in letters to Edward Dahlberg of the intellectual frigidity and merciless academic competitiveness of Harvard. He felt an "outcast" in Cambridge, recipient of "no sympathy or understanding, only the chill of jealousy and hate." Dahlberg wrote back to commiserate, recommending perseverance and advising Charlie to employ his personal charm in counteracting those hostile academic "blizzards and profound psychical wastes and moraines." He also continued to exhort his young protégé to get started on his Melville book, now beginning to show a friendly impatience with Charlie's stalling. It was imperative, Dahlberg advised, to ignore everything, even classwork, that posed a distraction from the one truly important task at hand. "Write!" he insistently admonished. Once Charlie had produced a manuscript, he promised, he himself would take care of the rest, doing whatever was necessary to find a place in print for it. This was no hollow assurance; Dahlberg still had the publishing contacts to back it up. One of them, Alfred Stieglitz' close companion Dorothy Norman, a wealthy young art patroness and aspiring poet, had lately offered him an editorial role in the founding of a major international literary magazine, *Twice A Year*. When Olson came down from Harvard to New York for a visit that fall, Dahlberg took him around to Stieglitz' Madison Avenue gallery, An American Place, to meet the owner and the cast of literary professionals who congregated there, including culture critic Waldo Frank, poet William Carlos Williams, novelists Theodore Dreiser, Sherwood Anderson and Ford Madox Ford. To Olson, rubbing shoulders with such longtime heroes seemed an exhilarating foretaste of triumphs to come.

Other escape routes from academia's frozen wastes were also opening up. Flight from the cruel God of the Calvinists led Charlie and John Finch into the more congenial haunts of goddesses of dance up and down the East Coast. At burlesque halls like the Old Howard in Boston and the Irving Place in New York they indulged a taste for sophisticated striptease, one shared, moreover, by certain of their academic superiors. It was not uncommon, for instance, for them to spy in the comfortable darkness of those theaters such dignified figures as Professors Murdock and Sedgwick, fellow connoisseurs of the "highbrow" art of strip dancing—a form that in fact seems to have contributed no little to Olson's conception of the dramatic arts, which would remain for him much less a matter of structure than of spectacle. (In an adult essay on the theater, he would hark back nostalgically to his infatuation with burlesque during these years, objectified in his memory by such significant images as "the scar on Ann Corio's belly.") Concurrently he and Finch also nursed a passionate interest in the ballet, a flame originally kindled during their Wesleyan days by close study of Lincoln Kirstein's dance articles in *Hound & Horn* and during this winter of 1936 heated up to new levels by attendance at performances of virtually every European touring company graced with Kirstein's critical imprimatur. One particularly enchanting evening spent under the spell of Léonide Massine's symphonic ballet *Les Présages* danced by the Ballet Russe de Monte Carlo was sufficient to make them devoted acolytes of the "luminous genius" Massine and of the Monte Carlo company's several star ballerinas, with all of whom they fell in love at once. Before long the ballet was making substantial inroads on Charlie's carefully calculated monthly budget. In November of 1936, for example, his solemnly irresponsible pact with Finch to pursue the Monte Carlo company "to Providence, to Worcester, to New York, Philadelphia, Land's End," set him back almost $30 in ticket costs, an amount equal to his half share of their rent for the month.

The roommates' balletomania crested in a series of encounters with Ballet Russe principals. They approached the company's male lead, Marc Platoff, while he was eating lunch in a Waldorf cafeteria. Much to their surprise, the dancer, whom they'd presumed to be Russian, turned out not only an American but an avid college football fan, who complained he had missed getting the scores of that day's games because of his matinee duties. The Harvard men offered to serve as gridiron heralds. During the final weeks of the college season they lingered in the wings to relay the latest scores every Saturday afternoon. The backstage friendship with Platoff led them in turn to the revered Léonide Massine, who spent a few minutes conversing with them. Massine spoke of what it meant to be an artist, "how hard it was, and how fine," and then invited them to tell him something about America. Charlie plunged into an effusive speech about Melville.

The roommates threw a cocktail party at their humble Cambridge flat to celebrate the completion of the company's American tour. They spent several days preparing. On the afternoon appointed for the momentous event there was a snowstorm, and the professional guests of honor were late. As Professors Murdock and Sedgwick looked on in amusement, nervous host Olson fretted by the window. Finally a cab crawled down the icy street and pulled up outside. Olson raced into the snow to greet his guests, neglecting, in his excitement, to don his overcoat. First to emerge from the taxi was the prima ballerina Danilova. While he stared agape at her silk-stockinged legs lithely unfolding from the backseat, the Russian dancer smiled up at her host and said, in a tone he mistook to be seductive, "Oh, you must be very *hot!*" When in the next moment it sank in that she was merely referring to his lack of a coat, the bottom dropped out of this near-climax to Charlie's most intense ballet season.

The several arts simultaneously beckoned, as he now settled into a phase of manic escapist dilettantism. *Les Présages,* for example, spurred a craze for Tchaikovsky—a composer Olson "never got over" after a few inspiring symphony concerts attended with Finch in Boston. At the theater, their tastes were generously indiscriminate, extending to every available play, whether "tryout or touring company, O'Neill or Odets, Shakespeare or Shaw [or] George Spelvin's soggiest triangle." At this time Charlie also succumbed to a romance with art films that would soon be consuming much of his time (and much space in his notebooks). He worshiped D. W. Griffith's poetic vision, making a temporary motto of a Griffith quote ("the task I'm trying to achieve is above all to make you see"), and idolized Charlie Chaplin, a "Homer of today" (to Black Mountain students, Chaplin would one day be cited as exemplar of a typically gnomic Olson axiom, "Simplicity is not simple"). Above all other film artists, though, he ranked the revolutionary Russian formalist masters. (Eisenstein's montage technique, discovered at this time, would later help guide him to a form for his first big modernist poem, "The Kingfishers.") He joined the Harvard Film Society, and, as its best public speaker, was soon delivering introductory talks before showings. While the movies ran, undergraduate music student Leonard Bernstein provided piano accompaniment. Afterwards there was socializing. One night at a screening of Pudovkin's *Mother* in the basement of a left-wing bookshop, Charlie was introduced to an attractive young Russian-born student named Elena Zarudnaya. Over coffee later in Harvard Square, he and the girl were joined by one if his academic sidekicks, Harry Levin, a Junior Fellow in English. The two graduate students vied to impress the girl. The energetic Olson was the "star of the occasion," but in the long run his more reserved colleague prevailed; Levin eventually married the young Russian woman (and like Jack Wells at Wesleyan, would one day loom in Olson's imagination as a secret symbolic rival).

For scholar-aesthetes Olson and Finch, the radical campus politics of the period could appear an extension of life's entertaining spectacle. "Left-wing politics, ballet, film—of course we were interested," Finch now says. "Everybody was." Entering through the gates of the Yard on his way to class any morning, Charlie would have been hard put to avoid symbols of a growing international drama. Pickets urged him to sign petitions to halt some "Red" professor's firing, canvassers begged quarters for Spanish Republican ambulances, barkers hawked the *Harvard Progressive* or passed out handbills announcing the latest Student Union agitprop theater production. With war fears on the rise in Europe and poverty still gripping much of America, the air was full of instant salvation ideologies. Politics, to Olson, meant mostly a chance to talk—over cigarettes on the Widener steps, coffee at Hayes Bickford's or beers at Clancy's. Most of the questions addressed were appropriately imponderable. What was the role of the engaged academic in society? Did the traditional isolated sanctuary of the campus cut one off from participation in a broader world? What was the meaning of Spain and the Moscow Trials? Charlie's earnest but unsystematic subscription to egalitarian and pacifist views left him aligned somewhere between the radical activism of the student Marxists and the only slightly more conservative political leanings of the English faculty, at that time a "nest of WASP gentility and literary fellow-travelling." Standard Popular Front causes of the day could provoke momentary strong feelings: in topical verses dashed off on the margins of English 7 survey quiz papers, he addressed the Siege of Madrid, the fall of French Socialist premier Léon Blum, Russian pacifist diplomat Litvinov's arrival in London. His relation to political ideas, however, remained emotional, an artist's response. His self-described "Guerre Civile crisis," triggered by the enlistment of a Harvard friend in the Abraham Lincoln Brigade, lasted only until the next Dietrich movie or Hurok ballet spectacular.

Over the winter of his first year in Cambridge, Olson underwent surgery to remove a number of infected teeth. During his recuperation he retreated to Harry and Eleanor Metcalf's Grey Gardens East home. A "great colorful invalid," he was looked after by Eleanor Metcalf with the kind of solicitous maternal treatment he was used to receiving at home from Mary. At this point such care provided him a sense of security and consolation even more valuable than simple physical healing. Recognizing their unusual houseguest's sensitivity and vulnerability—that he was a self-defined "quasi-monster" with a desperate need to belong—the other Metcalf family members, including Eleanor's two teenage sons, went out of their way to make him feel at home. It was no secret that Charlie longed to be somehow "a Melville," in spirit if not in blood. That longing was made apparent to John Finch when he was asked around to Grey Gardens East to have a look at the Joseph Eaton portrait of Melville in Eleanor's front parlor; he got the impression Charlie was introducing him not merely to a writer-hero, but to a lost father. "You can't escape those eyes," Olson told his roommate melodramatically, "wherever you go, they'll follow you." (Dahlberg, too, was brought to view the Eaton portrait, an image whose power over him Olson would still be acknowledging as late as the 1960s, when he had it placed on the cover of a reprint edition of *Call Me Ishmael*.) As if to secure his projected identity as a "neo-Melville," Charlie was especially eager to establish contact with Herman Melville's single surviving child, Eleanor's mother. This elderly lady, however, harbored ill feelings toward her father's memory, and had for years refused to speak of him to anyone. Still Charlie continued to besiege Eleanor with requests to arrange a meeting, until finally she gave in and with some reluctance revealed the address of her mother's Boston apartment house. Olson, by now sufficiently recovered to attend to such crucial business (if not to attend classes), found the building and crouched in the bushes outside until the frail old personage emerged for her daily constitutional. Casting a marveling eye upon her from his hiding place, he thus at last "identified with his grandmother."

As a houseguest he was no easy proposition. Having developed into a heavy smoker, he dismayed Eleanor by leaving cigarette smoke and ashes all over the house, even the bedroom. He made free with her kitchen even when this meant waking the household in the middle of the night. His engaging personality, though, was compensation for his faults. Among the growing cast of scholars who were in this season of Melville revival converging on the Metcalf home, Olson more than held his own. In this relaxed, informal salon atmosphere he began long-lasting associations with such fellow Melville admirers as biographer Raymond Weaver, the gentle, dedicated author of *Herman Melville, Mariner and Mystic* (henceforth his favorite book on Melville), and the distinguished psychologist Henry Murray, a cofounder of the Harvard Psychiatric Institute. Both Weaver and Murray would become supportive Olson patrons, and Murray a particularly important friend. (At work for many years on a massive but never-to-be-completed psychological biography of Melville, Murray had once discussed the subject at length with Carl Jung—who in the course of their conversations elaborated on his famous poetic description of *Moby-Dick* as "the flower.") Table talk in such company always came back to the same ever-inspiring topics, Melville, *Moby-Dick,* the sea, and whale stories. Of the last, one of the most notable was Olson's tale of a group of marine biologists examining the corpse of a whale beached on Cape Cod. On the occasion of its first telling, the Metcalfs' maid, a shy, quiet Irish Catholic girl, was in the midst of serving dinner. As the tale grew more and more involved, she paused from her task to listen. Slowly Charlie reached his punch line: the story's main figure, a vanished researcher, was discovered to have slipped into the beached whale's vagina. There were roars all around the table, from everyone but Eleanor. The lady of the house "turned pink with embarrassment, for the sake of the servant."

Charlie's health problems and proclivity for distracting himself with non-academic matters made a temporary casualty of the term paper for Matthiessen on Melville's democratic tragedy. Still incomplete at the end of the 1937 spring term, the paper had to be finished—with an extension from the professor—over the summer back in Gloucester. In the fall the wayward scholar returned to Harvard, taking up a new position as instructor and tutor in modern languages at John Winthrop House. One of seven residence halls established under a new Harvard "house plan," Winthrop was modeled on the colleges of Cambridge and Oxford, affording its undergraduates living and dining facilities, common rooms, library, and a staff of in-house tutors. Olson worked under the house master (a Mr. Ferry) and a staff senior tutor, directing the academic progress of those young men of the house who were majoring in English and American literature; he assigned and graded short essays on literary themes, suggested and monitored reading, and coached slow learners through the rocky passages of their course work.

At Winthrop House, Charlie shared a comfortable suite of rooms with Henry Guerlac, a fellow tutor, enjoyed access to the senior common room liquor cabinet, and at meals received personal motherly attention from Mrs. De Pinto, the house headwaitress. (He had by now become a consummate artist at charming women who served food, a gift that would come in handy throughout his adult life.) The privileged perquisities of the house system, however, were outward symbols of a patrician social status he himself did not possess, a factor that contributed to the distance he already felt from his housemates because of his intellectual eccentricity and general "bohemian attitude," both accentuated by contrast to the genteel young private-school aristocrats around him, uniform in not only their Harris tweeds and dark gray flannel trousers but their backgrounds, tastes and attitudes. His own casual rumpled look—on his spartan budget, finding clothes to fit his gargantuan frame was always less a matter of style than of basic necessity—caused him to stand out, as did his personal habits, in particular his habitual night-owl routine, alternating as usual with much daytime sleeping. Winthrop's Irish cleaning ladies were denied access to his sleeping chambers every morning throughout the entire fall term of 1937, creating house legend. By the following spring Henry Guerlac was letting it be known that "Charlie had not changed his sheets all year." Nonetheless, despite his oddball qualities, or perhaps in part because of them, Olson was a popular tutor, particularly a hit with a handful of progressive young literary men in the house—several of whom were eventually moved to present him with a copy of *Finnegans Wake* as token recognition of his "teaching and friendship," which, they avowed, had meant more to them than anything else they'd encountered at college. The gift symbolized Olson's Winthrop House image: verbally prolific if often obscure, brilliant but disorderly, generously outlandish and overall rather baffling.

Also subtly but perceptibly setting him off from the norm was his immi-grant ethnic background, especially his Hines ancestry. In the WASP atmo-sphere of the residential houses, the Irish were at this time regarded as a barely human servant subclass; more than one of the houses exercised invisi-ble discriminatory quota systems applying not only to Jews but to Irish Cath-olics. Winthrop, the significant exception, had a substantial Irish Catholic colony, including, in Charlie's first year there, his fellow tutor John Kenneth Galbraith, a young economist, as well as several undergraduate scholar-ath-letes who were contributing to Winthrop's standing as a "jock house." In the latter class were the Kennedy boys, Joe, Jr., a senior on the varsity football squad, and John Fitzgerald, a sophomore swimmer. Neither the Kennedys' athletic prowess nor their family wealth had proved sufficient to exempt them from Harvard's anti-Irish prejudice; even though their father was United States ambassador to England, and though they had come to college accompanied by their own personal servants, the boys were quietly yet firmly denied entry to Harvard's top social clubs. Fewer barriers faced them within the polite island of comparative tolerance that was Winthrop House, where new money was given much greater sway. Olson, with no such advantages, seems to have harbored a vague grudge against these children of Power. In the fall of 1937, Joe Kennedy, acting as chairman of the House Committee, invited his famous father to give a lecture as part of a Thursday-night speaker series. Joseph Kennedy, Sr., fondly recounted his tenure on the Securities and Exchange Commission in the twenties, waxing nostalgic over the bucket shops, wire houses and pools of the unregulated stock market. Though economist Gal-braith considered it a "wonderful talk," the Kennedy version of swash-buckling, main-chance free-enterprise capitalism left Olson cold—much as would what he later perceived as a similarly mean-spirited "economic comp-tometry" in the whole Kennedy clan. In the Kennedy "glories of egotism" he perhaps made out, as early as Harvard, an object lesson in the kind of aggres-sive Celtic overcompensating to which he himself often felt prey. Rich, hand-some, socially graceful—everything he wasn't—the Kennedy boys could not help but seem to him symbolic social rivals. Jack, furthermore, proved one of his hardest tutorial cases. The young swimmer seemed out of his water in the world of literature, and in Olson's view simply "hadn't yet learned to express himself" on paper; grading papers for Howard Mumford Jones' lecture course on the novel, he gave the future president "a 'gentleman's C.' "

When inspiration moved him, he himself was capable of being a far better than average student. Rarely, however, was he so moved at Harvard, where in his three years he found only one course that excited him as much as did Ann Corio's belly, Danilova's legs or Pudovkin's *Mother*. This was one of the

American Civilization program's codisciplinary offerings, History 62: The Westward Movement in American History, taught by Professor Frederick Merk. Merk, along with Samuel Eliot Morison and Arthur Schlesinger, was a dominant figure in American history at Harvard, a "fragile and saintly man" and notoriously exacting instructor, best known for the popular Westward Movement course (called "Wagon Wheels" by students), which he'd taken over from his own former teacher, Frederick Jackson Turner, and in which he was now extending Turner's original frontier theory. It was said he rarely gave more than one two-term A in the course. Competition for that A was intense. In the last of his big "show 'em" pushes for scholastic honors, Charlie secured it in his year of Merk's "Wagon Wheels" (1937–1938). he later boasted to Black Mountain students that he had done so without taking notes, but that was far from the truth; in fact his copious class notes, which he saved and consulted later during his own researches on Melville and the Pacific frontier, survive as a model of the "saturation" method of documentary accumulation which he was to claim as Merk's legacy, the gift that above all others had made Merk a "father" to him. The class notes reveal not only the rapid development of Olson's creative apprehension of history, but the germ of an idea that would almost a decade later flower into his first book. In one lecture, Merk described the inventive agricultural experiments of early High Plains farmers, driven by restless adventurousness into Western arid lands. Thrilled by this account of archetypal American hunger and energy operating in the grand theater of space, Olson scrawled across the top of his notebook page, "for M[elville] there was always a West in the spirit as well as fact." From this classroom insight would one day emerge the poetic historiography of *Call Me Ishmael*.

The history professor was the only one of his Harvard teachers Olson kept actively in touch with after leaving Cambridge. If he would over the years speak with reverence of Frederick Merk as a "master" and "intellectual disciplinarian," it was also in tones tinged with substantial affection, out of gratitude not only for what he had taken in intellectually, but for the attitude of loving respect for the past which he felt Merk to have inculcated in him. "My heart was taught by him," he said.

Edward Dahlberg meanwhile was still pressing Olson to get going on his Melville book. After two years, all Charlie had to show for it was the Matthiessen term paper, a scholastic attempt at relating Shakespeare and *Moby-Dick*. Dahlberg urged him to rewrite that into essay form for publication, and at the same time began lobbying hard to get it accepted, sight unseen, by Dorothy Norman for *Twice A Year*. Late in 1937 Dahlberg arranged a meeting between Olson and editor Norman in Cambridge. Olson's charm quickly persuaded the editor to reserve space for his piece in her inaugural issue, where it would be featured alongside work by, among others, Stieglitz, Bourne, Nin, Dreiser, Kafka, Rilke, Malraux, Cummings, Patchen and Silone. Projected as an international journal of the arts and civil liberties, *Twice A Year* was the sort of place in which an unknown could be proud to make his literary debut.

To Olson the prospect was at once flattering and daunting; the challenge of turning his academic prose into literary style of a level suitable to match such elite company—along with concurrent pressures of graduate school and personal matters, not to mention the chronic self-demand which kept him forever in dread of coming out second-best when the chips were down— made the rewrite job very difficult to get down to. Before long his reluctance to begin work on it had turned into a phobia. As the months went by, Dahlberg simmered with impatience—coaxing, cajoling, complaining of his "nefarious silence" when he didn't answer letters. Still Charlie stalled. A further complication entered his life: a sexual liaison with a professor's wife. The woman, named Joanna, represented trouble from the start. Attractive, headstrong, impetuous and possessed of the best of Connecticut country-school pedigrees, she had a husband who was a respected member of the Harvard faculty. For Charlie the affair quickly turned into a "hornet's nest." Joanna fled her Cambridge home, and her aggrieved academic spouse hired private investigators to track her down. She hid out at the Hotel Albert in New York. Charlie followed her to the city, camping at Dahlberg's apartment on 16th Street not far from the Albert. One night as Joanna joined him for dinner there, two private-eye types appeared mysteriously outside the building. They continued to linger there, causing Charlie to grow extremely nervous. Finally it fell to another dinner guest of Dahlberg's, the anarchist painter Ephraim Doner, to come to the rescue. While Charlie left by the front door, Doner conducted Joanna back to her hotel by a perilous backyard route. Though the guilty lovers escaped detection in this "real cops and robbers" episode, soon enough the clandestine romance came to an unhappy end, at least for Charlie. Joanna took off for Reno to obtain a fast divorce, ostensibly in order to marry him. While in Nevada, however, she hitched up with a cowboy, and did not return.

His own impulsive decision to go West in the summer of 1938 was probably instigated less by thoughts of catching up with her (it appears he didn't) than by the romance of the frontier as instilled in him that spring by Frederick Merk. Left in the lurch by Joanna, he decided their affair had been bred less of love than of the restlessness and pointlessness of his treading-water existence in Cambridge. He told Dahlberg he needed a break from Harvard's artificial environment—if only to be able to experience real emotions again,

to feel at least "the sadness and the repinings of having been somewhere."
He set off by bus at the beginning of July, bound first for Kansas City, gateway to the historic Old West. He had a contact there, of sorts: Dahlberg's
mother, Lizzie, whom he so far knew only as a fictional character. Edward
had suggested he look her up. Compelled by curiosity, Charlie made his way
to the specified address, where his "best postman's knock" drew no reply at
the front door. He went around to the side, taking advantage of his height
to peer in a high window, and inadvertently spied the former lady barber
splashing away in her bath. He beat a sheepish retreat.

Hitchhiking southwest along the old Santa Fe Trail, he stopped off to
explore every Spanish mission and trading post mentioned in Merk's course.
By the time he reached the Grand Canyon, his energy was flagging. The
canyon's heroic spaces, however, inspired him to outdo himself. He struck
up an acquaintance with a touring Cambridge University historian, with whom
he scaled the Bright Angel Trail at double time in an impromptu race. The
Britisher was an accomplished outdoorsman, and Charlie was left in the dust.
At the end of the climb he felt giddy and ill. He feared he had damaged his
heart, and for some time afterward lived in dread of cardiac or circulatory
failure. His having "not enough pump" for his size would henceforth remain
a permanent worry, added to the extensive list of his hypochondriac anxieties.

Still he soldiered on to the West Coast, avoiding further strenuous physical exertions to the extent of turning down a tempting sexual solicitation in
a Seattle waterfront bar, where he was offered his pick of white, black or
Chinese girls. In his journal he attributed his restraint to the "careful Swede"
side of his nature. California, the pioneers' imagined paradise, shocked him
most with its seaminess, the reality behind the dream turning out all "real
estate projects or decay." Heading homeward after only a quick glimpse of
this disappointing promised land, he spent a few days in Salt Lake City,
making notes on the strange behavior of the Mormon natives, "missionary
rubbernecks" who shuttled tourists around their Temple grounds like park-
ing-lot attendants. At Yellowstone Park, exhaustion again closed in on him,
bringing feelings of Olympian gloom whose influence made the "Park of
holes" appear a macabre spectacle, its gaping earth-lesions morbid reminders
of "death the diseased / presence on us." Mindful of Karl's premature demise,
he wondered unhappily whether fate would allow him to "break the fatal
[Olson] male small span." He arrived back in Gloucester a dusty, weary and
still unfulfilled voyager, more concerned than ever about "the persistence of
failure" in his life.

His state of mind hardly improved back at Harvard that September. Having neglected to take care of his previous term's unpaid Winthrop House
residence bill, he found his rooms locked up and his belongings summarily

deposited in the hall. He was virtually without funds as a result of the Western trip, and soon learned that a number of his friends and favorite touches, including the most reliable, Dahlberg, were themselves going through financial difficulties. It took him a few weeks to raise a small loan and straighten matters out with house authorities. With less than a month left before the October 1 *Twice A Year* printer's deadline, his essay still remained unfinished. He began to panic, dispatching to Dorothy Norman a series of "breathless, panting, pulsating" special-delivery letters, attributing his last-minute delaying to an urgent "crisis . . . one of those personal and intimate things which demand all one's attention instantly like death." Temporarily homeless and badly in need of moral support, he had no one to fall back on but Edward Dahlberg, who was currently taking shelter from his own career storms in a cheap Boston boardinghouse. The older man offered shelter, read the latest draft of his essay and suggested cuts. Charlie rushed back to Cambridge and attempted to retype his manuscript in the backseat of a borrowed car during a heavy rainstorm, an effort that ended in soggy defeat. With the deadline now only days off, desperation drove him home to Oceanwood Cottage, where a "crazy, not human" writing binge—seventy-two manic hours at the typewriter without food or sleep, talking to himself, sustained only by a carton of Philip Morris and a quart bottle of Vat 69—produced the essay "Lear and Moby-Dick," an ambitious sounding of the moral and political deeps of Melville's neo-Shakespearean "tragic world."

This taxing creative burst left Olson physically and emotionally drained. His essay reached Dorothy Norman just under the wire, and she responded with not only an immediate acceptance but even a small check, as payment advanced in recognition of his personal straits. The money helped settle his Winthrop House debt, but once moved back in there he remained in a distracted state, unable to concentrate on his duties. Instead of counseling American Civilization students, he found himself obsessively thinking about further revisions of his essay. Throughout October he pestered Norman with late corrections, continuing to fret even as the magazine went to press. The first copies had already been printed when he was stricken with sudden doubts over his punctuation, demanding that Norman make further small changes by hand in the published volume. (The patient editor balked at this last request.) His anxieties were only slightly allayed by the enthusiastic response his twenty-five-page essay received as the magazine was circulated. His nerves still raw from the recent writing ordeal, he felt unready to resume his academic chores. Once more he turned for consolation to Dahlberg, who attempted to soothe him with friendly conversation as they strolled the docks of Boston Harbor. Dahlberg advised an early exit from the exacerbating circumstances of academia, to be facilitated by a Guggenheim grant.

Charlie went back to Cambridge to begin work on an application, while his friend began a campaign to drum up support (he soon reported the enlisting of one useful reference, Waldo Frank). Olson's grant proposal, for a book on Melville, was completed by the beginning of November. Once it was sent off to New York, the weeks of tension and strain were over, but still he was not able to rebound. Flu attacked him before Thanksgiving, lingering on into December. Work was by now impossible. Around the winter solstice, the waning-time of his birth, there came another "crisis," much more alarming than the creative chaos of autumn. For several days he was subject to strange, wrenching feelings of alienation and internal upheaval. Then, one dark dawn, he lay dizzy and sick in the dead grass outside the house, unsure how he'd got there. He wandered the streets for hours, finally collapsing exhausted against a fence. During a light, giddy sleep in the thin noonday sun, he experienced a dazed vision of the sun "sinking into" his body. After this illumination he came back to consciousness feeling alert and aware for the first time in days. "I awoke free." This vision of a nature that "was in me, not out there" was the first of several epiphanic "sun-inside" experiences to mark his life. But at the moment he had little idea what to make of it.

The prolonged breakdown had reached its turning point. A period of withdrawal and recovery followed. For the next few months he went through the motions at Winthrop House, keeping up no more than a surface "concern with lectures, with courses, with jobs of work." In March a letter came from Henry Allen Moe, secretary general of the Guggenheim Foundation, informing him he'd been awarded a $2,400 grant to write his proposed book. First to congratulate him was the man most instrumental in getting him the award, Dahlberg, who upon hearing the Guggenheim news wired him in tribute: "DEEPLY HAPPY FOR YOU KNOW ONLY TWO IMAGINATIVE ARTISTS WHO HAVE RECEIVED THIS TRIBUTE HART CRANE AND YOU." Olson resolved to leave Harvard on the spot, abandoning his course work (forty-two hard-earned credit hours), his degree candidacy, and the Winthrop House appointment. He told friends at the university little about the sources of his abrupt decision to depart, hinting only that he had been suffering from nervous exhaustion caused by overwork and that a rest cure had been prescribed.

Throwing over his doctoral work was the most momentous act of Olson's first thirty years. Eight years later, when he had finally written his Melville book, he asked Harvard to award him a doctorate retroactively. The university's refusal remained a sore point with him for good. (Replying in the 1960s to a New York State University employee questionnaire, in the blank under "highest degree" he scrawled, " 'Ph D' . . . asked for . . . but not offered.") In the subjective analysis he applied to his own personal history, Harvard's withholding of the degree finally seemed to him not so much a result of his own failure to earn it as of the rigidity and narrowness of the "killer-place"—as he termed it in the 1950 poem "Diaries of Death," composed upon learning of the suicide of his old teacher Matthiessen and as testament to his own escape from a Puritan education system he'd come to regard as lethal.

> *O ground of death, o factory of wills for wheels, o killer-place!*
> *o Inheritor of wrongs! of values which are useless, o falsenesses!*
> *   . . . Give over*
> *New England, murder, suicide!*
>
> *There is cause, cause for effect, miseries unnecessary for a man*
> *who is, at best, his structures, fragile: go off, go off, go free*
> *from places where the strictures are too much, too much*
> *for you and me to bear!*

Alive Again
in This Burying World
(1939–1940)

Release from Harvard's strictures brought a general relaxation of Olson's tensions. With the welcome respite from the immediate pressures of academic work, there came a renewed interest in the opposite sex. Back at Oceanwood Cottage in the summer of 1939, he became involved with several women. One was the daughter of a local Portuguese fisherman; the affair proved short-lived, perhaps because of his mother's disapproval. A second liaison, with a young woman whose primary passion was riding, seems to have affected him more seriously. His blood stirred by this "Pasiphae"—as the myth-wise Dahlberg dubbed her—he lavished a substantial part of his first Guggenheim check on the purchase of a horse for her. The impulsive gift turned out to have been ill-considered; "Pasiphae" kept the horse, but rejected him. By midsummer his roving eye had turned toward a well-bred Irish Catholic girl, but after a few dates the courtship was thwarted by her parents, who found him an unsuitable match.

One of the summer boarders at Oceanwood, Doris Huffam, a pert, pretty Boston office worker, had aroused his interest, but Mary's maternal surveillance forestalled all thought of amorous approaches until the girl had left to return to her parents' home. At that point Charlie wrote to propose an assignation at the Parker House in Boston. Doris accepted, somewhat to his surprise. It was the girl's turn to be surprised by what happened next. He took a room, but spent the entire night talking about books and ideas. By dawn, he had still failed to make the anticipated advances. Doris departed in puzzlement. Though the towering, unconventional bachelor, with his artistic mustache and tousled hair, was not unattractive to women, he had problems dealing with them when the chips were down. His outward show of confidence could be mistaken for arrogance, but in private he remained painfully shy about his "monstrous" body, and overanxious about his "non-existent Big Cock." When the talking ended, he often found himself less inclined to press matters to a potentially disappointing physical conclusion than simply to return to his books. The mechanical "will to fuck" which impulsively drove him to seek sexual fulfillment remained in conflict with a fear of women that was at least equally powerful, and in the struggle between the desire to conquer and the urge to flee, a third distinct need that was stronger still—the need for love—went painfully unsatisfied.

By September, his conscience had begun to nag him over his lack of progress on the planned book. He resolved to resume his study of the Melville family papers, which by now—largely because his own earlier work had provoked widespread interest in them on the part of his fellow scholars—had been placed on deposit by the Metcalfs at the Widener Library in Cambridge. Less than eager to return to Cambridge, site of so many recent miseries, he instead moved to neighboring Boston, taking up residence in a cheap rooming house on Charles Street. Equipped with the most elemental of civilized amenities—hot plate, fold-down sofa bed, one balky radiator—these quarters provided fit setting for a new diversionary literary interest, the novels of Dostoevsky, on which at Dahlberg's bidding Olson now set out to compose a follow-up essay for *Twice A Year*. While at work on it he lived into the role of the Dostoevskian impoverished scholar, a self-conscious solitary haunting the shadows of the city's "bleak corners." His occasional encounters with those he'd known at Harvard only served to reinforce his isolation, bringing on a recurrence of the old unpleasant sensations of not belonging, of social "ineptitude and exposure." (Invited to a dinner party given by Matthiessen at the latter's posh Louisburg Square house, he was unsettled by the arch, effete tone of conversation—sexual innuendos about Auden and "Ahab's penis"—and found himself fixating on Matty's big, "vaginal" Georgia O'Keeffe orchid painting, mocking reminder of a female principle missing not only from the Matthiessen circle but from his own life.)

He continued meanwhile to rely on Edward Dahlberg's generous paternal support, escaping periodically to New York for brief stays with and fresh injections of confidence from his longtime literary mentor, and in low moments even prevailing upon Dahlberg to come to his rescue on Charles Street. Such a moment was occasioned, around the onset of cold weather, by the visitation of one of the mysterious flulike illnesses to which he remained susceptible at times of depression, loneliness or emotional distress. In this instance his SOS to Dahlberg was followed shortly afterward by an urgent-sounding phone call to Doris Huffam. Alarmed by his exaggerated report of his symptoms, Doris—with a friend, Jane Wilcock, in tow—was the first to arrive at his bedside. The girls found him in what appeared to be dire straits, flat on his back, pale, unshaven, and shivering noticeably despite heavy bedclothes, scarf, wool hat and overcoat. He raised himself up to produce a pint of Old Crow from under the pillow, but when the girls declined the proffered nip, slumped back down once again. At this point Dahlberg walked in, effecting a miraculous transformation in the invalid. Lazaruslike, Charlie sat up and pitched into animated talk with his friend. Ignoring the nonplussed females, together they polished off the whiskey. Olson then rose, shaved, dressed and swept the group out to dinner at a French restaurant, followed by a movie—*Algiers,* starring Hedy Lamarr and Charles Boyer. Strolling home afterwards he was in high form, raving over Lamarr's legs in a perfect imitation of Boyer's continental accent. While Charlie played the romantic clown, Edward was busy making time with the adventurous Doris, whom he had soon convinced to come to New York and take up cohabitation with him.

Inchoate, vulnerable, uncertain, the wavery image that stared back at Charlie from his journals of this "bleak corners" period was that of a young man ill-prepared for the big challenge facing him: "to create a personality in this world . . . to come into life, and make the potential real." Fully on his own at last after so many years of treading water in the comparatively protective environment of academia, he was entering the main act of what he would later think of as his Hamlet period. "Typical of me as I was," he would one day scrawl in the margin of his Shakespeare alongside the "What a piece of work is a man" soliloquy, "trouble with Hamlet he could never add anything to me, for I was he."

"Fathers & Sons," the theme that focused his imaginative identification with Hamlet, was also the one that he found drawing him into Dostoevsky. Reading *A Raw Youth,* he felt a close affinity with Arkady, a similar aching "hunger for identification" that defied all satisfying; as unfulfilled sons, each fated to forever suffer from a "continuing hunger to possess—(and devour!) his father," neither could be energized into effective action. Looking into the passionate world of Dostoevsky, and through its lens into his own life, Olson now perceived a new complexity in filial emotion. It involved not only respect and love but a strong urge to self-completion. The emotion, further, could easily become frustrated, warped and stunted. The son had to be permitted to rise and grow stronger in his own male powers, even if this meant aggression, intellectual violence, a symbolic unleashing of "the 'carnivorous' urge."

Yet even Dostoevsky, he sensed, had failed to account for one crucial element in the father-son drama, the crippling, "piercing & destructive" guilt that followed in the wake of the son's aggression, and could become an ego-destroying burden. As graphic evidence of such an outcome he had his own continuing dispirited state, the feelings of inertia, "deadness," "withdrawal" and "atrophy" he'd been subject to ever since his father's death—an event in which all the while he'd been half-conscious of a lingering complicity, as though by rejecting his father emotionally he'd been somehow indirectly responsible for it.

True to his habit of cutting out for himself more than he was capable of, he had soon allowed his concentration on Dostoevsky to grow into a scheme for a whole book-length "chain" of articles, taking in *A Raw Youth, The Idiot, The Brothers Karamazov, Notes from the Underground* and *The Possessed,* and addressing grand moral and philosophical issues, particularly two that were obsessing him at the moment: the nature of choice and the foundation of value. In the one link of the "chain" he actually managed to produce—the essay "Dostoevsky and The Possessed"—these issues were examined in depth, as essentially interrelated.

All values, Olson had come to think, proceeded from the ability to exercise free will by making moral choices. In his essay he pictured the world of 1939 as under immediate threat from an all-consuming "authority of the State," whose totalitarian encroachments could be limited only by a courageous and decisive assertion of moral resistance on the part of free individuals. The personal consequences of failing to make such an assertion could be seen in the character of Dostoevsky's Stavrogin ("he is the novel as Hamlet the play"), a figure who embodied the "tragedy of the inert, the neuter, the ahuman." With his "lukewarm" nature and inability to "live upon his pulse," Stavrogin was mired in a morally incapacitating "swamp of self," possessed, like a walking dead man, of only the external appearances of vitality. "He is his world's sun, but a sun without a fire and heat of its own. He gives life to others but in himself there is finally no life. He cannot generate himself . . . To choose it to take up the burden of life. But Stavrogin is suspended. . . ." To the essayist, such a condition could not but seem familiar. It is unmistakable from his notebook rehearsals for the essay that in Stavrogin Olson saw himself.

Beyond its veiled exploration of subjective urgencies, the essay had a historical topicality clearly reflective of outside-world pressures of the moment. The "State" power of which Olson hinted was clearly that of the Third Reich; the bombing of Warsaw and the assassination of the German National Socialist leader Roehm were held up as linked manifestations of the results of an apathetic Stavroginism, an abdication of moral responsibility by the free nations that remained content to look on without responding. And the drift of Olson's political fable was pointed up by his reference to the Biblical parable of the Demoniac of Gadara, from the gospel of Luke. "We are . . . as lost as Dostoevsky's people [but] we have gone so much further than the world of Dostoevsky that we do not need, as he did, the parable. . . . Our demoniac of Bavaria is alive and active and a palpable fact we are confronted by every midnight broadcast and every morning paper."

Dorothy Norman was delighted with the piece, which, after undergoing protracted revisions by its chronically indecisive author, appeared in her magazine's 1940–1941 double issue as one of a series of "Revaluations"—along with fresh contemporary estimates of Balzac (by Henry Miller), Gide, Mann and Dante.

Charlie gave up his Charles Street digs and went back to Gloucester, spending the winter there. (It was, in fact, after all those carefree summers, his first real experience of the lonely off-season existence of the shore community.) He moved in for a while with his mother, who was staying that winter in a boardinghouse on Middle Street, then took a room of his own in another boardinghouse on Kent Circle. The latter abode would be commemorated in his personal mythology as "Kunt Circle," an appellation perhaps unintentionally ironic in that his sex life during his months there seems to have been little more successful than during the preceding "bleak corners" period in Boston. An attempt at a clandestine affair with a "neurotic" young married woman living under the same roof ended unhappily, rendering him temporarily "neutralized . . . thus impotent." His winter's stay was barren in other respects as well. Holed up in his bare bachelor quarters overlooking the ice-blocked Annisquam, he felt exiled from life's flow—a morally sterile Stavrogin, able to recognize the precarious world situation in this winter of Phony War, with the European nations huddled under a frail "turtle shell" of false peace, and to sense the "pain of it and the terror of it," but not to overcome the feelings of futility, discouragement and "denial of common life" which kept him from emerging out of his own shell of cautious isolation. Writing that winter to Waldo Frank in the midst of new psychologically oriented Melville studies that would prove doomed by an excessive subjectivity, he spoke of being pinned down "grimly upon the cold table of self." It was at once a boast of sorts and a frank admission. While he had made up his mind that in the self alone lay the ultimate source of value and action, he was also conscious that given too much reflexive attention, the self could turn into a crippling thing, the "root of all evil."

His Melville of this winter, like his Stavrogin of the autumn, bore striking resemblances to his current self-image. No longer the shining epitome of manliness that had once inflamed him to reverence and emulation, the great

author now underwent a sea-change in Charlie's imagination, metamorphos-
ing into the epitome of Yankee repression—guilt-ridden, sexually inhibited
and, after the great early flowering of sea books culminating in *Moby-Dick,* a
fugitive from his own fertile discoveries in the archaic world of myth. Weakened by his fragile anchorage in the evasive havens of Christianity, nourished
only by the thin gruel of a New Testament that glorified Christ as a passive,
helpless son-figure, this Puritan Melville had been robbed of all creative vigor
by an attack of a midlife "sag of sex" Olson diagnosed as endemic among
New England males. Not that he was without assistance in producing this
revised portrait of the nineteenth-century master. By now Dahlberg had
acquainted him with the major outlines of his own concurrent sketches toward
an essay on Melville, tracing the deficiency of "pulse" in the later books to an
antilife strain of Puritan influence (there would one day arise some tension
between the two writers as to which had been first to develop such a view).
There was also a second important force shaping Olson's considerations not
only of Melville's but of his own psychic makeup during this time: the work
of Sigmund Freud, particularly *Moses and Monotheism,* a book that would
influence him profoundly.

Freud's controversial proposition of an archetypal tale of parricide and
guilt, leading to the institution of monotheistic religion as a reification of the
restless ghost of the murdered father, provided a mirrorlike confirmation of
Olson's latest "hunches" about both Melville and himself. He copied a large
portion of *Moses and Monotheism* into his journal, with many passages heavily
underscored for emphasis (among these, for instance, was Freud's definition
of the ancient mythic role of the hero, "a man who stands up manfully against
his father and in the end victoriously overcomes him"). Soon he had dashed
off an essay on Melville and myth, mingling speculative biography and hasty
literary criticism with undigested lumps of psychoanalytic terminology. Melville's supreme achievement in *Moby-Dick* had been made possible by a unique
sensitivity to myth serving as psychic pipeline for "one of the richest Ids
imaginable," allowing him to tap an "Ur world" of the imagination; the psychological backdrop had included a traumatic encounter with a whale in young
manhood, followed by an extensive latency period from which had issued
that "fragment of phylogenetic origin" his great whale-book, in which could
be found the keys to mankind's archaic heritage ("the autobiography of a
race") as well as the missing clues to his own personal life, "writ large" as if
in allegory. Charlie triumphantly identified the book's White Whale as "Nothing
but the Mother," and the crew of the *Pequod* as "impotent . . . exiled sons"
lorded over by the "Great Man" Ahab, representing *"Who else but the Father."*

The grim labor at his cold table continued with further exploratory readings. From Freud he moved on to a second discovery of magnitude, the *Joseph*

saga of Thomas Mann. Though eventually to dismiss Mann as "a great fatuity" (just as he would come to deny his debt to Freud, who became "Dr. Fraud" in his Black Mountain teachings), Olson undoubtedly borrowed many ideas from the German novelist's modern psychological reading of the Old Testament. In the early months of 1940 he worked his way through the saga's first two volumes, *Joseph and His Brothers* and *Young Joseph,* once more inscribing much of the text into notes for future use—most significantly, long stretches of Mann's Prelude, a slow, reflective descent into the "race past." In Mann's bottomless well of myth, Olson made out the familiar Freudian sons of the brother-horde, contending, consuming and prolifically begetting. Here was another paradigmatic source for the apprehension of Melville, a vivid unfolding of parricide and cannibalism themes, embodying a primal patriarchal archaic in images of ritual animal sacrifice, disguised birthrights and filial striving. After haunting his mind for some years, these images would reappear transmuted in the archaic vision of *Call Me Ishmael.* Fired by the *Joseph* books, he now decided that Melville's obsessive search for origins, a "fatal seeking [of] the First Day," signaled—like the relentless questing of Mann's Biblical sons—"an urge to kill the Father & be the Father." And he was especially intrigued by the novelist's handling of the figure of Ishmael, a primordial "son with the sickle" who had "actually played Zeus to Abram's Chronos & unmanned his father." It was *this* Ishmael, in his poetic conjecture the unconscious prototype of Melville's narrator, who would one day lurk behind the scenes of his own unique critical study, phantom protagonist of the hidden story-within-the-story.

By midwinter Olson had loaded down several thick journal volumes with notes, but his book still remained unwritten while his grant money was rapidly running out. He reported to Guggenheim Foundation secretary Henry Allen Moe that the work was proving unexpectedly exacting, and that he would need a year's extension in order to complete the book without having his "time of spirit eaten away by economics." But he could show no solid results for his efforts thus far, and his request was turned down. Persevering would require falling back upon his own insecure resources, a prospect that now seemed as intimidating as always.

He broke away from his solitary cold table for a while, fleeing the extreme severity of a prolonged New England winter that had buffeted Cape Ann with successive blasts of snow, wind and subfreezing temperatures. On St. Valentine's Day a great blizzard—part of the same massive Atlantic storm that also sank the schooner *Doris M. Hawes*—buried Gloucester under a foot and a half of snow. In a theatrical escape later described in a *Maximus* poem, Charlie executed a sweeping ballet leap from his mother's front porch into a deep snowbank, and then aboard the Boston–New York boat weathered an icy gale on the exposed deck, protected, from the top of his head to his overcoat collar, by a makeshift "upholstery fabric / hair mattress / headgear with eyes only / protruding."

In New York he was put up by Dahlberg, who was now living on West 8th Street with Doris Huffam. Doris had succeeded Edward's main flame of the previous fall, Ladine ("Deenie") Young, with whom Charlie himself now took up relations via an informal transfer of rights evidently authorized—if not in fact orchestrated—by his friend and mentor. A great womanizer, Dahlberg regarded Olson as a "gawk" with women. Coaching in sexual matters was regularly included in his multifaceted instruction of the younger man; Charlie's unhappy bachelorhood now inspired a gesture later itemized by Edward as one of a long series of such tutorial generosities ("I introduced you to Miss Young to ease you"). Not that the gift came without counsel of precaution. Dahlberg's appreciation of the opposite sex was accompanied by misogynistic reservations he did little to conceal—as he once informed Olson, he dwelt in agreement with the poets Homer and Euripides, neither of whom "regarded woman as a moral animal." And "Miss Young" was indeed a creature with the capacity both to enchant and distract literary men. Beautiful, intelligent and self-possessed, she had been the wife of a well-known novelist (Nathan Asch), the mistress of a famous foreign correspondent (Walter Duranty) and the sometime lover of many a New York bohemian artist and writer. Charlie became immediately infatuated and devoted much of his New York stay to this provocative siren of the cultural left. In subsequent visits to the city that spring he continued to pursue her, though with increasing wariness, as her spontaneity and caprice—the very qualities that he found most enticing—came to appear evidence of a Circean talent for turning men into "suckers." Years later, long after the affair was over, when he and Dahlberg became embroiled in an extended dispute over the complicated history of their friendship, "Miss Young" would become an issue between the two men, yet another point of contention in the "fixed mortgage" of unrepaid favors on which Dahlberg would attempt to collect.

Already Dahlberg was beginning to question the quality of Olson's affection and to doubt the sufficiency of emotional recompense he had received from his friend in return for his longtime support. Gratitude, or the lack of it, now entered their dialogue as a cardinal theme. Dahlberg's exacting attitude toward Olson's putative debt, says Ephraim Doner—then close to both men—became pronounced for the first time during this winter of 1939–1940, his expectations of repayment triggered by Olson's Guggenheim (though instrumental in Olson's gaining that award, Dahlberg himself had never received institutional assistance of any kind). With Olson's first assertions of independence as a writer, moreover, there came a threat to the balance of what had all along been an extremely dependent relationship. "Edward," recalls Doner, "demanded a price. He was like the God of the Hebrews—'Remember what I did for you?' Edward didn't want it to be equal. He wanted Charlie to go on playing his Grand Vizier while he himself got to be the Emperor." Before the end of Charlie's February visit, the first hard words were exchanged between them. Dahlberg accused Olson of selfishness, and of having manipulated the friendship for his own uses. Caught off guard, and no doubt shaken, Olson was unable to come up with a reply until he'd returned to Gloucester; then he drafted a letter of response revealing the confusion of his feelings—at once wounded, conciliatory and self-justifying. "I bear alive in my heart what a Host you have been to me, a Guest. If you must measure my power of giving beside your own generosity and find it less, even paltry and crass, then find me less than you. But do not conclude I have not generosity of gratitude. What you have done for me I measure beyond that of any other man. . . . [But] I will not trade in life, cannot. . . ." It is unclear whether the letter was ever sent. Surrounding it in Charlie's journal were a series of bitterly resentful sketches of his friend, in which Dahlberg was transformed into a demonic figure, an "anti-Christ," a "Destroyer." Yet in correspondence over the next few months Olson offered the appropriate gestures of appeasement, readily accepted by Dahlberg. A reconciliation occurred—but it would prove tentative, the first in a series of increasingly ineffective attempts at repairing an ever-widening breach.

While the Russian army advanced into Finland, Charlie, in frigid Gloucester, was assailed by waves of self-doubt. "Next year I will be thirty," he fretted in his journal. "I have wasted too much time." Nothing worried him more than being forced "to take up again the ugly necessity of earning a living." Yet he remained unable to get on with his book. The suspended, apprehensive drama of his life occupied him in extensive journal ruminations and self-conscious verses like "Purgatory Blind" (the title came from a line of Keats'), in which the geographical situation of his isolated Essex Avenue cloister, on its "jut of land" between the frozen tidal river to the east and the stark winter ocean to the south, became emblematic of his condition:

> *Between the river and the sea I sit writing*
> *The Annisquam and the Atlantic*
> *My boundaries, and all between*
> *The moors of doubt and self-mistrust . . .*

"Out of Joint," a title he'd thought up for the latest speculative mutation of his book, seemed to sum up the loose-ends psychic state in which he himself now toiled. Certainly the "dislocated," "psychotic," "desperately sick" subject of his current projections bore little objective resemblance to Herman Melville; indeed, on his latest visit to New York, a concerned Waldo Frank, after hearing the direction his work was taking, had warned him against placing excessive emphasis on the master's "pathology." And in truth the book he now had in mind was to be a sort of dual case study, implicitly joining himself with Melville in a cultural and psychological alienation imposed on each of them as writers "by [the] nature of his *temperament,* his *country,* & his time."

In his notes Melville continued to take on ever more surprising hues, as Charlie fished through further readings calculated at netting a vast American myth-book out of sources and subjects as various as Biblical apocrypha, Atlantis and the Lost Continent of Mu, the myths of Easter Island and Polynesia, and frontier folk heroes like Paul Bunyan, Kit Carson and Johnny Appleseed. Finally, in early spring, strongly affected by French Catholic novelist Georges Bernanos' mystical and uplifting *Diary of a Country Priest,* he began a "Christ essay," to be titled "In Adullam's Lair" and seemingly intended as an opening chapter for his book. In it he set out to show that the "utterly Protestant" Melville had secretly "sought Catholicism," and had sublimated his homosexual love for Hawthorne in a pallid devotion to a "hermaphroditical Christ." The essay was composed in an ornate, convoluted prose heavy with poetic inversions and other archaic rhetorical mannerisms, almost an unconscious parody of the highly sophisticated lapidary style of Dahlberg: "In Adullam's lair did Melville hide, a David, and made of each of his creations a psalm to absent Jonathan. . . . One Jonathan are they all, Pierre, Clarel, Billy Budd, neuters of desert, city, sea, outlaws from flesh who pass to and fro in a suffocate air mid between their earthly brother Hawthorne and Christ their heavenly."

In mid-April, Olson abandoned the "Christ essay" still in a fragmentary state and vacated his Essex Avenue room, going back to Boston to look for work. He had soon capitalized on old ballet contacts to pick up a small role in a Léonide Massine–Salvador Dalí production of *Bacchanale.* Though it was only a walk-on part, he enjoyed free lodgings along with the rest of the cast in a rooming house on St. Stephen Street near the Opera House. Rehearsals and performances went on for several weeks. The pay was minimal but for Olson it was a refreshing and exciting interlude nonetheless, allowing him the brief thrill of treading the same stage as such onetime idols as Marc Platoff (who was dancing the lead in the avant-garde surrealist production). John Finch showed up on opening night and found his former college chum perfectly typecast as a drowsy behemoth whose role was to wander onstage, taller than a dream giant, and lie down full length on the stage for a time, while tiny ballerinas in Dalí costumes swirled and swarmed above him. Then slowly, dreamlike, he was to rise and amble off. All this he did. . . . Where they found the tights to fit him, I never learned. And the ballerinas must have been warned about him, for prone and vast, he blocked off most of down-stage left and they detoured around him. But Charlie was very good, calm and poised, a dreaming presence. Motionless, he danced his best dance.

But offstage the sleepy giant felt less in place, and his rooming-house nights continued to be cold and lonely. It was on his way back from the Opera House to spend one such evening that a young woman with whom he would soon become close first laid eyes on him. Constance (or "Connie") Wilcock was living just across St. Stephen Street from his temporary home, sharing an apartment with her widowed mother and two sisters. One of the sisters was Jane Wilcock, Doris Huffam's friend. As Charlie hurried back from rehearsal that cool, wet evening, Jane, on her way home with Connie, spotted him on the dark street. She had already told her sister about this unusual man, and Connie was curious. For a lark, the two girls followed him to his rooming house. He disappeared inside, not to know till some weeks later that he'd just had his first brush with the love of his life.

When the ballet closed down, a footloose Olson wandered on to New York. This time he sought shelter with Ephraim Doner. The painter's top-floor flat at 137 Waverly Place, once the home of Edgar Allan Poe, was now the focal point of a Village "far-left group" and a day-and-night hotbed of political discussion in which the positions taken ranged from Doner's free-thinking philosophical anarchism through the more doctrinaire strains of socialism and communism then prevalent among downtown intellectuals. Inescapable topic of the moment was the recent, shocking Soviet alliance with Hitler, which had forced the Village Reds into a sudden isolationism. Olson's own instinctive pacifism notwithstanding, he now argued an opposing view consistent with the proposal he'd expressed in "Dostoevsky and The Possessed"—that in such times, a policy of nonintervention in the face of aggressive totalitarian state power, be it that of Hitler *or* of Stalin, could only be seen as amoral Stavroginism. *New York Times* accounts of Nazi advances into Denmark and Norway, neighbor nations to his father's homeland, had moved him deeply. With the specter of global war stalking ever closer, the proponents of noninvolvement among the Waverly Place group seemed to Charlie as blindly foolish as those revelers at the escapist midnight masque made legend by the flat's onetime resident short-story writer.

Back at Oceanwood Cottage in Gloucester for the summer, he received sobering confirmation of his historical intuitions—as well as a surprisingly hopeful projection of improved personal fortunes to come—from a new friend,

an exiled Italian surrealist painter named Corrado Cagli. A half-Jewish working-class follower of de Chirico and of leftist-anarchist thought, Cagli had
lately been forced to flee his homeland after an exhibition of his paintings
had been closed down by Count Galeazzo Ciano, Mussolini's son-in-law and
foreign minister. Now struggling to put together a new life as an art teacher
in America, the artist was at this point still quite ignorant of English, communicating instead in an "unspeakable" but uniquely expressive metalan-
guage composed largely of physical gestures mixed with a few well-placed
Anglo-Saxon obscenities. After meeting through mutual friends in Gloucester, Olson and the wiry, intense émigré passed a warm May afternoon together
sitting in the thick outfield grass of the baseball diamond at Cressy's Beach,
exchanging ideas and philosophies as best they could—with Cagli "speaking"
"via stones   a stick   sea rock   a hand of earth." Soon, by such imperfect
but inventive means, the artist had introduced Olson to a new world of arcane
knowledge, taking in a "fourth-dimensional" artistic geometry as well as the
mysteries of the ancient Italian tarot deck. Though their aesthetic dialogue
would prove among the most fertile of Olson's early years as a poet, it was
his new friend's mastery of the magic arts and proficiency as a "teller of tarots" that created a true shared spiritual ground underlying their relationship.
With Cagli, the superstitious side of Charlie's nature was for the first time
given full sway. Long obsessed by his peculiar personal apprehension of questions of self-determination and fate—his favorite brain-teaser since college
had been the triadic riddle of Milton's fallen angels, involving the relative
influence of "free will, fixed fate, foreknowledge absolute"—he had for some
time been secretly concerned that his habit for what he called "forecasting
yourself" was like a psychic equivalent of bad conscience, an indication of
some unfortunate doom awaiting him. The manipulation of the tarot cards
in which Cagli now gave him basic instruction seemed a direct instrument to
the actual decipherment of such destinies; and moreover, the cards hinted
that the fates were perhaps to be far more kind to him than he'd suspected.
To be sure, when his tarot fortune was first unfolded in the cards by the adept
Cagli, a "long bottomless period," marked by many slumps and setbacks, was
foretold. But beyond that were said to lie much better things—fame, great
achievement, even the accomplishment of "something unforgettable to man."
And Woman, too, was prominent in his fortune: the cards predicted he would
shortly find a significant new lover. He would mismanage the affair and attempt
to avoid marriage by escaping into work. She would nonetheless remain at
his side, and under her good influence he would in the long run grow
"streamlined, mature," and gain ultimate bliss in the conjugal state. Copying
down in a journal this sanguine picture of his romantic future, Charlie was

already moved to trust the veracity of the tarot's promise. "She will pull it out, & you will so long as you live be grateful to her."

War was in the headlines, with not only Dunkirk but civilization itself appearing on the brink of collapse, yet the long, hard Atlantic winter had been dispelled by warm shore breezes, and swelling buds dressed out Cape Ann in a rich sudden green that would remain in Olson's memory "the color of my true love." He decided on a whim that he would invite a girl to Ocean-wood. No one came immediately to mind, but then he recalled Doris Huf-fam's chum Jane Wilcock. He dashed off a letter out of the blue, asking her to spend the Memorial Day holiday with him at Oceanwood Cottage. Jane had no interest in the abruptly conceived "relationship." But when she read the letter aloud at home, her younger sister Connie surprisingly piped up that *she* wanted to go.

Twenty-year-old Connie, the family "intellectual," was intrigued by the idea of meeting a real writer. Forced by family economic straits to take a job straight out of Boston Latin School, she had kept up an interest in the world of books and ideas, lately even making an earnest study of the fashionable new Freudian psychology. She was currently engaged to a young business-man, but that arrangement was a rather tenuous one, the businessman having been for some months away in South America and Connie herself having meanwhile grown somewhat halfhearted about the whole plan. It was less the fiancé himself that attracted her than the image of security and stability represented by marriage. Having experienced the humiliation of watching her own family decline into genteel poverty after the death of her father, she was drawn to things that lasted. Overcompensating for a Depression child-hood, she was driven by a quiet, stubborn pride that caused her to seem self-possessed beyond her years, and to appear "patrician" even though by birth (or bank account) she was not. A young woman of fresh, delicate beauty, she was petite and slender, with brown eyes, a fine high forehead and silken, honey-colored hair that flowed to her shoulders. The few dollars she was able to put aside from her office-girl paycheck at John Hancock, the Boston insur-ance company, went into careful shopping for fine cashmeres and shetlands, alligator bags and shoes, silver jewelry. She had worked hard to develop her economic independence, and so was free to do as she pleased. Over her moth-er's mild protestations, she caught the train to Gloucester.

Bouncing toward the station in his banged-up, floorboardless 1929 Ford Model A roadster, Charlie felt abuzz with nervous anticipation. His expec-tations were more than matched by the lissome creature in straw hat and bright summer dress who got off the Boston train. Beaming, showering her with talk, he escorted Connie back to Oceanwood to begin a whirlwind courtship. Its decisive moment occurred in the midst of an outing later that day to the beach resort of Rockport. Dressed in a blue bathing suit that struck him as fetchingly coquettish, the lovely visitor leaped with "delicate strength" from a low stone wall into his arms. He was convinced the forecast fate was sealed. "It's her flesh," he would later explain in a fumbling attempt to relate this joyous episode to a male confidant, "[that] gives me the ultimate pleasure, the richness . . . the joy, the bones: her legs . . . look[ing] as rich as they did the first day i went for them (it was crazy, really, the way we went into it, her self, revealed . . . I was caught. . . ." That evening, once his mother was safely asleep, he slipped into Connie's bed in Oceanwood's sea-facing guest room. They spent the night in each other's arms, "two Buddhas of desire."

After their weekend idyll Connie returned to the prosaic reality of her city working life. Charlie was soon enriching it with charm and poetry. He wrote her almost daily, in ardent lyric tones: "Love is the only health, and love must be quiet, so silent no one hears its strong approach, and love must be intimate and intense in its closed, small circle of joy." That summer she came back several times for further weekends with him at the shore. In her company he at last felt freed of the crushing nutshell of self that had bounded his horizons all through the long, anxious winter. In a time "when horror followed fear in Europe," he was soon marveling to her, "we have spawned & created our love." A copy of Sherwood Anderson's *Winesburg, Ohio* he bestowed on her in June 1940 bore an inscription that reflected what he'd recently been through: he thanked her for "bringing me alive again in this burying world."

In July, Dahlberg showed up at Oceanwood with Doris Huffam. For several days the two writers labored concurrently in separate rooms of the cottage, Olson back at his Melville, Dahlberg also addressing Melville, among others, in the essays of *Do Those Bones Live*. The evenings were passed agreeably in literary talk. Dahlberg, though, grew impatient after a few days with what he perceived as unfair favoritism in Mary Olson's domestic management. One night at the dinner table she served up for her son a large platter of particularly appetizing pork chops, while Dahlberg was forced to settle for some leftover meat loaf, a "thin plate" as he found it. Charlie was used to such special treatment, and blithely ignored the disgruntled guest's baleful stare across the table ("glaring out of his one good eye to register / his notice of the preference"). After Mary had gone to bed, Dahlberg told her son that he was being "spoiled." Olson was embarrassed and upset. ("A mother," he would later write in recalling the episode, "is a hard thing to get away from.")

He ran his hands distractedly through his hair but said nothing to answer the challenge.

Dahlberg left shortly for New York, carrying a typescript of Olson's Melville work-in-progress, including the "Christ essay" and notes on myth. After a week or so, Charlie got back a letter of assessment containing the harshest criticism he'd yet had out of Dahlberg. His writing, he was told, badly lacked life and color. There were too many adjectives, "flattened verbs . . . barnacled fastenings of prepositions, redundant articles, and too many nouns." "The Seed of a Book" could be discerned in what he'd done, but nothing more. "For the moment," Dahlberg informed him, "you have lost your own Path, for everything you have done is against your blood." Detailed instructions for repairing and improving his faulty prose were also included, but were too much for Charlie to face at this disappointing moment. (Five years later, however, he would dig out this letter and adhere studiously to its directives in producing a much-altered Melville book.)

The ego blow would have been more damaging had it not been ameliorated by love. He'd decided by late summer that Connie was exerting a much more positive influence on him than Dahlberg ever had. That August, when she went off on a two-week vacation with her mother and sisters to Barnstable on the north shore of Cape Cod, he impulsively followed. The Wilcocks had the loan of a snug three-bedroom cottage nestled in a grove of locust trees near the beach. Several invited guests, including Connie's aunt and uncle, were already staying over, and Charlie's surprise arrival—with not only his big European-trip suitcase but his portable typewriter in hand—created a certain stir. Unruffled, the interloper barged off into the locust grove to set up his typewriter. Shortly drinks were served, and Olson engaged Connie's businessman uncle in an animated debate on the morality of real estate dealing. By dinnertime, the uncle was convinced Connie's beau was not only a freeloader but a "pinko." After taking Jane aside to reprimand her for her intermediary role in bringing such a man into the family, he left abruptly for Boston with his wife. Other guests also soon departed, leaving the field clear for Charlie to commandeer a bedroom.

He and Connie happily whiled away their hours together, lazing on the beach in the mornings and at night sneaking off to a deserted graveyard to make love. In the afternoons Charlie retreated into the trees to bang away at Melville. This ideal arrangement was too good to last. Tidying up his guest bedroom one morning, Connie's mother came upon a package of condoms. Denials and apologies proved fruitless, and Charlie had to make a quick exit.

The unfortunate denouement at Barnstable was only a temporary setback in his courtship. Letters shot back and forth between Gloucester and Boston.

Connie continued her weekend trips to Oceanwood Cottage in open defiance of her mother. By September, family tensions had reached a head. Charlie came to Boston, checked into the Hotel Buckminster in Kenmore Square, and asked Connie to join him there for the weekend. When she arrived, he was draped in scarves, blankets and overcoats, in the midst of another of his sudden mysterious flu attacks. The planned weekend of bliss turned into one of nursing and commiseration. Sister Jane showed up at the hotel, a dismayed emissary of the family. But Connie's feelings never wavered. When Charlie moved to New York in October, she faithfully caught the train every weekend to be with him. Thus began their shared life together.

A Boho in the Village
(1940–1942)

By his own amused later account, the winter of 1940–1941 was Olson's term as a "boho in the Village." Bred as much out of real poverty as of a self-conscious bid for artistic independence, the bohemian image quickly won confirmation among former academic associates. When a young Melville scholar from Yale graduate school, Merton Sealts, sought him out to discuss his work on Melville's reading, Charlie was discovered to have fallen into the state of some latter-day Pierre, making the best of the starving artist's life in a small unheated and unfurnished cold-water flat at 86 Christopher Street in Greenwich Village. The apartment was ankle-deep in a disorderly litter of papers, bottles, pipes, tobacco leavings, half-empty food cans; a makeshift work desk had been thrown together out of a plank propped between a table and a windowsill. Olson, bundled in long immigrant-style flea-coat, inspected the essay the visitor had brought to show him and handed it back with a solemn glare, declaring balefully, "I see that the WHITE DEATH has descended upon you too!" He then proposed adjourning to a nearby bistro.

Another unanticipated guest at Christopher Street was Marsden Hartley, celebrated modernist painter and noted dandy (Dahlberg, who knew Hartley well, had dubbed him "the superlative male bitch artist of the day"). To the hero-worshiping Charlie, Hartley was a figure of special importance because of his famous landscapes of Gloucester and his close friendship with Hart

Crane, currently ranked highly in the elite pantheon of the young man's favorite poets. Having previously exchanged only polite social chat with the fifty-three-year-old artist, Charlie was flabbergasted to find him at his door one day, resplendent in a "new beautiful sea-green suit" and clearly expecting to be asked in. Social graces gradually returning, he tried to compose himself and make tea for his guest, but in his excitement he neglected to add the tea bags. Hartley sat on in silence, sipping a cup of hot water, as Charlie proudly brought out his latest poem—an effusive but awkwardly rhetorical tribute to Hartley's erstwhile companion, Crane ("Fledged by the modern, / new Archeopteryx, you Hart Crane . . . I remember your death, reject all answers"). The painter slowly read the poem, then picked up his hat and left without a word, leaving his sensitive host "heart-broken."

Without income of his own, Olson was once again thrown back for support upon the generosity of Edward Dahlberg, who despite recent tension between them provided him not only a series of small loans (which were not repaid) but, through the auspices of a relative who owned the Christopher Street building, a place to live rent-free (collection of rental payments was deferred indefinitely, and in the end never took place). During the first months of his stay in the city, Charlie also regularly availed himself of carte blanche dining privileges at Dahlberg's 8th Street apartment. On the surface, their friendship continued as before. Early in 1941, however, a series of incidents occurred which indicated just how tenuous relations between them had grown. The trigger was a competitive dispute over their parallel work on Herman Melville, occasioned by Dahlberg's showing Olson the galley proofs of his forthcoming *Do These Bones Live*. One of the essays in the book contained insights on Melville which, as he read through the proofs in Dahlberg's living room, seemed to a crestfallen and envious Olson very much his own property. Beaten to the punch, he felt badly betrayed, and while unable to articulate his anger, he was also unable to conceal it. Dahlberg's attempts at conciliation, including the presentation to Olson of a copy of the published book with the Melville chapter now graciously dedicated to him ("originality is but high-born stealth," he suggested therein), resulted only in distrustful stalemate, with Charlie continuing to take advantage of his longtime benefactor's material kindness but remaining vigilant for further evidences of slighting.

The simmering emotions of rivalry could not long be kept from boiling over. Spurred to accelerate his own efforts, Olson had managed by early spring to come up with a final draft of his own Melville book. He carried the typed manuscript—a physically imposing object of some four hundred pages, easily dwarfing in bulk the slender *Bones*—immediately to Dahlberg. The book was inscribed to the older man, and branded throughout by unmistakable marks of Dahlbergian influence; while their ideas on the subject may have been held in common, there could be little objective question as to which man was the source of the prose approach both had taken, Olson's style miming his friend's right down to the pervasive Biblical analogizing present even in his chapter titles. Dahlberg was appalled. "I begged him to do something small," he was soon lamenting to Alfred Stieglitz, "not to essay a book in gaudy mural size."

> His MS . . . was written in a tumid bathetic Dahlberg prose, with all my worst faults. Aside from that it was vain and ambitious. The titles were Genesis and Exodus and Numbers and so on, and I felt this was just too vain-glorious. . . . I had to reject almost the whole of the MS. . . . And so I begged Olson to toil with his book to cast out the falsely vain titles and the mimetic Dahlberg dross, and find a prose and feeling and heart for himself. But he could not or would not do it, and naturally supposed that my judgement was in error.

Crushed at hearing Dahlberg's reaction, Charlie could spare himself the full brunt of its ego damage only by making it out as maliciously motivated. In a moment of bitter confrontation, he told the older man theatrically that he wanted to end their friendship because it had become too intense for him to stand. Dahlberg once again made efforts to appease him, but now had hurt feelings of his own. Recognizing the "hard demons that lay behind [Olson's] pedantic spectacles" as clear indication that his young friend "was resolved to go away," he soon gave up trying to reason—and it was six years before they would see each other again.

Charlie did his best to submerge his sense of rejection in denial, but it resurfaced as vague worries over his retarded development, his problem with father figures in particular suggesting a pattern of questionable attachments. A disturbing process of projection meanwhile continued in his dreams, which were densely populated by paternal images, "fathers" in the guise of powerful men of the world, from Franklin D. Roosevelt to Adolf Hitler. It occurred to him that perhaps behind those images the ghost of Karl was hovering, crippling him psychically, confounding all his earnest attempts at making a go of friendship or work. He still harbored strong, contradictory feelings about Karl, and could not help suspecting the move to expel Dahlberg from his life had been a subconscious bid to throw off those distracting emotions as well. He knew for certain, at any rate, that the bold expulsion of his surrogate father had finally been made possible only by the presence in the wings of a new female companion. "I rupture these friendships with men violently," he would soon be acknowledging. "I use women to do it . . . Connie with Dahlberg."

Dahlberg represented his negative connection with the past, Connie his "object of the future." In her company he was for once able to overcome those old rigid Yankee habits of "holding it all in the self." Teaching him to "share the flesh," to "live in the personal"—these were her gifts to him. Her weekend visits contributed the best moments of his New York stay. But the strain and expense of the long commute from Boston was wearing on her. She wanted to marry, settle down and have children. Marriage, he countered, was an empty social convention, made still more meaningless by the imminent prospect of world war. The passage of the Lend-Lease Act, authorizing transfer of U.S. supplies to the Allies, had made American involvement in the conflict inevitable: "Fear has come to America," he told her. In the face of a future so clouded, they should live completely in the present. Complaisant but not quite convinced, Connie quietly urged him to at least consider seeking work. Money, not a marriage license, was the immediate impediment to their moving in together.

The job he found required little sacrifice of his precious independence. It was a part-time publicist's position at the American Civil Liberties Union's Fifth Avenue office. He was hired by Dorothy Norman's friend Roger Baldwin, the organization's executive director (Baldwin and Olson were fellow *Twice A Year* contributors). Olson wrote press releases and edited a weekly ACLU news bulletin, duties which, he soon discovered, could be discharged with a couple of hours' effort during the late afternoon, leaving evenings free for his latest readings (Lawrence, Nietzsche, Prescott's Mexican history, Nijinsky's diaries), the mornings for sleeping in. His $25-a-week salary, however, was scarcely enough to get a household started. Cohabitation had to be postponed for a while longer. In the interim he agreed to share the burden of commuting, every few weekends coming up to Boston himself to stay with Connie. He found little difficulty making himself at home in the Wilcocks' apartment, its convertible living-room sofa becoming his personal domain. Surrendering the living room to him put something of a strain on the family's patience, however. Finally, during one early-summer visit he failed to yield his claim to the folded-down bed for an entire day. Connie's sister Jane made up her mind to initiate defensive action. When he and Connie went out for an evening on the town, Jane invited Doris Huffam, then in Boston staying with her parents, to sleep over. Coming in late that evening, Charlie found the two young women sitting up talking in "his" bed. Unfazed, he stretched his huge frame across the hallway floor and slumbered there, blocking all access to the bathroom. His departure for New York was a great relief to everyone but Connie.

The summer's first serious heat wave gave Olson ideas about a more extended New England vacation. He quit his ACLU job, and with Connie's help vacated his "boho" flat, sneaking his belongings down the back stairs while his landlord was playing cards in the basement. Returning to Gloucester, he moved back in with his mother at Oceanwood, and entertained Connie on weekends there. Things went well with that arrangement until the Friday evening in August when she stepped off the train with news that she was pregnant. Neither financially nor emotionally prepared for fatherhood, Charlie suggested an abortion. She was hurt and disappointed, they quarreled seriously for the first time, and the following weekend she didn't show up. When he called her in Boston, she refused to speak to him. He devised a diversionary strategy, phoning back to invite her sisters to Gloucester for a weekend as replacements. Jane and Barbara were treated to an evening of revelry along the docks. Not so much because she'd missed out on the fun as because she missed *him*, Connie soon decided to accede to his wishes and agreed to the abortion. For his part of the bargain, he proposed that they henceforth live together as man and wife—in nature's fact if not with society's legalities.

They embarked on common-law marriage immediately, catching a Boston–New York boat on Labor Day, and quickly finding a one-room ground-floor apartment at 3 Washington Place in Greenwich Village. Connie's medical procedure, performed in New York, proved unexpectedly trying, a source of serious problems in later years. But Charlie nursed her back to health, and once she was well, she returned his solicitude redoubled, adopting the role of quiet, self-effacing and adoring mate. Up early every morning, she combed the 8th Street produce markets for fresh fruit to prepare "ambrosial" breakfasts for him. He lounged in bed till late, then read and wrote in his cozy office alcove. After dinner he and Connie strolled the Village streets together in the soft autumn twilight, an obviously happy young couple. He introduced her to friends as his wife.

Within a few weeks Connie's savings had run out, and Charlie was left with no choice but to pursue gainful employment. By November he had turned up a full-time publicist's job at the Common Council for American Unity, a recently formed Carnegie Foundation–financed organization dedicated to protect the interests of immigrant citizens and combat a wave of xenophobia described by council founder Louis Adamic as "anti–Fifth Column hysteria." Hired by executive director Read Lewis as a $70-a-week editorial assistant, Olson wrote news releases for translation and distribution through the nation's foreign-language press and worked on *Common Ground,* the council's quarterly journal. *Common Ground* was edited by Adamic, a well-known immigrant author. (His books, including *My America, The Native's Return, From Many Lands* and *Dynamite,* were to become a strong influence on Olson's political thinking.) Outlining the democratic objectives of the council in the journal's Autumn 1940 inaugural issue, Adamic had called for a reawakening of "the old American Dream, the dream which, in its powerful emphasis on the fundamental worth and dignity of every human being, can be a bond of unity no totalitarian attack can break." It was that dream which Charlie now saw himself helping to bring back into reality. He threw himself wholeheartedly into the editorial work on *Common Ground,* including the canvassing of potential contributors. One night at an Almanac House dinner hosted by an old Harvard acquaintance, Pete Seeger, he approached folk singer Woodie Guthrie and solicited an article. The rambling guitar man produced a short, colorful piece about his life on the road, titled "Ear Players": "When you play music by ear," the article began, "it don't mean you wiggle your ears while you're playing it." (The Guthrie piece was seen by a Little, Brown editor who immediately commissioned the singer-turned-writer to make it into a book; the result was *Bound for Glory,* published the following year. "Charles Olson," Seeger recalls, "helped get Woody into being a published author.")

Also recruited to write for *Common Ground* were the likes of Waldo Frank, Van Wyck Brooks, Pearl Buck, William Saroyan, Sholem Asch, Langston Hughes. Another writer who was frequently seen in the magazine and in the Fourth Avenue council offices was the organization's Washington lobbyist, a bright idealistic young former foreign correspondent named Alan Cranston. This twenty-six-year-old Californian was already assembling a distinguished record for opposing repression and discrimination; he had viewed Mussolini's rise at close range while working for the International News Service in Rome, and later, upon the appearance of *Mein Kampf* in laundered form in the United States, had privately published an unexpurgated ten-cent pirated edition—a stunt successful enough to get him sued by Hitler for copyright violation. Cranston and Olson conferred frequently, and took a liking to one another. In the spring of 1942, when Cranston moved on to head a new government propaganda bureau in Washington, one of the first to be considered as an aide was energetic publicist Olson.

Charlie was not cut out to be a soldier. The interventionist stance he adopted in conversation belied a strong private dread of bloodshed and violence. Pearl Harbor put his convictions and his courage to the test. When America entered the war on December 7, 1941, he avoided military service, gaining a 3-A classification by stretching the truth in claiming both Connie and his mother as full dependents. (Currently able to help with Mary's upkeep for the first time in years, he did not let on that the total sum of his contribution came to only about $5 a week.) Terror of reclassification hung over him for the next few years, as he watched friends being marched off all around him.

Others, of course, were going to battle voluntarily. One of them was Mel

Atherton, a young man who had recently married Connie's sister Jane. When Mel was to be shipped out overseas, the Wilcock family convened in New York for farewells. For four days Charlie played the voluble host and guide, steering his in-laws around town. His affable behavior, along with Connie's radiant aura of contentment in her new domestic "caretaker" role, went some way toward winning over her doubtful family.

The Olsons' time of domestic tranquillity in New York was not to last. After a little over six months on the job, Charlie fell victim to "reorganization" at the Common Council. When summoned in to be notified of his discharge by his boss, Read Lewis, he became so upset that Lewis had to beg him "not to take it as so critical, or a *judgment*." Blown temporarily out of proportion by Olson's "exaggerated sense of event," the shock of the dismissal was soon superseded by the practical problem of paying for groceries. He sold off some books for cash. When his last money was gone, he and Connie approached Doris Huffam for a loan. By now separated from Dahlberg, Doris was out of luck herself and couldn't help them. Things looked dark until Charlie bumped into a distant acquaintance from Harvard, sociologist David Riesman. In a gesture that came as a pleasant surprise, Riesman provided not only enough cash to get them through July, but—as they were unable to come up with their own rent for August—the use of his 8th Street apartment until the end of the summer. When the sociologist left town for a vacation, they moved in. Olson's life in New York ended as he'd begun it, on somebody else's tab.

7

The Trick of Politics
(1942–1944)

In September 1942, the months of anxious unemployment ended for Olson when a long-hoped-for government job finally came through. His erstwhile Common Council colleague Alan Cranston, now head of the Foreign Language Division of the Office of War Information—a fledgling federal agency created out of the stopgap wartime Office of Facts and Figures—confirmed his appointment as assistant chief in the division, at a starting salary of $75 a week.

Charles and Connie left immediately for Washington. The city, until then a cultural backwater ("Washington was a village," as one exiled Parisian art dealer put it), had been transformed by the war into "the capital of the free world," magnet for creative people eager to lend a hand in the antifascist cause. While Connie hunted for a place for them to live, Charles reported to work at the Foreign Language Division, then quartered in the Library of Congress Annex. Looking out over the library's great Corinthian columns and historic green copper dome, the new agency's big, open office was as crowded, noisy, and bustling with activity as the city room of a large urban newspaper. It was an electrifying setting for Olson's entry to the arena of high-stakes political action. For the next few years he was to be not just a spectator but a player there. For him government service would indeed be a whole new kind of life, active, committed, and outward, a radical departure from the introspective absorptions of recent years. Acquiring "the trick of politics"—the knack of bluffing and then maintaining a commanding presence even in the toughest company, would during this period ahead permit him to "seem stronger" than he really was, "another man in the world of men."

At the OWI that world included individuals from the top echelons of communications, entertainment and business. Writers held key posts as well as rank-and-file jobs like Olson's own. Poet Archibald MacLeish, former head of the Office of Facts and Figures, was new policy director at the offspring agency. Playwright and movie writer Robert Sherwood was overseas director. Producer John Houseman was in charge of radio programming. Asian affairs expert Owen Lattimore headed the Pacific Bureau. Publisher Harold Guinzburg of Viking Press directed the agency's Outpost Bureau, and newspaper baron Gardner Cowles its domestic branch. The man selected personally by President Roosevelt to lead the agency was popular and widely respected CBS radio newscaster Elmer Davis, the "Walter Cronkite of his day." Behind his kindly public image the OWI director was a tough, no-nonsense character, held in awe by assistant foreign language chief Olson. Once, apprehensive about a morning appointment in the director's office, Charlie forgot to wear a necktie, and in his distraction compounded the breach of decorum by attempting to improvise one out of a shoelace. The last-minute loan of a tie from a fellow worker saved the day, but not before the episode had contributed to Olson's legend as office eccentric.

"We are not yet more than ankle deep in war," Elmer Davis warned his fellow Americans upon taking over the helm of the OWI. "Psychological warfare," in Davis' frank term, was to be the business of his agency. The Foreign Language Division functioned as a key component in the propaganda machine. Alan Cranston's staff people had been chosen for their ability not only to convey information but shape it in an imaginative, aggressive fashion. Cranston's second-in-command, and Olson's immediate superior, was associate chief Lee Falk, a witty, fast-talking Broadway writer-producer. Falk had collaborated with Cranston on a hit play about the latter's adventures as a foreign correspondent, *The Big Story,* and was also well known as creator of the *Mandrake the Magician* and *The Phantom* comic strips. Cranston's press chief was a young hotshot reporter from the *Brooklyn Express,* David Karr. Such writers as historical novelist Bradford Smith and anthropologist Ruth Benedict shared with Olson the role of "generalist" in the division, directing and coordinating the efforts of a battery of specialists, the ethnic-group experts and translators. Assembling the latter crew had been Cranston's largest organizational task, given the diversity of ethnic groups targeted as audience. ("We were working with thirty-nine languages," he says today, "some I'd never heard of—like Windish and Ladino.") Olson soon came to count a number of these ethnic specialists as friends, including the division's Italian expert Joe Facci, an idealistic exile from "Mussolini gangs" whose noble profile, Olson decided, bore a close likeness to Dante's; Iggy Lopez, Spanish-American expert from California's Central Valley, his collaborator on an OWI publication commemorating the battle of Bataan; Connie Poulos, the house Greek expert, a veteran journalist who would later return to his homeland to participate heroically in its freedom struggle; and Polish expert Adam Kulikowski, an Old World–style landed aristocrat who'd turned his exile into fortune by founding *Opportunity,* a business magazine for immigrants to America.

Olson's highly developed powers of persuasion quickly made him a success at his new job. Writing press releases and radio speeches on the draft and price controls, war bonds and gas rations, pitching in as pamphleteer and all-purpose troubleshooter of ideas, he threw himself with a passion into the task of interpreting and "promoting" the war for the benefit of the millions of immigrant citizens who were being counted on to populate the trenches and assembly lines. That reliance was highlighted most vividly by stirring minority performances in front-line action such as that of the bloody Bataan campaign of April 1943, occasion of Olson's most notable OWI assignment—a large-format pamphlet titled *Spanish Speaking Americans in the War.* Teaming up with Iggy Lopez (who supplied background data), he produced the agency publication's text, while house artist Ben Shahn (the well-known socially conscious painter, former assistant to political muralist Diego Rivera) contributed layout and design. Shahn's dramatic photomontage work provided perfect tonal counterpointing to Olson's understated eulogy of the brave Spanish-American soldiers from the border states who had risked—and in many cases given—their lives in the Pacific war. On one especially effective page, balancing bold-type stanzas of an Olson documentary poem faced one another above the starkly expressive photo image of a dark-veiled woman at a sun-bleached grave.

Bataan—   *Tejuan—*
old Spain's sun   *along white mud*
dries copper skin *black women lean,*
of Coronado child *cry, moan:*
holed up and killed *"Bataan battalion,"*
                    "Bataan,"
                    "Bataan"

Another powerful example of mixed-media presentation was a page on which the blown-up script of a soldier's longhand letter was collaged with snapshots of an innocent-looking youth in uniform and of a weathered-looking woman (his mother, the layout implied). The poetic conjunction of humanitarian sentiment with documentary image was capped by three quiet lines of Olson commentary: "Some have been cited, / some have died, / all fight for their country." In sum, *Spanish Speaking Americans* was a sophisticated manipulation of patriotic feeling that managed to convert sadness over great loss of life into a rousing call to arms, reminding the "fighters, workers, farmers" of the Southwest that—in the words of pamphleteer Olson—"ACTION was America's answer to Bataan."

A spirit of collaboration and camaraderie united Foreign Language Division staffers behind the war effort. Office fellowship was carried over after hours at local establishments like the Steak House or O'Donnell's, where Olson sometimes joined workmates for a drink or dinner. The atmosphere of team effort and the sense of sharing secrets made for a kind of group bonding he had certainly never experienced in academia. Though there were those at the OWI with whom he had serious political differences on non-agency-related matters—like Lew Frank, a radioman he shared desk space with and suspected of being a Communist—it was impossible to lose sight of the overriding fact that one enemy, that of Axis power, was held in common by all. "It was a war we believed in," remembers Lee Falk. "To Charlie and all of us, the enemy was crystal-clear, and it was really a fight to the death. There was none of the confusion and controversy of later wars."

His charm and verbal energy as well as his dreamy, poetic impracticality made Olson an office standout from the first, viewed by cohorts with a mixture of affection and amusement. He became famous around the office for his lack of attention to his wardrobe (the ancient corduroy jacket he wore every day was "rumored to have been in the family for centuries"). His "Rodin's *Thinker*" pose, one vast palm supporting his large head as he daydreamed at his desk in idle moments, was seen as evidence of the poet in him taking over; to the same source were attributed his barrages of verbalizing, usually entertaining though often "a little on the flowery side." His recollections of his ballet experience gave rise to stories about "Olson in a tutu," while his proud accounts of his maritime adventures on the *Hawes* convinced some he was "a real Viking." The most striking element of the Olson office legend, though, was his abiding reverence for Melville, whom he brought up constantly—even, as Alan Cranston recalls, in the midst of tense discussions about the war effort. Most times such effusions were humored or overlooked. On one occasion, however, Olson's enthusiasm almost got him in hot water. This was after the late-1942 Allied landing in North Africa, when his excitement overcame his caution for security and he dashed off a telegram from his desk at the Foreign Language Division to "General" Ephraim Doner in

New York, congratulating his friend for having astutely predicted the invasion site. The wire was intercepted by an FBI monitor, and an investigation ensued, in the course of which Doner dumbfounded federal agents who asked in *which* army was he a general by calmly countering, "Stonewall Jackson's."

Olson's usual high spirits around the office flagged markedly in the weeks leading up to his long-dreaded draft reclassification hearing in early 1943. As the scheduled date inexorably approached, he grew increasingly subdued, spending long periods locked in depression at his desk. His natural dread of violence, exacerbated by daily exposure to grim casualty reports from the various war theaters, had reached unmanageable levels, all but paralyzing him. One of his OWI colleagues recommended a hypnotist to help him conquer his fears. Olson submitted himself to a treatment session, but the fears remained undiminished. At his hearing he found they had been groundless: the draft board classified him 4-F, unfit for service due to his inordinate height. He returned to the office "amazed"—and elated.

His qualms about combat aside, Olson was soon convinced his new life in Washington's "world of action . . . world of men" was having salutary personal effects. After but a few months on the job he felt like a transformed being, newly decisive and assertive, "extremely clear, swift and all one piece." Connie concurred, letting him know she'd never found him so attractive— "handsome, all synapse, rhythm bones-making-straight-gestures & decisions, sex." Their life together, in the comfortable little studio apartment she had found for them, was happier than ever despite the ever-present ominous backdrop of the war.

The apartment at 217 Randolph Place, N.E., was a "two room jewel in brick, with garden," in easy walking distance of Charles' office in the Library Annex. Its two small rooms came with a sculpture studio that was currently vacant. Across an unkempt yard on the property there was a second and larger such studio; both structures were shielded from the street by a morning-glory-covered brick wall. The compound had been built for a sculptor of public monuments, Paul Bartlett, whose widow still owned it. The Olsons paid $50 a month to the aged widow Bartlett. (It soon became apparent to Charles that her advanced years would permit him to miss an occasional rent payment—but when he tested her attention by skipping payments over a prolonged period, she would turn into a dogged adversary, "all pepper, all iron.")

The place had great appeal as an artist's retreat. A low gateway in the brick wall opened on an unruly weed-and-wildflower-overgrown "jungle of a garden," whose state of natural disorder was a source of delight to Olson.

("I leave the grass wild," he would announce to a friend, "and the gate is gone, and the [coal] bin has given way from the rot. But the birds, bugs, cats, dogs like it—shit, screw, nest, sing.") Drifters wandering in from a Baltimore & Ohio railyard down the block sometimes took advantage of the broken gate at 217 Randolph to set up camp, drink muscatel all night and "have themselves a time" under the Olsons' french windows. Sequestered in his "hidden garden," the new tenant felt secure despite such invasions. He had been fortunate enough to discover "right rapture in this Dead City, like a rose among the broken bottles of the freight yard." The very seaminess of the neighborhood appeared to him a plus. The rear of the property was abutted by a block of row houses, one of which belonged to a government building custodian he dubbed "Missuz Maintenance." She tended her own casual jungle, which included a common geranium planted in a huge bronze foot. The foot was a discard of Felix De Weldon, a successful monumental sculptor who occupied the great barnlike main studio at 217 Randolph. A squat, autocratic man, De Weldon was little liked by Charles, who called him "the Papal Shit." (While De Weldon was directing construction of the famous Iwo Jima monument just next door to him, Olson took it upon himself to make known his aesthetic preference for Missuz Maintenance's planted foot.)

With its whitewashed walls, oak floors, casement windows and low-beamed ceilings, the Olsons' living space had a bright, cozy intimacy if very little elbow room. The small main room was made even more cramped by a king-size bed frame Charles hammered together in a rare stab at carpentry; it was eventually to collapse under the burden of his 260 pounds. A heavy wood work table bore his always-mountainous load of books and papers, and a brick fireplace warmed his back as he worked. The apartment's only other room was a tiny kitchen, from which, through a narrow Dutch doorway, a staircase wound down to a dark concrete-floored basement, where an elemental shower stall had been rigged up with so little overhead clearance that the towering new tenant found he had to hunker into squatting position to bathe. The miniaturist scale of these quarters, as one regular visitor recalls, produced an oddly appropriate "heightened sense of Olson's bulk. The place simply wasn't big enough to contain him, his gestures and his words, but somehow the setting was exactly right: seclusion, but walls and voids to wrestle with."

The B&O railyard became Olson's favorite refuge for reflective wanderings. Strolling the sun-and-wind-swept lanes between chains of chalk-marked boxcars, inhaling familiar "wharfish" fish smells, steering around ice mounds dumped from freezer cars and stacked-up produce crates, surrounded by a steady din of trucks and engines, he could almost imagine himself at home on Gloucester's waterfront. One day as he ambled ruminatively along, poking his nose into a boxcar every now and then, a vigilant railroad guard con-

fronted him to inquire what business he had in a place restricted to civilians
due to the movement of war matériel. He came, he replied, because the place
reminded him of the sea.

The OWI, originally a creative, freewheeling company known for its speed
of action and for such ingenious spur-of-the-moment propaganda stunts as
the dramatic Cranston-Falk maneuver to publicize Nazi atrocities by renam-
ing a small Illinois Slovak community after the decimated Czech village of
Lidice, had by the second year of its short life already begun slowing down,
slipping from ankle-deep in war to knee-deep in the war's red tape. Bureaucratic expansion was turning the agency into a sprawling administrative mon-
olith, with offices that had by now spilled over beyond the original Library
Annex confines to larger quarters first in the Social Security Building and
then in the old Railroad Retirements Building. Though the expansion was in
part a natural result of the steady growth of world conflict, it was also true
that as the war went on the OWI was becoming not only more cumbersome
administratively but increasingly limited in its movements by a changing
Washington political climate that threatened the entire New Deal policy agenda.
The incursions of traditional party politics were exerting a constricting effect
as early as the opening months of 1943, when complaints about the agency
first erupted from Republicans in Congress. Opposition party spokesmen on
the Hill charged that the OWI's domestic operation was mere camouflage
for a "New Deal publicity center" occupied with churning out what Oregon
Senator Rufus Holman termed "windowdressing" for a fourth-term Roosevelt reelection drive. To conservative congressional elements intent on a
methodical dismantling of radical New Deal social programs, the OWI appeared
less a cutting edge of the war effort than a last bastion of FDR's political
ambitions. Several agency pamphlets favorably depicting minorities in non-
combat settings, particularly the controversial *Negroes in the War* and also
including Olson's *Spanish Speaking Americans* (with its prominent publiciza-
tion of a friendly encounter between Roosevelt and President Camacho of
Mexico), came under fire from conservative lawmakers. Massachusetts Senator Henry Cabot Lodge, Jr., protested that such OWI propaganda literature
was not just antifascist but openly pro-Roosevelt, while a Southern Democrat, Representative A. Leonard Allen, lamented these pamphlets' federally
funded promotion of racial equality, "a philosophy that is alien to us."

The agency was meanwhile also being not so subtly undermined from
within. Throughout 1943, new executive personnel continued to flock on
board, no longer from literary and artistic fields but now from business, sales
and advertising. A new agency publications policy dictated tighter internal
controls, allowing staffers less freedom of individual expression in both text

and design. Content and tone would henceforth come from higher up, with new middle-echelon bureaucrats checking everything twice. Tensions between the old guard and the new inevitably arose. The image-conscious incoming salesmen and admen wanted to market the war like Coca-Cola (one new OWI program, for instance, was designed to educate America's merchants in making profits while helping the war effort), a tactic bound to repel idealists like Olson and most of the rest of the agency's writers. Domestic Bureau staffer Bernard DeVoto, Western historian and a friend of Olson's since Harvard days, came out in print with allegations that the OWI was getting "phony," with "too God-damned little straight talking over the table at an adult public." Liberal literary critic Malcolm Cowley, another Olson OWI cohort, argued along the same lines: new agency techniques of hard-selling the war in ways that appealed to public self-interest, Cowley suggested, could be used "to sell anything, good, bad, or indifferent," but were "based on distrust and contempt for the people." Resignations of disenchanted writers and artists became almost commonplace. The original chief of the Graphics Bureau, Francis Brennan, walked out because he believed the new crowd at the agency was trying to make the painful truth of Guadalcanal appear palatable for the sake of American business. In a letter directed to the White House, poet Archibald MacLeish, himself soon to go, told Roosevelt's special assistant Harry Hopkins that the OWI had lost interest in "the innards of war." And historian Arthur Schlesinger and several agency colleagues left as a group in April 1943, commenting bitterly that turning over the home front to "high-pressure promoters" had made the OWI into "Office of War Bally-hoo."

"Merchandise men" was Olson's personal term for the new kind of people at the agency. Their presence was rapidly taking all joy out of the job for him. "It was getting to be very hard on creative people like Charlie," says Alan Cranston of the 1943–1944 administrative pinch. Early in 1944, Cranston himself quit as head of the Foreign Language Division, forgoing deferment to enter the army as a private. A few weeks later, Lee Falk, who'd been working as a $1-a-year volunteer, did likewise. Cranston's recommendee, Greek specialist Connie Poulos, was named to replace him as chief, with Olson somewhat reluctantly staying on as Poulos' number-two man. Olson and Poulos were henceforth forced to fight two wars together: the continuing campaign against the Axis powers, and the losing battle against administrative interference from above.

The former struggle, the "big war," was in Olson's view now being turned into a "big lie," even as it was on the brink of being won. For him there was not only great irony but bitter disappointment in this realization, and to make things worse, the causes of his frustration and discontent appeared to him to extend from his own workplace upward to the highest levels. The sheer complexity of the wartime government, he believed, had perhaps over-matched even that most visionary of statesmen the far-seeing FDR; down the road could be foreseen a world in which major policy determinations would be guided no longer by such a trusty diplomatic steersman but by the unseen workings of insidious "charters and pacts." Looking out on the changed world of that spring of 1944, Olson was depressed to find prospective opportunities for postwar global advancement evaporating on every front. An America that possessed not only the energy and vision but the moral obligation to create "TVA on the Danube or on the Jordan or in China" was in his opinion rapidly sacrificing that chance, tragically mortgaging the future to petty busi-nessmen's ideas of empire-building. The administration's Pacific policy, an area of special interest to him because of his Melville studies, appeared partic-ularly vulnerable. The pro–Chinese Nationalist lobby in Congress, he feared, was about to tip the balance of America's influence against the popular rev-olution of Mao Tse-tung. In that historically momentous springtime his own work made such concerns far from theoretical; carrying his division's Far Eastern policy releases to the White House for checking by presidential Asian policy advisers, he saw and heard things that caused him to grow increasingly dismayed. On one of his courier visits he discovered that Vice President Henry Wallace—a hero to him as to all his fellow loyal "Appleseeds" in the dwin-dling idealistic liberal wing of the Democratic party—was about to leave on an official goodwill trip to China. To Olson the Wallace junket seemed an event of great moment for the whole future of Asian-American relations. The vice president, he learned, was to present the Chinese with a diplomatic gift: U.S. agricultural scientists working at Bethesda, Maryland, had developed a promising new hybrid strain of rice, and Wallace planned to deliver one sack of the experimental rice to Chiang Kai-shek and one to Mao. When the Air Force plane finally took off, however, only the sack destined for the Nation-alist leader was actually on board. At the last minute the one for Mao had got tangled up in those invisible "charters and pacts," and left behind. For Olson, this decision symbolized all that was myopic about the new breed of policymakers.

The low point came in May 1944, when censorship of his press and radio releases by new-guard superiors reached a level he could no longer live with. He and Poulos filed formal complaints against Domestic Bureau director George Healy and News Bureau director Dowsley Clark for obstruction and interference. The complaints were ignored. Poulos notified Olson he was about to resign. Next in line to take over the Foreign Language Division would be Olson himself. With the promotion would come another increase in his salary (which by now had almost doubled to $6,500 a year). The pros-pect of a pay hike, however, held little appeal for Olson in the face of a continued stifling of his conscience and freedom of action. He immediately made up his mind to join his colleague in leaving. On May 18 he and Poulos coauthored their last press release, which appeared in the following day's *New York Times*. In a joint statement of resignation, they charged that censorship by Healy and Clark had "hamstrung" the division. In a quoted response, Healy claimed he'd merely been editing stories for accuracy. The news item got half a column on page 14 of the *Times,* buried between an account of a presidential audience with the Campfire Girls and the final paragraphs of a report on neuropsychiatric stress in the navy.

While magnifying his distrust of the bureaucrats and businessmen, Olson's experience at the wartime agency did not deter him from continuing in political life. Leaving the war to the wielders of red tape, he turned to party politics, caught up in the ferment and fever of a presidential campaign.

The way was paved by social contacts during his tenure at the OWI, when he had met and been befriended by many prominent liberal Democrats. Two in particular, Secretary of Labor Frances Perkins, a fellow Worcester Classical graduate and political progressive, and Florida Senator Claude Pepper, influential leader of the congressional left, had become patrons of his political career, taking him into their homes and bringing him shoulder to shoulder with the big wheels of the party's national machine. Among the latter was Robert Hannegan, a big-city pol from St. Louis who had been boosted by his state's senator, Harry S. Truman, all the way up the party ladder to the chairmanship of the national committee—in which role he had latterly become, as Olson would one day put it, the last "good lever / us Appleseeds had." Hannegan, who had been apprised of Olson's energetic performance at the OWI, now offered him a job as director of the Foreign Nationalities Division of the Democratic National Committee. With the position came a $12,000-a-year salary. Olson accepted without hesitation and prepared himself to report for duty at the party convention in Chicago.

He entrained from Washington with an advance delegation of party officials in the second week of July. Connie soon joined him in Chicago for the opening of the convention, looking especially fetching in her new "Little Svenska" Russian-peasant braids. While she dutifully adapted to her role as self-effacing political wife, waiting patiently in the wings, he himself plunged headlong into the main action, covering the hotels, the Rush Street bars and the convention floor, pigeonholing inner-city ethnic-ward bosses, counseling caucus chairmen, consulting with backstage party strategists in smoke-filled rooms to push the interests of foreign-language groups in the shaping of the party platform.

With the nomination of FDR a foregone conclusion, the principal drama of the convention centered on the vice presidency. Its unfolding was of great interest to Olson, for personal as well as political reasons. The choice was made particularly sensitive by Roosevelt's questionable state of health. Henry Wallace, the vice presidential incumbent and Olson's own unqualified choice, was coming to be seen by many party regulars as a potential drawback for the ticket; in the changing political climate of 1944, the Wallace "quart of milk for every Hottentot" image had suddenly begun to look dangerously radical. Robert Hannegan, backed up by national committee treasurer Edwin W. Pauley, a California oil millionaire, had been pushing hard to replace Wallace with his crony Truman as FDR's next running mate. Another contingent favored Supreme Court Justice William O. Douglas. By the beginning of the convention, mainstream party support had shifted sharply away from Wallace. Olson was in the hotel-room headquarters of a fellow Wallace man, veteran labor leader Sidney Hillman—a Lithuanian-born onetime pants presser who now headed the powerful Amalgamated Clothing Workers Union—when Roosevelt phoned Hillman to get an opinion on Truman. Moments later Hillman let Olson know that the president himself was leaning toward Hannegan's candidate. Olson was crestfallen, but refused to give up hope for a last-minute reversal that might rescue "his" candidate.

Roosevelt came to Chicago on July 19 and, parked in his private railroad car on a siding in the midst of the city's fetid stockyards, conferred privately with party chairman Hannegan. On the 20th, FDR was unanimously renominated to embark on a fourth-term campaign, with Henry Wallace delivering the chief seconding address. For Olson the vice president's speech was the convention's emotional climax. At the end of it, a Wallace demonstration was initiated by Senator Claude Pepper. Adding his booming barrelhouse voice to the swelling commotion on the Chicago Stadium floor, Olson sensed a Wallace miracle was in the making. Wallace took a lead in the vice presidential voting on the first roll call, but on the second ballot the nomination was swept away by a Truman surge. While the stadium pipe organ blasted out "Happy Days," the ex-haberdasher from Missouri advanced to the rostrum to address the party. Olson looked away, sobered and disheartened by visions of a grubby republic run from slaughterhouse towns by greasy fund-raisers in Stetsons and shrewd merchandise men adept at "courthouse politics."

His commitment to the fading ideals of the New Deal remained solid nonetheless; he was resolved to go on pulling his oar as long as FDR remained at the helm of the democratic ship. He returned after the convention to Washington, then went on with Connie to New York to set up an office for himself in party campaign headquarters at the Biltmore Hotel. Ahead lay the work of getting out the ethnic vote. At his side was a trusted face from the OWI, Sally Almquist, a former aide of Alan Cranston's from the early days at the Library Annex. Summoned from her Virginia home to New York by Olson to serve as his campaign secretary, Almquist arrived to find him already in his element, furiously busy and "loving the excitement of it all."

By now he was gaining a real mastery of the "trick of politics." The network of contacts with foreign-language broadcasters, station managers, editors and publishers which he had established in recent years gave him a ready-made advantage; these past associations allowed him to bank in advance on the precious radio airtime and newspaper space that were essential commodities in any national campaign. Allies from his wartime work could be called on not only in the OWI's Foreign Language Division but in the Justice Department, the FCC Intelligence Service, and the Foreign Nationalities Branch of the OSS. His overall campaign plan was simple—"to operate full blast from national headquarters on the foreign nationality vote, and not leave the job to the local organization." Despite the multiplicity of disparate ethnic interests, there was a single emphatic message to be gotten across to the immigrant electorate: register and vote! With Roosevelt confronting New York Governor Thomas Dewey in a contest of clearly opposed political philosophies, basic policy positions on social and economic issues affecting the nation's ethnic minorities were easily formulated. Olson directed the assembling of foreign language "Digests" to determine voter reactions and the implementing of a Democratic master strategy aimed at bringing out big popular electoral numbers, especially in Eastern and Midwestern industrial cities. He worked closely once again with organized-labor boss Sidney Hillman. Hillman, now heading the CIO Political Action Committee, was overseeing a drive to set up registration booths inside the gates of every large factory in the land. "Every worker a voter" became the slogan. Olson's job was to see that slogan made an actuality.

The campaign was tense from start to finish. Republican opponents responded to the CIO-sponsored voter registration drive with mudslinging tactics. A *Time* magazine cover story on the Hillman drive left readers with the impression Jewish labor interests had taken command of the Democratic party. "With the aid of Sidney Hillman," candidate Dewey himself suggested, "Communists are seizing control of the New Deal . . . to control the Government of the United States." Racial and religious slurs in Dewey's speeches prompted FDR's interior secretary, Harold Ickes, to brand the verbal contest the dirtiest he'd ever seen.

Roosevelt's own team did not shrink from the fray. A vigorous counterattack was mounted, with polemicist Olson appointed to carry the battle to the enemy. He hammered out an aggressive article on legal rights of minorities, "People v. The Fascist, U.S. (1944)." In a thinly veiled reference to the discriminatory tone of Republican campaign rhetoric, he portrayed the nation as under grave threat from an international right-wing conspiracy bent on promoting "Hitler's lie" through a massive and subtle defamation program. Its targets, he suggested, were not only the obvious ones—Jews, Negroes and Catholics—but even "liberals" and "democrats." Group libel protection therefore ought to be instituted by the courts immediately as defense of Americans' civil liberties. These vital freedoms had no more sensitive refuge than the written and spoken word; it was there that the "fascist devil . . . works and there [that] he must be met." This effective piece of political argument owed some of its legal and sociological reasoning to a pair of 1942 essays by David Riesman (which Olson had evidently read while staying at Riesman's apartment that year). But its thrust and relevance owed more to the heat of the moment. It was published in *Survey Graphic,* a New Deal social policy organ whose pages regularly featured such politically related contributions as the prose of Henry Wallace, articles on TVA and racial integration in the army, and photo stories saluting America's fellow "frontier peoples" of the Soviet workers' republics.

To Olson, the candidate he served was more than just another politician. The imposing paternal "State figure" of his dreams, Roosevelt also embodied his warmest visions of a benign, humane America. "When Charlie talked about FDR," a later friend recalls, "his face softened, and his eyes became brilliant in affection." But his allegiance and admiration were offered mostly from a distance. Even in the course of the campaign, Olson's actual encounters with the president were infrequent and largely inconsequential, their conversational exchanges rarely going beyond a few polite sentences. On only one occasion did campaign staffer Olson take it upon himself to go further, putting in a word about the plight of Nazi-occupied Poland. (The "Polish Question" seemed of particular moment to him because of his discussions with Polish exile friends like OWI consultant Adam Kulikowski and Kulikowski's compatriot Oscar Lange, a University of Chicago economics professor later to become Poland's ambassador to the United Nations.) American intervention between opposing Soviet and Polish resistance elements then vying to liberate the war-ravaged nation was urgently required, Olson suggested to the president. Roosevelt listened sympathetically, but Charles was never to know whether his urgings had made a difference. He concluded uncertainly that the president seemed to want to continue "playing it by ear" on the issue of the fate of Poland.

There were also some less high-minded moments in Olson's campaign tour, if we are to believe his later stories of "dirty money" proffered him and his quandaries over what to do about it. One such tale involved a mysterious $100 bill that turned up in an envelope on his desk in campaign headquarters at the Biltmore. Another story concerned a wad of bills pressed on him by a lobbyist in evident anticipation of political favor. By Olson's account, he took the money back to his hotel room and spread it out on a table, where he and Connie counted it and found that it totaled $5,000. They sat at the table all night, talking about what to do. In the morning Charles took the money back to work with him and added it to the campaign fund, keeping a receipt as insurance against any future claims by the "donor."

Down to its final week the election's outcome remained very much in doubt. The campaign peaked with the production of a "Roosevelt All-Star Rally" at Madison Square Garden, which Olson helped organize. For this event E. Y. "Yip" Harburg, the popular songwriter, staged a musical revue that included many of the nation's best-known Democratic show-business figures. Frank Sinatra, George Jessel, and Charles Boyer showed up in person to praise the president, sing and dance. Robert Hannegan, Mayor Fiorello La Guardia and Harold Ickes gave speeches. The evening climaxed with Ethel Merman's rousing rendition of Harburg's "Don't Look Now, Mr. Dewey, But Your Record Is Showing." A throng of twenty thousand rose and sang along. For Olson, busy shepherding the entertainers backstage, the evening was a triumph. Twenty years later he was still proudly declaring it his greatest moment in political promoting.

On November 7 the long campaign grind came to an end. Olson waited anxiously with fellow workers around the big vote boards at the Biltmore as the national returns were chalked up. Not until the early hours of the morning did a narrow victory become certain. At three forty-five, the Roosevelt staffers heard loser Dewey concede on the radio. Olson was caught up in a victory celebration that spilled over into daylight.

Both he and his party superiors had every reason to feel satisfied with the job he had done. The race had been FDR's closest, with a strong turnout in ethnic and working-class communities proving decisive. Olson had earned a break, and in all probability a job for himself in the new fourth-term administration. In December he and Connie went south to join a detachment of vacationing party officials in Key West, unofficial Democratic winter headquarters.

8

To Begin Again
(1945–1946)

On vacation in Key West during the first months of 1945 the Olsons were hosted by Pauline Hemingway. The famous writer's ex-wife, one of the resort community's most prominent Democrats, loaned them the pool house behind her Whitehead Street villa in return for their keeping an eye on her two teenage sons when she was away from home. The extended holiday provided Charles an ideal opportunity to pick up his long-postponed literary career. In this tranquil setting he could spend long hours catching up with himself in his journals, working in an upstairs study overlooking the palmetto-and-banyan-shaded pool where the muscular "mesomorph" Ernest Hemingway had once churned out laps. For Olson, Hemingway's large shadow still lingered everywhere: the pool house under the palms had been the former resident's writing retreat, and the same desk where the temporary occupant now drafted poems and made notes had been the trying-grounds for *Death in the Afternoon, The Green Hills of Africa* and *To Have and Have Not*.

But despite the obvious enticements of the situation, resuming the disciplines of writing after the long wartime interruption did not come easy. The languor induced by Key West's warm, humid Gulf Stream breezes had soon lulled Olson into a listless, "static" state hardly conducive to sustained effort. A restless sense of false peace seemed to pervade the place. The navy submarine base discharged a steady nighttime flood of sailors into the local beer and fish dives, and the invasive din of low-flying Grumman fighters and dawn gunnery drills kept thoughts of war always anxiously at hand. Beneath the surface bustle, the town's seedy hothouse quality, an atmosphere of jungle lethargy and tropic decay bespeaking abandoned dreams, was equally unsettling to the visitor. At the legendary hangout of the Hemingway circle, Sloppy Joe's bar on Green Street, he found the denizens steeped in a cynical, alcoholic malaise. Once upon a time Papa's rugged-outdoors pals may have shared his fabled commitment "to do what men do / fish, hunt, fuck, fight, howl and die," but it appeared to Olson most of them were now resigned to a stagnant noncombatant retirement, "all tired people" with nothing particular to do but drink and play cards. And yet it was not long before he himself had fallen into similar habits. In a poem jotted down from conversation during a poker game, he sized himself up through the locals' eyes:

"Just the kind of a guy who
used to play the piano
in the whore houses
when I was a kid,"

was what Sully said.
He had me pegged.

"You'd think, from the size of him
he'd be a stevedore," was Canby's idea.
"But he don't know any more about low poker
than a hog does about the Bible!"

At first they figured I was F.B.I.
Ditto three sailors at the Cuban place
Where I went for bollos and fried salami.
"Listen, jerk, nobody don't work
in a dump like this in war."

One exception to Olson's hasty blanket judgment of the Key West cast was the "Sully" of his poem—J. B. Sullivan, a bald, chunky master mechanic who'd once had a hand in building the first railroad line to the Keys and now ran a local machine shop. This canny waterfront Irishman, who reminded him of a Gloucester wharf character, was credited in Olson's journals with a mechanical genius equal to the Wright Brothers'. The poem's second voice belonged to Canby Chambers, another Sloppy Joe's regular and former Hemingway drinking mate. Chambers' bourbon-sharpened barbs made Olson uneasy; always extremely sensitive to criticism, years later he would still be assailed by nightmares of Canby mocking his poetry. Poker player Chambers was also a Whitehead Street habitué, joining such prominent guests as Charles Thompson, former Hemingway fishing buddy and owner of several local waterfront businesses, and Thompson's wife, Lorine, in a seemingly endless cocktail hour that sometimes degenerated into a drunken squabbling Olson recorded in his journal with oblique distaste. Presiding over this indulgent salon was the rich, stylish, slightly faded but still boyish-looking Pauline, who owned the Whitehead Street spread outright (it had been a gift from her Arkansas perfume-baron uncle). Olson admired the lady of the house for her worldliness, but viewed her as a troubled and divided soul, torn between her devout Catholic beliefs and a repressed bisexuality; it was to the latter quality he came to attribute what he took to be her overly friendly attitude toward Connie.

In truth, the turbid emotional undercurrents at Whitehead Street were problematic for the Olsons as a couple. Left alone much of the time while Charles rambled the town or shut himself up to write, Connie soon grew restive, feeling alternately stranded and "smothered," and withdrew into herself. Charles, in a gesture of a kind that would become with his return to writing an increasingly integral element in the emotional rhythms of their relationship, attempted to woo her out of her mood with the intimacies of poetry—in one verse projecting her "smothered" feelings with some sensitivity: "His strictures tighten, bind my wonder. . . . Only in sleep do I belong to myself." He, too, in the change from active man to poet, was experiencing his delicate moments, and feeling the need of the tender handling only she could provide. "My spirit, like my body and my potency, is fragile," he confided to his journal. "C[onnie] makes firm my genitals, the South could strengthen my muscles, and life will toughen my spirit. [But] they all become fragile when my faith is low flame. How to have faith. How to assume the illusion of one's self!"

Assuming the "illusion of self" seemed crucial now, in the face of a challenging transition of life roles. Girding himself for it, he rehearsed old self-analytical notebook themes, urging himself to have faith in his instincts and to be wary of placing too much trust in his powerful intelligence, which had in the past led him too often into "despair." Pulling off the trick of politics had been all audacity and risk and intellectual bluff, "walking a silk thread across canyons." In a worldly sense it had succeeded, but his soul remained unsatisfied. The bluff could be carried no further; henceforth he must "insist only so far as my heart has gone." And it was just in those heart-places "where the writing strengthens."

For the Key West Democratic contingent the weeks leading up to the January 20 presidential inauguration were a period of great expectations.

With the division of electoral spoils now at hand, Olson's would be among the names sure to be considered for a place in the new administration. From some broad hints dropped by party cronies in a January poker game he drew the impression he was in line for a cabinet-level post—perhaps, he speculated, an assistant secretaryship in Treasury or State, or even the position of post-master general. The prospect of the latter job, offering a belated opportunity to avenge his father's mistreatment at the hands of the postal bureaucracy, could not but seem tempting; yet as he must have also known, it was at the same time highly remote, given his relative political inexperience. (Senator Alan Cranston suggests that in fact there was zero likelihood of Olson's actually being offered so elevated a post, and that any such expectations on his part can have been but a sanguine, highly unrealistic "poet's vision or dream.") Whatever job it was that was in the offing, at any rate, he soon resolved to turn it down in advance, making his refusal the subject of a self-consciously momentous poem of personal departures composed just after the inaugura-tion. To underline its importance as autobiographical statement he called the poem "Telegram" (a title too explicit to serve his later uses and changed by the date of its 1949 publication to the more suitably enigmatic "The K").

Take, then, my answer:
there is a tide in a man
moves him to his moon and,
though it drop him back
he works through ebb to mount
the run again and swell
to be tumescent I

The affairs of men remain a chief concern

We have come full circle.
I shall not see the year 2000
unless I stem straight from my father's mother,
break the fatal male small span.
If that is what the tarot pack proposed
I shall hang out some second story window
and sing, as she, one unheard liturgy

Assume I shall not.
Is it of such concern when what shall be
already is within the moonward sea?

Full circle: an end to romans, hippocrats and christians.
There! is a tide in the affairs of men to discern

Shallows and miseries shadows from the cross,
ecco men and dull copernican sun.
Our attention is simpler
The salts and minerals of the earth return
The night has a love for throwing its shadows around a man
a bridge, a horse, a gun, a grave.

Whatever its inherent opacities—for they were now less signs of mere awkwardness in expression than of the complex torsion of thought which would come to distinguish his most serious verse—this "go-away poem" marked a deliberate retreat from the public arena to the private sanctuary of language. Seizing his own tides at flood, choosing to ride subjective currents toward a belated realization of his tarot-forecast fate, he was forsaking for good the false pieties of the culture of Christ and Caesar, turning away from a public sphere now dominated by merchandise men to embark on an inward course whose exact trajectory he knew not—it was the act of going, alone, that mattered.

A good gloss of the poem is to be found in a letter written around the same time by Olson to a former OWI colleague, the anthropologist Ruth Benedict. He had, he told Benedict, made up his mind American political life was not suited to a creative person, and accordingly he had "left both politics and government again and gone back to writing." The political realities of this country, he had discovered, denied artists any vital influence on government policy, instead forcing them into severely compartmentalized roles that guaranteed futility. The modern democratic artist could never be more than just another cog in the bureaucratic machine. His own vision of big government in action had left him with a nostalgia for simpler forms, he told Benedict. "I have a feeling you will know what I mean when I regret we are not city states here in this wide land. Differentiation, yes. But also the chance for a person like yourself or myself to be central to social action at the same time and because of one's own creative work. I envy Yeats his Ireland." In some city state of the future, Olson allowed, he might return again to public life. But for now his calling must be to respond to an inner ordination, a concentrated self-divining akin to that of some ancient priest or augur. Fastening his "attention on the hot liver of myself like a haruspex must," he had now to follow what he took to be the way of "old peoples," like those native American tribes of the Southwest which were Benedict's specialty.

His fascination with the archaic figure of the haruspex or soothsayer, important both in affecting his immediate life course and in foreshadowing a later radical involvement with the shamanistic tradition, came directly from his reading of D. H. Lawrence's *Etruscan Places,* which he had discovered on the premises at Whitehead Street. The Etruscan priest-augurs of Lawrence's poetic study, Olson right away noted, had possessed a shrewdness equaling that of modern statesmen. Yet they had been far superior in spiritual power, stirred to illumination and revelation by a highly disciplined "religious concentration" that was based less on rote observance of prescribed routines of blood rite and animal sacrifice than on "an act of pure attention" directed inward. Lawrence's portrait of the Etruscan diviner was copied into Olson's journal, with heavy underlining for emphasis: "To him the blood was the red stream of consciousness itself. . . . the liver, that great organ where the blood struggles and 'overcomes death,' was an object of profound mystery and significance. . . . he gazed into the hot liver, that was mapped out in fields and regions like the sky of stars, but these fields and regions were those of the shining consciousness that runs through the whole animal creation." (Of all his own physical organs, the liver would henceforth occupy Olson as vividly primary, one in whose ultimate fatal dysfunction he would one day find multiple layers of metaphor—a personal image of life itself, in the Lawrentian sense.) Here, then, was the poetic path: it led back to an original human consciousness whose content had not survived, though its mode of connection to a universe—and a language—shaped by instinct and aura could still be grasped. "I am alone again working down to the word where it lies in the blood," Olson concluded the Benedict letter. "I continually find myself reaching back and down in order to make sense out of now and to lead ahead." In an early draft of another poem begun at this time, "A Lion upon the Floor," he put all this in a way that defined most succinctly his intended passage from political man to poetic writer: "To begin again," he proposed, meant "not to win / but sing."

Acknowledging an inner compulsion to start over in writing was one thing, finding a suitable literary approach another altogether. He felt driven to try for a work on the grand scale, something of sufficient scope to take the measure not only of his own spirit but of America's and man's, while at the same time reestablishing contact with the deep knowledge of myth. But what would be his subject? The quest for it first led him down a series of blind alleys. At least two had the value of indicating directions to which he would return in subsequent projects. Seeking to awaken in himself an inborn "Ur sense" ("I am Gilgamesh / an Ur world is in me / to inhabit"), he launched into a study of "tall critters" in American folklore, spending some weeks assembling notes on "the tall tale—from Bunyan down, in frontier fable—tales of space" (as well as a list of friendly experts to consult, including Benedict, Frederick Merk and Bernard DeVoto). Before setting aside the plan, he had expanded his lineup of potentially promising "American stories" to include Aztec, Mayan and Inca legends, Billy the Kid, and the Donner Party; this effort would form the basis of further researches over the next several years on the myths of the American West. A second scheme had soon evolved from the "tall critters" idea, this one aimed at a mythic elaboration of New England local history centered on the larger-than-life maritime figures of Gloucester, heroic seagoing men like Newman Shea, Lou Douglas and Carl Olsen. Also grinding to a halt in the early notebook-planning phase, the abortive Gloucester-book concept would eventually yield much more fertile long-term results as epic verse, in *The Maximus Poems*.

Still groping after a workable course and proceeding by the kind of unsystematic, instinctive associative swarming which for him took the place of the logical development of ideas that might have been the way of a more organized writer, he moved on from the foregoing considerations to essay a series of verse "translations" from Havelock Ellis' *The Psychoanalysis of Sex*, a book that attracted him mainly for its suggestion of man's saltwater origins. From Ellis' dream studies and psycho-allegory it was but a short step to reflections on his own sexuality, of which he next attempted a detailed notebook chronicle, starting out with confessions of secret childhood sex play and proceeding to analysis of confusing guilt feelings arising therefrom. Meanwhile his reading continued apace, the Whitehead Street pool house now serving less as a vacation resort than as an eccentric scholar's carrel. Sizing up his competition in the modernist *grand oeuvre*, he took on Pound's *Cantos* and Yeats' *A Vision*—works which, he'd quickly decided, clearly exhibited both the benefits and difficulties of intense focus on a single idea. Of the two great poets, only Pound had really stuck to his guns, showing the courage of his convictions by keeping on with his big poem in the face of all adversities; Yeats, on the other hand, in abandoning his vast occult-historical conflation of cyclic cones and gyres, had revealed himself "weak beneath all his beauty, all his power." The Irish poet's ultimate "failure to give himself up to a large piece of work" contained an object lesson for Olson, who was now more than ever inclined to view his own scattered, self-dispersing habits as his main nemesis in writing. "You start every morning as an original," he admonished himself in his journal. "It is not as productive as a continuous task."

By some six weeks into his Key West stay, such reflections had converged to make a single conclusion more or less inescapable. His interrupted Melville studies, source of so much excitement and disappointment in the past, must once again be resumed, this time with a new resolve and concentration. His subject thus determined, a form remained to be found. In the first week of February, reading Yeats' poetic plays gave him an idea for a *Moby-Dick* "dance mask" in verse. Again the idea came to nothing—it would be some years before he would actually try such a thing—but a few days later, on February

8, another notebook session found him closing in much more decisively. "The long work I ought to have to occupy my days so that each to each is a bead strung on a steady spring," he now saw, could not be undertaken in verse, a medium with which he still felt largely uncertain. Tackling Melville would require *prose*—but prose of a new kind, freer in form than anything he'd yet attempted, broad-ranging, deep, subtle and flexible enough to capture at once the geohistorical amplitude of "Ahab as American & Westerner" and the mythic wellsprings of "Genesis & the world of image & magic." Conceptually, the key would be enlarging the scope of his vision. The repressed Yankee patriarch Melville of his earlier psychobiographical studies must give way to a figure of more generous stature—poet and augur, Man of Space "long-eyed enough to understand the Pacific as part of our geography, another West," yet mythmaker as well, capable of sounding the primal ocean not only as physical fact but as symbolic cradle of creation. Extension in space ("the central fact of America to the writer"), depth beyond history ("In the beginning was salt sea"): here were Olson's twin themes, waiting to be explored.

Over the next three days he began work in earnest, producing several thousand words upon which he would eventually build Part One of *Call Me Ishmael*. Relieved to have a solid start at last, he went on to map out a rough scheme for the whole book before pausing to consider the practical scope of the research that lay ahead. He could push on no further with his first breakthrough, he decided, until he'd gotten back to Washington, reviewed his earlier writings on Melville, Shakespeare, Freud, Mann and the Bible, and dug up more facts on Pacific whaling history at the Library of Congress.

Meanwhile, with Yeats and Pound as exemplars, he returned for the remainder of his Key West stay to the concurrent effort of continuing his self-improvement in poetry. The Yeatsian "A Lion upon the Floor," a more playful variant on the theme of politics versus personal growth ("Power and the abstract / distract a man / from his own gain"), lacked the intellectual tension of "Telegram" but compensated with a lyric accessibility that made it a much more immediate candidate for publication. He sent it out to *Harper's Bazaar,* where it caught the attention of editor Mary Louise Aswell and won him his first acceptance in a mainstream magazine. An elegiac lyric called "Pacific Lament," commemorating the death of a U.S. Navy lieutenant, William Hickey, lost in the Pacific aboard the sunken submarine *Growler,* showed an almost academic mindfulness of "Lycidas" and Shakespeare's songs in *The Tempest,* yet managed to contribute something fresh to the sea-elegy tradition, articulating a palpable grief over the loss of the Billy Budd–like handsome sailor that was conjoined with a sense of real awe before the ancient mysteries of that "black deep / . . . water out of which man came." (Olson's feelings about the drowned "golden boy" were in fact strictly literary; he'd met but hardly known the young naval officer.)

"Pacific Lament" was rejected in turn by the *Saturday Evening Post* and the *New Yorker* before being sold to the *Atlantic Monthly*. Even so, one-for-three was well above Olson's poetry batting average for the period. Other verse written in Key West unsuccessfully went the rounds of not only the New York commercial magazines but literary journals like *Poetry* and *New Directions Annual* as well as major intellectual reviews like *Partisan, Kenyon* and *Sewanee*. To protect his tender literary ego from repeated blows of rejection, he experimented with pseudonymous submission. The most ambitious of his Key West poems, "The True Life of Arthur Rimbaud," a series of biographical vignettes in verse adapted from Enid Starkie's biography of the French poet, was sent out under the pen name John Hines (New Directions editor James Laughlin, whom Olson had known at Harvard, politely turned it down). Another Olson *nom de plume,* the self-shrinking "John Little," was attached to a poem called "Lustrum" (sent first to the *Nation* and then to the *New Republic,* it was turned down at both places).

Addressed in a brash tone to Ezra Pound, this latter poem betrayed Olson's conflicting emotions on a subject which at the moment was testing the objectivity of many a politically conscientious American writer. Pound, who had supported Mussolini in broadcasting for Rome Radio, was facing arrest and extradition from Italy on treason charges. Writers rallying to his defense included Williams, Hemingway, MacLeish, Frost and former OWI man Malcolm Cowley. Mailing off a typescript of "Lustrum" to Cowley, Olson volunteered—rather ironically in view of the poem's expressed disdain for Pound's fascism—to help out with any legal move to stave off the death penalty which was then generally assumed to be awaiting the accused traitor. He had signed the poem with a pen name, he told Cowley, so as not to compromise his future ability to "front with the Justice Department" on Pound's behalf.

This was more than mere hot air. His moral reservations notwithstanding, Olson felt compelled to make an effort to "save the scoundrel's skin." From Key West he also directed a letter to Attorney General Francis Biddle, another erstwhile Democratic colleague, urging clemency for the indicted poet. "Read his cantos and find out first," he beseeched Biddle, "before you order his neck broken. It is the movements of his dance not the dancer. The movements matter." Yet as his verses showed, his private feelings on the subject were far from simple. The Pound he described to Francis Biddle, a "large man" who'd "done much work, American work," bore little resemblance to the poem's "revolutionary simpleton," a more or less contemptible "lover of the obscene." In truth, Olson was torn; the New Dealer in him detested Pound's political attitudes, but he was dazzled by Pound's poetry, and perhaps even more affected by the energetic, aggressive authority of the literary and cultural criticism. That confident, cocky voice, firing out its certainties in brusque, telegraphic injunctions, had a ring Olson unconsciously associated with "the fathers." To him no voice—not even Dahlberg's—had ever seemed so powerful. Reading Pound's prose, he felt at once challenged, intimidated, provoked and awed. In his journals, Pound had already become a principal sparring partner, pervading his mind with a shadow presence that went well beyond mere influence. "Should you not best him?" he goaded himself. "Is his form not inevitable enough to be used as your own? Let yourself be derivative for a bit. . . . Write as the fathers to be the father."

The Olsons left Key West in early April, stopping off briefly en route north at Enniscorthy, the Keene, Virginia, estate of Charles' Polish exile associate Adam Kulikowski. If he was able to say in "Telegram" that the affairs of men remained a chief concern even in his new inward turn toward self and writing, it was largely because he retained strong lingering interests in specific causes, his Polish friends' cause foremost among them. He learned at Enniscorthy that Kulikowski and Oscar Lange were now supporting the post-Yalta Warsaw coalition government, an uneasy alliance of the Soviet-backed Lublin regime with the London exile group led by Stanislaus Mikolajczyk. Olson sympathized with their cause, and trusted that his sympathies were shared by his government—or at least by the man at the top. But back in Washington on Friday the 13th of April, he learned from his morning newspaper that all such assumptions of trust must be withdrawn: Roosevelt had died suddenly, and Truman's people would be taking over.

Any serious considerations Olson may have still harbored regarding a return to work in the present administration must now be "kissed off" for good, and along with them any hopes for a continuation of the enlightened global policy FDR had stood for. In the wake of the Sun King of Hyde Park would come that horde of petty Midwestern pork-barrel profiteers Olson most despised, trading the last shreds of enlightenment for the "swill" of a low mercantilism.

Immediately apprehensive over the fate of his Polish friends' interests, shortly after the president's funeral he went to New York and paid a call on Robert Hannegan at Democratic National Committee headquarters, presenting Hannegan with a letter to pass on to the newly inaugurated Harry Truman. Olson's letter urged Truman to "accept the Russian argument of security" on behalf of the shaky new Polish coalition government. The Polish nation, he suggested, was like a worried single girl who needed to " 'settle down' in comfort" with her Soviet suitor. In reply he received indirect assurances, relayed by Hannegan, that the new administration would possibly "do business with Warsaw." The vagueness of Hannegan's response convinced him he had been too guarded in his advocacy, "pulling the statement short" at a time when there was grave "danger in delay." The frustrating exchange with Hannegan confirmed his fears about the direction of policy. He advised Oscar Lange, who had just been offered the new Polish government's ambassadorship to the United Nations, that it would be wiser to return to Warsaw, where he would be needed more. Lange, however, accepted the ambassadorship anyway. Olson returned to Washington disappointed at his inability to act effectively and feeling a stranger in the public arena that had only recently seemed his own.

The news of Truman's cabinet appointments further depressed him: courthouse politics, it seemed, was now having its day. Edwin Pauley, the oil-millionaire fund-raiser, was rewarded with an under secretaryship of the navy. The postmaster general's job went to loyal party man Hannegan. Olson himself, meanwhile, toting up his own total earnings for the past three months of circulating his verse to magazines, found he had made just $25. In a wry journal note he remarked on the austerity of "the economics of poetics."

The return to Randolph Place required significant readjustments. He wanted to get right down to work on Melville, but the tiny apartment was temporarily mobbed. Connie's mother, Katherine, and younger sister, Barbara, both of whom had come to Washington to take war-related jobs, had been occupying the place in the Olsons' absence. They stayed on after the couple's return, a situation made marginally tolerable for Charles only by their significant contribution to the rent. Soon the crowd swelled further, when sister Jane, with her young daughter and father-in-law, showed up for a visit. The Olsons' landlady, Mrs. Bartlett, was meanwhile threatening to evict the whole ménage in order to sell the property. When she informed him that he would have to vacate the premises within thirty days, ex-politician Charles was stirred to battle. He fired back a sharp, crisply worded legalistic reply, intimating the eviction threats were endangering his work and upsetting his wife and guests, and implying he was considering retaliatory action. The "Old Bitch," as he termed his adversary, backed off, leaving him in comparative peace with his household of women.

The ladies were tutored *en masse* over dinner each evening, as Charles delivered impromptu lectures on topics ranging from ancient history to the news of the day. Connie had long since grown accustomed to these monologues, which she'd come to regard as a substitute for the college education she'd never had. Her mother and sisters, however, had less patience. One night as he discoursed at length, Barbara began to softly croon to the tune of "Old Man River": "Ol' Man Olson, he don't do nothin', he just keeps talkin', he just keeps talkin' all night long." At such moments, Charles felt "little touch" with his in-laws.

Jane soon moved out, to a new home in Hingham, Massachusetts. While Katherine and Barbara lingered on, Charles simply relocated his work from the house to the Library of Congress, to which he strolled or caught a trolley car every day. By early May he had gone through every book on whaling history in the library catalog, growing increasingly convinced "Oil & the Whaling Industry, America, 1844" held an important key to understanding Melville. He made a trip to see paleontologist and cetacean-fossil expert Remington Kellogg, who corroborated his impression that a fat shortage in the New England colonies had decisively affected the economics of nine-teenth-century whaling. "What Lies Under," his whaling chapter, came together rapidly out of these investigations of "natural history" and the "sociological aspects" of Melville's fable.

Further aspects of that multifaceted fable—the links with Shakespeare, Christ, "Freud & the prophets"—remained to be established. How to con-tain them all in the thread of a single discursive argument, when all along, going back even as far as college debating days, constructing formal argu-ments had always been his downfall as a thinker? The solution, he now saw, was to abandon the logic of argument altogether and follow the great mod-ernists in building instead a loosely constellated associative structure from which an unstated central thesis might be allowed to emerge as a strong cumulative pattern or sense. Of such a form there were three good models already at hand in works by modern writers on American cultural history: W. C. Williams' *In the American Grain,* Lawrence's *Studies in Classic American Literature* and Dahlberg's *Do These Bones Live.* All three were well known to Olson and served him as useful prototypes as he now began to reassemble, collate, edit and revise his own earlier writings on Melville, including the 1938 "Lear and Moby-Dick," his 1939–1940 "cold table" notes and the failed manuscript that had issued from them.

In late May, after celebrating the German surrender and the end of the war in Europe, he took off with Connie to visit the Kulikowskis at their rural estate. The many attractions of Enniscorthy had come to make it his favorite refuge from the city. Among these was the two-hundred-year-old property's history; one of its early owners, Isaac Coles, had been the private secretary of Thomas Jefferson, for whom Olson currently harbored a special respect bred of his reading of Pound's *Jefferson and / or Mussolini.* Here in the picturesque environs of Monticello, the recent world cataclysm could be put out of mind, the visitor relaxing into a calm Jeffersonian trust that "the earth belongs to the living." With its vernal ridges of oak, maple and pine, its flowering fruit orchards and wide fields of wheat and barley, the place radiated a timeless pastoral calm which prompted him during this two-week stay to compose a suite of nature verses whose Poundian imagistic style incorporated reflective after-echoes of the recently concluded conflict: "The sheep like soldiers / black leggings black face / lie boulders / in the pines' shade." (One section of the sequence, "Lower Field—Enniscorthy," would be taken by *Harper's*.) Most compelling of Enniscorthy's images for him, though, was the vigorous masculinity of his country-squire host, an Old World aristocrat and raconteur whose tales of a picaresque rake's progress through the boudoirs of central Europe the poet found endlessly diverting. The life and genealogy of this swashbuckling Original Adam would provide background for further Olson verse distinguished by an aggressive phallicism ("sex is the sword"). Such poems, written on this and subsequent visits, would include "Said Adam" and "For K," the latter sold to *Harper's Bazaar* (and eventually retitled "Trinacria").

Back in Washington in June, he and Connie were forced to come to some decision about finances. With his tribe of in-laws now dispersed, he was stuck with the nagging burden of the rent. It was agreed between himself and Connie that his slowly developing writing career was more important than immediate earnings. For the time being that left her as the household's main potential income source. Accordingly she set out to look for work, and found a secretarial job in the business office of a coal company. Over the next few years she would hold a series of such menial positions, later becoming a salesgirl in the women's clothing section of a large downtown department store, and then office manager of a nursing school. Connie's day jobs would not only provide their economic wherewithal, but reinforce the compartmentalization of their domestic patterns. Increasingly nocturnal in his habits, Charles now routinely remained at his desk over his books and papers until dawn, seldom stirring from bed before midafternoon and just beginning to come alive as Connie wearily trooped in from her long day of breadwinning. When friends dropped by to visit in the evenings he was not averse to talking all night long, creating a real challenge for the helpmate who was also his most attentive listener. During such verbal marathons Connie held out resolutely as long as she could keep her eyes open, staying to the sidelines, vanishing now and then to reappear bearing food and drink, always seeming to onlookers as quietly and serenely efficient as a Dutch wife in a Vermeer painting. "Charles himself did absolutely nothing but write, talk and read," says a friend who witnessed many of these sessions. "I do not recall his once washing a dish or sweeping the floor. Connie did everything."

The steady progress he was now making on the Melville book owed much to her devoted support, which was not limited to the practical money-earning and homemaking sphere. Less tangible but probably even more crucial for him was her contribution in terms of morale and self-confidence. The spells of insecurity and depression to which he remained periodically subject could be combated most successfully by turning to her and attempting to seek out in intimate conversation the sources of the mysterious moods that preyed on him. In dedicating his Melville book's last chapter "for Constance" he was expressing at least in token the real gratitude he felt toward this faithful companion and confidante. Her name itself, as the gesture suggests, had by now become symbolic for him of her ongoing role in his life allegory—a role which in the thoughtlessness of habit it was at other moments all too easy for him to take for granted.

That summer the writing went along "at a clip," his shaping of fact and conjecture now facilitated by the development of a confident prose measure aided by two late discoveries in the domain of style. The first was Ernest Fenollosa's provocative essay "The Chinese Written Character as a Medium for Poetry." He found the Pound-edited text of the essay in the latter's book *Instigations* and excitedly copied out its main arguments into his notebook that June. Fenollosa's account of the exhaustion of poetic qualities in modern discourse resulting from a degeneration of the original capacity of language to mime the physical energies in natural processes, and his implicit advocacy of a return to that state of primal verbal immediacy, with words once again becoming instrumental to the creation of "a vivid shorthand picture of the operations of nature," held for Olson the same appeal it had for Pound before him. But Olson, with his innate tendency to abstract habits of thought and expression, had perhaps even more to learn from Fenollosa than had his poetic predecessor. Pound, after all, had been working toward a direct, slashing, telegraphic prose style even before his discovery of Fenollosa, whose proposals about the ideogram he had applied primarily to poetry. For Olson, the impact and utility of Fenollosa's theories lay in the energizing of his approach to the prose medium which was his own principal engagement of the moment. (Five years later, he would return to his Fenollosa notes in laying the groundwork for his poetic manifesto "Projective Verse.") The "vivid shorthand" endorsed by Pound's scholar of Chinese now became Olson's stylistic goal in his Melville book.

In focusing that general aim on local contexts of his writing he was assisted by his belated attention to another instigation of "the fathers," this time the conduit being not the present master Pound but the superseded mentor Dahlberg. Dahlberg's letter critiquing his failed Melville manuscript of 1940, too painful to be addressed at the time, was now unearthed by Olson and given close inspection. Viewed in light of the Fenollosa / Pound insistences, Dahlberg's criticism made great retrospective sense. The thrust of that criticism was directed to the lack of color and solidity in Olson's prose, the "barnacled fastenings" of excess verbiage weighing down his sentences and robbing

them of vigor and action. The letter contained detailed line-by-line sugges-
tions which Olson now studied carefully and incorporated into the continuing revisions of his earlier writings. Though he had been out of touch with
Dahlberg for four years—and had moreover become accustomed to regard
the older man as a negative figure of almost allegorical dimensions, a "Demon,"
a "Hitler"—he was forced by this experience to acknowledge a hindsight
debt. Moved by conscience, he drafted a grateful dedication to his book,
hailing his estranged friend for having in effect brought it into being: "Beyond
all others, I took life from you and shall give it back as long as I write. . . ."
These words were drafted at the end of June, and not shown to Dahlberg.
Within a few weeks, however, the emotion (if not the usefulness of Dahlberg's advice) had passed; Olson at that point replaced the earlier dedication
with the much more ambiguous one that finally came to prefix his "Christ"
chapter in the published volume: "for Edward Dahlberg, my other genius of
the Cross and the Windmills."

That filial debts were not to be easily or simply discharged was hardly
news to Olson. With his manuscript approaching a final state, he reserved a
page in the front for a tribute to Karl, but as time went by no words came to
him. The page stayed a haunting blank until at last, nearly a year later while
preparing the final text for publication, he came up with a small epigraph of
lamentation voiced in an archaic idiom echoing ancestral origins: "O fahter,
fahter / gone amoong / O eeys that loke / Loke, fahter: / your sone!" Meanwhile the paternal shadow was lingering also in his text, particularly in the
still-progressing "Moses" chapter (now subtitled "The Book of the Law of
the Blood"). The chapter had become a pool of Oedipal images floating upward
from earliest memory and instinct; for Olson these images maintained a personal obsessive intensity that certainly exceeded any mere interest in literary
archetypes. While reworking old notes on Freud and the primal cannibalism
of the "First Murder," he fell prey to a series of nightmares whose most
troubling aspect was the residue of unresolved aggression toward his father
with which they left him. In one of them, Karl's siding with Connie to make
him feel "excluded . . . again!" roused up in him the old father-son rivalry
with renewed force.

The "Christ" and "Moses" chapters, both now rewritten to Dahlberg's
1940 dictates, and "Noah," a concluding fable of Pacific man as new Homeric
hero, occupied him into July. At that point he returned to the Library of
Congress in search of further documentary materials to balance out the psy-
chomythology which was threatening to take over the project. He began
research on early American explorers and traders like La Salle, attempting to
solidify his geohistorical theme (Melville as a "sea frontiersman"). But he
soon found his efforts frustrated by a lack of available data; in a letter to
Professor Frederick Merk written at this time, he begged his former teacher

to write a factual history of the frontiering instinct so as to satisfy the "hunger for knowledge" of "New Historians" like himself. Shortly after his July 28 letter to Merk, he presented his sister-in-law Barbara, who had offered to type clean copy, a rough typescript of his work to date. Then, still plagued by doubts about the objectivity of his psychic analogies, he drew up a list of potential last-minute factual insertions. The list came to forty-five items, each posing its own complicated research trail. In a rare concession to practicality, he reduced this total down to two, both of them nineteenth-century disasters involving Nantucket whaleships: the 1820 wreck of the *Essex,* and the 1824 mutiny on the *Globe.* These particular stories, he suspected, had strongly influenced Melville's conception of *Moby-Dick.*

In early August, he arranged a trip to Nantucket to inspect original records at the whaling museum there. On the eve of his departure, August 6, an American nuclear weapon fell on Hiroshima. Phoning ahead to his friend Ephraim Doner, whom he planned to visit in Newport, Rhode Island, en route, he revealed his shock and agitation over the news. He was with Doner in Newport a few days later when word of the Nagasaki bomb came. At the whaling museum in Nantucket he found indications of an underlying atavistic cruelty in human nature that could be traced back well beyond the present atomic horrors. The gruesome tale of the *Essex* provided the evidence. The ship had been struck by a whale in mid-Pacific, and cannibalism among the survivors had been documented in a graphic account kept by the first mate, Owen Chase. Chase's account confirmed Olson's suspicion: "Man devours man" was a fundamental rule of human behavior. He talked over the *Essex* incident with local whaling historian, Will Gardner, and then on board the boat back to the mainland sketched out a new section for his book, a documentary prologue to be called "First Fact."

There remained the story of the murderous mutiny aboard the *Globe*— the "psychic button," Olson speculated, which had specifically triggered *Moby-Dick.* Little detail of the *Globe* incident had survived, but it was known that two of the *Globe's* cabin boys had sailed the ship back to Valparaiso after the mutiny. Olson guessed the American consulate in that city might have retained some record of the affair. Upon his return to Washington he went directly to the National Archives. There he found consular papers that included eyewitness accounts from crew members of the *Globe.* The discoveries at the archive supplied him with "Fact #2," the story of how one of the *Globe's* harpooneers, Samuel B. Comstock, had split the captain's head in two with an ax, then slaughtered a ship's mate with a boarding knife normally used to cut blubber off a whale. This documentary insert became historical grounding for his "Moses" chapter, with its sickle-wielding brother horde of castrators and father-murderers.

A final injection of data was unexpectedly provided through the intercession of another Melville scholar, Howard Vincent, whom he ran into on a fact-checking foray to the Widener Library. At a recent Parke-Bernet auction, Vincent told Olson, a wealthy oil-company executive and book collector named Percival Brown had acquired a copy of Owen Chase's *Narrative of the Shipwreck of the Whaleship Essex*. The copy contained annotations in Herman Melville's hand. Olson implored Vincent to help him get a look at the book, and his fellow Melvillean duly complied, setting up a meeting at Brown's New Jersey home, in the course of which Olson was allowed to transcribe the treasured annotations. Melville's notes in the Chase *Narrative* confirmed the importance of "the whole Essex business." "These notes go in my direction," Olson was soon declaring in triumph to Melville scholar Jay Leyda. The transcribed annotations were turned to immediate use, as a last fact-insert called "Usufruct."

His "long work" had indeed taken years to produce, though the streamlined product would eventually yield but 119 book pages. (Not least among the benefits of the terse "vivid shorthand" prose method, he had discovered, was a new conciseness.) Finding a title was now all that remained to be done. Sorting through the several trial titles he'd listed in his notebook, from "I Take Space" to "My Country Is a White Whale," he finally opted for one of his earliest choices: *Call Me Ishmael*.

9 ～

Unresolved "Amours"
(1946)

Olson submitted *Call Me Ishmael* to John Woodburn, a Harcourt Brace editor recommended to him by Dorothy Norman. Getting a decision would take some time, since the manuscript was to be assessed not only by Woodburn but by a pair of academic readers serving as consultants to the publisher, Lewis Mumford and F. O. Matthiessen.

Olson's attention meanwhile turned to Ezra Pound, the absorbing figure whose influence had increasingly affected his literary thinking over the past year and who would engage him even more decisively in days to come. Pound, only lately removed from an outdoor cage in the U.S. military detention camp at Pisa, was flown from Rome to Washington on November 18, 1945. Olson read about his arrival in a *Washington Post* article that left little doubt about Pound's villainy; treason charges against him were summed up side by side with a story on revelations of Nazi concentration-camp horrors.

Even as the first movements toward a legal reckoning began, Olson was busy addressing the case in a polemical essay arguing that Pound should be judged not in the courts but in the eyes of fellow writers. Borrowing rhetorical authority from the only source he currently regarded as equal to Pound in eloquence, he cast its prose in a convincing imitation of the magisterial tones of W. B. Yeats, and titled it "This Is Yeats Speaking." The essay measured the achievements of the great moderns through the lens of a Yeatsian

cyclic view of history, with all save Lawrence coming off as failures, "enders
. . . out of phase." A revolutionary gambler in an age dominated by passivity
and orthodoxy, Pound had paid the price for opposing historical trends, for
ignoring the scientific and the practical in his "obsession to draw all things
up into the pattern of art," and for "reassert[ing] the claims of authority" in
a "leveling, rancorous, rational time." Before the sessions of "history present,"
Pound's work needed little defending ("I would undo no single word of all
he has published"), but the relevance of Pound's ideas, and of modernism
itself along with them, had passed. It remained to a new generation—Olson's
own—to move beyond, taking up the challenge of a postwar future. "You
are the antithetical men, and your time is forward, the conflict is more declared,
it is for you to hold the mirror up to authority."

The Yeats mask provided Olson an effective means for simplifying his
feelings on a subject that in truth appeared to him far more complex than his
essay indicated. His journals of the period reflect an almost schizophrenic
inconsistency of attitude toward Pound. Rewriting the Key West poem
"Lustrum," for instance, he reacted angrily to recent news of the death camps,
attributing to Pound's wartime propaganda the "smell of flesh in a furnace";
yet the same rewrite contained respectful nods to Pound's enlightened Jeffer-
sonianism and prosodic advances. In an assemblage piece titled "Your Witness" he diligently listed Pound pronouncements on American history, and
in a verse pastiche called "2 Propositions and 3 Proof" he incorporated a
Chinese inscription rifled directly from "Canto XIII." While contemplating
the prospects of undertaking a large-scale essay on *The Cantos,* he resolved to
attempt a reformation of his own style in keeping with Pound's example, a
superior image-making from which he himself hoped eventually to learn to
"manage an English which is a succession of objects rather than ideas."
Underlying all this assiduous discipleship, however, there remained an incipient sense of rivalry, an urgent drive to "outdo Pound, whatever his scholastic
power." Still too unsure of himself in poetry to challenge the great man in
that delicate medium, he decided he must for the present concentrate on
evening the balance by continuing to hone his most effective weapon: "Now
I take prose to be the place for me. . . ."

He persuaded Dorothy Norman to assign him to cover the Pound legal
proceedings as a *Twice A Year* reporter. Turning himself into a journalist was
no part of his intent; he merely wanted a press credential to get him into
Judge Bolitha J. Laws' district courtroom as a spectator. The arraignment
took place on November 27. While a clerk read out the nineteen counts of
treason, one for each of Pound's Italian radio broadcasts, the beleaguered
poet—"older and weaker than I imagined," Olson noted—sat silent and abject,
his eyes appearing to the curious onlooker "full of pain, and hostile." As the

accused man was led out, Olson checked an impulse to extend his hand and utter some expression of sympathy.

An insanity plea entered by his lawyer, Julian Cornell, won Pound a transfer from the D.C. city jail to Gallinger Municipal Hospital for psychiatric evaluation. Within a few weeks he had been moved again to St. Elizabeths federal hospital for the insane, where he went on awaiting a sanity hearing that would determine his legal fate. His publisher at New Directions, James Laughlin, with whom Olson had been in touch by mail, suggested to the latter that he visit the hospital. Pound, said Laughlin, was without allies in Washington and was starved for some friendly contact.

Olson had to put off visiting until after he'd returned from holiday-season trips to Enniscorthy and Hingham (where he and Connie spent Christmas with the Athertons and his mother). Back in Washington in the first week of January 1946, his first move was to follow up Laughlin's suggestion. He made the two-mile voyage across the river to the federal institution on its imposing hill overlooking the Capitol. The poet was being held in Howard Hall, St. Elizabeths' bleak, neo-Gothic penitentiary wing. There inmates in various states of dementia roamed dark airless wards and corridors, shut off from the outside world by a high surrounding wall. Olson could not help finding the place daunting. He was admitted through a black iron door into a holding room dimly illuminated by thin gray winter light seeping through barred windows. Overseen by the watchful eye of an armed guard, Pound came forward to greet him. The very bleakness of the setting made it all the more of a shock for Olson to find himself confronted not by the pitiable figure he had observed at the arraignment, but by a vivid, aggressive creature instantly recognizable as the author of all that incandescent poetry and prose. Grizzled, lion-maned, red-bearded, the Pound now before him projected the impression of a wounded animal tenaciously struggling for life. The prisoner launched directly into vehement complaint, railing against the conditions in the "gorilla cage" where he'd been kept, the shortcomings of his publisher, the enforced solitude of his present state. He lacked correspondence and company; his wife, Dorothy, couldn't get out of Italy to join him; nothing was going right. Olson, in awe, had little to offer by way of response, but Pound made it clear that at this stage a sympathetic ear was gift enough. He told his lawyer afterwards that the large stranger's fifteen-minute visit had saved his life.

For Olson, this brief first meeting seemed hardly less significant. Conscious that he was stepping into literary history, he made careful notes afterwards, giving these the auspicious title "First Canto, January 5, 1946" (later visits would be recorded as "Second Canto," "Third Canto," and so on). He had ensured a continued association by volunteering to act as Pound's informal literary secretary. In this capacity he now wrote James Laughlin to convey Pound's request for a copy of *Cantos 50-61* to present to one of the doctors at St. Elizabeths—a service less than entirely unselfish, since Olson also attempted to use the opportunity to forward his own literary interests, offering the publisher his Melville book, on which he still hadn't received a decision from Harcourt. (Laughlin politely passed.)

Before seeing Pound again he had to wade through considerable legal and institutional red tape, filling out and filing official papers at several government offices. During the resultant ten-day waiting period he was assailed by second thoughts about his emissary's role. It was sobering enough to have to state his motives in establishing relations with an accused traitor, and in this enforced hiatus between visits he also had an unsettling encounter with Michael Greenberg, a State Department Far Eastern policy adviser he'd gotten to know in his last months at the OWI. Greenberg had read "This Is Yeats Speaking," just out in the Winter 1946 issue of *Partisan Review*. Olson had given little concern to the ripples his advocacy of Pound might create in liberal political circles, in part because the *Partisan* editor who had accepted the essay, Philip Rahv, was Jewish—a nuance he'd rather naively taken as a guarantee of immunity from criticism. Greenberg brought him up short by reminding him that literary and moral criteria of judgment were far from identical; the State Department man hinted meaningfully that the essay might be interpreted by some observers as a clever whitewash job on behalf of an outright fascist.

The warning was still reverberating in his mind as he returned to St. Elizabeths for a second visit, this time much more wary. Though he successfully disguised them from Pound, his misgivings were in fact little relieved by the latter's behavior on this occasion. It seemed to him that Pound was presuming him to be an unquestioning disciple, a presumption he privately resented even as he continued to behave in a way that implicitly invited it. Pound, still under heavy attack from the press, now began to assign him fronts on which to mount a journalistic defense. Pound's idea of effective newspaper writing was that of Westbrook Pegler, a popular right-wing columnist regarded by Olson as a "fascist s.o.b."—exactly the kind of Red-baiting demagogue he himself most abhorred.

Pound moreover made no effort to conceal the deep-end views that had landed him in the loony bin. On Olson's third visit, January 24, the captive poet aired wild speculations concerning the effects of circumcision on the endocrine glands. While recognizing this as the "same god damned kind of medical nonsense Hitler and the gang had used," Olson couldn't help marveling at the force of conviction with which it was put forth: "It was so cockeyed for the moment it was funny, actually, absurd, and I was carried along by this swearing, swift, slashing creature." Despite all his resolutions of caution, he found Pound's tidal-wave energy all but impossible to resist. He came back to the hospital three times in the next three weeks, bearing gifts of dates, cigarettes and wine. On one visit he brought along Connie. These hospital days were now the big events of his life. Each was carefully accounted in his growing logbook of "Cantos," the entries saturated with Poundiana: literary trivia, reading tips, chance expressions of bigotry, everything—good *and* bad—that rolled off the tongue of the Master.

For Olson the high points came when Pound's monologue drifted into retrospect, touching on past acquaintances with such figures as the novelist Ford Madox Ford and the cultural anthropologist Leo Frobenius; at such moments he was able to sail serenely with the great raconteur on smooth seas of memory and enlightenment. In time he became adept at keeping conversation away from dangerous political shoals by exercising a little diplomatic steersmanship of the kind he'd learned during his days in government. A policy of calculated discretion, in fact, dictated his entire approach to this one-sided relationship in which his spectatorhood had been a given from the outset. Rarely did the shifting beam of Pound's attention turn toward him in any focused way.

One notable occasion when this did happen came on February 14, the day following the poet's final sanity hearing. After three months of anxious waiting, Pound had finally been determined mentally unfit to stand trial for treason, and was accordingly in unusually good spirits. Passing along to Olson some corrected typescripts of the *Pisan Cantos* for delivery to James Laughlin, he was full of confident plans for new work. Suddenly, in midsentence, he paused and glanced at his visitor as if for the first time, inquiring, "What exactly do you do?" Olson allowed modestly that he was a writer, but quickly added that he was also an unsuccessful one so far: he'd earned but $60 in the past year, his sole means of support was his working wife, his one completed literary work remained unpublished. Harcourt, he told Pound, had just turned down the Melville book because of the negative comments of academic advisers Matthiessen and Mumford; he felt particularly galled by this, Matthiessen having been his teacher. (He neglected to tell Pound he'd resolved to remove Matthiessen's name from a list of those whose help he was acknowledging in a prefatory note.) He had, he went on, recently submitted the book to another New York publishing house, Reynal & Hitchcock, on the recommendation of his former Harvard colleague Harry Levin; Levin had a contact there, editor Monroe Engel. Pound replied that he too had a connection at the firm, publisher Eugene "Kewpie" Reynal. He indicated willingness to intercede with Reynal, and also suggested that Olson send the manuscript to T. S. Eliot at Faber & Faber in London.

The next time Olson came to St. Elizabeths, on March 19, he brought the book for Pound's perusal. (Pound later commented he'd found it a useful shortcut to understanding Melville, an author he'd never had the patience to actually read.) He had meanwhile followed Pound's instructions and mailed a copy to Eliot, who had politely responded that while he had "greatly enjoyed" it, there was little market for Melville in the British Isles. The fact that both Pound and Eliot had taken an interest, however, had by now swayed Reynal & Hitchcock. In April, Olson received an acceptance from Monroe Engel. Pound's support had proved decisive.

The long-awaited news about *Call Me Ishmael* appeared to Olson a break-through that would not only vindicate his years of effort on the project, but launch him forward into further major advances. He went immediately to New York to sign a contract, discuss editing of the manuscript and propose further book ideas—for more Melville volumes, for a series of fables on the organs of the human body and for a big work on the West and its conquest by Spanish adventurers lured by gold—to not only Engel but editors at other companies as well. While in the city he made the rounds of foundation offices, seeking institutional grant support for the West project. "The precious circle I have lived and written in is broken, and I can now manage to settle the world," he reported optimistically in a letter home to Connie. When the grant "feedbag" did not yield instant funding, he turned to other potential sources of a quick cash strike, including a Buenos Aires millionaire who was allegedly inclined to lend philanthropic support to struggling writers. That scheme too fell through, but Olson did not want to return home without having achieved some measure of "private authority" as a breadwinner. He decided to stay on for a month or so to take up a temporary position as lobbyist on behalf of Polish interests at early meetings of the United Nations Security Council. The job came to him by way of Oscar Lange, now Poland's UN representative. It was behind-the-scenes work, a return to the "fast buck & easy blood" tactics that had caused him to withdraw in revulsion from politics in 1945. "I was being paid, in hotel corridors, by an unnamed foreign power, for, being their brain," he would later recall ruefully to a close friend. The experience merely confirmed his resolve to steer clear of such morally dubious activities in the future, and to continue his efforts to make a place for himself in the comparatively more conscionable—if for him much less lucrative—world of literature.

During this New York stay he was put up at the Second Avenue studio-loft of his Italian artist friend Corrado Cagli. He and Cagli hadn't seen one another since before the war, in which the latter had returned to Europe as a soldier in the U.S. Army. Their friendship now resumed with renewed intensity, the artist becoming an important influence on Olson both creatively and emotionally. For Charles the strength of this influence would in time give rise to serious self-questionings. While never openly sexual, and largely sublimated as professional fellowship, his relationship with Cagli was to take on dimensions similar in his view to those that had emerged with other strong male figures, Edward Dahlberg in the past, Ezra Pound currently: a pattern of excessive dependence, a conveying of powerful affect beyond the bounds of mere casual camaraderie. Along with Pound, Cagli would come to represent for him one of two principal "unresolved 'amours' " of the period, and his alliances with them to appear based—in his perhaps overly scrupulous judgment—on an almost rapacious imitative striving on his part; in both cases, as he would recognize in later reflection, "the love was covert, and the work posed as my own."

For the moment, however, no such doubts or complications could deflect the positive impact of the reestablished contact. Cagli's work had quickly inspired a major Olson poem, "La Préface." During the 1945 Allied liberation of Germany, the artist had been among the first G.I.s to enter Buchenwald. Hasty sketches he'd made of the death-camp inmates' graffiti had subsequently evolved into an extensive series of drawings, which Olson now viewed. No graphic art had previously moved him with the force of these harrowing images, signifying in their tortured figurations the destruction not merely of a civilization but—to his impressionable imagination, recently imprinted with multiple personal disillusionments about politics and history—of the entire humanistic proposition underlying it. In Cagli's Buchenwald drawings Olson saw the total past culture of Europe reduced to rubble. Out of this shattering vision of the Old World in ruins he began to assemble a poem of reconstruction, serious, allusive, modernist in form. He placed the Homeric figure of Odysseus at its center, as had Pound in embarking on the *Cantos,* and in procedure he had Pound's masterly Pisan poems, those consummate fragments shored against ruin, to follow as template. Even so, as the poem developed he could not but feel he was composing in what amounted to a primitive state, inscribing its post-apocalyptic images like "early recognizable facts on badly lit walls with rudimentary instruments." In "La Préface," the death-ground of Buchenwald became the birth-ground of a new archaic, a "new Altamira cave" whose walls were windows open on a future of indeterminate possibility. Olson invited his fellow survivors to "put war away with time, come into space," and emphasized his defiance of the temporal by echoing William Blake's "The Mental Traveller," transporting Blake's howling, time-entangled babe into a timeless present where Cagli's skeletal figures were still stretched in agony upon the barbed wire of their enclosure:

Mark that arm. It is no longer gun.
We are born not of the buried but these unburied dead
crossed stick, wire-led, Blake Underground

The Babe

  the Howling Babe

He gave Cagli an early typescript of "La Préface," and the artist returned the gesture with the gift of a tarot drawing depicting *il penduto,* the hanged man. Delighted, Olson proposed continuing the exchange by putting together a collaborative book of poems and drawings on the tarot, and Cagli agreed. Upon his departure from New York late that spring Olson began work in typical energetic scattershot fashion, immediately allowing the project to spill out well beyond its original parameters into a much more ambitious (and less practical) multiplicity of scope. Plotting not merely poems but a full-scale book on the occult mythic framework of the tarot (to include in its embracing scheme "major arcana-gods, minor arcana-demiurges, arcana-man"), he initiated a new offensive upon the catalogs and stacks of the Library of Congress, combing through all available readings on the history of hermetic magic. Inspired by the examples and directives of Cagli, he also soon began exploring a new line of interest in modern mathematical and geometrical theory, consulting especially the recent discoveries of Canadian geometer H. S. M. Coxeter (*Non-Euclidean Geometry,* 1942) and also looking into works on "time, the 4th dimension," "n-dimensional geometry" and "the unboundedness of space" by such nineteenth-century European mathematicians as Riemann, Cayley and Lobachevsky. His inability to grasp the technical fine points of such works took little away from the excitement of mental adventure, the sense of pushing beyond the frontiers of accepted definitions of reality, in which he felt quite able to share despite his scientific amateur's status. An 1823 comment of the Hungarian mathematician Bolyai Farkas to his son— "many things have an epoch in which they are found at the same time in several places, just as the violets appear on every side in the spring"—struck Olson as directly applicable not only to projective geometry but to the postmodern pursuit of knowledge in general; the quote became for him a touchstone statement on the process by which a plurality of minds may arrive unbeknownst to one another at parallel advances, and thus an image of a common intellectual "company" which he would always find particularly gratifying. No less appealing to him was the response, also found in Coxeter's book, of Bolyai Farkas' son Bolyai János: "I have created a new universe out of nothing." On the instinctive conjectural level at which he functioned best as a creative thinker, Olson's own later discoveries in open-field poetics, his aesthetic formulations of verse as "projective space," can in large part be traced back to these early Cagli-instigated inquiries of 1946.

That summer he and Connie went off on extended holidays to Enniscorthy and Gloucester, where he met again with Cagli to work out a mock-up version of their tarot collaboration. Olson offered this to James Laughlin, but the publisher showed little interest. Throughout the fall back in Washington he was still persevering with intermingled studies of the occult and of the new projective geometry, the big tarot-book plan having by now given way to a more realistic concentration on the smaller verse project. Hiking daily to the library, he keyed his walking route to the psychic mood of his latest poem, composing the lines in his head as he sauntered along. This superstitious "funny fetish trek" yielded the few finished pieces which were all that ultimately came of his tarot investigations. One was "In Praise of the Fool," a rather slight Yeatsian lyric provoked by Cagli's "fool" drawing (he sold this poem to *Harper's Bazaar,* and later retitled it "The Green Man"). Another, "To Corrado Cagli," interpreting one of the artist's abstract sketches, was an elliptical evocation of ritual rape, its anatomical "elements in trance" disposed in a tense configuration reflecting the recent mathematical interests he spelled out in an early draft: "Upon a moebius strip I saw this new geometry . . ." (while that line did not survive, he would later restore the poem's original title, "The Moebius Strip"). These two poems, together with the earlier "Trinacria," "The K," and "La Préface," made up Olson's contribution to the collaborative project.

Y & X, the chapbook that resulted, had found a publisher by the end of the year, once again thanks to the intervention of Ezra Pound. Pound had put Olson in touch with Caresse Crosby, cosmopolitan Washington hostess and founder of Black Sun Press. The connection was a by-product of one of Olson's secretarial errands; Pound, who, along with such fellow modernist luminaries as Crane, Joyce and Lawrence, had once been published by Black Sun, had dispatched him to carry to Crosby a message regarding some Gaudier-Brzeska drawings. Olson was soon accepted into Crosby's social circle, becoming a frequent dinner guest in her elegant Georgetown home, where "the demi-monde of art & politics" could be observed at close range. She expressed great admiration for his writing, and included his "Moebius Strip" poem in the latest edition of her deluxe *Portfolio* broadside series. Though Olson considered Crosby "empty" as a person, he was greatly pleased to have such a prestigious publisher for his first verse collection.

Despite his summertime absence from Washington and his absorption in Cagli-inspired studies, he'd managed to keep up regular attendance on Ezra Pound, making several brief pilgrimages from the Virginia countryside back to the sweltering city expressly to visit St. Elizabeths. On one of these visits, the subject of his association with Cagli came up. Pound, who had once sat for a portrait by the Italian artist, dismissed him contemptuously as a Zionist and purveyor of cheap gypsy magic. Torn between conflicting allegiances, Olson said nothing to defend the rival "amour," but later took out his resentment in his journal notes. He still considered the relationship with Pound too valuable to risk alienating him by direct confrontation.

During the remaining months of 1946 he went on laboring to track down Pound's books in an attempt to overcome his deficiencies of knowledge "of speech in relation to music," as well as of turn-of-the-century culture and letters, from Rémy de Gourmont to Henry James (following Pound's leads, he hoped, would provide him a ready-made "general summary of state of human consciousness in decades immediately before my own"). Under Pound's tutelage he also embarked on a serious study of the rhythmic cadences of Greek poetry—a longtime preoccupation of Pound's dating back to the early interest in Homer reflected in the *Cantos* and recently renewed at St. Elizabeths by collaborative efforts at translating Greek plays with a University of Maryland classics scholar, Rudd Fleming. On Pound's advice Olson read with close attention the writings of Victor Bérard and Jane Harrison on the *Odyssey*, examined historical works on the musical qualities of Greek choral verse and joined up with a group of fellow Pound disciples involved in the founding of a Washington-based poetic theater patterned after the early Greek model. Other participants in the group—later to take the name "the New Company"—included Fleming, whose living room provided an informal meeting place where performances of oral declamation were staged (there Olson himself was to make his first tape recordings, reading his own verse aloud in an approximation of archaic rhythms); Greek-American sculptor Michael Lekakis; Eva Sikilianos, a teacher of Byzantine vocal music; Greek scholar Michael Kyriakos, a visitor from Athens; and Frank Moore, a young New York musician who was at the time commuting regularly to Washington to confer with Pound on musical settings of the poet's translations of choruses from Sophocles' *Women of Trachis*. Moore, coincidentally also a friend of Cagli's and a student of tarot as well as a clever conversationalist in his own right, became quite close with Olson, a partner in Charles' marathon nocturnal verbal sessions and an occasional overnight guest at Randolph Place, where he improvised elementary sleeping quarters among the rusty gardening tools in the empty sculpture studio adjacent to the Olson apartment.

Olson's membership in the Pound circle had by this time come to be his principal literary association, not only in Washington but in the larger world beyond. Handling Pound's incoming mail, a service he'd undertaken to release the poet himself to spend more time on reading and writing, brought him into contact with like-minded aspiring literary types from all over the coun-try. On Pound's bidding, he attempted to set up an impromptu epistolary common front called the Committee of Correspondence, designed to circu-late the latest dicta of the Master, "fight the fake" and "promote the serious . . . Kung [Confucius], Frobenius, Ford, Gesell, Fenollosa." Among those included in the scheme were poet John Berryman, then teaching at Prince-ton; Harvard drama professor Theodore Spencer, whom Olson had known in Cambridge; and University of Iowa English instructor Ray West, editor of the *Western Review*. While some of his letters, most notably those to Ber-ryman, went ignored, and in the end the committee never really came together, for his assiduous efforts on behalf of the cause (or "for papa," as he put it) Olson once again reaped certain indirect rewards. The Iowa professor's mag-azine now became his best outlet for verse, providing space for several new poems that were too long or uncompromising for the commercial magazines (for example, an extended documentary piece on repression in Puritan New England, titled "There Was a Youth Whose Name Was Thomas Granger"). Though his reliance on the Pound connection was already engendering some inward doubts, it was not to be denied that this connection had useful aspects, both as ongoing instruction in poetics and as opening stake at the gaming tables of literary careering—an area in which, as he admitted in one of his Committee of Correspondence feeler letters, "the Olson hand is little played as yet."

During this period when Olson's involvements with Cagli and the Pound circle were dominating his time and attention, there came the first signs of strain in his relationship with Connie. After five years of common-law mar-riage, she had come to recognize certain patterns in his behavior that sug-gested the lifetime bond she'd hoped for might have elements she hadn't anticipated. She had a jealous side, and was easily roused to suspicion by his occasional indications of a roving eye, as when he became briefly enamored from afar of a high-wire performer in the Ringling Brothers circus (the inno-cent outcome of this infatuation was a poem he named after the lissome artiste, "Lalage"), but in truth his fidelity as a partner left little to be desired. Far more significant in Connie's view was the absorbing quality of his friend-ships with the men he admired. She had never appreciated Edward Dahl-berg's large and complicated role in his life, and had done her part to terminate it. Now, seeing a similar pattern of excessive influence and dependency devel-oping with both Cagli and Pound, she became determined to avoid a reprise of the painful Dahlberg situation. In her quiet, subtle fashion, she began to resist both these new rivals for all she was worth.

At the same time, Connie was now starting to suspect that in the long run she was perhaps facing an even more potent adversary than any individual contender for his attention. The phantom opponent was the intellectual coldness of his nature, an intangible but very real and obdurate force that lay beneath his surface charm and conviviality, seeming to permanently distance him from her. In moments of frustration she accused him of being completely without human warmth, of using his verbal mastery to cover over a terrible lack of intimate feeling. The absence of real emotional contact in their relationship was beginning to wear on her, she told him, making her less and less secure about her decision to commit her life into his hands without reservation. Even more disturbing to him was her further suggestion that he was spoiling their sex life by pushing it too hard, "straining it toward infinity instead of leaving it as use, as sensation."

He took such admonitions to heart, yet felt powerless to change himself. Moreover there were times when he couldn't help sensing that there were problems that went beyond even Connie's discontented analysis, that something essential was missing from his life, something he was not quite able to identify. He suffered continually from a nagging restlessness and from vague, nameless guilts. Falling back into old habits of unhappy self-scrutiny, he lectured himself ceaselessly in his journal about his need to integrate the dissociated halves of his personality, to force together the bluff, outgoing, eager public persona with the earnest, sensitive, moody private self. The division he felt in himself was now so radical, he secretly believed, as to actually produce two distinct "forms of behavior," and in effect two different Charles Olsons. The split in his personality was most clearly evidenced by his dealings with other people, in which two disjunct modes had become manifest: "to be alone with one other human being (for flagellation) or to be, when there are others, the preening, crowing, dominant cock (which I can only be via intellect)."

10 ❧

Arresting the West
(1947)

The drive to produce a "long work" which had two years earlier been a principal motive in Olson's return to writing—then however resulting only in the relatively brief and condensed book-length essay on Melville—had by the beginning of 1947 returned with renewed force, stirring him more urgently than ever toward the creation of an original opus on a grand scale, a work of sufficient amplitude to propel him forward from his present continuing state of apprenticeship to true equality with (and therefore independence of) those modernist "fathers" whose imprint still remained so powerful in his highly patristic imagination. Foremost among them, of course, was Ezra Pound. Instinctively Olson sensed that the only way to break through to the attainment of a creative identity of his own was to outdo Pound at the latter's own game, the epic construction form. Self-demand, always a spur for him, colluded with this growing sense of competitive rivalry to make the undertaking of some vast totalizing work seem not only a challenge but an immediate necessity. Well aware that by the age of thirty-six Pound had already left the preparing stage behind and launched forth in the *Cantos* upon an epic voyage over vast ranges of past culture and timeless myth, Olson resolved to do likewise, and moreover to outdistance Pound by expanding his own exploration to take in the New World, which the *Cantos* had largely ignored, producing an epic fable of the myths and history of the Americas.

Over the winter of 1946–1947 he began work at the Library of Congress, first envisioning a long poem centered on Indians, Spaniards and gold and bringing in as principals Ulysses, Columbus, Faust, Montezuma, Cabeza de Vaca, Cavelier de La Salle and Paul Bunyan, then on further deliberation opting instead to forgo verse and employ instead the conjectural, propositional prose style he'd developed in *Call Me Ishmael*—"assault" prose, as he now thought of it, a mix of bold assertion and documentary datum (short, factual sections, he speculated, could be inserted as in the Melville book, to "batten down" his major themes). By February 1947 he had arrived at a rough outline, with the working title "OPERATION RED, WHITE & BLACK": his focus would be "the acts and myths of the early Indian & White on this continent," specifically those of the Hopi, Kwakiutl and Cochiti tribes, of voyagers La Salle and Cabeza de Vaca, and of fortune seekers Cortez, Coronado, and the Donner Party (as for the third or "BLACK" factor in his equation, he'd so far been able to turn up only one likely frontier-era candidate—Jim Beckwith, mulatto war chief of the Crow nation). In the abstract, the scheme appeared to offer the breadth of vision he was after; already, however, it contained a serious drawback which he would not recognize until some years later, when he came to see that he'd been unconsciously attempting to imitate the form of another loosely structured work on the diverse national cultural heritage, W. C. Williams' *In the American Grain*. While Williams had succeeded in unifying his book by locating a "governing hero for himself" in the figure of Sam Houston, Olson's own plan lacked any such pivotal character. The resulting inherent lack of cohesion would ultimately doom the project.

But such sober hindsight was far away, and only the adventurous promise of the idea apparent to him, as he set out to sell it to New York publishers early in 1947. When Reynal & Hitchcock, made uneasy by his last-minute nervous fiddling over the final proofs of *Call Me Ishmael*, failed to exercise their option on the new project, he took it to Viking Press, where his enthusiastic pitch had soon won over the head of the firm, his former OWI colleague Harold Guinzburg. Viking awarded him a $250 advance, and a generous three-year period in which to produce a finished book.

Meanwhile, in mid-March *Call Me Ishmael* came out. Olson's exaggerated expectations for it, certainly disproportionate to any real chance so brief and eccentric a work had of making a significant impact in the conservative publishing atmosphere of its time, left him entirely unprepared for the predictably cool response it actually received from the nation's critics—particularly those in the academic sector from which he had departed with a lingering residue of ill feeling a decade earlier. The setback was temporarily devastating to him. "My interest in doing that book," he would later admit, "was to actually *arrest the West,* and I was so disappointed when everything didn't just stop that it knocked me out for five months after the thing came out. I couldn't imagine how the world could have this book and not catch up."

The most damaging salvo issued from an old nemesis, Lewis Mumford, in the *New York Times*. Writing in the *Times* of April 6, Mumford pronounced the book an anomaly and a failure, crediting Olson in passing for his contribution of some fresh knowledge about Melville, but severely faulting his lack of logical argument and scholarly procedure, and dismissing his "intuitive" approach as mere secondhand Lawrence and Dahlberg. This influential critic's negative verdict set a tone which would be followed in most of those establishment journals that deigned to bother with the book at all. Robert Berkelman of the *Christian Science Monitor* dubbed Olson a "poet laureate of eccentricity," "lost in the undergrowth" of Melville and unable to beat his way out with a style that alternated "fantastic and wilful prose" and "Sears-Roebuck cataloguing." In the *Saturday Review,* scholar Willard Thorpe challenged the book's underlying assumptions, especially those concerning whaling and Shakespeare. In *Accent,* conservative critic Stanley Edgar Hyman lamented Olson's "half coherent mumbo-jumbo." "Indefensibly wild, 'Freudian' and intellectual"—as a later observer would put it—was the summary judgment afforded *Call Me Ishmael* by the author's academic contemporaries. The maverick California historian J. H. Jackson, on the other hand, writing in the *San Francisco Chronicle,* expressed a friendlier view which would prove more indicative of the long-range perception of the book by those able to consider it in the larger context of American cultural history. Jackson found *Call Me Ishmael* "one of the most stimulating essays ever written on *Moby-Dick* and for that matter on any literature and the forces behind it." The *Chronicle* review would indeed prove useful, helping introduce Olson to a valuable potential readership on the West Coast. Still, it was far from enough to overcome the bitter taste of his rejection "in correct circles."

At the end of March he put in an appearance at the opening of an exhibit of Cagli's art work at the Knoedler Gallery in New York (a broadside featuring his "Moebius Strip" poem was produced as an announcement for the show). While in the city he let himself be drawn into a restless social whirl of appointments and parties, attempting to compensate for the insecurity he felt in a mainstream literary world by hyping himself up in nervous verbal exertions. It was a reflex he was disturbed by but could not control, the product of an irresistible urge "to hop it up, jerk it up . . . wooing in the way I have when I think I am being judged as less than I am." The disparity between the verbal performance or "wooing" and the literal *doing* could become the source of significant difficulties later. At a party thrown by his *Harper's Bazaar* editor, for example, he talked up the idea of a three-part feature article on a new interest of his, the comparative psychology of sleeping and waking states. He envisaged a study of his own dreams as the center of the piece, and was so convincing in his advance descriptions of it that he left New York with a $250 *Harper's* assignment; when it came to the actual writing, however, he was able to complete only the first section of the projected article, and that was rejected by the magazine as being far too abstruse for its popular audience.

His busy schedule of engagements on this New York stay included meetings with fellow Melvilleans Raymond Weaver, Henry Murray and Jay Leyda and with literary bigwigs Carl Van Doren, Van Wyck Brooks and Alfred Kazin. At a party he met the famous left-wing photographer Henri Cartier-Bresson, and was invited to take part in a political discussion group that gathered in Cartier-Bresson's apartment on the Manhattan side of the Queensboro Bridge; there he made another new contact who would be a significant friend over the years ahead, a twenty-seven-year-old French émigré businessman named Jean Riboud. Scion of a wealthy Lyons banking family, Riboud had fought with the Resistance, been captured by the Nazis, and survived the horrors of confinement in Buchenwald. Now an investment banker for an international firm, he was a soft-spoken, urbane advocate of all things progressive in politics and the arts. He owned an impressive collection of modern paintings and numbered among his friends such men as Alger Hiss, Langston Hughes, Max Ernst, Roberto Rossellini and Pierre Mendès-France; his artistic heroes were the photographers Robert Capa and Cartier-Bresson, his political idol Mao Tse-tung. To Olson, he appeared the prototype of a quality of "humanitas"—intellect, taste, culture and civilization raised to their highest levels. The two now talked at length, Olson taking away a vivid apprehension of "l'univers concentrationnaire," the fragile new world given birth in the wartime death camps. Riboud would later visit him often in Washington, and offer his own apartment on East 63rd Street as a stopping-off place for Olson on subsequent visits to the city.

Riboud's sophistication, gentility and patrician manners made him one friend of whom even Connie could approve (indeed, her soft spot for the Frenchman would occasionally stir Charles to moments of jealousy). In this sense their relationship would mark a hopeful turning point for Olson, away from the old paternal-substitution pattern toward a more balanced or "normal" kind of relationship with male friends. That transition was coincidentally underscored for him by the discovery of a letter from Edward Dahlberg awaiting him upon his return home from New York. The first communication from his former friend in six years, it contained profuse congratulations on the publication of *Call Me Ishmael*. When Olson did not immediately reply, he received a second letter, very different in tone. Now bristling and accusative, Dahlberg charged that Olson had become a "vain Absalom," selfishly and cruelly ungrateful to all his fathers. A brief, acrimonious epistolary exchange ensued, Dahlberg condemning Olson's recent writing style for a Pound-influenced descent into the vernacular, a wounded Olson replying angrily by suggesting his onetime mentor was trying to trade on affections "like money on a table," after the manner of a "Kansas City merchant."

But the Absalom allusion had hit home; Olson now once again fell prey to bad dreams about his dead father. In one of them Karl swung an ax menacingly over his head. In another the guilty son was warned about Corrado Cagli: Karl, speaking in Latin (the language of the classics, symbolic tongue of "the fathers"), questioned the "value" of his relation with Cagli ("ad valorem Cagli"). Afterwards Olson was left feeling vaguely resentful, "sore at the interference." But the message was unavoidable—"I continue to be a son, & fail to take up my perception & manhood."

Work on the West book meanwhile went slowly, progress repeatedly retarded by his tendency to pursue sidetracks into thickets of detail which he found personally absorbing but which proved difficult to integrate with his main historic theme, the lure of and appetite for gold in the early West. (An instance was his spending several library days on the story of the 1866 Fetterman massacre and related lore of Indian dismemberment rites, a topic much less relevant to the search for gold than to his own obsession with primal castration threat.) In late May he went off with Connie to Gloucester for a holiday. The return to New England produced his one memorable poem of the year, "Move Over," an emphatic rejection of postwar capitalism ("Smash the plate glass window. . . . The dead face is the true face / of Washington, New York a misery, but north and east / the carpenter obeyed / topography"). While in Gloucester he met for lunch with Cape Ann Historical Society director Alfred Mansfield Brooks, whose suggestion that he attempt a work on local history he took seriously enough to immediately follow up by interviewing his longtime Stage Fort Park fisherman-neighbors Lou Douglas and Frank Miles. The idea of a historical work on Gloucester was put back on hold for the time, but these informal interview sessions supplied material later to prove of significant use in *The Maximus Poems*.

He stayed on in the Northeast into the summer, preparing for a trip across country to appear at the Pacific Northwest Writers' Conference at the University of Washington in August. Before leaving he visited Frank Moore in New York, then joined Connie at Mel and Jane Atherton's new home in Weymouth, Massachusetts. After an unsuccessful (and semicomic) search for a used car to drive west, the couple were dropped off by Mel Atherton at the Boston bus depot, where a last-minute check of their baggage disclosed the absence of Charles' supply of hand-tailored king-size shirts, purchased in New

York specially for the trip. He wired Frank Moore with frantic instructions to express the shirts on to him in Seattle. Then, while waiting to board the bus, he struck up a conversation with a pair of college students who were about to head west by car; soon he'd cashed in his and Connie's bus tickets, having talked his way into a free ride for them both to Chicago. There he managed to pull off the same trick, this time hitching a ride all the way to Portland, Oregon, with a Chinese-American woman in return for his assistance behind the wheel. The Olsons reached Seattle with their carefully hoarded stash of traveler's checks virtually intact, but tired and squabbling from the long road stint.

Exhaustion was perhaps a complicating factor in Olson's erratic performance at the conference, as was his trepidation in the presence of a largely academic audience. He had been invited as a guest lecturer on the strength of *Call Me Ishmael,* but instead of addressing that book's thesis on Melville and the Pacific frontier, he elected to speak on the wider subject of writing and culture in a radically altered post-atomic world. His talk, titled "Poetry and Criticism," began with the contention that recent historical tremors had shaken loose all the old moorings of form and value, disrupting even the most fundamental principles of Western civilization and thought. This assertion was put forward in his current mode of abrupt conjectural "assault," relieved by neither logical development nor polite scholastic apology: "What bores me, and angers me, as much in writing as in foreign policy, are those who clutch old answers in a new, terrifying world. It is the act of the middle-aged, the reactionary . . . word-maker as well as policy-maker." Literature was under urgent obligation to come to terms with a redefined physical world, in which "experience, like matter, is discontinuous"; writing, like reality, must be broken down into its original components, the linguistic "elements and particles" of words, themselves like postwar man now "lost in a sea of question" and in need of resubstantiation through a new objectivism—a poetics based not on abstract ideas but on solid building blocks of fact and document. The process of change would involve less an innovation of technique than a return to archaic means, with document taking over the onetime role of magic in the human mystery, fact that of religious ritual. The neo-primitive writing on the cave walls of the future could be illuminated by discerning use of a handful of existing texts: *Moby-Dick,* Euripides' *The Bacchae,* Pound's *Cantos,* Freud's *Moses and Monotheism,* Fenollosa's "The Chinese Written Character" and the works of pioneers in cultural anthropology (Leo Frobenius, Franz Boas, Ruth Benedict) and in New Science, geometry and mathematics.

These remarks were in fact merely his introduction, a buildup to and gloss upon "La Préface"; he had intended to follow with a reading of that and other recent poems, clinching his proposal of an objectivist poetics by demonstrating it in performance. But the deadpan reaction of his listeners was daunting enough to cause him to lose his resolve, his confidence suddenly deserting him. He ended the show in silent, awkward embarrassment, walking off without reading a single line. (His strange behavior on this occasion would come back to haunt him in later years as a barnstorming poet, during which he was convinced his "objectionable" performance had made him permanently *non grata* on the Northwest reading circuit.) Afterwards, at a party for the conferees, he drank too much, and his verbal powers came back in an inopportune rush. While he ranted on against the errors of current American poetry and foreign policy to a bemused crew of young literature instructors, Connie, feeling neglected, ducked out with one of the conferees. He went looking for her, found them necking, and was thrown into "unruly terror." The next day the couple made amends, and agreed it was high time to hit the road again.

Following a restorative hike among meadows full of wildflowers on the foothills of Mount Rainier, they headed south toward San Francisco. Charles, eager to scout unfamiliar terrain, picked out a slow local bus stopping at every hamlet on the rugged Oregon coast. The urge to explore grew stronger as the miles went by, until at length he overcame Connie's sensible objections and they got off at a tiny logging burg in the middle of nowhere. It was getting dark and they were carrying neither food nor water, but he pointed out that they had brought camping gear and could buy whatever else they needed at the town's general store. At that establishment, however, some loitering lumberjacks' menacing comments about his bizarre appearance— bespectacled giant swathed in sweaters and shawl, toting portable typewriter—signaled serious trouble. The Wild West suddenly seeming much too close for comfort, he and Connie beat a hasty retreat into a grove of firs beside the highway, where they took apprehensive shelter until the arrival of the morning bus.

In San Francisco, poet and critic Kenneth Rexroth, with whom Charles had recently struck up epistolary contact, met them at the Greyhound station. Rexroth put them up at his apartment, and "did the turns" of introducing Olson to local verse luminaries like Muriel Rukeyser, William Everson and Mary Fabilli. On Rexroth's advice he also sought out Robert Duncan, perhaps the most flamboyant and certainly the most talented of the local poets. They met across the bay on the Berkeley campus of the University of California, where Olson was researching Gold Rush history at the Bancroft Library. He'd already heard quite a bit about the twenty-eight-year-old Duncan, who had achieved something of a reputation in the East Coast Pound circle: the Californian had only recently returned from a pilgrimage to the Master at St. Elizabeths, and had published some poems in *Circle,* a little magazine edited by Berkeley Poundian George Leite, that had impressed Olson considerably—an impression complicated by Duncan's simultaneous notoriety as "the Ambassador from Venus," a self-designed visionary Theosophist dangerously entangled in misty spirit worlds.

Their encounter dispelled most of Olson's fears on the latter count; Duncan's poetic visions, he quickly learned, were backed up by much solid historical knowledge. They talked at length on a lawn adjoining the library, with Connie as silent witness and Olson himself basking recumbent on a sloping bank of grass like some inquisitive Gulliver as the handsome young Berkeley poet matched him move for move in the kind of intellectual acrobatics that most delighted him. "I was interested in totally coordinating a time-space picture of the Earth, then zeroing in at some point of it, and so was he," Duncan has recalled. "That day I talked to him about the economic relation of cities to the surrounding landscape. It turned out he'd been thinking about the same thing himself." (Indeed Olson had, as evidenced by the poem "Move Over.") "He wanted to know about the Greek idea of *temenos*, which I explained to him. He'd just been back to Gloucester, talking to the fishermen. Even then the question of what it means to have a sacred place or precinct obviously interested him. And of course it would be *the* question for him—the whole problem of how to cultivate one's own locality in writing." Duncan took the Olsons home to dinner at his communal household on nearby Hearst Street, proudly displaying his in-progress *Medieval Scenes* poems, and introducing his attractive strawberry-blond female roommate, who intrigued Charles almost as much as the poetry. By his next visit to the Hearst Street house, however, the blonde had been dislodged by an equally comely male youth. Robert Duncan continued to surprise.

Olson's Berkeley sojourn brought him a second important future ally, the distinguished University of California geographer Carl O. Sauer. Though there was little poetry about Sauer—he was a polite, reserved academic, a scholar in the traditional sense—Olson would soon come to regard him as a creative "father" and forerunner in the intellectual adventure of earth history. Before coming West he had already used Sauer's *The Road to Cibola* (1932), a renowned work on the fabulous Seven Cities of Cibola, as a key source in his own gold studies. He now found Sauer in person at the latter's top-floor office in the earth sciences building of the university. Arriving armed with a notebook full of queries about Coronado, Cabeza de Vaca and the Spanish conquest, he was at first set back to learn that the geographer's main interest had lately shifted from New World explorations to prehistoric cultures of the Ice Age. But before long he had decided that the Ice Age, too, contained the stuff of myth; upon his return to Washington he would begin to bombard Sauer with questions about Deglaciation cultures, inquiring, for example, as to whether *Homo sapiens* had actually "started off as an omnivore."

His principal business in Berkeley, meanwhile, was his work at the Bancroft. In the library's Heller Reading Room, beneath historic paintings of California pioneer days, he combed through folios of old Gold Rush documents, seeking out in particular the facts of the infamous cannibalism episode culminating the ill-fated 1846 Sierra crossing of the Donner Party. In the journal of one George McKinstry, agent and sheriff at Sutter's Fort, he found what he'd been looking for—eyewitness accounts of the harrowing trip, straight from the mouths of the survivors. His excited discovery of those papers led him in turn to focus his attention on McKinstry's employer, the enigmatic Swiss immigrant John Sutter. He had soon turned up a significant "lost" document, the lease on Indian lands filed by Sutter and George Marshall after their 1848 discovery of gold at their sawmill near Coloma: between its lines could be made out the shrewdness and ingenuity of Sutter's attempt to stake first claim to the heart of the mother lode, as well as a foreshadowing of the tragedy that lay ahead for him after the claim was disallowed by the U.S. government. Olson resolved to devote the remainder of his time at the Bancroft to "trying to find out what was Sutter," and briefly entertained visions of a windfall of publications on the Gold Rush (including an edition of the journals of "Sutter's Clarke," McKinstry, and an ambitious "true chonology" of the Donner expedition), with himself as writer / editor. Only one of these was to become a reality: a two-page pamphlet edition of the Sutter-Marshall lease, released the following February in the California Book Club's centennial "Letters of the Gold Discovery" series.

In September the Olsons continued south by bus. The "shantied growth" of California coastal development, stretching the urban fringes of San Francisco and Los Angeles into one long funguslike growth of prefab bungalows and tract cottages, brought out in Charles the horrified reaction of the ingrained New Englander. Staring out the bus window at the cheap, fast, gimcrack America of midcentury, he felt the creeping encroachment of the cities spoken about by Robert Duncan becoming a dismal reality before his eyes. Yet this same spiritual no-man's-land was not without its allure. Like many an Eastern writer before him, Olson approached Southern California with highly divided feelings, torn between his instinctive distaste for the low culture of the place and his undeniable desire to partake of it professionally. If it was a citadel of Mammon, it was also the land of the Movies; and the cinema had possessed a magnetic attraction for him since even before his first inklings that he would become a writer.

In Los Angeles the couple spent a night or two each at the homes of a series of old political acquaintances of Charles', a form of "mooching" which came naturally to him when traveling, but which made Connie quite uneasy—particularly inasmuch as it had been their mode of existence for the better part of the past month. When they settled down for the duration of their stay at the Santa Monica bungalow of her newly married sister Barbara, she attempted to compensate for the embarrassment of being unable to help out with household expenses by pitching in with cooking and cleaning chores; to Charles such compunctions seemed mysterious if not slightly neurotic.

He arrived in town with a few advance studio contacts provided by his friend Jay Leyda, his main pipeline to the film world. Once the trusted personal assistant of Russian director Sergei Eisenstein, Leyda had sent on *Call Me Ishmael* to Eisenstein; just before leaving for the West, Olson had got back a congratulatory telegram from the famous director, a startling "shooting star" of a response that had convinced him there might indeed be work in store for him in the movies. Now, Leyda's letter of introduction got him into the Burbank studios of Warner Brothers, where, as his friend had informed him, John Huston was at work on a screen adaptation of *Moby-Dick* that was stalled by production problems. Olson met with Huston and offered his services on the project as writer/consultant. The director was cordial enough, but told him no hiring could occur in the absence of production chief Jack Warner, then off on holiday in the French Riviera until the beginning of October. Olson would have to cool his heels for several weeks.

While awaiting the producer's return, he met further with Huston, presenting him with a copy of *Call Me Ishmael*. They talked books; Olson got the impression the director was a frustrated novelist merely dabbling in the cinema, and that his taste for recent existentialist philosophy—"Camus and Sartre and that vision of life"—was hindering his apprehension of Melville. John Huston was "one of those people who might think that *Ishmael* has something to do with existenz." But before Olson had an opportunity to realign those views, the *Moby-Dick* production ran into some very unliterary technical problems. A mechanical monster built to simulate the White Whale stubbornly refused to float, sinking to the bottom of the tank in one test run after another. Returning a week late from vacation, Jack Warner blew up over the delays and gave orders to "kill that fucking whale." The movie, and Olson's chances of work, sank along with it (although Huston would revive the project as a British production nine years later).

The wait for Jack Warner had meanwhile given the aspiring screenwriter a chance to make the rounds of other studios. Olson blamed his continuing lack of success on an adverse political climate, with prevailing trade winds in Hollywood now blowing strongly from the right and writers' past political affiliations under close scrutiny by the House Un-American Activities Committee. Whatever the real reason, he found himself hard put to get past the front gates anywhere. Aside from the maverick Huston, the only man in town willing to listen to his ideas was visiting French director Jean Renoir, to whom he proposed a movie based on the *Essex* shipwreck story. Renoir gave it some thought, then said no. "As a Frenchman," Olson rationalized, "he really didn't understand it." He went back to Huston with a new scheme for a Sutter story to be developed from his Gold Rush researches (which he had been concurrently keeping up at the Huntington Library). Huston suggested he prepare a film treatment. Briefly encouraged, Olson headed back north with Connie to the Sacramento area, seeking further inspiration in the original gold country. He visited the state library, dug up old records in the historical museum at Sutter's Fort and inspected dusty files in sleepy little towns like Placerville and Coloma. The strongest impact of this foray was made by the terrain itself—the ravaged, strip-mined gold fields now reduced to "deserts" by hydraulic dredges seemingly conjured by some "Rube Goldberg / of Mars." Even as he looked on, the great dredges still pounded away without mercy at a landscape already spoiled for generations to come. The sheer scale of this industrial rapacity against the earth staggered him, further complicating the total meaning of the gold story.

He returned to the Bay Area, and there began sketching out longhand notes for a screenplay on Sutter and gold. Tiring, unsure of the medium, and out of money, however, he soon set it aside. While Connie went back East to spend the holidays with her family, he devoted his last weeks in California to the one work of real consequence he actually achieved there, an application for another Guggenheim. The "wretched, thin stage" of document-hunting and paper-shuffling he'd complained about in letters to friends underwent a vivid metamorphosis in his pitchman's prose, which announced his plans for an intensified program of "total research [to] crack down [on] the Donner-Sutter complex." He described the effort as requiring extensive travel expenses, not only for continued work on the West Coast but for further trips to Arizona, New Mexico, Mexico and even Europe.

The "dirty business" of grant writing out of the way, he said hasty farewells to Robert Duncan and a few other new friends and then, shortly after New Year's 1948, escaped the rain-soaked Bay Area aboard an eastbound Southern Pacific train. His "biggest survey of America on the ground" had been an interesting adventure, but by the end of it his planned long work on the West was no closer to reality than it had been when he started out.

11

The Broken Step
(1948)

Olson's course as a writer always obeyed inner currents. Upon his return to Washington he turned away from the West book to wrestle with old ghosts. The spring of 1948 was taken up with the psychic turmoil of renewed struggle with a specter of paternal authority which he felt he'd been shadowboxing for as long as he could remember. Blocking his full emergence into manhood, throwing him into torments of depression and self-doubt, this imaginal adversary would leave him no peace. His combat with it now became the main theme of a secret confessional journal aptly titled "Faust Buch."

Aggravating his problems were difficulties in his sex life, always an area of particular sensitivity. The slightest signal of impatience with him on Connie's part could precipitate a terrifying sense of "shame or intimidation." In such low moments he grew fearful of everything, "of women, of flesh, of event." He was having doubts about his effectiveness as a lover, and it didn't help that Connie diagnosed worrisome homosexual implications in his continuing dreams about men. In her view, much of the trouble came with his concentration on writing, a calling that had induced an increasing inwardness in his makeup; he had lost the "vigorous decisiveness, carelessness" that had made him so attractive to her in his years of active involvement in political life. Certainly Charles himself also related his present insecurities to writing, but in a reverse fashion. To him, the psychological woes seemed not the by-product of the cerebral, internalizing habits of the writing, but their cause. It was a vicious circle: he feared that his anxieties about his manhood were unconsciously creating a state of tension that in turn rendered him incapable of performing in a natural, relaxed manner, either in his interpersonal conduct or on paper. The self-demand which was so essential an element of his character was ironically the wellspring of both his prodigious energies and his crippling inhibitions. In his "Faust Buch," he warned himself over and over against "hopping it up," attempting to manufacture an artificial strength: "Don't try to talk and behave bigger than you are." And that spring he made a self-conscious decision to change his approach to writing, to stop evading his deepest concerns and instead confront them at their source. The first step would be a small book of true stories about his father, cast in simple, direct reminiscence form—not elliptical "assault" prose but a plain "mediocre humanitas" style, intelligible to any common reader. The book would be a kind of litmus test. If he was not cut out to be "an artist, genius or clever," the unadorned prose would once and for all reveal it. If, on the other hand, he really had something important and universal to say, that too would be allowed to come through unimpeded. Further, the effort would not be psychic therapy alone. Mastering the more accessible narrative form would, he hoped, bring him into range of a large mainstream audience so far closed off to him by his exclusively critical and intellectual concentrations.

The first story he tackled was a memoir of boyhood grape-picking and ice-fishing expeditions with his father. The tale, titled "Stocking Cap," portrayed Karl Olson as a driven, self-demanding man, fatally absorbed in obstacles and challenges; attractive, but ultimately tragic because of his "stubborn side," which had "killed him in the end." Awkward as fiction, "Stocking Cap" succeeded as reminiscence by virtue of its underlying honesty, Olson openly straining for terms to express his filial emotions, primarily guilt and sadness. Though its personal revelations would later make him "nervous," and its "weakness" embarrass him, the story felt like a breakthrough as he wrote it; he was encouraged to continue with the project, hoping to lay to rest Karl's ghost, and "relax me with him." He managed to finish two more tales—"Mr. Meyer," a rather static recollection of his father's tailor, and "The Post Office," a thumbnail biography of Karl Olson (the latter would become the title piece in the posthumous book publication of this sequence of tales).

The stories were written in February and March, and the project abandoned after the commercial magazines to which they'd been sent turned them down swiftly and without comment. For Olson, the most telling blow was the *New Yorker's* return of "Stocking Cap" within three days of its submission. The test of his new "relaxed" style seemed to have brought unambiguously negative results. The author's precarious self-esteem sagged even further as a consequence. In his "Faust Buch" he blamed himself for never having grown up, for his inability to break out of tedious filial dramas of his own insistent creation. The tales about Karl, he had soon begun to suspect, were less works of art than unsuccessful attempts at discovering "the path of love transposed." The effort to relieve the strains of his personal psychological burden through the mediation of fiction had been vain from the start. A better way to "cease to be a son" would be learning "to keep the experience of dominance" in himself.

An immediate opportunity to assert that dominance was provided him by Ezra Pound, whom he now returned again to visit after his eight months' absence from Washington. Upon his arrival at St. Elizabeths this time, Pound's wife, Dorothy, was on hand, though hardly a mediating influence. The poet had by now been transferred from Howard Hall to the slightly more comfortable environment of Chestnut Ward, the hospital's geriatric wing. Even so, the years of confinement had begun to wear upon his temper, and he was visibly out of sorts—"looks bad," Olson noted. When Dorothy Pound complained in bitter tones that her husband had been suffering unduly from the effects of a recent cold spell, however, the visitor's sympathy quickly evaporated. A loyal citizen, he resented the implication; the building and grounds of the institution in which Pound was receiving free housing were—he thought, but didn't say—"as good as anything in America, god help us." Thereafter his defensive hackles stayed up throughout the visit. Interrogated by Pound about his Western trip, pressed as usual to provide "particulars, not generalizations," he volunteered a "particular" bound to prove provocative—the fact that George Leite, the Berkeley Poundian who edited *Circle,* was of Portuguese descent, not the pure Aryan blood favored by the Master. The news triggered a series of xenophobic and racist comments out of Pound. Once capable of sitting impassively through such Mr. Hyde–like outbursts, this time Olson reacted by abruptly stalking out in disgust just at "the point of telling off" both the "bastard" Pound and his objectionably partisan spouse.

His show of feeling, he realized once he'd gotten home, was a product of his growing "resistance at any longer being a son." He became determined to immediately cease relying on Pound for "direction of work, decisions . . . to prime the pump." Making up his mind to force an ending by directly baiting Pound's anti-Semitism ("laying a trap to make the taker mad"), he went back one last time to St. Elizabeths. The bait was a misleading "admission." He casually announced that his father's mother had borne the Hungarian surname Lybeck; the suggestion, as he was aware, was that there was Jewish or gypsy influence clouding his own bloodline. Within moments, Pound responded with a pointed remark to the effect that William Carlos Williams—whose ancestry included a Spanish Jew—was "confused" due to "mixed blood." The indirect slur against his own hybrid background provided sufficient insult to spring Olson's trap. He went home, got drunk, and hammered out a sharp note in which for the first time he dropped his cloak of charm and actually "took on" the man who'd been the object of so much of his attention over recent years. His message addressed the issues of democracy and "mixed blood"—Williams', his father's, his own. Pound's answer was a succinct postcard message, reductively demolishing Olson's liberal moral arguments as "a lot of 2nd hand mass produced brickabrak." It was to be their last direct exchange.

Following the breakup, Olson wrote his epitaph to the relationship in the form of an essay called "GrandPa, GoodBye." It was both farewell to Pound and tacit declaration of Olson's latest switch of adoptive fathers. Proudly aligning himself with the democratic crossbreed Williams, he painted the aristocratic *claritas* of Pound as a thin strain of intellectual brilliance, one that failed to soak through to "roots." The Williams / Pound split, he suggested, was more than mere personal or literary disagreement. "Two contrary conceptions of love" were at stake, one operating from the head, via intellectual power, the other from the heart, by moral instinct. Olson himself would side with the heart, and with Williams. "Bill never faked and that's why he has been of such use to all of us young men who grew up after him. There he was in Rutherford to be gone to, and seen, a clean animal, the only one we had on the ground. . . ."

He circulated copies of "GrandPa, GoodBye" to James Laughlin and several other editors. All turned it down, but the piece did not go without effect. A copy he sent to Williams was predictably well received. The New Jersey doctor-writer—whose home he had once visited, and who had long commanded his respect as a rare voice of "belief" among poets, an American hero "like Kit Carson"—replied by telling him he was "one of the few men I take pleasure in reading." Williams would remain a helpful ally, never to be as dominant in Olson's life as Dahlberg and Pound had once been, but all the same a friendly and well-meaning, if sometimes irritating, "brother / father."

Olson's talent for ingratiating himself with others by "charm and wooing," once his prime asset as a politician, was now blamed in his "Faust Buch" for delaying his progress toward creative independence, not only from projected writer-"fathers" but from the world of cultural authority of which they stood as personal symbols. His challenge to the modernist fathers was an assault against that world, his "pathetic struggle to keep my ego above their water" a bid also to rise above the humanistic assumptions on which such authority was based. But so far, in his attempts to assert himself as a new voice, he was

still at the mercy of the prior vocabularies and structures which were all he
had at his disposal—chief among them the secondhand modernist devices
borrowed from those same predecessors. Tensions caused by this paradox
occupied him endlessly in the "Faust Buch." His inability to control his addictive
"whoring after culture," his involuntary adherence to the role of hopeful artist as past generations had defined it, brought him nothing but shame. Yet
he kept up dutiful attendance at poetry readings and lectures, sitting reverently at the feet of high modernism's visiting emissaries (like T. S. Eliot and
St.-John Perse, both of whom he heard read in Washington that spring) and
following with slavish attention the latest in progressive drama, art, even
music—a medium for which he possessed little natural sensitivity. (His tortuous attempt at achieving post-symbolist synesthetic effects in a verse hom-
age to Igor Stravinsky, written following a brief conversation with Stravinsky
after a Constitution Hall concert, remains as conclusive proof of an observation made by his composer friend Frank Moore that "music was mysterious
to him.")

Then there was his abortive foray into dance theater, inspired by a series
of shows put on that spring by a literary acquaintance, Robert Richman, at
Washington's Institute of Contemporary Arts. Richman's *Theater Dance Pieces*
featured, among others, the dancer Erick Hawkins, a leading member of the
celebrated Martha Graham company. After one performance Olson approached
Hawkins to air his own old scheme for a dramatic dance piece based on *Moby-
Dick*. Hawkins informally commissioned him to attempt a script for production by the Graham company. Olson spent much of April and May drafting
"Ahab: A Dance" (published posthumously as 'The Fiery Hunt"). He designed
the play for two dancers, who would act out Ahab's inner conflict in stylized
movements while reciting a mixture of prose and verse. As in all his attempts
at writing for the stage, however, he was handicapped by a lack of dramatic
conception. The result was a static echoing of "Faust Buch" themes. His
Ahab bellowed "Mountains are egos! Towers are egos!" while his Ishmael
crooned of "angels with hands in jars of sperm." When the play was adjudged
unsuitable for staging by Hawkins and the financially strapped Graham company, Olson doggedly tried other avenues, soliciting songs for it from New
York composer David Diamond and submitting it to the *New Directions Annual*,
but in the end got nowhere with any of these efforts. Like the book of stories
about his father, the dance play ended up a double disappointment—not only
a failure on its own terms, but a further waste of time and energy that might
better have been invested in his West book.

His original plan for the latter had meanwhile undergone a slow attrition
during its months of dormancy. Reading the *Divine Comedy* in May set him
off on renewed considerations of turning his material into a verse epic, cen-

tered on a mythic character named "Orpheus West" who would be a composite of Quetzalcoatl, Cabeza de Vaca, Ishmael and others. But these ruminations soon went the way of all his previous plans for the unwieldy work. He was, furthermore, now having serious doubts as to whether "the American experience" actually contained sufficient mythic amplitude to qualify it for epic narrative in prose *or* verse. His precious research discoveries had begun to feel "too stiff, historical, unfabled for use." More readings—this time in the works of the twentieth-century Norwegian polar explorer and chronicler Vilhjálmur Stefánsson, author of *The Northward Course of Empire* and *Great Adventures and Explorations*—intensified his misgivings. Stefansson's books, full of true-life encounters with geographical expanses not symbolic but real, made him painfully conscious of the limitations of his own library and armchair researches. In light of such an example, he could not avoid admitting to himself that "I am not (a) a traveler . . . and (b) am not an historian." By late spring, his momentum having dwindled to vanishing point, he had decided to abandon the work. At that time he got word he had been awarded a second Guggenheim. He gratefully accepted the money, regarding it as compensation for his long labors but at present little inclined to revive the West book project.

The weather grew warmer, Washington's trees broke into blossom, Olson had foundation cash to bank on. Yet his restlessness only increased. He went alone to New York for a session with Cagli. They discussed a new idea for a set of "American Tarot" playing cards with poetic text and graphics, but Olson was distracted by his qualms over potential homosexual signals in the relationship with his artist friend. Similar danger signs appeared to crop up everywhere he turned. In the course of a casual luncheon conversation during the same New York visit, Jungian psychologist and Melville expert Henry Murray brought him up short with a gentle but meaningful comment about figurative archetypes in *Call Me Ishmael*. The Father was obviously a dominant presence in the book, observed Murray, but there was a curious vacancy where the Mother should have been. Olson worried that his friend was correct. The feminine principle was eternally eluding him, leaving his sexual circuits sadly incomplete. Looking into the faces of women he passed in the crowded city, he imagined a carnival of missed sexual opportunities. On the train back to Washington, his eye was caught by a pretty and stylish young woman who reminded him of Connie in the early days of their courtship. Interpreting the woman's glances as a signal of invitation, he was thrown into a terrible quandary about whether to approach her. She suddenly got off the train at the 30th Street station in Philadelphia. After some moments of indecisiveness, he tried to follow her, but the imagined temptress had disappeared on the crowded platform. Desolate, he got back on the train just before it pulled out of the station. This crushing sexual "defeat" stayed on his mind all the way back to Washington.

There he fell back into his slough of notebook brooding. Convinced his own malaise was a symptom of the "whole deadness and vulgarity" of American culture, he blamed the repressive influence of "the family and righteous behavior." Yet such attempts at all-purpose explanation could hardly account for the specific and immediate phenomena of his decline into depression. He was feeling increasingly "inadequate" as a man—"disenchanted" was Connie's term for this depressed ego-state—and, in more or less direct ratio, washed out as a writer. "My arrogance and speech shreds away," he admitted grimly in his "Faust Buch," "and all I write is ashes in my mouth." His dreams meanwhile were flooded night after night with disturbing scenes of sexual transformation. In one, a stripper turned into Ephraim Doner's father-in-law, unexpectedly possessed of a pole-sized *membrum virile*. In another, an attractive woman turned into, of all people, Edward Dahlberg. Such nocturnal surprises made him wonder if his current flat, drained mood was caused by his willful efforts to cut himself off from the fathers. This counterfear over the enforced "absence of men I admire (love?)" even induced a conciliatory gesture toward Dahlberg, to whom he now directed a friendly letter out of the blue. Dahlberg replied cordially, remarking that he still believed with Keats in the friendship of men "passing the love of women," and sending along a typescript of *The Flea of Sodom*, his recently completed satire of Greenwich Village bohemianism in the thirties. In a telegram of congratulation, Olson lauded this as a "FIRST LEVITICAN FABLE"—an impulsive gesture that he would one day regret. He also mailed Dahlberg a belated presentation copy of *Call Me Ishmael*, inscribed in the extravagant words of Ben Jonson to his patron, Camden: "most revered head, to whom I owe all that I am in arts, all that I know." For a while after this sudden thaw, epistolary relations between the two men resumed in a reasonably temperate manner for the first time in nearly a decade.

In the "Faust Buch" Olson blurted out that at times he felt so frustrated by circumstance that he wished to "throw responsibility over" and start completely anew. A desperate desire for instant release occasionally seized him, but never at moments when there was real opportunity to act. How could he know what was ahead when he chose to reply to a fan letter from a female reader of *Call Me Ishmael*, who told him in no uncertain terms that he was himself her salvation, and that of "every lover of Melville"—"one of the ones we so urgently need"? This unknown admirer announced herself as Frances Motz Boldereff, a Pennsylvania State College book designer. Flattered and intrigued, Olson entered correspondence with her, at first in a tentative and exploratory fashion, answering her letters with rather guarded postcards and notes, his curiosity still hedged by caution. She, on the other hand, held back very little, allowing her volatile, independent character free expression in candid and direct letters that bespoke not only considerable intellectual sophistication but extensive life experience. (In fact she was nearly five years older than he was, had held various positions in the fields of publishing, visual arts and education, and had been married to a White Russian aristocrat, now deceased, by whom she'd had a daughter.) In one letter she recounted to him a conversation with the painter Philip Guston about the relation of artists' lives to their creations. The actual spiritual reality, she suggested, was rarely revealed in the biography, but always "given in the work." Consequently she and Olson should henceforth dispense with social preliminaries; in reading both *Ishmael* and his poem "In Praise of the Fool" (which she'd looked up in *Harper's Bazaar*), she had already seen his "spirit coming through so naked and uncovered" that any future attempts at concealment between them would be beside the point.

Such unusual openness at once unnerved and fascinated him. He began to draw out the exchange with professional-sounding queries, soliciting her opinions, for example, on the type design of Y & X. But when at the end of June, after some six months of intermittent mail contact, she put his discretion to the test by inviting him to visit her in Woodward, the Pennsylvania hill-country hamlet where she lived, he drew back, declining courteously with the excuse that he was busy on a new dance play. He had not yet let on a word to her about Connie.

The domestic status quo at Randolph Place, meanwhile, was shaken by another surprising development. Connie shocked and dismayed him by becoming pregnant. She herself was at first delighted to be bearing the child she had long wished for, but her joy soon turned to anxiety when she became unwell, evidently suffering lingering effects from the abortion of seven years earlier. They were told the pregnancy would not be an easy one. She was forced to leave her job, and to spend long hours resting.

With Connie indisposed and Washington's summer heat reaching "Afric" levels, his cooped-up, restive feelings spilled over in a new dance-play project, called "Troilus." Here, Shakespeare's tale of sexual infidelity provided a convenient mask for disguised self-analysis. The figure of Troilus, Olson told himself in planning the work, would speak in "your own voice." By "turning over his experience," Troilus would unhappily discover that "Love is not present now." The idea, true to recent form for its ever-tentative author, evolved no further than a fragment. Olson handed that over to Frank Moore to be set to music. Moore, however, had too little to work with to make a go of it, and "Troilus" joined Olson's growing roster of recent halfhearted and abortive works.

In midsummer, election-year politics briefly jolted him out of his doldrums. In one last effort to effect political change at the national level through traditional means, he revived old party connections to secure a delegate's spot at the Democratic convention in Philadelphia. Arriving shortly before the convention's July 12 opening, he quickly threw in with a small coalition of fellow former New Dealers and "Appleseeds" then attempting to mount a last-ditch challenge to incumbent President Truman. Acknowledged leader of this left-liberal faction was Senator Claude Pepper, one of the few men in government still holding Olson's unqualified respect. After failing in a bid to coax General Dwight Eisenhower to head the Democratic ticket, Pepper allowed himself to be "drafted" by a group of liberal congressmen and columnists at a breakfast meeting on the day preceding the presidential nomination. Caught up for the moment in the old excitement of power, "men and action," Olson pitched in on a thirty-six hour impromptu "campaign" organized from Pepper's hotel suite. But the desperate effort to rally delegate votes fell short. On the hot, humid nominating night of July 15, Pepper withdrew his name from the running even before the roll of the states was called. Drenched in sweat and noise amid the throng of Truman celebrants on the floor, a disappointed Olson bade his final farewell to politics.

For a few days at the convention, even in a losing cause, he'd felt "more whole" than he had in some time. Once back in Washington, he was again soon enmeshed in the familiar confusions and self-doubts. "The broken step continues," he lamented in the "Faust Buch." "Unable to work or figure out what to do with myself," he was hounded by strange dreams and recurrent, unsettling sexual fantasies. He dreamed, for instance, of losing several teeth and part of his jaw; the image of his empty mouth then elided frighteningly into one of his wife's disembodied vagina, and he awoke in the grip of "most unhappy sensations." The stifling, idle days at home with Connie, who was herself quite unwell, seemed endless. He wandered out to see friends, talked overmuch, came home uneasy and fell into long, nightmare-tossed sleeps. At the end of July he was to give a lecture on art at the American University in Washington. For his theme he had selected a current literary alter ego, the figure of Troilus. He made notes for a lecture, but lost his confidence onstage, and, as at the Seattle event a year earlier, found himself "tongue-tied" before a roomful of well-educated listeners. At once irrationally angry at his audience (for their imagined judgment of him and expected resistance to his ideas) and impatient with himself (for lacking the right words), he was simply unable to speak. This embarrassing incident left him shaken, mortified and more depressed than ever. He was already concerned about his male identity. Were the verbal powers that had been his mainstay now about to desert him as well?

In September, Connie's pregnancy ended unhappily. She had to be rushed to the hospital, and the baby was lost. She was spared further physical complications, but was emotionally shattered, and back at home had to spend several more weeks in bed. His attention abruptly pulled away from his own subjective miseries, Charles was considerably moved by her suffering, and became during her convalescence an ardent companion once more, bringing her ice cream and flowers, staying at her bedside for hours to talk in the old expansive way she loved. Cheered by this unanticipated development, she herself became again that "gay and foolish canary in the midst of trouble," willing to go through anything at his side.

Soon enough the couple indeed had new problems to face. There were big hospital bills to pay, and a stack of back-rent notices to be dealt with. A Guggenheim payment on which Charles had counted as a safety net was expected to come in early fall. But the check was held up, and would not in fact arrive until the beginning of November. Meanwhile something had to be done to make ends meet. After months off work, Connie still wasn't physically ready to return, and Charles himself had long since become accustomed to leaving the business of earning a living up to her. Now, faced with money problems that were obviously temporary but nonetheless very real, he stubbornly dodged the whole annoying work issue, squandering what little cash he had in compulsive book-buying sprees, sometimes spending whole afternoons prowling dealers' shops in search of the one line, lost in an obscure volume, which might spur him forward to new writing discoveries.

Aggravating matters further, his aged landlady, chronically neglectful of money, had lately hired a collection agent to pursue him for missed payments, and was now attempting to drag him into court. Though a $50 "bone" put up by his friends temporarily "stopped her yap," he soon received a second summons, informing him that he was being hit with an additional "175 slap." Again friends had to bail him out. When the weather turned cool in October, he bought wood to heat the house because he couldn't afford the cost of coal. His clothes were threadbare, at "that point from which there is no turning." Now appearing "as bohemian as I did in the village, aetat 1940," he feared he would fare poorly if he had to go to court. Yet a modest effort to raise a few dollars by reviewing some new books on Melville was as far as he was willing to go toward seeking actual work. (He did manage to produce the review, but it was decidedly uncommercial in nature, delving extensively into homoerotic themes, the "two levels of love operative" in both *Billy Budd* and the Melville-Hawthorne friendship; the piece took a year to reach print, in the *Western Review,* as "David Young, David Old.") Caresse Crosby, who had already generously advanced him $100 on $Y \& X$, played the good sport again by helping out with the tab for Connie's medical expenses. Still, in the weeks before the Guggenheim check finally came in, further stopgap measures had to be taken. Olson was forced to consider the offer of a substitute teaching position at an obscure North Carolina experimental arts college, less because he wanted to go than because he "needed their gold."

The college was Black Mountain. Dahlberg, who'd taken a job as writing and literature instructor at the remote Blue Ridge school, was already unhappy there. In a letter to Olson he gave as cause of his discontent a recent divorce, which by depriving him of his two young sons had left him feeling "bereft" and in no mood for combat with "pachydermatous students." (Not for some time would Olson find out that Dahlberg's initial aversion to the excessive "leafage and fetid earth" had soon developed into a full-fledged phobia, making Black Mountain seem a "devilish" breeding ground of "mania, suicide and avant-garde pederasty"—and that he had meanwhile become infamous among female inhabitants of the place on account of his relentless lechery.) Though he'd hired on for a year, within two weeks Dahlberg had handed in his notice to Josef Albers, the former Bauhaus painter who was Black Mountain's acting rector. As his replacement, he suggested Olson. Albers, badly in need of a writing teacher, dispatched a special-delivery letter to Washington.

Olson, who upon leaving Harvard had vowed he would never teach again, at first declined the offer, telling Albers he didn't want to leave Washington and his work. Albers countered by cutting back the job responsibilities. Olson remained reluctant, but his landlady's legal assault swayed him. At the beginning of October he agreed to come once and deliver three lectures. The option to return one week a month through the remainder of the year was left open to him. From his point of view these were appealing terms, affording him some small but immediate income—$120 per visit, plus travel expenses— while requiring little sacrifice of the precious freedom to write. Privately he couldn't help hoping Black Mountain would provide something beyond mere income. Randolph Place remained a secure island, but it had become a full-time effort to resist the stultifying effects of the "dead" city outside. His careful defenses had left him with a well-protected inwardness, but at its center there was little light or joy. Perhaps the change of scene would restore some of the missing "magic" in his life, and thus help him—as he put it bluntly in a letter to Dahlberg—"to solve what has, up to now, been a knot in which I was so bound I was unable to use my sword."

12

Domination Square
(1948-1949)

On October 11 the Olsons boarded a Southern Railroad train at Washington's Union Station. In Asheville they were met by some students in a jalopy. By the time they'd reached the sleepy dirt-road turnoff to the college, Civilization was no more than a memory. Beyond a dilapidated, yawing white picket fence and peeling gate bearing the Black Mountain sign, a heavily forested property sprawled uphill before them, thick with pine, oak, laurel, chestnut and hickory. The unpaved entry road wove its bumpy way up from the valley floor, skirting small irregular clusters of buildings scattered in dense woods, crossing several streams and gullies and coming at length to a sizable man-made lake, remnant of the property's summer-camp days. Overlooking the water were two mountain-style residential lodges, a large dining hall with screened-in veranda and, on the opposite shore, a low, oblong, modernistic wood, glass and stone box, the Studies Building, built during the 1940–1941 relocation of the campus from an earlier site at an old Baptist meeting hall across the valley and still the school's most impressive structure. Above the lake lay more woodlands, topped by a college farm and pasture. To the myth-seeker in Olson, this big, shaggy domain, nestled in a valley of the Allegheny Ridge—easternmost source of Gulfbound waters and historic gateway to the first pioneer settlements west of the mountains—immediately seemed "a strange spot, a holy place."

There were indeed elements in both the physical situation and the history of the small nonconformist institution that made it feel from the outset no accidental place for the eccentric, freedom-loving visiting lecturer to have landed. A tiny island of unconventional thought and behavior, moral and intellectual tolerance and political and academic liberalism, Black Mountain's principal distinction was its dramatic isolation—from the current narrow uniformity of American mainstream educational philosophy, as well as from the immediate sociocultural setting in rural environs whose conservative fundamentalist inhabitants, mostly descendants of the region's original Scotch-Irish tobacco-farming settlers, had little sympathy for either the Yankee-liberal / Jewish-intellectual / German-refugee blend that made up the college's faculty, or the freethinking godless communalism (if not actual communism) that was assumed to prevail among the student body.

Olson arrived bearing at least a passing acquaintance with Black Mountain history. While still toiling as a Clark University instructor in 1936, he'd read with some interest a *Harper's* article about the place written by Louis Adamic. Adamic's report, which was to influence many an idealistic and discontented young academic of Olson's generation, had focused on Black Mountain's downplaying of traditional educational "solidities" (like buildings, credits, grades) in favor of intangible spiritual and intellectual values—especially new ideas, no matter how advanced, "tenuous" or "imponderable." The unusual emphasis described by Adamic had been precisely the intent of John Andrew Rice, leader of a disaffected faction of instructors who had left Rollins College in Florida to found Black Mountain in 1933. It had been the design of Rice to enhance the role of creative inquiry by abandoning all conventional compartmentalized structures in the learning process. Demanding a new degree of risk on the part not only of students but of teachers, Rice's nonhierarchical, live-in, "round-the-clock" system of total faculty involvement permitted the latter no escape into familiar sanctuaries of rank and tenure (at Black Mountain, there simply weren't any). For everyone concerned, the school represented an educational experiment in all senses, requiring almost no reference to the past's prescribed ways and rules—but great commitment to an unknown future.

It was, in short, a place uncommonly accommodating to just such groundbreaking work as Olson himself had in mind, a fact he needed little time to recognize; from the outset he "threw [his] energies forward [to] pierce it to the root," for once held back by no self-conscious, tongue-tying inhibitions of speech. On this first visit he conducted several classes for writing students in the Studies Building and delivered three open lectures, generous, far-ranging "public goes" offered after evening meals in the college dining hall. Both classes and lectures were distinguished by a speculative expansiveness that would mark all his Black Mountain teachings. Drawing unexpected connections with breathtaking speed, he leaped across space and time, linking Troilus and new astronomy, Frazer and Freud, field physics and Frobenius, projective geometry's "gains of space" and epic poetry's timeless mythic archetypes, creating an open-ended architecture of knowledge that placed twentieth-century man in vivid relation to cosmic patterns of eternity. "We are a perpendicular axis of planes," he declared, "constantly being intersected by planes of experience coming in from the past—coming up from the ground, the underground tide—going out to the future. . . ."

Though one or two skeptical dissenters regarded him a "faddish *avant garde* charlatan," the majority at Black Mountain gave up all resistance. His evident personal involvement with his ideas, the experiential intensity with which his thoughts were being shaped even as he uttered them, the quality of challenge and adventure in the conjectural gamble he proposed, won from most of his listeners a trust that included considerable suspension of disbelief. "It was better to listen, let Olson carry you along," one of his first writing students remembers. "And he did. Circular, not linear. You ran along as best you could. It was not the pre-packed box of culture you'd get at Radcliffe or Harvard. Olson talked about some poem or story as though the person who made it really cared about it. He showed you how you DO it. We students were a motley crew, people were groping, it wasn't all clear or laid out or easy or comfortable, but we got his big message: STICK TO WHERE YOUR PASSIONS TAKE YOU." In such willing, attentive students, he had finally found his audience, after all those years of impatient preparation.

If the invitation to individual discovery was a keynote in his classes, there was nonetheless little question, even in these early meetings, as to where the classroom power was actually located. The visiting instructor took pains to establish a mystique that set him apart. "He was mythic," the same writing student recalls, "he cast himself that way and probably we students did so cast him. He had a way of surrounding himself with a special aura." Within that aura, he had little trouble maintaining the long-sought "experience of dominance." On those occasions when students did manage to get up the nerve to question him, his authority was usually further fortified. If Olson had learned anything at all from his years in politics, it was the knack of employing personal charisma to block argument. For the young, relatively inexperienced Black Mountaineers, there was no "squaring off with that guy [because] he was so devious, sly in his ways of sidestepping and moving himself back into domination square."

It was sweet conquest, and Olson came home delighted. "It is a lovely girl with whom I am in love," he reported to Dahlberg upon his return from the college. "In some karmic fashion, the place is very right on this prick of my time." Though relieved for the moment of financial need by the arrival of the Guggenheim payment, he readily agreed to return. In November and December, with Connie back at work, he went south alone, each time bursting with ideas, readings and theories, an "archangel" radiating new light. The physical exhaustion of the visits was a small price to pay for the influx of confidence and self-belief.

By the end of his first term as a visitor, he was already beginning to assert himself in college affairs beyond the instructional sphere. While he had little taste for sharing in the menial chores which were the collective responsibility of students and faculty, he readily pitched in on recruiting and fund-raising efforts that were no less vital to the survival of the perpetually underendowed school. In this area, he could draw usefully on his experience as a political publicist. At the request of rector Albers and college treasurer Theodore Dreier, for example, he produced a short promotional statement titled "Black Mountain as seen by a writer-visitor." While designed for distribution to prospective donors and students, this document also displayed the affection he'd already developed for the place. In it, he held up the winding "sidehill road" between the college dining hall and Studies Building—emblematic of Black Mountain's unique nonlinear, Moebius-like progression toward knowledge—as an image of "the traffic of human society" that would one day prove more important in the history of American education "than Mark Hopkins' log." In his choice of a renowned nineteenth-century New England educator as phantom competition there was special personal meaning, as there was in his designation of a discontinuous, post-Euclidean "principle of intensification" as Black Mountain's alternative to the entrenched humanistic education system: it was also his own first principle as both teacher and writer.

Not until his December visit did he really experience the full intensification of isolation which Black Mountain winters could exact. A cold spell found him "stuck on that sheer rise" in temporary cloister with fifty students and thirteen fellow faculty members, when one of the school's periodic administrative crises struck. To cope with the latest of the debt emergencies that were to plague the school throughout its twenty-three-year existence, Albers summoned in a panel of distinguished outside observers to form a board of trustees. By the second day of prolonged discussion sessions, however, the rector had lost his voice. Olson stepped into the breach to chair a climactic meeting. Addressing the panel of visiting dignitaries from New York City, Andover and MIT, he outlined his own plan for saving the college from imminent bankruptcy and closure. It was an imaginative scheme drawn from Pearl Buck's *All Men Are Brothers:* the nation's most valuable "mandarins"— artists, scientists and thinkers—would take off on "a broken pilgrimage to nowhere," touring the country to acquaint potential students and sponsors

with Black Mountain, and at length wind up back in North Carolina, thereby
rescuing from extinction not only the college but all useful culture and
knowledge. The impracticality of the proposal was lost for the moment in his
obvious enthusiasm. With seasonal cup of mulled Tokay punch held high,
eyes wide and brows lifted in challenging inquiry, he asked "what was wrong
with" fourteen seekers of truth wanting nothing more than to be "left alone
on a mountain"? His plan was politely ignored, and the college shortly saved
by other means, but this performance was an auspice of things to come: it
marked Olson's debut in a role later to become familiar, the crazy head monk
of the monastery. Afterward, he was so elevated by the cheap wine that he
"walked right down the hill without touching the ground at all." Soon he
had signed on to continue his teaching visits through the spring.

The appearance of *Y & X*, around this time, created an illusory flurry of
activity in Olson's life. Expecting big things of his five modest poems, he
talked Caresse Crosby into mailing out copies to an extensive list of literary
personages that included modernist father-rivals Eliot, Pound and Williams.
He himself sent dedicated copies to many writer friends. Results of this earnest promotion were, however, mixed at best. The book got but one review,
a perfunctory notice in the *Nation,* sold only a handful of copies, and lost
Crosby $1,200. Even Olson's friends were not very positive. Robert Duncan,
who'd impatiently discarded the book after a single skeptical look ("Oh, what
does the professor know about writing poems?"), didn't even bother to
acknowledge receipt of it. Edward Dahlberg, who did reply, had little good
to say: "too abstruse," "too cerebral," "too sententiously dried out." In Dahlberg's view Olson's poems sadly lacked the "darkling speaking heart."
    Their abstract intellectualizing rendered the poems difficult to the point
of opacity for other readers as well. In truth, Olson's private symbolism could
be comprehended only by a reader armed with the right kind of attention.
So far he had found only two such readers. One was Connie, long trained in
his codes. The other was his ardent Pennsylvania correspondent Frances
Boldereff, whose sympathetic response to the book seemed to reflect an intuitive affinity of vision. Her comments did much to offset for him the disappointment of others' coolness or silence. The poems, she told him, were "the
purest, hardest most perfect diamonds since Villon"; they placed him among
the ranks of "the bravest and the best," Rimbaud, Joyce, Blake, Michelangelo, Beethoven. "The K" was "the greatest poem which has been written in
this country in this century." Reading "Trinacria" made her feel as though
"an aristocrat [had] entered the door and left his armor there." In return for
Y & X she sent him her spiritual autobiography, a handsome self-produced
volume titled *A Primer of Morals for Medea* in which plates of Michelangelo

nudes faced a text stating her life philosophy of woman as prime nurturer, giving freely "to each who needs."

Like so much of his work in the years immediately ahead, a big, elliptical, multisourced new poem on which he began to work in the early months of 1949 owed its inception in some degree to the confidence-building exchange with Frances Boldereff. Commenting on the spiritual poverty of the postwar society around them, he had written to her of his hopes for a new America, hailing the emergence of "a green republic now renewed." She replied that in the current explosion of materialism she saw no evidence of such renewal, and challenged him to provide some. Before the year was over he would be able to do so, sending on to her a final draft of "The Kingfishers" as his "answer," the basis of his faith in the possibility of "survival in these States."

Its first embryonic movements came in February, with another of his epic-scale conceptions, a plan for a long poem to be called "Proteus." Only two fragments of this were actually committed to paper. One grew into "The Praises," an ambitious propositional poem in its own right, affecting an aggressive Poundian vernacular tone, reflecting wide reading (principally in the history of geometry and Plutarch's *Lives*), unwieldy enough to require eight months to "lock itself up," and even then less notable as verse than as a building block in that growing Olson didactic canon: "to dream takes no effort / to think is easy / to act is more difficult / but for a man to act after he has taken thought, this! / is the most difficult thing of all," he insisted. "What is necessary is / containment, / that that which has been found out by work may, by work, be passed on / (without due loss of force) / for use / USE."

Equally slow to come together but ultimately far more successful was the second poem developed from the abandoned "Proteus." Here Olson's drive toward large statement was contained and given figurative resonance by the vivid central image of the kingfisher, allusive symbol of the spiritual renewal which he'd forecast to Frances Boldereff. The image had its source in a seemingly trivial incident. At a party in the studio of a Washington artist friend, Olson overheard a drunken art curator mumbling semi-incoherently about "the blue of the kingfisher feathers." The episode lodged in his imagination to resurface—in typically cryptic and mysterious fashion—at the heart of his fable of cultural revolution. That fable was grounded in historical events of spring 1949, concurrently rehearsed by Olson in ongoing correspondence with Asian expert Robert Payne and in conversation with Jean Riboud, who visited Washington just as the poem was getting underway. The key topical figure of the poem was Mao Tse-tung, then winning the civil war in China by stages—his revolutionary army taking Peking in January, Nanking in April, Shanghai in May. Mao's call to action in a New Year's report to the Chinese

Communist Party, *"la lumière de l'aurore est devant nous, nous devons lever et agir"*—read aloud from a French periodical by Riboud to Olson—went directly into the poem in progress.

Mao's revolution was but one manifestation of a recurrent transformative energy Olson evoked by beginning his poem with an echoing paradox from Heraclitus:

What does not change / is the will to change

The line was to become a rallying cry for a generation of poets soon to follow up on Olson's bold cultural challenge. ("It is this change," Robert Creeley would comment, "and the force which it demands, which hold the only continuity possible . . . if a culture is to maintain itself.") Olson imbedded his oblique, discontinuous narrative with further archaic elements, details of Aztec and Greek rites taken from Prescott and Plutarch and arranged alongside tags from Eliot and Pound like tesserae in a complex mosaic. "The Kingfishers" was an impressive reconstruction of myth and history employing the major modernist juxtapositional mode and culminating with a first-person statement in which the poet at last rose above his modernist influences to position himself, like some ancient city founder planting his oar, at the jumping-off point for all his work to come:

I am no Greek, hath not th'advantage.
And of course, no Roman:
he can take no risk that matters,
the risk of beauty least of all.

But I have my kin . . .

Despite the discrepancy (an ocean   courage   age)
this is also true: if I have any taste
it is only because I have interested myself
in what was slain in the sun

    I pose you your question:

shall you uncover honey / where maggots are?

    I hunt among stones

In the hunt among stones—the search for renewable value in a rediscovered archaic—Olson was finding a valuable ally in Frances Boldereff. It was to her he now turned to share the excitements of his studies of the past.

When, for example, his reading of Sappho in translation led him to stumble on a reference to an obscure second-century author named Maximus of Tyre, she was the first to hear of it. Though his lack of "th'advantage" of classic Greek inhibited further immediate research on this heroic-sounding character, he managed to send on to her a few words of original script laboriously copied out from Maximus' *Dissertations* at the Library of Congress. (Never having laid eyes on him, she of course had as yet no way of guessing why the mere ring of the name "Maximus" held such special personal appeal.) She in turn began generously transmitting materials she'd gathered in her own archaic explorations, the surprising extent of which came as a welcome revelation to him. Egyptian and Sumerian cultures, it seemed, were a passionate interest of hers. That May she directed him to the ancient-history section of the library to examine French archaeologist Franz Cumont's color-plate reproductions of Mesopotamian frescoes at Dura-Europos in Iran, recommending that he pay particular attention to the strange, fixed gaze of the Babylonian priest-celebrant at the temple of the god Zeus-Baal, a "look the Christian world has not so far touched—the unworld brought to view." Olson did as advised, and came back to her a few days later with a poem of response called "Dura": "To come to the look in the sacrificer's eyes / the archaic sought, the harshness / unsought . . ." A creative vein had been struck, as they both sensed. She had soon sent along a treasured file of Sumerian poetic and religious texts translated by Samuel Noah Kramer, acquired by her on a personal pilgrimage to the University of Pennsylvania scholar's Philadelphia museum office. From these, Olson quickly produced a three-part verse series titled "La Chute," adopting the ritual hieratic voice of the Kramer fragments as vehicle for his own poetic descent into the underworld ("If you would go down to the dead / to receive my drum and lute . . ."). He declaimed the poems in a public reading at the Institute of Contemporary Arts, his breathy, percussive presentation ("half reading, half breathing") giving Frank Moore the impression he was acting out his study of Leo Frobenius' work by imitating African rhythms. He did nothing to correct Moore's mistaken impression. Connie, whose glimpses of the incoming mail from his Pennsylvania correspondent had given her a better clue, was made jealous by the "La Chute" poems. Not that she dared reveal to others what she knew about them; Charles, as she was well aware, felt "skittish as hell about anybody looking over my shoulder at my sources."

The mystery correspondent's importance in his life continued to grow. He took the surprising step of applying for a teaching job at the school where she worked, Penn State, getting Black Mountain and the Guggenheim Foundation to supply letters of recommendation (Black Mountain registrar David Corkran described his teaching as "imaginative and bold"). Frances Boldereff meanwhile lobbied school officials on behalf of his application and proposed that in the event of his hiring he make use of her three-bedroom "reconverted barbershop" apartment in rural Woodward. But he did not get the job, and as summer came on he began dropping hints about his uncertain housing situation in Washington. His landlady, he announced, was threatening to put the Randolph Place property up for sale. Worrying about it was taking his mind off his writing. The ideal solution, he suggested meaningfully to Frances, would be to have the property purchased "by one or more non-existent, or not yet dreamed up sponsors," then donated to him as a gift to be used as creative "BASE." She reported back that she was approaching some wealthy New York friends to put forward his ingenious proposal. His hopes briefly rose, and when the dream deal did not materialize, he was brought back to earth with a jolt.

On his teaching visits to Black Mountain in the spring of 1949 he found the college rife with discord. The faculty was split into opposing factions, on the one side the "revolutionists," as he called them, led by science teacher Natasha Goldowski and farm manager Raymond Trayer, on the other the "Germans," led by Dreier and Albers. Though as a part-time visitor Olson was not required to take sides, his own personal allegiances—and best sources of support—lay in the latter camp. By April he was reporting to Dahlberg that the Goldowski-Trayer group was taking command of the school; dissenters would be "going their separate ways." He himself was tempted to join "Albers & friends" in Texas at a prospective "reconstructed" Black Mountain to be financed by a rich student from Dallas. The Texas scheme, however, proved to be a pipe dream; soon thereafter, Trayer took over as acting rector and Goldowski as secretary, while Dreier and Albers left. Olson, who had remained an interested spectator to the struggle, was asked to return for the summer as writing teacher. In his view, the months of argument, tension and turmoil had "riven the atmosphere," threatened the feeling of "communitas," distracted the students; the whole business was "very stupid." But as warm weather came on, the sun and the natural attractions of the mountain springtime—astonishing growth everywhere, the air "alive with bees, birds & butterflies"—transformed the place into a temporary Eden. To Connie, back at her office desk in Washington, he wrote during his mid-May visit that he'd been thinking about the possibility of their making a home at Black Mountain—"the one back-to-earth you & I might both enjoy, an Enniscorthy for two."

Before heading to the college with Connie for the summer session, he took off on a solo trip to the Northeast, with literary business and a visit to his mother as his ostensible objectives. He secretly hoped to see Frances

Boldereff as well. After some wavering over whether to propose a rendez-vous, he finally got up the nerve to wire her directions to meet him in New York. But the wire was late, and when he got to the city he was disappointed to find they had missed connections. He hung around New York a few days, saw Jean Riboud and had a brief reunion with Edward Dahlberg. To cheer his former mentor, now toiling in unhappy obscurity as a freshman English instructor at a Brooklyn technical college, he reported he'd been touting the still-unpublished *Flea of Sodom* at Black Mountain and was making progress with getting a student printer to produce it in a limited edition. Before leaving New York he dashed off another wire to Pennsylvania, giving Frances Boldereff his mother's address. Then, borrowing Jean Riboud's car, he drove up to Gloucester.

Mary Olson, now in her late seventies, was aging rapidly, and it took him little time to tire of sitting around Oceanwood Cottage trying to make small talk with her. To get himself out of the house, he went off to look up a local poet whose verse he'd recently seen in a small literary magazine. When he stopped in to pay his respects, the poet, Vincent Ferrini, was away on day-shift duties at a local factory. The startled Mrs. Ferrini afterward told her husband they'd been visited by a giant. Olson came back the next night, found the man of the house on hand, and "made himself immediately at home as though he had been a member of the family." A General Electric assembly-line worker whose life in poetry was even more an affair of lonely moonlighting than Olson's own, the thirty-six-year-old Ferrini would provide him a loyal Gloucester poetic "brother" in years to come.

Getting no word from Frances Boldereff at Oceanwood Cottage, Olson moved on to Cambridge, and from there dispatched a note suggesting they meet at the Fifth Avenue Hotel in New York. She wired back that she couldn't make it to the city by his appointed time. He could dally in New England no longer.

He and Connie sublet their Washington home for the rest of the summer, and at the beginning of July they left together for North Carolina. There, the healing "back-to-earth" idyll he'd promised turned out a sodden interlude at best. Unusually wet and humid weather steeped the Blue Ridge days in a sweaty and oppressive haze and rendered the nights too hot and bug-infested for sleeping. Having sung the praises of "communitas" without fully considering its gastronomic implications, Olson found his first prolonged exposure to Black Mountain's "tantalian" dining-hall fare as unsatisfying as the gloomy weather. The realities of collectivism, moreover, kept sinking in all summer. The course he'd planned, an eight-week intensive workshop to culminate in a series of theatrical events, was cut back because of a funding veto by the college board. His original scheme for a stage production of the *Odyssey,* with Victor Bérard's translation as text and members of the Washington-based

New Company as collaborators and performers, had to be abandoned, and an impromptu program of alternate pieces, employing a makeshift cast, was put on in its place.

These "Theater Exercises" were Olson's attempted realization of the "stripped down," "plots gone" experimental drama he preached in his classes that summer. In them, his studies of archaic Greek theater and of African tribal rites collided head-on with the emergent avant-garde of Black Mountain, creating results resembling the reconstruction of a Southern folk pageant aboard a spaceship parked in the Olduvai Gorge. Performances were held over several stifling evenings at the end of August. Three low plywood platforms deployed around the college dining hall served as stages. Olson himself was the central actor in some of the "Exercises." In one, he boomed out "The Kingfishers" in his barrelhouse rhapsode's "Zeus-beat" while student volunteers performed ritualistic interpretive dance gestures and executed a prepared-piano musical score. Another, titled *Kyklops,* featured an Olson text adapted from Euripides' play about the Homeric giant, sets by a student abstract expressionist painter and polyrhythmic drum-beating by a writing student. (Olson's personal identification with the mythic one-eyed man-eater moved one summer student to dub him "Kee-Klops.") In the main event, *Wagadu,* his adaptation of the Soninke folk tales collected by Frobenius and Douglas Fox in *African Genesis,* Olson chanted a neo-primitive monologue, student painter Dan Rice flashed slide projections on the dining-hall walls, and a pulse beat of archaic-sounding drums throbbed out across the dark sleeping waters of Lake Eden. Only the small crowd of perspiring white faces betrayed the missionary effect, Black Mountain's actual black population at the time being strictly limited to kitchen staff.

Incessant rains having turned the college grounds to a "jungle & humid" swamp, Olson looked forward to the summer's close. The Trayer-Goldowski axis, he'd decided, were "barbarous & vicious creatures" who meant him no good (he had not been asked back for the fall), and the summer faculty included few people he felt inclined to talk to. Fellow instructor Buckminster Fuller pressed on him some very long, and equally long-winded, poems, which left him unimpressed. The voluble dome guru provided his main competition for students' attention, but Olson was convinced his own contingent of followers was larger (his "oraculizing" had won him several new disciples). He liked much better two of Fuller's protégés, artist Emerson Woelffer and wife Diana, a photographer. Over cold beers with Connie and the Woelffers, he killed long, hot August nights with discussion of a grand scheme for the following winter—a trip by both couples to the Yucatán. The voyage, as he pictured it, would be a sort of group quest for the truth behind such archaic practices as "the Indian ceremony of cutting out the heart of the sacrificial victim."

It took a September holiday in New England to clear the effects of the

sluggish Black Mountain summer out of his system. After a visit to Gloucester, he and Connie continued up the coast to Maine. They stopped for a
awhile with Washington friends who had a country house in Damariscotta,
and he got a chance to tour the local side roads, "those places where the
carpenter was the agent of grace." The down-east stay revived his spirits and
senses, bringing back the sharp "delight [of] what New England was." By
the end of the month he and Connie had moved on to Connecticut, where
Jean Riboud and his new Indian companion Krishna Roy (the niece of poet
Rabindranath Tagore) were getting married at the spacious estate of the bride's
wealthy guardian. Olson, resplendent in hired tuxedo and "lovely public airs"
rarely displayed of late, served as Riboud's best man at the October 1 wed-
ding, rubbing shoulders during the ceremony and reception with high-toned
guests including the bridegroom's future employers, the oilfield-engineering
family of Schlumberger. Clearly the primitivist in him hadn't taken over altogether. Heading back to his plebeian home base in Washington, he felt refreshed
and ready for the future.

13 🙙

Riot in My Soul
(1949–1950)

The midcentury year went down in Olson's private self-mythology as one
of "riot in my soul," a time of confused intensities and disruptive excitements opening up important new directions. The period actually began a few
months before the end of 1949, its outset marked by his first meeting with
the muse and lover whose intervention would help him effect a self-transfor-
mation from "slow nordic emerger" to "new man Olson." Years later, charting his personal history in a journal, he set down this encounter as a watershed
in his life as a poet:

> 1949 Frances / result: 1950
> 1950: spring   the writing starts

The turbulence of his life during this period stirred conflicting psychic images—
of "flight from woman" and strong attraction to a female projection, of
encapsulation in self and creative release in a frenzied flood of language. In
that effusive torrent, old habits and inhibitions in poetry would be shaken,
especially that stiff "posing of the self on the surface of the poem" which had
always made him feel awkward in the verse medium and which now began
to give way to a new mode, one in which the self could be accepted and made
at home, "most presently if anonymously *inside*." But if the new self-centering

would yield a much more personal strain in his poems, it would also force them to become more opaque, as he reacted to his own impulsive exposures by clothing them in increasing layers of private coding.

Early in November he went north to assist his mother's annual move from Oceanwood—and to make personal contact with his mystery correspondent at last. After the crossed signals of the trip five months earlier, he was careful this time to phone ahead to Pennsylvania, confirming the arrangements and instructing Frances Boldereff to meet him at a specific hour in the front lobby of the New York Public Library. He got to the city a day early, and stayed over with Edward Dahlberg. They engaged in a late-night dialogue on the subject of women. When Dahlberg, complaining of recent misfortunes in love, took a mysogynistic position, Olson rallied to the philosophical defense of females. In the morning, borrowing Jean Riboud's Mercury, he drove on to the library. He waited for several hours in the lobby, growing increasingly restless as second thoughts multiplied.

Frances, meanwhile, was hurrying to the appointment with no real knowledge about what to expect; showing typical reserve about his person, he had not even let on anything to indicate he was physically out of the ordinary. "We both disdained any identification signs," she says now, "and all I knew was that on the telephone he'd sounded like a New England sea captain." She had missed her train, and, with small daughter in tow, was four hours late getting to the city.

> I entered the library on the 42nd St. side with Lucinda. As I came into the front lobby, I saw a large man in a raincoat disappearing through the revolving door. I asked the attendant at the front entrance if the man who had just disappeared had been there long and he said, "Yes, miss, he was waiting here all afternoon." I was too stunned to make any reaction. I did nothing, just stood there, stunned.
>
> While I was standing there the revolving door began to move and back in came Charles. He looked at me and said, "Frances," and then said, "Something forced me to come back."

They exchanged excited greetings in the warm glow of the brightly lit lobby. Her appearance took him by surprise: in anticipatory imaginings, her Russian married name and evident life experience had combined to summon an image dark and exotic, but confronting him now was a small, comely figure, fair and almost girlish, possessing a pale Celtic clarity of complexion that reminded him of his mother in early photographs.

After dinner and intense conversation at a quiet restaurant in Brooklyn Heights, he dropped Frances and her daughter at a brownstone in the neighborhood, home of old friends of hers. The moment she left him, he was plunged in gloomy "despair," and paced damp Brooklyn streets as far as the East River, an "angel who tasted then like ash to himself." He spent a fretful night at the nearby St. George Hotel. In the morning he phoned her and invited her to breakfast. She came alone. He ran off at the mouth "like a giddy boy," but was too nervous to propose ascending to his room. A few hours later she left him, announcing plans to depart by train for a visit to a friend in Tarrytown, a small village upstate on the Hudson. "Losing" her once again rendered him even more disconsolate than on the previous night.

He went to Grand Central and boarded a train headed toward Glouces-ter, but, a few miles out of the station, experienced a sudden change of mind. At the first opportunity he got off and took the next train back to New York. Once there, he raced across town to Penn Station. Each of these maneuvers was attended by feelings of great risk, as he sensed his fate unraveling further with every step. At a whistle stop on the Hudson he got off and stood on the platform peering into each passing coach for a glimpse of her face.

Frances was meanwhile nearing her own destination. "Around two or three o'clock in the afternoon Lucinda and I were riding on the train and had not very many stops before we were to reach Tarrytown. The coach door opened and in comes Charles. He plunked himself down beside me."

In Tarrytown, Frances' friend took charge of Lucinda. The couple pro-ceeded to an exclusive local inn. There, recalls Frances,

> A most ladylike woman was seated at a tiny table near the entrance and she was the registration desk. With her Charles made arrangements that we would share a room which turned out to be very large and lovely with very far apart twin beds and he said, "You don't mind, do you?"
>
> Next morning we took a stroll down a steep hill, at the bottom of which runs the Hudson River. But before you reach the river you come to the roadbed of the New York Central RR and before that space, another, which had a business—indiscriminate industrial look. We strolled along and came to a very large circle of trees. What was it doing there? Planted by man? Happenstance? It was too small in diameter for the kind of house to be found in the neighborhood on the top of the bluff (Washington Irving's home, for instance, not too far off), there were no signs of a foundation of any kind of building—it did not look cared for but never-theless had a fairly smooth surface, whether covered with green or not I cannot remember. It did seem to us faery. It was truly round, the trees were fairly good size, deciduous of some kind, and fairly like to one another in size. Around out-side was the most casual spread of RR ties, junk, earth, etc. Who planted it there? How could it have possibly remained there?
>
> Dunno.
>
> For us, birth and magic.

Charles, for his part, felt moved and inspired by her adventurous, expres-sive ways in love—and particularly by her openness toward sex. She was, he had decided by the end of their brief tryst by the Hudson, not merely an exceptional woman, but, in personal terms, a "wizardess," capable of transforming him.

His trip on to Gloucester was like a dream. Once back in Washington, he wrote to Frances to exultantly proclaim his rebirth in that "magic ring" at Tarrytown—"Woodhenge," druidlike sacred ground of their union. The riverside "hidden wood" became the stage of a new poem, "Epigon." Vivid testimony that the recent whirl of events had been more than a mere adulterous escapade, and marker of his first step toward the determination of a personal self-measure in writing, it would remain a closely guarded private document, unpublished in his lifetime. "Birth," he declared, "is a euphemism,"

> *. . . it is the mortal which matters,*
> *from which I now spring*
>
> *intent,*
> *the measure*
>
> *Nature,*
> *is proved again*
>
> *I am*
> *of use*
>
> *blood has to be spent, this boreal heath warmed*
> *out from this faery circle (in the November sun*
> *creatures present, including the angelic orders, ordering)*
> *to take on the demons, to regain*
> *first principles, crying*
> *redeem, redeem*
> *the dead*
>
> *you,*
> *who art awake!*

The metaphor of resurrection and "second birth" here expressed would sustain him through the first months of soul riot ahead.

This verse invocation of his new, alert oracle, as well as the prolific letter exchange which soon followed, was sped along to Pennsylvania via a recently instituted same-day postal service. Also conducive to his stage management of the epistolary romance was Connie's being out of the house six afternoons a week (she now ran the office of a nursing school). Arrival of the daily mail during her absence kept Frances' distinctive blue stationery safely out of her sight.

One morning, however, the postman showed up inconveniently early with a special-delivery letter. Charles was still sleeping, and Connie, who hadn't yet left for work, was present to answer the door. She immediately recognized the telltale stationery, confirmation of her instinctive suspicion that his recent trip had been less than routine, and refused the letter. The subtle rift between them created by the interloper now for the first time widened sufficiently to begin seriously affecting domestic relations. Tentative plans for a winter trip to the Yucatán with their Black Mountain summer neighbors, the Woelffers, were dropped. It took Connie—"quiet, angry, determined, proud"—some time to get over the special-delivery-letter episode. A somewhat sobered Charles meanwhile instructed Frances to restrict herself henceforth to regular mail.

Within days of the Tarrytown idyll he was at work on setting up a sequel in Pennsylvania. After a first attempt to get there by way of New Rochelle, New York—where he had to appear on Dahlberg's behalf at a child-custody hearing—was thwarted by inconvenient bus timetables, he hatched another scheme. This time nonexistent literary business in New York provided a cover story. He took off by bus on December 8 and wafted into tiny Woodward, a dreamlike landscape of silence and snow made ethereal by twilight "greys of houses, stone, pines, highway." Frances awaited him at the bus stop. Following a hike through falling snow to her cozy "reconverted barbershop" apartment, they talked much of the night before a potbellied stove. Agreeing on their shared affinity with a generative archaic, they spoke excitedly of space and geometry in art, of form and design in print, and finally of ancient mysteries to be brought back to life not as thoughts and words alone—and it was precisely this last element that had been eluding him through twenty years of anxious self-doubtings—but as liberated, vital "acts."

Back in Washington, Connie's suspicious questions about the trip forced him into revelations, left however deliberately incomplete. He admitted that he'd been in Pennsylvania, but painted the encounter with his epistolary friend as strictly platonic, describing Frances to Connie as "middle-aged and ill." His distracted state, however, belied his disavowals. For Frances, meanwhile, he had a slightly different version of the situation. "Constanza," he announced, "speaks your name now, almost as i might, and struggles with every ounce of her strength to deal with this thing, and to move ahead with it." (If Connie was in fact now speaking Frances' name, it was with no such earnest goodwill.) To Frances' repeated urgings that he return for another visit, he responded with repeated admonitions to "hold." Together they would "create acts for men and women to come," but not just yet. In truth the initial heady rush of the affair had now subsided sufficiently for his natural caution to set in; he could see that Frances, for all her vibrancy, was too independent ever to take the place of Connie, his self-abnegating supporter and indispensable "rock." From this point on, between the lines of even his most effusive letters to Pennsylvania, the hedging of bets was clearly audible.

The "life unmodified" he assured Frances he foresaw for them would meanwhile have to take a backseat to his literary routines. A week after the Woodward trip he introduced an American University exhibition of Corrado Cagli's "Drawings in the 4th Dimension" with a lecture on projective geometry, Cagli's Moebius experiments, space and poetry. (The artist himself was absent, having moved back to Italy the previous year.) With the local art cognoscenti on hand in the university's Watkins Gallery, Olson experienced the predictable stress, and the event did not go well. The ranging and abstruse talk met with polite stares of incomprehension, and his reading of "The King-fishers" and "The Praises" went over little better. Afterwards he lamented to Frances that the occasion of public speaking, and particularly the traditional lecture format, had become simply too confining for the private intensities of his thought. All such attempts at discursive speech now felt "futile" to him, he said, because of "my utter lack of interest in discussing things publicly what do i care to argue or to explain that which moves me all i wish to do is to use it . . . people are lazy, that's why they take personality as a pill of force, i feel nothing but contempt, and it is an emotion which i do not like, for it assaults my faith, & drains me." The aftermath was one of his cyclic flu bouts, driving him to bed for a week.

Frances administered healing texts, Egyptian love poems he had soon reshaped into some secret verses wherein she became a vestal-maidenly "flow-ering sib" with Mary Hines' cheeks, priestess in some sacred incest rite bear-ing for him the "essence of you, / who are woman." But she was soon revealing personal difficulties of her own, especially as regarded the "holding" pattern he had charted for her: her role in it, he acknowledged in a Christmas-present poem ("The Babe"), remained one of continuing isolation ("you / who are alone"). Frustration and impatience on her part now began to show. The pain of not seeing him, exacerbated by battles with "enemies" at work, was sometimes almost intolerable, she told him early in the new year. She described her emotional state for him in a vivid metaphor: "I am the most alive giant Sequoia which has been torn out ruthlessly roots and all by a hurricane, turned upside down and made to brush top down against the dirt of the world." Her anguished outcry drew from him only an oblique literary response—his own "roots" theory of poetics. "A man must somehow leave that connect, as you'd say, that bunch of roots and dirt hanging down into himself, or the thing is DEAD." This was soon reduced to a small, amulet-like poem, "These Days" ("Whatever you have to say, leave / the roots on, let them / dangle . . ."), which he circulated to writer friends as a sort of miniature credo. (One recipient, William Carlos Williams, was moved to forward it on to a little magazine, *Imagi,* which published it.)

Not long afterward a second Olson position-poem, "The Advantage," was developed from another of her letter images. Writing to encourage him in his works, she had emphasized the redemptive mission she envisaged for him, enjoining him to force open "all the inherited puffballs" of a fallow culture, thus releasing "spores to beget new life." Her image brought to mind Bolyai Farkas' observation that parallel discoveries in thought had a way of springing up like violets. "The Advantage" combined the two figures in a touchstone statement on the natural propagation of new ideas, a pollenization process which Olson with unwitting irony described as exclusively male (Frances, for once, did not receive a copy): "Where do these / invisible seeds / settle from? / And how are men able / to spore them / into air? / For the gains are / thus communicated. / Shall you say there are not Powers / when men spring up (like violets, sd Bolyai Farkas) / on all sides, to the need? / Men have their proper season. . . ."

For effective literary propagation, however, the Lawrentian male solar energy this poem posed against humanism's "old device, the making / domestic abstract gods / of paled-out humans" would have to be provided historical framing. Once again Frances obliged. He must, she told him, look up an obscure 1923 text by an Austrian art historian and scholar named Josef Strzygowski. Olson obediently trekked to the Library of Congress for Strzygowski's *Origin of Christian Church Art,* in which he found a ready-made, well-documented dismantling of the received "history of art history." The idea of a dominant naturalistic tradition in Western art was dismissed by the revisionist historian as mere myth ("a tissue of the imagination spun by church, court and Humanism"); the true central line, Strzygowski contended, was nonrepresentational and austere, and ran not through Greece and Rome but Egypt, Mesopotamia and Islamic Iran and over the medieval trade routes into Eastern Europe, Scandinavia and the British Isles. This iconoclastic reversal of the classic humanist view held considerable appeal for Olson, not least because of the obscurity of the source. A bizarre "Lake Van measure," putatively derived from proportions of bas-relief sculptures on a tenth-century Armenian cruciform church on the island of Achthamar in the middle of Lake Van—as depicted by "Doctor Strzygowski"—would one day not only afford him a convenient, half-spoofing poetic rule of thumb, but also dictate one of the most distinctive poems in the final *Maximus* volume, a belated tribute to Strzygowski titled "AN ART CALLED GOTHONIC." Illustrations of such sculptures in *Origin of Christian Church Art* already appeared a potential gold mine, acquainting him, as he told Frances, with a blending of primal Bible imagery and the formal austerity of Islamic art that suggested a perfect figure of "the archaic myth of the baking of man—my objectivism right under my nose!"

Cooking up a myth of neo-archaic man to fit the present had become an obsessive preoccupation for him, so all-consuming that he could not allow himself even a day or two away to see her. Keeping him compulsively chained to his typewriter for eight and ten hours at a stretch like "some manacled mad thing," this "desperate job, this business of words, words, words," was a discipline requiring absolute "exclusion and privacy, with no other human being but oneself." Such apologies and rationalizations notwithstanding, however, the lonely Frances could find little solace in his disciplines when they necessitated breaking dates to come and visit her. Several times he postponed promised trips to Woodward in deference to imagined urgencies of work, leaving her with the justifiable suspicion her own role in his life had been reduced to that of "just some damned note-taker."

She abruptly quit her job, and declared she was about to arrive on his doorstep. She needed to come to an understanding with Connie, she said. Charles shot down the idea by return mail. He was, he assured her, already "doing the very maximum in all directions"—in the moment's "unbelievable pitch," relations between himself and Connie were strained to breaking point and could bear no added pressure. At the same time, he begged her to continue writing: "About your letters . . . I have to have them." She succumbed to his persuasions, backed off her demands, stayed put in her backwoods hamlet, kept on writing to him—there were sometimes two and three letters from her in a single post—and took on free-lance design work to support herself and her daughter.

Meanwhile the spate of words from his end continued undiminished. He, too, often wrote several times daily, supplying her a running account of that "hammering of oneself out on the anvil of oneself" which was now his full-time engagement. She was invited to participate from a distance not only in the development of his writing and thought but in its occasional extensions beyond his work desk into real life—such as his acquisition of an original painting by D. H. Lawrence, an author they both regarded as a prophet of the psychosexual "living flame." In the course of the habitual bookstore browsing that was his principal relief and escape from the daily bouts of reading and writing, he spotted a Lawrence collection containing a small watercolor of a naked man urinating into a bank of daffodils. The boldness and candor of the image, so indicative of the sort of Lawrentian openness to which he imagined himself and his Muse together aspiring, provoked him to engineer a deal involving the purchase of the Lawrence collection by the Library of Congress, from which he emerged with the watercolor as his middleman's bonus. He proudly mounted it above his writing desk, where it would prevail as symbol of the creative "root of universe" energy he sought to tap in himself.

For Frances, however, long-distance life-sharing was an increasingly difficult proposition. Inevitably misunderstandings arose. An example was her misreading of his report on a rare public foray that February, to lecture on Melville at the Institute of Contemporary Arts. After the second of his two lectures, he told her, he'd been approached by a member of the audience, a young Italian sculptor. They'd talked at length, and ex-Catholic Olson had been much impressed by the young man's passionate advocacy of the aesthetic canons of the Roman church. Frances, fiercely anti-Catholic after the manner of her hero William Blake, took this as a sign of potential relapse and rebuked him sternly for "turning Catholic on me." Taken aback, he protested by return mail that he'd merely been interested—not tempted. To support his avowals of a continuing aversion to the "filthy faith" of his childhood, he produced a pair of long, breezy letter-poems, "A Po-sy, A Po-sy" and "The Morning News." These were demonstrations of a new free-form poetic mode at once loose and arcane ("truly hermetique / nothing catholique")—conscious imitations of her irreverent, "terrific laugh and down, down, derry down throat speech, sex-all-over-the place," and incorporating a series of her recent letter-gifts, from Strzygowski to Meister Eckhart. Along with these conciliatory garlands of verse he reiterated his thanks to her, for once again "delivering to me up clean out of the delicate sure fingers of your mind such things."

Charm and wooing merged subtly into a real acknowledgment of debt. He was, he now told her, still very much in her tutelage—learning all over again how to write, "from the inside, from the working along with the self." Each new day at the typewriter inundated him with fresh poetic discoveries, advances that seemed enormously promising yet at the same time frustratingly elusive. The impulse to contain them in some total formulation was becoming at least as strong as the urge to go on creating. He began drafting a manifesto to announce the emergence of a new open verse. "PROJECTIVE," he called it, using a term derived simultaneously from new geometry, psychology and the cinema. This first typed version of his ground-breaking essay—dated February 9, and on the following day sent off, with extensive revisions inserted by hand, to his "mistress printer" Frances—opened with a schematic delineation of the dichotomy between open and closed verse forms:

PROJECTIVE   VERSE
                (projectile   (prospective   (percussive
                                    vs.

the NON-projective, what we have had, pretty much (outside Pound & Williams), what a French critic calls the "closed," the visual verse, the lyric, if you
like, the "personal" . . .

The oppositional staging of the argument—only slightly qualified in later
drafts, which borrowed a phrase from Keats to shift the focus of attack from
"lyric" and "personal" to an inherited Wordsworthian-Miltonic "Egotistical
Sublime"—was a characteristic Olson tactic. Impact, in his theoretical pronouncements, was to be attained not by logic but by the posing of abstract
resistances, and the overcoming of them by sheer force of propositional thrust.

The proposal which followed defined the incipient verse revolution in
terms primarily physical, involving the poet's voice and breathing; Olson's
poetics here took shape as a reflection of anatomical and organic models that
dictated much of his current thinking about human capacity in general. Pre-
scribing a compositional adherence to idiosyncratic "rhythms . . . personal to
the composer," he likened the emergence of the poet's voice from his "drum
of a body" to the ceremonial priest's in the coronation scene from Eisenstein's
Ivan the Terrible: a powerful, incantatory filling-up of space "one by one noun
after another breasting out and up." Highly expressive of the poetic self-
image of a verse performer who to some listeners seemed all breath, this
revealing figure was edited out of the published essay—as were some accompanying remarks on musical composition in verse, which Olson evidently
came to find too derivative of the Poundian doctrine of *melopoeia.*

For the representation on the page of his expansive voicing, the open-
verse poet was dependent on the typewriter, mechanical extension of the
physical voice. ("The irony is, from the machine comes deliverance. . . . For
the first time the poet has the stave and bar a musician had.") Samples of his
own verse—the opening line of "The Kingfishers" and the first three lines of
"The Advantage" (in later drafts to be replaced by a passage from "The
Praises")—provided instructive illustrations of proper projective space nota-
tion and page design ("if a contemporary poet leaves a space as long as the
phrase before it, he means that space to be held an equal length of time . . .").
Such empirical specifications, he allowed, were less his own contribution than
an attempt at summarizing an ongoing, collective modernist effort, as observ-
able in "the already PROJECTIVE nature of verse as the sons of Pound and
Williams are practicing it."

Larger moral and philosophical implications of the projective occupied
him in the third and final section of his draft. Here he stated his own version

of basic modernist tenets regarding the elimination of subjectivity as a means to a more direct grasp on the world.

> It is no accident that both Pound and Williams were involved in a movement which got called "objectivism." But that word was then used in some sort of necessary quarrel, I take it, with "subjectivism." . . . What seems to me a more valid formulation for present use, is, "objectism," a word to be taken to stand for the kind of relation of man to experience which a poet might state as the necessity of a line or a work to be as wood is, to be as clean as wood is as it issues from the hand of nature, to be as shaped as wood is when a man has had his hand to it. It is the getting rid of the lyrical interference of the individual, of the subject and his soul, that peculiar presumption by which western man has interposed himself between what he is as a creature of nature with certain instructions to carry out and the other creations of nature which we may, with no derogation, call objects. For a man is himself an object, the moment he achieves a humilitas sufficient to make him of use.

A second key passage, added by hand in the draft sent Frances, marked the center of the essay, and also heralded his advance beyond the modernist canon to his own special contribution, the poetics of self-measure.

> It comes to this: the use of a man, by himself and thus by others, lies in how he conceives his relation to nature, that force to which he owes his somewhat small existence. If he sprawl, he shall find little to sing but himself, and shall sing, nature has such paradoxical ways, by way of artificial forms outside himself. But if he stays inside himself, if he is contained within his nature as he is participant in the larger force, he will be able to listen, and his hearing through himself will give him secrets objects share. . . . It is in this sense that the projective act, which is the artist's act in the larger field of objects, leads to dimensions larger than the man. For a man's problem, the moment he takes speech up in all its fullness, is to give his work his seriousness, a seriousness sufficient to cause the thing he makes to try to take its place alongside the things of nature.

Visions of a limber, physical, muscular new poetry were still dominating his thoughts when he attended a Dylan Thomas reading at the Institute of Contemporary Arts in early March. "A wretched rabbit, fat and seedy," the much-publicized touring Welshman appeared to him a sadly deteriorated person. At a reception afterwards, fellow Washington poet Karl Shapiro (a Pulitzer Prize winner and poetry consultant to the Library of Congress) launched into praise of Thomas' rich language. Olson countered that the verbal beauties camouflaged a deep weakness at the center: "He is all language, there is no man there." Shapiro's puzzled stare of response—as if to say, " 'What in Christ's name is Olson talking about?' "—was, as Charles told Frances afterward, a "look I am so well acquainted with." The obvious difference of opinion was implicit proof of how far he had come from accepted establishment views of poetry. "They dream too easily," he commented to her apropos of both Thomas and his mainstream followers, "they dip themselves too readily in the sensuous. The bones are not there. . . . a man must fight every instant to keep himself vertebra, bone from the neck to the tip of his cock."

The overtly sexual tenor of his reaction to the Thomas reading carried over into a poem written to Frances a few days later, "Of Lady, of Beauty, of Stream." In it he likened himself to a golden fish rising through clear water to be caught in her delicate "directive hand." Delighted with the poem, she directed him to Graves' *The White Goddess* to read up on the Salmon of Wisdom in early Irish myth. Once again, as with Strzygowski, her chance tip opened up for him a rich imaginative vein. He seized on the salmon image as a poetic metaphor for their ecstatic soul-identification. She would reappear as his "sweet salmon" in letters and poems at intervals over the years, and in the *Maximus* he would write of "the salmon of / wisdom when, / ecstatically, one / leaps into the Beloved's / love . . ."

As Frances' March 26 birthday approached, and there still seemed no convenient way for them to see each other, he tried to bridge the distance with a "birthday present" letter in which he compared their love to that of Pericles and Aspasia, and rehearsed again their first meeting and its subsequent impact: a dramatic loosening of that "visored grip on his flesh" which before then had so impeded all his attempts at self-expression, not only sexual but creative. Within days this feeling of gratitude and release was informing a new long poem in her honor, "The She Bear," the ritual invocation of an empowering archaic goddess. Upon reading it, Frances told him that they were now working in such close psychic conjunction that she could instantly "understand everything as though I were the blood pushing the ink."

Receptive to his work and pleased with her status as its generative Muse though she may have remained, she was, however, also a woman and not completely immune to the predictable effects of being left alone indefinitely. "I am a passionate woman who has given herself once and for all into your hands," she reminded him in early April. "I make no stipulations or inquiries or halfnesses . . . [but] if you think it is likely that I may not see you for a long time—it would be kind of you to tell me—so that I may prepare myself." At times the precariousness of her position made her feel as naked and vulnerable as a friend who had "bought Bergdorf Goodman's best dress and hat—rode uptown on a New York bus—undressed to nakedness—left the clothes on a bank and walked naked . . . in the greatest loneliness and insanity the earth has to show—and drowned herself in the Hudson River." Though moved by these words—he incorporated them almost verbatim into a poem, titled "here i am, naked"—he was unable to offer her the emotional security she so obviously craved. Their love at such moments seemed to him an impossible dream, destined to cause only pain: "there is no sense in any business which leads you to such a pitch as this, that you be torn like this, that you write me such notes as these." Yet at the same time he continued to do everything in his power to keep it alive—even resorting to the simplest forms of sympathetic magic as practiced by lovesick adolescents, chalking the names of the wall-separated lovers Pyramus and Thisbe on the sidewalk outside his house.

Ironically it was a breakdown in his careful secrecy routines that led to their first meeting in almost five months. At the beginning of May he was to go off on a two-week Southern tour, taking the Cagli exhibit on the road. Several days before his departure a package from Pennsylvania arrived in a new and unforeseen morning mail delivery. The unsealed oversized envelope contained an art poster, accompanied by a note from Frances urgently exhorting him "to put off, to voyage" along with her into the unknown and concluding with an image of their souls as twin rafts on the open sea. Connie was at home to intercept the package. Armed with this fresh evidence the affair was still alive, she threatened to leave him unless the clandestine correspondence ceased immediately. He rushed to instruct Frances to withhold all further mail until he had been able to secure a post office box. For Frances this was the low point of "the most difficult winter I have ever had." She lashed back: "I believe it is wrong to enter a house by the back door, something your subconscious knows I am not able to do." Her tone hinted of extreme consequences. Desperate to appease her for this transgression, he phoned her to suggest a meeting, dictating a complex railroad itinerary that would place her in Knoxville, Tennessee, in time to meet up with him between stops on his Southern trip. He then departed from Washington himself, heading for Alabama.

At Alabama College, a state school for women in Montevallo, he was hosted by his friend Robert Payne, English-born Chinese scholar and editor of the *Montevallo Review* (in which "The Kingfishers" was soon to appear). The evident success of his lecture—a free-ranging consideration of man's natural place in creation, drawing on the *Pisan Cantos* and *King Lear*—merely added to the elation he already felt in anticipation of seeing Frances again. She, meanwhile, had borrowed money and journeyed south at breakneck pace. His train from Alabama pulled into the Knoxville station just as she was stepping off hers from Washington, a piece of synchronicity that seemed to him to bless the whole plan. His booming laugh rang out across the platform, alerting her to his presence. They spent the night at an old wooden hotel near the railroad tracks. In the morning, when they parted, he kissed her goodbye with a magnanimous "You deserved this, baby."

While leaving his Muse feeling somewhat diminished and used, for Olson the hurried Knoxville interlude had exactly the opposite effect. Sex and language were no longer distinct, compartmentalized realms of experience for him, but superimposed levels of a single thrust of self into the world ("potency man's measure, all, ALL he liveth for . . ."). Success as a lover brought with it renewal in other expressive areas. Out of the carefully timed rendezvous in Tennessee came a fresh surge of verbal confidence, a "wild fool" energy that carried over to his next stop, Black Mountain, where the tour climaxed with a series of talks and readings in which the lingering heat of erotic contact allowed him to "pour on [his] blood" as never before. This time his principal text was Blake's "The Mental Traveller," a poem long held sacred by Frances, and a secret key to the cyclic view of history he'd proposed in "La Préface." He was, as he told Frances in a note from Black Mountain, still savoring love's "sweet, sweet taste."

"My mind is aswarm," he announced to her on May 17, a few days after his return to Washington. "It is the coming back, to work, after the affirmation of you, and the flooding of speech of two weeks." The fortnight's vivid rush of language and feeling had produced, he said, a "change in my sounding of, verse." Already the confident certainties of his "Projective Verse" essay (now in the hands of a literary magazine, *Poetry New York*) seemed premature, "only scratching the skin of it." The practical problems of achieving a "music-contained" poetry still remained to be confronted. The closest he'd come to realizing that praxis, he felt, was in a few passages of letter-poems to her. Primitive starts, at best—and yet, what with the paradoxical calculated spontaneity of approach, the quality of deliberate uncertainty that seemed built into the projective, how could he know such things might not turn out to have been the sum and extent of his accomplishment?

> I am scared i shall never write another! It is the craziest sort of feeling, this, of not being able to match the done! . . . I suppose this plane is the sex of writing art, the underpart, the nervousness because love is not born. One loves only form, and form only comes into existence when the thing is born. And the thing may lie around the bend of the next second. Yet, one does not know, until it is there, under hand.

Retyping this passage for her as verse, he unconsciously proved his point ("one does not know, until it is there . . ."), mistakenly hitting "s" for "x," making "next" into "nest," and then, in keeping with the serendipity of the projective, retaining the error as a fortuitous twist in the poem. From the "nest" mischance issued a key image: "the bird! the bird!" This bird in turn became the poem's principal incarnation of his poetic persona, Maximus—first appearing in the guise of Anthony of Padua, patron saint of the local fishermen, swooping low over the rooftops of Gloucester (metaphorical parallel to the ancient hero's Phoenician sea-city of Tyre) and later returning to the sanctuary of the home nest bearing a feather as love token.

> *the thing may lie*
> *around the bend of the nest*
> *second, time slain, the bird! the bird!*
> *there, strong, thrust, the mast, flight, o kylix!*
>
> > > > *o Anthony*
>
> *of Padua sweep low and bless the roofs,*
> *the gentle steep ones on whose ridge*
> *gulls sit, and depart,*
>
> > > *the flake racks,*
>
> > > > *o my city*

This early draft, "I, Maximus," unwitting inauguration of his master-work-to-come, was, like most of his poetry of the period, composed in two intermingled languages: one public and literary, one private and coded for translation only by his directive Muse. The poem went on to address a "lady of good voyage" who represented, on the one hand, the statue of the Virgin cradling a schooner on the Church of Our Lady of Good Voyage in Gloucester, and on the other, Frances, whose recent invitation to voyage, in the letter intercepted by Connie, had made such a powerful impact. It was boldly sexual, thrust forward on images of phallic masts, beaks and lances directed with propulsive energy toward receptive female nests. He proffered the draft poem itself to Frances as a kind of love token in its own right, a "jewel . . . flashing more than a wing," intended to make up for their separation. He took pains to make its deepest sources clear. "Despite troubles," he assured her at the conclusion of the poem-generating letter,

> these webs which spin, get spun across the space, the wild
> and at times intolerable space, are flowers of life, are
> facts to bow to, gentle maitresse. Anyhow, I give you the
> deepest sort of recognition, speak out from hidden islands
> in the blood which, like jewels and miracles, you invoke.
> And I, as hard-boiled instrument, as metal hot from boiling
> water, tell you, he recognizes what is lance, obeys
> the dance
> > mio chorego,
> > > eros, eros eros!

Beneath his signature ("a kylix, charles") he reshaped this last passage of prose into the lines of verse that would become his epic's opening:

Off-shore, by islands hidden in the blood
jewels & miracles, I, Maximus
a metal hot from boiling water, tell you
what is lance, who obeys the figures of
the present dance . . .

It was only fitting that the grand poem of his life, summation of all his intellectual gambles, was to begin in a lucky accident instigated by Eros and the Muse. After mailing off the letter to Frances, he revised the verse, expanded the title ("I, Maximus of Gloucester, to You" it now became), and sent a copy of the completed poem to Vincent Ferrini—whose solicitation of contributions for a new Gloucester magazine, *Voyager,* had indeed played some part in determining its thematic direction and local color. He had, he was soon able to declare to Dahlberg, at last pulled off a "long verse." "The howling way i was"—he added enigmatically—"i have continued to be, roaring from a storm which heaves up from the hidden places. . . . are they forever sexual?"

The storm raged on. The week following the writing of "I, Maximus" was one of much domestic strain, as Connie had little trouble fathoming the actual cause of his turbulent state in the wake of the Southern tour—and he had little heart left for the effort of concealment. During that week he made the first of a series of day trips to inspect Civil War battle sites in the Washington area, a junket that contributed thematic battlefield imagery to another important and difficult new poem-in-the-making, this one about forces in conflict on multiple levels from the military to the psychological and metaphysical.

"In Cold Hell, in Thicket" was an exacting and all but impenetrable conundrum of a work. Shifting metaphorical vocabularies were drawn variously from early industrial-age warfare ("lead soldiers," "spit-hardened fort") and its modern remnants (a deserted battlefield, "this / rotted place where men did die"); from projective geometry and its figurative moral extensions ("high mind," in these times of great stress and tension, was called upon to remain "abstract" and "strong . . . as strut or wing, as polytope"); and from the mathematical field theory of modern physics (persons, in such complex behavioral fields, had to be viewed with neutral objectivity as "particles," actions plotted as "traceries," human situations determined by precise "fix"). A background landscape—the archetypal forest of the mind—was supplied by Dante's *Inferno.* Only one thing was clear: that the action was being played out in the poet's own midlife dark wood, one thick with bewilderment and dilemma, a foreboding, impassable "selva oscura" of impossibly complicated, insolubly tangled networks of intention and relations.

Once again, only a reader privy to the poet's secret codes could decipher his true burden: a formal refusal of that old Olson nemesis, choice. As he'd admitted to Frances in a letter a few days before mounting this latest ambitious assault on the projective, he'd never been easy in dealing with personal decisions of any serious dimension, much less one as momentous as that now facing him—the choice between two women, each of whom was in her own way essential to his life. At such critical moments, he said, his natural inclination was to "rest action on risk . . . to throw it out there in space and come what may." (A second letter expanded on this, broadening the context from personal relationships to the course of events in general: "I prefer to stay, in a sense, fluid, as though the SUM was not to be of my doing . . . but to be taken care of by others.") His point, for once, was obvious. If decisive action was to resolve his quandary over whether to opt for wife or Muse, it would have to be action taken by one or the other of the women involved. Not that this withdrawal from choice provided immunity from the pains that came with dwelling in cold hells of the mind. Evidence of such torments, of thought's harsh "knivings" and of raw "nerves laid open," permeated the poem.

The verse, he told Frances, "was a letter . . . to you." Trusting her grasp of the codes, he made little attempt at explanation, supplying only an oblique gloss of a section which evoked "the sister" as "necessary goddess," with "awkward stars drawn for teats to pleasure him, the brother, / who lies in stasis under her." (This tribute, he confided, came out of the Egyptian cosmology they both held sacred, but by way of an unlikely intermediary source— the seventeenth-century metaphysical poet Richard Crashaw.) To Connie, meanwhile, he passed the poem off as a statement specifically directed to their recent marital trials—"these hells and thickets we['ve] been thru." His most revealing comment on the poem, however, was made to a neutral outsider, Vincent Ferrini. "What we call guilts—or pleasures," he told Ferrini in a letter written the same day the poem was begun, "remain, forever, ambiguities." In the guarded third-person discourse of the verse itself, the same thought was inscribed like a talisman of his palpable uncertainty: "he will forever waver / precise as hell is."

Certainly the verse was, in its tortuous, halting carriage, as irresolute and difficult, tense and abstract, as the poet himself was. Its relentlessly intellectual formal strategy proved daunting, even to a reader as trained in the intellectualism of Ezra Pound as Olson's fellow explorer of open verse Paul Blackburn—who subsequently complained to him of difficulties with the poem's overbearing rhetorical procedures, lack of *claritas,* and "real dearth of concrete imagery." Later generations of scholars and critics, as unsuspecting as Blackburn of the real personal divisions it concealed, would be equally baffled, if impressed, by "In Cold Hell" 's propositions and haunting, mysterious structures of figuration.

Hung up in those complex projective structures, Olson had a hard time making out the human reality behind distress signals that were now coming in from Pennsylvania with nearly every visit of the postman. His explosion of poetry in the wake of their Southern tryst was all but blinding him to that brief meeting's evident effect on Frances. Not that she didn't outdo herself in exposing her redoubled pangs of loneliness. But her *in extremis* life messages merely became more source material for verse, their highly charged personal content not only distanced but obscured by the kinetic impetus of the projective form. The late-May cycle begun with "I, Maximus" and "In Cold Hell," certainly his most productive outburst of poetry thus far, showed him learning to sustain a new intellectual energy and formal poise, in verse that at the same time betrayed a surprising detachment from the intensities it set out to register. "For Sappho, Back" and "Help Me, Venus, You Who Led Me On," both derived directly from her letters to him at this time, completed the cycle.

One urgent missive from Frances informed him that recent events had convinced her to "stop all thought of love, to abandon the whole concept." In its place, she told him in her usual metaphorical style, she aspired to attain the impassive serenity of a copperhead snake she'd encountered in her Pennsylvania woods. "I look out on you with the innocent cold eye of a serpent," she wrote in lines laid out as verse, "I will draw close and reside in your hand not because of love but because of the music." In a subsequent letter she again invoked Nature's redemptive but "cold fierce law," offering a vivid account of a painful abortion without anesthesia she'd once undergone—an experience, she said, that had relieved her of her belief in God, and taught her that there was "nothing to touch the beauty [of blood] straight out of the womb of a mother." Once more Olson was shaken by recognition: she was indeed a "sibyl." For his poetry's sake he could not afford to lose her. "O Frances," he pleaded, "just because you have been so clear ab[ou]t what got born between us, do not, at this high time, desert the Cause." The epistolary appeal soon yielded to the verse of "For Sappho, Back":

> *With a cold eye, with her eye she looked on, she looked out, she*
> *who was not so different as you might imagine from,*
> *who had, as nature hath, an eye to look upon her makings, to,*
> *in her womb, know*

how red, and because it is red, how
handsome blood is . . .

Frances not surprisingly took the poem to be a "very accurate portrait" of herself. "That I am your actual flesh sister I now know," she told him. "That our terrible oneness creates incest I know . . . our paths so unlike and [yet] the blood-beat so precisely the same." If their life roles kept them apart physically, the communication of souls would remain intact. It was the tending of that dialogue to which she must now give herself over. "I have no choices," she told him candidly. "What has assigned the parts? Is it great to obey—or is greatness a childish concept? I will continue to obey." In another letter she quoted from Blake's *The Visions of the Daughters of Albion,* assuming the selfless generosity of the maiden Oothoon to declare her renunciation of physical claim to him: like Oothoon for Theotormon, she would, in the extremity of her love, deny herself to "catch for thee . . . girls of mild silver, of furious gold." Replying to his latest confessional flourish on the figure of incest which obsessed them both—"i am your male," he'd told her, "yr brother-father, i am strangely the son of, as well as the man of, f[rances] m[otz]"—she produced a startling revelation of her own.

> I have never really had a father. . . . all his life-long cruelty to me I did not remember and I gave love. . . . I have always always been absolutely alone—But I have thrown out tenderness and belief to life—that is true—and now I am naked—your letter makes me absolutely naked, but I trust you with all my soul—Yesterday when I was bathing I also thought "I am his teacher—God teaches me and I teach Charles and he teaches the world"—I did not think "teaches"—I *felt* the connect—the path, whatever it is—but I mean the son business you speak of and I believe this is the direct true thing as God meant—for woman to be absolutely Pure and a receptacle and to be open to one man—her son and lover—who instructs life—I mean her sibyline knowledge open to one man—the part to be hidden by her from everyone else. . . .

The raw poetry of this effusion fueled the concluding poem of his two-week run, "Help Me, Venus." Frances here appeared as a beguiling Blakean "silver girl," inciting the poet to sexual pursuit even as she seemed to flee it. Once again the chase led him back toward archetypal phallic power sources ("If you would guess, fond man, the secret . . . why your beloved . . . still doth stir the root . . ."). And once again his poem served double purpose, as private message to both Muse and spouse (it contained an oblique reference to his first Rockport encounter with Connie, when she had played "hare" to his "tortoise").

If on this course, as she is, as she runs, as she too looks for love
as she, a daughter, seeks a lover,
forever seeks the lover worthy to undo the obdurate father

If, as she leads you, as she outruns you in this racing,
as you pursue both her and some more stubborn, abstract tracing,
you who go as tortoise and as hare do,
as you, slow, in search for source, and then so quickly furious

If you and she both race uncertain,
palpably uncertain . . .

His conditionals hung in midair, neither completed nor resolved by a chain of rhetorical questions that followed in the second half of the poem. He was keeping himself open to the Heisenbergian fates.

By June "the connect" was hanging by a thread. Frances was out of work and money, and experiencing some alarm over the prospects of continuing the sacrifice of her own interests to those of a man who had long since demonstrated his inability to commit himself to her. ("He had the kind of personality that simply could not clarify and decide," she observes in hindsight, "and I'm just not that way.") She left Woodward for New York, hopeful of finding work with a commercial publisher. But despite her experience and qualifications—over the years she'd held several responsible positions in the design and production end of publishing—her age, sex and exceedingly forthright demeanor were not in her favor, and the search proved fruitless. Soon she was not only jobless but truly impoverished, scraping by in a series of borrowed apartments on loans from friends. A promised visit by Olson in mid-June was canceled without explanation, yet he continued to send her huge letters—and poems in a steady stream: "Other Than," "The Story of an Olson and Bad Thing," "ABCs (3—for Rimbaud)," "Adamo Me," "The Cause, the Cause." The internal tension, and the quality, of the verse had already begun to ebb after the crest of the May poems. Still he steamed away through Washington's withering summer months at the typewriter, forcing the dry vein, prodding Frances for archaic materials that might trigger a fresh spring.

She made an obedient visit to the Oriental Room of the New York Public Library to look up a Jane Harrison book he'd prescribed, and there accidentally encountered an eminent Sumerian scholar, Columbia University professor Edith Porada. Following up on Porada's tip, she went on to inspect a collection of ancient Sumerian cylinder seals at the Pierpont Morgan library. Olson received a full account, and pressed for more details on one particularly intriguing figure, a "King with the Breast of the Hanging Lions," who reminded him of the Gilgamesh-like city-founding hero of his latest poem-in-progress, "Bigmans." For her "present" of Porada's monograph on the cylinder seals, Frances received from him confirmation of her status as his "SUMER GIRL," "LADY OF THE WILD THINGS." Tracking down archaic prototypes for "my boy BIGMANS" at the Library of Congress, he had soon turned up a discovery of his own in Scottish historian L. A. Waddell's *The Makers of Civilization in Race and History,* an account of the Sumerians as a seagoing race with Aryan origins. He synopsized Waddell's dubious theories for Frances in an excited eleven-page single-space blow-by-blow covering all twenty-six centuries of the Sumerian kingship chain. She made valiant efforts to keep up, reporting back her progress in wading through Waddell even as Olson continued to "discharge the whole Mesopotamia mess" in her lap.

The shared Porada and Waddell enthusiasms, together with several earlier ones—Dura Europos, Kramer, Strzygowski—as well as longtime Olson interests like Fenollosa, Frobenius, Victor Bérard, Carl Sauer and Vilhjálmur Stefánsson, were bundled together into his second major essay of the year, "The Gate and the Center." Herald of much boldly assertive (and variably coherent) prose to come, the piece was less rational argument than sheer explosion of thought. Like much of the dogmatic propositional writing that would follow it, "The Gate and the Center" began in the form of a letter— this time not to Frances but to a new literary contact, Robert Creeley. Aiming to restore a mythic dimension to modern life, Olson called for a return to the cultural consciousness of Sumerian civilization.

> . . . From 3378 BC . . . until date 1200 BC or thereabouts, civilization had ONE CENTER, Sumer, in all directions. . . . this one people held such exact and superior force that all peoples around them were sustained by it, nourished, increased, advanced . . . a city was a coherence which, for the first time since the ice, gave man the chance to join knowledge to culture and, with this weapon, shape dignities of economics and value sufficient to make daily life itself a dignity and a sufficiency.

In modern times, and under the "American and Western education" system, by contrast, knowledge itself had become a "State Whore." Out of touch with "primordial & phallic energies and methodologies," the diminished human creature was cut off from earth, nature and cosmos. Heroes of the essay were the Sumerian god-kings he'd found listed in Waddell, impressive "archaic figures [such] as dreams produce" which had been haunting his imagination for weeks; it was time, he proposed, for man to assume once more an active role in the larger scheme of creation, to become, by emulating these "archetype figures," a "participant thing, to take up, straight, nature's, live nature's force."

There was a certain irony in this closing injunction: Olson himself was at this point more than ever caught up in the sedentary life of the intellectual, participating far less in the natural world than in that diminished one of words and ideas. It was not until the third week of July that he broke away from his work desk and papers to New York and his "SUMER GIRL." He quickly saw that he had waited too long to come. Frances, still jobless and camping in a borrowed flat, seemed tired and defensive. She accused him of ruthlessness in his treatment of her, and told him he'd never really tried to understand her. Words alone were not enough to satisfy a passionate woman, she said; life was more important than art, and the two should never be confused. Her unexpected resistance stepped up his wooing efforts. Back in Washington, he wrote ardently to reaffirm his gratitude for all her instruction. "You seem to me the strongest, most beautiful expression of *what life is* that I have ever known. If I have been able to *commit* myself to the fate I think now I was born for, it is because you have proved, you do prove by being, something which was my vision. . . . I should not have been able to take up belief except as you proved me right!" Her faith and allegiance, long crucial to his morale, were now more indispensable than ever, he said. He refused to view her sudden coolness toward him as anything but temporary, a result of the recent strains of her life. The renewed physical communion had restored the pulse of poetry to his life. "The smell and taste of you carried away is always so sweet, so stands in the mind. . . . [you have] the fragrance of a Pistis-Sophia (who is a mimosa). . . . you prove to me, for example, why Cavalcanti and Dante made, as they did—and there is no question there was a woman behind it—an image, a Beatrice, a Mathelda, to stand, in a phrase dove sta memora. . . ." A final amorous poem addressed to her in this season of soul riot, "Of Mathilde," was drawn on the twenty-eighth canto of the *Purgatorio,* in which Dante's pilgrim is overcome with love for a miraculous, flower-gathering maiden, Matelda, or Mathilde. Like "In Cold Hell, in Thicket," the enigmatic "Of Mathilde" had double currency, applying with equal plausibility to either of the women in his life. Mathilde was Connie's middle name. He persuaded her the love poem, a celebration of "what she gives off / what love gives off," had been written expressly to her. "There was a woman behind it," indeed. But which one?

In this summer of difficult truce in their relationship, Charles and Connie's only relaxed times together each week came on Sunday, her day off from the nursing school. They spent many of those holidays on Charles' historical expeditions, which, with Frank Moore's girlfriend Ibby von Thurn as chauffeur and Connie as picnic preparer, were turned into full-scale recreational outings. The foursome bounced up and down the dusty back roads of Maryland and Virginia in Ibby's battered jalopy every free weekend through the summer months—visiting Manassas, Harper's Ferry, Antietam, Fredericksburg, Chancellorsville, Spotsylvania Courthouse, as well as a number of lesser-known sites. Charles' reconnaissance of places long ago made mythic for him by Mathew Brady's photographs was prefaced by close study of history books and maps; once out on the road he kept up a nonstop volley of comment, pointing out the strategic significance of each passing nook and hollow with such extensive animation that in one memorable monologue he managed to completely uproot the old car's front seat from its moorings. Connie's "frugal but elegant" picnic lunches were "devoured" largely by Charles himself. They stoked him to uncommon outputs of physical exertion: he breast-stroked across flooded quarries, crashed through thickets long vacated by rebel sharpshooters. Not that certain dangers didn't remain. While stalking through thick woods at Spotsylvania, he just missed stepping on a guerrilla-style "abatis" or sharpened-stick fortification, still poised, after the better part of a century, "to impale a Fed coming in from the forest." (This artifact was carried off as an objectivist souvenir to decorate his mantlepiece.) Other finds were reported to the U.S. Park Service, which at that time had not yet cleared the overgrown battle sites. In the midst of dense brush at Manassas dauntless explorer Olson came upon a sizable cairn with an inscription revealing it had been erected by a company of Union soldiers. The cairn was obviously too large to cart away, so he proudly tipped off the Park Service.

In the evenings, back at Randolph Place, he kept his weary little company up late with exhaustive rundowns on the deeper meanings of the day's adventures. Ancient psychic forces, he suggested, were always the true underlying causes of aggressive civil conflicts. "One of the most vivid recollections I have of Olson," says Elizabeth von Thurn Frawley, "comes from one of those evenings."

What was being discovered and said came forth in rhythmic rages, red faced, with a distant-vision glaze to the eye, staccato. As always there was the blasting through, the pounding, the possessing need to attain the unattainable synapse. With great arms waving and punching, he bellowed about the need to kill one's father in order to come into being oneself. His point was that one's father's death is not enough in itself; a person, he said, must overwhelm, wrestle down, kill his father within himself before the son can become free. By his own account, he was struggling with that need / problem at the time and felt that having verbalized it and begun the struggle, was part way there. It was not a question of hate or even dislike. It was a question of cells becoming truly separate.

There it was again, oldest threat to his identity, too often prematurely laid to rest. Every time he was tempted to think he'd emerged from under the long paternal shadow, it fell anew over his dream life. By now, however, its impositions had become much less menacing. A letter to Frances related one night's "wondrous visitation from my father." The dream, "confirming maestro Freud," stranded Charles on a death-bound train with a very ill-looking Karl. (His father's face was covered with terrible skin sores, as his own had been on the day of the breakwater fishing trip, their last outing together.) They stood on the speeding train's observation car, discussing, of all things, poetry. Karl unexpectedly praised his verse accomplishments ("You have done more with it than I would have said you might have"), and he felt flooded with great relief and satisfaction. Then his father vanished, and he himself was released from the death train. The dream next took a sudden "clear woman-turn," as he described it to Frances. He awoke feeling "full of strength, physical strength," a feeling he attributed in part to the dream's removal of some psychic burden and in part to a larger "swelling of strength inside the body" which he'd been blessed with through the "tremendous months" just past. It all seemed to him somehow "mythic," as though his personal history were unfolding not only in time but in larger dimensions as well. "It is amazing to me," he told her now, "how the parable of my existence is working itself out, as on a stage, before my eyes."

14

The Big Year Shift
(1950)

B y the middle of 1950, Olson had taken up a second correspondence that would soon rival in sheer volume if not in emotional intensity the abundant exchange with his Muse. This time the correspondent would not be a lover but a fellow writer, a cohort and "co-agitator" in the struggle for a foothold on the literary scene. Robert Creeley would become not only a sympathetic ally and sounding board, much as Frances had been, but one whose special relation to language, as uniquely intense, compulsive and idiosyncratic as Olson's own, would provide an immediate basis for friendship; it allowed him a degree of tolerance for Olson's peculiar reliance on words— as both validation of experience and substitute for action—which Frances had understandably never been able to manage.

Olson's juggling of the two long-distance relationships was testimony of his ability to compartmentalize his life. In the several thousand pages of his letters to Creeley, no mention of Frances would be made. To the projective Muse herself, meanwhile, he would make but a single substantive reference to the new friend, and that only in passing, apropos the latter's appreciation of the "mystery" poem "La Chute"—"first of our investigations," as he reminded Frances. An unnamed young man, he said, wanted to publish the poem in a little magazine. Not that the newcomer was cognizant of the mysteries. What Creeley liked in "La Chute," Olson reported to Frances, was the percussive tribal rhythm, the "real crazy beats in that / bongo . . . too much: shows what yez can do with rhythms in an open form." As if slightly embarrassed by the hipster diction of such a comment, which she might take as a profaning of the archaic sacred ground, he tried his best to account for the source.

> You will understand, that this nut (a former peddler of narcotics, a former drinker, a former musician, now a hen-farmer, and the best young writer I know here where the language & the energy of the earth is pounding, here and / or anywhere, this lad, speaks funny because he is trying, and right he is, to get dialect in without localism: crazy—too much (if you know bands, is such talk . . .

Not that Olson himself "knew bands" of the new bop variety or was at all easy with "such talk." In fact, Creeley's occasionally esoteric streetwise diction was at first as mystifying to him as it was intriguing, and his own casual use of the hip term "too much" was made possible only by his having come right out and asked for a translation. (Creeley had patiently explained that it was in the same class with "goofed," "gone," "dig" and other expressions employed by black musicians as "a shortcut to speech, understanding.") That initial linguistic barrier, implying a certain sociological disparity, reflected one of age as well. Creeley was at the time only twenty-three, the author of a handful of small poems published in fugitive periodicals and of a few eccentrically distinctive but unpublished short stories. In terms of literary experience and accomplishment he was not nearly as far along as Olson, yet it took Olson little time to realize that there was much to be learned from the younger man. Creeley was already a painstaking formal craftsman, with developed and exacting tastes. He was also aggressively concerned with finding a place as an antitraditional writer in a cautious, conservative time, an aim Olson certainly shared. In this endeavor, indeed, Creeley had the advantage of traveling light, without Olson's top-heavy burden of cultural-intellectual reference to weigh him down. (A particularly striking example of this was their respective attitudes toward libraries, citadels of formal learning where Olson felt naturally in his element while Creeley, as he was soon confessing to his new friend, was made uncomfortable to the point of panic.) A general practitioner's son, Creeley was attracted by writing as a trade that could be practiced with basic tools no more burdensome than a doctor's little black bag—an approach the bookish Olson couldn't help finding enviable.

Creeley's youth, furthermore, could be viewed by Olson as in some sense complementary to his own situation as "slow emerger," his coming only in his fortieth year to what he saw as his belated second birth as a writer. Increasingly unable to identify with his own literary generation, he was, as he'd more than once lamented to Frances, in desperate search of a new one to which he might belong. In some real sense, Creeley, who had already begun establishing his own small network of hopeful but disaffected or at least left-out writers, would be able to supply a generation ready-made. And beyond these things, there was also a certain basis of affiliation in simple coincidences of birth and background that on an intuitive level related the two writers from the outset. For Olson, to whom New England had long seemed "enormously his field of interest and endeavor" in an almost proprietary way, it was important to know that Creeley, who had grown up in West Acton, Massachusetts, and was living at present in the White Mountains of New Hampshire (where he was supporting his family on his meager earnings as a poultry farmer, supplemented by his wife's small trust fund), was a New England native son. Each man, too, had attended Harvard and left in less than happy circumstances—Creeley in 1947, before the end of the final year of an undergraduate career interrupted by wartime service during 1944–1945 as a U.S. Friends ambulance driver in Burma. (There, much to the detriment of his academic future, he'd discovered marijuana, which had in turn upon his repatriation led him into hipster jazz circles in Boston, source of that obscure "dialect" so fascinating and baffling to Olson.) Both Olson and Creeley, finally and perhaps most significantly, had served a period of apprenticeship as disciples of Ezra Pound; Creeley's acquaintance with the teachings on the Master dated from his discovery of Pound's *Make It New* while editing a 1946 issue of the *Wake,* a subversive publication founded in protest against Harvard's established literary journal, the *Advocate.*

The attempted founding of another little magazine, one Creeley was hoping to start up with a former Harvard friend, led to the contact with Olson. The intermediary was another modernist forerunner they both looked to as a renegade master, William Carlos Williams. Williams wrote to Olson in late April 1950, "Drop a note to Robert Creely [sic], Littleton, N.H.—he's got some ideas and wants to USE them. Maybe you've already heard of him. Write. Send him anything you think is worth perpetuating." Olson had indeed already heard of the aspiring editor. On his behalf (but without his knowledge), Vincent Ferrini had passed on copies of the 1945 Key West piece "Pacific Lament" and of a more recent Olson poem, "The Laughing Ones," to Creeley, who'd unceremoniously rejected them. Ferrini relayed back to Olson the negative verdict: Creeley had commented that the poems' author seemed to be "looking around for a language." Getting Williams' endorsement of Creeley soon thereafter, however, Olson was prompted to overlook this setback and try again. He sent Creeley a copy of *Y & X* plus several other poems, along with an argumentative letter ("i says, creeley, you're off yr trolley: a man god damn well has to come up with his own lang., syntax and song both, but also each poem under hand has its own language, which is variant of same"). This time the would-be editor quickly fell in line, accepting "The Morning News" and "Move Over," expressing interest in "La Chute" as well, and following up with a series of friendly and flattering letters that gave Olson his first real taste of recognition for his poetry achievements from someone he considered a fellow in the art. These responses set the stage for their imminent concerted push beyond the frontiers of the modern. "I take you to put down here," Creeley wrote of *Υ & X,* "movement beyond what the Dr., Stevens etc., have made for us. . . ." Olson was invited to participate in the prospective magazine's "open forum . . . on *methods* of blocking [out] what few IDEAS this country possesses." He declared himself eager to take part, confident, as he told Creeley, that "poets are the only pedagogues." Creeley's planned magazine soon fell through, but it hardly mattered. The alliance thus begun had a life of its own. Within a year Olson was introducing Creeley to Robert Duncan—by letter, of course—as "my running mate, my tandem."

In strategic terms, for Olson the greatest value of his association with Creeley lay in the simple fact of having someone with whom to promote a shared agenda. One could not start a revolution alone. And Creeley was no mere passive partner. He, too, refused to settle for simply keeping his head above the modernist waterline. "I dont think we can get to an exact 'program' which will embrace with sincerity the present concerns of Williams, Pound," he wrote to Olson in May. "In the case of the Dr.: we come close because we take him to be a focus for these matters. But always, our own way, has to be it." These closely resembled Olson's own sentiments. "Right, right," he agreed, "love the Dr, love the Master, still, even they, are in the way." Pound, especially, remained stubbornly "in the way." Though Olson hadn't set foot in St. Elizabeths for over two years, friends like Frank Moore, Michael Lekakis and now even Creeley—who corresponded with Pound—had lately been carrying back tales of vindictive cracks made by the Master at his expense. When Creeley snitched that Pound had recently in typically summary fashion pronounced him "FUNDAMENTALLY (not superficially) wrong," it was enough to enrage Olson on that old score all over again. He had to be restrained by his more diplomatic running mate from launching an all-out reciprocal attack on Pound. "We will outlive him," Creeley shrewdly pointed out. "That is our function, to go beyond."

To outflank the masters, solidarity would first have to be established among the rebel ranks. "Let's you and I, by God, write for each other!" Olson proposed to Creeley in the wake of the Pound blowup. "It's the only deal." As part of that "deal," they would pool their literary contacts and try to commandeer as many publishing venues as possible. The procedures of annexation, Olson suggested, should be swift and brutal. "I swear—what we have to do is, quick, intimidate 'em. And then go right ahead sans regard, sans anything, but, make use of 'em."

So far, however, the confrontational approach he advocated couldn't very well be advertised by his own success in applying it. Though he was still busily submitting his poetry to aboveground journals ranging from the *Hudson Review* to *Poetry New York,* he was still regularly striking out with it. When James Laughlin of New Directions finally accepted an Olson poem—"The Praises"—for the house annual, it was, after all those years of trying, a major career event, but there were few scores to match it. A Japanese Poundian, Katue Kitasono, was bringing out "La Préface" in a little magazine called *Vou,* and Olson's friend Robert Payne of the *Montevallo Review* was to publish "For Sappho, Back." But the poems Olson sent out to mainstream journals came back to him with little evidence they'd even been read, and only a fraction of them could be channeled to his few existing outlets. Creeley's extensive network of outlaw literary connections consequently held great interest for him. He was soon tapping it.

Early that summer one Creeley contact, Richard Emerson, young publisher-editor of Columbus-based Golden Goose Press, offered to print an Olson poetry chapbook. Olson spent long hours that summer combing through his extant poems—"getting ready for the new print-push," as he explained to Frances—to come up with what he expected would be his second book of verse; when Emerson came to visit at Randolph Place in August, he read some of them aloud for a tape recording the publisher was making. As it turned out his hopes for Emerson and for this early phase of the "print-push" were in for a slow deflation. Emerson delayed production for eight months, during which time Olson suffered a hundred small attacks of annoyance and impatience before actually withdrawing the book in exasperation and settling for having a few poems—including "In Cold Hell"—represent him in a Golden Goose anthology. Another Creeley contact, however, proved far more reliable in the long run, if occasionally just as maddening along the way. This was Cid Corman. Host of a weekly poetry show on Boston radio, Corman would soon take up Creeley's stalled magazine project and turn it into *Origin,* the first Olson / Creeley showcase periodical. And it was also through Creeley that Olson's work received its first exposure to European audiences. On Creeley's advice he got in touch with Rainer Gerhardt, editor of the avant-garde magazine *Fragmente.* Before his death by suicide at age twenty-eight in 1954, Gerhardt would become the first serious European translator of Olson's poetry, and out of their short-lived association by mail and print would issue two major Olson poems, "To Gerhardt, There, Among Europe's Things" and the elegy "The Death of Europe"(in the latter piece the young German writer was viewed as a postwar tragic figure, and "the first of Europe / I could have words with").

In the formation of a literary common front no instrument could be more useful than a punchy, concise, well-circulated manifesto. Olson conveniently had one in the making: "Projective Verse," now awaiting a final rewrite for *Poetry New York*. During the late stages of revision, Creeley replaced Frances as his audience. Creeley, less temperamental than the Muse, could be much more constructively critical. It was here, on the actual compositional ground even more directly than in helping expand his publishing horizons, that the new friend could be of use to Olson. He mailed off a copy of the essay-in-progress and got back much helpful advice. The sharp-eyed Creeley suggested several small but strategic amendments, which he duly adopted.

The idea of an open form, now overwhelming Olson's poetic imagination, was characteristically oppositional in its historical context. "The New Criticism of that period was dominant," as Creeley has said. In theoretical terms—as well as, certainly, in terms of literary politics—the New Critical academic establishment which then controlled the nation's English departments could appear a uniform repressive force, standing, with its forbidding phalanx of "poems patterned upon exterior and traditionally accepted models," directly in the path of all modes of poetic experiment. "What confronted us in 1950," Creeley observed some fifteen years later, "was a closed system [which] would not admit the possibility of verse considered as an 'open field.' " Olson's essay, as it took final shape, distilled his prescriptions for the writing of verse into three basic elements, each essential to the creation of the new open form which would follow the overthrowing of that closed system. He termed these essential elements "simplicities"—necessary to be learned by any "man . . . if he works in OPEN, or what can also be called COMPOSITION BY FIELD, as opposed to inherited line, stanza, over-all form, what is the 'old' base of the non-projective."

First there was "the *kinetics* of the thing."

A poem is energy transferred from where the poet got it (he will have some several causations), by way of the poem itself to, all the way over to, the reader. . . . the poem itself must, at all points, be a high energy-construct and, at all points, an energy-discharge. So: how is the poet to accomplish same energy, how is he, what is the process by which a poet gets in, at all points energy at least the equivalent of the energy which propelled him in the first place, yet an energy which is peculiar to verse alone and which will be, obviously, also different from the energy which the reader, because he is a third term, will take away?

This is the problem which any poet who departs from closed form is specially confronted by. And it involves a whole series of new recognitions. From the moment he ventures into FIELD COMPOSITION—puts himself in the open—he can go by no track other than the one the poem under hand declares, for itself. Thus he has to behave, and be, instant by instant, aware. . . .

A second principal emphasis was borrowed from a casual but catchy observation dropped by Creeley in the course of a June 5 letter: "form is never more than an *extension* of content." Olson, then in the midst of his revising, immediately seized on the tag line and incorporated it into the essay at a crucial point. After "kinetics," in his three-stage description of the projective, came

> the principle, the law which presides conspicuously over such composition, and, when obeyed, is the reason why a projective poem can come into being. It is this: FORM IS NEVER MORE THAN AN EXTENSION OF CONTENT. (Or so it got phrased by one, R. Creeley, and it makes absolute sense to me, with this possible corollary, that right form, in any given poem, is the only and exclusively possible extension of content under hand.)

Every poem, by the dictates of this "law," would have its own shape: the closed system had been exploded; there was no pattern left to adhere to but that of the poet's own psychological and physical reality in the moment. This moment-to-moment quality was defined in a third and last step in the proposition—once again borrowed from a close ally, this time of years gone by:

> Now (3) the *process* of the thing, how the principle can be made so to shape the energies that the form is accomplished. And I think it can be boiled down to one statement (first pounded into my head by Edward Dahlberg): ONE PERCEPTION MUST IMMEDIATELY AND DIRECTLY LEAD TO A FURTHER PERCEPTION.

The nod to Dahlberg in this July rewrite of "Projective Verse" was to be his last public gesture toward his on-again, off-again friend. Correspondence between the two men had been at best sporadic in recent times, with letters from Olson growing increasingly infrequent during the season of soul riot just past. Throughout that absorbing time much that was connected with his former life had simply ceased to engage him. Now, not long after the completion of his essay, he received by mail an inscribed copy of Dahlberg's *The Flea of Sodom*, which had just been published in London. The inscription bore lavish tribute to Olson's "Genius and Understanding." Once, this would have been a proud moment for him. But associations had changed, and at this point his earlier promises to Dahlberg about reviewing the book returned to haunt him, killing off what remained of their friendship. Dahlberg, unpublished for almost a decade and hungry for that promised review, began pestering him relentlessly about it. Regarding this desperate appeal as psychological blackmail—the extortionate demand of an abandoned father—Olson resisted stubbornly. Complicating matters further was the appearance in the published text of *The Flea* of a chapter he had not previously seen. This chapter was formally dedicated to him. Its subject was the mythological hero Bellerophon, a Herculean warrior and grandson of Sisyphus. Dahlberg's Bellerophon closely resembled Olson. A cautionary fable of solitary intellectual pride, the new chapter echoed Dahlberg's old lament about the cold, selfish side of the Olson nature. Unable to bring himself to tell Dahlberg he considered this characterization sufficient grounds to retract his promise, Olson instead adopted a tactic of calculated evasion. He sent the anxious author extensive results of his own studies on Bellerophon conducted at the Library of Congress, meanwhile continuing to slyly dodge the review question and declining even to supply so much as a short blurb for the jacket of the upcoming New Directions American edition of the book. At the same time, Frances and Creeley received long, resentful letters about the pressure of "wily intimidation" Olson felt Dahlberg was exerting. Creeley himself had just read *The Flea;* he told Olson he thought it "dismal . . . unreadable, [a] sick, sick book." When Dahlberg continued to nag, Olson, in a late-September letter, instructed his one-time mentor to "just fuck it, my fine-feathered friend, fuck it." Dahlberg did not pass by the opportunity to get in a haunting parting shot of his own: "I guess I am your Father-image."

The acrimonious farewell exchange with Dahlberg marked another crossroads in the parable Olson was accustomed to make of his existence. Writing to Creeley six months later, when things had stabilized considerably in his personal life, he was already looking back with the simplified hindsight of self-mythology on "this big year . . . shift, with you coming in, and three others going out . . . my mother, Ed (thru my purposeful default on his book), and another, which, to my bewilderment, had to be gone by." The transition was at the time not at all so simple or clear-cut for him, however. Ambivalent afterthoughts about those "going out" stubbornly persisted. Dahlberg was indeed gone, but certainly not forgotten. His mother—who had in the past year suffered a rapid physical decline because of a persistently advancing chest infection—now more than ever represented for him psychic and emotional demands that he felt incapable of fulfilling and that would remain a source of guilt for years to come. And Frances, the mysterious bypassed "another," would linger as a tantalizing possibility in his imagination long after his chronic wavering had caused her to distance herself from him.

Absorbed in his own interior operations, he was slow to adjust to the dawning recognition that his Muse would not always be available to him as a psychic safety valve. Early in September, after experiencing one of his cyclic slumps—"could find no peace," he told Frances, "was tormented, terribly, angry, at the way I had used my life"—he abruptly wired her to announce he was about to arrive for a visit. She immediately wrote back, putting him off and—even more surprisingly—informing him that a new man had entered her life. Within hours of receiving her letter he was on a train to New York. He hurriedly booked into the Hotel Shelton, and rushed by taxi to her new apartment on Monroe Place in Brooklyn. "He got my letter at two o'clock," Frances says now, "and that same evening, after months of stalling about coming to see me, he was knocking at my door. The fact that he got there so quickly burned me up. He just didn't know anything about women." She told him she had another date, and turned him away.

The rebuff left him—as he would soon let her know by letter—"stunned, astonied." In a daze, he went on to Gloucester to visit his ailing mother. From Oceanwood Cottage he put in a late-night long-distance call home to Washington. The "depth and tone" of Connie's voice, at once unknowing and reassuring, seemed to him "very tremendous" in this weak moment. The next morning he wrote passionately to her, declaring a renewal of love and swearing that the past year's "fires and false fires" had but firmed his resolve to "be with you and go forward." He then canceled a planned trip to New Hampshire to meet Creeley, and flew directly from Boston back to Washington. He had soon swept Connie off for a weekend holiday at a favorite trysting spot, a small shoreline hotel in Oxford, Maryland.

The maritime atmosphere of the Chesapeake Bay lobster-fishing and resort village—always reminiscent to him of Gloucester—helped generate a first draft of one of his most seagoing poems, "Maximus, to Gloucester: Letter 2." Adopting for a second time the projective voice of Maximus addressing his city, he held up the commercialized "pejorocracy" of current culture, with its "deathly mu-sick," against a prior ethos represented by the heroic exploits of veteran Gloucester fishermen like Lou Douglas (whose Stage Fort Park home he had visited during his recent trip), Frank Miles, Howard Blackburn and Carl Olsen. True to his own projective axioms, he began headlong in mid-thought, with a self-directed statement that referred back to the first *Maximus* poem's confident opening declaration, "I, Maximus . . . tell you / what is lance, who obeys the figures of the present dance." Buffeted by the vicissitudes of life's dance, Maximus / Olson was now temporarily less certain about his authority in such matters.

> . . . *tell you? ha! who*
> *can tell another how*
> *to manage the swimming?*

he was right: people

don't change. They only stand more
revealed. I,
likewise.

The poet had come around, at least for the moment, to agree with Edward
Dahlberg, whose "argument" regarding constancy of character—"we never
change . . . same agonies, same urges, same aberrations, same pains at 40 as
at 20"—he'd inscribed into his journal ten years back. (It was "one of the
finest pieces of wisdom i acquired from you," he'd told Dahlberg later.) Recent
events in his life had reminded him there was no easy way of shedding his
own difficult intensities and complexities of character.

Despite his assurances to Connie, once back in Washington he was overcome by an impulse to patch things up with Frances. If people didn't change,
he implied to her, at least they could recognize their mistakes. Words, he
now told her, had become a source of trouble for them: "they did you damage . . . ran ahead of acts." Yet he couldn't help employing words to try to
win her over again. While expression had evidently betrayed him—for his
mistreatment of her, he claimed, had never been "a question of loss or lack
of love & affections, but of the way they are expressed"—this was merely the
symptom of a larger betrayal to which all persons were now subject. The
culprit was the false culture in which they lived, and its false values. As D. H.
Lawrence had prophetically suggested, old notions of love and feeling had
become obsolete in the modern world ("the adhesive is rotted"), and emotions were continually being distorted for lack of a new, honest mode of
expression between people. "The situation," he insisted in a long letter to her
written a few weeks after the Monroe Place showdown, "is OPEN. It may
have been blown open, sure. But it is open. And that's what we have, to work
with. / Write me again, and, recognize, / this is love. . . ." Clearly prepared at
this point to shoulder some responsibility for the breakup (if only to get her
back on the hook), he had arrived at a forced apprehension of the need for
new terms in sexual relationships. In its literary aspect, the revelation returned
him directly to Lawrence. The conciliatory appeal to Frances, together with
a letter to Creeley on Lawrence written the same week, were soon spliced
together into a brief essay exploring themes of love, reality and language.

"The Escaped Cock: Notes on Lawrence & the Real"—destined to appear
in Cid Corman's magazine, *Origin*—proposed Lawrence as a writer of intense,
unrelenting struggle, one whose experience of an ongoing combat between
self and world, a vivid "contesting with reality," yielded all the drama of his
work. In *Etruscan Places,* the adversary reality was locality, or "ideal place";

in *Lady Chatterly's Lover* it was "the FIRST SENSE, sex"; in *The Escaped Cock* it was the totality of feeling, "THE WHOLE SENSES." As to the last-named work, Olson faulted it for Lawrence's misperception of his heroine, a "goddessissing [sic] the actuality" which distracted attention from her substantial reality as woman. For contemporary lovers, he suggested in the essay as in the letter to his ex-Muse, it was imperative to throw off cultural conditioning, to abandon preconceived romantic conceptions, to "stay OPEN." "Love, as they have it, is . . . dead. . . . We are, all of us, now, essentially guerrillas . . . EVEN in the intimate."

But literary matters had before long replaced love at the center of his own attentions. The "Projective Verse" essay came out in *Poetry New York* that October. Over the years no work of his would make more impact. William Carlos Williams wrote him within weeks of its appearance to proclaim it a "keystone"—"the most admirable piece of thinking about the poem I have recently, perhaps ever, encountered." This acknowledgment from the "brother-father," a vindication of all his own years of obscure apprenticeship, pleased Olson enormously. Williams soon gained his permission to reprint four entire pages of the essay's text in his *Autobiography,* and in a prefatory note praised it for contributing a new way of "looking at poems as a field."

Others fell in behind the essay's theoretical banner. Cid Corman, assembling the debut issue of *Origin,* announced plans for an editorial charting the magazine's future course "along the PROJECTIVE TRAIL." For the twenty-six-year-old Corman, an aspiring poet still living with his parents in the Boston suburb of Dorchester, intent on making his mark with the magazine but with no solid program of his own, the Olson agenda had much to offer. He invited Olson to participate as contributing editor. Olson wasted no time on preliminary courtesies, snowing the would-be editor under an extended set of directives thrust forward with a mixture of dictatorial bluff and generous conjecture. To start with, Corman was put on notice he would have some adjusting to do. When he reported attempts to negotiate subsidy for the magazine from Brandeis University, it was suggested by Olson that he was dangerously soft on academia. And when Corman confessed to harboring certain residual sympathies for the middle-of-the-road poets of the day, Olson sniffed at the idea of colluding in the creation of just another predictable forum for the "well-made poems" of such "decidedly impressive" contemporaries as "o, say, Harvey Shapiro, or Richard Wilbur . . . or, Stephen Spender (intimate) or who[ever] else . . . you think of publishing." Olson's banned list took in all present poetic strains in any way linked with the flaccid, humanistic "cultural tradition," from the "weary-or-howlyrically lovely" lyricists like Barbara Gibbs to the "lazy leftists" like Muriel Rukeyser, the "backtrailing colonialists" like W. S. Merwin to the "high level sources" like T. S. Eliot. He nominated for inclusion in their place not only open-verse poets but fellow "wandering scholars," investigators doing breakthrough work in various sectors of a broad new "American PUSH" to discover the "going reality culture-wise": Frederick Merk, Norbert Wiener, Edith Porada, Owen Lattimore, Vilhjálmur Stefánsson, historical botanist Edgar Anderson (author of *Plants, Man and Life*), and archaeologist Robert Barlow, an expert on the pre-Columbian cultures of the Americas. Though the writings of such explorers of the earth and its past would never actually appear in the magazine, Olson's own quest for first things would be deeply imprinted on the project—most visibly in Corman's choice of a title, *Origin,* and in his inside-cover epigraph, an injunction drawn from Olson-inspired reading of Samuel N. Kramer's Babylonian genesis texts: "O my son, rise from thy bed . . . work what is wise." (Ironically, the epigraph infuriated Olson; as he told Creeley jealously, Corman had "gone to my sources"—violation of a sanctum more fiercely protected than any possession.)

There was little doubt as to who would head the magazine's initial lineup of contributors, or how. Inevitably, it would be Olson, in his own disorderly creative fashion. "If you are already ready to put one man forward in his (approximate) totality," he advised Corman, "give a shot at his reach by way of fragments and putsches, go by spontaneous guerrilla forms." He would supply the editor as a kick-off feature "the best 40 pages of, Olson YET." This turned out to include, first, a substantial selection of verse, dominated by "I, Maximus," a poem for which he already had large if hazy further ambitions. To the poetic salvo he added "The Gate and the Center," which he considered his major culture-statement to date. The essay occasioned a certain amount of haggling of a kind soon to become common in the writer-editor relationship. Corman distrusted its heavy reliance on the half-baked theories and chronologies of Waddell, and also feared the four-letter words in Olson's first draft might offend potential supporters. A compromise was struck: Olson, after complaining bitterly behind Corman's back to Creeley (to whom he conspiratorially sent on Corman's letters, heavily annotated with contemptuous comments), retyped the piece *sans* the offending terms, while Corman agreed to swallow the Waddell material and publish Olson's revised draft intact.

With no financial support for the magazine forthcoming beyond a one-time-only contribution of $550 from a wealthy art patroness, Olson offered Corman his aid in fund-raising. This consisted of sending on an address list of potential $10-a-head prepublication "guarantors." It was, as Corman later remarked, "a *fantastic* mailing list including [Charlie] Chaplin—a Hemingway wife—several senators, etc." As it turned out, however, only a few of those on Olson's elite mailing list actually responded. Of those who did—

like Eleanor Metcalf and Pauline Hemingway—fewer still knew what to make of the publication. ("People like Mrs. Metcalf," the editor would subsequently report to Olson, "said frankly that your writing was over their heads.")

In December, while Olson was still in the process of working out his final submissions to *Origin,* surprising news came in the mail that had a dramatic effect on his life plans. A change in government regulations would allow him to prematurely withdraw several hundred dollars of retirement funds, due him for time put in at the Gloucester post office years earlier. He immediately decided to spend the money on a trip to the Yucatán. The Woelffers had returned from their holiday the previous winter with glowing reports about a tiny Gulf fishing village called Lerma, where they'd been able to rent a beach house for just $15 a month. Supplied with their Mexican landlord's address, Olson began to prepare for his own vacation in the same spot.

He and Connie had sublet 217 Randolph Place to Frank Moore and were set to leave for Mexico when an urgent wire arrived that put the trip in doubt. Mary Olson, who had been staying the winter in Worcester with old friends, was seriously ill and not expected to live more than a few days. Charles rushed to Worcester with Connie, arriving just in time to see his mother before she died on Christmas Day. He arranged a Roman Catholic funeral, and stood by as she was laid to rest beside his father in Worcester's Swedish cemetery. It was a bitterly cold, snowy day. "He would howl," he wrote in a poem soon afterwards, "confronting / the wind which rocks what was her, while prayers / striate the snow. . . ."

His mother's death, and his fortieth birthday following two days after, prompted a return of all his earlier fears that he had mishandled his life. He felt superstitiously guilty over a tarot reading he'd done which had predicted her death—"to the minute and the hour," he later claimed—and renounced the cards forever. Less easy to put aside, however, were his ambivalent emotions toward her. She had, he feared, brought out in him an irrational aversion, a "mother freeze" that permanently affected his relations with all other women. To become a "free thing," he was coming to see, he had to lift himself out from under the stifling maternal influence:

> *Rise*
> *Mother from off me*
> *God damn you God damn me my*
> *misunderstanding of you*

15 ～

A Human Universe
(1951)

In the first weeks of 1951, Charles and Connie saw to the disposition of Mary's things. After cleaning out Oceanwood Cottage they returned to Washington and prepared once more to depart for the Yucatán. For Charles it was none too soon to be going. He longed for the sun and for escape from the "worn-out frame" of American culture.

They set off by bus to New Orleans, whence they embarked for the ten-day Gulf voyage on the Norwegian merchant vessel *Bennestvet Brovig*. (They made up exactly half the passenger list, the other half consisting of a Connecticut couple, historian Bernard Knollenberg and his wife, Mary, who became hosts and friends to the Olsons on return to the States.) Life aboard the freighter revived Charles' old appetite for the sea. The skipper, who reminded him of "the great Carl Olsen of Gloucester," gave him the run of the ship, a privilege he enjoyed to the hilt, poking his nose into everything from the loaded cargo holds below deck to the bridge house, where he spent hours studying navigation and cloud charts. The fresh sea air also had invigorating effects on connubial relations. When he later learned Connie had become pregnant, he traced the conception back to the fertile rocking cradle of the Gulf—though Connie herself held the less poetic view that the source of their future child had been a rather sordid moment on a deserted end of the beach at Veracruz, where during a port call they'd got off the boat to have lunch and Charles had drunk too much beer and become amorous. (The fact that the pregnancy had begun at least in close proximity to the ocean was taken by the erstwhile reluctant father as an auspicious sign, augury of a fresh start in the relationship.)

They went ashore on the Yucatán peninsula at Progreso, Charles seething with bottled-up energy and emotion, the distillation of those "22 years in the Pen" of Yankee ways of life and language (a term he now dated to his emergence from the family cocoon in Worcester). Indeed his quest for the deep past had been so far almost entirely theoretical. Confrontation with ancient Mayan civilization would, he hoped, correct that. Here at last was a chance to make a reality of the long-envisioned "hunt among stones" for evidence of the Old Ways.

His first stop was Merida, an Americanized "shit town" where he was dismayed by news that awaited him at Carnegie Institute headquarters: the expert he'd counted on to guide his researches, University of Mexico archaeologist Robert Barlow, had just taken his own life. Without any substantial knowledge of Spanish, the Mayan culture, or archaeology, the ill-prepared "documentarian"—always a gambler in his investigations—was thrown back on the mercy of chance. The local Carnegie field representative, a bluff veteran digger named Gustavo Stromsvik, told him of a young Maya expert at the provincial museum in Campeche who might be able to help. Following a side trip by tourist bus to the Mayan ruins at Chichén Itzá (it was a letdown because of the absence of any present-day Maya to lend the dead stones a living color), Olson went on to Campeche and looked up the man Stromsvik had recommended, Hippolito Sanchez. Sanchez, an assistant director at the Campeche Archaeological Museum, had done hundreds of large, accomplished drawings of the stairway glyphs at the Mayan pyramids in Copán, Honduras. Inspecting these, Olson felt he was getting his first vivid sense of the Maya. Equally a pleasure was Sanchez' cooperative attitude. Over beers at a local cantina, the Mexican researcher expressed generous interest in sharing his work with an American audience via Olson. After inviting the young man to come and see him in Lerma, Charles boarded a bus with Connie for the four-mile ride down the coast from the provincial capital to the tiny fishing village which was to be their home for the next five months.

The Woelffers had shown them tantalizing photos of the house they were to rent. The adobe *casa,* surrounded by palms and with stone terraces facing on the rocky beach, proved to be at least as large and romantically situated as it had appeared in the pictures. But neither Woelffers nor photos had prepared the Olsons for the derelict condition in which the place had been left by the last set of tenants. The floor tiles were covered by mounds of crumbling limestone wall plaster that had to be attacked with pail and scrub brush.

The toilet, a modern ceramic fixture covering a crude hole in the floor and flushed with buckets of salt water, was blocked, and a local handyman had to be summoned to clear it. The rooms were bare. For sleeping the Olsons supplied themselves with hammocks from Campeche, and for their only furniture, a table and a few chairs from the local cantina. Water had to be drawn from a well, and as there was no electricity, kerosene lamps had to be used after dark. Doing without American-style amenities, however, was more of a strain for Connie than for Charles, who for philosophical reasons counted the primitive aspect of their accommodations a plus. "We are that close to the beginning of life," he marveled to Cid Corman, "even on the skirts of such a civilization as the Maya!"

The cultural transition was still more abrupt on the social front. For a few days the new arrivals were shadowed by a pack of small children, whose insistent mocking chorus of "griing-GO, grrrriiing-GO" echoed an "unbelievable underground hate for Americans." To "extricate myself from the antagonism [of] the mass" became an early Olson priority. Drawing on natural reserves of charm, he had soon made a friend of one of the Lerma fishermen. Before long the local man, whose name was Martinez, took to stopping in regularly to drink with Charles and to exchange his wife's tortillas for water from the house well. Their informal, rum-and-Dos-Equis-lubricated "maya-espanol" sessions, while failing to provide Olson much solid grounding in either language, made him feel less of an outsider. Martinez, he soon raved to Creeley, was a walking, talking "clue to what the Maya were," "a live object to spark it all." Martinez' wife and eldest son, fifteen-year-old Alvaro, also came around to meet the *norteamericanos*. The boy set out every morning with several other youths in his own *cayuco* just beneath the Olsons' terrace. The fearlessness with which these apprentice fishermen confronted the open ocean much impressed Olson, who had already made up his mind that despite centuries of colonialism, poverty and "pitiful cultural inertia," the local descendants still possessed blood-traces of the ancient Maya's original nobility.

He became swept up in that archaic magic, particularly while resting on his terrace of an evening, listening to distant dogs bark in the stillness and contemplating the illuminated spectacle of the tropical night sky. "I am like a kid," he enthused to Creeley one night—"saw Venus lay down a path of light on water . . . enough . . . to make me wild." No less enthralling were the birds he watched wheel above his terrace in the daytime. To the poet who believed it "better to be a bird, as these Maya seem to have been," the majestic *zopilotes* (vultures) and *chii-mi* (frigate birds) seemed emblematic of some cosmic force, the energy of nature in its purest state. He delighted in their sweeping flight, and was horrified to see that the small boys loitering on the beach below—the same "little bastards" who'd made up his raucous reception party—had a habit of targeting these proud birds with slingshots. On one occasion the urchins managed to knock a *chii-mi* out of the sky and were pelting it to death in the shallows. Charles, overcome by the sight, could only look on speechless, but Connie had the presence of mind to order an older boy to wade in and rescue the injured bird. The Olsons sheltered it on their terrace until it recovered and swooped off again from the top of the seawall. Watching it move out over the water gave Olson the uncanny sensation he was being lifted through space himself. This momentary "sense of a bird's strength, inside strength," filled him with awe of the power of creation.

His life in Lerma made him realize just how dramatically he had been divorced from nature during all those sedentary years at his Washington work desk. A series of predictable "nits in Eden"—minor, exotic ailments—briefly complicated the transition to life in the Yucatán. After the first few weeks, however, the heat rashes, tick bites and intestinal disorders had ceased to bother him. He began to thrive on the fresh air and physical activity. In less than six months, he slimmed down from a ponderous 265 pounds to the 215 he'd weighed as a stripling soccer player at Wesleyan. He lost his scholar's midnight pallor and grew lean and tanned on a regimen of daily swims in the Gulf followed by amateur archaeological expeditions that sometimes involved not only long hikes but much hard labor under the equatorial sun.

His first impromptu digs were within walking distance of his house. Ignoring property boundaries in his eagerness, he risked being caught red-handed, trespasser's "pockets bulging with potsherds like a kid who had stole the farmer's apples." In fact, one of his early excavations was interrupted by the owner of the land he was digging up, a farmer named Vasquez. Diplomatic measures were required to get him out of this tight squeeze. In exchange for permission to work on Vasquez' land, he made a spur-of-the-moment offer to locate the best spot for a new well to replace an old one that had gone dry. His hydrogeological estimate failed to locate water, but the farmer, convinced by the sincerity of the effort, let him continue to dig anyway. This "secret ruin" produced several interesting artifacts. A carved owl's head found there was soon presiding over his work table in Lerma. (It subsequently adorned many an Olson domicile back in the United States, even becoming a dope stash in the 1960s.)

Luck, as usual, ruled the search. One day in March, riding the bus to Campeche, he spied a promising heap of stones and later went back to investigate, overcoming his fears of encountering a deadly snake out there "in the wilds with no one to suck the wound." His daring paid off in the discovery of his first hieroglyphic stone. "The run's on: and the joy," he exulted to Creeley. "The excitement, the loveliness . . . I am wild for it." He rushed the stone to the Campeche Museum. There it elicited only a ho-hum reaction from director Raul Pavon Abrue. Abrue, Hippolito Sanchez' boss, was a noted authority on Maya. Still, his condescending coolness did little to quench the amateur's enthusiasm, merely convincing him he was dealing with an administrative time-server and "horse's arse."

Olson's most precious find, however, was turned up not in the field but on the black market: a human thighbone carved with hieroglyphics so "perfect" that from the minute he obtained it—after much haggling over price with a local entrepreneur in artifacts—he was certain it was a rare treasure, a "unique survival of the Maya." Back in the States, he would proudly display it to selected friends as "Quetzalcoatl's own knee-to-hip." Despite failure of long-distance efforts, with Gustavo Stromsvik as intermediary, to locate and negotiate purchase of the missing section of legbone (the femur, evidently broken off by an earlier trader), Olson remained confident that the piece he retained was itself of incomparable archaeological value, nothing less than "the Rosetta Stone of Mayan studies."

The hunt among stones spanned an ever wider geographical radius. An early April solo trip to Mayan ruins at Uxmal and Kabah involved some two hundred kilometers of bus travel. A few weeks later, accompanied by Connie—who was thriving on their new life and enjoying a surprisingly trouble-free pregnancy—he journeyed by sea to inspect Mayan burial pyramids on the isle of Jaina. Though the island was only twenty miles north of Lerma, the trip took a grueling four hours by primitive *cayuco,* leaving time for nothing but the most cursory examination of the remotely located pyramids. Olson made up his mind in the wake of this frustrating junket that uncovering a lost culture demanded resources he could not presently marshal. Yet, somehow, a "total reconaissance of *all* sites" had to be done before it became too late. And indeed, as he told Creeley, the moment was already slipping away: vital traces of Mayan civilization were disappearing daily. Just down the road from his own *casa,* a construction supply company was busy grinding up the stone columns of a small Mayan city into "white cement in bags," destined for a new apartment complex in Campeche. Such senseless destruction was at least partly attributable to the neglectful complicity of the professional archaeologists, who had ignored dozens of such unexplored satellite sites in order to maintain a few tourist-attraction "Maya Metropolises."

These myopic, irresponsible professionals—the "Peabody-Carnegie gang"— were by now a constant object of Olsonian wrath, condemned for their "intellectual carelessness, stupidity & laziness" in letter after letter to his associates back home. The ill feeling was not without traces of envy. His own haphazard researches lacked all the professionals' material advantages. Rustling up a Maya dictionary, for example, proved a significant test; he was finally supplied one by Cid Corman, who shopped Boston used-book stores for Alfred Tozzer's *A Maya Grammar*. Robert Creeley, called on to provide information about the stars and planets—urgently needed by Olson for his studies in Mayan astronomy—did his best by forwarding listings on Venus and the constellations taken from the farmhouse encyclopedia. This mail-order method was at best slow and error-prone. On one occasion, seeking confirmation of his hunch that the Mayan deity Kukulcan / Quetzalcoatl had been a "SEA-HORSE" god (a key assumption underlying his latest idea for a book about "THE SEA, in MAYAN ECONOMY, and ITS EFFECTS on THEIR CULTURE AND ART"), Olson received from the obliging Creeley some encouraging evidence—drawings of sea horses copied by a hipster friend from pre-Columbian mythological codices. Olson's elation was considerable, but a few days later there was a deflating second letter reporting that the codices had unfortunately turned out to be Aztec, not Mayan.

For Olson, such experiences caused a hard truth to sink in. Without the advice and backing of those same institutional bogeymen he spent so much of his time castigating, he might as well give up the idea of doing serious research on the Maya. "My only hope," he wrote to Creeley in late March, "would be to convince one of these professional Maya outfits in the States that what I am doing would pay-off, to them, in some form or other. Which, it still strikes me, is small chance, they are so backward in admitting culture-morphology as a discipline (my premise being, of course, that only a poet, now, can be said to possess the tools to practice culture-morphology at its best . . .)." He made at least two vigorous bids to enlist top people in the "professional outfits" as allies, approaching Robert Wauchope of the Middle American Research Institute at Tulane and Samuel K. Lothrop at the Peabody Museum at Harvard. Extensive letters of proposition and inquiry, however, earned him slim returns. The sum total of the response was a map of known digs in the Campeche area (supplied by Wauchope). Olson resolved after this strikeout to skirt the established academicians and aim instead at the foundations that were their institutional overseers.

To attract attention, his work would have to have a single clear focus. He settled on the aspect of his studies that both interested him the most personally and seemed to offer the best fund-raising potential—the picture language of the hieroglyphs. Here, he declared to Creeley, lay "the real pay-off, the inside stuff." The drawings of his original would-be collaborator, Hippolito Sanchez, now emerged in a new light, as a hole card in the game of funding. Meetings with Sanchez at the Campeche Museum and in Lerma yielded a scheme for a joint study of hieroglyphs. Olson proposed to Cid Corman an *Origin* feature on the Sanchez drawings to be timed with a major U.S. exhibit. He even dictated a site for the show's opening, the Boston Institute of Contemporary Art. He himself would provide catalog copy. The event, he promised Corman, would produce a sensation, perhaps outdoing the 1913 Armory Show or Leo Frobenius' famous cave-art exhibition at the Museum of Modern Art. It would simultaneously release the subject of picture language from stuffy academic confines, "clear the GLYPHS of archeology, of professionals." The inevitable result would be an outpouring of financial support for further research. When Corman indicated a restrained interest, Olson immediately went into high gear, attempting to hustle the necessary permissions. Rights to ship, display and reproduce the Sanchez drawings, he soon found, could be obtained only through his nemesis at the Campeche Museum, Sanchez' boss Pavon Abrue. After two weeks of exasperating "pushing" and "maneuvering," Olson out of desperation finally agreed to include the museum director in the deal as consultant. In exchange for this piece of the action, tentative permissions were granted. Back in America, meanwhile, Corman was now experiencing doubts. He suggested the actual drawings be sent on as proof of Olson's promised "golden egg." "I can't print dreams, no matter how entrancing," the editor insisted.

Impatient with subsequent delays and red tape, Olson let the *Origin* exhibit idea slide. He decided to avoid further time-wasting sidetracks and instead mount a full frontal assault on the grant feedbag. His advances to the Bollingen and Peabody foundations were unsuccessful, but the Wenner-Gren Foundation for Anthropological Research—a little-known money source to which he'd been tipped off by his former Wesleyan teacher Cornelius Krusé—proved more receptive. Informed he might be able to qualify for aid from the Wenner-Gren's Viking Fund, he had soon put together a challenging proposal for "The Art of the Language of Mayan Glyphs," a book project to entail intensive on-site studies at Copán, Yaxchilán, Piedras Negras and Palenque. Both Sanchez and Abrue—men with imposing archaeological credentials—were written into the project as collaborators. An even more grandiose version of the plan, combining the Mayan proposal with one for investigations of Sumerian clay tablets in Iran (the outcome would be a vast opus on "the force of ORIGINS"), was simultaneously submitted to Henry Allen Moe of the Guggenheim Foundation. Moe, meanwhile, was named as a reference on the Wenner-Gren application.

Satisfied that he'd played all possible angles to find cash support for further explorations of the archaic, Olson turned his attention to more immediate literary matters. The arrival in Lerma in late April of the inaugural issue of *Origin*, showcasing his poems and essay as well as a sampling of his letters to Vincent Ferrini, brought him, he told Corman, "the fullest satisfaction i have ever had from print." The pleasure was tempered only by his mixed feelings over "I, Maximus of Gloucester, to You." Writing to the editor upon receiving the magazine, he confessed, i don't like the poem at all, this morning: crazy, isn't it, that the poem i wanted so hard, 1st, and out there, seems, now that i see it, altogether bad, altogether sliding, slippery, wrong: somehow, the fish, got out of his element, and is just slimy, to the touch, on land.

The real source of his "huge disappointment" in the poem was of course largely personal, and not easily conveyed to literary associates who were unaware of the unsettling relationship which had produced it. (That relationship was now temporarily in abeyance: he had not corresponded at all with Frances since his departure for Mexico.) The passages from his letters selected by Corman, on the other hand, came as a pleasant surprise, confirming what he'd already half suspected—that he was a more direct and unself-conscious writer in personal correspondence than in much of his more formal literary composition. The letter passages, in fact, made up the "highpoint" of the magazine for him. Though in some of them he seemed to be mimicking the aggressive propositional prose of his essays ("we have to kick sentences in the face here, if we are to express the going reality . . ."), in others he found hints of a deeper soul-revelation for which he'd long been aiming in poetry. Certain passages recorded dreams about his Gloucester youth—of cart-pushing on the wharf, bathing in an "ancient tub," and being involved in some mysterious death-doings "down back of Lufkin's diner" (a dream scene later to be resurrected in one of his finest poems). Taking the lesson of his own prophetic intuition ("injuns . . . they knew how useful dreams are"), he would henceforth allow dream material an increased role in his poetry.

His letters from Lerma, he now sensed, held the actual logbook of his voyage to Maya. Without delay he asked Creeley to annotate and return them. He had already taken the trouble to keep careful carbons; what he wanted from his friend was the editing and arranging of a book, a chore he felt too subjectively involved (and too busy) to perform himself. Creeley would within two years complete not only the editing job but the further task of personally publishing the results as *Mayan Letters,* one of Olson's most influential books. To Creeley, it seemed there was no mistaking the work's importance.

> The problem [for Olson] was, to give form, again, to what the Maya had been— to restore the "history" which they were. For in the Maya was the looked-for content: a *reality* which is "wholly formal without loss of intimate spaces, with the ball still snarled, yet, with a light (and not stars) and a heat (not androgyne) which declares, the persistence of both organism *and* will (human). . . ."

The overall impact of the *Origin* appearance was to whet Olson's creative appetite. He felt hungry to write, "possessed of that kind of taste, or drive towards a hot world, which is called creative power." Shut up in his *casa* to escape the brutal "Heat Equator" sun, he had by June begun work in earnest on the large cultural statement which would be the fruition of his Mexico stay. Aimed once and for all to "set my cultural position . . . my base . . . the body, the substance of my faith," this statement would have at its philosophical core a pair of related beliefs, both immeasurably strengthened for Olson by his sense of contact with the ancient Maya: that for any culture to survive and flourish, it must contain a mythological dimension; and that once active in such a dimension, an individual must thereby come to participate in a vibrant, interconnected larger nature. Like so much of his thought, its impetus would be in some degree reactive, in this case the desire to qualify and amend a tendency he attributed to Ezra Pound. Whereas Pound, sustained by sheer ego force, had "turned time into what we must now have, space & its live air," Olson himself, as he told Creeley during the conception of the piece, would now exploratively extend his own reach *backward,* "to fill a mythological space." His new range was owed to the Maya, who had taught him to comprehend the gods of archaic myth as "not at all inventions, but . . . disclosures of human possibilities, in other words, human necessities." To rediscover a viable cosmology for the modern world would require a heightened sensitivity to these original imperatives of the human creature—one no longer set off from all other creatures, but a part of nature's "given," "the given organism, both in itself, and its obedience to laws evident as part of all organism, including nature as creation."

The composition of "Human Universe"—as this ambitious essay was to be titled—found Olson once again struggling to transmute the intensity and fervor of his personal epistolary style into an expansive and vital public discourse. Working from the carbons of the correspondence to Creeley, he reshaped one particular March letter into the essay's centerpiece. The letter recounted his experiences not amid the ruins but on his way to them, riding local buses up and down the coast, and his democratic pleasure in the familiar jostlings of his fellow passengers, Indian sugar factory workers and field cane cutters on their Sunday outings. In editing the letter prose he distanced himself only slightly—at one strategic point, for instance, turning "me" into the more remote "a man." Here was Olson's image of the insecure giant at home in his own skin at last.

> I have been living for some time amongst a people who are more or less directly the descendants of a culture and civilization which was a contrary of that which we have known and of which we are the natural children. The marked thing about them is, that it is only love and flesh which seems to carry any sign of their antecedence, that all the rest which was once a greatness different from our own has gone down before the poundings of our way. And, now, except as their bodies jostle in a bus, or as they disclose the depth and tenacity of love among each other inside a family, they are poor failures of the modern world, incompetent even to

arrange that, in the month of June, when the rains have not come far enough forward to fill the wells, they have water to wash in or to drink. They have lost the capacity of their predecessors to do anything in common. But they do one thing no modern knows the secret of, however he is still by nature possessed of it: they wear their flesh with that difference which the understanding that it is common leads to. When I am rocked by the roads against any of them—kids, women, men—their flesh is most gentle, is granted, touch is in no sense anything but the natural law of flesh, there is none of that pull-away which, in the States, causes a man for all the years of his life the deepest sort of questioning of the rights of himself to the wild reachings of his own organism. The admission these people give me and one another is direct, and the individual who peers out from that flesh is precisely himself, is a curious wandering animal like me—it is so very beautiful how animal human eyes are when the flesh is not worn so close it chokes, how human and individuated the look comes out of a human eye when the house of it is not exaggerated.

The ancient Mayan way, a mythic consciousness operating through energized organs of perception to produce a keen attention to the totality of the cosmos, was held up by Olson in dramatic apposition to the passive, subjective, physically alienated Western spectator-commodity culture of the present. Fragments of that lost attention remained to be learned from, lingering evidences of the creative genius of the Maya's arts and sciences, their innovations in astronomy, pottery, agriculture—and above all, language. In the Mayan as in other regions of the archaic, suggested Olson,

Men were able to stay so interested in the expressions and gestures of all creatures . . . that they invented a system of written record, now called hieroglyphs, which, on its very face, is verse, the signs were so clearly and densely chosen that, cut in stone, they retain the power of the objects of which they are the images.

To account for the disappearance of this signifying power, Olson briefly traced the cultural degeneration that had succeeded it, first set in motion by Socrates, Aristotle and Plato, with their invention of a discourse system based on logic, generalization and classification.

We have lived long in a generalizing time, at least since 450 B.C. And it has had its effect on the best of men, on the best of things. Logos, or discourse, for example, has in that time, so worked its abstractions into our concept and use of language that language and language's other function, speech, seems so in need of restoration that several of us got back to hieroglyphs or to ideograms to right the balance. (The distinction here is between language as the act of the instant and language as the act of thought about the instant.) . . . The Greeks declare[d] all speculation as enclosed in the "UNIVERSE of discourse." It is their word, and the refuge of all metaphysicians since. . . . We stay unaware how . . . means of discourse the Greeks

appear to have invented hugely intermit our participation in our experience, and
so prevent discovery. . . .

The bad habits bred by this system of discourse, Olson contended, had cut
man off from elemental contact with the phenomenal world, integrating and
unifying embodiment of the "only two universes which count . . . that of
himself, as organism, and that of his environment, the earth and planets."
These two grand processes together formed a total creation whose harmo-
nies—"post-logical, as is the order of any created thing"—would remain forever inaccessible to Logos.

As he moved into technical particulars, his practical case against the
"inherited" discourse system came to rest in his critique of two specific established modes of thought, the symbolic and the comparative.

> These are the false faces, too much seen, which hide and keep from us the active
> intellectual states, metaphor and performance. All that comparison ever does is
> set up a series of reference points: to compare is to take one thing and try to
> understand it by making its similarities to or differences from another thing. Right
> here is the trouble . . . such an analysis only accomplishes a description, does not
> come to terms with what really matters: that a thing, any thing, impinges on us
> by a more important fact, its self-existence, without reference to any other thing,
> in short, the very character of it which calls our attention to it, which wants us to
> know more about it, its particularity.

As antidote to this conditioned and reflexive identifying of a thing by
saying what it is not, he proposed an emphatic, dynamic new kind of linguistic cognition, moving as directly and accurately as possible toward what some
aspect of reality *is,* in the full vividness of its processual unfolding; which
brought him back to the principle of mimetic dynamism, foundation of his
projective aesthetics.

> There must be a way of expression . . . a way which is not divisive as all the tag
> ends and upendings of the Greek way are. There must be a way which bears *in*
> instead of away, which meets head on what goes on each split second, a way
> which does not—in order to define—prevent, deter, distract, and so cease the act
> of, discovering.

One indicator of the nature of that pioneering "way of expression" was
the form of the essay itself, the shape of its argument fully as much an intensive unfolding (or as the Creeley tag went, an "extension of content") as
anything Olson had yet attempted in open-field verse. The very method of
his challenge to identity thinking and the logical discourse system was the
best validation of his contentions. Instead of being subjected to comparison

and analysis, Western and Mayan cultures and styles of thought were juxta-posed for the reader's inspection much as images in a work of art.

Stripped of all mechanics save those hidden in the nature of his subject, Olson's scattershot argument came out curiously true to its intent: "A thing . . . impinges on us by . . . its self-existence." His serial, accumulative style in the essay served to accent that point, highlighting the individuating, anti-identifying quality of his thought. The rhetorical form employed was one of simple parataxis—or as he would later define it, the placement of "words or actions . . . side by side in the order of their occurrence in nature, instead of by an order of discourse or 'grammar.'" This appositional or "dream syntax" would dictate the internal ordering of much of his major work to come. His delighted discovery, in a book read a decade after the writing of "Human Universe" (Eric Havelock's *Preface to Plato*), that a paratactic method not unlike his own, uniquely suitable for containing "an experience of experience, vision dream seeming," had actually reigned supreme in the poetic expression of pre-Socratic times, would strike him as the ultimate confirmation of the legitimacy of his entire approach in writing.

Along with the previous year's essay on poetics, "Human Universe" would remain a linchpin of Olson's theoretical work. That sweeping totality of view, a generous summoning of all knowledge to an exacting yet imaginative inquiry, which had long been his main aim in writing, now came close to realization for the first time.

On June 17, copies of the essay's first draft were sent to Cid Corman, for submission to his magazine, and Robert Creeley, for editorial comment. Both recipients cautioned Olson about an occasional overaggressiveness of tone, especially in a passage attacking the "collectivists," "existentialists" and "homosexuals" who were his fellow contributors to the latest New Directions annual. Heeding their politic advice, he deleted the potentially embarrassing section, and also slightly moderated his assault on humanism and "Greek-ism." For some months he continued to revise and trim the entire essay with an unusually assiduous attention to detail. Its importance was already obvious to him; in the larger perspective of his work, it would have to stand up as "a piece of huge & simple Mosaic stone." The finished product would not finally go off to Corman until mid-September, to appear in the Winter 1951–1952 issue of *Origin*.

But as absorbing as the "Mosaic stone" was, it remained as difficult as ever for Olson to focus his attention exclusively on a single project. Long late-June mornings over breakfast were spent discussing and dissecting his dreams with Connie, feeling around for "a metric proper to myself." One night his father appeared to him in the guise of a "heavy-jowled Indian," lamenting Mary's death and the family sorrows. Charles worried superstitiously that the dream might contain grim foreshadowing of failures of his own. This visitation was soon incorporated into "To Gerhardt, There, Among Europe's Things," a rambling, portentous poem in which the impatient American son rejected the accumulated European cultural burden. Here, taking on the dream form of a ghostly New World specter, Karl was barely recognizable—not only wearing the wrong face, but emanating a body odor Charles did "not know as his, as his was meadow-sweet." Contributing to increasingly frequent "pissed off, jumpy" moods was the realization that his time in Mexico was finally running out. The postal retirement windfall was long since used up, and a money order from the Creeleys, supplied out of Ann Creeley's trust fund, had gone into the last round of field trips to remote Mayan sites. The Wenner-Gren Foundation, furthermore, now notified Olson that to be eligible for support he would need institutional affiliation, and that could hardly be gained in Mexico. Ironically, to buy more time there, he would have to leave.

He decided, in view of the foundation's affiliation requirement, to reconsider an offer that had come in from Black Mountain. A new regime was in control at the school, his enemies Trayer and Goldowski having cleared out (the former for good, the latter for a year's leave). Mary Caroline Richards, a popular literature and drama teacher now acting as administrative coordinator, had asked him back for the July-August summer session. Proposed terms sounded spartan even by Black Mountain standards: Olson's former students had chipped in $93 toward his and Connie's boat fare back to America, but the college itself could offer no solid promise of cash remuneration. Still, even $93 was more than he could hope to scrape up in Mexico. Reluctantly, he accepted the offer. The last days in Lerma were emotional ones. Watching the Lerma fishermen paddling their *cayucos* in the rain, he found himself "weeping, to leave." The regret was evident in his final letters to Creeley. "God, but we shall miss what we have wrought here," he told his friend on June 28—"damnest thing, how I have come all the way over, and do not care for anything but this day of work precisely here, and the evenings."

Pinching every last centavo, he and Connie hooked up with a Campeche timber dealer who offered them free passage to Pensacola. On July 5, Charles' drinking partner Martinez ferried them by *cayuco* to the pier in Campeche, where they boarded the lumber boat *Lucero di Alba*. Midway across the Gulf, looking out from the boat's stern to far horizons where the sun sank amid massed clouds "brilliant as Titian's," Olson's mind was as full as always of language, and of thoughts of further exploratory seas. At the moment they seemed suitably limitless—"and is there any end, to that energy?"

16 ⟨⟩

Lawgiver
(1951)

F or Olson, the return to Black Mountain was a strange leap from the
baked-earth archaic to a disorienting "paradise . . . suspended like a Swiss
Lake Village of post-Cenozoic time in the midst of waters no human with
sense would cross." There was little time to prepare for the transition. He
and Connie dropped off their bags in their upstairs flat in South Lodge, the
men's dormitory building, and then he went directly to work. An audience
of some fifty summer-session faculty and students was gathered in the college
dining hall to hear him lecture on his Yucatán adventures. Exhausted by the
long, rattling bus trip north from Florida, he abandoned his original plan to
talk extempore and instead read aloud the latest draft of the still-in-progress
"Human Universe" essay. His opening sentence rang with the authoritative
tones of an archaic lawgiver coming down from his mountain to deliver truths
revealed: "There are laws . . ."

"These 'laws' I am talking about so much these days"—"priorities of
succession & importance" governing all natural and human process—were
also to be a central insistence in his propositional writings of the first months
back at the college. Revising "Human Universe," that "huge & simple Mosaic
stone," he gave serious consideration to retitling it simply "The Laws," and
before long he would be making a hasty pass at a second such sweeping
pronouncement on culture in a piece called "The Law," advocating a retreat

from the "BOX 500 BC–1950 AD" back to a prior "old phallic wisdom." In his summer-session instruction likewise the harmonic orders of man and nature, and retunings thereof necessitated by recent historical and perceptual developments, would receive heavy stress. Expounding his antihumanist corrective code for his faithful writing-student followers ("my tribe"), Olson would now take on not only the textual emphases but the teaching style of some ancient patriarch, oracular, dogmatic and utterly committed to the significance of his message. So intensely had he come to identify with the ideas he represented, in fact, that in students' eyes he now seemed a living image of his own absorptions, dominating classroom discourse without challenge ("I go so fast I am so far ahead, what is there but, a monologue?"). As he lectured he produced speedy notational hieroglyphs graven not on stone but on slate, a snakelike trail of blue-chalk scribblings that uncoiled across and beyond a white chalkboard onto an adjacent wall, his mustache and fingers in the process becoming smudged a chalky blue as his thought and hand raced ever on, interrupted only by periodic deep puffs on a cigar or a cigarette. Hypochondriac as always, he permitted no windows to be opened while he taught, and by a few hours into the four- and five-hour evening meetings the atmosphere in the room came to resemble that inside a factory chimney (one female student, in a vain gesture of protest, showed up at class one night armed with Airwick). A Moses come back from the Yucatán—as one of his students noted—like "a man liberated . . . brimful of fire," he surrounded himself with a hazy aura of far-flung vision, saturating his listeners' open, willing minds with dense, swirling nebulae of diverse thought and knowledge, much of it posed with the urgent immediacy of commandment.

Sometimes when these marathon sessions ran on past midnight, Connie, tired of being left alone in South Lodge, drifted up to the Studies Building to fetch home her man, materializing in the smoky classroom in her flowing Mexican maternity dress like some impatient fertility goddess. Despite Charles' earnest resolutions, the precious bond of intimacy they'd established in the isolation of Lerma inevitably began to relinquish its hold on him with the return to America. At the college he was quickly pouring so much effort into the emergence of thought and self as language, both in the classroom and at the typewriter, that there was little left over for his increasingly neglected mate. "I shall more and more narrow myself to my own life, this machine, and my wife," he wrote to Creeley just ten days into the Black Mountain stay. Yet it was not Connie but writing partner Creeley—relocated in Aix-en-Provence—who was actually now his closest confidant. And though he spoke of aiming "to see as much of Con as I damn well can, away from, them all," in fact as the weeks went by he let himself gradually be lured into center stage of the "three-ring circus" that was the 1951 summer session.

Ben Shahn, his wartime fellow propagandist at the OWI, was on hand to teach painting. They had soon resumed amicable relations. For Olson, reencountering a familiar spirit in the midst of Black Mountain's disconcerting "paradise" led to "a sort of combustion." The two men, joined by Bernarda Shahn and Connie, took off together several times on social excursions into town, and soon were plotting out a new collaborative venture, the instigation supplied by an Olson poem called "Glyphs." This developed into a full-scale multimedia production, staged in the college dining hall. A student artist converted glyph drawings done for the project by Shahn into large stage backdrops. Black Mountain dance teacher Katherine Litz choreographed and performed an expressionistic interpretation of Olson's poem. Musical accompaniment was provided by resident composer Lou Harrison, whose prepared-piano score called for "someone's pressing firmly against all the low strings, & at a 'nodal angle,' a heavy piece of wood, as perhaps, $2'' \times 2''$, on the sharp edge." While the resultant intensely modernistic spectacle was received with general baffled approbation, some in the audience found it rather difficult to sit through. Poet Edward Dorn, at the time a relatively unsophisticated twenty-two-year-old summer student from rural Illinois, was struck most by the unintentional comedy of "Katy Litz squirming out of a burlap bag." Olson himself was delighted with the event, confirmed in his conviction not only that the svelte blond Litz was "the best dancer now alive," but that dance was of all the arts currently the most "forward."

Inspired by the success of "Glyphs," he had shortly embarked on a further series of dance plays intended to utilize the talents of a repertory of student performers. He sketched out *The Born Dancer,* a poetic play based on the life of Nijinsky, and *King of the Wood,* a Frobenian "African shadow-play" after the manner of the 1949 *Wagadu.* Neither work, however, was actually staged. Nor was a third, more ambitious dance play of the summer, *Apollonius of Tyana,* conceived as a vehicle for student poet and dancer Nicola ("Nick") Cernovich. The gifted and attractive young man had been a favored student during Olson's earlier period at the school (it was Cernovich who as Black Mountain printing apprentice had at the writing teacher's behest taken on the ill-fated production of Dahlberg's *Flea of Sodom* in 1949). For a college choreography project Cernovich had put on a solo show based on "Pacific Lament," Olson's wartime poem about the drowned "golden boy," performing it first at Black Mountain and then by special invitation at Randolph Place just before the Olsons' departure for the Yucatán. That July at the college the student debuted a new piece, a dance version of the life of Saint Francis of Assisi. Olson was moved to write a poem in response, "Applause," in which the student performer was hailed as a godlike "cold dancer / in the sun." Accordingly, when the poet came to conceive what he regarded as his major work of the summer—the Apollonius play—it was with Cernovich in mind as soloist and himself as narrator.

His script of some ten thousand words chronicled the spiritual growth and travels of the first-century wandering Greek sage. While he would describe it to Creeley as a bid to map out "the whole known world of the 1st Century," the play was actually focused on its protagonist's inward voyage, the journey toward self-knowledge; the main themes of its narrative monologue—the development of personal ethics through self-inquiry, the rejection of arbitrarily imposed social sanctions and the establishment of alternative cultural codes—reflected less the interests of the historical philosopher Apollonius than the personal obsessions of playwright Olson, ever intent on the projection of an image of the questing self. "A sudden geometric and annunciative man measurer and to be measured," Olson's Apollonius was "loaded with an appetite for the real world . . . the world as we love it—the world of other men. He craved to talk . . . in fact, he was one of those who talked to live."

In the volubleness of Apollonius there was not only autobiographical but psychological resonance. Questions of orality were now coming into increasing prominence in Olson's writing, particularly clouding his communiqués on cultural matters. What else but a testament of oral compulsion is the "sheep's heart" letter, a mid-July epistle to Creeley which last-minute misgivings kept Olson from ever sending? The letter, as he informed his friend in a series of fumbling later efforts at paraphrase (which in fact merely heightened the mystery of his withholding it), was a "long go on Jews, oral, phallic, and EATING," "historic" in its import yet so precious to him as personal "fetish" that he "dare[d] not let it out of my hand," feeling constrained to keep it "hidden, like an Omaha's dream." It had been precipitated by a confusing emotional scene brought upon him—importunately, he felt—by his friend Ben Shahn. The artist, plainly in a distraught state, had approached him with the distressing news of Bernarda's just-diagnosed breast cancer. Shahn thought his wife was dying and wanted to share his grief. Fond as he was of the man, Olson found himself repelled. The intensity of the emotional demand was more than he could deal with, and its imposition all too reminiscent of the pressures he'd once had exerted upon him by Edward Dahlberg. Struggling to articulate this in his unsent "long go," he began by complaining bitterly of "that goddamned restless eating unhappy way that great Jews have always dogged my tail." Later in the letter Shahn and Dahlberg emerged as co-bearers of an ancient tribal burden of unconscious guilt, seeded in all Jews as part of their original monotheistic legacy, an "Arabian desert wrongness" inherited from a "God that herding people picked up." Jews, according to Olson, were irreversibly marked by that early cultural imprint, "from the beginning chosen to be the corrupters by the very burden of the heart, the heavy heart they carry, which is no human heart, but is an enlarged sheep heart, the heart of sacrificed animals." Not Shahn or Dahlberg personally but the whole history of the Judeo-Christian humanist tradition, still viewed by him as the main impediment to his own as well as the culture's healthy development—and embodied here in imagery that went all the way back to the Father Murder recounted in *Moses and Monotheism* and the Jewish ritual eating scenes and animal sacrifices described in *Joseph and His Brothers*—was the real target of Olson's attack. The obsessive emphasis on the eating theme in his letter also mirrored subjective concerns predating even those influential early readings of Freud and Mann. (The same insistence was to come forward in far less mediated form in his late poetry: "I have eaten my father / piece by piece I loved my cannibalism.") "The oral is profoundly phallic," he would eventually confess to Creeley apropos the deeper sources of this "fetish" letter. But in trying to sum up the conclusions of his wandering cultural exegesis, he could only signal his powerful instinctive sense that from Abraham and Isaac to the Crucifixion, the Judeo-Christian patriarchal tradition had been one long disaster, issuing ultimately in "such collapsings as those of Jesus," a stultifying weakness in men, and a fear of women instilled by the threat of a Biblical God who "punishes man for his sexuality."

Another characteristic document of this lawgiver phase is "Letter for Melville 1951," a verse polemic composed by Olson soon after the "long go." The poem was provoked by an invitation to a Williams College conference organized by the Melville Society in celebration of the hundredth anniversary of the publication of *Moby-Dick.* Consciously conceived in what its author took to be the spirit of Elizabethan verse pamphleteering, "Letter for Melville" was actually less a message to the literary hero of his youth than an act of posturing performed for the benefit of his present legion of disciples. It contained angry assaults against both the academic conference itself (a "false and dirty thing") and the reputations of the organizers ("a bunch of commercial travelers from the several colleges"). Much of its rather intemperate satire was personal, directed at fellow Melville scholars who had in Olson's opinion betrayed and cheapened the great writer by reducing him to a clichéd banquet commodity. "Please to carry my damnations to each of them," he rhetorically commanded Eleanor Metcalf, who had dared to forward the invitation on to him. The gentle Mrs. Metcalf was puzzled and hurt, put off by the startling aggressiveness of his poem. (Indeed, the Metcalf family was by now getting the impression Charlie Olson had turned into a "megalomaniac.") The same inflammatory anti-academicism, however, made the Melville Letter a big hit at Black Mountain, where by popular acclaim—and at student expense—it was produced as a pamphlet on the college press.

Since *Apollonius of Tyana* was also in production that summer as a chap-book, Olson became a frequent visitor at the print shop, overseeing the efforts of college lithographer Larry Hatt and student typesetter Ed Dorn with typical vigilance. During his shop visits the radio Hatt and Dorn kept on while setting type and running the presses had to be switched off as a dangerous electronic intrusion of "viral input" from American popular culture. In Olson's neo-archaic domain, an atavistic distrust of technology went hand in hand with the patriarchic drive to reinstate ancient cultural foundations.

The zeal of his quest for origins could blur discrimination, that nagging practical carryover of rationalism. A critical article on William Carlos Williams by Yale English professor Louis Martz which Olson read that August occasioned a monumental confusion when he misread Martz' reference to Williams as a *Pelagian* (subscriber to a fifth-century Christian heretical sect opposed to original sin), incorrectly taking the word to be *Pelasgian,* applicable to members of a cannibalistic tribe of aboriginal inhabitants of pre-Mycenean Greece. (He'd been reading excitedly about the Pelasgians in Pausanias' account of Arcadia.) He directed an enthusiastic eleven-page letter to Martz, based entirely on his erroneous assumption. They had, he told the Yale scholar, independently stumbled upon the same momentous discovery: Americans were indeed latter-day Pelasgians! Recognizing his error at the last minute before posting, Olson simply readdressed the letter to Creeley, offering his extended commentary as of value regardless of the provocation.

For the resourceful projective theorist even apparent mishaps could prove creative—perhaps especially so in this instance, as it provided Olson coincidental occasion, in his postscript to his friend, for the coining of a new and useful piece of jargon, meant to describe the historical aftermath of sixteenth- and seventeenth-century world voyaging and the nineteenth-century machine age. The term he came up with was "post-modern."

But the hazards of a headlong approach to cultural revolution could not always be so blithely sidestepped. His precipitate reactions could get him in trouble, as in the difficult moment he created for himself over a relatively innocuous secondhand remark about the imperfect clarity of his thought, made in a private letter by William Carlos Williams and passed on to him as gossip by Cid Corman. Williams had suggested to Corman that Olson's ideas ought to be "pulled together in firmer terms." Perhaps in part because it hit so close to home, Olson let the reported criticism get under his sensitive skin, and decided on the spot to mobilize his polemical heavy artillery against his erstwhile champion. As a first shot he declared emphatically to Creeley that Williams now seemed to him "the most valueless enthusiast of our time." A somewhat shocked Creeley quickly wrote back cautioning him against allowing the "too easy recognition" of Black Mountain disciples to cloud his judgment on so important a matter. Olson was given pause. Anger fading, he sheepishly acknowledged his reversion to an old bad habit, setting up a dispute with a father-surrogate merely to rouse his own oppositional energies. The Williams he was using to rev up his creative tensions was not a real person but a projective figment. "I honestly don't *know how to act* toward anyone," he admitted in some embarrassment. "What a goddamned little baby the Strong Man comes out!"

In the presence of his students, however, he remained the forceful, opinionated Strong Man. "His great conflict as a teacher was democracy," Ed Dorn has shrewdly observed. "He got his method from his predecessors, Pound, Eliot, and they were all such fascists. The method was the problem—all knowledge is elite." Notwithstanding the reservations Olson professed in his letters to Creeley about "the dogmatism [of the] JUDGE . . . [the] old logical fallacy, of, appeal to, authority," the actual context of his teaching regularly dissolved such doubts. While he was ready to aver in theory that "even he who made the laws, does not necessarily, therefore, have the right to state them in discourse," in practice he did not hesitate to claim that right.

Olson's enthusiastic and impressive recommendations of prescribed works from Homer's and Jane Harrison's to Victor Bérard's and Robert Creeley's was balanced by the perhaps even more notable formulation of a corresponding roster of proscribed texts and authors, to become known irreverently among his student protégés as "the Index." This extended list stretched from the humanists' classics (Plato, Aristotle, Thucydides, Virgil) through the seventeenth- and eighteenth-century Puritans, Rationalists and Transcendentalists (Milton, Johnson, Emerson) on up to the reigning eminences of twentieth-century modernism (Hemingway, Eliot, Joyce). Not only Olson's considered intellectual resistances but the instinctive blind spots and spur-of-the-moment lapses in his judgment were thus inscribed as law. That summer, when visiting music teacher David Tudor performed Pierre Boulez' Second Piano Sonata in a college recital, both Tudor and Boulez were instantly enshrined in the writing teacher's canon of approval, and Boulez was solemnly proclaimed "the first composer since Bach." Dismissed to the Index, on the other hand, were the experimental all-black and all-white canvases of student painter Robert Rauschenberg. Rauschenberg was not "destined for fame," nor to rank among the "truly great."

"Resisters" among his writing students were rare but not unknown. One was Francine Du Plessix, a young woman whose European background and private-school education made her perhaps better armed to defend herself than some of her classmates. Du Plessix found his "iconoclastic" views intriguing, but his methods unpleasantly "dictatorial." Olson, evidently sénsing potential opposition, was hard on her from the first: his initial instruction, delivered in his writing class while digging his fingers into her scalp as if to pull out thoughts forcibly by their roots, was that she must immediately rid herself of the lingering effects of "highfalutin Yurrup and *poh-lee-tess* and stuck-up schools," and "start playing Gringo ball." Few of his women writing students, indeed, made much progress under his tutelage. According to another of them, Mary Fitton Fiore, in both his classes and his private circle of followers he tended to perpetuate the standard Black Mountain "straight" male view of women as alluring but largely vacuous creatures—"Me Tarzan heap big intellect you Jane full of mysteries."

His male students won him over more easily, and, in great ceremonial sharings of after-dinner moonshine and cigars, were much more easily won over, as he fell naturally into the comfortable role of "a father of sorts to the guys in the class"—a number of whom had in fact lost their real fathers through death or abandonment. One student writer, Joel Oppenheimer, later commented that Olson "handled me the way I wish my father had handled me." And Fielding Dawson has spoken of Olson as "my other father." On the occasion of insecure rookie writer Dawson's turning twenty-one that August, Olson loaded his birthday poem with paternal coaching, advising the young man "to bear in, to bear / down," for only thus could a "bush league man" be "made major." The intensity of the teachings was carried over onto the playing field, where, however, a democratic leveling tended to even things up. In the school's Sunday softball games, as in the classroom, Dawson recalls, Olson "gave it everything he had," but on the ball diamond, the Strong Man's prerogatives weren't automatic, as they were in class. Once Dawson, a crack softball hurler, faced slugger Olson at the climax of a tightly contested game. With two out and the tying run in the person of Ben Shahn standing on third base, Olson swung enormously at his student's slow deliveries and struck out.

Despite Olson's oft-stated plan of returning to the Yucatán that winter, by the end of the summer the hoped-for Wenner-Gren grant had not yet materialized to provide the requisite funding, disposing him positively toward Black Mountain's offer of an extension of his temporary summer post into an open-ended appointment as writing teacher. At $50 a month (with food and housing thrown into the bargain) he would hardly be overcompensated— nor, in view of the school's perpetually shaky finances, could there be any consideration of permanence in the position. But what the school had to offer him could now less than ever be measured in simple terms of job security or dollars and cents. Black Mountain had a way of stirring him, confusingly but powerfully. "I am like a tiger, with my energy," he told Creeley in September, "the place invokes so many forms of it." While he fretted over the steady waste of time and energy, and while his private letters lamented the run-off into teaching and into "profound useless talk" with "just-too-spoiled-for-their-own-good-students" of inspiration that might better have been saved for his writing, still it was difficult for him to do anything with restraint—least of all anything so connected with his compulsive sources as talking. He would for the time throw his full verbal powers into the school, beginning to mold it into a new shape defined by his energetic imagination, in the process transforming the college into "Olson's University."

If not exactly crying out for transformation or even reformation, Black Mountain was indeed ripe for rescuing at this time. Growing educational uniformity in the postwar nation at large had pushed the tiny progressive school farther than ever out onto the precarious economic fringe. With few graduating high school seniors—and fewer of their parents—shopping for nonconformist alternatives, enrollment had been dropping steadily in recent years, hitting a new low of thirty-five by the end of 1951. Money was short, and for the faculty there was no forgetting the practical exigencies of survival. It was not, therefore, unusual for Olson, soon after his faculty appointment that fall, to be putting his shoulder to the recruiting wheel, touring black high schools in the region to drum up minority enrollments. The tour was something short of a success, his rhetorical assault on the Truman administration's Korean policy being probably better suited to a national political campaign. Plying the other end of the socioeconomic spectrum in college fund-raising appeals to the Ford Foundation and other philanthropic institutions, he attempted to "sell the place like the Brooklyn Bridge" on the strength of his "Chinese plan," by which scholars and experts from all fields would join up at intervals to revitalize Black Mountain with a free exchange of "ideas, forms and energies." Though his foundation approaches yielded little better results than his high school recruiting tour, such activities strengthened the bond of his involvement with the college and his sense of his own fate as converging increasingly with Black Mountain's.

He now moved by force of circumstance if not of will into an administrative vacuum at the school, where the position of rector had continued to remain vacant since Josef Albers' departure. The ranking official at the moment was college board chairman and treasurer Wes Huss. Huss, who also doubled as drama instructor, had no interest in being rector. A Quaker, a former conscientious objector, and a person of meticulous attention to detail, he was little disposed to power and by nature much more comfortable in the role he now took up at Olson's side, that of trusty administrative support man, and—once they had begun teaming up to handle official college correspondence—grammarian. Olson wrote the rough copy, and Huss, mediating with formal business language the poet's wilder paratactic leaps, supplied the copy-editing. "I actually had the temerity to take each college letter he wrote and correct it—I put in the capitals and format, the ands and ors and howevers," says Huss. "Charles looked the letters over, and always accepted my changes with complete good grace. He said, 'Okay, you're my connective.' "

Olson's election to the college board of fellows in October was uncontested, perhaps because of the absence on leave of the one colleague who might have been expected to rally opposition, his old nemesis Natasha Goldowski (the following year, after making ineffectual efforts to enlist Buckminster Fuller and others in an Olson ouster, Goldowski would be gone for good). Languages instructor and college secretary Flola Shepard, who had voted against Olson's faculty appointment, had evidently resigned herself to his accession to the board (her paperwork protocols, "stiff things" that drove him to furies of impatience, would, however, continue to be an annoyance for some time to come), as did such other Olson nonfans as the founder's ex-wife and current college librarian, Nell Rice. And the elderly math teacher Max Dehn, who this fall registered a quiet protest over the writing instructor's growing "tyranny," within six months would be dead.

Minutes of the faculty board and board of fellows suggest that meeting-table skirmishes kept Olson on his toes throughout the period of his informal rise to para-administrative control. Adversaries included a pair of natural scientists, biologist Victor Sprague and anthropologist John Adams. Sprague on one notable occasion hit a nerve in expressing his distrust of Olson's autocratic teaching approach, stating flatly, "I'm not convinced you believe in the many." And Adams, even though outside the boardroom a spirited participant in "Olson's dionysiac symposia"—trading late-night opinions on American Indian myths and Jungian archetypes, Akhenaton and Quetzalcoatl—would more than once insert deflating commonsense interpolations into Olson meeting-monologues. In a November meeting, for example, Olson was rather longwindedly calling for the immediate replacement of all prior educational concepts by a completely revolutionized form of pedagogy adapted to the altered condition of post-modern man when Adams interjected dryly that he "doubted anybody here knows what Mr. Olson is talking about." And when in another meeting Olson hit a similar risky note, declaring it essential "to go blind in education as in other areas," Adams put in succinctly that such policies were bound to land the college in "chaos." In the long run this would prove hardly an inaccurate prophecy, not that the skeptical anthropologist would stay around to see it fulfilled. By the end of 1952, both Adams and Sprague would join in a general faculty exodus from "Olson's University."

With Olson's increasing involvement in college business the inner tension between opposing pulls of self and community was inevitably aggravated, the chore of administration gradually becoming even more of a burden for him than that of teaching. In rare idle moments he was already daydreaming escape routes back to creative freedom. His confidence in the imminence of a "Medici time" of grand-scale arts patronage now spurred fresh efforts to "tap some dough" from the grant feedbags. In an application for a Fulbright Lectureship in American Civilization at the University of Teheran, he laid out ambitious designs for a book on Maya, Sumer and the role of hieroglyphic language in the morphology of culture, with field work to be accomplished at ancient Sumerian valley-city sites in Iran and Iraq. To the Fulbright as well as the Wenner-Gren officials (from whom he still awaited a decisive word), he offered the same justification for the urgency of his present pleas for funding of field studies: to have any real validity, explorations of past cultures had to be done *in situ,* invested with "the live sense that only the actual ground gives"—and that took money.

His planning of escapes had to be put aside as Connie's pregnancy reached its term, bringing, for him, the momentous and absorbing attainment of fatherhood. His most powerful wish was to see her produce a son. Confiding to Creeley his anxious hopes for a boy-child, he added that among the potential names he'd been pondering were Obadiah (after the Old Testament prophet, descendant of David, majordomo of the House of Ahab) and the simple patronymic "Son of Olson." Connie, in her turn, was made so acutely aware of his preference for a male offspring that upon emergence from anesthesia after giving birth to a healthy infant in the Asheville hospital on October 23, her first words were "A girl—how terrible." (In sad hindsight she would later reflect that "a boy could have *helped* us.") The patriarch's evident disappointment over the interruption of the Olson male line notwithstanding, the child's arrival occasioned much excitement and celebration back at the college, where the Olson apartment in South Lodge was festooned with tinfoil streamers. And Charles' initial dismay over having fathered a female was shortly replaced by a pleased fascination. The child, after all, was "very beautiful," as he proudly told Creeley. Connie, too, was soon being notified of his growing delight with "this lovely being we made." The baby was called Katherine Mary, a combination of the first names of their own mothers. It did not take much time for the engaging, demanding Katherine—"so alert and hungry for company"—to become Kate, after the lively heroine in *The Taming of the Shrew,* one of the Shakespeare plays Olson was at this time rereading. The affinity of life and poetic fable gave him confirmation that he had selected a name to perfectly "interpret" the character of his daughter, who like the girl in the play was "somewhat handsome, & shrewish as she shld be, having her mother & her name!"

Connie's preoccupation with motherhood, an eventuality he'd failed to anticipate, shook him more than the birth itself. Feeling neglected and "let

down" once thrown back on himself, he fell into a depression, waxing "grim
& tired." The stress of overwork became suddenly no longer tolerable. "The
drainage of this place is beyond belief," he told Creeley. The onset of cold
weather drove him into one of his periodic withdrawals from the world. He
missed a class or two, trying to sink back into his writing. As snow blanketed
the hills and the mercury dropped past freezing, an eerie sense of isolation
closed in at South Lodge, the edgy silence broken only by the clatter of his
typewriter keys competing with his daughter's hungry wails.

He took to his bed for some days, then was beset by cabin fever. To chase
off sudden, untoward longings for "sun & sex"—and "to get away from Con"—
he hiked far out over the frozen mire of back roads into surrounding farmers'
fields. Back home, still seeking a cause for his continuing restlessness, he
turned inward. "Can't lick this feeling of unexpressed life," he moaned to
Creeley at the end of November. "[It] tears at me, beats me, that I am barricaded, cut off, have been, as long as I have lived." The basis of the trouble,
he suspected, was, as so often before, sexual—the kind of problem Shakespeare had located in the "root metaphors" of lust and repression.

Dammed-up emotions broke through in verse when he sat down to compose a seasonal message for the college Christmas party. The result, "An Ode
on Nativity," served not only the immediate occasion but less timebound
poetic purposes as well. Its moving presentation of the poet's personal origins
and imaginative growth incorporated autobiographical details from his earliest Worcester years, especially a haunting, emblematic "moon of pain,"
glimpsed in boyhood through the flames of a stable fire. A record of his
family's history in the city of his nativity, of his daughter's birth, and of his
forty-first birthday, Olson's "Ode" commemorated his perilous passage through
a dark, "bare winter time," and affirmed an endless process of hunger and
renewal, one which could, like his newborn child, finally be accepted as a
redemptive gift, part of the continuity of life's strange beauty.

> *All things now rise, and the cries of men to be born*
> *in ways afresh, aside from all old narratives . . .*
>
> > *is there any birth*
> *any other splendor than*
> *the brilliance of the going on, the loneliness*
> *whence all our cries arise?*

17 ⟿

In the Dark Stall
(1952)

The Olsons journeyed north to the Athertons' in Weymouth for Christmas, and stayed on into the New Year. Jane and Mel had acquired a television set, affording Olson his first close-up experience of the new electronic medium. After several evenings of gazing raptly into it until the test patterns took over, he abruptly concluded that the picture-box was an "obscene thing," and ordered it turned off, stalking out of the Athertons' living room when his command was ignored.

While new mothers Connie and Jane compared notes on child rearing, Charles went off by himself to meet Cid Corman. At Corman's family home in Dorchester he quaffed schnapps and quoted Shakespeare to impress the editor's parents and sister, and talked Corman into devoting the whole of a forthcoming *Origin* to Olson poetry (the scheme would eventually issue in his second collection of verse, *In Cold Hell, in Thicket*). But the visit also revived Olson's earlier misgivings about the editor's personality and character. Corman, he reported back to Creeley, was a mother's boy, too soft to be trusted with a man's work; to become of real use, he would have to be forcibly reeducated ("If I could hold him while you punched some sense into him!").

Back at the Atherton's, Charles found his welcome wearing thin, among other reasons because of his casual commandeering of the master bedroom every morning shortly after Mel's departure for work. Hints were dropped, and he failed to respond. Jane, however, was a practiced adversary. One morning shortly after New Year's, she headed off his anticipated invasion by stripping the bed down to a bare mattress and flinging open the windows to flood the room with cold air. Getting the message, the disgruntled guest took off again, this time for New York.

It was officially a business trip. He saw editor Robert Giroux at Harcourt to discuss publishing prospects, and met with experimental composer John Cage to extend an invitation to Black Mountain. But once in the city it was hard for him to keep his mind off the thought of seeing Frances. (He had not been alone in New York since his last unhappy visit to her sixteen months earlier.) He showed up unannounced late one chilly evening at her door in Brooklyn Heights. Frances, having long since given up expecting of him anything but the unexpected, calmly asked him in. A woman friend who had been visiting her was shocked by the sight of the gaping holes in his shoes, and beat a hasty retreat, leaving them alone. Frances sat patiently through his involved account of his life since he'd last seen her. He touched on every event in which he'd felt her influence affecting his behavior, even going so far as to suggest she had been at least partially responsible for the birth of his child. Connie, he told her, had been made more receptive to conception by reading *A Primer of Morals for Medea.*

His emotions still aswirl from the encounter as he navigated a borrowed car northward out of the city, he was pulled over for speeding by state police in Manchester, Connecticut. Only an automobile club card (also borrowed) saved him from a night in jail. The next day, with Connie and Kate in tow, he returned to Manchester for a court appearance. The brush with the law was unsettling, but it proved an indirect stroke of fortune. Dropping in, since he was in the neighborhood, at the home of Bernard and Mary Knollenberg—the couple he and Connie had befriended on the boat to Mexico—he became the recipient of an automobile of his own, a gift of the generous historian (who explained that he had two other cars and didn't need a third). This gesture of spontaneous patronage facilitated the Olsons' return to North Carolina.

The physically and emotionally "dragged" state into which he relapsed once back at the school in mid-January 1952 was the product in part of a nagging intestinal bug and in part of continuing stress over the issue of community involvement. The virus would eventually relinquish its hold, allowing him to climb out of his sickbed late that month to entertain a visitor—his English friend Robert Payne, the Chinese scholar from Montevallo College. Less easily dispelled was his conflict of mind on the community question;

unable to resolve it, Olson would go on oscillating indecisively between periods of emergence as college patriarch and withdrawal into the creative self.

A single frightening incident, the near-drowning of Robert Rauschenberg in Lake Eden on a snowy night at the end of January, threw his own divided position into dramatic relief for Olson. Summoned away from draining his car radiator by a sudden commotion coming from around the dining hall (where a party had been going on), he arrived at the scene to find an evidently disturbed Rauschenberg had waded into the dark, frigid water and was submerged up to his neck, moaning helplessly, while Cy Twombly, his fellow student painter and closest companion, struggled out to attempt a rescue. Held back from assisting in the lifesaving effort by the uncomfortable "thought of going in to that damned cold water, and the mud," Olson instead set off with student Joel Oppenheimer in the opposite direction, toward the dam at the other side of the lake, in search of a raft to serve as lifeboat. Later, once Rauschenberg had been brought ashore, an agitated Olson again shrank back from the action, withholding from the soaked, shivering near-victim his own warm wool overcoat while instead giving orders for blankets to be found— another "curious failing of myself," as he would afterwards assess it. Then, hurrying the bedraggled youth back toward the warmth of the dining hall, he recoiled from "the wetness of his clothes against me (I do not like him)." The episode left Olson strangely shaken, as if he'd unconsciously drifted in range of some obscure sexual temptation. The "feminine . . . endocrine creature" Rauschenberg, he concluded, had intended his action not as suicide but as "some gesture some posture some infliction of the sexual continent, of that geography I know in the other hemisphere of myself." He was moved to recount the entire episode in detail for Creeley by letter. But he was attempting to articulate to his friend something he still did not sufficiently understand. Even the bottom of Lake Eden could hardly approximate the "muddiness of the underlying homosexuality" that made Black Mountain's psychic landscape so ambiguous.

The Rauschenberg incident was followed within a few days by another that was at least as disturbing. An official-looking black Chevrolet, far too clean and new to belong to anyone at Black Mountain, pulled up at the college registrar's office and discharged two solemn, black-suited strangers, "white world men" whom the registrar recognized as agents from the regional FBI office. They asked for Olson and were told he was unavailable. He was then alerted. It was not his first warning. The FBI, Frank Moore had reported, had been looking for him at Randolph Place during his absence in Mexico. In a time when he had only to glance at the front page of a newspaper to see former OWI colleagues falling from public grace because of their political pasts—one, Owen Lattimore, had even been indicted for perjury after being accused of espionage by Senator Joseph McCarthy—Olson had not been able to resist the occasional temptation to ask himself if his own former involvements might contain similar dangers. Late the next afternoon the vague apprehension became acute when he was awakened from his customary day-long slumber by the agents, who had refused to accept Connie's protestations of his absence. He emerged barefoot and tousled from his bedroom, and over a late breakfast of bacon and eggs was grilled by the FBI men about his work with labor and ethnic groups during the 1944 presidential campaign as well as his postwar activities as a lobbyist for Polish interests at the Security Council.

The most difficult questions were those regarding specific individuals. Olson was careful not to incriminate onetime coworkers, even some of the "most 'Red' men I had to do with in my political posts." By the time the interview was over, however, the growing realization of how well the agents seemed to know *his* past had made the threat to others' fates seem somewhat less urgent. His most immediate fear concerned his chances of getting away to the Near East or Central America; in fact he would soon be denied an expected Fulbright to Iran, a rejection he would attribute directly to the FBI's interest in him. But other potential alarming consequences also ran through his head as he was being interrogated: "The import of it, the danger . . . of jail, say, the moment war came." Afterwards, his fear was replaced by anger against the violation of his privacy and outrage against the interference with his fate by the blind hand of history. To Creeley, whose ignorance of his political background made a few basic autobiographical disclosures necessary, he expressed what he could of that anger and outrage.

> THIS, is the way HISTORY, is a LIE right there in front of me in my own parlor . . . I was of the Roosevelt administration, and played the time straight. . . . was not Red, and god knows the 30s gave hotter men than I reason to be, but also I did not play it safe, as, goddamn them, the men did who now inherit the Western world—
>
> that is, it just may turn out these ten years after that I may be restrained *inside* the country . . . my life (my fate) is herewith interfered with:—*I have had to feel that shadow.* . . . (Yet these absent wings must be felt, to experience, citizenry: no tax-collector, or draft board, has this force; not even the police,—tho, they are closer: this must be the old European thing anew: the SECRET police).

Three days later he came back from getting some car repairs done in Asheville to learn that the agents had returned in his absence, and would be coming around again. He had to chalk up another lost, "fucked day" to the continuing intrusions of the "fucking FBI." After a second round of questioning he was left alone, but in psychic terms the damage had already been done. Following these ominous events Olson would be forever vigilant to the point of paranoia about the invasive authority of state power. It was "the first time I have felt that modern business of investigation—of anonymous creatures suddenly playing with the counters of one's own life, off there, a file, and certain unknown people pawing you over." Up until this moment, he had assumed he would never have the knowledge of what it was like to exist "in a fascist state." Now that assumption had been irrevocably shaken; henceforth state power would be defined in his imagination in absolute opposition to the authority of self in which he placed all faith.

Olson's latest run-in with outside systems of law and order provided a further spur to his reactive onslaught against the moribund civilization the humanists had wrought, increasing his haste both to dismantle it and to erect an alternative base of value and thought. His sense of the urgency of the task, partly the result of recent personal experience and partly the symptomatic impatience of a mind obsessively and "forever bugged by time," strongly influenced the evolution of his prose style during this period. In the interests of projective velocity he was experimenting with a newly aggressive "presentation prose"—"not written but thrust." This was in fact but an accelerated version of his peremptory, dogmatic, propositional essay style of the past few years—itself an outgrowth of the Fenollosan telegrammatic style developed for *Call Me Ishmael*—done at the pace and with the immediacy of letter-writing (its products, indeed, were mostly worked-up versions of letters). It was pressed into service that February on a pair of ambitious but hasty, rambling and uneven essays.

The first, "Culture," lived up to its subtitle—"A Stab at Its Present Shape The Wild Guesses Necessary Fully Admitted To Be Such, Done To Get Things Started"—with a burst of highly provisional thinking. Here, after an introductory nod toward archaic heliocentric religions, the two main strains of humanism, "Hellenism & Hindooism," were dismissed with little difficulty; a third, "Hebraism," took more time, as the suddenly tentative essayist found himself once again immersed in quicksands of cultural conjecture about "that sheep-thick world" of ritual sacrifice and ceremonial eating explored in the previous summer's withheld missive to Creeley. The "Culture" essay's most animated moment came when the topic of cannibalism, always among Olson's favorites, was introduced by way of Jane Harrison, Pausanias and the Pelasgians—whose chieftain Lycaon had been a great exponent of human sacrifice. "The dimensions of [his] acts sound like the acts of a Founder, of a City-Founder and of a Religion-Founder," Olson commented. After sacrificing a baby to Zeus, Lycaon had been transformed into a wolf. Here was a vivid example of "the purer type" of leader, the wise ruler-priest whose acts become "LAWS."

Somewhat more cogent was a companion essay, "History," begun as one of Olson's sprawling letters to Creeley. The most extensive of his efforts in "presentation prose," it documented the latest chapters in his ongoing struggle to adapt projective methodology to the study of man's myths and past. Here he proposed a totalizing, in-the-round, Herodotean-"mythic" approach to history, one tailored to the atomic consciousness of post-1945 *Homo sapiens* and rendering obsolete the one-dimensional linear-discursive tracing of past event as practiced in classic Thucydidean analytical history. The atomic bomb itself, Olson suggested, was the product of a divisive historical tension between opposing and equally faulty analytic modes, the "twin lies" of "truth" as defined by the Platonists and the Christians and "fact" as defined by the Marxists. This crucial disjunction, the original decisive rationalist "SEPARATION . . . which has run us down," had eventually culminated in such uncomprehending intellectual errors as the attempt "to slide out any plane from a sphere and have anything more than a plane" (which was the chronic mistake of conventional cause-and-effect history) and the antinatural, suicidal unleashing of the destructive force of the atom.

To reverse the dissociated rationalist trend of Western thought and make history true to the post-modern experience of the world would require a radically revised historical methodology. In "History," Olson advocated abandoning such standard nineteenth-century historical concepts as teleology, "universal monotony" and the Marxist-Darwinist hobbyhorse "evolution," and at the same time replacing the traditional categorical "divisions of reality and investigations of same divisions" with an all-over "presentation" method that allowed the event to stand forth "as round and as multiple in its planes" as the world itself. By way of example he offered the farsighted geopolitical vision of Brooks Adams' *The New Empire* (a onetime Ezra Pound assignment, which he was now rereading), and demonstrated the continuing applicability of Adams' ideas by training them on recent manifestations of U.S. imperialism, from Far Eastern policy disasters like Hiroshima and Korea to the capitalist manipulation of consumption and promotion in stimulating the growth of markets ("a principle of pumping up wants and turning them into cravings, of creating artificial or superabundant human wants"). His primary commendation, however, was reserved for Herodotus, the poetic mythmaker-as-historian, whose procedures had lately been illuminated afresh for him by the commentary of J.A.K. Thomson in *The Art of Logos*. Herodotus' verb *'istorin,* Thomson showed, meant "finding out for oneself." " *'Herodotus is looking for the evidence'*—is it ever anything else that we such men who listen to Stories, *who make them up,* are looking for?" Post-modern poets like himself, Olson suggested, had to proceed as Herodotean explorers of reality, creatively annihilating the Platonic dissociation of *muthos* and *logos* ("fictitious narrative" vs. "fact") which had been so detrimental for so long.

Olson sent "History" to the ultraconservative journal *The Freeman*. While the essay was quickly rejected, his attempt had not been completely devoid of calculation. A recent issue of the same publication had contained Edward Dahlberg's impressive tribute to him as an "unsung pioneer" of Melville studies. Dahlberg, latterly descended to the meanest of free-lance wastelands yet no less than ever on the lookout for windmills to tilt, had put aside his bitterness toward Olson out of loyalty to the book he felt their failed relationship had fostered, and came now to its defense in the wake of an alleged plagiarization by an academic scholar. Smith College English professor Newton Arvin, contended Dahlberg, had made extensive unacknowledged borrowing of ideas and even phrasing from *Call Me Ishmael* in writing a recent National Book Award–winning Melville biography. Dahlberg supplied carefully prepared collations of comparable passages from the two books as evidence, and also made a point of protesting his own disinterestedness in championing his ex-protégé's out-of-print work, insisting he was not merely "trumpeting a friend" ("let it be known that Olson and I are strangered"). At once pleased, embarrassed and moved by the unexpected gesture, Olson allowed himself to fall into another sporadic round of correspondence with his onetime mentor; but the inevitable backwash of unresolved hard feelings doomed it to end once again in mutual recrimination. Nothing beyond a few old ideas remained to connect the former friends, and at this point in his life Olson had neither time nor intention to burden his mind with the ghosts of a personal past he had put so much energy into trying to bury.

The controversy created by Dahlberg's article stirred some belated interest in Olson as a Melville expert. Out of the blue he received an interesting assignment from the *New Republic,* to review several recent publications on Melville along with a centennial edition of *Moby-Dick*. Writing the piece, however, took months of grief and stalling. Engaging the daunting formalities of public discourse had never been easy for him, and for this occasion clearly the speedy headlong "presentation prose" wouldn't do. The April assignment was not completed until August. "The Weights and Measures of Herman Melville," which would appear in the magazine in two parts that fall, was nonetheless worth the trouble. Olson's identification with Melville remained a source of creative motivation for him, and it was quite possible to read his review as an illuminating progress report on his own ongoing experiments with employing language to register the "physicality" of space, the "actual experiencing of [its] *dimension* . . . its kinetic." That "non-Euclidean penetration of reality" here identified as the great prophetic advance of

Melville in *Moby-Dick* had previously been achieved in such degree by no other writer save Homer, Olson asserted. But the coming post-modern advances, he also implied, had to go even further, past Melville's Christ-obsession and Rimbaud's questioning of the other side of despair toward a new "totality, the condition of the Hero"—whose epic narrative, Olson now seemed to be signaling through the restraints of a relatively subdued prose, it would fall to him one day to undertake.

The call to solitary creation constantly beckoned, weakening Black Mountain's hold on him. Yet though he talked much about wanting to be left alone to write, he actually wrote little. "I would prefer to be alone," he told one correspondent, "but I love the young too much." Still he was becoming increasingly protective of his privacy, declaring his South Lodge flat off-limits to all but a few favored students and resisting even the most basic communal duties, making himself "damned unpopular by refusing to carry my lift of the stick . . . washing dishes, attending lunch, cutting wood." In March he managed to put in a few appearances at college board meetings to pitch his Institute plan. A small congregation of "men who in the present are pushing knowledge to the edge of the unknown," he proposed, would proceed on over the border into the unknown together, at once cracking open the known universe and elevating Black Mountain's academic status (the school would become a "twin" of the Institute of Advanced Studies at Princeton). In reality, however, the place was being kept going from one month to the next only on a wing and a prayer. The prayer, currently, was invested in a former student named Paul Williams, whom Olson estimated to be "worth untold millions." In 1952 Williams would supply the college with three emergency loans of $5,000 each, covering not only operating costs but the first of Olson's Institutes, yet still falling short of the patriarch's million-dollar expectations. Soon Olson and Williams were in a dispute over educational philosophy, with the ex-student challenging the "Great Man" concept implicit in Olson's plan for importing outside scholars.

The harried administrator's first thought upon getting word in April that the Wenner-Gren Foundation had finally granted him $2,500 was to use the money to "buy" himself some free time away from Black Mountain. He immediately asked Robert Creeley to return from Europe to substitute for him at the college, but understandably Creeley could not come on the spot. Forced to stay on at the helm, Olson continued to grumble unhappily about his teaching and administrative chores. He was too "fucking fatigued" even to answer Creeley's letters. He felt stale, thwarted. Worse, he was taking his tensions out on Connie, and she in turn was acting unresponsive, setting him off on new cycles of self-doubt. Casting around for any pretext to get away, he took a leave of absence to see to absentee rental problems with the Randolph Place apartment. After a brief stop in Washington, he went directly on to New York, where he stayed several nights with Frances.

His former Muse had lost little of her mysterious appeal. After months of feeling something was missing from his life, these latest "tremendously beautiful" days with her were for him a reconnection with the "real reality" of flesh and self. Once back in Washington he wrote to thank her for her renewed sexual instruction. "The sun of the body," sex was a deep principle or "logic" which had once moved archaic people to embrace the mysteries of cosmic rites; "sexual energy [was] absolutely the measure of the amount of life in a human being." Love, he promised Frances, was now "stay[ing] so alive" in him that he would not be able to do otherwise than to come to her "as soon, and as often, as I can make possible."

In his absence Connie had experienced much apprehension. One evening she and Mary Fiore were talking on the dining-hall porch when there was a brief spring shower, and then a rainbow appeared. "God's promise," Mary observed. "Don't say that," Connie admonished superstitiously. *"Charles* is God to me. And he *is* coming back." He had not been home long, however, before the telltale blue envelopes from New York started coming in again, mocking reminders for Connie of his distracted escapades of two years earlier. Though she revealed the reasons for it to no one, in the small, isolated community her unhappiness was hard to conceal. The more sensitive of their friends tried to help her through what was visibly a difficult time. In May, the thoughtful Wes Huss arranged to have her taken onto the college staff as registrar. Though the extra contribution to the family income was a minimal $25 a month, Connie was given the first indication she had a real place of her own at the college—where faculty wives, as one of them later commented, were customarily conceded only a "limited consciousness," like the women's choruses in Greek drama.

Charles' relations with Frances must meanwhile henceforth be "a matter of presences," he told her from Black Mountain; his current grueling "16 hour day" made letter-writing too much of a strain for him. Yet her letters had once again become a source of immediate inspiration. Responding to his latest ideas about sun worship and sexuality, she directed him to Rimbaud's poem "Credo in Unam" or "Soleil et chair," "Sun and Flesh." This "perfect response" gave him the makings of a lecture to his Black Mountain writing class. The gender shift from *unum* to *unam* in Rimbaud's Latin title transformed "God the Father [into] a goddess," Olson told his students. He was soon soliciting from Frances a complete translation of the French poem, which she dutifully supplied.

Questionings of his sexual identity returned once he had been away from

the Muse a few weeks, however. "He / in the dark stall," a rather awkward
and confused poem drafted in late May, hinted of sexual repression in symbolic terms. "Stalled" and blinded like the bull on the college farm, the poet
was in the dark about his own deeper motives, especially in playing the surrogate father to his youthful male charges. A figure of his own curbed power,
he was "randy, / and left, in the end, with young men."

He dreamed of ambiguous sexual encounters involving male students like
Nick Cernovich and a new favorite, Dan Rice, a handsome young apprentice
painter whose "real Western Levis and tough way with a cigarette" made him
the epitome of Black Mountain machismo. In Olson dreams Rice turned
from adoptive son into an enigmatic and menacing rival, blocking the frantic
patriarch's access to his own wife's bedroom. The "passion for men" Fielding
Dawson made out in the Olson of these years was driven by a strong, highly
sublimated "wish to engage," to at once befriend and lock horns with other
males.

Olson's continuing private worries over his "troubles of Androgyne" were
kept secret from everyone but Connie, however. In public he was capable of
crude displays of homophobia. When New York writer Paul Goodman,
notorious for his open advocacy of homosexuality during a Black Mountain
teaching stint two years earlier, returned to the college as an outside examiner
that June, Olson made a great show of snubbing him. Goodman returned to
New York and composed some arch verse on his unpleasant sojourn at Olson's
University. In response Olson pushed the debate a further unedifying step
with a loud, low vernacular blast of his own, "Black Mt. College Has a Few
Words for a Visitor," sarcastically crediting his adversary with the ability to
"corrupt an army." That it was *his* army threatened with corruption by the
outsider-seducer was of course the college patriarch's principal concern.

The Arts Institute Olson had set up for the summer was scheduled in two
sessions, during the first of which he himself was freed from teaching. The
break allowed him to get away alone to Washington. He claimed he wanted
to get some writing done, but Connie suspected ulterior motives. They had
a fight the night before he was to leave. He was following his own feelings
and ignoring hers as always, she said. She'd "never felt recognized" in their
relationship, and was having thoughts of terminating it. He defended himself
feebly, and in the morning caught a bus north.

Sharing Randolph Place with the "unbearable" Frank Moore in 98-degree
heat soon reduced Olson to the state of a "fried bug." He gave up all thought
of planned writing projects and headed straight for New York, where the
reunion with Frances was even more heady than that of the spring. "By touch,
and a new nakedness," as D. H. Lawrence had put it in a poem Olson sent

on to her in advance of his arrival, she once again helped him achieve the "Resurrection of the Flesh." On the bus back to Washington he experienced a recurrence of mystical solar "illumination," sensing a "sun inside" transforming him with a radiant inward heliotropism. ("The moment you love, there is a SUN born, a sun inside yourself.")

His visions of creative immanence ever more in conflict with a looming exchange society that would soon elect a Republican administration, he found himself opposing the spreading pernicious and vulgar influence of "massman" in a third verse letter for his *Maximus* sequence, written shortly after he got back from the Washington–New York trip. The outrage of "Letter 3" was directed at a sweeping wave of commercialism that was inundating with cheapness even Gloucester, the place that had been since his boyhood Olson's beloved emblem of what remained of value in America. "O tansy city," the poet exhorted, "root city / let them not make you / as the nation is." But in fact the real city of Gloucester was shown by his poem to be as much a lost cause as the rest of the culture, all its individuality washed out by the pervasive mediocre mass-market totality. Between the lines of the poet's hortatory address to his sea-city one makes out vague outlines of the neo-archaic stronghold of his imagination, the projective city-state Black Mountain, last sanctum of idealistic dissent within the cultural wasteland of "Big Boy, the emerging World State" and a place where it was still possible "to invert totality—to oppose it—by discovering the totality of any-every-single-one of us."

Ironically, Olson's backwoods nation-within-a-nation, his self-created "Polis [of] a few," seemed at times to make more desperate sense as an idea in proportion as it became less manageable as a reality. This summer session of 1952, though to be remembered by some as the last great summer of Black Mountain, was for him a time of conflict and withdrawal, with his postmodern dominion and position as "King of the Mountain" coming under implicit challenge from outsiders he'd brought in for his Arts Institute.

Foremost of these projected rivals, and like Olson himself a charismatic figure with strong ego and imposing physical presence, was the New York abstract expressionist painter Franz Kline, whose hard-drinking, intense personal style, easily as mystique-laden as Olson's own, won him an immediate awed following among the lawgiver's cadre—for whose attentions he briefly bested even Olson. Kline appears to have quickly recognized Olson's anxious projection of a competitive tension and to have taken a certain mischievous pleasure in exploiting it. Once, with students looking on, the painter bluntly asked Olson his age, then confidently asserted, "I am older than you are." In truth the discrepancy in ages was a matter of mere months, but the visiting contender's point had been scored. On other occasions Kline engaged with evident delight in subtly undercutting the college patriarch's abstract intellectualizing, sinking one Olson monologue in midstream by interjecting an off-the-wall comment about how a nearby parked car looked like a bakery truck. Behind the apparent non sequitur lay all Kline's powerful attention to the real world of things. Here, it was obvious to students, was a down-to-earth, no-nonsense alternative version of the creative mind in action: an artist who could see the world as bakery trucks clearly had the jump on one who habitually saw it as a mere provocation to cerebral activity. Kline's unpredictable, regular-guy instinctiveness, moreover, was problematic *per se* for Olson, who despite his high theoretical valuation of nonlinear behavior was made very uneasy when anyone "didn't behave according to plan." In a predictable defensive reaction, he attempted to dismiss Kline, Jack Tworkov (a painting instructor in the first Arts Institute session) and the rest of their New York painter ilk as "space cadets," brilliant yet deficient in intellectual foundations. But the damage-control effort had only limited success. "A man had come to the school," as one student noted, "a guy . . . who would not let Olson manipulate [him]." Olson might still reign supreme as thinker and talker, but for a month or two at least "Franz was the man."

John Cage, the avant-garde composer and Zen philosopher, represented a threat of a less obvious kind. Each a noted proponent of artistic indeterminacy, Olson and Cage were nonetheless quite unlike personally, with Cage much the cooler-headed of the two, by nature disinclined to heavy gestures and somewhat puzzled—if not put off—by Olson's sudden heats and mood swings (the composer later commented on the "softness" of Olson's character, as well as on his shortcomings as a college administrator). Olson, for his part, seems to have regarded Cage with much the same mixture of respect and distrust that had earlier marked his relations with an innovative guru of another artistic medium, Buckminster Fuller. He suspected Cage, like Fuller, of a fundamental lack of seriousness. And notwithstanding his own expressionist's faith in improvisation, he felt a certain contempt for the mechanical reliance on chance as a compositional element that lay at the basis of Cage's aesthetic, finding it altogether too programmatic and technology-bound. Indeed, the progressive composer's facility with "anecdote," "magnetic tape" and other "tricks" came under oblique attack this summer in Olson's poem "A Toss," addressed to Cage and allied avant-garde experimenters.

Cage's indirect reply came in an evening of ultimate show-stealing that culminated the summer Institute, when he drafted the poet-host to play the straight man in a performance piece that would become legendary as the world's first "Happening." Olson's verse, distributed among students in the audience and recited earnestly by the poet himself from a stepladder perch, was drowned out in the ambient informational context, a chaotic sea of seemingly unrelated activity and noise that included Edith Piaf records played at double time, crying babies, barking dogs, David Tudor on piano performing a Cage chance composition, and the composer himself calmly cruising through an all but inaudible lecture on Zen. As entrepreneur of the overall summer proceedings the evidently puzzled Olson had to keep to himself any misgivings inspired by these proceedings, but those few of his remaining faculty colleagues to harbor traditionalist aesthetic leanings were at less pains to conceal their view of the event as the nadir of his Institute. Halfway through it, his friend Stefan Wolpe, college music teacher, a respected composer in his own right and onetime theatrical collaborator of Bertolt Brecht, stomped out in disgust. Later, as the Cagean cacophony droned on, Johanna Jalowetz, teacher of bookbinding and voice, widow of former music teacher Heinrich Jalowetz, lamented that Black Mountain had sunk "deep in the Middle Ages."

The most comfortable moments enjoyed by Olson around any of his professional guest talent that summer seem to have been spent with dance teacher Merce Cunningham, whose classes he attended as an informal student, participating in prescribed exercises and rehearsals. "Merce of Egypt," an Olson poem in which the dancer becomes a figure out of an Egyptian fresco, is a testament of this involvement, as is Cunningham's memorable comment on his large pupil's surprising physical agility—that of a "light walrus." In a period of many repressions and frustrations, the dance became Olson's "therapy, one of the very few means of sexual approach he allowed himself."

18

Inland Waters
(1952–1953)

Olson's 1952 summer Arts Institute lost the school $7,000 and left him feeling wrung out and strangely unfulfilled. Around Labor Day, seeking a break before the resumption of his college labors—and perhaps also seeking the peace of mind to decide whether to return for the fall session at all, or to buy writing time with the Wenner Gren money, or even to follow through on his grant promise and actually return to Central America—he withdrew with Connie and Kate to Washington, where they repossessed the Randolph Place apartment from Frank Moore.

Moore moved out in a cloud of acrimony. He and Charles got in an argument over unpaid utility bills, and then after Moore had gone, some gentian-violet athlete's-foot medication he'd left behind was discovered and swallowed by the "oral as all get out" eleven-month-old Kate, inducing convulsions and emergency hospitalization. Olson blamed Moore for the accident, and, close though they'd once been, refused to forgive his former friend, henceforth dismissing him as "a part of me I won't keep acquainted with." He also disdained paying the sizable hospital bill.

The medicine-swallowing episode convinced Connie that confinement in a one-bedroom inner-city apartment was not the right thing for Kate. She would prefer to see their child raised at Black Mountain, where there was at least some space and convivial company, like her friends the Husses and the

Fiores. Charles' late-night Washington social rounds left her alone with the baby too often to suit her, and she could feel the emotional distance between them widening. She lobbied for an early return to North Carolina, but he delayed, claiming literary projects demanded his attention.

Discussions of same with publishing contacts—as he explained his intentions to Connie—took him off to New York in late September. The contact, he didn't, however, add, was with Frances, who was now working as a book designer at Doubleday and had been trying to talk editors there into undertaking an Anchor paperback reprint of *Call Me Ishmael*. But the venture led to nothing, businesswise, and once back in Washington he quickly saw that going had been a serious tactical mistake. Connie, accurately guessing the real motives of his trip, confronted him in an emotional scene that ended with her in tears, begging his help in arranging that they separate, and him in a state of guilty confusion, understanding only that they had reached the low point in their marriage.

The new fall session at Black Mountain was to feature a Crafts Institute Olson had labored to set up, but when the time came for leaving, he felt too edgy and depressed to go. He phoned instead, offering excuses involving problems with his landlady. A week later the college board notified him that his presence was required immediately. He wired back pleading his need for a "REST." Another prod in mid-October also failed to stir him. "STILL FINDING I NEED RESTORATION AS WRITER AND EDUCATOR," said his telegram of reply. Connie at that point took Kate and went back to Black Mountain without him, resuming her registrar's duties as he lingered on at Randolph Place, eventually winning the college's official acquiescence in the leave of absence he had already taken. (Poet Hilda Morley, the wife of Stefan Wolpe, was appointed Olson's temporary substitute as writing teacher.)

Left alone, Charles had trouble actually finding the rest he'd sought. Though it had been mutually agreed-upon, there could be little comfort for him in what amounted to a trial separation from Connie, who in the strained last days just before her departure had brought him up short by pointing out to him that he'd never been able to "rest in a close relationship," a truth he now had to unhappily acknowledge. Yet he was no sooner deprived of her stabilizing influence than his depression and confusion grew deeper than ever. Something seemed radically wrong. While a psychological study of poets in which he'd taken part a few years earlier had confirmed his unusually "high tolerance for disorder," he'd never undergone formal analysis, an omission he decided to correct forthwith by attempting a thoroughgoing psychiatric self-examination. Performed with the aid of select analytical texts, it would probe the hidden roots of feelings of self-estrangement that had long plagued him.

The pursuit of self was soon all-absorbing. He began to sort through his "whole life back to backwards," trying, if not to restore order, then to see what sense could be made of the chaos. "What I am in," he enigmatically informed Cid Corman, "is something only I could get into. . . . it is one of those central crucial engagements some men do, I suppose, walk up to (in the dark, &, I guess, in the middle of life). Anyhow, it is wholly exclusive & excluding—allows nothing in but itself." The only person entrusted with the "crucial privacies" thus discovered was Connie, who became the recipient of long confessional letters secured from prying eyes at the college by special postal-tape seals he'd devised. These epistles recounted the day-by-day and hour-by-hour tracking-down of his "UNC," or unconscious, the final quarry in his self-investigative hunt. Written immediately upon waking in early evening after all-day "huge sleeps," they were a collation of various evidences: a turbulent and abundant dream life which he'd begun recording in a special journal, solitary nocturnal meditations on sexual and family history, and consultations of classic sources like Otto Fenichel's *Psychoanalytic Theory of Neurosis* and Carl Jung's *Psychology of Religion* and *The Integration of the Personality*.

His experimental self-analysis was soon taking an increasingly sober turn, as it dawned on him that much of what he considered unique in his own psychic makeup could appear as mere common neurotic symptom when seen in the hard clinical light of a basic Freudian casebook like Fenichel's. The latter's chapter on character disorders became a particular mine of grievous revelation for him; atop its first page, he scrawled "Fear Shame Disgust Guilt," and inside he heavily underscored and annotated the psychiatric commentary on " 'bossy' authority types," individuals whose excessive display of verbal powers as a defense against anxiety masks a sexually passive state. These "actors of reality," suggested Fenichel, tended to believe themselves the cause of everything that happened to them, and thus unconsciously evolved from actors into directors. "Stage Manager Olson dies hard," the amateur psychic sleuth was meaningfully reminded.

Absorbed in his personal campaign to become "President of his own Disunited States," on election day, November 4, he slept through most of the Eisenhower / Stevenson presidential contest, his disturbing erotic dreams—in one his mother was sitting on his knee in a provocative way, in another he discovered Connie *in flagrante delicto* with a stranger—lending him the text for a series of letters to Connie concerning the current "paralysis" of their sex life. He poured out in painful stages his analysis of the "unconscionable deadlock" that had befallen them as lovers, blaming much of the trouble on his own inability to reconcile the "living act" of his writing life with the "living fact" of flesh and feeling—yet ironically reduced, even in his gentle and contrite arguments, to putting forward that writing self in place of actual emotional contact with her.

At some point in the evening he went out to mail the letters to his wife, and on the way home stopped off to glance without much interest at the Eisenhower celebrations on a friend's television set. Back at Randolph Place, he returned his attention to the business of self-analysis, producing the one piece of published writing to come out of this most introspective of times: "The Present Is Prologue," a brief note on his growing consciousness of the influence in his own life of those "founders who [lay] buried" there, his parents. The short essay served a double use, in extending his self-investigation a further step and as his response to a biographical questionnaire from a forthcoming reference work on twentieth-century authors. He dispatched a copy to Connie to follow up on his election-night letters.

This time the mail brought back an unexpected disclosure: she, too, had been doing some reviewing of the past. To get to the bottom of their marital problems, she now suggested, perhaps her experiences as well as his own ought to be taken into account. She proceeded to offer a history of her unspoken doubts and frustrations in the relationship, culminating in the crushing—for him—revelation that as a result of her failure to be made emotionally "complete" by him, she had sought fulfillment in a secret love affair with a Washington artist friend of theirs.

A totally devastated Charles retroactively experienced the jealous husband's gamut of emotions, becoming first irrationally angry ("This is the end. . . . this proves all women are betrayers"), then remorseful and self-pitying, finally abject and conciliatory. The more he mulled over Connie's abrupt revelation, the more he was led to the difficult but unavoidable admission that he'd brought the "betrayal" on himself by unreasonably expecting her to tolerate his own infidelity—and by all along unfairly depriving her of any real feeling of self-worth. His "will to power" and compulsion to manage other people's lives were purely destructive. His disgust with himself, however, could only lead him deeper into destruction. Cruising the city streets in a distracted stupor, he ran over a young black girl who seemed to appear out of nowhere in front of his car. The accident left him in a shaky state, and he had to call on Rufus King, a radical lawyer friend of Caresse Crosby's who had helped him out in the past, to get him through a court hearing. Fortunately, the victim's injuries were not serious, and her parents agreed to sign a waiver releasing him from liability. Relieved, he pressed on the child a doll given him by friends as a Christmas present for Kate. Afterward, nearly overwhelmed by his humiliation and shame over all that had been happening, he could articulate to Creeley only a strangled complaint about the string of "damned days" he'd come into, during which everything in his life seemed to be rapidly "accelerating down hill."

The near brush with automotive manslaughter seemed to mark a turning point in his personal crisis, and he began to pull himself together, aided by a new expert guide, one Connie had been strongly recommending—the Swiss psychologist Jung, whose alternative mode of analysis did not take long to prove more suitable to Olson's poetic tastes than the "biological and evolutionary" approaches of clinicians like Freud and Fenichel. (Their influence, he now began to suspect, had led him down a dangerous blind alley in his first round of self-investigations.) His newfound enthusiasm for Jung represented a complete turnabout from the peremptory estimate he had made upon their one personal meeting at Harvard in 1938. On that occasion the distinguished visitor had been dismissed by the immodest graduate student as "soft," "pretentious," a "lazy fraud." But events in the interim had made Olson much more receptive to a psychology of the soul, as well as to Jung's cosmic philosophy of archetypes. Within a few weeks of his first serious look into the texts, he was calling Jung a "great man," one who, he was further elated to find, seemed to have "done all his work just to meet me now." He was even sufficiently roused by the discovery to consider Black Mountain business for the first time in some months, dashing off a letter to Jung in Zurich to invite him to a spring 1953 New Sciences of Man Institute, the "true center or radix" of which would be—Olson had just made up his mind—"the morphology of what you alone have with precision called the soul." (Jung declined to attend in person but agreed to send a trusted assistant as his personal emissary.)

Jung's structural model of dream analysis greatly facilitated the progress of interior examination. It did not take long for "hidden myths" to begin emerging. One night in late November, Olson's sleep returned him to a "buried scene" which—as he would shortly explain to Connie—contained hints of a childhood event underlying his present problematic condition of sexual passivity. In this "source" dream, he found himself back at Norman Avenue in Worcester, listening in terror as from his parents' bedroom there came what seemed his "father's cry." Creeping up to their door to investigate, however, he got a peek not of his parents in their bed, but of Connie, aggressively libidinous, straddling the passive, "helpless, & 'used' " figure of Frank Moore. This unsettling dream projection of Moore as his "doppelganger" would not be soon forgotten, hanging on in his imagination at least long enough to supply the otherwise mystifying conclusion to one of his most enigmatic as well as one of his finest poems, "The Librarian"—"Who is / Frank Moore?"

Jungian theory would also prove helpful in persuading his wife to forgive his extramarital affair. (The matter of Frances, after all, remained the biggest single issue between them.) In his letters to Connie he now referred to that affair as a "sickness," even justifying a quick trip to New York to see Frances as an attempt to rid himself of his debilitating habit of anima-projection— that is, of identifying his own "inward face" or "feminine soul" with a real woman whose autonomous identity was thereby obscured for him. "She was only some vehicle," he retroactively rationalized Frances to Connie. "She was an anima, and until I'd dealt with my unconscious, I'd more and more exaggerate this person until all possible harm would be done—I would be destroyed, and you too."

As it was, the strain of the trial separation and the emotional upheavals that had come with it had been no easier on Connie than on him. In mid-December the experiment ended suddenly, when she suffered a stress-induced nervous collapse and he was urgently summoned to Black Mountain to be at her side. It took her several weeks of bed rest, attended by a hired nurse while Kate was looked after by Charles, to regain the strength to pick up her registrar's duties—and even then, as her newly considerate husband reported to Creeley, she remained for some time "a very shaken lady."

In whatever capacity—father, lover or nursemaid—Charles himself was greatly relieved to be back with his brood, thankful even, as he indicated in the January 1953 "Songs of Maximus," for "the blessing / that difficulties are once more"; in such fat times, after all, the material austerities of Black Mountain became almost salutary, and resistance to easy solutions a necessary virtue: "In the land of plenty, have / nothing to do with it."

"Man is estranged from that with which he is most familiar," the Heraclitus paradox he'd made a motto in personal and historical investigations of the past year, was again the keynote of his latest and most extensive effort to refound from archaic makings a culture for the "mythological present": a series of eight lectures for his New Sciences of Man Institute, delivered on Sunday nights in February and March to highlight the new college session. The lectures, drafted hurriedly in the first weeks of 1953, offered "a chance for me to draw together all the sort of 'research' I've started the last five years." With characteristic long reach he set out to address "the totality of the problem of the phenomenon of man" through the related "sciences" of archaeology, culture morphology and mythology. For the hard evidence to back up his ambitious conjecture he had hoped to be able to rely on a panel of distinguished experts, including Carl Sauer talking on Place, English archaeologist Christopher Hawkes on Culture, Carl Jung on Mythology. Instead he had to make do with a pair of replacement guest lecturers, neither one much to his liking in the actual event. Jung's proxy, the Austrian folklorist Marie-Louise von Franz, bored him with her typological interpretations of fairy tales (and at the same time won over his students sufficiently to provide a new source of competitive distraction), while the fastidious field reports of Robert Braidwood, a Near Eastern specialist from the University of Chicago Oriental Institute, impressed him most as further proof that though archaeology was still a far "cleaner" discipline than psychology, "even . . . an archaeologist [was] a very dull knife to have to work with."

Following the close of his New Sciences Institute at the end of March, Olson was free of teaching until the summer. With over half the Wenner-Gren money already spent, he made up his mind against attempting another Central American venture, and instead stayed on at the college as writer-in-residence, drawing a minimal salary. "Hopped up and put deep" by the arrival from Mallorca of the first copy of *In Cold Hell, in Thicket,* the volume of his poems nominally published as *Origin* 8 but in fact obligingly (and tastefully) produced and edited by Creeley as "stand-in" for Cid Corman, he was eager to start on a new writing project. (Even a disheartening response to the verse from William Carlos Williams—"I was reared an imagist and if the image is not put down clearly I tend to become lost"—could not spoil Olson's pleasure in the more or less homemade Creeley family production, particularly his delight with Ann Creeley's cover drawing of Paleolithic cattle, "utterly Indical" of his current intentions in writing.)

That spring, a former student, Jonathan Williams, wrote from Germany (where he was stationed with the U.S. Army) asking for some Olson verse to print as a book. The request "pushed the button" for a "run" of *Maximus* poems. In the first three weeks of April, Olson drafted six new pieces which, added to the four already completed (including his recent "Songs of Maximus"), would make up *The Maximus Poems 1–10* to be issued that fall from Williams' fledgling Jargon Press. An initial wave of excited composition soon gave way to extensive revision done before the typescript was sent on to Williams in early May. The main problem was establishing tone and voicing, to a large extent a matter of trial and error. The forward "tracking" of the work involved abrupt leaps in the narrative: "displacements are the bloody life of it," as Olson soon discovered. Yet sustaining the tactic of narrative displacement, characteristic mode of the single projective poem, over the longer stretches of the "serial universe"—he hinted to Creeley he had the musical experiments of Boulez in mind as a possible formal model—was clearly not going to be easy. In extending the *Maximus* sequence even as far as ten interconnected pieces, "hooked to hook," he quickly sensed the "field play [of] the single poem get[ting] too jazzed up," and found himself once again impeded by his lack of strategy just at the brink of a breakthrough, faced with a "damn delay due to developing difficulties of this new form biz, this Max thing, now that it is clearly running ahead toward some length of act." The potential epic dimensions of the project prompted heroic metaphors of the creative quest. None came more naturally than Ahab's pursuit of the great whale, a chase with which Olson in his own obsessive drives had always strongly identified. "Very much am caught by the bastard," he put it to his friend on April 24, "but, after i [thought I] had the final mss done . . . it almost pulled me over-board! that is, i was so damn pleased i had a big one, i forgot the oars! . . . and for this week i have been writing, to pull in, and at the same time allow more line."

By May 3, however, with the manuscript revisions for Williams now dispensed with, the wind was up again and he was once more off and running, feeling a "damned good break" opening the way for him as he sped forward through the thirteenth "Letter" of the open-ended set, "The Song and Dance of." "This thing keeps looming," he reported with a certain awe to Creeley, "looks as tho it is the vehicle [I've] been looking for so fucking damn long, to keep me at it day in & year out. . . . What rides me is, that it does damn well invoke all the damned dispersions I have been so busy abt practically the whole of [my life]. . . . the appetite, just now, is to keep whaling the hell out of it in a steady go, drive it, and see. . . . I have started so many birds of it not yet brought down I have to watch that the gun don't haul me up into the air, from firing itself dizzy." He worked on through many frustrations in a confident unknowingness, pushing ahead as far as "Letter 22" by the end of June.

On two consecutive Sundays in August he crowned that summer's Arts Institute by reading aloud from printer's proofs of the first ten *Maximus* poems, as well as from in-progress manuscripts of numbers 11–30. (Of the latter, many would eventually be rewritten or discarded.) For his audience of students and friends in the college dining hall—those loyal "islands of men and girls," the discrete persons of his tiny model *polis*—there was predictably a general bafflement in the face of the work's referential and allusive onslaught, "all those nouns and dates, the histories . . . that constant obsessive fix on details." But as Fielding Dawson remarks, there was also great power in the image of Olson's poetic commitment to intellectual adventure, an evident "massive singleness" of purpose compelling all that difficult material into some grand shape of impressive size if as yet largely imperceptible outline. This was the poet Olson had made of himself, the artist as reality-maker, "like a creative child, rearranging his life and the world so that it will all be at his fingertips."

The willful, idiosyncratic nature of the undertaking was evident in the sometimes conflicting multiplicity of the "dispersions" incorporated by Olson into his unfolding epic. A major division of mode and intent that would continue to generate tension for the work as a whole appeared as early as these spring and summer 1953 pieces, in which the disjunctive narrative oscillated somewhat unstably between, on the one hand, a paratactic dispos-ing of seventeenth-century New England and Gloucester factual history, rendering emblematic specific actions and instances by the force of a hortatory ethical tone; and on the other, a lyrical figuration of personal "inner" history instanced as dream revelation.

The first of these two approaches, which dominated, furnished his poem's geohistorical background and moral landscape, as he encapsulated within his poetic critique of seventeenth-century "nascent capitalism" (seen in the Puritan settlers' proclivity for the profitable exploitation of the earth and human exchange) the germ of his larger cultural charge against the prevailing "pejorocracy" of the American present. His experiments with the second, inner-historical approach—arguably the outcome of his recent intensive self-analysis—represented the real breakthrough for him, however, particularly in the eighteenth Letter, "The Twist," a kind of pivot poem in which the *Maximus*' first astute critic, Ed Dorn, would detect "a turning of the human attitude," a new modulation of feeling in Olson's poetry as a whole.

> *Trolley-cars*
> *are my inland waters . . .*
>
> *As dreams are, when the day*
> *encompasses . . .*
>
> *I run my trains*
> *on a monorail, I am seized*
> *—not so many nights ago—*
> *by the sight of the river*
> *exactly there at the Bridge*
>
> *where it goes out & in*
>
> *I recognize*
> *the country not discovera*
> *the marsh behind, the ditch that Blynman made, the dog-rocks*
> *the tide roars over*

"The nouns seem to calm themselves here, and take on the sheerings and simplicity of immediate knowledge which resides together in what is more felt, the searching substances of the inscribed field of Gloucester," Dorn would observe in his essay "What I See in *The Maximus Poems.*"

After writing "The Twist," an elated Olson indicated to Creeley his sense that he'd made a quantum leap as a poet. The verse of *In Cold Hell*—that is, the best of the poems he'd written up to now—would henceforth cease to be the measure of the possibilities of his art. Suddenly his "song [was] so much deeper, & wilder . . . a real razzle-dazzle. . . . No holds. And freedoms all over the place."

For the poet who had felt "barricaded" all his life, the creative release in an access of actual production had to be exhilarating. At the same time, he was moving forward into uncharted territory, and the confusions and mysteries of the advance were unsettling, particularly to the frustrated scholar and fact-seeker in him. Unsure and seeking guidance in his Cape Ann studies, he addressed a letter of inquiry to his former history professor and patron saint in the art of "saturation" research, Frederick Merk, deliberately concealing the fact that it was a poem he was working on—"aware I'd scare him / off," as he put it in "Letter 23," "*mutbologos* has lost such ground since Pindar." But the gods of Olson's myths, thus far at least, were *men*, the presumed agents of history. And the mythic ground of his poem so far was equally unconventional, a compound of fact and dream blurring the demarcations between them, defying the accepted boundaries of history and fable. "I would be a historian as Herodotus was, looking / for oneself," he announced in "Letter 23," a sort of declaration of purpose composed after his Merk correspondence and concurrent discovery of English historian Frances Rose-Troup's *John White, the Patriarch of Dorchester and the Founder of Massachusetts*—an invaluable data-source on the Dorchester Company's efforts to settle a "fisherman's ffield" at Stage Head on Cape Ann in 1623.

Yet despite such proclamations he was prey to lingering uncertainties about how to proceed. In late October, he wrote to Frances, whose judgment he continued to trust on essential creative matters, that "Letter 23" was "the hump, of the book. . . . I have stayed unsatisfied that the movement of the poem from that point is right." He was stymied by what would for some time remain the overriding formal question of his epic, a poem including history that already stubbornly refused to stay simply that: "the dilemma of history versus art. . . . It is 'history' (and of my own front yard, Gloucester) which has me engaged blindly, stupidly. . . ." Although at least the ten poems that had just been published by Jonathan Williams in Stuttgart still appeared to him "solid," he had growing doubts about much of the later work done in summer and early fall, and would delay publishing the next volume, *11–22*, for three years. Even then, looking back over both early volumes, he would reject the historical and economic focus not only of the withheld poems but of some of those he'd chosen to publish. They represented "an unlived area . . . a numb point" for him, insistences on themes that in hindsight he felt he'd have "better [kept his] mouth shut on." After the productive burst of 1953, the creative quandaries suggested by such remarks conspired with life events to impede further progress on the epic until the poet's return to Gloucester.

19

Chinese Monastery or Hill-fort
(1953–1956)

The last man of the place
dreamed
of 14 persons on this hillside
like the mountain in the Chinese classic
to whom all those repaired who were useless,
the empire had become that good it was impossible
it was so dull, the court had no use
for the imperial instructor in fencing,
the greatest wrestler in the nation . . .

In his poem "Obit," Olson would address the increasingly fugitive condition of life in the last years of Black Mountain. The disparate citizens of the place may have disagreed about many things, but they had one essential thing in common: in a centralizing time, all were wanderers of life's side roads, conscious dissenters from the monolithic secular empire that America was rapidly in the process of becoming. The test of exile and isolation was to grow even more severe, significantly thinning the renegade ranks at Olson's "Chinese monastery or hill-fort."

What one can say, is . . .
                    there are people
who ran, when others stayed, and some
got down

For those who stayed, Black Mountain became less a college than a refuge, gradually shedding the last vestiges of conventional academic form. One puzzled visitor from the outside world in the fall of 1953 came away with an impression of having stepped into an anachronistic, run-down "company convent," with a mountain-man of a poet presiding as crazy head monk. All around Olson, his "monastery" and its hilly grounds were slowly reverting to a natural state. Quail and wild mountain aster were repossessing the college grounds. Mountain lions were said to lurk the winter hills, foxes ran the main road and rattlesnakes nested in the bushes along its margins; copperheads and kudzu vines were infiltrating the foundations of the cottages. Leaves littered unused type cases in the print shop. The coal bin had caved in, and trash piled up in unsightly mounds in abandoned Studies Building cubicles whose missing windows were covered over with cardboard and tape. Still Olson stayed, and got down.

By fall 1953 the student body had dwindled, according to the best estimates, to fifteen. Nine faculty members remained: Olson, Wes Huss, Flola Shepard, Stefan Wolpe, Nell Rice, painting teacher Joe Fiore, ceramics arts teachers Karen Karnes and David Weinrib, and farm manager Doyle Jones. (Shepard, Rice and Jones, none particularly friendly to Olson, would be the next defectors from his *de facto* regime.) To save on operating costs, the surviving college population retreated from the communal dining hall and dormitories on the lower property to disperse into the hillside cottages—where meals were now separately taken, enhancing the general sense of isolation. For firewood to heat the cottages, Breughelesque bands of student woodsmen fanned out into the college forests, gradually depleting venerable stands of oak, hickory and pine. By the end of that school year, the woods had suffered even more sweeping reductions, as logging rights were sold off to lumber companies for cash to prop up Olson's shaky little *polis*—thus establishing a precedent soon turned by continuing exigency into a routine, as by the middle of the following winter the college beef herd and farm were also sacrificed to auction and leasing.

Distracted from his writing by the school's unending money troubles, Olson found himself throwing much time and creative energy into fundraising schemes. To his perpetual chagrin, these schemes ended for the most part in futility. At Meadows Inn, the cottage whose upstairs apartment he and Connie had been allotted in the first stage of the fallback to the hills, he arranged to have as downstairs neighbor the affluent ex-student Paul Williams, whom he'd lured back to the school in the informal capacity of resident architect. Already the holder of a $25,000 interest-free mortgage note secured by the college farm, Williams was at this point largely responsible for Black Mountain's survival. Olson, however, had dreams of far more. Never quite able to get his mind off the tantalizing prospect of "Williams, with his wealth, under me!" he was greatly disappointed when, a few weeks into the term, the architect not only walked out on Black Mountain but did so in order to join John Cage, David Tudor, M. C. Richards and others in founding a rival experimental community venture outside New York.

In November, after the Williams departure, the Olsons relocated to the "Jalo house." Built in 1941 according to the architectural and acoustic specifications of former college composer and music teacher Heinrich Jalowetz (and made available by another recent departure, that of Jalowetz' widow, Johanna), the house was rigorously modernist in design, with "phoney spaces" that were a slight embarrassment to the neo-archaic chieftain in Olson. Still he could not deny that he now had the "fucking best house" at Black Mountain.

He would need it, in the winter of desperation ahead. By the beginning of December the cash shortage was bad enough to force the faculty into voting to close down the school through the rest of the winter. Salary payments would be deferred, and the faculty would exist on subsistence food rations provided from the farm's last season of production. During the period of closure, which continued until late March 1954, Olson, with the assistance of Huss and Fiore, worked to put together a major sale of college landholdings, but was constrained at the last minute by the intervention of Flola Shepard and Stefan Wolpe, who had been away attempting to raise money in New York and not privy to his proposal. When the big sale plan collapsed, immediate debts had to be met with the proceeds of a much smaller transaction involving a few unused acres on a remote corner of the property. Shepard was meanwhile making a bid to have control of the school turned over to outside trust officers. "I am not practical," Olson admitted to Creeley; on the other hand, no one else was willing to step into the breach. To consolidate his own authority, one day he informed Wes Huss, more or less casually, "I'll be rector." With the treasurer's help, his informal control of the school thus became official. He now was, as he boasted in a note to Frances, "monarch of all I survey . . . 550 acres, a farm of 175 acres worth 50,000 dollars, a stock of Herefords larger than Kulikowski's."

The school's operating budget for the new spring term was virtually microscopic. Still, out of it, and as one of his first priorities in rectorial capacity, Olson apportioned $500 for starting up a literary magazine to be edited by Creeley—the *Black Mountain Review*. The first issue, which arrived a few months later from Mallorca, introduced a group of writers of which, as Creeley later said, "Olson was to prove [the] center almost singlehandedly." It was kicked off by one of the best of the 1953 *Maximus* pieces, "On first Looking out through Juan de la Cosa's Eyes," a stirring projective summoning of a geomythic New World "mappemunde . . . out of the mists . . . out of mermaids & Monsters." Following the ambitious lead, the magazine proposed a whole new mapping of the American literary landscape. "We felt, all of us, a great distance from the more conventional magazines of the time," Creeley says. All the major contributors, in this initial issue as in the half-dozen to follow—whether student writers, like Edward Dorn, Joel Oppen-heimer, Michael Rumaker and Fielding Dawson; or unaffiliated but clearly aligned sympathizers and Creeley contacts from the alternative poetic fringes, like Denise Levertov, Paul Blackburn and Larry Eigner; or comparatively senior figures like Robert Duncan and Olson himself—were cultural out-siders, disqualified by lack of social, academic and professional standing from the mainstream literary life of a time of extreme monocultural dominance. The *Black Mountain Review,* with its tough-guy ethic of resistance, was the self-conscious declaration of an opposing front, alienated but assiduous in its attentions and concerns. The evident seriousness of its counterstatement, together with the elegant reductiveness of Creeley's editing and design, made it the most effective vehicle to date for Olson's post-modern agenda.

While snow accumulated on the pine boughs and icy mists hung over the lake, there were long, difficult nights at the Jalo house. Sensing he'd once more lost the momentum of his energies and was stuck in a bleak "hole in the pavement" as real life passed him by, Olson had trouble concentrating and quarreled pointlessly with Connie. The cooped-up hours were made tenser by further intrusions of the federal government's fell shadow. FBI men came "snooping" again, and there was also an unwelcome guest from the U.S. Treasury Department, demanding to know why Olson hadn't filed a tax return for his Wenner-Gren grant money. Though Wes Huss helped him through the immediate anxiety of these latest ordeals, Olson, left with a troubling "general sense the enemy is up to something," grew increasingly agitated and distracted. The time lay heavy on him in his mountain lair, and when he let on as much to his businessman friend Jean Riboud (who had gone to work for the Schlumberger oilfield-equipment firm, giving Olson dreams of "oil money from Houston" for his needy school), Riboud offered a promising escape, proposing to take him and Connie off on a holiday to Mexico. But business came up that forced Riboud to cancel the Mexican trip, leaving Olson more restless and frustrated than ever.

Not long before the scheduled late-March college reopening, he was flushed out of his anxious isolation by a court-ordered eviction notice from his Wash-ington landlady, the final rout in his twelve-year "guerrilla war" over delin-quent rent payments. He drove north with Connie to clear their belongings out of 217 Randolph Place. In Washington, however, Connie found the job of packing left entirely up to her, as he made a hasty exit—over her impas-sioned objections—to catch a bus on to New York. Frances had been on his mind again, and he'd been equivocating for some months about seeing her. But this time, instead of the relief and release he sought, the flight to his Muse brought an ironic and sobering recognition of the nets of betrayal into which he had descended with his wife. The suitcase into which he'd hurriedly thrown together his overnight things for the trip—he found when he opened it up to get out his shaving kit in the New York bus station lavatory—contained, stashed away in a side pocket, a packet of romantic letters written to Connie by her ex-lover. After the experience of reading through the letters in a feverish "heat of ferreting," his visit to Frances in Brooklyn was something of an anticlimax, and he was soon on a bus back to Washington. At Randolph Place, Connie confronted him all over again with Frances, the "Anima" he had so vehemently claimed to have forsworn. Old resentments spilled out on both sides. Finally Connie declared she was walking out on him—to return, she said, only once there had been "changes made."

Left at a loss by this sudden turn of events, Charles sadly piled their accumulated possessions of the years into a moving van to be hauled away for storage at the Chevy Chase home of Robert Creeley's sister. Connie rode back to Black Mountain with him, silently adamant about her decision. She stayed only long enough to pack up clothing and then leave again with Kate, this time bound for her sister Jane's in Weymouth. He was left on his own indefinitely.

Creeley, whom Olson had for some time been politicking to bring in as a teacher, finally showed up for the new session's opening, just on the heels of Connie's departure. After the five years of letters, it was the two writers' first physical encounter, and doubtless Olson was anticipating the arrival of his longtime literary running mate as an event of great moment. No one had helped as much as Creeley in making a reality of his conjectural pushes, a fact only lately brought home to him anew by his getting an advance copy of his *Mayan Letters,* edited and produced by Creeley, in the mail from Mallorca. Few first meetings could have measured up to the years of long-distance buildup that had preceded this one, and in fact the long-anticipated occasion proved somewhat of a letdown. Exhausted after an all-night drive from New York, Creeley made an early-morning appearance at the Jalo house: a shy, nervous, rumpled apparition in work clothes and navy-blue beret, with black eye patch masking the vacant socket of an eye lost in a childhood accident. Olson, roused prematurely from his customary daylong slumbers, came to the door dressed only in a bath towel, but did not let his informal attire diminish the enthusiasm of the expansive bear hug in which he enveloped the disconcerted visitor. Creeley, ingrained beneath the hipster veneer with a strong Puritan restraint, was "shocked." After being inundated with talk throughout an extended breakfast, he was herded over to the nearby Studies Building and assigned a ground-floor studio apartment that lacked glass in one of the windows; within a few hours, still reeling from the effects of several days without sleep, he was facing the intimidating prospect of his first writing class.

The students, for their part, had little idea what to make of the new teacher's intense, understated, halting manner. Nor, more significantly, did Olson himself. The respective privacies of the two men were to be far more of a barrier in person than on paper. As often for Olson, there was little actual correspondence between his subjective perception of another person's figurative role in his life and the objective reality of that person. With the most important characters in his life allegory or self-myth—like Frances, the Muse or Anima, and Creeley, the "Figure of Outward" to whom he had dedicated his first *Maximus* volume—the subjective distortion was most extreme; Olson found himself more comfortable with the projection than with the real person. Despite all the recent "volubleness when we were 500 miles off [or] 5000," now that they were neighbors—he was soon finding—he and Creeley "never talked in a large sense."

While Creeley took care of the literary end of the curriculum that term, Olson himself conducted a current-affairs class on "the reasons, causes and consequences of the present." The *Asheville Citizen-Times,* copies of which were picked up by a student at the highway turnoff every morning, supplied his text for an exploration of the hidden themes and motives behind the face values of the daily news. The course was designed to show how timeless mythic patterns could be made out even in the blank public history of the present. An item on Carolina hill-country Christian fundamentalist snake-handling cults, for instance, sprang Olson back on wide arcs to Greek religious rites described by Jane Harrison, while the mythic archetype of Moses and the Great Man was found reemerging in such front-page figures of the day as Senator McCarthy (whose hearings the students were dispatched to view on the farm manager's television set) and Chairman Mao. Olson's impressively up-to-the-minute lecture on Mao was the climax of the course: students were duly dazzled, and it was only later learned by one of them that Olson had actually cribbed the whole thing from the latest issue of the *New Republic,* snatching the college copy before anyone else could get a look at it. As ever, a halo of mystique hung inviolate around his sources.

Life without Connie required some domestic adjustments. As it developed that the job of keeping Olson fed would have to be taken over by somebody, a sort of round-robin standing invitation system was established, with the honors of hosting the hungry but helpless rector shared around among the college community. He ate most often with immediate neighbors Wes and Bea Huss and Robert and Helen Hellman. (Hellman, a friend of Creeley's, had taken over as languages teacher from the departing Flola Shepard.) Stefan Wolpe and Hilda Morley also figured in his dinner rotation, until one evening when he sternly pointed out a stray fragment of Brillo pad in his serving of Morley's *paella.*

One dinner invitation of this bachelor period—from writing students Michael Rumaker and Tom Field—set up the circumstances for an unexpected episode of violence. Before the meal at the students' Meadows Inn apartment, Olson was treated by his hosts to numerous beers at Ma Peak's tavern in town. Driving back, he stopped his car to confront three trespassers he'd spied fishing off the dam on Lake Eden. The burly intruders—local rednecks—ignored his command to leave. Olson appeared to be "storming for a fight . . . to prove his authority over the place." When he gave the biggest of his adversaries a tentative shove, the man surprisingly reacted by punching him in the nose, breaking his glasses. Shorn of his vision like a blinded Samson, the humiliated rector was reduced to groping around on his hands and knees for pieces of the shattered lenses. A vivid and unsettling reminder "that I am timid and have known physical fear," the incident compelled him to prove his masculinity to himself all over again; and since trespassing was now common on the disused lower property, an opportunity was not long in coming. A motorcycle daredevil caught doing show-off stunts on the college road "got aggressive" after being ordered off the grounds. Olson "took steps," knocking the rash biker off his vehicle with one enormous blow to the forearm, and authority was restored.

The trial separation from Connie remained open-ended, but the letters back and forth between Massachusetts and North Carolina were a tacit acknowledgment that the present arrangement represented a hiatus in their life together rather than its terminus. Even as he was supposed to be "making changes" in himself so that their domestic relations might resume, however, Charles began seeing another woman—a twenty-eight-year-old Black Mountain music student, Augusta Elizabeth ("Betty") Kaiser—and had soon fallen for her in a big way. The young woman, who lived in the Olsons' former flat above the Rumaker and Field apartment in Meadows Inn, was generally perceived in the community as the quiet, pleasant, somewhat aloof "housemother" of the cottage household, hardly a *femme fatale,* and seemingly a highly unlikely candidate for an affair with the intimidating poet-patriarch (who appeared, after all, so secretive and withdrawn in his own hermetic privacies as to have no personal life at all). Somewhat older than most of the other students, Betty was obviously serious about her music studies, which had been conducted at the extensive expense of her parents (middle-class Catholics from Queens) and had included Juilliard School training under Stefan Wolpe, by whom she was now being tutored in advanced piano. She was well liked but had no real close friends at the school; tall, slender and quite attractive, she'd nonetheless had little to do with the available swains (her most interested pursuer, Fielding Dawson, had been drafted into the army before making any significant progress with her). The mysterious, enigmatic Betty Kaiser brought out the troubadour in Olson, who was before long sitting at the foot of her bed pouring out deep talk well into the night, and pining over her in poems of a moonstruck lover's "helplessness / asking her / to unclasp / her knees." Once begun, the affair gathered a momentum of its own, rendering futile all Olson's efforts at secrecy. If nothing else, his telltale heavy tread as he attempted a stealthy nocturnal ascent of the rickety wooden staircase above Rumaker and Field's flat invariably gave him away. In so tiny a community, even the creak of a wooden step could echo mightily as gossip.

Any lingering doubts about whether the surprising couple were really in love were dispelled by a summer-session college theatrical production of Ibsen's *Peer Gynt*. Director Wes Huss cast Betty Kaiser as the gentle maiden Solveig, Olson as the hulking, menacing Button Moulder. In the climactic final scene, Betty performed Stefan Wolpe's haunting, ethereal setting of Solveig's Song. To those in the audience it was clear that though it was Peer Gynt—Robert Hellman—she held in her arms as she sang, it was Button Moulder Olson, crouched behind a hut on one side of the stage, who bathed in the radiance of her loving glance, and after his fashion returned it.

The new entanglement was as risky as it was sweet. Following his heart was unfamiliar behavior for Olson—but then again, as he wrote in a June poem titled simply "Love," "there is no intelligence / the equal of the situation." Connie, as if sensing at long distance that there had indeed been changes made, but not the kind she'd hoped for, was now dropping hints by mail that she was ready to return. He was forced into some adroit juggling and feinting, which if not in the long run "the equal of the situation" at least provided him a chance for further seizing of the moment. In midsummer he went north, stopped off in Weymouth to see his wife and daughter, but instead of picking them up as expected, rushed on to Gloucester for a few days of hasty *Maximus* research before heading back to North Carolina to take care of what he described to Connie as urgent college business. Though a push to win back the school's lapsed G.I. Bill accreditation took up some time and necessitated another encounter with government authorities (this time on their turf, as he descended to federal agency offices in Raleigh, armed with an optimistically inflated—and ultimately convincing—prospectus of future Black Mountain course offerings), the actual urgent business of the rest of his summer was prolonging the romance with Betty. Its early idyllic phase came to an end in September, when she learned that she was carrying his child and decided to leave school to think matters over. Reluctant to reveal her condition to her family, she went to stay with a married sister, Jean Radoslovich, in New Brunswick, New Jersey. There, after a few weeks, she made up her mind to go ahead and have Olson's child.

The time had come for the patriarch to reclaim his brood. Shortly after Betty's departure he returned to New England to do poetry readings in Boston and Gloucester. A big blow heralded his arrival: Hurricane Hazel, with its hundred-mile-an-hour winds. On the day the storm came ashore, he delivered a reading and talk at the Charles Street Meeting House, and afterwards pitched the college and distributed copies of the *Black Mountain Review* to some curious witnesses, including a twenty-year-old waif of the night named John Wieners who would not only follow him back to Black Mountain but one day develop into a lyric poet of importance in his own right, the most accomplished (and Olson's acknowledged favorite) of the many would-be practitioners of projective-verse principle. ("Big Charles put his hand on me," Wieners later avowed, "and ordained me a priest.") In Gloucester, Olson weathered a double-barreled emotional scene at the home of Vincent Ferrini: he had to both patch things up with Ferrini after a cruel blast at the latter's expense in the *Maximus* and pull off a public rapprochement with Connie, who'd come to join him. Following a fresh assault from Hazel that knocked out the power, he read his poems by candlelight. Afterwards he gathered up wife and child and returned to the hill-fort.

But for the temporarily reconciled couple the emotional waters stayed choppy. As always, Olson's work reflected his private life obliquely, through baffles of abstraction that revealed the pressure of feeling if not its source. "Love is pitched where you haven't found it," he wrote in an essay on verse quantity in Shakespeare's late plays. "It is not at all a fluent scene. There are pure awkwardnesses. Women and man say things." It was one of his most thoughtful critical efforts, a revaluation of Shakespearean themes—innocence and lust, chastity and candor—that gained considerable intensity from his current personal involvement with these same themes. During times of historical "change in the discourse system"—times such as Shakespeare's and his own—love became capable of a special condition of innocence, he proposed. "Its size and power increase again, and innocence emerges with a thrust much more than sensuality ever gave."

With Betty's return to the school in October, however, he found the actual exercise of innocence in a complex situation to be little aided by theory. They once again became lovers, and now he was faced with more serious questions of duplicity and concealment. Inevitably Connie found him out, receiving the fresh injury with a fatalistic resolve to "stick it out" this time. The tensions of the love triangle were multiplying, and despite his avowals in a letter to Frances that "I am life's neophyte, at 43 thrown from naivete into a fragile opening innocence," his conscience was uneasy when he attempted to analyze what was happening. Momentous importance seemed attached to everything he did, yet it all seemed an immense gamble to him, and he had no real plan. He was not sure of anything except that things were changing in ways he did not yet understand, and that an attitude of innocence must be maintained. "I live an unconscionable life these days," he told his longtime soul-tutor with the earnest bewilderment of one reborn, "I have this sense, that I have left the shores of privilege, & am for the first time swept into the currents of life . . . following you in that sense and it is all so unknown to me."

The "currents" shifted as rapidly and confusingly as dream landscapes. At the closing of the fall session in December, Betty left once more, this time for New York. Charles held his ground, occupying himself on the surface with the business of writing, but finding himself confronted by his divided feelings in his dreams—where Connie and Betty now sometimes interchanged identities, or took similar roles, conspiring against him with various real or imagined sexual "rivals," like Wes Huss, Jack Wells (his onetime Rhodes scholarship nemesis) and Connie's erstwhile lover. Since much of the dream action occurred in the childhood landscape of 4 Norman Avenue, Olson concluded that the threatening male images represented Karl.

> Isn't it all a struggle to get through to woman without my father in the way?
> *two women*   the tendency is to keep Con individuated as my Mother . . .
>   & the "other woman," who is Mother *after the Fall,* that is, after
>   Father has done her in . . .

Such private questionings of the sources of his sexual identity provided the instigation for and yet were largely camouflaged by a Creeleyesque lyric mask in a December sequence of short poems called *O'Ryan.* Punning in his title on the name of that prototypical male adventurer, the ancient hunter of the skies, Olson here adopted a persona which—as Robert Duncan suggested—reflected not only "the poet in Creeley [but] the rueful figure any of us is as men we are." "Don't fool yourself," enjoined the surprisingly knowing "innocent" lover here, "it's night / you got a hard on / and it's to be made." During the between-sessions break of January 1955, Olson performed the sequence at the college for a few faculty friends. Also in attendance was Duncan, who had dropped in on his way to Mallorca and stayed to hear the new poems read in a "bare room at Black Mountain, with its cold night and the blazing winter sky at the window" (a scene that would be evoked on the cover of a San Francisco small-press edition of the poems by the black-and-white star-chart figurations of Duncan's companion, artist Jess Collins). For Duncan and Olson, the encounter involved a wary reconciliation of sorts, Olson having less than gracefully dismissed the entire San Francisco literary scene as a nest of soft-headed mystics in the essay "Against Wisdom as Such," a piece of muscle-flexing showmanship included in the first issue of the *Black Mountain Review*. Duncan, more tolerant in judgment, amicably forgave, but came away from the visit with a clear sense that his friend was in some domestic bind. There was an almost palpable state of tension in the Olson household, the San Francisco poet noted; Olson seemed edgy and indecisive, and the obviously unhappy Connie "a caricature of the disgruntled shrew."

The crisis in Olson's marriage coincided with the nadir of Black Mountain's fortunes. The piecemeal financing measures he had so far employed having proved inadequate, he set out early in the new year to raise an urgently needed $75,000, firing off to prospective donors a salvo of appeal letters cosigned by Harvard mathematician Norbert Wiener (the father of cybernetics and a longtime Black Mountain sympathizer). The letters advertised a new college advisory council comprised of Wiener, Carl Sauer, Franz Kline, William Carlos Williams and Albert Einstein, and were sent out with an enclosed promotional affidavit attributed to Einstein but actually written by Olson himself, the famous physicist having permitted him to say whatever he wanted. The mailing failed to raise even a fraction of the needed sum. At this point Olson's remaining faculty colleagues, Wolpe, Huss and Fiore, acceded to his wishes and voted with him to sell the lower property, including the dining hall and North and South Lodges. Before a sale could be made, however, news of the decision reached former faculty members to whom deferred salary payments were long overdue. Rumors were going around that Olson intended to abscond to the Yucatán with the sale proceeds. Stephen Forbes, a former major backer of the college who still held $5,000 in outstanding mortgage notes on the property, moved to block the land sale. The Forbes notes were bought out with borrowed family money kicked in by Mary Fitton Fiore. No sooner had that challenge been met, however, than Olson and the school were faced with a new one—lawsuits for recovery of back salaries filed by former faculty member Natasha Goldowski, Nell Rice, and former photography teacher Hazel Larsen Archer. Olson and Huss, working with the college lawyer, negotiated a compromise: all contingent salary claims would be paid off upon the final closure of Black Mountain. Once legal maneuverings were out of the way, a lease with option to buy was taken up by the sponsors of a Christian boys' camp, which would soon occupy the lower property. The deal netted the school $65,000, in three annual rental payments to be followed by a $25,000 final payment for the exercise of the purchase option.

Negotiating his personal problems was even more complicated for Olson. Fifteen years of "close husbandish marriage" with Connie had given way to an impasse of mutual disaffection and distrust (learning she'd taken a measure of revenge by engaging in a casual flirtation with a dashing student artist, sculptor John Chamberlain, was further cause for discouragement, made all the more irritating for Charles because he was in no real position to object). Betty, meanwhile, living in solitary and anonymous poverty in Manhattan, had checked into New York Women's Hospital and on May 12 given birth to a boy, whom she named Charles Peter Olson. She brought the baby back home to her bare one-room midtown apartment, to be kept in a dresser drawer because she had no money to buy a proper bed for him. She let Olson know he had at last become a father of a son, but that fortifying news could not resolve his larger problem. Creeley, who came back in July to take over again as substitute writing teacher, found him in an emotionally "inchoate state," deeply involved with two women at once and "just totally flummoxed" as to what to do about it. For the first time in their relationship, Olson dropped his reserve and asked the younger man for advice on a personal matter, but Creeley, who was himself suffering through the throes of a failed marriage, hesitated to comment. ("I certainly couldn't help him decide.") Shrinking from public contact in his time of private trial, Olson withdrew to the Jalo house and dealt only with a few tutorial students, communicating with them mostly via the school mailboxes. (*A Bibliography on America for Ed Dorn,* a hurried but provocative compressed manual on the methodology of poetic history, was a product of this time: "late one night he delivered the thing to my window," Dorn recalls, "so it came to me for breakfast.")

An atmosphere of tension and desperation—or, as student Michael Rumaker later put it, of "underlying or hidden malevolences"—prevailed that summer not only in the Olson household but in the college community at large. Creeley, roaming the hills spilling out the alcoholic lamentation of the wounded lover, seemed to be sowing a mood of manic discord that spread from cottage to cottage. His and Olson's were not the only marriages on the rocks. Another summer-session instructor, Robert Hellman, took an overdose of sleeping pills after breaking up with his wife. A contagion of suicidal nihilism seemed to have been loosed in the hill-fort. Rumaker, receiving his degree that summer, had to accept it with his wrists bandaged after slashing them in an apparent suicide attempt. Things reached bottom when student Tom Field, after a night out drinking with several Black Mountaineers, rammed his fully loaded Buick sedan headlong into the massive stone chimney of Meadows Inn. It appeared he'd been goaded to the act as a gesture of defiant self-destructiveness. While Field and Dan Rice suffered serious injuries, Creeley, who'd been a backseat passenger, walked away from the crash with only a wrenched shoulder. He was seen wandering near the wreckage in a daze, amazingly still trying to find someone to listen to his continuing pained narrative of failed marriage. Though the demolished Buick ended up a long way from the nearest road, Olson managed to talk puzzled state troopers into accepting his unlikely reconstruction of the event as an accident caused by a jammed gas pedal, and to get Field and Rice, as service veterans, admitted to a V.A. hospital in nearby Swannanoa. But it was some time before even the routine abnormal normalcy of Black Mountain could be reestablished, and as head monk Olson had to bear much of the strain of psychic rehabilitation. Still administering to his banged-up congregation when his old friend Ephraim Doner showed up some weeks after the Meadows Inn crack-up for a surprise visit, he appeared to Doner a sad parody of his former brilliance, an *"enfant terrible* guru" reduced to preaching nonsense philosophy to an audience of juvenile delinquents who seemed to have just been through a mass motorcycle collision ("Everybody in the place was on crutches").

Convinced by late August that the wave of bad drinking and negativity that had impacted Black Mountain all summer was a serious threat, Olson responded authoritatively in poetry. Creeley, he had decided, was a sort of pied piper of nihilism whose involuntary but potent influence had to be counteracted after the fashion of ancient Greek religious practices. Ghosts set loose on earth to fill men's hearts with nameless dread, he learned from Jane Harrison's *Themis,* had been expelled by the people of Athens with traditional rites of exorcism. A hortatory verse proclamation designed to ward off evil in a formal way, "A Newly Discovered 'Homeric' Hymn," served a similar function for his own endangered *polis,* putting the community on guard against the morbid spells of the intruder who, "drunk from the pot," had come to undermine morale, spread drunkenness and talk everyone "blue / in the face."

His temporary exasperation over his friend's erratic behavior that summer did not, however, prevent Olson from turning to Creeley when his own private problems became intolerable. By the fall of 1955 it was evident that he could no longer perpetuate the pretense of marriage. Acting on impulse as during the previous crisis of 1952, he called on Creeley to hold the fort as writing teacher and company agent while he himself went off to New York to join his true love and the son he'd never seen. With Betty and Charles Peter he moved in on a former Black Mountain student, Peter Stander— nephew of the blacklisted actor Lionel—at an apartment on 9th Street in Greenwich Village. Financially unprepared to support his new family away from the college, he had some thoughts of writing for money, but his attempts to work in the cramped circumstances of the shared flat soon came to grief; his "offices," he reported to Creeley, were now "bars & libraries & museums." Word had gotten around town that he'd walked out on Connie, and former friends he ran into on the street were cool to him, making him feel "truly cut off." In December, the ironic conjunction in his and Creeley's romantic fortunes landed him in a Manhattan courtroom as witness for his friend's divorce proceedings. His own fate's course was at the same time being hurried along by Connie, who had given up on waiting things out in North Carolina and come north to the city with Kate to find him and force a resolution. Olson immediately packed them into the family Ford and set out on a frigid 250-mile drive to deposit them at her sister's present home in Scituate, Massachusetts. In a harrowing goodbye scene at the Athertons' he showed a firmness of decision that Connie saw to be final. At the last minute she pleaded with him not to go. "Baby, I *have* to go," he said with death-knell seriousness, donning his overcoat for the road.

Connie stayed on at the Athertons', suffering a prolonged nervous collapse; it would take her some months to get back on her feet, find an apartment and begin to seek work and an independent life for herself and her daughter. The way, meanwhile, was now cleared for the patriarch's return to his domain. He headed south in mid-February 1956 with Betty and Charles Peter, stopping off en route at the New Jersey home of Betty's sister Jean, where the Kaiser family had gathered to inspect the prospective new relation. He had so far not exactly gotten off on the right foot with the in-laws by influencing Betty to abandon her grand piano and music in her 72nd Street apartment, after making her an unwed mother (although she now adopted the surname Olson, there was never a legal marriage). This interview did little to improve the impression; all but Jean gave him a chilly reception, refusing even to talk to him. He was greatly relieved to be off again, bound for the hill-fort and—at last—home.

20 ～

The Last Man
(1956–1957)

Olson was greeted upon his return to Black Mountain by a backlog of undone college business that soon had him caught up all over again, as he reported to Frances, in the "24 hour miseries of trying to keep a little polis alive in the monstrous bland quantitative present." But on the eve of Washington's Birthday, meeting his writing class for the first time in nine months— he was filling in during the hiatus between Creeley's departure for the West Coast and the arrival of Creeley's successor in the job, Robert Duncan—he "caught fire," making up for lost time by conducting his remaining handful of student disciples and a few new ones on a seven-hour lecture tour through the origins and history of language and culture, accounting for recent advances into the post-modern ("what went out in 1945 and has come on since") by reaching all the way back to the Sumerians. His reliance on the Samuel Noah Kramer materials passed on to him by Frances made the lecture "sound as much y[ou]rs as mine," he told her.

The dispatch to his ex-lover in the wake of his exhausting teaching stint contained only vague hints about the recent changes in his personal life, however. "I despair to tell you what my life now is," he said. "You knew pain before I did because you knew love, which I had to learn . . . and now I know a little." Though he added in the bittersweet tone that increasingly characterized his communications to her that he "ought to have known better, that I loved you from the start," the pain and love he now spoke of were the product of a situation of which Frances could know next to nothing. The pain of the final separation from his family was fresh, and in his conscience Connie's last emotional "Don't go!" still echoed. Yet he had brought on the whole terrible upheaval quite willingly, responding to the new, more powerful call from his future which Betty seemed to represent. In the sexual realm, which had always been pretty much a morass of confusion for him, the certainty of his present response could seem a positive beacon capable of illuminating everything else. He celebrated the physical union with his young wife as an event of ultimate moment, affirming with great seriousness in poetry Betty's casual comments that the act of love "goes straight to the / heart" and "puts one / in touch with / the universe."

Having little luck in his ongoing efforts to lure such experts as Sumerian scholar Kramer or Hittite specialist Hans Guterbock to the college for an "Institute of the New Ancient Literature," Olson did manage to bring in as visiting lecturer for the 1956 spring session another expert on ancient languages whose services he'd been wooing for three years, Martin Sprengling of the University of Chicago's Oriental Institute. Sprengling, author of *The Alphabet,* a study of the early development of writing from hieroglyphs, was an acknowledged authority in the field. To get him, Olson found himself forced to make exaggerated representations about the school and its curriculum, facilities and resources. (In fact it took a certain amount of optimistic portraying to make Black Mountain seem appealing to any prospective instructor, not to mention one who already held a distinguished position at a respectable institution.) It took the elderly German-born scholar only a day or two to see that he'd been enticed on false pretenses. He departed abruptly, leaving the dismayed rector to take up the slack. Fortunately Olson had his own passionate amateur's contribution to the Institute up his sleeve. In March, while Duncan came in to take over the writing-instructor chores, he himself turned to the bigger conjectural picture, highlighting the session with ten days of lectures on "The Special View of History."

The expanded philosophical outlook of the lectures was largely the result of Olson's reading in recent months of Alfred North Whitehead's *Process and Reality,* a work in which he found sketched out the cosmic dimensions of an enlarged creation—a "park of eternal / events" in which matter, space and time were essentially interrelated and in which there was ample allowance for the poet's habitual disposition to "stay fluid" because there were no partitions and no closure, only the continuous revitalizing flow of process. Olson recognized at once the majestic setting of a cosmological poetics as well as a new view of history. And like Carl Jung, the other thinker most influential on his own later writings (and, ironically, like Jung a Great Man with whom he'd had a disappointing personal meeting while a Harvard graduate student), Whitehead seemed to offer a figurative or allegorical frame of reference in which the poet as *muthos*-maker could easily feel at home. The British metaphysician who had "cleared out the gunk / by getting the universe in" was now to become for Olson the "great master and companion of my poem[s]."

His initial excited encounter with *Process and Reality* would be followed by intensive further studies over the next few years (his own copy was to become one of the most densely annotated volumes in his library), those studies eventually yielding the more sober hindsight judgment that in his first ambitious foray into Whitehead's thought he'd actually "known nothing, nothing about it." But for Olson the pioneer of projective forwarding, never certain of, yet forever committed to, whatever lay around the next bend, to be working out ahead of himself intellectually when the inspiration was running hot was quite in character. Audacious, precipitate, yet at the same time compelling in the peculiar challenging way that was uniquely his own, the "Special View" lectures offered a stirring glimpse of him as creative thinker. Here was the "great intellectual punter, constantly at the gaming tables of thought and literature" (as Ed Dorn called him), proposing the adventure of the mind as an activity of worth in its own right, no less to be valued because it was also so openly a gamble. Along with Whitehead, Olson parlayed an impressively and predictably diverse field of primary authorities: Heisenberg, Heraclitus, Jung, even John Keats, whose "proposition that a man's life . . . is an allegory," long an Olson touchstone, was here cited as indicator that one's path through the world was to be viewed as a thing of "scale," "not as a 'lifetime,' not as flesh going toward death and resurrection, but as *history:* that you live." Keats' life of continual allegory amounted to a Whiteheadian dynamic: "History is the intensity of the life process." "MAN IS A CONTINUOUS CHANGE IN TIME."

The first of Olson's many grand duels with the metaphysics and cosmology of Whitehead, the lectures struck audience member Robert Duncan as the ultimate in messianic totalizing, an impatient but heroic effort "to produce a new and redeemed man" out of the sheer energy of ideas. It was the same urgent use of ideas that had made Olson's Black Mountain such a heady, disorienting environment throughout his onslaught of conjecture in these years, an ongoing campaign of "education as spiritual attack."

A gentler brand of education by spiritual persuasion was dispensed by visiting instructor Duncan, whose subtler, more reflective teaching approach served to point up by contrast the headlong, assaultive quality of Olson's own conjectural pushes. Never completely immune to competitive stimulus, Olson was too proud to actually attend Duncan's classes, but took pains to keep up with them by means of a student "spy" network. He was brought up-to-date accounts of the proceedings, including news of both the outsider's casual heretical recommendations of "Indexed" works and authors (*Finnegans Wake*, Eliot, Stein, Zukofsky, H.D., even Edith Sitwell) and of other more intriguing assignments, such as Rimbaud's *Illuminations* and *A Season in Hell*, texts soon to spark new developments in his own poetry. Well aware that the punctilious Duncan met his classes at eight o'clock in the morning, Olson went out of his way to extend his own marathon lectures well past midnight, forcing the San Francisco poet to conduct a daily wake-up call in order to muster a quorum. Duncan took this as a deliberate if amusing affront, and responded by teaming up with Wes Huss to produce a dramatic farce, *The Origins of Old Sun*, in which "Old Sun" was portrayed as an oversized, demanding infant in diapers. It was performed in the Studies Building basement before a small audience that included Olson, for once stony silent as he watched himself spoofed. "My little farce scared him," Duncan was delighted to see. "He both wanted to know and did not want to know that the big baby was himself." Duncan's *Medea: The Maiden Head*, a more serious verse drama put on as a college production that summer, was also attended by Olson, who did little to conceal his jealousy over the fact that his friend and rival possessed such a mastery of the dramatic medium for which he himself lacked all gift. On opening night he made an early and apparently chagrined exit, uttering "nary a word" and afterwards delaying delivering his customary and expected pontifical verdict until he'd regained his diplomatic composure. Then, in politic fashion, he complimented Duncan, telling him, "You're our dramatist."

The fusion of lyric vision with "primary images" in a burst of poetry Olson produced that spring owed a certain debt to Robert Duncan's visit, if only in his picking up effectively on certain of the visiting instructor's key insistences. Along with the euphoric fecundity of new love and of the Southern mountain springtime, and with his concurrent intellectual passions for the cosmology and typology of Whitehead and Jung, the final decisive influence on his April-May 1956 verse advances was a "magic view" of the poem as spiritual alchemy, which he found—following up on Duncan's advocacy— in the work of Rimbaud.

Olson had been interested since 1945 in the French poet's life and legend, for him an emblematic image of the post-humanist artist as iconoclastic anti-hero. But though he'd once borne a copy of the Pleiade edition of Rimbaud's poems to Frances as a love token, he'd so far actually paid them little close attention. Under his Black Mountain visitor's indirect influence, he now set out to remedy that oversight, rising to the perceived challenge by "making his way earnestly" (as Duncan later put it) through the poetry in both French and English that spring. In March he introduced Rimbaud into a lecture of his own on Stance, citing the poem "Ô saisons, ô châteaux" and also bringing up "Soleil et chair / Credo in Unam" in the translation he had solicited from Frances. He'd now recognized an affinity of confrontational stance that linked Rimbaud and himself, he reported in a letter to her. Both were poets of the "double-axe," engaged on the cutting edge of "mercy versus justice." In the poetic justice of Rimbaud's Time of the Assassins Olson could make out a sense of urgent cultural-revolutionary necessity akin to his own. That the grimness of such justice should not go unrelieved was the lesson of "Ô saisons, ô châteaux," a poem in which the progression of Rimbaud's season in hell reached a turning point, "restor[ing] Beauty and Charity." The "pivot," Olson told Frances, was the poet's crucial hermetic term "le bonheur," connoting not only happiness or joy but an alchemical elixir, the marvelous "poison" whose traces never left the blood of the intoxicated initiate.

In Olson's springtime rush of poems, vivid celebrations of love, nature and "the powers that be," Rimbaud's image of a miraculous alchemical potion provided a key figurative harmonic relating love with cosmic process: it became, in "The chain of memory is resurrection," a "green poison" announcing at once the fullness and "the death of spring"; in "The Perfume," a "poison / of desire" saturating the poet's bedroom at night; and in "Variations Done for Gerald Van De Wiele," an "elixir" demanded by the body as it "whips the soul" into a state of great desire. At the heart of the lyric "Variations," a poem animated by the pastoral immediacy of the flowering time of year (dogwood, plum and apple in blossom, the hum of bees and tractor diesels, a whippoorwill's song at full moon), lay an inspired reworking of Rimbaud's "Ô saisons." In his American post-modern version, Olson updated the alchemical metaphor of the original, enlarging its allusive scope by means of a Jungian psychological perspective.

I have no longer any excuse
for envy. My life

has been given its orders: the seasons
seize

the soul and the body . . .

              The hour of death

is the only trespass . . .

can you afford not to make
the magical study

which happiness is?. . .

        do you know the charge . . .

     that no body and soul are one
if they are not wrought

in this retort? . . .

In the roar of spring,
transmutations.

In "The Writ," another poem of vernal awakening, he pursued the "secret of correspondences" with Rimbaudian fervor. Correspondences and secrets of renewal in mythic and chromosomal dimensions were explored in "The chain of memory is resurrection," a magisterial affirmation of process. Here Olson once again evoked Jung and Whitehead, summoning his reader to participation in not only the great genetic flow of being but its perpetual spiritual combat:

rise into being: the onslaught,
he calls it,
resurrection

The being of man is resurrection, the genetic flow
of each life which has given life, the tenderness
none of us
is without. Let it come back. Let it be
where it is . . .

        Desire
is resurrection

The soul
is an onslaught

In this poem of grand cyclic sweep—a hymn to endless life forces—he traced the gene-stream or chain of souls through personal forebears buried in Worcester's Swedish cemetery back to the Cro-Magnons and the Venus of Willendorf and forward into new generations yet to come, finding genesis mirrored in his infant son's face ("All that has been / suddenly is") and death overthrown in the spiritual uplift of springtime ("I Adonis / Lift me, life of being / the shape of my soul").

Finally, in two powerful poems based on dream transcriptions, the enduring primary characters of his imagination reemerged in scenes of much psychic resonance. In "The Lordly and Isolate Satyrs," members of a motorcycle gang appeared on a beach as monumental figures like Easter Island monoliths. "The Androgynes, / the Fathers behind the father," these "awkward boddhas," hyper-dimensional giants with "huge third leg like carborundum," evoked "no feeling except love." But if such gods still figured the male as Father, Mother remained for the poet a link with difficult entanglements of being human. "As the Dead Prey Upon Us," a poem of painful but redemptive disclosure, was provoked by a dream encounter with his mother in a living room of dead souls. Out of the poem's imagistic transformations arose Olson's vision of "the poverty / of hell": his mother's unfulfilled life, with its "ghastliness / of going, and forever / coming back, returning / to the instants which were not lived." Entrapment in tortuous nets of being, beguilement by the "false cause" of a Catholic concept of eternity—such a "death in life" had been only narrowly missed by the poet himself. "O mother, if you had once touched me / o mother, if I had once touched you . . . O souls, burn alive, burn now / that you may forever / have peace."

In May, Olson's attention was diverted from poetry by new demands of college business. A Veterans Administration inspector's unexpected visit to the closed-up and nearly deserted school during the rector's midwinter absence had resulted in the cancellation of Black Mountain's G.I. Bill accreditation. The ensuing loss of government benefits was a serious blow to the school, the prospective damage to recruiting potentially fatal. The V.A. official was scheduled to return for a follow-up visit. Olson, showing he'd lost none of his gift for stage-managing reality, organized a phony curriculum on the spot, trumping up courses in subjects as conventional-sounding as French and landscape drawing and seeing to it that classrooms were filled up on cue with eager, attentive students, decked out in clean shirts and ties for the inspector's arrival. The impromptu performance was convincing enough to earn the school a provisional restoration of benefits.

The hard truth behind the charade was that such occasional temporary victories could do no more than delay the inevitable. To help keep up with costs, Olson and Huss jettisoned more property—this time the college farm, which had already been leased a year and a half earlier. Faculty morale had meanwhile fallen to a new low, hardly surprising given the relentless asperity of Black Mountain life. Stefan Wolpe, who quit that spring, complained that the school had degenerated into "the garbage heap of the world." In August,

Robert Duncan would depart for good, and Wes Huss was planning to follow Duncan to San Francisco to work on further *Medea* productions. Joe
Fiore wanted a leave of absence and was about to take it, and Olson himself
was emanating unmistakable signs of being fed up with teaching. He appeared
at times to be merely going through the motions, approaching the end of his
patience with his loyal but unknowing charges: "Why do we have these fleas?"
he roared to Robert Duncan in one "shocking blowup" of private frustration
and anger against his own disciples. Complaining of migraines, more often
than not he had Wes Huss post "class canceled" notices in the Studies Building. He actually stepped into a classroom only "three or four times all that
summer," according to Robert Hawley, who had traveled from California for
the privilege of being his student. (Not that Hawley went away disappointed;
informal talks with Olson yielded tips on books about the West that would
open up to him a lifetime interest in the field.)

At the end of summer, in a final unrealistic bid to float a new, visionary
Black Mountain tailored to his hopeful imaginative design—less a school than
an artists' and scholars' retreat, that ultimate "Chinese monastery" of his
dreams—Olson drafted one last promotional prospectus. Between the lines
he admitted that formal instruction would henceforth no longer be taking
place: students were invited to come for sanctuary from a pernicious American higher-educational system ("a dread and dangerous featherbed of nepo-
tism, deadness and the club of colleagues and gerontology") as well as for the
opportunity to rub shoulders with real working artists and craftspeople. It is
not clear whether the prospectus ever went out to potential students and
supporters, but the point is probably moot. Olson's University was effectively out of business, due not only to outside-world stresses but to growing
pressures within the rector himself to move on to a new phase of his creative
life, into himself and away from all demands of community or *polis*.

He took off with Betty and Charles Peter for a two-week vacation at the
shore in Myrtle Beach, South Carolina, getting back in time for the scheduled
September 27 opening of the fall session to play out what he resignedly termed
"the final act of Black Mt." The place had by then become a virtual ghost
town, populated only by a handful of ex-students and stray newcomers who
were hanging around on the chance Black Mountain might undergo a last-
minute phoenixlike resurrection. But Olson had no more miracles in store.
The day after his return he took Wes Huss into Asheville for a late breakfast,
and as they lingered over coffee he aired his feelings about the future, finding
his trusty sidekick largely in agreement. "Neither of us wanted to go on,"
says Huss. "For the last year or so we had been moving, psychically, into
something new but undefined. If Charles and I were sure of anything, it was
that this was the time for a change." Before the cups and ashes were cleared

away, they had decided to close down Black Mountain. A few evenings later in an open meeting at the Jalo house Olson announced the decision and delivered a short valedictory talk, appearing to those on hand quite casual, even "cheerful," as he outlined the situation. To all present it was obvious that he had made up his mind, and when one or two of the students piped up with proposals to "write to Grandma" for emergency donations to save the school, he brushed the well-meaning offers aside without discussion.

A breaking of camp and general exodus followed. Olson himself, as he would later point out with some pride, had resolved to see things through to the finish, and now settled into doing so, occupying the abandoned school grounds as caretaker and overseeing necessary repairs and maintenance as well as legal business prior to closing of the final sale. In truth less a hardship than a relief for him, a welcome period of relative peace in solitude, this last year of his tenancy gave him his first real liberty to wander at his ease around his beloved hillside domain. The "last man" of the place, he let his neat mustache burgeon into a full grizzled salt-and-pepper beard, thus taking on a bewhiskered mountain-man look to suit the role. Basking in what he conceived as a state of elemental wildness "at the heart of the world," he passed idle hours watching hornets nest-building in the grille of an abandoned truck, dawn mists rising off the lake, or steely clouds chased across a vast night sky by "the wind off / the oldest mountains." He puttered around the property, unhurriedly discharging final chores. He brought in painters to spruce up the empty buildings, and, with winter coming on, pitched in himself to install storm windows. The spell of handymanism came to an end when he cut his hand on a pane of glass as he unloaded it from his prized new 1956 turquoise-and-white Chevy "beach wagon." (Wes Huss, in his last act as treasurer, had purchased the car out of college funds and then turned it over to Olson, who officially "sold" it to himself for a nominal sum.)

The injury and the cold weather drove him indoors, and poetry returned to the center of his attention. The second volume of his epic, *The Maximus Poems 11–22,* had recently come out from Jargon, allowing him to assess the work's direction and progress to date and also prompting him once again to consider ways of bringing it to a close. A September effort to get the project going again had only deepened his self-questionings, leaving him with four more failed "Maxies" and a good deal of confusion. The epic at this point seemed to have ground to a halt, a conclusion confirmed by his estimate of the three-year-old work in the new volume. While those poems sourced in the ahistorical propositional immediacy of a self-mythological present, like "Maximus, to Gloucester" (Letter 15), "On first Looking out through Juan de la Cosa's Eyes," and "The Twist," still held up for him, he saw serious flaws in the others, especially in the more strictly historical attempts at narrative, which seemed pushy and overreaching, "high fallutin big shot stuff fancy & *wide* . . . 'Historie,' instead of *live* warm *stupid Gloucester*."

Olson's own misgivings were hardly relieved by the general absence of response to the new volume. "So far not one god damn word on it has appeared in the public press," he complained to Ed Dorn in a January 1957 letter. The one review he'd seen, written and sent to him by William Carlos Williams, had been "scorned" by the *New Republic*. And in fact the Williams review was mixed at best, on the one hand crediting Olson with an attempt of major dimension (the second book of his unfolding "American poem" was "much better than the first and when it comes off . . . brilliant, breathtaking . . . a thrilling experience") and on the other faulting his "wrongheaded" and "vicious" aggressiveness of tone and the paratactic "disconnectedness" of his method ("one of Olson's chief faults which he shares with Ezra Pound"). Olson was greatly disappointed with the review, describing it to Dorn bitterly as "damning." (Williams, far more perceptive a judge of life and letters than Olson was at this moment ready to allow, had pointed out that another of his flaws lay in an inability to learn from criticism: he was "not modest.") Dorn, now an itinerant worker in the Pacific Northwest and quite able to sympathize with his former teacher's feelings of literary isolation, offered the fortifying comment that for his part, he'd found "the language a little more slender and dry" in the second volume of the poem: "it departs a bit from 'by ear' and comes, delicately, out of the mouth again." (Asked by Olson to elaborate, Dorn in time produced "What I See in *The Maximus Poems*," which remains the most sensitive critical judgment of this phase of Olson's work.) Olson told his ex-student the impasse the poem had come to was the result of his problem with form. To start with, there was the apparent conflict between his drive toward the substantive, "the noun . . . as language," and a more purely poetic impulse to concentrate on sounds, vowels especially ("orotund, with round mouth"). In theory, each appeared a "possible source of form," but in practice they seemed mutually contradictory. And beyond that immediate dilemma lay further, evidently insuperable difficulties in finding a larger "Form, [for] the poem as a segmented length of all the 'letters.' " Compounding the struggle, he was working totally in the dark due to the lack of useful feedback on what he'd already done.

> Have had very little simple honesty abt Max II. Nor do I figure there is any reason why it shldn't be most problematic / It was to me: I held it three years, trying to figure where the hell I'd got to. And the answer's still unknown to me. . . . Am in one of those periods verse-wise when I don't know my way. I suppose it always follows when I am intimidated by the "failure" of a book or some failure I take it I am, with or without that measure. In any case I want to write like everybody else. . . .

But for Olson as poet, the condition of unknowingness often paradoxically proved the most fertile. Two weeks after his bewildered letter to Ed
Dorn, he deflected the sensitive "middle voice" of the best of the *Maximus*
into a shorter offshoot poem of haunting enigmatic power. Its landscape was
the self-mythic Gloucester, its text his dreams, in specific one in which his
father had appeared first as a Gloucester bookseller, vending "materials for
Maximus," and then in the guise of "the young musician" Frank Moore,
"intimate with my former wife." This father / false friend became "the Librarian of Gloucester," then later turned into the poet's stillborn brother. The
endless burden of dreams, a complex encoding of inner process with memories of being in time, was Olson's subject in "The Librarian," a poem whose
terminal riddles explored that *penetralium* of "black space," awe and mystery
he'd so often sensed at the inarticulate center of his life. "The best poem I
ever wrote," he would come to call it.

> *The places still*
> *half-dark, mud,*
> *coal dust.*
>
> *There is no light*
> *east*
> *of the Bridge*
>
> *Only on the headland*
> *toward the harbor*
> *from Cressy's*
>
> *have I seen it (once*
> *when my daughter ran*
> *out on a spit of sand*
>
> *isn't even there.) Where*
> *is Bristow? when does I-A*
> *get me home? I am caught*
>
> *in Gloucester. (What's buried*
> *behind Lufkin's*
> *Diner? Who is*
>
> *Frank Moore?*

Tying up loose strings of college business occupied Olson intermittently
through the rest of the winter. He shipped off transcripts to ex-students who
had requested them, generously awarding retroactive extra credit as needed—

and showing no prejudice even against nonstudents, like Creeley, who was given twelve free units that enabled him to complete a bachelor's degree. Anticipated income of $45,000 from the imminent sale of the upper property presented further fuel for creative fiddling. Olson schemed of investing any surplus in a sort of Black Mountain road show, a touring "Institute in Pre-Homeric Texts and Literature" that would feature Samuel Noah Kramer lecturing on Sumerian, Cyrus Gordon on Phoenician, Hans Guterbock on Hittite texts, and himself as "anchor man." The show would be kicked off a year hence, in San Francisco "or anywhere else anyone wants it," and run for eight weeks as a "caravan traveling around the country" after the Chinese wandering-scholar model. (The college lawyer eventually shot down this imaginative fund-diversion plan.) He was also at work again on Whitehead and the "Special View" lectures, which he was soon going to reoffer in San Francisco. He planned to lecture "flatly on history," as he wrote to Ed Dorn, "just to set it down, once and for all, try to empty the thought out."

The late-February westbound trip began in hair-raising fashion. Paul Metcalf, now living in a small town not far from Black Mountain, was instructed to meet the Olsons at the Asheville railway station on the day of departure so as to take possession of the beach wagon in their absence. Olson, with wife and small son in tow, roared into the station a quarter hour after their train had pulled out, and announced that they must race it over the mountains to its next stop in Knoxville. Negotiating the narrow high road over the Great Smokies in the beach wagon, passing a pint of whiskey back and forth with the anxious Metcalf, he "fishtailed around the S-curves at insane speed" to make the 111-mile drive in barely over two hours, reaching the Knoxville depot just ahead of the train.

Pressure of self-demand, always a factor in his public appearances before unfamiliar audiences, was intensified on Olson's San Francisco visit by his awareness of the city's formidable cast of poets, a cast he'd furthermore previously made the object of juridical opprobrium in "Against Wisdom as Such." The first of several events set up for him by Robert Duncan—now assistant director of the San Francisco State College Poetry Center—was a reading at the city's Museum of Art. To calm his shaky nerves, Olson began drinking some hours before the event, and when the time came to go, could not rouse himself to leave the apartment where he was staying. Betty phoned Duncan, who rushed over. "He was huddled under the covers, drunk. Here was this big man, scared to death by the occasion of performing verse before his peers, so exaggerating it that he had become totally intimidated. I had to reassure him—'Charles, you're just reading your poetry among friends, it won't have to last four days.' " Fortified by Duncan's commonsense ministrations and several cups of black coffee, the panicked poet emerged to do the job. His reading went over well, and afterwards he was toasted by an assembly of bards at a local eatery, the Spaghetti Factory.

There was another reading at the Poetry Center, but the traveling show-man's main act was the Special View of History. Duncan had arranged for the lectures to be given on a private subscription basis at the homes of inter-ested local citizens, the first talk taking place in his own Potrero Hill apart-ment, the others in a series of living rooms around town. Poets Philip Whalen, James Broughton, Jack Spicer, Richard Duerden and Michael McClure were among the subscribers, as were relocated Black Mountaineers Wes Huss, Tom Field, Joe Dunn and Michael Rumaker. Olson's brainstorming, received and construed with "a tone of adoration" by the survivors of his *polis,* proved a much harder sell with the local poets. Whalen, who had actually read *Process and Reality,* created an awkward moment by challenging the lecturer on his sources, raising some pertinent questions about Whiteheadian "historiogra-phy" which the reverent Black Mountain contingent considered out of line. Olson's phenomenal cerebralism stunned many of those who hadn't encoun-tered it before, quickly becoming a topic of controversy. Poets Spicer and McClure, among others, reacted negatively to the wholesale intellectualism of the lectures. (McClure was reported to have gone out and "sold his whole library.")

Following a classroom visit at the University of California—where he was disconcerted to bump into a onetime graduate school colleague and rival, and now a self-conceived academic nemesis, Henry Nash Smith—Olson's junket continued on with stops down the coast in Carmel, where he gave another reading and dropped in on Ephraim and Rosa Doner, and Albu-querque, where he and Betty spent a few days with Creeley and Creeley's new wife, Bobbie Louise Hawkins. By the time they got to New Mexico the Olsons were not getting along; the toils of traveling with a not-quite-two-year-old were wearing on Betty, and Charles' own nerves had been stretched thin by too much talking and drinking. He cut the overland return short by putting down the rest of his cash for a first-class Pullman sleeper berth out of Santa Fe.

Back in North Carolina he was immediately beset by new problems atten-dant to the dissolution of Black Mountain. He had to appear in court as assignee of the college at hearings on the contingent salary suits brought by ex-faculty members Rice, Goldowski and Larsen, the "three horny cows" as he exasperatedly termed them. Since the legal situation appeared to be about to distract him indefinitely, Betty left with Charles Peter to spend the summer in Gloucester with her sister Jean (who was now living there). Her departure probably also owed something to the personality conflict that was already beginning to complicate their relationship. A radical difference in temperament was emerging, his intellectual aggression sometimes seeming to batter the quiet, intuitive Betty into a state of sullen resentment. "At this stage in my life," he confided in great disappointment to Creeley, "I believe I better live alone, at least for awhile. Very sad."

He pushed on dutifully with the sale business, sending out dozens of form letters to former faculty members to notify them of their eligibility for a share in forthcoming revenues. Then, at the end of May, he took a break and went north to Washington and New York, dropping in overnight at Frances' new place on Clinton Street in Brooklyn. This time the reunion was a happy one. "For me too it is now the opening of the flower of my insides because I was with *my own*—you," he told her afterwards. Frances was now writing a book about *Finnegans Wake*. Though he hated and "insulted" Joyce— "and begged me to turn my attentions back to *him*," as Frances recalls— Olson grudgingly yielded to her determination, and before long was even making at least a show of helping out with the project. In the course of "gutting" the college library before its sale, he appropriated several volumes that he thought might be of use to her. Among these were some books on Celtic art and history. Going through L. Russell Muirhead's *Ireland* before turning it over to her, he came across a reference to an ancient sailor-hero who had died of a bee sting and been buried in a Bronze Age cairn at Knock-many in County Tyrone. Researching the subject further for his own as well as for Frances' benefit, he found this prototypical mythic mariner identified with both Manes, founder of the Egyptian First Dynasty, and Minos, King of Crete. The same "handsome sailor" figure would within the next few years become a new persona of Maximus, introduced in a gnomic lyric section titled "All My Life I've Heard About Many" ("He went to Spain, / the hand-some sailor, / he went to Ireland / and died of a bee: / he's buried, at the hill / of KnockMany")—a piece Olson would hold up as prime exemplum of his "atavistic" use of image, or "letting the thing stay back where you find it, and going back there . . . very much [as in] magic practice."

Renewal of creative dialogue with his elective Muse stirred a fresh ripple of curiosity about what might possibly be made of the connection on a life level. He paid her a late-June visit in Woodward, where she was building a rudimentary cabin. Being back in the tiny Appalachian hamlet brought back strong emotional memories. Ironically, however, the memories served mostly to remind him of the passage of the years, and his strongest feelings while in Pennsylvania were of missing his young wife.

It was to see Betty that he ventured north again in early August. She met him at South Station in Boston, appearing tanned and rested after the time on her own. He stayed long enough to talk her into putting their differences aside, then returned to Black Mountain to pack up and be present for the sale closing. From the latter event, which occurred on September 21, 1957, he came away with a sizable stake for his future: a payment of $8,000 for his services as legal assignee, on top of several years' worth of back salary. It was the first week of October before he'd finished loading up the beach wagon with everything he hadn't already shipped off to Betty in Gloucester. His hill-fort monastery, the sanctuary and refuge of his last seven years, would henceforth be but "a speck in the dust of eternity."

21 ~

Isolato
(1957–1960)

The trip to rejoin his family gave Olson strong inklings that his move from Black Mountain to Gloucester would be less a going into the world than an exchange of sanctuaries. In a real sense it was only in the isolation of places and conditions that were somehow spiritually separate that his poetry could now thrive. And it was to his poetry, a private covenant largely exclusive of public realities, that he was henceforth to be giving over his life.

So invested with the mythology of private significances had the poet's life become that its quality of magic resonance or allegory could never be far from his mind. On the way north in the book-laden beach wagon he tried a back route that would allow him to check out Civil War sites in Virginia, but was arrested near Appomattox Courthouse for straying across the white line while rubbernecking and fined $16.25 in a traffic court not far from the spot where Lee had turned the South over to Grant. In a stop at a Maryland county fair he viewed a lurid hootchy-kootchy act, the "dirtiest girlie show" he had ever seen, and stock-car races during which beer-swilling spectators gobbled hot dogs and cheered " 'death' & 'killer' laps" replete with violent crashes. Repelled by this "unbelievable new junk America," he found that crossing over the Annisquam River on Highway 128 had never seemed more a relief, nor Gloucester more a refuge.

His residence during the years ahead would be a second-floor apartment

in a big, weathered white clapboard house at 28 Fort Square. Betty had
found the place in a late-summer house-hunting expedition with her sister
Jean. The best thing about it, in Charles' opinion, was the spectacular, commanding seven-window southward sweep, taking in what were for him sacred
spaces—the whole stretch of water from Eastern Point to Western Harbor,
over whose "golden life, golden light" it would be his daily ritual to gaze into
the setting sun; from Ten Pound Island, "a floating / cruiser or ironclad /
Monitor, all laid out on top of the water," with its "dusky old Light" and fog
bells, to the far lighthouse at Dog Bar on the tip of the outer harbor breakwater, with its whistle buoy. From the kitchen at the rear of the apartment,
furthermore, he could look out and see Half Moon Beach, Tablet Rock and
the rocky bluff at Stage Head—where as a young boy he'd gone rowing, and
where, as a younger one, he'd hidden behind the rocks to listen to those
fishermen's yarns that had "made [him] a poet." One *Maximus* outtake reg-
istering a silver sunset making "Stage Head / a pure Tsukiyama-sansui" he
would title "The Intended Angle of Vision is from My Kitchen." Such brilliant views, laying out "the whole / full landscape a / Buddhist message," would
constitute a "sharp drawn / lesson" for him as poet of the visual world and of
its visionary lights. Whether working from a Chinese or Japanese landscape
painter's perspective or "[Fitzhugh] Lane's eye view," he would henceforth
ground his poetry's image of the physical world upon the literal scene that
rose up before his eyes as he sat at "my fair window."

   The locale, inspiring as it may have been to him, was socially "much
scorned." The "Fort" neighborhood, so named because of the eighteenth-
century fortification and cannon on the point, was home mostly to working-
class Sicilian families, whose paint-peeling bleached-wood frame houses
resembled the one Olson himself inhabited. Many of his closest neighbors,
like the Tarantinos and the Randazzas, came from the same small town of
Terrasini, west of Palermo. In an ethnic community so tightly knit Olson
would come to think of it as almost tribal ("Algonquin-Sicilian"), the huge
and eccentric newcomer immediately stood out, acquiring the nicknames "The
Jolly Green Giant," from the children of the neighborhood, and "The Professor," from their parents. Many of his neighbors were fishermen. For the
poet who had long revered men of the sea, moving among them, being surrounded by the "fish stink" and "shabby old fish-houses" of the Cape Ann
Fisheries wharf—a constant haven for gulls noisily scavenging fish scraps, just
across the street from 28 Fort Square—was a passage into personal myth.
Time would sober him little in this regard, as was to be evident to literary
visitors who would catch him "staging" friendships with the fishermen. (Olson's
compulsory tour of the fishing docks left guest Paul Metcalf, for instance,
with the clear impression the poet's attempts at engaging the net-mending

sea dogs in manly talk were being humored at best—"the fishermen were never warm, and after awhile became quietly hostile: they stopped speaking English and spoke among themselves in Italian. Charles was slighted, and we moved off . . .") To complete the maritime ambience of Olson's immediate environs, on a rise at the rear of his unkempt backyard—whose tall grass, sunflowers and wild poppies grew knee-high to a large plaster statue of the Blessed Virgin—a weathered wood fence was usually draped with fishing nets belonging to the Gloucester Net and Marine Supply Company.

For a family with a small child—not to mention a vast pack rat of a poet— the apartment was rather cramped from the first, and the deluge of Charles' books and papers would before long be overflowing his trestle-table work desk, flooding bookcases, closets, cardboard boxes, dresser drawers, and finally the floor, where they competed for space with Charles Peter's toys. The walls too were soon to be covered, Charles' annotated maps tacked up edge-to-edge with large "petroglyphic" canvases done by Betty (who now took up painting, renting a studio a few doors away). When all available space was occupied in the living room and bedroom, Charles took over the kitchen, turning the kitchen table into a second work desk upon which a further epic confusion of papers swamped dishes, food and ashtrays. Becoming Charles Peter's playroom as well, and the place where Charles and Betty entertained guests, the large kitchen was usually the most crowded room in the apartment. In wintertime Charles often passed his nocturnal work vigils there, since it housed the big "Cape Ann" range-style oil stove that provided the apartment's main source of heat.

As the approach of cold weather soon revealed, the number-one physical problem for him at 28 Fort Square was to lie not in finding room for his poetic disorder but in keeping himself warm enough to work. With "winter / staring me in the face" and not having spent one in Gloucester for nearly twenty years, he had forgotten just how much colder the North Atlantic shore could be than even the chilliest of times in the mountains of North Carolina. By Thanksgiving heavy snow had fallen, and he was already insisting that despite the cost the apartment's "two heats"—the oil stove and a basement furnace—had to be going at full blast so as to keep the room temperature at a stable 85 degrees. This was a regime he maintained much of the year even though others at times found the resultant atmospheric conditions "suffocating." Even when the windowpanes were ice-cold to the touch, the stale air inside stayed warm enough to keep the poet's juices going through the frigid small hours that were his most creative time. ("Night construction, day constriction" was still his compulsive pattern.) With little traffic outside and no television or radio to disrupt his concentration, in the still of the night while he worked the silence of the apartment was nearly total, interrupted only by his breathing as he pulled deeply on his cigarettes, the tapping of his old Royal typewriter, and the occasional clicks of the thermostat.

Out the window on clear, icy nights during the first deep cold spell of that winter, the shining of the lighthouse beams and stars and moon over the water could not but beckon him to poems. Inevitably the latter were affected by the emotions of his return to Gloucester. Evoked with particular strength were feelings about his mother, mixed as ever. One chilly evening with Christmas on the way, his habitual gesture of bundling himself up in an afghan made for him by Mary brought suddenly to his mind "my dearest mother, / in the grave" ("Just Inside the Vigil of Christmas"). Yet in another poem he asserted emphatically that "we grow, and act, away from / the mother" ("What's Wrong with Pindar"). In a third, "Moonset, Gloucester, December 1, 1957, 1:58 AM," he staged the tensions of achieving outward growth and action with greater particularity. Like many of the finest poems of his later years, this one began with the view out his window.

> *Goodbye red moon*
> *In that color you set*
> *west of the Cut I should imagine*
> *forever Mother . . .*

When Cape Ann Historical Society director Charles Brooks asked him what he was doing back in Gloucester, Olson answered simply: "to thicken the soup." He was talking about his *Maximus*. "The advantage of a long poem," he noted in his journal shortly after the return to Gloucester,

> is [that] like pot au feu, it creates its own juice . . . Or put it formally: the long poem creates its own situation. Which is its gain over the small poem, which, each time, must make its own way, and thus loses, to itself, a character of reality which the long poem creates for itself—a continuity in time which is both massa confusa and the prolongation of life itself.
>
> When you got that meat stock the poem's got more to work with.

A Poundian conception of epic as associative accumulation of historical materials still ruled Olson's imagination of the form. In compositional terms, this method had the obvious attraction of offering a way around having to start up from scratch with each new writing session. His dread of the blank page remained strong, a residue of his fear of the formal occasion of composition, whose challenges awakened in him old demons of self-demand. In the increasingly improvisational works ahead, he would sidestep the problem by doing his writing elsewhere, on quite literally any scrap of paper—placemats, napkins, bills, the backs of letters—which came to hand at the moment of inspiration.

The thickening of the stew via historical researches began as soon as Olson got to Gloucester that fall, and kept up over a data-laden stop-and-go historical "run" of the *Maximus* that would extend to the end of the third "book" of the poem with the spring 1959 "April Today Main Street." The section showed that he'd as yet failed to hit on any original alternative to the Poundian epic formula. In his journal he acknowledged as much to himself.

> The error of the epic at this point in time [is] that with the long poem you get something into which you can throw anything (as though we were looking for some hole in the ocean or earth in which to deposit atomic waste—a silly search & a silly goods . . . we've known enough of a universe whose laws don't turn out to apply in the domain of the infinitely small. . . .

The element of self-critique in these remarks is clear. Olson had only a few days earlier begun his historical "run," drafting the poem "a Plantation a beginning," a tribute to the "fourteen spare men" of the Dorchester Company who had spent their first New World winter "huddled above Half Moon Beach"—just across Western Harbor from his apartment windows. The poem was drawn largely on current favorite sources like nineteenth-century writer John Babson's *History of the Town of Gloucester* and the dependable Frances Rose-Troup, whose biography of John White, employed earlier for "Letter 23," would prove invaluable throughout the ensuing "run" (for "a Plantation" he unearthed a primary account to which Rose-Troup had led him, White's *Planter's Plea*).

In the practical sphere, it now made some sense to get his epic back into gear. For once there was active interest from publishers. Jonathan Williams was intent on doing a third set of *Maximus* pieces. And Donald Allen, a Grove Press editor who was now seeing *Call Me Ishmael* back into print, wanted to follow up on that book with a two-volume selected Olson, poetry and prose. The attentions of Allen in particular aroused Olson to attempt new writings. During his first weeks in Gloucester, the editor journeyed up from New York to see him. The flattered poet entertained at a favored hangout, the Tavern—a big old restaurant-inn on Pavilion Beach just below his Fort Square flat—treating Allen and traveling companion Robin Blaser to several hours of expansive conversation and a reading of his poem "Letter 5." Writing to Robert Duncan in the first week of November, Olson attributed his getting started on the new series of historical poems to "the impetus of Don Allen's coming."

Within a few months, though, it was apparent to him that the going was

to be intermittent at best. "Off my pace," he would report to Duncan by
March 1958. At this point the very different way in poetry taken by Duncan
could not but affect his judgment of his own present efforts, particularly as
his West Coast colleague was currently turning out poems Olson had to
acknowledge as "magnificent," "beautiful"—and which made his own documentary approach appear dull and overly literal to him in comparison. He
was particularly envious of the magisterial reflective sonorities of Duncan's
"A Poem Beginning with a Line by Pindar," sent him by his poet friend in
late October 1957. Tacitly conceding his dismay with the way *Maximus* was
now getting caught up in the fact-meshes of the "materials," he told Duncan
he had no comparable grand work to send in reply. "Like a fool instead of
plunging into words when I landed back here I went into local research. And
have spent myself, like an idiot . . . hungry, after all these years, to find out
facts abt my place . . . instead of doing what is wiser, contemplating through
a glass darkly. . . . Down with materials, and moving parts!"

The danger of the accumulation method was that the processing of historical material into the long poem could become mechanical, a matter of
mere "moving parts"; finding this to be the case in some fifteen of his attempted
Maximus pieces of these years, Olson would eventually lay them aside as misdirected efforts. An essay done on Melville for the *Chicago Review* at this time,
"Equal, That Is, to the Real Itself," reflected his ongoing thinking on the
central formal questions posed by his long poem. How would the post-modern epic creator, swamped by a universe of boundless energy and motion,
deal with the mass quantity of data before him? How, further, could he include
history at all without succumbing to the hypermaterialistic supermarket culture of the present, image of the "exact death quantity does offer, if it is
[merely] numbers, and extension, and the appetite of matter"? Addressing
quantity and measurement as his themes, the poet-turned-critic betrayed the
intensity of his own quest for a new "metric means," a formula for "the new
equation, quantity as expansive." Also its frustrations. For while acknowledging the value of Melville's legacy of radical procedures—a "point-by-point
mapping" of the "elliptical and hyperbolic spaces of topology and congru-
ence"—Olson left the impression he felt later writers, himself included, had
so far failed to fully explore and develop those post-Euclidean projective spaces
so tantalizingly opened up in *Moby-Dick*. The future of form, in an open,
processual Whiteheadian universe, itself remained an open question:

> What did happen to measure when the rigidities dissolved? . . . What is measure
> when the universe flips and no part is discrete from another part except by the
> flow of creation, in and out, intensive where it seemed before qualitative, and the
> extensive exactly the widest, which we have also the powers to include?

The search for a measure would occupy Olson increasingly over the next six years of withdrawal and isolation in Gloucester. He told Robert Duncan in a letter from his new home: "I am hungry to be one thing again." In the larger scale of things, he had long believed, a special power was conferred upon the poet by his priestly function; but his role was not so much to live that power as to project it, "to make our image of a union of ourself," an image of perfect wholeness amid chaos. The creation of such an image of self-integration was the purpose of the figuration of poetry. "It is not I, / even if the life appeared / biographical," Olson would come to declare through the allegorical mask of Maximus. "The only interesting thing / is if one can be / an image / of man." It was the allegory of the poet's life, its figurative aspect, which alone mattered; all other concentrations and considerations of a merely personal nature had to be put aside. "You can work on the life, or you can work on the work; you can't do both."

The human consequences of that choice remained to be reckoned with. The poet's young wife, his "captive caretaker," would be affected most strongly. Betty, little attracted to the "footnoter" role Connie had once filled, did not take long to grow impatient with the exclusivity of his involvements in the life of the mind. Every further advance into his work seemed to be won at the price of a proportionate impoverishment of their personal relations and social life. In an effort to justify his reclusive self-absorption as a reaction against and compensation for the draining of energies that had been the most negative aspect of his Black Mountain experience, he explained to her that he was actively engaged in "getting up my own waters, or water level (life-level)." The demands of the restorative process supplied him also with a reply to charges of selfishness, which in such circumstances could hardly be avoided. "Charles is the most selfish person you'll ever meet," Betty advised her sister succinctly, "so don't expect anything but that." He himself naturally saw the matter as less simple. The spiritual energies which in one note of domestic apology he told his wife he was allowing himself to build up were akin to the originary cosmic "stuff" he was simultaneously investigating in archaic poets and thinkers from Hesiod to Heraclitus, and beginning to write poetry about. Describing it to Betty, his metaphors were those of alchemy, evidently influenced by his readings in Jung: "What I'm speaking about is . . . fluids . . . liquid things which got lost, talking & all that being 'gross,' in respect to some distillation which gathering (like dew) the matters one is interested in—cares about—does bring about." For "putting in, and keeping in" that vital fluid, nothing but solitude would do. "I'm storing up," he told her. "For so long there [at] Black Mt., I gave it away—you know, spilled it ('wasted it,' in some respects, too, no doubt). The point is, simply, that it did get 'used up' . . . [like] scraping the bottom, as Archie McCleod sd they were doing, fishing out the

Atlantic." By such tenuous arguments he attempted to reassure her that the storing-up and brewing stage was only a passing one, and that "there is an end somewhere . . . to give you some sense it's not all, hammer, hammer!"

But the relentless, obsessive time- and life-consuming work binges in fact had no terminus, being far more a matter of expressing compulsive inner drives than of completing external projects. Of necessity the resulting poetic product was, like the notes of the alchemist seeking perfect conversion, encoded in a private vocabulary of symbols which in personal terms could only serve to further isolate the poet. Yet despite his extraordinary self-involvement, Olson remained capable of great emotional intensities and sensitivities, and there is evidence of his guilty awareness of the sufferings his eccentric habits caused for his loved ones. Most telling is a letter to his daughter written late in his life and at his death left behind in the pages of Otto Fenichel's *The Psychoanalytic Theory of Neurosis*. The letter was an apology not only for his failure to spend more of his time with Kate in her maturing years, but for his entire life, that of a man who had made "constant use of all the time he could squeeze . . . for what he had not even good reason to know." It was also an acknowledgment of his compulsive phobic relation to temporality.

> I have been "rushing" sort of, stealing all the time I could get all my life. . . . It has always been a race. . . . I had so much to learn. . . . [it] was compelling enough for me to continue along the same course even without interruption. . . . almost any time lost from the pursuit was more than I could stand.

Olson's terror of the flight of time was not mere literary convention, the poet's traditional comment on the fleetingness of temporal passage, but an urgently felt emotional reality. In his battle against time, family perennially lost out. Rebuked by Connie for neglecting their daughter, he announced in May 1958 that he was "not going to set any record" for fatherly behavior. The issue of how often and with what degree of scheduling he was to see the seven-year-old Kate became a matter of bitter dispute between himself and his estranged spouse, from whom he was now physically separated only by the waters of Massachusetts Bay. Connie preferred a strict regulation of paternal visitation by formal appointment, while he insisted that he should be allowed to have Kate at his disposal on a spur-of-the-moment basis. To test things, he made a surprise visit to Scituate; Connie herself refused to see him and permitted him only a few hours with Kate, who was deposited by Mel Atherton outside the town's general store for a forlorn picnic with her father. After this episode, he agreed to Connie's terms: Kate would come to Gloucester to stay a few times a year, during school holidays. In the actual event, however, he often found these scheduled visits occurring in the midst of work drives. When that happened, he either canceled out or showed up woefully late to pick up the girl at South Station in Boston. The experience of waiting for hours in a crowd of strangers for him to appear became a particularly traumatic chapter in the prolonged disappointment of Kate's relations with her father, "one repeated broken-heart story" to unfold over the decade to come. From his point of view as well, there was much heartache in the situation. When in September 1959 Connie married George Bunker, an independently wealthy Philadelphia art teacher, and Kate thereby acquired a stepfather, Olson ruefully reported the news to friends: "Kate now Katherine Mary Bunker, to my dismay." Lacking the ability to provide child support himself, however, he had no choice but to surrender control of his daughter's future.

As the Black Mountain money gradually ran out, he was hard put to support even his own small brood. And there were growing tensions in the household. Ironically, having long wished for a male heir, he now found he "didn't know how to be a father to a son." With Charles Peter he was an "autocrat," flying into rages over having his daylong sleeps interrupted or his books and papers disturbed. Betty, as temperate intercessor, was continually occupied with simply keeping peace in the poet's creative sanctum. One 1959 visitor to the Fort, former Black Mountain student Fielding Dawson, got the impression the former college patriarch was flopping as a family man. The Olsons were by then clearly in difficult financial straits; Betty seemed to be "trying her best to live up to a tough scene," though "disillusioned" by the narrowness of their life—and Charles himself appeared "indeed guilty." At the same time, Dawson and other visitors found Olson susceptible, on very little provocation, to fits of paranoid jealousy involving Betty and various imagined rivals. (Something of this is betrayed in his poem "The Distances," a consideration of the possessive love of the eternal siren-goddess, written shortly after Dawson's visit.) As time went by, friends noted a mysterious elusiveness in Betty. Pale, thin, she seemed like some evanescent phantom on the run, "a luminescent Moon speeding away from Olson." When things got too confusing at the Fort, Charles, following the suggestion of his gnomic little poem "All Havens Astern"—"I'm going to swim for my life / to another shore. The human shore's / too much / You can speak. You're on safe / ground, you mandala, you. I'm / getting out of here"—simply took off on his own, heading out for a few hours to the Tavern or to Vincent Ferrini's frame shop on nearby East Main Street, or for a few days to drop in on poet friends like John Wieners in Boston and Robin Blaser in Cambridge. A scrawled note to Betty from this time hints of Olson's inner turmoil: "Don't mind anything— I just feel such a load of bullshit I'd like to hide out somewhere until I can believe in some part of me again."

A not insignificant element in his crisis of confidence of these years was a growing sense that progressive literary tides had turned, leaving him (and his beached epic) high and dry, just "an old schlumpf from Gloucester," while younger and more accessible revolutionaries—particularly the Beats—enjoyed the ride on a media wave of unprecedented intensity. The jealousy and chagrin Olson felt at having his own work and "movement" passed over were undoubtedly exacerbated by his awareness of such historical ironies. It did not escape him, in the *Time, Life* and *Newsweek* hullaballoo over the 1957 *Howl* obscenity trial and publication of *On the Road,* that the youthful and enthusiastic Allen Ginsberg, one-man publicist of the Beats, had been briefly an adman before winning notoriety in poetry; nor that the sudden fame of the Beat phenomenon as a whole owed much to a sophisticated updating of the same packaging and promotional techniques whose proliferation twenty-five years earlier had been largely responsible for his own departure from government service and political life. At the same time, he could not suppress in himself a powerful hunger for at least some taste of the same wide exposure the Beats were getting now. He resolved to study their formula, however distasteful. Vacationing in Provincetown in the fall of 1958, he laboriously copied into his notebook long passages from Kerouac's *On the Road*—despite his misgivings about the naturalistic dimensions of the book ("Jack with his 'pictures,' " he commented in a letter to Creeley, "Saroyan will catch him if he don't watch out").

In 1959 he showed up for a much-touted Harvard appearance of Beat bards Ginsberg, Gregory Corso and Peter Orlovsky. The occasion left him ambivalent over whether the author of *Howl* was a real poet or merely a crowd-pleasing publicity hound and "Rowser." In his estimate of Corso he was less uncertain, disdaining the neo-romantic ex-con's verse and falling into a protracted argument with him over post-reading drinks. Corso, who in a recently published interview had called him a "hip square" and "mental gangster," kept up his needling until Olson became "bugged" and put an end to the discussion by walking over to his adversary and wordlessly knocking him out of his chair with a vigorous head-butt. Corso "had a big lump on his head for days." Olson, for his part, also went away sore. He felt the Beats were "hexing" him. Back at the Fort after the Harvard event he hammered out a spell-reversing *Maximus* poem (which, upon striking up better relations with some of the Beats in later years, he would withhold from the published epic), "A Maximus Written to Throw Back a Hex on Allen Ginsberg and / or Gregory Corso." But sour grapes did not make for good poetry. In the wake of events at Harvard, Olson became more depressed than ever, encased in a gloomy competitive resentment over having been displaced at the top of the poets' mountain by men he didn't consider serious. For a while he even contemplated desperation schemes of setting up a common front to co-opt the Beats by including them in the faculty of a projected "moral university" at Venice, California. But at this point it was not his bandwagon to drive. His grudge lingered, nursed over the isolation of the next several years. "I sat in Gloucester," he would confess at the 1965 Berkeley Poetry Conference—his ultimate up-close tilt-for-power with Ginsberg et al.—"suffering, suffering that the world had been captured by Allen and Peter and Gregory and their own master (like my Pound), Burroughs."

Holed up at his shore retreat conserving and renewing energies that might or might not ever be used, preparing himself like a woodshedding jazz player for a triumphant return that was being indefinitely postponed, at times it was all Olson could do to resist the fear he'd wasted his life. An occasional note of self-pity now crept into his private correspondence, especially to the small band of Black Mountain survivors on whom he had implicitly counted as apostles to extend his sphere of influence in thought and poetry: so far, in their various dispersions and migrations across country, they had failed to do much more than mirror back to him his own isolation. To Ed Dorn, he remarked with some bitterness that in an age of affiliations-of-convenience he himself belonged to "the school of few to talk to, or visit." The single greatest deficiency of the current progressive cultural scene, in Olson's envious sideline view, was its lack of a flexible periodical outlet for his own work and views. He had long since given up on Cid Corman and *Origin,* and in the two years following the 1957 demise of the *Black Mountain Review,* only Donald Allen's *Evergreen Review,* where he published some prose and a poem or two, offered any prospect of relief from the frustrating deprivation of expression. But *Evergreen*'s obvious commercial purpose severely limited its utility as an organ of intransigent dogmatic resistance; and while Olson put considerable trust in Don Allen, he could not but feel that much like any clever mainstream editor, Allen was less a gambler or risk-taker than simply an astute student of the stock market of literary trends—as reflected by the growing presence in *Evergreen* and the Grove Press lists of the "holyroll-ers . . . Ginzy McClure Burroughs." If another editor as ideally congenial as Creeley was to be found, clearly it would have to be outside the media main-stream.

Not until 1959 did Olson find a likely candidate. He was contacted then by LeRoi Jones, a bright, energetic young New York black writer / editor in whom he was quickly able to make out a fellow cultural revolutionary, one just as quick on the draw as himself, and, most important, one willing to offer him carte-blanche publication. Jones, later to espouse Black National-ism and, as Amiri Baraka, to become a force in the unfolding of American history in the Newark riots, was at this stage of his career still involved mainly with aesthetic insurgency, seeking to promote a redefinition of poetry and art and in specific a "popular-oriented" poetic language that "moved toward American speech" in the tradition of Whitman and Williams. To him Olson was a figure of "awe." Editing the landmark little magazines *Yugen* (where Olson's first appearance came in 1959, with "The Librarian," a poem previously rejected by several other editors), *Kulchur* (begun in 1960) and *Floating Bear* (1961), Jones would provide a hip-culture forum for much of the poet's highly unsystematic speculative writing of the early sixties, including the majority of the short pieces collected by Don Allen in the 1965 Four Seasons Foundation pamphlet *Proprioception,* prime documents of the unrestrained conjectural skeet-shooting that characterized Olsonian "thought" during these years. Without Jones' standing offer to publish literally anything he wrote, Olson's urgent if fragmentary sketching of a philosophy of proprioceptive Immanence, a positioning of self and soul inside the living "cave" of the body, would probably never have been articulated at all. "Jones was in New York City," he would later remark of these campaigns of intellectual guerrilla warfare conducted long-distance from the Fort in Gloucester, "I was lobbing 'em. It was like the Civil War. . . . He was in Richmond, and I was in the redoubt at St Petersburg." Jones had too much else going on in his life ever to be as reliable a correspondent / aide-de-guerre as Creeley had once been, but Olson was inclined to overlook occasional communication lapses in light of the editor's total commitment to the Push in all its adventurous creative disorder. "I go easily with LeRoi," he declared in a December 1959 letter to Creeley, now briefly employed as an English tutor on a Guatemalan coffee finca. "In fact the past year he has 'saved' my life in publishing by just being scattered . . . as against the horrible managed biz it all has been since you and the Review."

The impulsion to begin a new movement of the *Maximus*—with self and cosmos as poles, ocean or Okeanos as integrating metaphor, and the rocky, half-wild glacial moraine called Dogtown Common on the outskirts of Gloucester replacing the harbor community itself as sacred precinct ("my 2nd 'town' ")—came late in 1959, a few months after Olson had mailed off to publisher Jonathan Williams the first major collection of *Maximus* poems (containing all three extant sections), and immediately following an energizing November visit from a carload of New York friends, including LeRoi Jones, Don Allen and San Francisco poets Philip Whalen and Michael McClure. Particularly eager to impress the touring West Coast luminaries, who in his perennially competitive imagination represented the challenge of the poetic moment, Olson proposed a hike through the waste expanses of Dogtown. Feeling out of sorts after a week of hard traveling, Philip Whalen begged off.

Olson was convinced (with no evidence) that Betty was secretly "pretty gone on" the California Buddhist "holy doctor," and felt anxious about leaving them alone together in the house. (In fact Whalen spent the afternoon flat on his back on the Fort's living-room sofa, ill with intestinal flu and totally unaware of his host's paranoid suspicions; "I didn't catch any vibes from Bet," he recalls, "I was raised by old fashioned people, and thought of another man's wife as being completely 'off limits,' so I didn't come on to her in any way.") Though also unwell, McClure held up the visitors' side by submitting gamely to the Dogtown expedition, and was led by Olson through a landscape of scrub pine, overgrown blueberry brambles, rocky granite outcroppings and cavernous holes in the earth (the ruins of old cellars, from eighteenth-century settlement days), past weeds, junk and a pile of stinking, rotting fish, on to Dogtown Meadow, the spot where in 1892 a brawny six-foot-seven-inch "handsome sailor" named James Merry had been torn to pieces in a drunken wrestling match with a bull. In his telling of this elemental tale, tour-guide Olson breathed dramatic life into each archetypal detail. "Around us in the cold rocky fields where once farms and houses stood," remembers McClure, "women, far away, bent picking ground growing evergreens for Xmas florals. Charles told me the story of the handsome stocky man—pointing to a rock & patch of ground—'Here' he said 'where the bull's enclosure was . . . ' "

Back at home that evening after the poet pilgrims had left for the next stop on their tour, the same narrative of male hubris, shown in its cosmic aspect as an overreaching appetite for experience and knowledge, became the basis of "MAXIMUS, FROM DOGTOWN—I," foundation stone in the construction of the second main movement of Olson's epic. The poem here attained a new level of analogical vision. Splicing Memphite theology conned from Erich Neumann's *The Great Mother* with Greek cosmogony cribbed from Hesiod's *Theogony*, Olson transposed Dogtown's Ice Age granite and diorite masses into the body of a great archaic earth / sky goddess like the Egyptian Nut, and, in lines of a persistent rhythmic power echoing the slow heaving motions of the sea beneath his window, narrated the birth of Okeanos, the river-god of genesis, figure of the self-measured generative process of creation.

> *The sea was born of the earth without sweet union of love Hesiod says*
>
> *But that then she lay for heaven and she bare the thing which encloses*
> *every thing, Okeanos the one which all things are and by which nothing*
> *is anything but itself, measured so*
>
> *screwing earth, in whom love lies which unnerves the limbs and by its*
> *heat floods the mind and all gods and men into further nature*

Vast earth rejoices,

deep-swirling Okeanos steers all things through all things,
everything issues from the one, the soul is led from drunkenness
to dryness, the sleeper lights up from the dead,
the man awake lights up from the sleeping

The mythic Okeanos Olson saw out his seven windows bore increasing likeness to the self reflected back at him by the light glancing off the panes. In this chapter of the poet's allegory, Oneness was all. "When Maximus looks out to sea," critic J. H. Prynne comments of the epic's next stage, *Maximus IV, V, VI,* "he looks out through the sea, down into the sea, out to the cosmos, we have the whole of Okeanos, we have the whole of the void, the whole of the condition of that circular curve to the condition of space." The challenge posed by the poem, as it expanded outward like the developing universe, was more than ever to find a form of containment—a task approached in this stage, as Prynne accurately suggests, by means of a radical "mythography" based on "the writing of where one is," the poet's instinctive way of keeping the self securely at the gravitational center. As well as first philosophies and cosmic views, Maximus / Okeanos was prone to extremes of subjectivity in vision. "You look out to sea, recognizing that you do what Melville did, and you make the excursion in such a way that the land becomes enlarged behind you and occupies your dreams. The sea occupies your vision, and in between the two you whirl. . . ."

Whirled in dreams one night at the Fort, Olson heard a low voice intoning a single gnomic sentence, with "a strange down-fall of the last phrase": "Everything issues from the Black Chrysanthemum, and nothing is anything but itself measured so." Upon waking, he inscribed the sentence in his journal as an omen of potentially great portent, a dogmatic "message" or "instruction." It was evidently meant for him as poet: the final phrase, "measured so," identified the mysterious dream-statement as "from the start a principle, may I call it, of measure." The dream's cosmos-originating Black Chrysanthemum came from a Jungian text he had been reading, the ninth-century Chinese alchemical tract *The Secret of the Golden Flower.* Looking back over the esoteric text, he found the line that had triggered his dream: "that which exists through itself is called meaning." The planting of this message in his psyche, he quickly decided, was a direct oracular dictation, a "receiving [of] a 'gift' of the truth." His subsequent thorough investigation of the Jungian symbolism of the Chinese text amplified the original impact of the dream. The Golden Flower, he learned, represented a mystical solar quality; its botanical equivalent was a magical plant described by medieval alchemists as akin to Homer's *moly,* a drug capable of inducing shamanic spells. "The Black Chrysanthemum / Ocean . . . the Black Gold Flower" became a kind of spell or rune for him, a potent source of poetic associations—and the "measured so" dream, intensely self-mythologized over the years to come, a talisman of the immanent or "autonomic" condition he was now about to enter in his writing.

"MAXIMUS, FROM DOGTOWN—II," a "twin" to the first poem, written immediately on its heels, was in Olson's conception a "backward face of the other." It marked a pivoting of the epic as a whole, a turning away from the literal shore to view the "protogonic weather" of "the other side of heaven"— the mythic boundary-zones of Gaia, the earth goddess: "Dogtown the under / vault heaven—the 'mother' / rock: the Diamond (Coal) the Pennsylvanian / Age the soft / (Coal) LOVE." The establishment of a topography of archetypes for Dogtown and Ocean and in the process for Earth itself, as well as the sketching of a multi-dimensional "mappemunde . . . to include my being"— with the poem in the process taking on a strongly analogical quality, like the early world maps which also functioned as cosmological charts—would constitute the main action now to unfold in the *Maximus*.

As the poem changed, so too did Olson's writing habits. His verse was now coming not in poems but in *pieces,* improvisational, notational, fragmentary. Further, the secondary compositional stages of editing and revision, once a routine element in any Olson writing project—and indeed the source of much painful and protracted labor—had all but ceased to take place. As a result, the *Maximus* began to fill up with the raw stuff of the creative process: found notes, journal musings, the ongoing log of the raging immediacy of the experiential moment. Not all the ore contained gold, of course; much of what he wrote—and kept—was cryptic, wayward, or uninspired. It was the improvisational conceiving of the whole, as opposed to the formal mediation or "composing" of the parts, that now received paramount consideration. This development, as he struggled to explain to Ed Dorn in an early 1960 letter, at once puzzled, troubled and intrigued him.

What "kills" me is—like not being able to "compose" or not in and of the *single* poem. It all either comes of itself, in a rush, or it isn't—& I can't figure how to "tinker" with it thereafter. (Which seems like what one means by "creative" power: wld like so much to be able to sit over it *afterward,* and snap my whip *anywhere* where—like—it can be "improved." That cool

Finally

give up, and continue—like—to "push on" Mush Seems as though there is this way of "conception": as against, say, "composing," I can find some confidence of going on, both by test of hindsight and present burst, like But miss that other *"proof"* Had a "big" sensation a couple of weeks ago say—on a Maximus layed

in this crazy place back of the city called Dogtown . . . had crazy feeling like this
is the way it felt 5th century BC this writing that "verse" they did for "plays"!

It was the precognitive irrational power of the verse impulse which moved
Olson to compare the activity of writing as processual "conceiving" with the
practice of Greek poetic dramatists like Euripides, but in fact the action of
his own poetry was increasingly *non*dramatic, an unfolding self-mythology
that was by its nature ahistorical, circular and unplotted. "Life," he had long
insisted, "*is* preoccupation with itself." The work ahead on the epic would be
largely an effort "to bring this thing [the poem] closer and try to talk as
though it was I rather than some creature . . . I call Maximus, who's been the
person that's previously presided." The Olson who was forever departing
into himself—his long poem was already a chart of the successive unfoldings
and castings-off of all those earlier trial selves—thus began his final departure,
heading "straight into himself, leaving everything behind" in his quest for a
paradoxically impersonal mythological vision of individual identity.

It was a quest that would gradually make a religious poet of him, though
hardly one of any recognizable or conventional persuasion. Adopting a religious attitude he ascribed to "the ANCIENTS" (that "world outside and before
Christianity" plus such isolated "EXCEPTIONS inside it circum 1200 A.D." as
the alchemists and Arab and Vedic philosophers), following the semimystical
autonomic discipline of self-measure, and intent to "write a poem simply to
create a mode of priesthood in a church forever," Olson became during these
years an intuitive dogmatist of private vision, a shamanic votary as committed
to his own spiritual exercises as the Greek poet-priests to the mysteries of the
earth goddess they guarded at Eleusis. ("All night long / I was a Eumolpidae /
as I slept / putting things together / which had not previously fit.") The "voice
of a sense of religion" which he had projected to student disciples at Black
Mountain was now to find its ultimate home in a fetishlike analogical poetry
transmitted as runic spell, inaccessible to the point of incomprehensibility to
the general public, but to a small audience of acolytes nothing less than necessary data, the hermetic doctrines and protocols of "secret rites practiced by
the initiates alone, just like mysteries."

In late 1960 Olson found a new spiritual guide to the ritual work of verse,
a French scholar of medieval Arabic thought, Henry Corbin, whose essay
"Cyclical Time in Mazdaism and Ismailism" he discovered in a Jungian yearbook. Corbin's formulation of medieval Muslim mystical belief offered a fresh
response to "that question of a poet's images and his coming into possession
of them leading to . . . cosmology," increasingly the central question of poetics for Olson. In Corbin's description of the Ismaili angelology of person,
each personified angel or spiritual adept, observing a particularized "total

Time of his own measure," rode the cyclic homing-beams of a cosmic "thought that is thought through him" back into soul origins in a timeless paradise of genesis. The process of spiritual exegesis or perpetual return, called by the medieval Ismaili philosophers *ta'wil,* was identified by Olson—as hinted in his largely baffling essay "Grammar—'a book,' " published in LeRoi Jones' *Floating Bear* in 1961—with his own idea of a poetic "middle voice," syntax of autonomic measure. The concept of *ta'wil* also provided him a talisman of the personal meaning of eternity: on the page margins of Corbin's definition of the term he scrawled an exultant "WOW," and beneath it the underscored summary comment *"history."* Like Corbin's Arabs, he himself had long stubbornly construed history not as a linear progression but as an endless circling back to an "obdurate, or . . . *archaic* time or condition." To see, and experience, history as cyclic return allowed one to simultaneously escape its power "as a 'fate,' " in these years as much a motive in Olson's poetry as (he now learned from Jung) it had once been in archaic mystery rites designed "to break the 'compulsion of the stars' by magic power." The cosmological imagery derived from Corbin entered Olson's epic in 1961, with "Maximus at the Harbor." Written during a dramatic early-winter storm on Cape Ann, it was an anthem of the "progressive rise" of self and soul through the chaotic whirl of natural process: "Paradise is a person. Come into this world. / The soul is a magnificent Angel. / And the thought of its thought is the rage / of Ocean. . . ."

A book of heaven, earth and sea, and of the elements whipped into trance, *Maximus IV, V, VI* would achieve a kingly "land skope view" of the local weathers of creation as setting for an image of immanence or lived self-union, ensconcing its vast, shaggy, analogically minded Egyptian-Algonquin-Norse-Arab hero on the hump of Cape Ann, astride the Great Mother, the "protogonic" landscape of Dogtown at his back, at one with his angel in his obdurate archaic condition, "overlooking / 'the town' / sitting there like / the Memphite lord of / all Creation."

22

In Tenebris
(1960–1963)

Writing comes from the darkness of one's own initiation.

—OLSON, *Causal Mythology*

What art does is to seek to do justice to accident by groping
in the dark, which darkness is the trajectory of necessity. . . .
Its immanent process has something divinatory about it.
The idea is to follow the divining rod in the direction in
which it is being pulled.

—ADORNO, *Aesthetic Theory*

The sixties began for Olson in a state of darkness, poverty and humiliation little relieved by the radiant black-gold flower of self and creation which illuminated his visionary poetry of this time.

"*Dark* at 3.30," he lamented to Creeley at the nadir of the winter of 1959–1960, "no fucking place to go." A mood of boredom, frustration and depression, increasingly routine for him during the midwinter "birthtime" doldrums, gripped him on into the early months of 1960. He felt lonely, ignored, passed by as an artist and thinker, and even worse, insulted by continual material difficulties. After some years' frugal nursing of the nest egg from the college closure, he was now virtually without resources, and had no idea how he was to go on subsisting as an independent poet in Gloucester. In January he put in for another Guggenheim, proposing a year's work on the *Maximus* and supplying backup letters from Duncan, Creeley and Dorn. He was turned down, reminding him anew how far he'd drifted from the official mainstream of culture. Since he now found it "impossible to even conjure up [the thought of] working for anybody, or, for that matter, for money"—as he told Creeley upon reporting the bad news from the foundation that spring—he had little choice but to transfer his hopes to the private patronage system, one he anyway liked to think of as less demeaning than kowtowing to institutions. He explained as much to Robert Duncan, who stopped off in Gloucester while in the East that spring on a reading tour. Duncan found him all but destitute, yet still belaboring old schemes for a cultural resuscitation of the nation via enlightened philanthropy. This time Olson envisaged the endowment of specific writer-thinkers by a board of private donors. "What's needed," he insisted, expanding on the plan as he and Duncan drove south to visit John Wieners in Boston, "is twelve men each independently supported, backed, in such a way that they form flanges of a hierarchy." Skeptical, Duncan suggested he consider a return to teaching for his livelihood. "Awww, come on, Robert," Olson sighed.

His income during these years consisted largely of unrepaid personal "loans" from friends and supporters of his work. Yet he fiercely resisted any sense of debt. Paul Metcalf, by this time a struggling writer himself, was struck on visiting the Fort by the tension between the "grubby poverty" of Olson's present life and the surviving pride of the earnestly aspiring old Charlie— apparent when he refused to be asked out to dinner without reciprocating in some way, if only by buying ice cream for his friends' children. "It was a battle gesture, not simple generosity. He would never allow himself to be placed under obligation to another; and when, inevitably, such a relation became necessary, he was extremely reserved about it, even sharp at concealing it. When he had no money at all, and someone was supporting him, we never knew who it was." Prospective secret supporters, however, tended to greatly outnumber the real ones.

This was to be the period of Olson's most prolonged and painful campaign of feedbag-wooing. Its object was local millionaire John Hays Hammond, Jr., a seventy-two-year-old retired inventor. Hammond, who had made a fortune by developing underwater guidance systems for the navy, inhabited a neo-Gothic castle he'd had built for himself (by Finnish masons, using stones taken from actual European ruins) on the heights above a notorious reef called Norman's Woe on the Magnolia Shore of Cape Ann, just two and a half miles southwest down the coast from Olson's own rented home. An expensive prop out of an Aleister Crowley adaptation of a Poe tale, this Hollywood-Medieval spread, known locally as "the Castle," contained an underground crypt (or "Pseudo-Vault," as Olson called it in a poem) hewn from the rocky cliff in occult inverted-pyramidal shape and connected to water's edge by sixty-nine "Aztec steps," which the eccentric inventor had designed as his last resting place. Inside the Castle, Olson would find "another tomb"— a sumptuous but claustrophobic environment "like the Masque / of the Red Death," kept only by various artificial disguises ("green dye to make the pool not corrupt . . . gum from Araby to make it smell right") from appearing in its true deathly light. Introduced to Hammond's salon by local poet Gerrit Lansing, Olson became a Castle fixture, standing by the massive ebony doors

to hand out leaflets before the rich man's cultural evenings (he got a percent-
age of the take), splashing under skylights and hanging tropical plants in the
turquoise-tinted swimming pool (other guests would occasionally "hop in
from the balcony"), eating steaks off banquet tables draped with "red Cardinal's cloth," and spouting his poetry in the fake-thirteenth-century "High
Mass" auditorium (where he contended for breathing room with a huge 8,200-
pipe organ).

Amid the leopard-skin couches and collections of hermetic arcana, the
poet could appear merely another curious appurtenance, seemingly being
used—as outsider Ed Dorn observed—"like a cigar store wooden Indian."
Indeed, the demeaning aspect of his economically motivated tenure as glorified court jester to Hammond and "the faeries of Gloucester" was hardly lost
on Olson himself. His role as "Thy Gleeman Who Flattered Thee" was
acknowledged with cutting self-irony in his private writings, particularly after
the failure of his protracted attempt to "put the pinch" on the millionaire had
become apparent. Counting on "some sort of poet-grant-in-aid" as the ultimate outcome of his attendance at Hammond's court, he was held back by
pride from making an outright solicitation until 1962, by which time his
financial troubles had become extreme (he had been summoned to court over
unpaid medical bills). Vincent Ferrini at that point stepped forward as intermediary to present Hammond a request for subsidy of five years' work on
the *Maximus* at $10,000 per year. Once the ice was broken, Olson followed
up with approaches of his own—promising, in hopes of at last tipping the
old man's check-writing hand, to put part of the subsidy money into the
establishment of a local "lay monastery" where he would instruct adepts in
proprioceptive exercises performed "on a spirit level." Hammond agreed to
consider the idea, but then stalled indefinitely. Olson, coming to suspect he
would never see a cent and increasingly uncomfortable with his position as
beggar, decided eventually that "my Milliardaire is not a King of Hell but
solely a stupid selfish greaseball," and gave up his pursuit. But angry feelings
on his part were slow to fade. When Hammond died in 1965, leaving his
castle to be turned into a public museum and his money to the Catholic
Church, those feelings spilled out all over again: even in death, Olson's millionaire was still eluding the long awaited reckoning.

> John Hays Hammond Jr
> faggot inventor & friend of all us
> half-assed FAGGOTS OF GLOUCESTER
> GAVE, $15,000,000 AND HIS
>   "MUSEUM" (LIE, turned his home
>   into a CASTLE TO Evade

Federal Income Taxes————
& now after his death MAKES SURE
the AVOIDANCE

Ironically, in the years 1960 to 1962, during which Olson's material fortunes descended to their lowest point, his work received its first widescale
national exposure, bringing him, if not financial security, a growing recognition as poetic revolutionary and leader of an emerging underground movement in writing—and in the process starting a literary civil war of sorts. The
sheer unanimity of the ensuing critical rejection of his art and ideas by the
ascendant academic establishment of the time appears in retrospect not so
much a considered aesthetic or intellectual judgment as the defensive campaign of a threatened orthodoxy against an iconoclastic cultural assault far
broader in implication than mere tactical poetics. It was now to become clear
beyond all mistaking that Olson was bent on tearing down the old orders of
language control; but if that deconstructive project would be opposed almost
universally by those in entrenched power positions, to another audience of
the young, interested and relatively disenfranchised it would hold great appeal.

The recruitment and first forming of ranks in Olson's new model army of
poetry and thought owed much to Donald Allen's Grove Press anthology
The New American Poetry. The anthology hit the stands in spring 1960, with
a bold American-flag cover design and text kicked off by "The Kingfishers,"
that ringing Olsonian incitement to perpetual revolution: "What does not
change / is the will to change." There was a copious forty-page selection of
Olson verse, including three early *Maximus* pieces as well as such sizable self-
contained poems as "A Newly Discovered 'Homeric' Hymn," "The Lordly
and Isolate Satyrs" and "As the Dead Prey Upon Us." (Always working out
ahead of his critical reception, Olson privately lamented Allen's conservatism
in choosing poetry that in comparison with his more recent and experimental
efforts might come off seeming "too consistent—or rhetorical.") The book
was anchored at the back by "Projective Verse," heading a section of "interim
reports" from the various fronts on which new American poets were engaged;
Donald Allen, in a brief, sober introduction, held up Olson's 1950 essay and
an additional later statement on poetics as benchmark definitions of the new
poetry's "dominant double concept: 'composition by field' and 'stance toward
reality.' " Allen's editing left little question that Olson was the thinker of the
bunch, principal spokesman and authority figure of a "long awaited but only
slowly recognized . . . strong third generation" of postwar American poets
represented in four prevailing underground "schools": Olson's own "Black
Mountain" bloc (including his running mate Creeley and a number of his ex-
students, Dorn, Wieners, Oppenheimer, Williams); "San Francisco Renais-

sance" (Duncan, Whalen, McClure et al.); "Beat Generation" (Ginsberg, Corso, Kerouac et al.); and "New York Poets" (O'Hara, Ashbery, Koch et al.). That Olson alone among the contributors was actually of an age not with the "third generation" of postwar poets but with the one preceding—i.e., that of Lowell, Bishop, Rexroth—was an anomaly which the editor's introduction did not address, but which was indirectly accounted for by the poet in one of his contributions, "Maximus, to himself": "I have had to learn the simplest things / last."

A cornerstone of American post-modernist poetics, the Grove anthology would also prove a strong seller, eventually going into some twenty editions and achieving worldwide readership. Quite a bit less successful commercially but no less significant in establishing Olson as a poet were two major books of his published the same year, a volume of selected poems, *The Distances,* also issued by Grove, and the first substantial trade edition of the *Maximus,* from Jargon / Corinth. All three volumes came under heavy fire from mainline quarters.

The Allen anthology, as most visible, took the brunt, with Olson's contributions and influence singled out for particular dispraise. Harvey Shapiro of the *New York Times Book Review* identified him as mastermind of the movement—"an Ideologue of the New Poetry"—and one of the more contemptuous of the reviewers, poet Louise Bogan, writing in the *New Yorker,* made a point of bringing up his age, as if, being the senior member of the group, he ought to have known better. Poets, indeed—mostly of the academic persuasion—became the main instruments of summary critical justice in the Olson Case. X. J. Kennedy, in *Poetry,* was the voice of common sense, exposing mechanical contradictions in the typewriter and breath theories of "Projective Verse." James Wright, in the *Minnesota Review,* suggested neither Olson's theories nor his poems were worth discussing, and called into question his position of preeminence in the anthology. In the *Sewanee Review,* Southern white-hope poet James Dickey aimed an *ad hominem* dismissal of the new poets directly at the upstart group's central perpetrator, Olson, portrayed as a jargonizing, irrational wild man whose offensive notions licensed the demise of all discipline and structure in verse. Finally, reviewing the Grove anthology for the *New York Herald Tribune,* veteran modernist particularist Marianne Moore, named in Donald Allen's introduction as among the forerunners of the new American poetry, contributed a last shot that was at once more subtle and more wounding. Her discreet assessment of Olson's theories contained an implicitly damning reflection on the overly cerebral quality of his verse, for which she obviously had little taste. "Mr. Olson advocates open form or 'composition by field,' projective or field composition being offered as an improvement on inherited or non-projective form," Moore wrote.

"Inherited form can be projective, I would say, and projective form may be weedy and colorless like suckers from an un-sunned tuber. . . ."

Reviews of Olson's own two poetry books merely exaggerated the negative profile the anthology had engendered. James Dickey made both books the target of a fresh onslaught in the *New York Times Book Review*. Samuel French Morse in *Poetry* could find little but oracular aggressiveness in *Maximus*, and Robert Bly, in *The Sixties*, termed *Maximus* the work of "a Babbitt in verse," the "worst book of the year." *The Distances*, in its turn, came in for attacks from the likes of Thom Gunn and Louis Simpson, in the *Yale Review* and *Hudson Review*, respectively. And British critic Anthony Thwaite, reviewing the Olson phenomenon in separate *Spectator* articles, blamed Olson for the rampages of the latest horde of destructive New World poetic "redskins." His work displayed a combination of all the worst national characteristics, from Whitman's democratic lack of discrimination to the ranting abstruseness of Pound.

Any satisfactions Olson may have taken from the flattery of the handful of youthful admirers who now made their way to the Fort as a result of his recently published writings hardly compensated for the discouragements of the bad reviews. Concentrating too much of his attention on his public image could sink the beleaguered poet into "daily depression." "This was bound to be a 'bad' time for me," he wrote Creeley as the toll of the critical verdict mounted, "simply that 'the world' doesn't succumb completely."

The sudden mass circulation of his work occasioned Olson's emergence from the Fort "to go whoring around the Universities selling myself." It was his first venture into poetry-circuit performing, a new field which would over the next few years become the source of a fair share of his small income; also of much psychic strain, brought on by the pressures and demands of exposing his poetry to audiences made up largely of strangers.

To suit the allegory of his life, his reading-circuit debut came at the site of his first "show 'em" drives and pushes of thirty years earlier. At the Wesleyan Spring Poetry Festival in the last week of April 1960 he appeared on a two-man program with Hyam Plutzik, an academic poet published by Wesleyan University Press. Robert Duncan, also on the festival bill, and Norman O. Brown, Wesleyan's resident pop psychologist, led a demonstration of allegiance by a small but committed "pro-Olson claque" at the Plutzik / Olson event. As Plutzik's opening reading wore on, a subdued but audible rumble of impatience from the "claque" gradually turned into "sounds of muffled mockery." It was plainly the view of Olson's supporters that he deserved an evening to himself. When his turn came, the prodigal-son alumnus felt bound to pull out all the poetic stops, but found himself crippled once again by the ancient nemesis stage fright. His reading "consisted in great part of false starts," recalls poet Richard Wilbur, then a Wesleyan professor of English. "He would say, 'The lordly and isolate satyrs . . .' and then stop, apparently unsatisfied with the rhythm he had given to the words; he would stand and think for a time and then try it again and again. . . ." Afterwards, however, when his friends and fans gathered in the more relaxed surroundings of Brown's home for a second, private reading, with the pressure off and a few drinks under his belt Olson was transformed into a confident, forceful reader. He had managed in one evening to live up to both the low estimate of the academic majority in the festival crowd and the much higher expectations of his followers.

Olson and Wilbur, nominated in a recent article as leaders of contending schools of verse, were formally introduced at a cocktail party later in the festival. Olson, outwardly "hearty" but immediately on his guard, lost no time in interjecting a note of challenge. Wilbur was struck by the confrontational energy with which his fellow poet seemed to address the occasion. "He greeted me as a coach or quarterback might greet the coach or quarterback of a rival team. There was no implication that my school of poetry was a wrong or misguided school; he was more generous about that than I have known some other Black Mountain poets to be; but it was clear that he *did* think in terms of rival schools and aesthetics."

A more appealing side of Olson's character was revealed after the "rivals" bumped into each other again in the student cafeteria and Olson, brandishing a bottle of whiskey, cheerfully proposed that they pay their respects to his old mentor, "Wild Bill" Snow. At the Middletown home of Wesleyan's longtime poetry father-figure, Wilbur was witness to an affectionate reunion of teacher and pupil.

> We had a long and rambling talk in Bill's living room. When Bill found that Charlie had not read Frost for years, he asked me to read aloud "Home Burial." Olson said that he had forgotten how good Frost could be, and also remarked that the poem was an expression of "scarcity." That remark remained mysterious though Bill and I urged him to clarify it; it seemed to have something to do with the poverty of the people in the poem. Later, Bill and I got going excitedly about Keats, and Charlie, having listened for a time, said, "Do you know what you guys are talking about? Subject matter!" Subject matter, I suppose, as opposed to poetic form. It amused me that, since Bill and I were classified in the 60's as traditional formalists, Charlie should reproach us for discussing words and themes rather than poetic structure. Throughout our visit, I was struck by Olson's gracious, warm and filial behavior toward Snow.

Reading directly afterward at an art gallery in Toronto, poetry phenom Olson was written up in the local *Daily Star* as an "intellectual Paul Bunyan."

He was invited on a Canadian Broadcasting Company television show, sharing the spotlight with a lady safari guide from Tanganyika and an American baseball umpire. Feeling like a man in a freak show, he couldn't get out of the studio fast enough. But once back home again, he soon found the walls of his refuge at the Fort closing in on him. A cash gift from one of his secret sponsors enabled him to get away that summer for a few weeks' vacation in Maine and Nova Scotia with Betty, Charles Peter and Kate. Though the sea voyage aboard the coastal liner *Blue Nose* was bracing, tensions between himself and Betty put a damper on the trip.

Work on the *Maximus* in the fall of 1960 narrowed his home life to a fine point of drudgery, with no real end in sight. The conditions of its creation seemed increasingly obsessive and claustrophobic, and the effects were being felt by everyone in the family. It was, as Olson reported to Ed Dorn with the annual trial of the winter solstice nearing, "the damndest time."

> The fucking "subject" . . . leads me, and sucks like mud. . . . A dreadful sort of slavery actually—not free in any imagination sense whatsoever; and if I were, I'd do nothing, I'm sure, [but] look off into space. That's the drag of it, like a stone . . . sea anchor, in fact. . . . [Besides,] we're sick of these three rooms, with Charles Peter now 5½ and solid hell in the house—no space for him, or us . . . and the kids outside all gangs of large families, and agin him, sort of, he's such a damn indoors creature anyway—by inheritance, no doubt.

In his isolation he couldn't tell whether the world had shrunk or his imagination was shrinking, from "sitting out" the activity of public life too long. "Nothing seems to me going on out there," he told Dorn, "except world politics again for such as LeRoi Jones and Ginsberg." His own disinterested sideline attitude was laced with a certain envy. Both Jones and Ginsberg were at the time actively engaged in the emergence of an international cultural underground. Jones had recently sent Olson an enthusiastic report on a visit to Cuba, a communiqué that could hardly fail to remind the ex-politician how far he himself had drifted from his onetime idealistic commitment to a global political vision. His own political action of the period was limited to one not very successful polemical poem, "The Hustings," which he dedicated to Jones. Composed on the occasion of the Soviet moon shots and the election to the Presidency of Olson's former student John F. Kennedy, this rather gloomy diatribe discovered in the Space Age and the New Frontier only an evolved form of the same rampant materialism which had driven the poet out of politics fifteen years earlier. "Democracy en masse" now meant not the populist openness of Whitman's dream but a technological society's international marketing strategy for selling watches and transisters to "the youth of the world" while promoting a worldwide cheapness in "the use / of human beings." "The Hustings" reflected Olson's bleak view of the possibilities of any further political involvement.

Allen Ginsberg, meanwhile, had been busy extending the frontiers of world politics into consciousness expansion and the administration of visions—a move which Olson, whose recent poetry showed his own growing curiosity on the subject of ritual mind alteration ("We drink / or break open / our veins solely / to know"), found quite a bit more promising. In December 1960, once again prey to the depressed moods which had affected each winter of his life, he was lured by Ginsberg without much coaxing to take part in experimental tests of psilocybin-39, the hallucinogenic-mushroom derivative. He drove to Cambridge, met with Harvard Psychology Department researchers Timothy Leary and Frank Barron at the Center for Personality Research, and was taken to the "Mushroom House" in nearby Newton. He immediately proved himself a unique test subject in terms of sheer capacity alone, astounding the renegade-academic experimenters by casually tossing back several dozen of their little pink two-milligram psilocybin pills like "peanuts." Then it was his turn to be astonished. Instead of merely getting high, he found he had "literally tak[en] a bite straight out of creation." Activating the prodigious analogical capabilities of his imagination, the drug induced in him a euphoric mimesis of a Mohawk "peace sachem" conducting a traditional ritual longhouse ceremony. Suddenly wise to "the great truth of the Indians of this territory," he spent the rest of the evening playing chief, while Ginsberg (who had a vision of him as Santa Claus) and session guide Leary looked on in awe. "It came popping out of my mouth," Olson later recounted the experience. "The moment the peanuts affected me I started talking longhouse talk. And created, because I was the responsible person . . . I was the tone, I created the tone of the evening. And it was absolutely a pure ceremonial set." The revelations of the magic mushroom confirmed the role cut out for him as poet of the autonomic condition. This instruction was moreover accompanied by a vast sense of relief, a temporary letting-go of all his drives and pushes. "The startling & unbelievable first impression of going under the mushroom is that everyone & everything is nothing but itself so that all—everything—is therefore well, and there's no push, there's no fuss, there's nothing at all to worry about, or press at, no sweat of any sort called for, it's all too real and way beyond any attitude or seeking some greater or bigger answer. . . ." These initial illuminations "under the mushroom" would join the Black Chrysanthemum dream of a few years earlier in Olson's private mythology of self-measure, instated as authoritative proof that "God is no longer 'out there' somewhere, but He is within you, and you are one with Him."

Two months later, he received a telegram from Leary requesting his participation in another mushroom session. This time, in recognition of his demonstrated prowess under the drug, the poet would serve as guide or *cur-andero,* accompanying Arthur Koestler—the renowned novelist and journalist, then in America gathering material for the updating of a book on neuropsychology and creative thinking—through the ritual. Leary, with a significant stake in "selling" his miracle drug, had picked on "the father of modern poetry" as perfect person "to introduce Arthur Koestler to the open-brain and its ecstatic possibilities." Upon reaching Cambridge, Olson was made aware that "it was a very crucial act for Leary and the group because they wanted to capture Koestler." His own part was to perform as a sort of psychic downfield blocker, running interference "rather like a football player" for the celebrated European guest. ("I'm supposed to be euphoric under the drug, and to make him feel he could be comfortable and confident.") But the well-laid plans immediately started to unravel. Waiting for the researchers to bring Koestler back from a dinner party in Boston, Olson got caught up in kitchen-table conversation with Leary's children, one of whom offered him a pair of realistic-looking toy six-guns to try out. Just then Arthur Koestler was ushered into the kitchen by Leary.

> The giant poet turned, and looked down at the small figure of the novelist, and beamed out of his jolly eyes that really were animal's eyes, except that animal's eyes are always serious, while his always laughed and turned into human eyes.
> Olson was holding a toy pistol in his hand.
> Arthur Koestler's eyes went up, up, up to look at Olson and then dropped quickly to the pistol. He paled and pulled back. There he stood face-to-face with what he feared.
> Olson roared out genial greetings.

The author of *Darkness at Noon* never quite recovered from his disconcerting initial shock. Psilocybin pills were brought out and duly consumed, and in Leary's words, "the ship cast off." But session leader Olson soon found his "Mohawk Sachem funny chiefness" was rubbing the serious, reserved visitor the wrong way. Koestler's resistance continued to grow, until after an hour or so he exited, glowering, and ascended to a dark room where he spent the remainder of the night awake, refusing all inducements to rejoin the party. This was the classic, dread "bad trip." Still feeling the aftereffects of the drug himself, Olson was assigned to chauffeur the shaken guest back to the Center for Personality Research the next day. Koestler's stony silence made him so anxious that he backed his car into a brand-new Cadillac, incurring $75 in damages. He billed the center for repairs, "because I'm transporting your host's customer and he's given me such a terrible day after the mushroom that all the benefits of the benefit have been lost!" He'd been driving without a license, and briefly feared, as he confided to Creeley, that "now that god-damn mushroom is going to cost me plenty." A thoroughly disenchanted Arthur Koestler subsequently returned to London to write up his mushroom nightmare for the *Sunday Telegraph*, calling Olson's "pressure cooker mysticism" an "ultimate profanation" of what had been cracked up as serious research. Olson was somewhat amused by the negative publicity, making a joke of being portrayed as "a horrible American hot-rod gunman."

The poet remained an enthusiastic advocate of psilocybin, proposing that it ought to be legalized and made available "in the common drugstore as a kind of beer, because it is so obviously an attractive and useful, normal food." (He would also extend this endorsement to other psychoactive drugs like marijuana, peyote, mescaline and LSD, all, in his experience, effective creative tools. "He never met a substance he didn't like," suggests Ed Dorn.) The Koestler debacle did not significantly affect his friendly relations with Leary's psychedelic movement. When shortly afterwards the drug guru and family showed up in Gloucester with religious philosopher Alan Watts, looking for a house in which to establish an LSD research center, Olson acted as a one-man welcoming committee, promoting the acquisition of property on Dollivers Neck belonging to Jack Hammond's sister. The deal did not go through, evidently in part because Gloucester was not yet ready. "The whole town blew up" over the appearance of Leary's fifteen-year-old daughter Suzanne in a bikini on Pavilion Beach, an event Olson himself viewed as an archetypal return of the "utterly beautiful" Phryne, model of Praxiteles' Cnidian Venus. He would publish cosmological poetry from the *Maximus* in Leary's *Psychedelic Review*, and later, after Leary and Suzanne had received federal sentences for crossing the American border from Mexico with a small quantity of marijuana, volunteer that he still considered acid's High Priest "the most beautiful *brujo* that we've had in this country."

The drug experiments were relatively vivid interludes amid what was otherwise "as dark [a] winter as I ever knew." "Been dragging like never before," he complained to Creeley in mid-February 1961, a week or so after the Koestler episode. "Bewildered, and all other desperate experiences . . . have exhausted money and have about two weeks left, at the most—and not a bloody step taken or any expectation of what then will come [nor] even care what it is: have had it so far as this time and sort of work. . . ." Creeley responded with a small check. Such emergency gestures on the part of those of his friends who could manage now kept Olson's unstable economy afloat from one month to the next. Living on immediate income had become a habit. Most often he did not know what would be the next source. In March, it was Brandeis University, where he appeared in the Lewisohn Lecture Series. To earn the

Brandeis check he had to undergo another dismaying brush with the academic humanists, his long-standing shadow antagonists. Hearing his professor hosts reverently sing the praises of such popular writers as novelist Norman Mailer and journalist James Wechsler—"like John Keats being quoted at funerals"—got on his nerves, and when it was hinted that his own performance had not elicited as much local interest as that of the poet who had preceded him in the series, Robert Lowell, he raged secretly against both his loathed academic rival (a turncoat "goyim [brought in] to spread a little of the immense & increasing ignorance of phyloSemitism") and the whole tone of academic "PHYLO-JUDAISM—like a Universalist Church" by which he felt oppressed at Brandeis.

By May, when Creeley stopped in at the Fort on a break during an East Coast reading tour, Olson was out of money again—quite literally. He had exactly $1 to his name. It was Charles Peter's sixth birthday, but there was no money to buy even a cheap toy for him as a present. Creeley peeled off a $10 bill out of his modest tour earnings. Olson accepted the gift with the wry comment that what he really needed was not $10 but $10,000. Charles Peter was then taken out to a local sundries store, where he picked out a large cap pistol for himself. Outside the store, the pistol was discovered to be defective. When Creeley's wife, Bobbie, suggested a replacement could be obtained, Olson, who retained a primitive distrust of the mercantile trade, merely shrugged and inquired, "What's that, the new anthropology?"

Creeley, who'd recently made a few hundred dollars by selling archival papers to Indiana University, suggested that Olson might be able to do likewise. Assuming his own papers would be worth quite a bit more, Olson dug into a box of weathered and sodden manuscripts that had been slowly returning to nature in the trunk of the battered beach wagon. He came up with the original annotated typescript of "Projective Verse," a document whose historic value, he was sure, made it worth thousands. He contacted Indiana. But when the library offered only $150 for the precious script on which his poetics was founded, he decided to hold on to it after all. Though he was destitute, currently lacking money not only to buy kids' toys but to meet even such basic requirements as dental care for Betty—who badly needed bridgework following the loss of an eyetooth—he was not about to part with his literary legacy for cheap.

The pressures of poverty, all too routine during these years, did, however, drive him into accepting a cash advance for some unlikely literary work that fall. The commission came through a representative of the drama department of Manhattanville College in New York, Kindred McDade (an admirer of his poetry, and the wife of a former FBI agent). Assigned to write an original Christmas drama suitable for production at the exclusive Catholic women's school, Olson procrastinated for some time before finally coming up with a hastily sketched-out miniplay called *Telepinus,* featuring a muscular Hittite fertility god, who trundled on stage "carrying Mary & Joseph before & behind like a Japanese wrestler" while a chorus proclaimed the Nativity with neo-pagan candor ("man's only born / for a ball"). Though benefit performances over the winter holidays had already been scheduled and advertised, upon inspection of Olson's script school officials abruptly canceled the program.

Poetry once again drove Olson back to old haunts early the next year, when he was invited by a Harvard faculty committee that included his former associates Monroe Engel and Harry Levin to deliver the annual Morris Gray reading. The prospect of returning to the "killer-place"—and particularly under the sponsorship of his onetime graduate school colleague Levin, now a professor of comparative literature and the university's reigning arbiter of modern writing—carried a private allegorical resonance far more important than a mere paycheck. For Olson the circumstances of the present invitation were significantly complicated by rumors that had come to him of the influential Harvard critic's low estimate of his poetry; Levin, he'd heard, thought the *Maximus* lacking in style and coherence, so much watered-down Ezra Pound. Approaching the occasion as though the success of his whole challenge to the New England academic fathers were at stake, Olson worked himself into an extreme state of prereading jitters. On the night before the February 14 event his peaking anxiety resulted in a nasty drunken tussle with a young visiting poet from New York, John Keys. Getting the impression Keys was trying to make a play for Betty by upstaging him verbally, Olson threw his weight around the kitchen of the Fort in an angry, confused pushing-and-shoving match that ended inconclusively when the younger poet fled. In the bleary light of dawn, further unnerved by finding out that his glasses, which had been knocked off during the fray, had been broken, he made a desperate bid to overcome the chain of negative auspices by enlisting the support of his empowering Muse, wiring Frances in Brooklyn to request her presence at his reading. (Given only a few hours' notice and not having heard from him for years, she neither came nor answered.)

Without having slept, he then drove on apprehensively to Cambridge for the Boylston Hall event. During Monroe Engel's introduction, he noticed Harry Levin attempting to slip unobtrusively into a front-row seat. There was a moment of tense, uncomfortable silence in the hall as Olson, clearly ill at ease, tried to gather himself to begin. Several false starts merely increased his agitation. He pulled up short at last and glared at his former friend. "Harry, could you be excused?" Slightly hard of hearing as well as understandably baffled, however, Levin was "not very quick on the uptake," and stayed in his seat. When Olson stiffly repeated his request, the still-puzzled professor finally got the message and left. Having dramatically captured the audience's attention by publicly ejecting—and humiliating—the man who had invited him, Olson somehow managed to recover and pull off a "rousing" performance. Afterwards, encountering Levin's wife Elena, he seemed moved to a certain degree of contrition. He mumbled an awkward explanation, telling her he'd been hurt to think Harry did not respect his writing. At Engel's post-reading cocktail party, he appeared chastened and made efforts to apologize personally to Levin. The following day he sent a mysterious note, attributing the embarrassing incident to his having been "under duress."

Shortly after the Harvard ordeal, feeling stifled again by life at the Fort and responding once more to impulses welling up from places in himself which even he did not fully fathom, Olson lit out without warning for New York, leaving Betty only an enigmatic note announcing that he "just went— to break it" ("it" being, evidently, his latest psychic slump). The mechanism of escape and the direction of the trip were strangely familiar, as if from a dream of another life. In the city he immediately sought out Frances, but the late hour of his unexpected visit, compounding the years of noncommunication, won him a cool reception, and he was not invited to stay the night. For once at a loss for words with his Muse, he cast her only a haunted, "desperate glance" as he departed. The trials and griefs of a poet's life were still foremost on his mind a few days later when he showed up in Toronto to give a reading. Local Canadian poet Margaret Avison, "a real person" who evinced a certain empathy regarding the vocational woes of the verse trade—she suggested he look into Johnson's *Lives of the Poets* as a primer on the subject—consoled him with platonic but "genuine tenderness." To drink and lament his troubles was one stock element of the touring poet's act which Olson was unable to resist.

On an April reading swing through upper New England he took Betty along, but her presence did little to curb his need to force the public moment with artificial spirits. At Dartmouth, English professor John Finch, who had set up Olson's reading, could not help noticing his former eccentric roommate was acting "more rambunctious" than ever before. At Goddard College in Plainfield, Vermont, Olson's next stop, he was at his outgoing best for the first few days of a week-long reading / lecture visit, helping a young but receptive student audience through his latest mythohistorical *Maximus* run by airing his views on the poet's role as mythmaker—reformulated, he said, following discussions a few days earlier with Dartmouth French poetry expert Ramon Guthrie. (Guthrie had pointed out to him that the medieval French verb *trobar* meant *to find,* allowing word-root fanatic Olson to link the troubadour poets with Herodotus, Homer and himself in the tradition of the investigative storyteller, "the man who finds out the words.") But by the end of the week, both the poet himself and his wife had been summoned before the college Judiciary Committee, reprimanded for taking part in a wild drinking party on campus, and sternly "told to abide by community laws while there."

When Ed Dorn came East from Idaho to visit Olson at the Fort in July 1962, he found his friend and former teacher living in conditions of abject poverty. The Olsons' broken refrigerator stood marooned beside the plaster Virgin in the tall grass of the backyard. Betty fished off the pier to supplement the family's thin food rations. From the same spot, under cover of darkness, Charles himself threw out the household trash. Though intended to avoid the collection charge, this garbage-disposal ritual was invested with the seriousness of archaic ceremony. "He went down to the water at two o'clock when the tide went out," recalls Dorn, "just like Maximus in a sort of bullshit ceremonial way. That's what he loved, it was ancient to him—as if to say, that's what the tide's *for*." The pride that had made Olson cling fiercely to his poetic independence through these hard years now seemed to lend him an odd nobility despite the ignominy of material deprivation. During the local fisherman's festival, the Fiesta of St. Peter, he took his guest out on the town to drink beers at the Tavern and then wander through carnival streets bathed in the glow of colored lights and the brassy din of John Philip Sousa. Dorn would memorialize the evening in "From Gloucester Out," a moving verse tribute capturing the pathos and paradoxical dignity of Olson's heroic isolation at this time: "so bold / on his ground / and so much / lonely anywhere . . . only / he who worships the gods with his strictness / can be of their company."

Olson confessed to his friend that he had no idea where his next dollar was going to come from. He spoke vaguely of trying to "make a buck" in the old-fashioned workaday way by getting a job in a local fish-processing plant, but clearly his heart was not in it. As Dorn packed up to set out with his wife, Helene, and family for New York City to visit LeRoi Jones, Olson decided he didn't want to be left behind. Dropping their son with the Radosloviches, he and Betty piled into the back of the Dorns' car for the big-city trip. Suddenly brightened to be getting away, he was in commanding form during the ride south, smoking and talking up a storm. But once actually in the city his energy soon began to dissipate. He and Betty joined the Dorns as guests in Jones' suddenly overcrowded Cooper Square apartment, where he made a game effort to get with the unfamiliar, confusing urban pace. The flat was situated in the inner circle of a vivid, pulsing downtown avant-garde scene. On hot open-window afternoons above the street busy with stickball games and traffic, progressive horn player Archie Shepp, who lived below, could be heard working out in high-energy improvisation. The Five Spot, just down the block, kept the nights thick with new jazz, a wild noise spilling over into early-morning hours. Accustomed to the gentler music of foghorns and sea birds, Olson felt distinctly old-schlumpfish after a few nights of trying to sleep on Jones' floor. There was much partying going on, with hard drugs like heroin and cocaine in evidence. Black Mountain survivors John Wieners and Dan Rice were on hand, and Olson had one unsettling encounter with Rice, who seemed disapproving of recent changes in his life. After several days he "wandered off" semimysteriously, proving himself the poet who could be lonely anywhere by taking a room for himself at an uptown hotel while Betty went back to Gloucester. He stayed on for some weeks, looking up, and attempting to put the touch on, people from his former life; his poetry friends caught only occasional further glimpses of him, in places like the Russian Tea Room. Upon his return home he admitted the whole trip had been a mistake. He'd had a "terrible time."

As the days narrowed and the dark time of year closed in, he tried again to lose himself in the inner life of language. Returning to the archaic world in which he now felt most at home, and to the poet of cosmos and creation, Hesiod, whose *Theogony* he was hopeful of one day being able to read in the original, he made scattered attempts, with the help of a young local scholar, to learn Greek. He also pressed ahead with *Maximus IV, V, VI,* mailing off chaotic bundles of disorderly hand-corrected typed scraps of verse across the Atlantic in irregular installments to a new fan and secretarial volunteer, a young Cambridge don named Jeremy Prynne, who faithfully deciphered and returned them, transformed as if by magic into clean, neatly typed copy. (Prynne proved a loyal, assiduous poetic research assistant as well, supplying a copious package of documents copied from the London public records office and containing, as the astounded recipient put it, "all the goddamned records of all the boats that crossed the Atlantic Ocean after Columbus that might have bearing on entering Gloucester Harbor"; increasingly scattered and hasty in his own creative researches, however, Olson was never able to muster the patience to sit down and inspect the contents in detail.)

If Olson's poetry, like his scholarship, was growing more elusive and fragmentary than ever, a matter not of grand architectures but of disjunct bits like *tesserae,* "those little pieces they use in making mosaics," it was little wonder. Psychic unrest and physical ill health conspired that winter to prevent him from concentrating on anything for very long. His sedentary life, and the heavy smoking and drinking of recent years, had taken a toll: there were new and ominous if fleeting reminders of the fatal Olson small male span. Rambling aimlessly one day through the wastes of Dogtown in search of inspiration for poetry, he was overcome by dizziness and vertigo, became disoriented, and for some hours was unable to find his way home. "Here I am," he would relate the episode later, "the big pro of the Memphite theology and the whole of creation, and I can't even get the fuck out of there." The frightening "loss of space control" left him shaken. A doctor advised him to cut down on alcohol and tobacco and to get regular exercise. But his appetites and habits of intake were essential elements of his creative makeup, now ingrained past all uprooting. And his nocturnal ways left little opportunity for venturing out of doors. There was anyway not much inducement to do so, during these cold months. He went on living as he had been, and was sick on and off through the rest of the winter, plagued by attacks of "flu" both psychosomatic and somatic in origin.

23 ~

Instructing the Angels
(1963–1964)

With the return of the sun came a revival of spirits. In the spring of 1963 Olson sensed hopeful intimations of a fresh creative season. "We live at the beginning of a new millennium," he announced sanguinely to fellow experimentalist Stan Brakhage when the moviemaker dropped in at the Fort that May. "God, what an exciting time . . . how much there is to do. . . . How much we must here instruct the angels, who are at this time running around being very busy, needing our Instruction." That summer at the creative counterculture summit of the Vancouver Poetry Conference he got a chance to do so, publicly assuming the weighty mantle of senior poet-savant and bringer of cosmic knowledge to the new generation of poet-angels of America.

Though University of British Columbia English professor Warren Tallman, putting together the Vancouver event with the help of temporary instructor Robert Creeley, had drawn in most of the major lights of the new poetry—Allen Ginsberg, Robert Duncan, Denise Levertov, Philip Whalen, Margaret Avison joined Creeley and Olson on the bill—from the outset of the five-week summer school event it was clear to Olson (as he reported to Betty, quoting Margaret Avison) that in fact it had been set up as "a *Festschrift*—for me!" Host Tallman, quickly becoming a convinced Olsonian, allowed the honored guest special privileges befitting Maximus. At the faculty club dining hall on the staid, English-style UBC campus, patriarch Olson was given the run of things, setting up free-wheeling court on a scenic balcony overlooking the majestic peaks of the North Coast range and expansively "ordering everything, just everything," as Tallman remembers. "He wanted a stack of sandwiches. He wanted to know, 'Do you have milkshakes in this club? What kind of cigars do you have now?' He didn't want a *glass* of Scotch; he said, 'Why not bring the bottle!' And the staff did as he said. The academic faculty were sitting inside with no one to wait on them, because all five waiters and waitresses were out on the balcony with Charles." Tallman was reminded of the wild hungers hinted at in Olson's poem "As the Dead Prey Upon Us": "We must have / what we want . . ." "That was Olson: he must have what he wants, he cannot afford not to! That ultimate protest against the Puritan pinch of things."

During the conference Olson was put up at the Tallman home, residing among—and somewhat nervously presiding over—a household of poet guests that also included Whalen and Ginsberg. He lost no time taking over the main bedroom, displacing onto separate couches Tallman and wife Ellen (who was kept busy stocking up the refrigerator against the hungry visitor's late-night onslaughts). The cramped communal quarters, however, proved far too much "like a fraternity house" to suit Olson's highly individualized tastes and habits. He was kept perpetually on his guard by Buddhist wise guy Whalen's "pious smart aleck" humor, and prevented from obtaining peace of mind by the nosy sociability of Ginsberg, who was forever putting him on the spot with difficult questions about God or interrupting his matutinal slumbers to pump him about his dream life. ("Get that guy outta here," an exasperated Olson at one point pleaded to his hosts, "he's trying to steal my dreams!") Despite Ginsberg's sly efforts to rouse him, Olson's Vancouver days routinely did not begin before noon, an observance of personal custom that also provided him a convenient excuse for skipping almost all of the morning conference panel sessions—which he anyway disliked. Dealing with the give-and-take of argument, if only about verse measure, appeared to him too much like work, something he considered it sacrilegious to attempt before midday. While lesser mortals (like Ginsberg and Duncan) toiled on campus, he himself lingered over prolonged breakfast and many cups of coffee at the Tallmans', sometimes indulging with Creeley in the elaborate, convoluted "late Henry James style" discourse found so mystifying and intriguing by their followers. His afternoon workshops at the university, runaway-train-of-thought talk-solos described by one amazed student observer, East Coast poet Carol Bergé, as a collision of "hip modern lingo, Hittite, lightning and the oracle of Delphi," were fueled by handfuls of Dexedrine, the "forward pills" that would get him through many a public show in these years. The talk kept up well into festive social evenings, abetted by whiskey consumed in large quantities as Olson strove "to slow himself down." But as witness Philip Whalen adds, "of course he never really slowed." On one night of conference legend, the Royal Canadian Mounties showed up to check IDs at a student apartment after a noise complaint and walked in on a congenial poetry "bacchanal" ruled over by the benign satyr Maximus, who disported on a bed with four or five comely female conferees, "giggling and mildly feeling each other." It was, Olson would later proudly declare, "the best I've ever done."

"An American," the poet announced paradoxically in the previously "withheld" *Maximus* "Letter 27," a much-requested poem which seemed to strike the thematic keynote of the conference, "is a complex of occasions. . . . I have this sense, that I am one / with my skin." Projecting an image of comfortable singularity in scraggly salt-and-pepper pony tail (Robert Duncan suggested it made him look "like one of the signers of the Declaration of Independence"), stubby gray sea captain's beard, buckskin shoes, battered sportcoat and well-worn army-tan chinos, Olson gave the impression at Vancouver of being at ease with himself, one with his skin. But appearances, as ever in the poet's life of self-allegory, were carefully stage-managed to protect his precious privacies. A few of the more sensitive of his summer students were able to make out vaguely, behind the beaming, round-eyed mask of Olson-Maximus, the restlessness of a "solitary animal." But the true scale of the unseen labor required to keep the aura and mystery of the image intact, as well as the multiplicity of personal complications concealed behind the powerful singleness of the projection, could only be guessed at.

Outwardly seeming a relentless juggernaut of verbal energy, inwardly Olson was growing more fatigued every day with the sheer effort of maintaining his position as "#1" at the conference. He felt self-consciously constrained by the static mechanics of the patriarchal hierarchy. "I am grandaddy or something," as he put it succinctly in a letter to Betty, "& it's a pain in the ass. . . . Everyone pussyfoots around me, or I do [around] everyone. . . . Feel like some walking machine. Can't fall or open my mouth." Yet the competitive tightrope he was walking, he also honestly acknowledged to her, had been spun largely out of his own inhibitions and distances. The self-imposed struggles of the pecking order kept him, at most times, cut off even from friends—"like a fucking New Englander, & scaredy cat I stand above and away from [everybody]." He nursed a secret envy of his housemate Ginsberg, who seemed, ironically, the one poet on the scene sufficiently possessed of the "life message" to steer clear of the tiresome territorial pussyfooting and "go straight." Rendered suddenly unsure of the subjective creative advances which had been achieved and so far tested only in solitude, Olson admitted to his wife that he'd been asking himself with sinking heart all through the

conference whether he was really "a *poet* at all," and not just "a figure . . . some creature of Duncan and Creeley's long years of admiration."

His anxious doubts about his new poetry were largely allayed, in the long
run, by his conference-closing reading. The August 16 event, a four-hour
marathon finally shut down by the arrival of janitors to clean the hall, was a
total triumph—the best reading, he later told Betty, that he'd ever done. As
successful as it was, however, the climactic show, one last push culminating
a season of epic pushing, took a great deal out of him, and in the immediate
aftermath the accumulated exhaustion of the whole trip hit all at once, leaving
him with a vast sense of letdown. Adjourning to the faculty club, he hid out
from his followers in a reading room, where Warren Tallman eventually found
him standing among the magazines with tears streaming down his face. Tallman attributed his emotional state to missing Betty.

For Olson the inner tensions of the conference appeared to have had issue
in the somatic realm when a small lump emerged on the side of his neck at
Vancouver. Secretly fearing it to be cancerous, he was approaching a state of
panic by the time a specialist to whom he was referred by Ellen Tallman's
physician finally removed it. The outpatient surgery took place after the last
of the other conference guests had cleared out. Tests showed the growth had
been merely a benign lymphatic cyst. One last worrisome challenge out of
the way, the greatly relieved poet headed home.

Olson had been prevented from "getting a vacation" at Vancouver, he
had told Betty, by his continual consciousness of having to perform up to
expectations so as not to jeopardize his $900 paycheck. The largest one he
had earned since the closing of Black Mountain, it represented a much-needed
contribution to the depressed family economy. But the money, he was also
aware, would be gone before winter, leaving himself and his family once
again in desperate poverty. It was consideration of that prospect which disposed him, despite his vows never to return to teaching, to give serious thought
to an offer of work relayed on to him while at the conference. The position,
to be filled immediately, was a $15,000-a-year distinguished professorship in
English at the State University of New York at Buffalo. By the time Olson
left Vancouver he had notified Buffalo department chairman Albert Cook—
a liberal classicist and scholar of Greek epic who had just taken over the
department, and was pursuing the author of *Maximus* as one of his first actions
in command—that he would be coming.

Subduing his own qualms about the fallback to academia turned out to
be somewhat easier for the poet than overcoming those of his wife. Generally
perceived by acquaintances—especially those whose principal interest was *him*—
as being withdrawn, self-effacing, "shy, quiet, polite," Betty had in fact grown

increasingly capable of showing Charles another side, a serious, stubborn will of her own expressed in spells of mute sullenness punctuated by quick flashes of anger. Given a first clear issue on which to make a stand against him, she turned the proposed move into a pitched battle that lasted several tense weeks. She and Charles Peter would stay on at the Fort, she told him; he himself could go on to Buffalo without them if he liked. Regarding that solution as unthinkable, he continued to press hard for the move. The stalemate was not broken until the moment of departure. Betty, after several changes of mind, was still holding out against going even as they stood among their baggage in Boston's South Station. Charles had to resort to melodrama, going down on his knees on the station platform to coax her aboard the train to Buffalo.

The Olsons' first weeks in their new hometown were spent at Albert Cook's house. Cook, soon also to prove a tolerant employer who considered himself more a friendly "facilitator" than a boss, was just the kind of generous host the visiting poet-professor most favored. He and his wife, Carol, cheerfully reshaped their own domestic routines to suit those of their unconventional guest: late sleeping, extended midday brunches and long, informal evening dispensations of "the cosmic vision, and personal wrenches into it" for the benefit of whoever dropped by. Betty spent the days resting in bed or going out to get her teeth fixed while Carol Cook bore the brunt of shopping and cooking for Charles.

When the strain of group living inevitably began to wear on everyone, Olson withdrew with his brood to the relatively palatial sanctuary of an Old World–style country manor house situated in gently rolling hills near Wyoming, New York, some forty miles east of the city. The place belonged to the Hooker family, owners of Hooker Chemical, one of the area's major industrial presences as well as an important source of endowment revenue for the university. The latter fact, indeed, caused Olson to assume the house was to be his gratis as a fringe benefit of his connection with the school, and when the first month's $150 rent bill arrived he became "furious." His aristocratic tastes—Carol Cook thought of him as "lordly"—were otherwise not disappointed, however. Since some of the region's solidest landowning families were now his neighbors, he was "amongst the gentry" at last. The two-story stone mansion had canopied beds, leaded windows, lofty ceilings, a huge country kitchen and a glassed-in sunporch. Both his obvious satisfaction with such circumstances and Betty's apparent lack of interest in them are recalled by Olson's daughter Kate. "Papa loved eighteenth-century things, elegant things. That house was elegant, beautiful, livable and full of light. But Betty was miserable in that house."

Being stuck in the wilds of Wyoming as country wife indeed left Betty cold from the outset. She had no way to get around, and no friends in the neighborhood. With Charles Peter off at school, the long days alone in the big house weighed heavily on her, and the many nights when Charles stayed late in town, lingering in restaurants and bars to kibbitz with his students after hours, were even worse. He would later come to lament his "mistake [of] taking over [Betty's] power . . . by authority" during this last year of her life, and remind himself in bitter hindsight of her negative reaction to the conditions of enforced solitude in Wyoming ("*as Bet said horrified*—'no social life' / solely alone"). It did not help that on those infrequent occasions when he invited her to join him in town, she felt left out and ignored. Betty, says her sister Jean, "hated Buffalo" every bit as much as she'd feared she would. "The whole environment, all those students with slack jaws listening to Charles . . . she didn't want it."

He, conversely, was in his element, conducting a small, reverent band of acolytes through the complicated rituals of the mystery-religion of his thought. Although he complained to Vincent Ferrini shortly after taking over his new duties that "to get a perfectly obvious advantage of income, & some means" entailed "quite a struggle" for him, in reality he was afforded by both the easygoing department chairman and a loyal core of student disciples the freedom to operate largely as he pleased, making the job of teaching much less of a strain than it might have been in a more rigid academic environment. To start with, he was permitted to convene each of his two classes—Modern Poetry and Myth and Literature—but once a week, and then not until quite late in the afternoon, so that his daytime sleeping habits could be maintained. The sessions, attended by some twelve to fifteen students, were held in an unventilated basement classroom on the old downtown campus. Surrounding himself in a cloud of smoke and aura, Olson was, in the words of one stunned graduate student, "fascinating and indecipherable at once." He adopted an informal challenge system to "weed out" of his classes the less venturesome students by making seemingly impossible demands. Some of the demands were actually "legitimate, some eccentric," one friendly observer suggests. "He only accepted resistance from those who could tell the difference." More than once those ejected—for inadvertent acts of "resistance" in some cases as trivial as eating candy—were women, who remained Olson's particular weakness as a teacher. If they were not actually dismissed, it was often made very difficult for them to stay. In the notorious first meeting of his fall 1963 Modern Poetry seminar, Olson started class by having students identify themselves. When it came the turn of one rather small and delicate-seeming young woman, the new distinguished professor interrupted, "I once knew a woman who looked like you: one brown eye, one blue." He then casually added, as an aside to the men in the class, "The only thing you can do with a woman like that is fuck her." The young woman rose to her feet, replied flatly, "You couldn't," and stalked out.

The thinning-out process left him with an almost entirely male coterie of "angeloi," graduate disciples who were, as Albert Cook puts it, "enraptured and oblivious" in their uncritical awe and admiration of him. There was nothing particularly new for Olson in the intense, selective master-student relationship, the pleasing security of "being surrounded by a very tight, very small retinue" having always been close to the heart of the teaching situation for him. But in his post-class holding of court at Buffalo night spots like Onetto's, an eatery conveniently located just across the street from the university, there was a definite secret-society tone that reflected just how exclusive his dream of *polis* had latterly become. John Clarke, a friend, colleague and follower from these years, remarks tellingly that Olson "simply didn't bother himself with engaging most citizens, feeling more comfortable with 'those few' he could and thus did engage." In the poet's little Buffalo "company" of the few, Olson doctrine became article and verse of a private faith, and Olson terminology—no matter how abstruse—basic vocabulary. (Ironically, Olson's doctrinal line on and definition of parataxis, that disjunctive mode of thinking and writing which he now saw as the key link between archaic "oral" bards like Hesiod and Homer and post-modern ones like himself, came by way of two of his "angeloi," former Harvard classics majors Charles Boer and Charles Doria, who acquainted him with his primary source on the subject, Harvard classicist Eric Havelock's book *Preface to Plato*.)

As the frigid darkness of the Wyoming winter locked in, Olson's nights out in the city got later and later. When after evening sessions with his students he stopped in at the Cooks' to drink wine and talk, Carol dropped tactful hints about his wife being out in the country all by herself. But the footloose poet himself seemed oblivious. The week before Christmas, Betty, who had been feeling increasingly desolate, took an impulsive step to improve her condition, going out without his knowledge to purchase an automobile. She registered the black Volkswagon "bug" in his name because she lacked a valid license of her own, and, though unaccustomed to driving long stretches alone, took off for Gloucester through a heavy snowstorm. Eleven hours later, she was at the Radoslovich home. She told Jean she was terribly unhappy in her new existence as neglected faculty wife. She wanted to come back to live in Gloucester. But she had left Charles Peter behind, and did not feel comfortable letting the eight-year-old boy stay long in the care of his roaming father. She intended to go back for him. But she feared Charles would stand in the way and once again talk her into staying. "I'll see if I can get out again," she told her sister uncertainly. After a day or two, she drove back to Wyoming.

At Christmas the thirteen-year-old Kate arrived to spend the holiday with her father. Unaware of the reasons, she felt the subdued, withdrawn Betty was casting a pall over the festivities. When a wealthy neighboring family, the Gratwicks, came by with their team of Arabian horses to take the Olsons on a romantic "midnight picnic in Bavaria" sleighride through the snow, Betty refused to go. "The whole two weeks I was there," Kate remembers, "Betty did nothing but mope."

In January 1964, Olson returned to teaching and the care of his student flock. Betty, who had agreed to stick things out at least through the spring semester, meanwhile retreated further into silent depression. On March 28, deliberately or not, she took a further, final step away from him. Leaving a half-cooked chicken on the stove, she drove to Batavia, the nearest large town, bought an Easter basket for Charles Peter, then went to a movie. The roads were slick with ice when she headed back toward Wyoming. On a narrow country road her black "bug" swerved into the headlights of an oncoming truck. The collision left her unconscious, her chest crushed. Rushed to St. Jerome's Hospital in Batavia, she did not regain consciousness. She had not yet reached her thirty-ninth birthday.

Roused out of bed by the police, an "incredulous" Olson went into psychic shock. His first dazed gesture was to phone the Cooks. The department head was away in Europe, but his wife was at home to receive the bad news. To Carol, the staggered poet "sounded very far away as he talked." Olson asked her to help him keep the fact of the accident quiet so there would be no further immediate ordeals to face. Inevitably, however, the local media reported the fatal crash, and word quickly spread. Friends and faculty colleagues stepped in to help organize a wake at the Wyoming place. A Catholic funeral mass was said over the open casket in the living room, and the body, laid out in a long black dress, viewed by a gathering of local Olson sympathizers (joined by Vincent Ferrini, who had driven all the way from Gloucester). The day's most painful moment came when Betty's young son approached the casket and stood over her last remains. The clear resemblance in their features struck Carol Cook as "unbearable somehow." After the boy had placed roses around his mother's body, he was left to wander like a lost child among the drinkers. Betty's family, meanwhile, had avoided the service, a tacit statement that they felt the responsibility for the tragic loss was at least indirectly Olson's. ("His demands were enormous," Jean Radoslovich still believes. "They could actually kill.") The bereaved husband himself seemed completely overcome, whether with guilt or grief alone it was impossible to tell. "Well enough plastered to weep unashamedly," he broke down when a faculty colleague who was Catholic attempted to console him in terms of the faith of his childhood. He "talked openly and passionately about his loss," recalls Laurence Michel (Cook's stand-in as department chairman at the time, and thus the presiding university representative in attendance), "in that vocabulary of profanity-scatologyobscenity-mild blasphemy one uses to appease the demon of grief." The last mourners adjourned for dinner to the Gratwick estate in nearby Pavilion. One of the Cooks' sons was assigned to ride over with Charles Peter and his father in the beach wagon. The boys hung on for their lives as Olson slalomed the beat-up old wagon around the icy curves at breakneck speed.

Betty's body was held in "deep freeze" pending solution of a dispute between Olson and her family over the choice of a burial site. He favored letting her be laid to rest without further ceremony in a Batavia cemetery; the family wanted her back in Gloucester. A second battle was soon being waged over custody of Charles Peter. Olson was determined to keep the boy by his side, but from the first it seemed a lost cause. Father and son retreated to the Cooks', where Charles Peter immediately came down with chicken pox. "Gloomy and not quite sure of how his life had changed or would change," Olson killed the days sitting around chain-smoking cigars and playing poker for pennies with his son and the Cook boys. When Robert Duncan showed up in town, a few days late for the wake but eager to be of use, Olson turned over his classes to the West Coast poet. "I don't want to live to be sixty," he dejectedly informed his old friend. He prowled the site of Betty's crash, studying the landscape for signs that might make the meaning of the event come clear, and appeared in the dead of night at the homes of friends and acquaintances in an evidently distracted state. After a few weeks he brought Charles Peter back with him to Wyoming, where emergency volunteers, mostly young women, were sent in to help him cope with child care and housekeeping. Coping with *him,* in his unstable condition, proved an even larger challenge. After attacking the untouched kitchen, where Betty's chicken had been collecting mold in a pot for three weeks, the first recruit cooked dinner for the master of the house and guest Robert Creeley, who happened to be in town for a reading. As the two poets sat down to dine, Olson questioned the kitchen volunteer as to whether the cooking pot had been fully sterilized. Dissatisfied with her replies, he flew into a violent rage, thundering, "You're trying to kill us with botulism!"

Life, he told Creeley, now seemed to him "utterly impossible without *staff.*" Yet he found it hard to abide sharing his living space with virtual strangers. At the beginning of May he checked himself into Buffalo's Millard Fillmore Hospital for two weeks, nominally for treatment of chronic emphysema brought on by years of chain-smoking. In fact he simply knew nowhere else to go to get the kind of special care he required. Once out of the hospital, he had to acknowledge defeat in his struggle to keep Charles Peter at his side. Arranging to deposit the boy with the Radosloviches, he headed toward Gloucester in the beach wagon, but got only as far as Albany before collapsing. "I can't go any further," he told Jean by phone. She had to drive to

Albany to pick up the boy, who by this point had reason to welcome the change of guardians. Henceforth, even upon Olson's subsequent return to Gloucester, father and son would see relatively little of one another.

He doubled back to the northwest by way of Rochester, where he fetched a visitor at the airport. This was Gladys Hindmarch, a Canadian writer he'd met and liked at Vancouver and lately invited to keep him company at the Wyoming house in his hour of need. Getting in at dusk, they sat up late drinking beer; he talked all night, then ushered her at dawn to a second house on the property, where she would sleep during her visit. Over the next several days, he continued to spill out his troubled soul, dwelling at length on the circumstances of Betty's death—which he'd been replaying obsessively in the weeks just past. Preying particularly on his mind was the question of whether the "accident" had really been that. To Hindmarch he admitted his gnawing suspicion that it had been suicide and that he himself was to blame for the loss of his wife because he hadn't paid enough attention to her. And there were further anxieties relating to the matter of the ultimate disposition of the body. Could Betty be administered the last rites of the Catholic religion in which she'd been raised, given that he'd deprived her of the state of grace by living with her without actually marrying her? He spoke also of guilts of an even deeper strain, seeming unconsciously to elide Betty with Connie. "I felt he confused the two of them, that the 'she's' were interchangeable," Hind-march says. One balmy evening they walked through a barley field under a full moon, discussing the "woman question." Olson cited the views of D. H. Lawrence. His guest in turn brought up Betty Friedan's recently published *The Feminine Mystique,* which he at first peremptorily dismissed as "The Feminine Mystery or Mistake." Later in the conversation, however, his ridicule gave way to a grudging admission that the domination of women by men might not be such a good thing after all, and that "maybe Bet felt that [way] too."

Following the departure of Gladys Hindmarch, Olson returned to Gloucester for the rest of the summer, occupying the Fort Square flat alone. His poetry, as ever, became the field in which the deep experience he was undergoing found its allegorical figuration. It reflected his continuing failure to find rest in his own mind on the subject of his late wife. He was shaken by the realization that he had in effect been "forecasting" her death in myth-ological poems even during the last year of her life, when in what at the time had seemed no more than routine plunderings of Hesiod he had described at length the abduction of Earth-"daughters" into the underworld by Pluto, the chariot-jockeying "King of Hell," "God of the Black Sun." Similar images returned, with a hallucinatory vividness of personal obsession eerily distort-ing the mythic context, in strange, tormented, dreamlike poems composed during the months when Betty's body lay unburied in a cold-storage vault in Batavia. These mythological externalizations of responsibility for the "crime" of inflicting Betty's premature demise may well have served as a release mechanism, a transferring of guilt that relieved the poet himself of some of the psychological burden he was carrying at this time. In one poem, "Grinning monster out side the system," death, the ravisher in his automotive chariot, ran down the lost woman with unexpected violence; "slammed in the night" like a bird ripped from its nest, she was abruptly seized away "right down through the highway blacktop / slicing." Another, "barley or rye," pointed the finger of blame at a mythic, truckdriving Pluto:

King of the Ravished Bride
Black One-Eyed King
who lay with my wife . . .

> *seen by the eye of my Angel*
> *swept by him coming through*
> *on his black 4-wheeled vehicle . . .*

> *oh Bride of my Life*
> *Whose secret I do keep*

As priest and keeper of his unwed bride's secret, there could be no peace for the poet until that dangerous secret—of the underlying causality of her death—was exorcised or sublimated in self-mythological transformation. This process was less one of creative "escape" than of wrenching, bewildering emotional upheaval. The poems just quoted, left out of the *Maximus* by Olson's posthumous editors, are complemented by passages the poet unequivocally intended for incorporation in his epic. In "Maximus to himself June 1964," a poem of bitter loss, the shattered narrator stands at the exhausted wellsprings of personal myth ("no more, / where the tidal river rushes"), announcing the reversion of his life to himself—not as power but as mere property ("the ownership / solely / mine"). Here the poet finds release from the ravaging of self by savage fates that like wild dogs "tear anything apart" only in the simultaneous loss of all sense of "wonder."

On the 3rd of July, Olson looked on with Jean, her three children and Charles Peter as Betty's earthly remains were at last laid to rest in Beechwood, the fishermen's cemetery of Gloucester. Still acceptance of the loss and of its personal meanings were slow to come. His imagination remained haunted by his mythic nemesis, the hard-driving King of Hell, though with time this figure became more complicated, a teacher as well as a raptor, even a sort of cosmic spiritual guide. In a 1965 *Maximus* poem, Olson would recall locating the stars of the chariot in the night sky only a few years earlier, in the winter before the fatal crash, when he'd been "happy, on my hill, in the clear cold / of the best of my life." Now he rediscovered the same constellation in the summer night, "my instructor at last": "You also were Pluto, you did take my girl, you are / triumph . . . I hail you, Driver, / in your place upon the sky."

24

Life Solely to Be Lived
(1964–1965)

> . . . driven as a Christian out onto
> the highways, suckered into the present as a soul
> forced out of fortune, with no lead but myself,
> with no love, with life solely to be lived . . .

The poet missed his late wife, and the married state, more than he would have imagined. The flood of elegiac fragments that filled his notebooks following her death show the emotion he retroactively invested not only in the lost partner but in the condition of conjoined souls which their relationship, lent the softer lighting of hindsight, had belatedly come to represent. Released from the world of confusion, trial and petty difficulty their life together had become, Betty took an idealized place in the Olson self-allegory. "Her skin covered me, illuminated / my nature . . . kept me / (at least at night) free . . ."

"The World gets into position," he suggested to himself in one poem-note, "only when the dialogue is with a 'wife.'" Out of kilter on his own, he had before the summer of 1964 was over sought to reestablish contact with Frances, the one woman he considered a feasible potential replacement for Betty as spiritual companion and helpmeet. After a brief exchange of letters, he talked her into coming in to New York City from Princeton—where she now worked as a book designer—to meet him for dinner at the Waldorf Astoria. As in the old days, he inundated her with talk for several hours, lingering over drinks until they were alone in the room except for the impatient waiters. Finally Frances made a move to leave, but, she says, "he refused to let me go." He led her upstairs to an expensive suite, assuring her that everything had been paid for with a borrowed credit card, and there went on talking and talking in the complicated analogical discourse to which his later disciples were accustomed; Frances herself could gather only that he was a physical and nervous wreck. "He was in terrible psychic suffering, but I couldn't respond. There was no contact between us. I felt, there's no human being there, just a husk. He was experiencing a real loss of his own identity, which he was hoping to get back through me. Alas, it did not work."

Olson was not so easily discouraged. Back in Gloucester, he wrote his former Muse a desperate letter, asking her to take him back into her life. In her reply Frances laid her cards on the table. She had a new man, and had, since last seeing Olson, become engaged to be married. Her fiancé, she told him, was "someone more truly Maximus than yourself." Temporarily blinded by jealous rage and lonely drunken suffering, he responded with a wild nineteen-page screed of irrational accusation and rebuke. She had taken the name of Maximus in vain, a corruption and misuse, as he told her, "of *my creation my work* [by making it] the measure of your true new man."

Frances ignored his letter, but within a few months she had broken off the engagement with the "interloper" and resumed their intermittent correspondence. Thereafter, though Olson periodically declared his rediscovered love for her, she carefully sidestepped all but strictly intellectual expressions of passion. She wrote him about her own esoteric studies (pursuits that would yield several unique books), remarking at one point on "the times without number we have found ourselves tossing back and forth the same ball—the quick of the universe." But all the knowledge in the universe could not compensate Olson for the special melancholy of loneliness which he now felt. His loveless solo existence stale in his mouth, he persisted in the impossible project of raising the dead affair. "I have loved you," he avowed, "with all my life. . . . And I don't know now where in fact to place that life or what in fact to do with it in all those ways at least you were my dream of it."

A crash course in domestic readjustment was in store for him at the Fort that summer. Suddenly forced to shift for himself, he had to develop a whole new set of habits. Cooking for himself was too much trouble, and his eccentric inner clock seemed to defy synchronization with the business hours of favored eateries like the Cape Ann diner in town or the Surf in nearby Magnolia. When he could manage to get himself out for dinner before closing time, he sometimes followed the meal with a nocturnal constitutional stroll through the deserted streets, afterwards retiring to the Fort to work until dawn. With no one else's life pattern to modify the vagaries of his own metabolism, his work-pushes now could and often did overlap into the following evening. After forty-eight hours of intensive writing and reading, time-bending exacted its price, as he collapsed into bed for the next twenty-four. "Like a cave bear, he knew how to hibernate," a friend observes.

Foremost among the few visitors allowed into the Fort during the reclusive time following Betty's funeral were Harvey Brown, a young jazz aficionado from Cleveland who had dropped in on one or two of his Buffalo classes earlier that year, and Brown's wife Polly. Wandering scion of a wealthy Shaker Heights industrial family, Brown had survived an American upbringing that included spells in both exclusive boarding schools and the U.S. Marines, becoming a dedicated pilgrim of the new improvisational music and poetry and befriending many progressive East Coast jazz players as well as writers like LeRoi Jones. He was now devoting as much of his inherited fortune as possible to the attentive study and generous furthering of just such cutting-edge cultural advances as Olson's. "We're on the same belt transmission," the poet was soon declaring of this important new friend. Already the invisible backer and soon to take over as editor of an Olson "company" journal out of Buffalo, the *Niagara Frontier Review*—whose inaugural issue this summer had a cover photo of the poet-master in aggressive teaching stance, and featured his recent writings—Brown would within a year, acting on Olson's instigation, begin selling off family trust fund holdings to subsidize Frontier Press, conceived and designed as a venue for Olson-approved texts.

The remainder of the summer of 1964 was otherwise devoted mostly to poetry, now to be Olson's final, enduring close companion. Working from Jeremy Prynne's typescripts, he assembled, and in September sent off to Jonathan Williams, a text of *Maximus IV, V, VI,* the difficult, unwieldly, cosmic-exploratory midsection of his epic, representing the central effort of the past six years of his life. Meanwhile new verse of the summer, variously somber and agitated in reflection of the psychic trauma of recent months, yielded fragmentary groundwork for the epic's third and last volume. Most notable was the muted, ominous "COLE'S ISLAND," document of a dream run-in with an allegorical specter of death in the wilds of Essex Bay backcountry. In the dream Death was dressed up as a country gentleman strolling his property, encountered by the wandering poet in the midst of investigations of local topography. The dream poem seemed an omen, another tacit warning of the dangers of infringing carelessly on the domain of mortality—something the obsessive researcher had been doing much of his life, though only lately had he learned something of the stiff penalties such trespassing could bring. In "COLE'S ISLAND," when landowner Death and intruder Maximus sized one another up, Death seemed much less unsettled than the poet by their sudden, chilling propinquity.

Ironically, the unmistakable intimations of a narrowing personal future which haunted Olson after Betty's death not only failed to ameliorate his compulsive work drives, but actually intensified them; it was as if, since his own time was about to be foreclosed, absolutely no more of it could be wasted. In one verse fragment he attempted to articulate his feeling that the loss of his wife had somehow derailed him from his own forward track in life, increasing the pressure on him to drive ahead harder than ever now: "I went full tilt / and then she was killed / in her automobile / I need every bleeding minute now / I don't have any time for new life." His brain teemed with schemes for new projects, but at the same time the patience and perseverance required to sustain such projects and complete them was less than ever his. While he marshaled "every bleeding minute" for new poetic creation, translation and compilation projects were left in the hands of often-bewildered trustees. French, Italian and German editions of his work were now underway, as were two major book-length American trade selections, the responsibility for both of which Olson was farming out to old reliable satellites: Robert Creeley was being counted on to edit a New Directions *Selected Writings,* and Donald Allen had been for some time entrusted with seeing a *Selected Essays* through the works at Grove Press. With both these books, as with *Maximus IV, V, VI*—which, after a bitter dispute over what the poet perceived as the imperfections of the typesetting job, would be withdrawn from Jargon / Corinth and subsequently go unpublished until picked up outside the country, by London's Cape / Goliard, three years later—there would be serious foul-ups, to some extent the result of the poet's insistence on retaining an Olympian detachment from the prosaic practical realities of authorship. The volume of essays lingered on the back burner at Grove until Olson rerouted it to another erstwhile protégé, his former Black Mountain student Robert Hawley, then a San Francisco fine printer; there was to be yet another squabble over publishing details before the book finally came out in a limited edition from Auerhahn Press in 1965 (as *Human Universe*). The actual outcome of the New Directions *Selected Writings,* meanwhile, appearing a year later, would be greatly disappointing to Olson, Creeley's cautious choices of the poetry—concentrating almost exclusively on the earlier, more expository work—puzzling him almost as much as his friend's apparent ignorance of his life, as betrayed in an error- and omission-filled introduction. (Olson, it must be said, had steadfastly ignored Creeley's requests for corrective biographical data at the book's proof stages, preferring, with characteristic backhanded pride, that the mistakes be kept in so as to "increase the *mysterium*.")

In the second week of September, Olson left Gloucester to return to Buffalo and resume his teaching chores. This time around, however, he was deliberately traveling light, making no bones about his independence of the conventional academic way of life. Even such assertions of permanence as the Wyoming house had represented were now out of the question for him. He converted his paychecks into traveler's checks and spent the money immediately "on sleeping and moseying around." Instead of renting a house or apartment, he installed himself in the University Manor motel on Main Street, conveniently adjacent to his workplace. It was to the motel room that he retreated between his two midweek classes; it was there that he entertained his students following evening sessions at Onetto's, and even held his office hours, such as they were. Graduate student Stephen Rodefer, arriving at the University Manor for an appointed midafternoon consultation, was taken aback to find the motel room's blinds still down and his teacher not yet fully awake; he was offered the room's second bed as Olson climbed back into his own and conducted the conference from a horizontal position in the darkness.

There were periods in the winter months when the motel dweller did not see the light of day for weeks at a time, emerging from his lair to teach his dinner-hour classes or to take sustenance at nearby joints like Onetto's or Bill's Luncheonette. Smoking heavily, and making only occasional attempts to keep up an exercise regime consisting of brisk pacing through the streets around the motel after midnight, he was conscious of but unable to arrest a continuing slow decline in his health. One visitor to the University Manor, his friend and department colleague Jack Clarke, found him stalking around the room unclothed and complimented him on maintaining a relatively trim physique. Olson seemed visibly cheered. Ambling over to the floor-length mirror, he struck a mock Charles Atlas pose, inspected his sucked-in gut and expanded barrel chest, and declared convincingly, "Anyone who talks as much as I do has got to stay in shape." In private, though, he was finding nature harder and harder to fool. The physical and mental slumps to which he'd always been prone were multiplying in both frequency and severity. He sometimes holed up incommunicado for extended periods, posting a succinct notice—"DO NOT DISTURB / THIS MEANS YOU"—on the motel-room door. It was then, indeed, that much of his actual work got done. When the urge to withdraw became extreme, he jumped into the beach wagon and retired to the tiny town of Clarence, a few miles east of Buffalo, where he was able to lie low in anonymous rented rooms, reading and writing for days without being found. Books and papers were now his only essential baggage; for the furnishings of a writer's life he'd come to depend on whatever lay immediately at hand, be it a bartop, restaurant table or any other available flat surface. His poem "The Lamp," a complex reflection on the passage of time, self and universe, was first written out—with a restaurant placemat as his spur-of-the-moment paper—on the roof of the beach wagon, parked on the side of the road en route to one of his country retreats.

Olson was more than ever an interesting anomaly in his capacity as distinguished professor. In the classroom he pounded the table, swore, wooed, pontificated and set fire to $20 bills, making his students witness to the spectacle of the state's money literally as well as figuratively going up in smoke. His consistently "mind-bending talk" awed such new student followers as McGill University graduate Albert Glover, an aspiring poet and Gurdjieff devotee who was quickly moved to a transfer of allegiances, earnestly inquiring of spiritual mentor Olson "if he was, in fact, Gurdjieff." Other recently enrolled graduate students now entering the inner circle included George Butterick, one day to join Glover as an Olson bibliographer and editor; Fred Wah, a promising poet from Vancouver; and a bright young English poet / editor from Cambridge, Andrew Crozier. Also on hand, and the evident favorites among this year's crop of disciples, were Harvey Brown, sitting in on classes as an unenrolled auditor, and the poet John Wieners, for whom Olson had arranged a teaching assistant's position in the English department. Wieners, a fellow wanderer of the night, shared talk and sometimes drugs with him, providing "a comfort like the Irish say," sensitive and tolerant company that more than once kept him from "coming to grief" during this difficult year. There was also a growing recognition on the older poet's part of equal fellowship with his longtime student in the difficult vocation of verse; Wieners' own emotionally forthright poetry of "affect" had come to seem to Olson "elemental," a force to be reckoned with and learned from.

Another poet out of Olson's past, the Beat troubadour Gregory Corso, was hanging out in Buffalo that fall, and occasionally making his unreconstructed presence felt in "company" circles. As on a few notable past occasions, Corso represented for Olson a sort of truth test, introducing an element of challenge, seemingly only half playful, that made their encounters unnerving for him. One day Corso dropped in midway through the mythology seminar, disrupting the proceedings to announce knavishly that he was "Captain Poetry" and demand a kiss from a visibly ruffled Olson. Moments later, a library Special Collections curator stepped into the classroom to make a routine announcement. Corso, refusing to be upstaged, turned his attention to the librarian, calling him a "faggot." Both men soon exited. In the hallway, the angry librarian flattened the abusive poet with one punch. Olson led his students "in a fast Elephant Walk" to investigate the ruckus, and once satisfied that his tormentor had escaped with nothing worse than a bloody nose, paraded his little flock back to the classroom and "resumed the 2nd Millennium as though nothing had happened."

Corso's habit of showing up late at night at the University Manor had before long forced Olson to temporarily switch rooms, retaining his old one as a "blind" to throw off the unwanted guest. But confrontation was not always avoidable. On a snowy night in November, after a reading at a local coffee house that had been a real trial for him—in his first attempt to read his poetry in public since Betty's death, despite the encouragement of the faithful he simply hadn't been able to get all that grand epic machinery off the ground—

he was sitting in a bar unwinding when Corso, apparently drunk, appeared out of the night and sat down beside him. An unsolicited critique of the reading and of his poetry followed. "Gloucester is shit!" declared the Beat jester with intoxicated recklessness. "Maximus is shit—and you, Professor Olson, are shit!" Instead of rising up in wrath, as onlookers perhaps expected, Olson dropped to his knees, thrust his face into his assailant's, and implored, "What do you *want* me to do? *Change?*" After the encounter, he sat on for several hours brooding and silent with his friend Jack Clarke, obviously "in a great state of disappointment."

At Thanksgiving, Olson went back to Gloucester for a break. Kate came from Philadelphia to stay with him at the Fort. He also attended Charles Peter's baptism into the Roman Catholic faith that was practiced in the Radoslovich household. The boy was already going to a Catholic school. Though having a child of his raised in the religion he'd once blamed for his own painful repressions was something Olson formerly would have been hard put to tolerate, he accepted it now with a combination of resignation and provisional approval. His current worship of cosmic gods of creation had ironically brought him around to consider the Catholics' God of Creation in a more sympathetic light; in teaching and conversation, in fact, he had lately taken to quoting the Lord's Prayer as a sort of esoteric mystic mantra. Back in Gloucester again at Christmas, he returned to Our Lady of Good Voyage Church once more, for his son's First Communion, and this time took the unprecedented step of staying for Mass. His first experience of the liturgical ritual performed in English, rather than in the familiar Latin, was entirely negative, however, dispelling his illusions about an easy rapprochement with the mystic Catholicism of his childhood. He walked out in mid-service.

At the end-of-year holiday Kate joined him in Gloucester, this time staying with him at the Tavern, where, in order to avoid the housekeeping headaches of the Fort, he'd taken up quarters for the duration of the six-week interim between Buffalo semesters. After years in which there had been little but chore and guilt for him in fathering, he found that he now enjoyed Kate's company considerably. She was becoming old enough to sustain a serious conversation, and when they talked he was delighted to make out evidences of his own strengths of mind emerging. In view of his otherwise unfortunate track record as a family man, it was a real pleasure and relief to him to know that, as he reported proudly to friends, he and his daughter had arrived "in an independent relation with each other finally." And too, with Kate around to look after him and keep him occupied, he felt much less helpless and alone.

After Kate left, the midwinter doldrums set in as usual. He wrote off to the Guggenheim and Rockefeller foundations asking for support of travels to Crete and Ireland, where—ostensibly, at least, for the sake of the *Maximus*—he wanted to retrace the mythic voyages of Manes / Minos on which he'd been reading up in Robert Graves' *Greek Myths*. Once back in icebound Buffalo for the new term, the daydream voyages looked ever better to him in comparison with the increasingly distasteful reality of "this working for a living," a mode of existence in which—as he told Frances—all his energy was being drained off into externals while "so much piled up" inside, all that unexpressed life. The foundations denied him his epic travels, but he stuck to the Graeco-Celtic myth-trace in verse like a "sweet salmon" *Maximus* poem directed to Frances on the occasion of her fifty-ninth birthday. As if drawn to the shifting analogical ground of Olson's self-allegory, where cosmic congruences were less the exception than the rule, the great myth expert Graves himself arrived in Buffalo around that time to appear on a poets' panel. Olson was using *Greek Myths* as a text that spring, and was so wrapped up in it that he'd gone through several paperback copies, and the well-worn latest of them was held together by rubber bands. Anticipating a climactic meeting, he approached the snowy-haired, diminutive British poet-mythologist after the panel presentation at the Albright Knox Museum, enclosed him within one vast arm, leaned down close and beamed, "You're just like a loaf of bread right out of the oven, and I'm going to take you home and eat you right up!" Graves, appearing unaware of the identity of the friendly giant who was accosting him, acted confused and quickly changed the subject.

A highlight of the spring 1965 semester for Olson was a poetry reading at the university in which he performed with two poets of his choosing, in effect delivering not only a statement of his own progress after twenty years of practice but his vision of the American poetry of the future. Rising to the occasion, he put on a memorable show, as did his two appointed poetic heirs, John Wieners and Ed Sanders. Sanders, twenty-five-year-old college-dropout classics scholar, artistic renegade, Poundian, Egyptologist, peace activist, emissary of the new electronic rock generation, had been corresponding with Olson since his 1961 discovery of "MAXIMUS, FROM DOGTOWN—I"—an event which, as he later put it, "changed my life" (he had since set a section of the poem for musical performance by his radical folk rock group, the Fugs). *Poem from Jail*, Sanders' rhapsodic testament of his attempt to sabotage the commissioning of a Polaris nuclear submarine and his subsequent incarceration, was already being touted by Olson as the herald of a "new metric," its neologistic lyric diction commended as an advance "in a direction . . . which probably isn't even guessed at." On this first actual encounter, the older poet was bowled over by the younger one's "new public style," and greatly flattered by being asked to translate Hesiod's *Theogony* for publication by Sanders' Fuck You Press, sentinel of the underground mimeograph new wave, though, put on the spot, he had to admit sheepishly, "Well, look, Ed, I don't have any Greek." The work of younger followers like Sanders and Wieners, Olson would make a point of remarking whenever the subject of the poetry stock market came up after this Buffalo reading, now actually seemed to him of more interest than that of "men whom I have been attached to in early years, such as Mr. Creeley, Mr. Duncan. . . ."

Wieners, Olson's closest companion of that spring, became his traveling partner on a summer trip to Europe to take part in the Spoleto Festival of Two Worlds and the P.E.N. International Congress in Bled, Yugoslavia. (Olson owed this first reading invitation abroad to two touring poets who had lately stopped in to read at Buffalo, New Yorker Frank O'Hara, an adviser to Spoleto organizer Gian-Carlo Menotti, and Englishman Stephen Spender, a P.E.N. official.) In late June, after Olson transferred his University Manor life-cargo into the beach wagon and stowed it in Jack Clarke's garage, and following a goodbye scene at the Buffalo airport in which the departing poet acted as if he'd never be back (he got rid of all his U.S. currency by stuffing $20 bills down the dress front of Clarke's wife Sue), he and Wieners flew to Rome. For Olson, his entry to the Mediterranean world, cradle of ancient mythic sources, was a momentous event. Even the roads into the city from the airport seemed infused with a "close beautiful condition of every possible matter, trolley cars, solid dirt walls, hay (made into perfect solid houses on the edges of fields)." From the Hotel Atlantico he dispatched to Frances a vivid account of his arrival, making it clear he'd landed in a human universe that felt like home to him. "Love you more than Ever, Having flown through the Empyrean and Arriving here in the Host of Human beings—Incredible . . . Ancient Human Life, the light. . . ." For a few days in Rome, the two poets dwelt in the thrall of personal mythology, Wieners enchanted merely to be traveling with the teacher he adored ("with you, father, I have found delight . . ."), Olson himself entirely carried away by the romance of tourism. They made pilgrimages to the Vatican Library and to one of Rome's best tailors, Olson shelling out $120 in traveler's checks to have a stylish white linen suit hand-made for his debut as a world poet. Then they moved on to Spoleto and checked into a small hotel overlooking the town's thirteenth-century aqueduct.

At the festival they joined an American poets' delegation that included Allen Tate, Lawrence Ferlinghetti and John Ashbery, among an international cast of bards featuring such famous names as the Chilean Pablo Neruda and the Russian Yevgeny Yevtushenko, as well as the main attraction, the seventy-nine-year-old American expatriate Ezra Pound, making a rare public appearance to attend the staging of his ballet *Villon*. Pound, whom Olson hadn't seen or communicated with since their acrimonious breakup of 1948, hardly seemed to remember him—much less want to carry on their old quarrel. The Master was a changed figure, frail, remote and mute, his mind and spirits obviously affected by age and an advancing condition of abulia. A wispy "Umbrian angel" with absent "eyes of stone," Pound stymied Olson's energetic efforts at bringing about a "summit conference" by almost completely ignoring them—as well as everything and everyone else at the festival. The only two comments Olson managed to elicit from the older poet in several days of trying were so minimal as to amount to almost nothing.

One night he and Wieners accompanied Pound and his companion / protector Olga Rudge to the Theatro Caio Melisso for a performance of LeRoi Jones' play *Dutchman*. Jones' tense and timely drama of racial confrontation held a packed house breathless, though Olson inadvertently broke the spell at one point by dropping and breaking a glass in his front-row seat. As they slowly negotiated a flight of stairs afterwards, he got up the nerve to ask Pound for an opinion on his friend's play. "Tremendous," Pound murmured as if from another dimension, and then again fell silent.

The following day it was Olson's turn to perform in the ornate old theater. Introduced by John Ashbery, he led off a program that also included New Yorker Bill Berkson and Italian Communist Pier Paolo Pasolini by delivering a breathy rendition of his "Song of Ullikummi," a free adaptation of a Hittite / Hurrian creation myth ("and five times he took her / nanzankan 5-anki das / and again ten times he took her / namma man zankan 10-anki das . . ."). He seemed to be aiming the poem—not at all an easy one for anyone who hadn't taken the Buffalo "company" tour of the Second Millennium—directly at Pound, who sat motionless in a dress-circle royal box adjacent to the stage. To Olson's dismay the long poem "fell dead," and Pound made no sign of acknowledgment. Having to sit through an ensuing enthusiastic demonstration of support for Pasolini by the leftist poet's claque of "Roman boys in fuzzy sweaters" hardly relieved the sting of the defeat for Olson. After the show, in an outdoor café, he made one final unsuccessful bid to engage Pound in conversation—this time trying an opening gambit borrowed from Ed Sanders, who had described to him a sanguine vision of Pound at eighty, entering upon "a revival of life [and] fifteen further years of power." Pound listened indifferently to the reported "vision," and, in a voice barely audible, replied to the café at large, "Sanders has a sense of humor."

Caresse Crosby, Olson's former patron and publisher, was living in the region and attended several festival events. Crosby was one old ally whose faith in Olson hadn't wavered; over the years she'd maintained an intermittent but highly idealistic correspondence, keeping him posted on her "Humanist and Utopian" thirty-year-plan for saving the planet by the collective efforts of an avant-garde think tank of geniuses—in which he was to figure prominently. Now, once he'd concluded his Spoleto obligations, he was conducted along with John Wieners to Roccasinibalda, Crosby's seventy-two-room, solid-rock medieval castle in the Abruzzi hills, where she renewed her efforts to enlist him in the future Utopia, offering him extended refuge at the Cinque-cento fortress-palace. (She explained the place had been designed as a war stronghold by a competitor of Michelangelo; strategically impregnable for five centuries, it was, she said, "the only spot that will survive atomic war.") But Olson did not have time to tarry. He and Wieners hurried across the Yugoslav border to the P.E.N. Congress at Bled, where, this time eschewing Hittite for English, he was proclaimed by playwright Arthur Miller "more Russian than the Russians" in honor of his profligate verbal intensities. Much drinking and talking and little sleeping, however, at the congress as at the festival, had reduced the great talker to a state of severe energy debt by the time the continental fling was over. Still there was no immediate rest in store for him at the end of the big push. He flew directly back from Europe to California for an event that would demand even more of him, the Berkeley Poetry Conference.

Overstressed, jet-lagged, battling fatigue and competitive tension, wired on artificial energy provided by amphetamines and increasingly muddled by heavy counterdoses of brandy, Cutty Sark and pot, at Berkeley Olson was brought to admit he'd "arrived at a point where I really have no more to feed on than myself." By his frenzied consumption he gave Robert Creeley the impression of a man intent on "working his way through the whole history of drugs in America in about two weeks." At whatever physical cost and by whatever chemical means, Olson felt driven to achieve and maintain the peak of his form. He approached the Berkeley show, an alternative-culture all-star affair, as an event of no less historical magnitude than the national political conventions in which he had once taken part—and in personal terms if anything even more significant, since this time the man at the head of the ticket was himself. The latter view was not entirely a subjective delusion. Times were changing in America, as the Dylan song suggested; at Berkeley Olson's hyperbolic vision of the importance of poetry politics was reflected back to him in surprisingly literal terms by new followers like Bay Area poet Kirby Doyle, who after attending a July 20 seminar talk on "Causal Mythology"— Olson's most lucid presentation of the conference, delivered within hours of his arrival—was moved to declare that "Olson is Freedom of Speech," as well as old ones like Ed Sanders, who proposed, with at least some degree of seriousness, an Olson for President campaign.

Olson joined the proceedings halfway through, missing a first week that had included appearances by Wieners (who had flown back ahead of him), Ed Sanders and conference cohost Robert Duncan, but taking in a second week that was highlighted by nightly main-event readings: Dorn on Tuesday night, Ginsberg on Wednesday, Creeley on Thursday, all leading up to his own "anchor man" reading on the final Friday night. Perhaps more appealing to him than his friends' readings, which actually produced much secret competitive envy over everyone's supposed recent advances, was the attendant sociological context—young, attractive, liberated. Lonesome and loveless for too long, Olson felt a powerful urge to take the implicit invitation of the Love Generation at face value, to leap into the exciting cultural moment and experience firsthand "the whole terrestrial angel vision," in all its physical as well as spiritual manifestations. His choice as personal guide was a female conferee from Vancouver, Suzanne Mowatt. A UBC poetry student of Warren Tallman's, the tall, shapely Suzanne, with long streaming golden hair and skimpy white miniskirt, was the acknowledged "bombshell of the conference." Sanguinely mistaking her expressions of affection as indications of love, Olson made up his mind after one night with her that she would be, in the sphere not only of spiritual allegory but of real life, his new angel bride. He appointed a particularly trusted younger poet protégé, Drummond Hadley—a rancher and cowboy from Arizona, whom he'd proclaimed the "most important person" he'd encountered at Vancouver, and who had since been to visit him in Buffalo—to provide travel arrangements for a romantic elopement and Southwestern desert honeymoon commencing directly after his reading. (Though Olson expressed his preference for a private jet or at least a helicopter, the best Hadley could do on such short notice was the promise of a pickup-truck ride to Arizona.) Seeing that he was serious, Suzanne hesitated to let him down until the reading was over. He had confided to her that the public act of maintaining his dominance had always been difficult for him, and that now in particular he feared "all *my boys* have got ahead of me," since he himself had no new poems to offer.

His drunken performance that night offended a few older friends—especially Robert Duncan, who as master of ceremonies felt personally insulted and walked out in protest at the first available break, some hours into things—but left most of the younger spectators in Wheeler Hall merely puzzled. Few understood the real pathos of the spectacle—the lonely, aging and insecure man, desperately running for the offices of President of Poetry and Great Lover at once. Loaded on Dexedrine and gulping liberally from a fresh fifth of Cutty Sark, Olson managed only two poems before the "reading" degenerated into a wandering, confused monologue on politics and poetry. Only intermittently coherent, laced with personal references that were largely obscure to his present audience, the long, swaggering confessional speech was actually more like a filibuster. He bragged that he belonged "where I have been, in Madison Square Garden," and only half playfully proposed appointments to his poetry cabinet: Allen Ginsberg, for instance, was "going to be my Secretary of State for Love." One impatient audience member, poet Lew Welch, called out for poems to be read. Olson overruled the suggestion, claiming he was "addressing the convention floor. The only convention I care of in the whole earth is occurring tonight." When Welch repeated his request, Olson shot back that there was plenty of time: he'd made it clear, hadn't he, that "we stay here all night." As the odd evening wore on and defectors began to file out, his tone took on an edge of challenge. "If you don't know, brother, that poetics is politics, [that] poets are political leaders today, and the only ones," he jeered at the back of one escaping spectator, "you shouldn't have come." The "nonreading," conference co-organizer Professor Thomas Parkinson noted, had turned into a painful "loyalty test" for those who'd respected Olson's work: "Duncan left at the Moscow trials, I left at the Finnish War." Finally even the poet's close friends were squirming. "Is *this* the Charles Olson we all know and love?" Creeley asked Ed Dorn. At the end, Olson looked for support to his "cheering section," where Ed Sanders was keeping Suzanne company. But his prospective bride, too, was by now just looking for somewhere to hide. "I have to run away," she notified Sanders in a frantic message scrawled on a matchbook. "Should I just leave?" Soon two university policemen entered the hall, tapped Olson on the shoulder and politely stopped the show.

At the post-reading party, while the dazed poet continued to hold forth, Suzanne made her getaway, fleeing into the night with a young man to protect her. To the Creeleys and the Dorns fell the unenviable task of attempting, in the ensuing bleak light of dawn outside a Shattuck Avenue gas station, to console the bewildered, hungover and desolate President of Poetry. Olson's chagrin and humiliation were complete.

The fifty-four-year-old widower's infatuation with his angel lover died hard. Back in his solitary bed at the Fort after returning from California, he addressed a series of forlorn invitations to her, conveying his visions of her as his "Fly By Night Jefferson Cart-Wheel," beseeching her to join him in Gloucester to share "loving spoonfuls" of stored-up feeling. When Suzanne didn't come, he phoned her parents in Vancouver, unsuccessfully trying to enlist their collusion in his wooing.

His loneliness was intense; since Betty's death, he admitted to himself, he'd been like a ship adrift without an anchor, a fact which the California fling had merely underscored. When it came time to return to Buffalo for the fall semester, he talked his sister-in-law into accompanying him back to the University Manor for a few days. But Jean had her family to get home to, while he had only his "ailing Buffalo herd" of disciples. In class he began to shepherd them as planned through the Pleistocene epoch, with road maps provided by Gertrude Rachel Levy's *Gate of Horn*. After two weeks, however, he was already bored with the enterprise, and feeling gloomier than ever in his motel room. He approached Albert Cook to propose a readjustment of the terms of his professorship: he would retire forthwith to Gloucester to live and work, continuing to draw his salary for periodic Buffalo teaching visits. When Cook informed him that the job couldn't be restructured in mid-semester, Olson made his anger plain by pounding the office table. To those of his followers who were closest to him, there could be little doubt that the poet now badly wanted out of Buffalo. As if providentially, his friend and student Harvey Brown stepped in to make his departure possible, setting up for him, on the quiet, an open-ended $20,000 annual "editorial" stipend as an adviser to Frontier Press. The grateful and relieved beneficiary lost no time in getting out of town, flying home by way of Boston as soon as he'd cashed Brown's first check. His abrupt exit was thoughtfully smoothed over at school by friends like Cook, who officially euphemized his absence as "sick leave," and Jack Clarke, who took over his classes (the door was thus left open for him to return, though he had just been deprived by enlightened private patronage of his only reason to consider doing so). Clarke also helpfully volunteered to ferry the beach wagon, groaning with Olson's books and papers, back to Gloucester. When the road-weary old Chevy suffered an engine fire and burst into flames outside New Canaan, Connecticut, Clarke—fully cognizant of the vehicle's fetish status for its owner—searched used-car lots until he had found and purchased (for $300) a same-color look-alike wagon. Olson's sacred archives, right down to the "gum wrappers with writing on them," were carefully transferred into the replacement vehicle, which was then safely delivered to the Fort. His treasures secure, the poet turned his back on academia, and once more started his life over.

25

The Conventual
(1966–1967)

Only my written word

I've sacrificed everything, including sex and woman
—or lost them—to the attempt to acquire complete
concentration. (the con-
ventual.) "robe and bread"
not to worry or have to worry about
either . . .

—"Maximus of Gloucester"

I really do prefer the soul to society; and think that the
conventual is now solely the imagination which applies.

—Olson to Edward Dorn, September 1965

Forsaking with little apparent reluctance the security of his Buffalo "company" for a sanctuary more private still, that isolated condition of subjective innervation which he thought of as "the conventual," in the solitary winter of 1965–1966 Olson turned more dramatically than ever away from the public world that had brought so much tension and confusion. In his effort to transform himself he was saying goodbye to not only the social world but—it sometimes seemed—the material world as well. The poet of self-measure, making the best of the corner he had painted himself into, was becoming "Captain Over-Soul" (as he signed himself in a 1966 letter), shaman and priest in his own mystical religion.

"Follow Bet," he'd urged himself in one fragment written after the calamity of his wife's death, "into the colors of her dress / and up the weak ladder / to the Face of God." The image of approach to godhead in his writings now metamorphosed from an ascent to an inward spiral, a furling of being into the sunlike vortex of the soul. In a powerful winter-solstice *Maximus* poem titled "The winter the *Gen. Starks* was stuck," he hailed the year's turning from his frozen vantage at "the end of the land," invoking the alchemical Golden Flower, image of self union, as he welcomed the new sun: "the tightest Rose is the World, the Vision / is the Face of God." Other poems now took a roseate conformation on the page. In his journal he enjoined himself to "Pray *Read Read Read ReRead work*," and in a cryptic verse meditation he implicitly declared his allegiance to a spiritual *"Modus* / absolute . . . as a Prayer." By February 1966 it was clear that for Maximus *work* and *prayer* were rapidly converging.

> *Bottled up for days*
> *in great sweat of being, seeking*
> *to bind in speed—petere—desire,*
> *to construct knowing back to image and*
> *God's face behind it turned as mine*
> *now is to blackness image shows*
> *herself, desire the light*
> *speed & motion alone are, love's*
> *blackness arrived at going backwards the rate*
> *reason hath—and art her beauty God the Truth*

The spiritual illuminations produced in seclusion did little to relieve the intense psychic needs and ravening hungers also bespoken by Olson's poems and notes. Not that he was entirely without contacts in Gloucester. Jean, acting out of consideration for what she imagined Betty would have wished, had committed herself to looking out for him as best she could; and he had stayed in touch with a few local friends, like painter Harry Martin, poet Gerrit Lansing and Vincent Ferrini. But in a lonely moment he told his journal he'd "never in fact except for Ferrini had anyone here . . . [and] Vincent is— and was and always has been a fool." In truth his most meaningful connection with the world remained his poetry, which continued to draw the curious to his door. Inevitably such casual encounters were forced to fill a great social void for him; his longings for someone to talk to, built up over the nights alone, led him to greedily consume drop-in guests. A case in point was the visit paid him by a young English poet. The most recent of several Cambridge University Olsonians to seek him out in person, John Temple had arrived as a graduate student at Buffalo only to find nothing left of Olson but the legend. Tracking the Great Man to the Fort, Temple chanced to knock at the kitchen door on one of those occasions when the DO NOT DISTURB sign wasn't posted, a stroke of fortune he may have shortly come to rue. For forty-eight hours held a virtual captive, deprived of sleep and fed nothing but cigarettes and whiskey while his indefatigable host talked, Temple was finally reduced to crawling across the floor in a vain attempt to keep up as the discoursing Olson, forging the disjunct paratactic links of one long open-parenthesis chain of thought, stalked from room to room of the apartment. Prostrate and "olive green" in complexion by the time Jean Radoslovich mercifully walked in to revive him, the unprepared young Englishman appeared to have survived his fifteen rounds with heavyweight poetry champ Olson only by the skin of his teeth. "Charles would just *do* that," Jean says. "He'd *take you*. . . . He really collapsed people."

Olson proved only slightly easier to keep up with when his sanctuary was invaded in March 1966 by a production crew from the NET documentary series *USA: Poetry*. He allowed himself to be filmed amid a cloud of smoke in his unventilated kitchen, reading "The Librarian" and then talking extempore, with great good cheer and characteristic poetic disconnectedness, of Catholicism and fishing, the history of Gloucester and Tim Leary's drug bust, the writing of the *Maximus* and a recent bizarre neighborhood episode in which he'd hoisted a boy who'd flung dirt at him onto the roof of the beach wagon and, in lieu of administering a spanking, taken a bite out of him. Afterwards he dragged producer Dick Moore and cameraman Phil Green out on the town, proudly showing off landmarks of his poems like Lufkin's Diner, and conducting an informative but potentially hazardous tour of the harbor while "stumbling around in his big coat talking about a million things at once" with such evident abandon that Green feared he'd misstep and plunge through the rotting boards of the ramshackle old wharf. (When the show appeared five months later, with his several hours of monologue squeezed into a fifteen-minute segment, the TV-star-for-a-day sent out notices instructing old friends as disparate as Frances and James Laughlin to tune in.)

The voracity with which Olson greeted outsiders reflected just how sparse his day-to-day existence was becoming. In May, after the loneliest winter of his life, he wrote Creeley that the time since his Buffalo walkout had been "unrelieved . . . & mostly or almost entirely without human company—most of all that 1 million %, no private company." Social needs could be met, but those for more intimate relations were "unanswerable." His one immediately pressing desideratum was "simply a lady fair!" "Find me a woman," he charged Creeley. The same injunction was also now being issued to other friends, with growing urgency. It was, says Creeley, impossible to underestimate the seriousness of Olson's request. "He didn't mean it at all casually. It was almost like someone on the frontier saying, '*Find* me someone with whom I can have a life.' "

The love-starved poet had his own lines out. A fan letter he received that spring from a thirty-nine-year-old Ohio college English teacher named Joyce Benson, who'd encountered his propulsive "MAXIMUS, FROM DOGTOWN—II" in the *Paris Review*, led to a quickly burgeoning correspondence. Benson shared her poems and her sense of a bond of creative affinity and spiritual sympathy between them, as well as extended reports on the ups and downs of her emotional life, while he responded with much free intellectual instruction that was dispensed in an increasingly ardent tone as the weeks went by. Hearing that his correspondent was, like Betty, a Scorpio, had a powerful effect on the highly superstitious Olson. He was before long signing his letters "Yr Tutor & faithful lover." But in July their intense epistolary exchange was abruptly suspended when Benson was hospitalized for a nervous breakdown.

Olson himself had by then other interests closer at hand to divert him. Chief among them was a second prospective "lady fair," this one a glamorous, sophisticated New York City social hostess and art patroness who had taken up residence for the season with her small daughter at an old stone mansion in Riverdale on the fringe of Dogtown. Possessed of the slim, elegant bearing of a clothes model and an aura of class and money, Christine Kerrigan (as we shall call her here) was said to be descended from European royalty, a supposition which her aristocratic style seemed to confirm as fact. The style and glamour indeed were a major part of Kerrigan's appeal for John Wieners, her summer consort at the "Dennison house" (as the historic old Riverdale place was known locally). Wieners, who had resigned himself to a life without intimate knowledge of the society and celebrity women he worshiped from afar, had finally found himself in a love relationship with one of them, and was basking in the unaccustomed role. Olson, as Wieners' fatherly spiritual adviser, did some heavy hanging-out at the Riverdale manse, whose woodsy setting provided landscape inspiration for a June *Maximus* poem on pathfinding as a way of knowledge, "AN ART CALLED GOTHONIC." Another *Maximus* of the same time, "[to get the rituals straight," written after a day with Wieners and Kerrigan "up where Gloucester thins out," explored inner paths of love among the little company of poets. It was a fine thing, Olson suggested in the latter piece, to "live in a World on an Earth like this one we / few American poets have / carved out of Nature and of God." Among his beloved poetic brethren he singled out especially "the careful ones I care for . . . John Wieners, / Edward Dorn & the women they love. . . ." The poem also mentioned Joyce Benson, but it was the woman John Wieners loved upon whom Olson was already focusing his closest attention. In a letter to Ed Dorn, who'd gone off to England to teach, he hinted mysterously of sudden dramatic complications in his emotional life, with Christine Kerrigan at "the center of the web." Similar veiled disclosures reached others. Soon enough tales of the Dennison house love triangle had traveled to the West Coast, where Robert Duncan, a friend to both poets involved in the Riverdale *ménage*, got wind of the situation. Duncan considered it "disastrous": "Wieners thought he had fallen in love and been redeemed from his homosexual fate," while Olson, in his zeal to latch onto the coveted prize, was not only cruelly disregarding the feelings of his longtime friend and protégé, but setting himself up to be the next man turned into the wealthy socialite's "kept monkey."

As the three-way romantic entanglement took its course, the Dennison house became the site of a sort of serial bardic congress, or "Gloucester Poetry Conference" as Olson termed it. First Creeley came through; the two old friends spent an evening together drinking and talking, and at the end of it, over coffee at bleary dawn in Lufkin's Diner, Olson betrayed something of his current state of emotional turbulence, breaking into apparently unprovoked tears as he lamented "that the mountains can diminish and the seas dry up" (initially mystified, Creeley later fathomed Olson had been speaking analogically of the diminution of his own powers, to him a process obviously of no less magnitude than the literal deterioration of the world). Next came Ginsberg, making like a gypsy family circus with his wild "troupe" of Orlovsky brothers (having latterly "in some way at least" scaled the Olson hierarchy ladder, Ginsberg too now took his place among those favored with positive mention in the *Maximus*). And last but hardly least, in September, at a point when the activity of the "Conference" had been lagging slightly because of the temporary absence of Wieners and Kerrigan, Ed Sanders arrived, accompanied by his Fugs drummer Ken Weaver.

It was Sanders' visit, Olson later declared, that "did me the most good." Olson's key contact with the youth culture, or perhaps more accurately with his hopeful dionysiac imaginings of it, the young poet-musician was in the midst of a "hot year" that had contained off-Broadway stage success; a top-forty album, featuring Olson verse set to electric-rock strains; and an English tour, on which he'd tried in vain to get Olson to come along. (On one occasion around this time, the older poet was set up by matchmaker Sanders on a date with Janis Joplin, and took her out for a Chinese dinner on Grove Press' tab; his extensive remarks on Sutter and the Donner Party, however, completely failed to impress the California singer, who aborted his monologue, and the evening, by inquiring, "Where's the pool table?") Now, as on most of those occasions when the world he thought to be passing him by actually stopped to include him, Olson lost no time catching up. He helped Sanders' companion Weaver, a long-haired, hard-drinking ex-marine from Texas, to polish off a fresh fifth of bourbon out of the latter's traveling kit (Weaver, he immediately decided, was a "spontaneous non-poet poet"), then dug out his stash of souvenirs from the Leary experiments and offered to share them around. "Everybody's high on bourbon already, and Olson shows up with this *bottle* of LSD," Sanders is still amazed to recall. "He says, 'Here, want a swig?' What is it, five hundred micrograms to get high, and he's proposing twenty *million* micrograms. . . . You know, enough for Manhattan!" When his guests passed on this first offering, Olson pulled out a jar containing his home supply of psylocibin "peanuts," tossed down two dozen of them himself, and began to count out equal amounts of the tiny orange pills for Sanders and Weaver. Once again the rock musicians' appetites for chemical adventuring were beggared in comparison. Despite deciding after a little quick calculation to try no more than a few of the pills ("I'm flagging out on twenty-four . . . I'm skinnier than him, I'm this quasi-ectomorph, you know—and he's *Maximus*"), Sanders nonetheless soon found himself afloat in visions in the backseat of the beach wagon as "guru" Olson—maneuvering the vehicle down the road at a snail's pace so as to better enjoy his own magic mushroom ride—transported the party to the Dennison house. En route, Sanders hallucinated that their shaggy autonomic navigator was actually the mythic Poseidon, "a horse with a sea-green mane, and chestnut-colored hair and kelp swirling around him." Olson, meanwhile, was causing traffic to back up as he slowed the wagon to a virtual halt in order to ogle a trio of large gray roadside boulders which were apparently taking on analogical dimensions: "Whee, look at the elephants!" Once at the Dennison place he sat Weaver down over further drinks to hear his longhouse visions from earlier mushroom trips, as Sanders, dressed up "in full Fugs regalia"—an all-red suit—crashed off into the wilds of Dogtown, eventually to be found and rescued by puzzled police in the early hours of the morning. The entire "mad 24 hours" seemed to Olson a marvelous time.

Learning upon Christine Kerrigan's return that she'd become pregnant with Wieners' child, Olson counseled an abortion (an action that would be regarded as a serious betrayal—leading to a tragic loss of "good blood"—by the prospective father, once he found out about it). Soon afterward, in a strained telephone call between Gloucester and the Chelsea Hotel in New York—where Kerrigan herself, Creeley and several other witnesses stood by the phone—he broke the news to his fellow poet that he himself was about to sail off with their mutual paramour to England.

On October 28, Olson, Kerrigan and the latter's small daughter embarked from Montreal on the *Empress of Canada*. They landed in Liverpool and went on to London, where Olson immediately split off from his consort to dive into intense socializing with English followers. Ed Dorn, summoned in from Essex, conducted him around town to pick up Barry Hall and Tom Raworth, Goliard Press copublishers who had lately issued a handsome little Olson chapbook of poems titled *West* (it was Hall, working with the London commercial house Jonathan Cape, who would also bring out Olson's posthumous selected poems, *Archaeologist of Morning*). By the time the growing party of welcome reached Raworth's flat in suburban Barnet it was two in the morning, but the guest of honor still showed no sign of flagging. The discovery that Raworth's wife, Val, was Welsh prompted an Olson monologue on the previously unremarked correspondences between the Welsh and the Mandan Indians that went on until the break of dawn. The whole group was then taxied down the hill into the city for a "massive" breakfast charged to Kerrigan's bill at the Hilton. After a few more hectic days of entertaining with Kerrigan in a rented flat on Half Moon Street, Olson entrained by himself to Colchester to be hosted by the Dorns. Sleep-lack and overuse of liquor and stimulants were by now beginning to catch up with the speeding traveler; assailed by a violent migraine in the Colchester railway station, he was forced to lie down for some minutes on the platform, and then, toiling up the long, gentle incline to his friends' home with an armload of gift cheeses, an emphysema attack struck. He had trouble regaining his breath and "was in bad shape, wandering and at a loss" by the time he made it to the Dorns' front door. Still he refused to stop forcing the moment, continuing to abuse his health throughout the next few days. "All the drinking and the pills were torture for his system, and he was in sweats a lot," recalls Dorn, "yet he could still whale a Camel in about two drags."

After another month of high living back in London—first at the Connaught Hotel on Carlos Place, then at a Mount Street flat of Kerrigan's—Olson moved on alone to Berlin, where, ignoring menacing signals of increasing exhaustion, he continued to behave as if intent only on fresh worlds to conquer. Appearing as part of the Literarisches Colloquium, he did a reading at the Akademie der Kunstes that was well attended but stiff, as his overly polite audience, seemingly "too attentive" to respond, could not be made to "come off their arse" despite all his pushing. Afterwards, at loose ends in the unfamiliar city and still full of compulsive nervous momentum, he roamed around trying to look up his few local contacts. During a visit to the widow of the German poet Rainer Gerhardt, he experienced a sudden systemic "turn," accompanied by strong chest pains, and immediately concluded he was having a heart attack. A physician who was called to the scene had him admitted to a hospital, where a cardiogram revealed a palpably "weakened heart." He was prescribed medication—a new kind of pill to take—and told, "You must feed your heart, Mr. Olson." Having stumbled deeper than ever into death's shadow terrain, the voyager was left badly shaken. For some days after the cardiac episode he lay abed in the Hotel Steinplatz, meditating upon his life and writing letters to women he knew in a new effort to recruit someone to care for him in his "protectionless" remaining days. The list of candidates, however, was by now sadly short. Joyce Benson was sounded out about a rendezvous on the isle of Crete. In a more thoroughgoing proposal, he offered Frances a permanent share in "my bed and life," making it clear that despite— or because of—present circumstances, he was still hungry for more of the latter: "My heart lies at your feet, poised here on the tilt (of the East) only to gather strength (I hope) to go into those places my mind has fed on, as has yours. And which now lie open before me—casements, wasn't it, Keats called magic casements opening on seas forlorn. . . ."

Watching thickening snowflakes fall and merge into the first light of the new solar year outside his window, he spent a solitary Christmas day composing one of his most emotional and powerful later *Maximus* poems. A dramatic enactment of the ancient theme of poetry as ritual self-sacrifice, "Hotel Steinplatz, Berlin, December 25 (1966)" tacitly reflected the extremity of the poet's personal situation by raising self-allegory to the level of myth, the pain in his side evoking a mimetic identification with his fellow martyr-shaman Odin, the hero of the Norse *Eddas* who had surrendered his person for poetry by hanging nine days on the World Tree. As if his own life hung in the balance along with that of the mythological hero—his own being reduced to a devouring mouth sucking at the "hungry tits" of "the female in the boughs"— the poet continued to want *more*. Five days after writing the Hotel Steinplatz poem, continuing to be absorbed with themes of hunger and appetite as motive forces in creation, a still-convalescent Olson observed in a letter to Robert Duncan that "Truth is the mouth." (Duncan himself, one of the most astute critics of Olson's poetry, has commented that in the late stages of the *Maximus,* and beginning with this poem in specific, the poet's "thought went toward life and death, and while the angel of the poem now appears, it is an angel if not of death then of passage, and Olson himself becomes suddenly a baby, hungry for the sources of poetry—as in that famous canvas of Rubens where the infant figures are not just nursing, but tearing at the tits and wildly sucking the substance out of the mother, so that the whole thing turns into a rape of another kind.")

In January 1967, Olson was back in London with Christine Kerrigan, who had by now taken up residence in the former Chinese embassy, one of a row of elegant neoclassical Nash town houses on Hanover Square. Friends quickly noted a change in him. "He was way slowed down, more reflective," recalls Ed Dorn. "I think he saw the future in some way, that all his habits of intake, his weird hours, just couldn't be maintained." A subdued Olson was indeed reviewing his life in light of the close call in Berlin, which he was already seeing in terms of his life allegory, interpreting it as yet another aftershock of the rupture caused by Betty's death. "Life's long path has uneven Sioux hills after 50," he wrote to Robert Duncan. "Time also has its bumps, horribly, & unhappily, and I have never recovered from the last one, alas. . . ." He received the company of London poets from the semirecumbent, shawl-swaddled throne of a reclining lounge chair in Kerrigan's drawing room, obviously unwell yet just as obsessively verbal as ever. Inundated by his "nonstop" talking, well-wishing friends were hard put to keep up, or in some cases even to keep awake. Anselm Hollo, a Finnish poet temporarily expatriated to England and new to the Olson Experience—"swirling 'Northern mists' & mushrooms, Algonquin & Ullikummi"—found it "way over my head." Tom Raworth, bringing his daughter to play with Kerrigan's child in the afternoons, got the benefit of the invalid poet's seemingly interminable daily wake-up thoughts, but despite his best efforts, was "bored" much of the time. Olson's language motors were running on habit. In the still of the night he made long-distance telephone calls to American friends, once keeping poet Robin Blaser on the line in California for half an hour to listen to a Debussy record in its entirety, with running commentary. His relations with Kerrigan were meanwhile rapidly deteriorating. "I'm here with a human vampire from Transylvania," he complained in a letter to his daughter. "I can't deal with her." Harvey Brown, arriving from the States for a visit, got the impression after only one night amid the Olson / Kerrigan ménage that "it was over."

Olson escaped into "hiding" in a Mayfair hotel for some weeks, then, without informing any of his friends, took off for the West of England. On May 8 he reached Dorchester and booked into the Antelope Hotel. The next month or so he spent lying low in Dorset, poking halfheartedly through local port records and rummaging idly in antiquarian bookshops. This was the long-awaited research expedition he had ostensibly come abroad to accomplish; after all the years of anticipation, however, the jumping-off place of the Gloucester fishing settlement seemed only a dull English provincial town, and he passed far fewer hours in actual research than in sitting around the hotel bar drinking, playing the slot machine and wondering what to do with himself. He wrote, then wired Suzanne Mowatt, extolling the beauties of the Dorset countryside and asking her to fly over and join him as he pursued a historical enterprise he had "always wanted to be in England for"—yet offering, in the same letter, to "torpedo the whole matter & come there" if she preferred and would have him. He was "at crossroad," he told her honestly. When the weeks went by and nothing could be arranged with her, the time grew heavier on his hands. He responded to an ad taken out by Harvey Brown in the London *Times* for information as to his whereabouts, and was shortly retrieved from the country by his concerned friend and benefactor.

Back in the city he checked into a room at the Adelphi Hotel and wired Joyce Benson to set up a rendezvous with her in Gloucester. But actually getting himself aboard the homebound plane took him longer than expected, and they missed connections on the first attempt. By dogged phone sleuthing from the Fort, he traced her to Maine and talked her into returning to Gloucester. They met at last, drank Black Horse Ale and chatted at Vincent Ferrini's frame shop, then retired to the Fort to begin what Benson calls "the event of my life, a terribly romantic courting in the old-fashioned sense of the word." A few days later, she and Jean Radoslovich escorted him to Logan Field for a flight back to England to appear at the International Poetry Festival.

He read on July 12 at the Albert Hall on a program that included W. H. Auden, Stephen Spender, Allen Ginsberg, Patrick Kavanagh and Giuseppe Ungaretti. Characteristically viewing the proceedings as "a kind of contest to determine the world's best poet," Olson felt one-upped by Ungaretti, who "stole the show" and afterward drew an admiring audience off to one corner of the post-reading party; and by Allen Ginsberg, who attracted even greater attention at the party by ostentatiously tutoring rock star Mick Jagger in Hindu mantras.

Joyce Benson was there to meet him at the airport on his return. She accompanied him back to Gloucester, where he was soon finding the reality of steady proximity with this latest "angel of aid" not quite what he'd hoped. While Joyce was farmed out to stay with Jean, he threw himself into a last-ditch epistolary campaign to stop the demolition of a historic local house as ordered in a city council–approved street-widening program. Like several other quixotic Olson lobbying efforts to preserve Gloucester's historical landmarks in the later 1960s, this one was a failure, serving only to further depress the poet—a self-described "WHITE guerrilla" when it came to local politics—about human nature in general and the present Gloucester citizenry in particular. ("I believe in God and creation," he would tell a local journalist after the house was bulldozed, "and it doesn't matter to me what the human species as a bunch of—what we call midges, coming off the marsh—do to it, do even to themselves.") When Benson flew back to her Ohio home, he was quickly at loose ends and impulsively followed her, flying from Boston to La Guardia, phoning her from there, then flying on to Dayton to be picked up and driven on to her place in Oxford. For some weeks he stayed on with her, taking turns reading *A Vision* and experimenting in medium transmission à la Yeats. A wild anomaly on his nocturnal strolls through the quiet streets, the wandering giant in the mohair blanket soon became the talk of Benson's middle-class residential neighborhood. He felt no less strange than he looked. "I don't understand what I'm suffering for anymore," he observed in his journal on August 25. "Equally I am literally *stuck* on *where,* other than G[loucester], to settle; and how to accomplish a successful working and living life. . . . Night time? Any person possible at all?" That Joyce Benson was not destined to be the "person" was made more apparent than ever by his sojourn in Oxford. In the first week of September he restlessly hit the road in a rented white Mercury sedan. Following his instinctive compass rather than any real plan, he took off to the northeast and revisited Betty's death site in Wyoming County before doubling back to Gloucester.

Soon he was off again on a holiday trip to Maine with Ferrini and the twelve-year-old Charles Peter. They stayed at Cranberry Island, the property of Connie's husband, George Bunker, where Kate, now a fifteen-year-old Massachusetts boarding school student, was spending the last days of her summer vacation with her mother. Olson's first extended meeting with his first wife since dropping her at her sister's place on that cold day in early 1956 was not easy for him. "There was a lot of tension," his daughter recalls. In a loud quarrel at water's edge that was overheard by the children, he repudiated Connie's charge that he'd never recognized her emotionally, finally breaking off the argument by bursting out emphatically, "That's *dead*, Con!"

Another unsettling reunion awaited Olson in October at Cortland, New York, where he addressed a state university poetry convocation and encountered his estranged comrade John Wieners, whom he hadn't been able to face since the previous summer's indelicate double cross. Obviously intent on peacemaking, he gave over his keynote talk before the big banquet crowd to a lavish if rambling tribute to Wieners and Ed Sanders. By the end of the convocation he had managed, by old-fashioned charm and wooing, to patch things up sufficiently with his wounded fellow poet to appease his own conscience on at least that one touchy point.

With the onset of the 1967–1968 winter, a dark, monkish solitude once more closed in at the Fort. All his angels gone, Olson had no one to fall back on for spiritual sustenance but himself. Every afternoon upon waking he stared over the flat western harbor waters into the rosy blaze of the setting sun, meditating on the solar "message" and inviting it to fill up his being. But the long nights that followed were lonelier than ever. "I shall be 57, so many years / on the lookout and no further than here," he conceded sadly in his annual verse on the turning of the sun. Unfulfilled cravings were becoming no longer an occasional problem but second nature. "Gather a body to me," he began "The Telesphere," a *Maximus* poem that was a lament for his sexual deprivation. Without the enjoyments of the flesh his own body felt as tense as a "hoop / empty and like steel." It required an "impossible effort," he suggested to Frances in a miserable midwinter letter, "for a man like myself, finally *compulsive,* to live alone." The Fort had come to feel less like a sanctuary than a prison of the imagination, with himself as sole inmate—a sort of latter-day "Count of Monte Cristo."

26 🙠

The Subterranean Lake
(1967–1970)

I n January 1968, some verses sent by Robert Duncan prompted an intense
response out of Olson, who filled up the margins of his friend's typescript
with very revealing personal reflections on the theme of Time's passage. Duncan had pictured the poet as priest-timekeeper, a servant in the temple of the
oracle charged with announcing the hours to the goddess. The faculty for
such patient observance of life's "HOURS," Olson noted, was reserved for the
great "Protestants"—like Duncan, Frances and William Blake. "Frances—&
Duncan"—he now recognized them as a tandem in his allegory—those two
friends had always been "so alike in their striking the Hour," their willingness
to tune the spirit life to everyday temporal measures without forever pushing
and rushing, their sensible attention "Always on the BIG THING while I, in
my refusal, will run out the MINUTES only UNLESS, now, I do catch up. . . ."
(He added in a parenthetical aside to himself, "Do I want to?") In truth, for
himself no such wise waiting-out of the hours had ever been possible. Life,
in his experience of it as far back as he could remember, had always been a
self-consuming ritual, a mimetic playing out of "the minutes of Christ! of his
realisms!!! Love's realisms." In his own "Catholic" observance of time, there
had been only the anxious, agonized consciousness of each passing moment
as a further loss to possible creation.

The obsessive project of self-union, encompassing all other interests and excluding all distractions, now came near completion as time grew short for Maximus. In the face of "Time's / unbearable complexity—as though our souls / could never be the equal of our bodies its / devouring," the poet's bid to at once integrate and internalize all things in the myth of self became ever more urgent. In notebook mappings as well as in the cryptic figuration of his epic he employed a pair of oceanographic ridges off the Maine coast as allegorical emblems of his purpose: "To internalize my / Schoodic to make Inner / or Outer / Schoodic one piece from conception . . . all one." And in March 1968, in a poem he represented to a Beloit College audience as a sort of personal talisman of the poetics of self-measure—"the poem of the narcissism of the narcissism . . . written from the inside"—he plotted that drive to an immanent condition more exactly than ever before.

> *Wholly absorbed*
> *into my own conduits to*
> *an inner nature or subterranean lake*
> *the depths or bounds of which I more and more*
> *explore and know more*
> *of, in that sense that other than that all else*
> *closes out and I tend further to fall into*
> *the Beloved Lake and I am blinder from*
>
> *spending time as insistently in and on*
> *this personal preserve from which*
> *what I do do emerges more well-known than*
> *other ways and other outside places which*
> *don't give as much and distract me from*
>
> *keeping my attentions as clear*

In the last week of March he emerged from his Beloved Lake to fly to Wisconsin to deliver the annual Beloit Lectures in Modern Poetry. "He was dressed in what I took to be old clothes, and looked as though he had literally been sleeping on a haystack," recalls English department poet and lecture series organizer Chad Walsh. "His fly was half open. He wore his long hair in a pony tail fastened with a rubber band. The man was grotesque to look at, and at the same time majestic, even with a compelling beauty." In Olson's three lectures, his outlandish appearance (comically counterpointing his somewhat portentous Goethean billing, "Poetry and Truth or the Dogmatic Nature of Experience"), his improvised delivery (he gave the impression of "wrestling with some demon of language, trying to put into words the ideas that already existed in the preverbal state") and "non-Euclidean" style of thought ("the faculty, mostly registered Ph.D.'s and trained in common logic, could not make heads or tails of it") invited speculations that "the inhabitant of another planet [was] paying a visit." For those few who could follow him, however, the poet had much to say, laying down an intriguing trail of clues that led directly to the philosophical center of his mysterious later work. Introduced to the mysticism and dogma of thirteenth-century Old Norse poets and Muslim angelic philosophers, the bewildered Midwestern college crowd was in effect being shown Olson himself in his own latest creative incarnation, as absorbed in what he was doing as the Sufi mystic Ibn' Arabi "writing the Meccan Revelations for twenty years around the black meteoric stone at Mecca," and as "strictly theological . . . traditional and metaphysical" in his attitude toward poetry as the authors of the *Eddas*. And the audience was treated to a rare autobiographical exposition of the private story behind the poet's doctrines of spiritual analogy: he recounted his "helio inside myself" vision on that 1952 New York–Washington bus, and harked back to his Gloucester adolescent days and "the first cigarettes I ever smoked"—a pack of Player's, featuring the image of "His Majesty's Ship *Heliotrope*"—to complete the associative circuit.

Leaving behind a Beloit dormitory legend for his terrorization of the cleaning ladies (one of whom he had scared half to death for waking him), Olson flew out at the end of the week in his usual cloud of awe and enigma. The labors of the visit had left him worn, but instead of heading home he continued west to California to join fellow poet Joanne Kyger and several other artists in a KQED San Francisco experimental television project. His role in the proceedings, as he conceived it, involved the use of his voice as instrument, after the manner of the ancient poet-musicians or rhapsodes. But chronic emphysema, exacerbated by excessive talking and smoking in his recent performing travels, had robbed his voice of much of its onetime projective power, leaving him with an instrument more breathy than booming; his earnest attempt to "keep a Zeus beat" in his videotaped improvisational monologue tailed off into desultory rambling drowned out by electronic feedback. (Soured further on the creative prospects of technology, he privately concluded after this experience that the futuristic video medium was a good thing "to stay away from.") Friends like Kyger noted that his emphysema also made it difficult for him to scale the city's hills without great effort, spells of huffing and puffing interspersed with small rests. His range of mobility pretty much limited to the insides of cars and the sofa in Don Allen's Jones Street apartment, he had a hard time enjoying himself, and eventually, on a side trip to the fogbound West Marin poets' village of Bolinas, caught a cold which he couldn't shake. After two weeks in the Bay Area, he escaped to the warmer and drier climes of Arizona for what was planned as a recuperative stay at Drummond and wife Diana Hadley's ranch in the mountains near Tucson. The literal high point of the desert sojourn came when his host transported him, perched Buddhalike atop the storage rack of a four-wheel-drive International Travelall, down out of the hills into a sweeping valley that stretched south to Mexico and west to Baboquivari Peak, held by the Papago Indians to be the sacred center of the world. For Olson it was exhilarating to be even momentarily back on top of creation.

In Arizona as on his previous stops, however, he continued to burn up verbal energy, bending Hadley's ear with compulsive rehashings of events out of his "secret" past, descriptions of the suitcase-loan refusal preluding his father's death and of the final breakup with Connie, and even some tantalizing, mysterious comments on his "old Muse" (he'd actually spoken of Frances by name to none of his friends save Robert Duncan, to whom he'd had her send copies of her books). By the end of his six weeks on the road he had barely the strength to climb aboard a plane. Ill and exhausted, in sober hindsight he confided to Frances in a letter from the Fort that his days of poetry barnstorming were behind him: it had been a "wretched trip." After celebrating Charles Peter's fourteenth birthday, he collapsed into the hospital with various complaints, including, in a particularly disturbing development, the loss of his voice. He spent two weeks resting and going through tests. When one day his voice came back to him out of the blue, he got up and walked out on a bill of nearly $1,000. The exhaustion resulting from the spring tour lingered on, however. Unable to resume bachelor housekeeping, he went to the Radosloviches', where he was given an attic room and the special attention he craved. "He loved it," Jean remembers. "He could look out over the ocean and the bay. He'd sit in bed all day. I'd bring him juice and coffee, and just give my time away to him." Inevitably, after some weeks Jean's husband, Bill, grew impatient with the arrangement, and the semi-invalid Olson had no choice but to return to his Fort Square digs.

Having rented a second apartment next door to his own as a catch-all for his overflowing books and papers, he assigned it as servant quarters for the summer to a temporary housekeeper, a young woman student from Buffalo who had been enlisted by George Butterick, one of the most loyal and assiduous of the poet's former graduate-student "company." A steady trickle of summertime visitors was led off in June by Butterick, who was taking notes from the horse's mouth for a Buffalo Ph.D. thesis on the *Maximus*. Another researcher, Ann Charters, at work on a study of the Olson / Melville affinity, came through next. Alasdair Clayre of the BBC showed up in July to make a tape for the Third Programme. But the climax of the season for the lonely bachelor was definitely the August visit of Inga Loven, an attractive Swedish journalist. Falling over himself to be a helpful interview subject, Olson spiced

his remarks with Scandinavian references, from Snorri Sturluson to Vilhjálmur Stefánsson. With the tape recorder turned off, he stepped up his wooing
efforts, in his eagerness to impress even at one point breaking the glass frame
enclosing his prize D. H. Lawrence painting so as to afford his comely guest
a better look at it. He invited the interviewer to stay on at the Fort with him,
and after she flew back to Stockholm, pressed her by telegram and mail to
meet up with him somewhere in Europe. But all his overtures—including a
last-ditch visionary love letter, written, as he later claimed, "in Icelandic"—
were doomed to failure. "Hairy honkie- / hard and horny too," he was forced
to settle for the emotional consolations of long, late-hours talks with his friend
and "legendary phone man" Harvey Brown, lamenting his lovelorn state deep
into the sultry August nights. (One of their "ten league calls" was documented in a *Maximus* poem, "I'm going to hate to leave this Earthly Paradise.")

The Browns drove down from their current home in West Newbury to
keep him company, sometimes accompanied by Ed Dorn and Dorn's new
English wife, Jennifer. Dorn's ex-wife, Helene, was now living in Gloucester
and had joined Jean and a few other thoughtful friends in a sort of volunteer
Olson soup brigade, occasionally stopping by the Fort—now that the departure of Olson's summer domestic helper had left him with no one else to
cook for him—to drop off prepared meals. But truly keeping body and soul
together, Olson still believed, required the ministrations of the heart, something he increasingly despaired of ever again receiving. "Despite the size of
this human race," he complained in a September note to Connie, it now
seemed to him the hardest thing on earth to find a truly sympathetic partner,
someone who could "give one anything like the turns and tones of oneself's
sense of the experience of life."

After a surprise late-October visit from his fellow solitary writer Jack Kerouac—chauffeured in a black limousine by Greek brothers-in-law from nearby
Lowell, the erstwhile King of the Beats hailed Olson with diplomatic camaraderie, but passed out drunk before the poet could even crank up a decent
monologue—the encroachment of cold weather and early darkness narrowed
life at the Fort down to an anchoritic condition of solitude all too familiar to
Olson from the past few winters. At his annual winter-solstice dinner with
Jean Radoslovich, the gnawing question of mortality was more on his mind
than ever. Jean tried not to let on that this time her premonition confirmed
his apprehensions. "I knew then, a year ahead of time, that he was going to
die. I could see it. I believe that he knew it too." Olson's inner consciousness
that the alchemy of creation was escaping him, and life itself along with it,
was indeed now a source of much dread for him. Most of all he feared the
loss of his essential language powers, the precious "Gold-making machine"

in which his poetry was fused: "in loneliness & in such pain I *can't* / lift the bottom of the alemb the gold- / making juices lie in sounding the / striking of the surf & waves. . . ."

His isolation was relieved only briefly in January 1968 by the arrival from England of Apple Records representative Barry Miles to tape poetry for a long-playing album. Olson's reading of recent *Maximus* sequences (eventually released posthumously by Folkways) was unusually reflective and subdued. Immured in the stale, dusty stillness of the Fort—where for the five days of Miles' stay there were no other visitors and the phone rang only once, with a call from Kate—he seemed curiously out of touch with reality. At one point, illustrating a lecture to his guest, he tried to point out local fishing channels on a Gloucester Harbor map affixed to his bedroom wall, and when he noticed it had long since been yellowed by time and sunlight practically into invisibility, became disoriented, as if not only the map but the world of everything that was most familiar to him was fading from view. "How long was it since he had actually looked with interest around his own bedroom?" his British visitor wondered. "He made a joke but I could see deep down then that he knew he was dying."

Liquor deliveries to the Fort remained frequent, and Olson's medicine cabinet was well stocked with prescription stimulants and sedatives. But food was becoming a serious problem. It was more than the poet could do to make himself remember to buy groceries. His notebook attempts to keep track of his eating habits were documents of entropic futility: "not having eaten properly now since when? . . . last outside meal Tuesday? . . . Wednesday? *nothing at all!*" Spiritual sustenance meanwhile came intermittently and unpredictably, in occasional flashes of momentary clarity illuminating the inner blackness and confusion; his poetry, limited now in its means to a notational, fragmentary immediacy that made it hard to separate from his ongoing journal meditations, reflected the practical extremities of his condition through the glass of self-allegory with a stark, tremulous "shamanistic shimmer."

> *Full moon [staring out window, 5:30 AM March 4th*
> *1969] staring in window one-eyed white round clear*
> *giant eyed snow-mound staring down on snow-*
> *covered full blizzarded earth after the*
> *continuous 4 blizzards of February March 5 feet*
> *of snow all over Cape Ann [starving*
> *and my throat tight from madness of isolation &*
> *inactivity, rested hungry empty mind all*
> *gone away into the snow into the loneliness,*
> *bitterness, resolvedlessness, even this big moon*

doesn't warm me up, heat me up, is snow
itself [after this snow not a jot of food left
in this silly benighted house all night long sleep
all day, when activity, & food, And persons]
5:30 AM hungry for every thing

Synchronizing his eccentric timing with anyone else's schedule was now almost beyond his attempting. He enforced his privacy by regularly posting notices on the door saying he was sick and warning off potential visitors. In April, *Paris Review* interviewer Gerard Malanga had to come back several days running before finally rousing him up to participate in a wandering, gnomic dialogue composed largely of punning, paradox-making and leg-pulling on the poet's part. Once Malanga was gone Olson lapsed back into touchy, irritable seclusion. "Fussy, ill-tempered tired—exasperated" much of the time, he was no less difficult with old friend Robert Creeley, who that summer was renting the Dennison house in Riverdale. As they'd seen each other only occasionally over recent years, Creeley was looking forward to the opportunity to make up for lost time, and soon after settling in came by the Fort for a visit. He was unprepared for the nonreception he got. "Charles seemed cool, and I remember being surprised. He said, 'Jeez, I'm all packed in. Lousy time for company. But no rush, see you later!'" But later there was little evident change in Olson's standoffish attitude. As if nursing some paranoid grudge in his solitary competitive imagination, he continued to play mysteriously hard to get all summer, keeping his friend at arm's length. Creeley grew increasingly puzzled, especially in light of a secondhand report that his new book *Pieces* was about to be honored with a review by Olson. After some time went by and Olson himself never uttered a word on the subject, Creeley, overcome by curiosity, confronted him about it as casually as possible—and learned that his erstwhile running mate remained as sly as ever in his inexplicable personal distances. "He said, in an offhand way, 'Yeah, Robert, I wrote a review.' And he smiled and pointed to his head. 'Yeah, it's all in here.' And there it stayed."

His daughter's boarding school graduation early that summer was a bittersweet occasion for Olson, who had reason both to glory in the sight of the poised, grown-up-looking young woman he had somehow managed to father—in long white Victorian gown with fresh flowers in her dark hair, Kate cut almost as striking a figure as he himself did in his sprawling Olympian girth and unlikely yellow-gray ponytail—and to mourn her childhood, which seemed to have gone by while he was looking away. Immersed in his compulsive writing pushes, constantly "occupied (or driven?)," he had missed the experience of seeing the girl grow up. But then in truth—he now asked himself—hadn't his habit of "stealing time" for work amounted all along to robbing himself of the important emotional occasions of his life?

His guilts concerning Kate merely compounded his sense of the larger "enormous / tremendous error" of his accumulated failures with the significant women in his life, all of them variously "wronged" by him over "the hours the days the years the decades." In "She-Bear Re-Visited or Re-taken 19 years later," a confused, turbulent confessional poem invoking the matriarchal goddess whose protection he'd first sought in the 1950 poems of soul riot (it was alternately titled, in his notebook, "For Woman, Who Is Loved / & Hated if she say so & She Be"), he now begged the forgiveness of those women—and God's "Impossible Forgiveness" along with it: "Oh my mother wife daughter . . . may I ask you in the name of Heaven to / forgive me having held so much / away from all of you . . . My God exert / in my behalf / from now throughout Eternity my / Shame / Exhibit me as / example." Taking up several July nights and spilling over many notebook pages in a disorderly torrent, the poem was a regretful catalog of what seemed in retrospect his complicated lifelong transgression against the natural orders of the cosmos. "In the double lamp light of my own isolated bedroom / in the heat of a summer night in 1969 / God save my soul because it needs it for the harm it's done / for almost 20 / years by being sightless when it had / its eyes & didn't have its beautiful fishlike / scales of sight itself to / lay on a bed & be / as bound to her as man when / [he] is lying in the arms of the Serpent Goddess Hell herself . . . Poor woman in an age when / daughters have not had their / fathers' loves / Or discipline because / the fathers themselves are / not the stars they should be hung along the night / the Anchors of the sky / now / Shiva has again ascended & shone forth . . ." The same theme was amplified in the journal notes into which such wild verses now often merged, further testimony to the poet's absorption in the "Oedipean" world tale he now made out at the heart of his self-allegory: the story of "the eternally unique who has died before us as she in another guise gave birth to us and in her womanness who has been wife mistress goddess & sister as well to man-ness selves . . . who can exact the sense or pay such a Piper?"

Sick and miserable, he drank heavily for solace in the difficult Fort nights. "Frightful loneliness yet some increase of purification," he noted one night this summer, "I drink to live to go further." He fantasized trips to Lake Van, Crete, Egypt, but in fact rarely left the house. At the end of the summer, hoping a change of scene might restore him, he flew to Maine with Kate. They spent two weeks at Robert and Helen Hellman's place in Isleford. Given the low-ceilinged attic as his bedroom because it was the warmest room in the house, still Olson could not seem to keep himself warm. Instead of the anticipated return to health, the holiday left him feeling even sicker than before. On the return flight from Bangor to Boston, he felt a sudden, sharp pain flashing through the left side of his face—the region, he would later learn in a moment of chilling recognition, of the *maximus* nerve. The sensation lasted only a moment, but it alarmed him enough to prompt detailed description to Ed and Jenny Dorn when they visited the Fort the following week. In hindsight, he would term it ominously "the invasion."

As if trying to deny to himself the instinctive knowledge that something was seriously wrong, totally bewildered by the future and at immediate loose ends, in September Olson turned the Fort over to the care of a young woman who had been his latest live-in helper and went off on a spur-of-the-moment expedition to Mansfield, Connecticut, to pay a call on Charles Boer, one of his former Buffalo *angeloi* now teaching at the University of Connecticut. He made it by train as far as Boston, whence he was fetched and ferried on by his obliging ex-student to the latter's hilltop hideaway home. Commanding a grand view out over miles of forest, the place came supplied with an interesting store of miscellaneous books and fresh groceries, and—most important to Olson now—an attentive audience for the all-night talks that kept him from having to dwell too much with his dark thoughts alone. Oblivious to the gradual eroding of the patience of his host (who was putting in fatiguing double duty between Olson Watch and classroom), within a week he had made clear his intention of staying on for the duration. Leisurely investigations of the surrounding woods and stone-walled back roads yielded the last substantial *Maximus* poem Olson would write, "I live underneath / the light of day," a time-obsessed meditation on earthly and spiritual transit that confirmed what those few who had known him well had long ago discovered: "My life is buried / with all sorts of passages." The infinitely honeycombed underground complexities of final passage much on his mind, the poet now kept an eye out for eternity around every allegorical turning. During one backwoods ramble he buttonholed his host and strenuously insisted the latter was actually an angel sent to guide him to paradise. Boer demurred, but with the stakes now so high, Olson refused to take no for an answer. The reluctant angel, a sleepless wreck by the end of their second week together, managed to set up a job for him in the English department, but far from moving him to seek out permanent lodgings of his own, this latest service seemed merely to confirm Olson's current state of dependence; he refused to budge. It took an unpleasant showdown, following some days of tense mind-war, to force him out again onto the roads of life.

After enduring a night of semicomical humiliation and trial in a bleak rented room—where the flimsy bed collapsed beneath his bulk—he rented a Plymouth Fury at the Avis outlet in Willimantic and drove to Gloucester;

then, paratactic as only Maximus could be, he turned around and drove right back. This time he installed himself at an expensive weekenders' inn near the U. Conn. campus, the Altnaveigh, where he could command the twenty-four-hour room service that was now a basic necessity for him. So compliant with his wishes did the inn's staff in fact prove—allowing him to call for meals from the top of the dining-room stairs while clad only in a casually draped sheet, for example—that he briefly toyed with the idea of buying the place, a not altogether ridiculous consideration in view of the fact that he now had a university salary matching that of prestigious writer-in-residence Stephen Spender (he'd insisted he wouldn't work for less) to add to the stack of Harvey Brown's $5,000 subsidy checks sitting uncashed in a safe-deposit box back in Gloucester.

"Like a mammoth aroused from the tar pits of La Brea," a shaggy archaic revenant battling the phantom chills of the New England Indian summer with heavy sweaters and clutching wicker baskets bulging with the mysterious fetish articles of his trade, profane, difficult and "electric" as ever, Olson returned to the classroom one last time. Given liberty under the terms of his visiting professorship of English to teach whatever aspect of the discipline he pleased, he characteristically chose to subvert its basic premises altogether, proposing for recent American poetry—particularly that following the indigenous line of Williams as opposed to the classical line of Pound—a radically new set of sources and lineages. The current impulse to use language "to register the bite of immediate condition," he suggested, had its origin not in the exhausted English tradition but in North Atlantic currents flowing down to American from Icelandic and Norse through the skalds, runes and *Eddas*. And the present revival of the autonomic poet's spiritual way of life and vision, likewise inexplicable if viewed as a development out of the mother tongue's literary mainstream, was actually a ripple stirred by breezes blowing in from the mystic thirteenth-century Arabian deserts, a recurrence in postmodern context of Ismaili and Mazdaist philosophies of cyclic time and paradisal angelology.

But the "retardation of eternity," a spiritual discipline devoted to "the practicing of the thing that gives you control over time & space" which he preached in the Connecticut lectures, soon proved to be of little use to the poet in his personal struggle against the encroachment of mortality. By November, his health had deteriorated to an extent that could no longer be ignored. Troubled by a persistent pain in the left side of his face, at a Thanksgiving party he described the symptoms of the distressing "earache" to a professional physiotherapist, who recommended a prompt visit to a physician. A week later he checked into Manchester Memorial Hospital for tests. The pain was growing worse, yet he seemed able to at least partially deny it by dwelling on the analogical dimensions of the moment. He told friends who came to see him that the body scan he'd been given was proof of his proprioceptive theories: he'd had a look at "the inside of me / printed direct," incontrovertible evidence at last that "my soul really exists." But when no one was around, the poetic significance of what was occurring faded quickly into a sea of pain so severe that by the end of his eighteen-day stay in Manchester Memorial he was crying out at night for more medication—and receiving morphine in eight times the normal dosage. Not until his third week in the hospital did a liver biopsy reveal the diagnostic verdict: "Hepatoma—Grade 1," a primary cancer of the liver.

"It's curtains," Olson flatly informed shocked visitor Charles Boer. Getting immediately down to business, he charged Boer with a short list of essential duties: the ex-student was to serve as his literary executor, guide the third *Maximus* volume into print, and return the rented Plymouth Fury to Avis (Boer was relieved of the last task by the rental company, which had already repossessed the car from the hospital parking lot). Then, on a night of particularly heavy pain—December 15—he composed a will that was, as his daughter would later suggest, "more like a poem": calling for her to become a "foster mother" to his son, and to eventually receive equal share in his estate ("it is my anxious belief that my son and daughter become me, as my work"), this uniquely Olsonian document, yet another product of the chaos of his life, would go unwitnessed and ultimately be declared invalid by the state of Connecticut in the course of a protracted estate settlement. The next day, improvising stationery out of a roll of hospital hand towels, he wrote out "The Secret of the Black Chrysanthemum," a compulsive, cryptomystical "solution" to all his work which he sealed in an envelope marked " 'Secret' notes," requesting that it be kept by him as long as he remained alive.

On December 18, Harvey Brown transported the sick man in a rented ambulance from Manchester to New York Hospital, where, it was hoped, he might be able to receive a liver transplant. The four-hour ride to the city through heavy snow and traffic was a tremendous ordeal. Fortified by Demerol at the outset, Olson fought gamely to maintain his spirits, at one point breaking out in a dramatic emotional recitation of the "Poor naked wretches" speech from *King Lear*. But when his supply of painkillers ran out, there ensued several hours of an agony equal to Lear's or worse; he was reduced to pathetically asking over and over, "Are we there yet?" as if the universe indeed held no compassion.

In New York, harrowing abdominal punctures proved the whole trip had been pointless: the cancer had metastasized and was definitely inoperable. While awaiting the test results, Olson suffered a fresh wave of losses and indignities. His dental plate disappeared, the hospital staff dropped hints about his sanity, and, once his terminal condition had been established, it was even suggested that he might be evicted from his bed so that it could be released to some patient who had a chance to be saved. But within the alien domain of the medical technicians, Olson would nonetheless for as long as he was able continue to assert his own sovereignty. Taking over a sunny solarium on the hospital's twelfth floor, he held court for friends and followers in diminished but determined fashion, conversing in intermittent snatches and staring out over a sea of skyscrapers that through the morphine haze could at times take on an illusory resemblance to the floor of heaven, or to his beloved North Atlantic expanses.

The social rituals were presided over by Harvey Brown, who put in extended shifts by the patient's door, screened visitors and established protocols for the paying of last respects. Brown also footed travel and hotel bills to bring in Olson's closest associates from as far away as California and England. First-class suites at the Plaza filled up with poets. Ed and Jenny Dorn, late arrivals from London, walked into a scene like a death ceremony out of some medieval allegorical pageant: corridors of both hotel and hospital were awash with Olson friends, disciples, scenemakers, bookdealers, literary groupies, "everybody lined up in order to get a piece of the manna." Creeley came in; and Jack Clarke; and Butterick and Boer to discuss editing the *Maximus*. (Cognizant he was leaving the editors an overwhelming *massa confusa* of papers—he'd begged his doctors for "ten more years" in which to sort out and somehow finish the work—Olson could give them no guideline beyond the directive to include as the last poem a compressed inventory of recent and coming losses composed around the time of his cancer's Thanksgiving advance: "my wife   my car   my color   and   myself.") Ed Sanders, a faithful observer of the rituals, showed up bearing a plaque of Egyptian hieroglyphs, while Vincent Ferrini brought from the Fort a wicker basket full of things Olson had specifically asked for—his wall map of the Atlantic seafloor, a photo of himself on his back steps, an Indian blanket, two oranges, a Russian spoon, some wrapping paper and a crystal ball. The poet was deliberately surrounding himself with personal sacred objects, setting up a force field of magical aura-action against eternity.

Robert Duncan, flying in just before Christmas, found Olson cadaverously thin, talking half coherently of poetry, fate and the multiple mysteries of the cosmos, and lamenting through his ever-present curtain of pain, above all else, a lack of priestly solace. Reality's outlines now evidently blurred for him by pain and drugs, the dying man gave the impression of having fallen back on an exclusively analogical view of things as a last refuge against the conclusion that could no longer be in doubt. He told Duncan meaningfully that his particular strain of cancer had been called a "female disease," and appeared obsessed with the possibility that an injection of female hormones might somehow release his female principle or Anima—"Lady Live-Her"— and allow him / her to live on. Finally, exhausted with the effort of their last meeting, Olson told his old friend in a pain-racked "oracular voice" of his desire to be ministered to by a spiritual doctor who would be able to tutor him in "holy things." "These are holy things," he insisted, "but no one here knows these are holy things." Duncan was struck by the extremity of Olson's physical state. Naked except for a sheet, he had wasted away to a sort of radiant skeleton—"a truly magnificent and very Nordic looking crea- ture . . . some kind of Wotan [or] Okeanos."

The eighteen-year-old Kate, matured by grief, remained constantly at her father's side, often staying on when other guests were gone, soothing him with quiet conversation: visitors sometimes found them lying side by side, a "royal pair," the loving, fiercely loyal Cordelia and the dwindled, suffering Lear. She was with him to the end, joined by her mother, who had been in Europe and learned of his condition too late to reach him until he was slip- ping into a coma. At one forty-five in the morning on January 10, 1970—an hour he had often used for poetry—Connie was weeping over him and gently calling his name, "Charlie me boy, oh Charlie," as he was taken by eternity.

Jean Radoslovich arranged a Roman Catholic service for Olson in Gloucester. On the day of the event, a light dusting of snow lay on the frozen ground of Beechwood Cemetery, covering the adjacent plot where Betty lay. Charles Peter looked on with Jean, Kate, Connie and a smattering of the dead man's poetry friends, including John Wieners, Ed Sanders, Harvey Brown, Vincent Ferrini and Allen Ginsberg. Ginsberg, accidentally triggering the coffin-release mechanism, sent Olson's mortal form, laid out in his Italian white linen suit, plunging through the portals of the underworld with a head- long precipitate rush akin to that of his poetry.

Notes

Abbreviations:

AP Charles Olson, *Additional Prose,* ed. George F. Butterick (Bolinas: Four Seasons Foundation, 1974).

CMI Charles Olson, *Call Me Ishmael* (San Francisco: City Lights, 1967).

CP *The Collected Poems of Charles Olson, Excluding "The Maximus Poems,"* ed. George F. Butterick (Berkeley: University of California Press, 1987).

CtU Olson Archive, University of Connecticut.

FH Charles Olson, *The Fiery Hunt and Other Plays,* ed. George F. Butterick (Bolinas: Four Seasons Foundation, 1977).

Guide George F. Butterick, *A Guide to "The Maximus Poems" of Charles Olson* (Berkeley: University of California Press, 1980).

HU Charles Olson, *Human Universe and Other Essays,* ed. Donald Allen (New York: Grove, 1967).

MAX Charles Olson, *The Maximus Poems,* ed. George F. Butterick (Berkeley: University of California Press, 1983).

MR "A Gathering for Charles Olson," *Massachusetts Review,* Vol. XII, No. 2 (Winter 1971).

MUTH I, II Charles Olson, *Muthologos: The Collected Lectures and Interviews,* Vols. I and II, ed. George F. Butterick (Bolinas: Four Seasons Foundation, 1978, 1979).

Nation	Charles Olson, *A Nation of Nothing but Poetry*, ed. George F. Butterick (Santa Rosa: Black Sparrow Press, 1989).
O&P	Charles Olson, *Charles Olson and Ezra Pound: An Encounter at St. Elizabeths*, ed. Catherine Seelye (New York: Grossman, 1975).
O / CC	*Charles Olson and Cid Corman: Complete Correspondence 1950–1964*, Vol. 1, ed. George Evans (Orono: National Poetry Foundation, University of Maine, 1987).
O / D 1, 2, 3	"The Letters of Edward Dahlberg and Charles Olson," ed. Paul Christensen, *Sulfur* 1, 2, and 3 (Pasadena: California Institute of Technology, 1981–1982).
OJ 1–10	*The Journal of the Charles Olson Archives*, Nos. 1–10, ed. George F. Butterick (Storrs: University of Connecticut Library, 1974–1978). .
O / RC 1–9	*Charles Olson & Robert Creeley: The Complete Correspondence*, Vols. 1–9 (Santa Barbara and Santa Rosa: Black Sparrow Press, 1980–1989).
PM	Merton M. Sealts, *Pursuing Melville, 1940–1980: Chapters and Essays* (Madison: University of Wisconsin Press, 1982).
PO	Charles Olson, *The Post Office: A Memoir of His Father*, ed. George F. Butterick (Bolinas: Grey Fox Press, 1975).
SVH	Charles Olson, *The Special View of History*, ed. Ann Charters (Berkeley: Oyez, 1970).
WUSL	Creeley Archive, Washington University in St. Louis.

Chapter 1: Trinity

p. 3   *"I was . . . point"*: "Great Washing Rock . . ." *MAX*, p. 579.

p. 3   *"love . . . us"*: Olson to Robert Creeley, November 12, 1967. WUSL.

p. 3   *"the state . . . heat"*: Olson to Frances Boldereff, April 1952. CtU.

p. 3   *"Well . . . year"*: Jean Radoslovich interview, February 10, 1987.

p. 3   *"Eternity . . . infinity"*: Olson to Robert Duncan, February 8, 1950. CtU.

p. 3   *"The End . . . Turn-About"*: "—the End of the World / is the Turn-About . . ." *CP*, p. 591.

p. 4   *"Across . . . Time"*: "Across Space and Time," *CP*, p. 508.

p. 4   *"master builders"*: "The Post Office," *PO*, p. 30.

p. 4   *"My father . . . steel"*: " 'I know men for whom everything matters': Charles Olson in conversation with Herbert A. Kenny," *OJ* 1, p. 30.

p. 4   *"unknown . . . Maine"*: "The Post Office," *PO*, p. 31.

p. 5   *"the farthest outpost"*: ibid.

p. 5   *"laziness . . . energy"*: Olson notebook, "May 6, 1934–1936." CtU.

p. 5   *"incredible showman"*: Kate Olson interview, February 21, 1987.

p. 5   *"He had . . . concentrated"*: "Mr. Meyer," *PO*, p. 19.

p. 6   *"My old . . . jaw-tackle"*: Olson to Robert Creeley, October 9, 1951, *O / RC* 8, p. 35.

p. 6   *"old fashioned . . . respect"*: "The Post Office," *PO*, p. 47.

p. 6   *"had . . . fault"*: Olson notebook, "#4, Cambridge & N.Y. Winter–Spring 1940." CtU.

p. 6   *"oh my . . . dad"*: first draft of "ABCs: For Arthur Rimbaud," enclosed in Olson to Frances Boldereff, June 8, 1950. CtU.

p. 6   *"the best . . . was"*: Robert Creeley interview, November 13, 1986.

p. 7   *"a five-petaled . . . it"*: "The Thing Was Moving," *CP*, p. 263.

p. 7   *"pushed . . . insistence"*: Robert Creeley interview, November 13, 1986.

p. 7   *"protectors"*: Norman Solomon interview, March 20, 1988.

p. 7 *"What . . . attachment"*: Olson to Constance Olson, November 8, 1952. CtU.
p. 8 *"no sexual . . . undressed"*: Olson notebook, "Key West 1, 1945." CtU.
p. 8 *"liver . . . flesh"*: "Anubis will stare . . ." *CP*, p. 381.
p. 8 *"tidy . . . man"*: Olson to Constance Olson, November 8, 1952. CtU.
p. 9 *"island"*: "Letter 3," *MAX*, p. 15.
p. 9 *"my front yard"*: Olson to Frances Boldereff, October 27, 1953. CtU.
p. 9 *"henhouse"*: "proem," *MAX*, p. 306.
p. 9 *"with . . . woman's"*: "The NEW Empire," *MAX*, p. 433.
p. 9 *"form . . . Park"*: ibid.
p. 10 *"bloated . . . wind"*: fragment from 1952–1953 among the poet's papers. CtU.
p. 10 *"the painted . . . war"*: "The Post Office," *PO*, p. 26.
p. 10 *"busted"*: ibid., p. 36.
p. 11 *"more . . . gay"*: ibid., p. 32.
p. 11 *"To 'plant' . . . country"*: Olson to Robert Creeley, April 10, 1953. WUSL.
p. 11 *"Tragabigzanda . . . collar"*: ibid.
p. 11 *"a great . . . poor"*: Robert Creeley interview, November 13, 1986.
p. 11 *"a no-nonsense school"*: Faye Rosenblum to author, December 15, 1986.
p. 12 *"definitely . . . hurry"*: ibid.
p. 12 *"inspiration"*: ibid.
p. 12 *"a Senate . . . Whip"*: ibid.
p. 12 *"a charming . . . mind"*: Classic Myths, n.p.
p. 13 *"the beloved . . . Ireland"*: "The Present Is Prologue," *AP*, p. 39.
p. 13 *"Fear . . . sex"*: Olson notebook, "Key West 1, 1945." CtU.
p. 13 *"amniotic cocoon"*: "The Post Office," *PO*, p. 36.

CHAPTER 2: Show 'Em

p. 14 *"a small . . . minority"*: Wilbert Snow, *Codline's Child* (Middletown: Wesleyan University Press, 1974), p. 279.
p. 15 *"left out . . . laughed at"*: Olson notebook, "1947–1948 Faust Buch." CtU.
p. 15 *"the womb . . . Avenue"*: Olson to Constance Olson, November 15, 1952. CtU.
p. 15 *"coat . . . fellows"*: Olson notebook, "March 1, 1932–March 25, 1934." CtU.
p. 15 *"was . . . 'human' "*: Olson to Frances Boldereff, March 28, 1950. CtU.
p. 15 *"It is . . . need"*: Olson notebook, "March 1, 1932–March 25, 1934." CtU.
p. 15 *"deal with others"*: Olson to Constance Olson, November 15, 1952. CtU.
p. 15 *"to show . . . etc."*: ibid.
p. 15 *"With . . . else"*: Wilbert Snow, "A Teacher's View," *MR*, p. 42.
p. 15 *"Wild Bill"*: Olson to Henry Allen Moe, April 23, 1951, *O / RC* 3, p. 215.
p. 16 *"Irish Indian"*: "Bill Snow," *AP*, p. 41.
p. 16 *"father"*: Charles Boer, *Charles Olson in Connecticut* (Chicago: Swallow Press, 1975), p. 87.
p. 16 *"thorough . . . thesis"*: Wilbert Snow, "A Teacher's View," *MR*, p. 41.
p. 16 *"I love . . . food"*: Olson notebook, "March 1, 1932–March 25, 1934." CtU.
p. 16 *"true . . . , ex-winner"*: ibid.
p. 16 *"lean . . . tragedy"*: ibid.
pp. 16–17 *"My imagination . . . express"*: ibid.
p. 17 *"To be . . . great"*: ibid.
p. 17 *"an intellectual pygmy"*: ibid.
p. 17 *"mechanical summarizer"*: Olson notebook, "#4, Cambridge & N.Y. Winter–Spring 1940." CtU.
p. 17 *"whoring after culture"*: Olson notebook, "1947–1948 Faust Buch." CtU.
p. 17 *"preparing . . . her"*: Olson notebook, "March 1, 1932–March 25, 1934." CtU.

p. 18   *"ridiculous . . . nonsense"*: Olson notebook, "Key West 2, 1945." CtU.

p. 18   *"convulsion"*: Olson notebook, "Key West 1, 1945." CtU.

p. 18   *"instinctively a solitary"*: Olson notebook, "March 1, 1932–March 25, 1934." CtU.

p. 18   *"havens of gossip"*: ibid.

p. 19   *"ability . . . acting"*: FH, intro. p. vii.

p. 19   *"thin . . . ruined"*: Olson to Henry Allen Moe, April 23, 1951, *O / RC* 6, p. 215.

p. 19   *"The ham . . . there"*: Paul Metcalf interview, May 10, 1987.

p. 19   *"endless dreamer"*: Wilbert Snow, "A Teacher's View," *MR*, p. 42.

p. 19   *"Carrier . . . table"*: *Gloucester Times*, June 11, 1931, quoted in *PO*, p. ix.

p. 19   *"Chaalie . . . Woos-tah"*: Fred Buck to author, November 14, 1986.

p. 19   *"Cut . . . bummaging"*: "The first of morning . . ." *MAX*, p. 605.

p. 19   *"walking myself down"*: Olson to Constance Olson, November 13, 1952. CtU.

p. 20   *"coffee & gab"*: Olson to Robert Creeley, March 9, 1951, *O / RC* 5, p. 61.

p. 20   *"Stage Manager . . . Around"*: Olson to Constance Olson, November 10, 1952. CtU.

p. 20   *"It is . . . arguments"*: Olson notebook, "March 1, 1932–March 25, 1934." CtU.

p. 21   *"sickness"*: Olson to Constance Olson, November 15, 1952. CtU.

CHAPTER 3: To Tell of Ishmael's Father

p. 22   *"monumental task"*: Wilbert Snow, "A Teacher's View," *MR*, p. 41.

p. 22   *"bad pun"*: Olson to Ann Charters, January 10, 1968, Charters, *Olson / Melville: A Study in Affinity* (Berkeley: Oyez, 1968) p. 5.

p. 22   *"debonaire aesthete"*: Harry Levin to author, May 18, 1987.

p. 23   *"clerk . . . do it' "*: John Finch, "Dancer and Clerk," *MR*, pp. 38–39.

p. 23   *"starved . . . entry"*: Olson to Ann Charters, January 10, 1968, Charters, p. 5.

p. 23   *"stutterer . . . stars"*: Wilbert Snow, "A Teacher's View," *MR*, p. 42.

p. 23   *Professors . . . Charlie"*: ibid., p. 41.

p. 23   *"the first . . . attempted"*: Charles Olson, "The Growth of Herman Melville, Prose Writer and Poetic Thinker," p. 1. CtU.

p. 23   *"original estimate"*: Wilbert Snow, "A Teacher's View," *MR*, p. 41.

p. 24   *"read . . . others"*: CMI, p. 36.

p. 24   *"confirmed . . . 1847"*: Olson to Ann Charters in conversation, June 14, 1968, Charters, p. 8.

p. 25   *"glorious great type"* Herman Melville to Evert Duyckinck, February 1849, quoted in Charles Olson, "Lear and Moby-Dick," *Twice A Year*, No. 1 (Fall–Winter 1938), p. 165.

p. 25   *"usable . . . Shakespeare"*: "Lear and Moby-Dick," p. 165.

p. 25   *"some . . . Brooklyn"*: Olson to Merton Sealts, March 2, 1963, *PM*, p. 138.

p. 26   *"castrated . . . flair"*: Olson notebook, "March 1, 1932–March 25, 1934." CtU.

p. 26   *"Even . . . humbled"*: Olson notebook, "May 6, 1934–1936." CtU.

p. 26   *"road into life"*: ibid.

p. 26   *"The task . . . usher"*: Pittsfield Address, *OJ* 2, p. 71.

pp. 26–27 *"terrible . . . revolutionists"*: Olson notebook, "May 6, 1934–1936." CtU.

p. 27   *"loose backbone . . . sky forever"*: ibid.

p. 27   *"middle class . . . wasted"*: Olson notebook, "Key West 2, 1945." CtU.

p. 27   *"well-diseased biscuit"*: Olson notebook, "May 6, 1934–1936." CtU.

p. 27   *"incoherent"*: Olson notebook, "#4, Cambridge & N.Y. Winter–Spring 1940." CtU.

p. 28   *"innocent . . . sea"*: "the clashing rocks . . ." *OJ* 9, p. 71.

p. 28   *"too soon"*: "My Father," *Nation*, p. 29.

p. 28   *"pathological disappointment"*: Olson notebook, "May 6, 1934–1936." CtU.

p. 28   *"came through sexually"*: Olson notebook, "1947–1948 Faust Buch". CtU.

pp. 28–29 *"nympho . . . white"*: Olson notebook, "1952–1955 Dream Journal." CtU.
p. 29   *"unorganized life"*: Olson notebook, "May 6, 1934–1936." CtU.
p. 29   *"A Man's . . . allegory"*: John Keats to George and Georgiana Keats, February 14, 1819, quoted by Olson in various contexts, e.g. in letters to Robert Creeley (June 29, 1953) and Robert Duncan (August 24, 1955), and in lectures, such as *SVH,* p. 17.
p. 29   *"keeping . . . Melville"*: *OJ* 7 [Swordfishing Journal], p. 3.
p. 29   *"true sailors"*: Olson notebook, "March 1, 1932–March 25, 1934." CtU.
p. 30   *"as close . . . whaling"*: *OJ* 7, p. 3.
p. 30   *"college feller"*: ibid, p. 8.
p. 30   *"piss . . . taffrail"*: Olson draft letter to John Finch, August 3, 1936, in notebook, "May 6, 1934–1936." CtU.
p. 30   *"first . . . joy"*: *OJ* 7, pp. 6–7.
p. 30   *"borne . . . divided"*: ibid., p. 9.
p. 30   *"character heroic"*: Olson notebook, "March 1, 1932–March 25, 1934." CtU.
p. 31   *"talked . . . fault"*: "Letter 20: not a pastoral letter," *MAX,* pp. 95–96.
p. 31   *"the sort . . . garden"*: "Maximus, to Gloucester: Letter 2," *MAX,* p. 11.
p. 31   *"a giant . . . man"*: "The Death of Carl Olsen," *MAX,* p. 475.
p. 31   *"Hyperion"*: "Letter 6," *MAX,* p. 31.
p. 31   *"brutish . . . stupid"*: *OJ* 7, p. 15.
p. 31   *"the geography . . . God"*: "Olson in Gloucester, 1966," *MUTH* I, p. 197.
pp. 31–32 *"Melville . . . civilized"*: *OJ* 7, pp. 24–25.
p. 32   *"Elizabethan vigor"*: ibid., p. 24.
p. 32   *"nervous notes"*: ibid., p. 12.
p. 32   *"the sea's vocabulary"*: ibid., p. 24.
p. 32   *"mug up . . . teeth"*: ibid., pp. 16–18.
p. 32   *"put . . . force"*: "Projective Verse," *HU,* p. 57.
p. 32   *"cunts . . . syphilis"*: *OJ* 7, p. 27.
p. 32   *"The more . . . quietly"*: ibid., p. 28.
p. 32   *"hell . . . life"*: Olson notebook, "May 6, 1934–1936." CtU.
p. 33   *"the belly . . . women"*: Olson draft letter to John Finch, August 3, 1936, in notebook, "May 6, 1934–1936." CtU.

CHAPTER 4: Killer-Place

p. 34   *"out of joint"*: ibid.
p. 34   *"intellectual war"*: Olson notebook, "March 1, 1932–March 25, 1934." CtU.
p. 34   *"vitiated will"*: *OJ* 7, p. 13.
p. 34   *"sprung . . . educators"*: Olson to Frances Boldereff, January 11, 1950. Ct U.
p. 34   *"taught . . . write"*: Olson to Ann Charters, January 10, 1968, Charters, p. 5.
p. 35   *"canonized . . . philosophy"*: Edward Dahlberg, *Because I Was Flesh* (New York: New Directions, 1963), p. 143.
p. 35   *"repulsive consciousness"*: D. H. Lawrence introduction to *Bottom Dogs* (San Francisco: City Lights Books, 1961), p. xvii.
p. 35   *"literary Marx Brothers"*: Olson notebook, "May 6, 1934–1936." CtU.
p. 35   *"city-nomad . . . Ishmael"*: Olson to Frances Boldereff, July 14, 1950. CtU.
p. 35   *"victim . . . head"*: Edward Dahlberg, *Do These Bones Live* (New York: New Directions, 1941), p. 96.
p. 35   *"obscure youth"*: Edward Dahlberg, *The Confessions of Edward Dahlberg* (New York: George Braziller, 1971), p. 257.
p. 36   *"near . . . spectacles"*: ibid., pp. 257–58.
p. 36   *"knew . . . advantage"*: ibid.

p. 36   *"a demi-god . . . literature"*: Edward Dahlberg to John Cech, January 27, 1972, Cech, *Charles Olson and Edward Dahlberg: A Portrait of a Friendship* (Victoria: English Literary Studies, University of Victoria, 1982), p. 38.

p. 36   *"porous . . . life"*: Edward Dahlberg to Alfred Stieglitz, August 12, 1936, Cech, p. 12.

p. 36   *"I should . . . butter"*: Edward Dahlberg to Alfred Stieglitz, August 23, 1936, Cech, p. 13.

p. 36   *"love . . . unresolved"*: Olson notebook, "1947–1948 Faust Buch." CtU.

p. 36   *"Dahlberg . . . naivete"*: Olson notebook, "Journal begun September 1, 1936." CtU.

pp. 36–37 *"Timon-like . . . faces"*: Olson draft letter to Edward Dahlberg, September 1936, ibid.

p. 37   *"Inaction . . . you"*: Edward Dahlberg to Olson, September 14, 1936, *O/D* 1, p. 120.

p. 37   *"thorn . . . flesh"*: Olson notebook, "March 1, 1932–March 25, 1934." CtU.

p. 37   *"slight hypochondria"*: John Finch interview, May 28, 1988.

p. 38   *"democratic prose tragedy"*: "Lear and Moby-Dick," p. 188.

p. 38   *"the cause, the cause"*: Diaries of Death," *CP*, p. 144.

p. 39   *"re-write Moby-Dick"*: Olson to Merton Sealts, March 7, 1952, *PM*, p. 115.

p. 39   *"Young El"*: *O&P*, pp. 79, 87, 130.

p. 39   *"tragedy . . . mind"*: William Ellery Sedgwick, Jr., *Herman Melville: The Tragedy of the Mind* (New York: Russell & Russell, 1962).

p. 39   *"rat race"*: Harry Levin to author, May 18, 1987.

p. 39   *"romantic . . . Hemingway"*: Henry F. May, *Coming to Terms: A Study in Memory and History* (Berkeley: University of California Press, 1987), p. 64.

p. 39   *"a much . . . influence"*: Henry Nash Smith, "A Texan Perspective," *Political Activism and the Academic Conscience: The Harvard Experience 1936–1941*, ed. John Lydenberg (Geneva, N.Y.: Hobart and William Smith Colleges, 1977), p. 50.

p. 40   *"new englandism"*: Olson to Frances Boldereff, March 17, 1950. CtU.

p. 40   *"outcast . . . hate"*: Olson recalling his Harvard years in a draft letter to Edward Dahlberg, notebook "#4, Cambridge & N.Y. Winter–Spring 1940." CtU.

p. 40   *"blizzards . . . moraines"*: Edward Dahlberg to Olson, January 27, 1937, *O/D* 1, p. 121.

p. 40   *"Write!"*: Edward Dahlberg to Olson, January 21, 1937, *O/D* 1, p. 121.

p. 40   *"highbrow"*: John Finch, "Dancer and Clerk," *MR*, p. 35.

p. 41   *"the scar . . . belly"*: "Notes on Language and Theatre," *HU*, p. 74.

p. 41   *"luminous genius"*: John Finch, "Dancer and Clerk," *MR*, p. 37.

p. 41   *"to Providence . . . Land's End"*: ibid.

p. 41   *"how . . . fine"*: ibid.

p. 42   *"Oh . . . hot"*: John Finch interview, May 28, 1988.

p. 42   *"never got over"*: John Finch, "Dancer and Clerk," *MR*, p. 37.

p. 42   *"tryout . . . triangle"*: ibid., p. 35.

p. 42   *"the task . . . see"*: Olson notebook, "#5, March 1940." CtU.

p. 42   *"Homer . . . simple"*: Olson notebook, "April 19, 1941." CtU.

p. 42   *"star . . . occasion"*: Harry Levin to author, May 18, 1987.

p. 42   *"Left-wing . . . was"*: John Finch interview, May 28, 1988.

p. 43   *"nest . . . fellow-travelling"*: Irving Howe, quoted in May, p. 249.

p. 43   *"Guerre Civile crisis"*: Olson notebook, "Friday July 15, 1966." CtU.

p. 43   *"great colorful invalid"*: Paul Metcalf, "Charles Olson: A Gesture Towards Reconstitution," *Where Do You Put the Horse: Essays by Paul Metcalf* (Elmwood Park: Dalkey Archive Press, 1986), p. 24.

p. 43   *"quasi-monster"*: ibid.

p. 43   *"You can't . . . you"*: John Finch, "Dancer and Clerk," *MR*, p. 40.

p. 44   *"identified . . . grandmother"*: Metcalf, p. 25.

p. 44   *"turned . . . servant"*: Paul Metcalf to author, June 17, 1987.

p. 45   *"bohemian attitude"*: Harry Levin to author, May 18, 1987.

p. 45 *"Charlie . . . year"*: ibid.

p. 46 *"jock house"*: Doris K. Goodwin, *The Fitzgeralds and the Kennedys* (New York: Simon & Schuster, 1987), p. 477.

p. 46 *"wonderful talk"*: ibid., p. 507.

p. 46 *"economic comptometry"*: "The Hustings," *CP*, p. 530.

p. 46 *"glories of egotism"*: Charles Olson, *Some Subtlest of All Possible Trail-Back* (Buffalo: Institute of Further Studies, 1969), n.p.

p. 46 *"hadn't . . . himself"*: Olson in conversation, quoted by Peter Anastas in "Olson's Beef with Homer Stamp," *Gloucester Daily Times*, February 19, 1987, p. 5.

p. 46 "a 'gentleman's C' ": Olson in conversation with George Butterick, *Nation*, p. 207 (editor's note).

p. 47 *"fragile . . . man"*: May, p. 227.

p. 47 *"saturation"*: "A Bibliography on America for Ed Dorn," *AP*, p. 11.

p. 47 *"for M . . . fact"*: Olson notebook, "Merk #1, February 8, 1938." CtU.

p. 47 *"master"*: "A Bibliography on America for Ed Dorn," *AP*, p. 8.

p. 47 *"intellectual disciplinarian"*: Olson's entry in *20th Century Authors*, ed. Stanley Kunitz and Howard Haycraft (New York: H. W. Wilson Co., 1941), p. 742.

p. 47 *"My heart . . . him"*: Olson to Edward Dorn, May 22, 1966. CtU.

p. 48 *"nefarious silence"*: Edward Dahlberg to Olson, February 9, 1938, Cech, p. 38.

p. 48 *"hornet's nest"*: Ephraim Doner interview, February 9, 1987.

p. 48 *"real . . . robbers"*: ibid.

p. 49 *"the sadness . . . somewhere"*: reported by Edward Dahlberg to Dorothy Norman, June 30, 1938, Cech, p. 39.

p. 49 *"best postman's knock"*: Terence Burns recalling Olson's account of this visit in Charles DeFanti, *The Wages of Expectation: A Biography of Edward Dahlberg* (New York: Gotham Library of the New York University Press, 1978), p. 167.

p. 49 *"not enough pump"*: Edward Dorn interview, March 17, 1987.

p. 49 *"careful Swede"*: loose notes from 1938 trip, folded into Olson notebook, "Journal begun September 1, 1936." CtU.

p. 49 *"real estate . . . decay"*: Olson to Dorothy Norman, August 14, 1938, Cech, p. 39.

p. 49 *"missionary rubbernecks"*: loose notes from 1938 trip, folded into Olson notebook, "Journal begun September 1, 1936." CtU.

p. 49 *"Park of holes . . . us"*: "Maximus, to Gloucester, Sunday, July 19," *MAX*, p. 158.

p. 49 *"break . . . span"*: "The K," *CP*, p. 14.

p. 49 *"the persistence of failure"*: Olson to Dorothy Norman, July 27, 1938, Cech, p. 39.

p. 50 *"breathless . . . pulsating"*: Edward Dahlberg to Olson, February 9, 1938, Cech, p. 38.

p. 50 *"crisis . . . death"*: Olson to Dorothy Norman, circa October 1938, Cech, p. 40.

p. 50 *"crazy, not human"*: Olson to Robert Creeley, October 25, 1950, *O/RC* 3, pp. 131–32.

p. 50 *"tragic world"*: "Lear and Moby-Dick," p. 188.

p. 51 *"sinking into"*: Olson to Robert Creeley, May 20, 1952. WUSL.

p. 51 *"I awoke free"*: "Diaries of Death," *CP*, p. 143.

p. 51 *"was in me . . . there"*: Olson to Robert Creeley, May 20, 1952. WUSL.

p. 51 *"concern . . . work"*: *Rat and The Devil: Journal Letters of F. O. Matthiessen and Russell Cheney*, ed. Louis K. Hyde (Hamden, Conn.: Archon Books, 1978), p. 260.

p. 51 *"DEEPLY . . . YOU"*: Edward Dahlberg to Olson (telegram), March 18, 1939, *O/D* 1, 122–23.

p. 51 *"highest . . . offered"*: questionnaire reproduced in *The Horn of Ulph: Charles Olson Letters*, narration by Ralph Maud (Barnaby, B.C.: privately published, c. 1970), n.p.

p. 52 *"O ground . . . bear!"*: Diaries of Death," *CP*, p. 144.

Chapter 5: Alive Again in This Burying World

p. 53 *"Pasiphae": Confessions of Edward Dahlberg,* p. 258.

p. 54 *"non-existent Big Cock":* Olson notebook, "1952–1955 Dream Journal." CtU.

p. 54 *"will to fuck":* Olson notebook, "#1, Summer and Fall 1939." CtU.

p. 54 *"bleak corners":* ibid.

p. 54 *"ineptitude . . . vaginal":* Olson notebook, "#3, December 1939–Spring 1940." CtU.

p. 55 *"To create . . . real":* Olson notebook, "#1, Summer and Fall 1939." CtU.

p. 55 *"Typical . . . he":* Olson marginal annotation in his copy of *The Complete Works of Shakespeare,* ed. George Lyman Kittredge (Boston: Ginn, 1936), p. 1163.

p. 55 *"Fathers & Sons":* Olson notebook, "#1, Summer and Fall 1939." CtU.

pp. 55–56 *"hunger . . . chain":* ibid.

p. 56 *"authority . . . suspended":* Charles Olson, "Dostoevksy and The Possessed," *Twice A Year,* Double Number Five-Six (Fall–Winter 1940 / Spring–Summer 1941), pp. 233–37.

p. 57 *"We are . . . paper":* ibid., p. 232.

p. 57 *"Kunt Circle":* "Wrote my first poems . . ." *MAX,* p. 299.

p. 57 *"neurotic . . . impotent":* Olson notebook, "#3, December 1939–Spring 1940." CtU.

p. 57 *"turtle shell . . .terror of it":* ibid.

p. 57 *"denial . . . life":* Olson notebook, "#1, Summer and Fall, 1939." CtU.

p. 57 *"grimly . . . self":* Olson to Waldo Frank, December 1939, Cech, p. 57.

p. 57 *"root . . . evil":* Olson notebook, "#1, Summer and Fall, 1939." CtU.

p. 58 *"sag of sex":* Olson notebook, "#3, December 1939–Spring 1940." CtU.

p. 58 *"hunches . . . Father":* ibid.

p. 59 *"a great fatuity":* Olson notebook, "#4, Winter–Spring 1940." CtU.

p. 59 *"Dr. Fraud":* Olson to Robert Creeley, November 28, 1951, *O/RC* 8, 192.

p. 59 *"race past . . . Father":* Olson notebook, "#3, December 1939–Spring 1940." CtU.

p. 59 *"son . . . his father":* Olson notebook, "#4, Winter–Spring 1940." CtU.

p. 59 *"time . . . economics":* Olson draft letter to Henry Allen Moe, ibid.

p. 60 *"upholstery . . . protruding":* "Letter 41," *MAX,* p. 171.

p. 60 *"gawk":* Edward Dahlberg to Olson, November 10, 1950 *O/D* 3, p. 167.

p. 60 *"I introduced . . . animal":* Edward Dahlberg to Olson, November 16, 1949, *O/D* 2, p. 130.

p. 60 *"suckers":* Olson notebook, "#1, Summer and Fall 1939." CtU.

pp. 60–61 *"fixed . . . Emperor":* Ephraim Doner interview, April 14, 1987.

p. 61 *"I bear . . . cannot":* Olson draft letter to Edward Dahlberg in notebook, "#4, Winter–Spring 1940." CtU.

p. 61 *"anti-Christ . . . Destroyer":* Olson notebook, "4, Winter–Spring 1940." CtU.

p. 61 *"Next . . . living":* ibid.

p. 61 *"jut of land":* Olson to Waldo Frank, March 25, 1940, *Guide,* p. 415.

p. 61 *"Between . . . self-mistrust":* Olson notebook, "#4, Winter–Spring 1940." CtU. (Cf. revised version of "Purgatory Blind," *CP,* p. 3.)

pp. 61–62 *"Out . . . time":* ibid.

p. 62 *"Christ . . . Catholicism":* Olson notebook, "#5, March 1940." CtU.

p. 62 *"hermaphroditical . . . heavenly":* Charles Olson, *In Adullam's Lair* (Binghamton, N.Y.: Archetypes, 1975), pp. 12–13.

p. 63 *"taller . . . dance":* John Finch, "Dancer and Clerk," *MR,* p. 38.

p. 63 *"far-left group":* Ephraim Doner interview, February 9, 1987.

p. 64 *"unspeakable":* Frank Moore interview, May 25, 1987.

p. 64 *"via . . . earth":* "La Préface," *CP,* p. 46.

p. 64 *"teller of tarots":* "Maximus, to Gloucester, Letter #29," *OJ* 6, p. 19.

p. 64 *"free will . . . absolute":* John Milton, *Paradise Lost,* bk. II, l. 557. Quoted frequently by Olson in conversation, as recalled in Duncan McNaughton to author, November 26, 1986; and Drummond Hadley interview, May 4, 1987.

p. 64   *"forecasting yourself"*: Olson annotation on the endpapers of his copy of Otto Fenichel, *The Psychoanalytic Theory of Neurosis* (New York: Norton, 1945).

pp. 64–65   *"long . . . grateful to her"*: Olson notebook, "#3, December 1939–Spring 1940." CtU.

p. 65   *"the color . . . love"*: "Move Over," *CP,* p. 67.

p. 65   *"relationship"*: Jane Atherton, "Memories of Charles Olson" (an unpublished memoir), p. 11.

p. 65   *"intellectual"*: Jane Atherton interview, March 28, 1987.

p. 65   *"patrician"*: Mildred Harding, "My Black Mountain," *Yale Literary Magazine,* April 1985, p. 83.

p. 66   *"delicate . . . caught"*: Olson to Robert Creeley, October 1, 1950, *O / RC* 7, p. 220.

p. 66   *"two Buddhas of desire"*: Olson to Constance Olson, undated letter circa spring 1946 (recalling their courtship). CtU.

p. 66   *"Love is . . . love"*: Olson draft letter to Constance Wilcock, in notebook, "April 19, 1941." CtU.

p. 66   *"bringing . . . world"*: Olson inscription on flyleaf of Sherwood Anderson, *Winesburg, Ohio* (New York: Modern Library, 1919).

p. 66   *"thin plate"*: Edward Dahlberg to John Cech, January 27, 1972, *Guide,* p. 299.

p. 66   *"glaring . . . from"*: "for Robt Duncan . . ." *MAX,* p. 207.

p. 67   *"flattened . . . blood"*: Edward Dahlberg to Olson, July 16, 1940, *O / D* 1, p. 123.

p. 67   *"pinko"*: Jane Atherton, "Memories of Charles Olson," p. 15.

CHAPTER 6: A Boho in the Village

p. 69   *"boho . . . Village"*: "Paris Review Interview," *MUTH* II, p. 145.

p. 69   *"I see . . . too"*: Olson in conversation with Merton Sealts, *PM,* p. 94.

p. 69   *"The superlative . . . day"*: Edward Dahlberg, "My Friends Stieglitz, Anderson, and Dreiser," *The Edward Dahlberg Reader,* ed. Paul Carroll (New York: New Directions, 1967), p. 226.

p. 70   *"new . . . suit"*: Olson to Robert Creeley, June 23, 1950, *O / RC* 1, p. 145.

p. 70   *"Fledged . . . answers"*: "You, Hart Crane," *CP,* p. 4.

p. 70   *"heart-broken"*: Olson to Robert Creeley, June 23, 1950, *O / RC* 1, p. 145.

p. 70   *"originality . . . stealth"*: Edward Dahlberg, *Do These Bones Live,* p. 104.

p. 71   *"I begged . . . error"*: Edward Dahlberg to Alfred Stieglitz, April 3, 1944, Cech, p. 58.

p. 71   *"hard . . . away"*: *Confessions of Edward Dahlberg,* p. 258.

p. 71   *"fathers"*: Olson to Constance Olson, November 5, 1952. CtU. (Also Olson to Robert Creeley, April 12, 1951, *O / RC* 5, p. 136).

p. 71   *"I rupture . . . Dahlberg"*: Olson notebook, "1947–1948 Faust Buch." CtU.

pp. 71–72   *"object . . . personal"*: Olson notebook, "April 19, 1941." CtU.

p. 72   *"Fear . . . America"*: Olson draft leter to Constance Wilcock in notebook, "April 19, 1941." CtU.

p. 73   *"ambrosial"*: Olson to Constance Olson, November 4, 1952 (recalling their first months of living together). CtU.

p. 73   *"anti–Fifth Column hysteria"*: Louis Adamic editorial, *Common Ground,* Autumn 1940, p. 68.

pp. 73–74   *"the old . . . break"*: ibid., p. 103.

p. 74   *"When . . . it"*: Woodie Guthrie, "Ear Players," *Common Ground,* Spring 1942, p. 32.

p. 74   *"Charles . . . author"*: Pete Seeger, letter to the editor, *Exquisite Corpse,* Vol. 7, Nos. 10–12 (October–December 1989), p. 3.

p. 75   *"not . . . event"*: Olson to Constance Olson, November 15, 1952 (recalling his firing from the Common Council). CtU.

Chapter 7: The Trick of Politics

p. 76   *"Washington . . . world"*: Anne Conover, *Caresse Crosby: From Black Sun to Roccasinibalda* (Santa Barbara: Capra Press, 1989), pp. 85, 82.

p. 77   *"the trick . . . men"*: Olson to Constance Olson, November 4, 1952. CtU.

p. 77   *"Walter . . . day"*: Lee Falk interview, March 15, 1987.

p. 77   *"We are . . . warfare"*: Allen M. Winkler, *The Politics of Propaganda: The Office of War Information 1942–1945* (New Haven: Yale University Press, 1978), p. 55.

pp. 77–78 *"We were . . . Ladino"*: Alan Cranston interview, March 13, 1987.

p. 78   *"Mussolini gangs"*: Olson to Robert Duncan, December 31, 1956. CtU.

p. 78   *"Bataan . . . 'Bataan' "*: *Spanish Speaking Americans in the War* (Washington: OWI Foreign Language Section, 1943), n.p.

p. 79   *"Some . . . to Bataan"*: ibid.

p. 79   *It was . . . wars"*: Lee Falk interview, March 15, 1987.

p. 79   *"rumored . . . centuries"*: Sally Almquist interview, March 14, 1987.

p. 79   *"Rodin's* Thinker"*: Lee Falk interview, March 15, 1987.

p. 79   *"a little . . . tutu"*: Sally Almquist interview, March 14, 1987.

p. 79   *"a real Viking"*: Lee Falk interview, March 15, 1987.

p. 80   *"Stonewall Jackson's"*: Ephraim Doner interview, February 9, 1987.

p. 80   *"amazed"*: Lee Falk interview, March 15, 1987.

p. 80   *"world . . . men"*: Olson to Constance Olson, November 4, 1952. CtU.

p. 80   *"extremely . . . sex"*: Olson to Frances Boldereff, June 27, 1950 (recalling his years in politics). CtU.

p. 80   *"two . . . garden"*: Olson to Robert Creeley, June 22, 1950, *O/RC* 1, p. 186.

p. 80   *"all pepper, all iron"*: Olson to Frances Boldereff, October 17, 1949. CtU.

p. 80   *"jungle of a garden"*: Olson to Robert Creeley, May 30, 1950, *O/RC* 1, p. 59.

p. 81   *"I leave . . . time"*: Olson to Robert Creeley, June 22, 1950, *O/RC* 1, p. 136.

p. 81   *"hidden . . . yard"*: Olson to Robert Creeley, May 30, 1950, *O/RC* 1, p. 59.

p. 81   *"Missuz Maintenance"*: Frank Moore to author, May 26, 1987.

p. 81   *"the Papal Shit"*: Frank Moore interview, May 25, 1987.

p. 81   *"heightened . . . wrestle with"*: Elizabeth von Thurn Frawley to author, July 12, 1987.

p. 81   *"wharfish"*: Olson to Frances Boldereff, August 21, 1950. CtU.

p. 82   *"New Deal . . . windowdressing"*: Winkler, p. 66.

p. 82   *"a philosophy . . . us"*: ibid., p. 68.

p. 83   *"phony . . . people"*: ibid., pp. 62–63.

p. 83   *"the innards . . . war"*: ibid., p. 64.

p. 83   *"high-pressure in Bally-hoo"*: ibid., p. 65.

p. 83   *"Merchandise men"*: "The Song and Dance of," *MAX*, p. 58.

p. 83   *"It was . . . Charlie"*: Alan Cranston interview, March 13, 1987.

pp. 83–84 *"big . . . pacts"*: *O&P*, pp. xix–xx.

p. 84   *"TVA . . . China"*: Olson notebook, "Friday July 15, 1966." CtU.

p. 85   *"hamstrung"*: "Two OWI Aides Resign," *New York Times*, May 19, 1944, p. 14.

p. 85   *"good . . . had"*: "Maximus Letter #28," *OJ* 6, p. 16.

p. 85   *"Little Svenska"*: Jane Atherton, "Memories of Charles Olson," p. 33.

p. 86   *"quart . . . Hottentot"*: Ted Morgan, *FDR: A Biography* (New York: Simon & Schuster, 1985), p. 727.

p. 86   *"courthouse politics"*: Olson in conversation, recalled in Frank Moore interview, March 25, 1987.

p. 87   *"loving . . . all"*: Sally Almquist interview, March 14, 1987.

p. 87   *"to operate . . . Digests"*: Olson to Robert Hannegan, January 23, 1946 (recalling their work together on the 1944 campaign). CtU.

p. 87   *"Every worker a voter"*: Morgan, p. 738.

p. 87   *"With . . . United States"*: ibid., p. 739.

p. 88   *"Hitler's . . . met"*: Charles Olson, "People v. The Fascist, U.S. (1944)," *Survey Graphic,* Vol. XXXIII, No. 8 (August 1944), p. 356.

p. 88   *"frontier peoples"*: Henry Wallace's Foreword, *Survey Graphic,* Vol. XXXIII, No. 2 (February 1944), p. 41.

p. 88   *"State figure"*: Olson to Constance Olson, October 28, 1952. CtU.

p. 88   *"When . . . affection"*: Fielding Dawson, *The Black Mountain Book* (New York: Croton Press, 1970), p. 22.

p. 88   *"playing it by ear"*: Olson notebook, "Washington Spring 1945." CtU.

p. 88   *"dirty money"*: Frances Boldereff Phipps to author, February 3, 1987.

p. 89   *"donor"*: John Clarke to author, February 13, 1987.

CHAPTER 8: To Begin Again

p. 90   *"mesomorph"*: "Poetry & Criticism," Olson's 1947 Seattle Writers' Conference lecture notes. CtU.

p. 90   *"static"*: Olson notebook, "Enniscorthy June 1946." CtU.

p. 91   *"to do . . . die"*: Olson notebook, "Key West II, 1945." CtU.

p. 91   *"all tired people"*: Olson recalling Key West stay in notebook, "Enniscorthy June 1946." CtU.

p. 91   *"Just . . . war"*: "Key West," *CP,* p. 23.

p. 92   *"smothered"*: Olson notebook, "Enniscorthy June 1946." CtU.

p. 92   *"His strictures . . . myself"*: "She, Thus," *CP,* p. 17.

p. 92   *"My spirit . . . self"*: Olson loose notes from early 1945, in Cech, p. 88.

p. 92   *"despair"*: ibid.

p. 92   *"walking . . . canyons"*: Olson's characterization of his political career, in a letter to Frances Boldereff, March 10, 1950. CtU.

p. 92   *"insist . . . strengthens"*: Olson loose notes from early 1945, in Cech, p. 88.

p. 93   *"poet's . . . dream"*: Alan Cranston interview, March 13, 1987.

pp. 93–94   *"Take then . . . grave"*: "The K," *CP,* p. 14.

p. 94   *"go-away poem"*: Robert von Hallberg, *Charles Olson: The Scholar's Art* (Cambridge: Harvard University Press, 1978), p. 6.

p. 94   *"left . . . peoples"*: Olson draft letter to Ruth Benedict, January 12, 1945, in notebook, "Key West I, 1945." CtU.

p. 95   *"religious . . . attention"*: D. H. Lawrence, "Etruscan Places," *D. H. Lawrence and Italy* (New York: Penguin Books, 1972), pp. 54–55.

p. 95   *"To him . . . creation"*: ibid. (Passage copied by Olson into notebook, "Key West I, 1945." CtU.)

p. 95   *"I am . . . ahead"*: Olson draft letter to Ruth Benedict, January 12, 1945, in notebook, "Key West I, 1945." CtU.

p. 95   *"To begin . . . sing"*: Olson notebook, "Key West I, 1945." CtU.

p. 95   *"Ur sense . . . American stories"*: ibid.

p. 96   *"weak . . . task"*: Olson notebook, "Key West II, 1945." CtU.

p. 97   *"the long . . . magic"*: ibid.

p. 97   *"long-eyed . . . West"*: ibid. (cf. *CMI,* p. 12).

p. 97   *"the central . . . sea"*: ibid. (cf. *CMI,* p. 13).

p. 97   *"Power . . . gain"*: "A Lion upon the Floor," *CP,* p. 12.

pp. 97–98 *"black . . . boy"*: "Pacific Lament," *CP,* pp. 15–16.

p. 98   *"front . . . Department"*: Olson to Malcolm Cowley, April 26, 1945, *Nation,* p. 173 (editor's note).

p. 98   *"save . . . skin"*: ibid.

p. 98   *"Read . . . work"*: Olson draft letter to Frances Biddle, in notebook, "Key West 1, 1945." CtU.

p. 98   *"revolutionary . . . obscene"*: "Lustrum," *Nation,* pp. 26–27.

p. 99   *"Should . . . father"*: Olson notebook, "Key West II, 1945." CtU.

p. 99   *"kissed off"*: Olson in conversation with Ann Charters, June 13, 1968, Charters, p. 9.

p. 99   *"swill"*: "Paris Review interview," *MUTH* II, p. 110.

p. 99   *"accept . . . comfort"*: Olson reconsidering his letter to President Truman, in notebook, "Washington Spring 1945." CtU.

pp. 99–100 *"do business with Warsaw"*: Olson draft letter to Oscar Lange, in notebook, "April 1945 en route north–May 1945." CtU.

p. 100   *"pulling . . . delay"*: Olson notebook, "Washington Spring 1945." CtU.

p. 100   *"the economics of poetics"*: ibid.

p. 100   *"Old Bitch"*: Olson to Frances Boldereff, February 10, 1950. CtU.

p. 100   *"Ol' Man . . . long"*: Jane Atherton, "Memories of Charles Olson," p. 31.

p. 100   *"little touch"*: Olson to Robert Creeley, October 23, 1951, *O/RC* 8, p. 86.

p. 101   *"Oil . . . 1844"*: Olson notebook, "Key West II, 1945." CtU.

p. 101   *"natural . . . aspects"*: Olson notebook, "Washington Spring 1945." CtU.

p. 101   *Freud . . . prophets"*: Olson notebook, "Key West II, 1945." CtU.

p. 101   *"the earth . . . living"*: Olson notebook, "Washington Summer 1945." CtU.

p. 102   *"The sheep . . . shade"*: "Lower Field—Enniscorthy," *CP,* p. 24.

p. 102   *"sex . . . sword"*: "For K," *Nation,* p. 36.

p. 102   *"Charles . . . everything"*: Frank Moore to author, May 26, 1987.

p. 103   *"for Constance"*: *CM1,* p. 112.

p. 103   *"at a clip"*: Olson to Ann Charters, February 14, 1968, Charters, p. 9.

p. 103   *"a vivid . . . nature"*: Olson notebook, "Washington Spring 1945." CtU.

p. 103   *"barnacled fastenings"*: Edward Dahlberg to Olson, July 16, 1940, *O/D* 1, p. 123.

p. 104   *"Demon . . . Hitler"*: Olson notebook, "Key West II, 1945." CtU.

p. 104   *"Beyond . . . write"*: draft dedication in notebook "Washington Spring 1945" (June 26 entry). CtU.

p. 104   *"for Edward . . . Windmills"*: *CMI,* p. 88.

p. 104   *"O fahter . . . sone"*: ibid., n. p.

p. 104   *"The Book . . . Blood"*: ibid., p. 81.

p. 104   *"First Murder"*: ibid., p. 83.

p. 104   *"excluded . . . again"*: Olson notebook, "Washington Spring 1945." CtU.

p. 104   *"sea frontiersman"*: *CMI,* p. 117.

p. 105   *"hunger . . . Historians"*: Olson draft letter to Frederick Merk, July 28, 1945, in notebook, "Washington Summer 1945." CtU.

p. 105   *"Man devours man"*: A concept Olson borrowed from Edward Dahlberg, who reiterated it often, e.g. Dahlberg to Dorothy Norman, December 14, 1937, Cech. p. 30.

p. 105   *"psychic button"*: Olson in conversation with Ann Charters, June 14, 1968, Charters, p. 10.

p. 106   *"the whole . . . direction"*: Olson to Jay Leyda, January 27, 1946, in Robert Bertholf, "On Olson, His Melville," *An Olson-Melville Sourcebook,* Vol. 1, *The New Found Land* (Io/22), ed. Richard Grossinger (Plainfeild: North Atlantic Books, 1976), p. 22.

p. 106   *"I Take . . . Whale"*: Olson notebook, "Enniscorthy Summer 1946." CtU.

CHAPTER 9: Unresolved "Amours"

p. 108 *"enders . . . phase"*: "This Is Yeats Speaking," *HU*, pp. 100, 102.
p. 108 *"obsession . . . authority"*: ibid., pp. 98–102.
p. 108 *"smell . . . furnace"*: "A Lustrum for You, E. P.," *CP*, p. 39.
p. 108 *"manage . . . ideas"*: Olson notebook, "October 25, 1945." CtU.
p. 108 *"outdo . . . power"*: "Again the sense the forms we have are conventions . . ." *OJ* 5, p. 45.
p. 108 *"Now . . . for me"*: Olson notebook, "October 25, 1945." CtU.
p. 108 *"older . . . hostile"*: *O & P,* pp. 35–36.
p. 109 *"gorilla cage"*: ibid., p. 38.
p. 110 *"fascist s.o.b."*: ibid., p. 44.
pp. 110–11 *"same . . . creature"*: ibid., p. 55.
p. 111 *"What . . . do"*: ibid., p. 75.
p. 112 *"greatly enjoyed"*: T. S. Eliot to Olson, March 20, 1946, *O / RC* 6, p. 237.
p. 112 *"The precious . . . authority"*: Olson to Constance Olson, undated, circa spring 1946. CtU.
p. 112 *"fast buck . . . blood"*: Olson to Frances Boldereff, August 5, 1950. CtU.
p. 112 *"I was . . . brain"*: Olson to Robert Creeley, April 17, 1951, *O / RC* 5, p. 168.
p. 113 *"unresolved . . . own"*: Olson notebook, "1947–1948 Faust Buch." CtU.
p. 113 *"early . . . instruments"*: "Poetry & Criticism," n.p.
pp. 113–14 *"new Altamira . . . Babe"*: "La Préface," *CP*, pp. 46–47.
p. 114 *"major . . . arcana-man"*: Olson notebook, "Enniscorthy June 1946."
p. 114 *"time . . . nothing"*: Olson notebook, "Washington Nov. 1946." CtU.
p. 115 *"projective space"*: "Equal, That Is, to the Real Itself," *HU*, p. 120.
p. 115 *"funny fetish trek"*: Olson to Frances Boldereff, March 24, 1950. CtU.
p. 115 *"elements in trance"*: "The Moebius Strip, *CP*, p. 55.
p. 115 *"Upon . . . geometry"*: Olson notebook, "Washington Nov. 1946." CtU.
p. 115 *"the demi-monde . . . empty"*: Olson to Constance Olson, November 8, 1952. CtU.
p. 116 *"of speech . . . own"*: Olson notebook, "Washington Nov. 1946." CtU.
p 117 *"fight . . . as yet"*: Olson to John Berryman, February 24 and March 19, 1947, in Paul Mariani, *Dream Song: The Life of John Berryman* (New York: Morrow, 1980), p. 183.
p. 118 *"straining . . . sensation"*: Olson notebook, "Enniscorthy June 1946." CtU.
p. 118 *"forms . . . intellect"*: ibid.

CHAPTER 10: Arresting the West

p. 120 *"assault"*: "Again the sense the forms we have are conventions . . ." *OJ* 5, p. 44.
p. 120 *"batten down"*: "OPERATION RED, WHITE & BLACK," *OJ* 5, pp. 30–31.
p. 120 *"the acts . . . continent"*: "November 20, 1946," *OJ* 5, p. 20.
p. 120 *"governing . . . himself"*: Olson to Flossie Williams, March 6, 1963. CtU.
pp. 120–21 *"My interest . . . catch up"*: audio tape of Olson lecturing at Goddard College, April 12, 1962.
p. 121 *"intuitive"*: Lewis Mumford, "Baptized in the Name of the Devil," *New York Times Book Review,* April 6, 1947, p. 4.
p. 121 *"poet . . . cataloguing"*: Robert Berkelman, "On the Melville Trail," *Christian Science Monitor,* April 18, 1947, p. 16.
p. 121 *"half coherent mumbo-jumbo"*: Stanley Edgar Hyman, "The Critic as Narcissus," *Accent,* Vol. 8, No. 3 (Spring 1948), p. 187.
p. 121 *"Indefensibly . . . intellectual"*: Richard Chase, "The Real Melville," *Nation,* December 1, 1951, p. 479.

p. 121 *"one . . . behind it"*: Joseph Henry Jackson, "Bookman's Notebook," *San Francisco Chronicle*, March 20, 1947, p. 16.
p. 121 *"in correct circles"*: Olson to Merton Sealts, March 5, 1952, *PM*, p. 115.
p. 121 *"to hop . . . am"*: Olson notebook, "1947–1948 Faust Buch." CtU.
p. 122 *"l'univers concentrationnaire"*: "The Story of an Olson and Bad Thing," *CP*, p. 180.
p. 122 *"vain Absalom"*: Edward Dahlberg to Olson, April 17, 1947, *O/D* 1, p. 131.
p. 123 *"like . . . merchant"*: Olson to Edward Dahlberg, April 23, 1947, Cech, pp. 79–80.
p. 123 *"ad valorem Cagli"*: Olson notebook, "1947–1948 Faust Buch." CtU.
p. 123 *"sore . . . manhood"*: ibid.
p. 123 *"Smash . . . topography"*: "Move Over," *CP*, p. 66.
p. 124 *"What . . . question"*: "Poetry & Criticism," n.p.
p. 125 *"objectionable"*: Olson to Edward Dorn, January 14, 1957. CtU.
p. 125 *"unruly terror"*: Olson to Constance Olson, November 4, 1952. CtU.
p. 125 *"did the turns"*: Olson to Robert Creeley, June 17, 1951, *O/RC* 6, p. 59.
p. 126 *"the Ambassador from Venus"*: Olson in conversation with Harvey Brown, recalled in "The Correspondences: Charles Olson and Carl Sauer," *New World Journal*, ed. Bob Callahan (Berkeley: Turtle Island, 1979), p. 136.
p. 126 *"I was . . . writing"*: Robert Duncan interview, November 6, 1986.
p. 126 *"father"*: Boer, p. 87.
p. 136 *"started off . . . omnivore"*: Carl Sauer to Olson, November 17, 1949, *New World Journal*, p. 142.
p. 127 *"trying . . . Sutter"*: Olson to Robert Duncan, May 31, 1965. CtU.
p. 127 *"Sutter's Clarke"*: Olson to Edward Dorn, May 5, 1966. CtU.
p. 127 *"true chronology"*: "Guggenheim Fellowship Proposal, 1948," *OJ* 5, p. 35.
p. 127 *"shantied growth"*: *O&P*, p. 93.
p. 127 *"mooching"*: Jane Atherton interview, March 28, 1987.
p. 128 *"shooting star"*: Olson to Ann Charters, February 14, 1968, Charters, p. 11.
p. 128 *"Camus . . . existenz"*: audio tape of Olson lecturing at Goddard College, April 12, 1962.
p. 128 *"kill . . . whale"*: *O&P*, p. 93.
p. 129 *"As a Frenchman . . . it"*: audio tape of Olson lecturing at Goddard College, April 12, 1962.
p. 129 *"deserts"*: Olson to Robert Creeley, February 18, 1951, *O/RC* 5, p. 24.
p. 129 *"Rube Goldberg / of Mars"*: "Letter #72," *OJ* 4, p. 8.
p. 129 *"wretched, thin stage"*: Olson to Frances Boldereff, December 29, 1947. CtU.
p. 129 *"total . . . complex"*: "Guggenheim Fellowship Proposal, 1948," *OJ* 5, pp. 34–35.
p. 129 *"dirty business"*: Olson to Robert Creeley, June 3, 1951, *O/RC* 6, p. 50.
p. 129 *"biggest . . . ground"*: Edward Dorn interview, December 2, 1986.

CHAPTER 11: The Broken Step

p. 130 *"shame . . . carelessness"*: Olson notebook, "1947–1948 Faust Buch." CtU.
p. 131 *"hopping . . . clever"*: ibid.
p. 131 *"stubborn . . . end"*: "Stocking Cap," *PO*, p. 8.
p. 131 *"nervous"*: Olson to Robert Creeley, June 21, 1950, *O/RC* 1, p. 123.
p. 131 *"weakness"*: Olson to Robert Creeley, June 21, 1951, *O/RC* 6, p. 61.
p. 131 *"relax . . . him"*: Olson notebook, "1947–1948 Faust Buch." CtU.
p. 132 *"the path . . . dominance"*: ibid.
p. 132 *"looks bad . . . bastard"*: *O&P*, pp. 92–93.
p. 132 *"resistance . . . pump"*: Olson notebook, "1947–1948 Faust Buch." CtU.
p. 132 *"laying . . . mad"*: Olson to Robert Creeley, May 27, 1950, *O/RC* 1, p. 51.
p. 133 *"confused . . . blood"*: *O&P*, p. 101.

p. 133 *"took on . . . blood"*: Olson to Robert Creeley, June 17, 1953. WUSL.
p. 133 *"a lot . . . brickabrak"*: Ezra Pound to Olson, February 12, 1948, *O / RC* 6, p. 225.
p. 133 *"roots . . . love"*: "Grandpa, Goodbye," *O&P,* p. 102.
p. 133 *"Bill . . . ground"*: ibid.
p. 133 *"belief . . . Carson"*: Olson to Flossie Williams, March 6, 1963. CtU.
p. 133 *"one . . . reading"*: William Carlos Williams to Olson, spring 1948. CtU.
p. 133 *"brother / father"*: Olson to Flossie Williams, March 6, 1963. CtU.
p. 133 *"charm . . . water"*: Olson notebook, "1947–1948 Faust Buch." CtU.
p. 134 *"music . . . him"*: Frank Moore to author, May 26, 1987.
p. 134 *"Mountains . . . egos"*: "The Fiery Hunt," *FH,* p. 17.
p. 134 *"angels . . . sperm"*: ibid., p. 19.
p. 135 *"Orpheus West"*: "The Long Poem, May 27, 1948," *OJ* 5, p. 38.
p. 135 *"the American . . . use"*: ibid.
p. 135 *"I am not . . . historian"*: "Post-West," *OJ* 5, p. 57.
p. 136 *"defeat"*: Olson to Constance Olson, November 4, 1952. CtU.
p. 136 *"whole . . . mouth"*: Olson notebook, "1947–1948 Faust Buch." CtU.
p. 136 *"absence . . . love"*: ibid.
p. 136 *"passing . . . women"*: Edward Dahlberg to Olson, July 29, 1948, *O / D* 1, p. 151.
p. 136 *"FIRST . . . FABLE"*: Olson to Edward Dahlberg, undated telegram, *O / D* 1, p. 153.
p. 136 *"throw . . . over"*: Olson notebook, "1947–1948 Faust Buch." CtU.
p. 136 *"every . . . need"*: Frances Boldereff to Olson, December 22, 1947. CtU.
p. 137 *"given . . . uncovered"*: Frances Boldereff to Olson, circa May 1948. CtU.
p. 137 *"Afric"*: Olson to Frances Boldereff, June 23, 1949. CtU.
p. 137 *"your own . . . now"*: "Troilus," *FH,* p. 43.
p. 138 *"more . . . sensations"*: Olson notebook, "1947–1948 Faust Buch." CtU.
p. 138 *"tongue-tied"*: Robert Creeley interview, November 13, 1986.
p. 139 *"gay . . . trouble"*: Edward Dahlberg to Olson (recalling his visit to the Olsons during Connie's recuperation), March 17, 1949, *O / D* 2, p. 96.
p. 139 *"bone . . . 1940"*: Olson to Edward Dahlberg, circa October 1948, *O / D* 2, p. 77. [Misdated therein as "December?"]
p. 139 *"two . . . operative"*: "David Young, David Old," *HU,* p. 107.
p. 140 *"needed their gold"*: Olson to Edward Dahlberg, circa October 1948, *O / D* 1, p. 78.
p. 140 *"bereft . . . students"*: Edward Dahlberg to Olson, September 16, 1948, *O / D* 1, p. 155.
p. 140 *"leafage . . . pederasty"*: Edward Dahlberg to Olson, April 5, 1949, *O / D* 2, p. 99.
p. 140 *"dead"*: "Move Over," *CP,* p. 66.
p. 140 *"magic . . . sword"*: Olson to Edward Dahlberg, October 1948, *O / D* 1, p. 166.

CHAPTER 12: Domination Square

p. 141 *"a strange . . . place"*: "On Black Mountain," *MUTH* II, p. 68.
p. 142 *"solidities . . . imponderable"*: Louis Adamic, "Education on a Mountain," *Harper's,* April 1936, quoted in Mary Harris, *The Arts at Black Mountain College* (Cambridge: MIT Press, 1987), p. 52.
p. 142 *"round the clock"*: John Rice, quoted in Harris, p. 53.
p. 142 *"threw . . . goes"*: Olson to Edward Dahlberg, circa October 1948, *O / D* 2, pp. 103–4.
p. 143 *"gains of space"*: "Man Is Prospective" (Olson lecture notes), *Boundary 2,* Vol. II, Nos. 1 & 2 (Fall 1973 / Winter 1974), p. 1.
p. 143 *"We are . . . future"*: Olson to Frances Boldereff (recalling his first Black Mountain lectures), August 10, 1950. CtU.
p. 143 *"faddish . . . charlatan"*: Mel Mitchell Kelly, in Martin Duberman, *Black Mountain: An Exploration in Community* (New York: Anchor / Doubleday, 1973), p. 391.

p. 143 *"It was . . . YOU":* Mary Fitton Fiore to author, January 26, 1987.

p. 143 *"He was . . . aura":* Mary Fitton Fiore to author, February 10, 1987.

p. 143 *"squaring off . . . square":* Mary Fitton Fiore to author, January 26, 1987.

pp. 143–44 *"It is . . . archangel!":* Olson to Edward Dahlberg, October 1948, *O/D* 2, pp. 103–4.

p. 144 *"Sidehill . . . intensification":* "Black Mountain as seen by a writer-visitor, 1948," *Credences: A Journal of Twentieth Century Poetry and Poetics,* Vol. 2, No. 1 (Summer 1982), pp. 89–90.

p. 144 *"Stuck . . . rise":* "On Black Mountain (II)," *OJ* 8, p. 78.

pp. 144–45 *"mandarins . . . at all":* ibid.

p. 145 *Oh, what . . . poems":* audio tape of Robert Duncan at New College of California, October 9, 1985. (Also Robert Duncan interview, November 6, 1986.)

p. 145 *"Too abstruse . . . heart":* Edward Dahlberg to Olson, circa November–December 1948, *O/D* 2, pp. 85–86.

p. 145 *"the purest . . . Villon":* Frances Boldereff to Olson, January 1949. CtU.

p. 145 *"the bravest . . . best":* Frances Boldereff to Olson, January 8, 1949. CtU.

p. 145 *"the greatest . . . century":* Frances Boldereff to Olson, January 20, 1949. CtU.

p. 145 *"an aristocrat . . . there":* Frances Boldereff to Olson, circa April 1949. CtU.

p. 146 *"a green . . . renewed":* Olson to Frances Boldereff, June 23, 1948. CtU.

p. 146 *"answer":* Olson to Frances Boldereff, October 26, 1949. CtU.

p. 146 *"survival . . . States":* Olson to Frances Boldereff, August 20, 1950. CtU.

p. 146 *"lock itself up":* Olson to Frances Boldereff, December 29, 1949. CtU.

p. 146 *"to dream . . . USE":* "The Praises," *CP,* pp. 98, 100.

p. 147 *"la lumière . . . agir":* quoted by Olson in letter to Frances Boldereff, October 26, 1949. CtU. (Cf. "The Kingfishers," *CP,* p. 87.)

p. 147 *"What . . . change":* "The Kingfishers," *CP,* p. 86.

p. 147 *"It is . . . itself":* Robert Creeley, "Charles Olson: *In Cold Hell, in Thicket,*" *A Quick Graph: Collected Notes and Essays* (San Francisco: Four Seasons Foundation, 1970), p. 154.

p. 147 *"I am . . . stones":* "The Kingfishers," *CP,* pp. 92–93.

p. 148 *"look . . . view":* Frances Boldereff to Olson, May 10, 1949. CtU.

p. 148 *"To come . . . unsought":* "Dura," *CP,* p. 85.

p. 148 *"If . . . lute":* "La Chute II," *CP,* p. 83.

p. 148 *"half . . . breathing":* Frank Moore to author, May 26, 1987.

p. 148 *"skittish . . . sources":* Olson to Constance Olson, November 10, 1952. CtU.

p. 148 *"imaginative and bold":* David Corkran to Pennsylvania State College, April 4, 1949, *Credences,* p. 79.

p. 149 *"reconverted barbershop":* Frances Boldereff to Olson, May 8, 1949. CtU.

p. 149 *"by one . . . BASE":* Olson to Frances Boldereff, May 23, 1949. CtU.

p. 149 *"revolutionists . . . Germans":* Olson to Edward Dahlberg, July 18, 1949, *O/D* 2, p. 117.

p. 149 *"going . . . stupid":* Olson to Edward Dahlberg, circa April–May 1949, *O/D* 2, p. 110.

p. 149 *"alive . . . two":* Olson to Constance Olson, circa May 12–16, 1949. CtU.

p. 150 *"made . . . family":* Vincent Ferrini, "A Frame," *Maps #4: Charles Olson,* 1971, p. 48.

p. 150 *"tantalian":* Olson to Edward Dahlberg, August 16, 1949, *O/D* 2, p. 119.

p. 151 *"stripped . . . gone":* "Notes on Language and Theatre," *HU,* p. 75.

p. 151 *"Kee-Klops":* Fielding Dawson to author, November 26, 1986.

p. 151 *"jungle & humid":* Olson to Edward Dahlberg, August 16, 1949, *O/D* 2, p. 119.

p. 151 *"barbarous . . . creatures":* Olson to Edward Dahlberg, July 18, 1949, *O/D* 2, p. 117.

p. 151 *"oraculizing":* "On Black Mountain," *Maps #4: Charles Olson,* p. 39.

p. 151 *"the Indian . . . victim":* Olson to Florence Glessner Lee (explaining his interest in the Maya), May 1, 1951, *O/RC* 6, p. 217.

p. 152 *"those . . . was"*: Olson to Edward Dahlberg, October 6, 1949, *O / D* 2, p. 124.

p. 152 *"lovely public airs"*: Jonathan Williams, "AM-O," *Parnassus: Poetry in Review*, Spring-Summer 1976, p. 249.

CHAPTER 13: Riot in My Soul

p. 153 *"riot in my soul"*: Olson notebook, "Monday January 18, 1966." CtU.

p. 153 *"slow nordic emerger"*: Olson to Frances Boldereff, August 10, 1950. CtU.

p. 153 *"new man Olson"*: Olson to Frances Boldereff, December 3, 1949. CtU.

p. 153 *"1949 . . . starts"*: Olson notebook, "Monday January 18, 1966." CtU.

p. 153 *"flight from woman"*: Olson to Constance Olson, November 9, 1952. CtU.

p. 153 *"posing . . . inside"*: Olson to Frances Boldereff, December 8, 1949. CtU.

p. 154 *"We both . . . back"*: Frances Boldereff Phipps to author, January 20, 1987.

p. 155 *"despair . . . Losing"*: Olson to Frances Boldereff (recalling their first meeting), March 17, 1950. CtU.

p. 155 *"Around . . . magic"*: Frances Boldereff Phipps to author, January 20, 1987.

p. 156 *"wizardess"*: Olson to Frances Boldereff, November 18, 1949.

p. 156 *"magic ring"*: "Epigon," *CP,* p. 93.

p. 156 *"Woodhenge"*: Olson to Frances Boldereff, June 26, 1950. CtU.

p. 156 *"hidden . . . awake"*: "Epigon," *CP,* pp. 93–94.

p. 157 *"quiet . . . proud"*: Elizabeth von Thurn Frawley to author, July 12, 1987.

p. 157 *"greys . . . highway"*: Olson to Frances Boldereff, December 16, 1949. CtU.

p. 157 *"acts"*: Olson to Frances Boldereff, December 14, 1949. CtU.

p. 157 *"middle-aged . . . ill"*: Frances Boldereff Phipps interview, February 24, 1987 (recalling conversation with Constance Olson after Olson's death in 1970).

p. 157 *"Constanza . . . with it"*: Olson to Frances Boldereff, December 22, 1949. CtU.

p. 157 *"hold . . . come"*: Olson to Frances Boldereff, December 14, 1949. CtU.

p. 158 *"rock"*: Olson to Constance Olson, November 4, 1952.

p. 158 *"life unmodified"*: Olson to Frances Boldereff, December 14, 1949. CtU.

p. 158 *"futile . . . drains me"*: Olson to Frances Boldereff, December 16, 1949. CtU.

p. 158 *"flowering . . . woman"*: Olson to Frances Boldereff, December 19, 1949. CtU.

p. 158 *"you . . . alone"*: "The Babe," *CP,* p. 101.

p. 158 *"enemies . . . world"*: Frances Boldereff to Olson, January 9, 1950. CtU.

p. 158 *"A man . . . DEAD"*: Olson to Frances Boldereff, January 10, 1950. CtU.

p. 158 *"Whatever . . . dangle"*: "These Days," *CP,* p. 106.

p. 159 *"all . . . life"*: Frances Boldereff to Olson, January 2, 1950. CtU.

p. 159 *"Where . . . season"*: "The Advantage," *CP,* p. 105.

p. 159 *"old . . . humans"*: ibid., p. 106.

p. 159 *"history of art history"*: Josef Strzygowski, *Origin of Christian Church Art*, translated by O. M. Dalton and H. J. Braunholtz (Oxford: Clarendon Press, 1923), p. 251.

p. 159 *"a tissue . . . Humanism"*: ibid., p. 250.

p. 159 *"Lake Van measure"*: "An Art Called Gothonic," *MAX,* p. 551.

p. 159 *"Doctor Strzygowski"*: "The Morning News," *CP,* p. 118.

p. 160 *"the archaic . . . nose"*: Olson to Frances Boldereff, April 10, 1950. CtU.

p. 160 *"some . . . thing"*: Olson to Frances Boldereff, circa January–February 1950. CtU.

p. 160 *"desperate . . . oneself"*: Olson to Frances Boldereff, March 2, 1950. CtU.

p. 160 *"just . . . note-taker"*: Frances Boldereff to Olson, March 2, 1950. CtU.

p. 160 *"doing . . . pitch"*: Olson to Frances Boldereff, February 13, 1950. CtU.

p. 160 *"About . . . them"*: Olson to Frances Boldereff, undated, circa February–March 1950. Letter in the possession of Frances Boldereff Phipps.

p. 160 *"hammering . . . oneself"*: Olson to Frances Boldereff, March 2, 1950. CtU.

p. 160 *"living flame"*: Frances Boldereff to Olson, February 17, 1950. CtU.

p. 161 *"root of universe"*: "The Advantage," *CP,* p. 106.

p. 161 *"turning . . . me"*: Frances Boldereff to Olson, March 2, 1950. CtU.

p. 161 *"filthy faith"*: Olson to Frances Boldereff, March 2, 1950. CtU.

p. 161 *"truly . . . catholique"*: "The Morning News," *CP,* p. 118.

p. 161 *"terrific . . . -place"*: Olson to Frances Boldereff, January 16, 1950. CtU.

p. 161 *"delivering . . . things"*: Olson to Frances Boldereff, March 10, 1950. (Also Olson to Frances Boldereff, circa January 11, 1950). CtU.

p. 161 *"from . . . self"*: Olson to Frances Boldereff, March 10, 1950. CtU.

p. 161 *"mistress printer"*: Olson to Frances Boldereff, February 13, 1950. CtU.

p. 162 *"PROJECTIVE. . . up"*: February 9, 1950, first draft of "Projective Verse," sent to Frances Boldereff February 10, 1950. CtU.

p. 162 *"The irony . . . practicing it"*: ibid.

p. 163 *"It is . . . nature"*: ibid.

pp. 163–64 *"a wretched . . . cock"*: Olson to Frances Boldereff, March 9, 1950. CtU.

p. 164 *"directive hand"*: "Of Lady, of Beauty, of Stream," *CP,* p. 127.

p. 164 *"sweet salmon"*: Olson to Frances Boldereff, April 14, 1950. CtU. Also Olson to Frances Boldereff, March 20, 1965. Letter in possession of Frances Boldereff Phipps.

p. 164 *"the salmon . . . love"*: "the salmon of . . ." *MAX,* p. 581.

p. 164 *"birthday . . . flesh"*: Olson to Frances Boldereff, March 17, 1950. CtU.

p. 164 *"understand . . . ink"*: Frances Boldereff to Olson, March 29, 1950. CtU.

p. 164 *"I am . . . myself"*: Frances Boldereff to Olson, April 9, 1950. CtU.-

p. 164 *"bought . . . River"*: Frances Boldereff to Olson, April 18, 1950.

p. 165 *"there is . . . these"*: Olson to Frances Boldereff, April 17, 1950. CtU.

p. 165 *"to put off, to voyage"*: Frances Boldereff to Olson, circa April 30, 1950, recalled in Olson to Frances Boldereff, May 15, 1950. CtU.

p. 165 *"the most . . . do"*: Frances Boldereff to Olson, April 28 and April 30, 1950. Letters in possession of Frances Boldereff Phipps.

p. 165 *"You . . . baby"*: Frances Boldereff Phipps to author, January 26, 1987.

p. 166 *"potency . . . for"*: Olson to Frances Boldereff, June 26, 1950. CtU.

p. 166 *"wild . . . blood"*: Olson to Frances Boldereff, May 12, 1950. CtU.

p. 166 *"sweet . . . taste"*: ibid.

p. 166 *"My mind . . . music-contained"*: Olson to Frances Boldereff, May 17, 1950. CtU.

p. 166 *"I am . . . hand"*: ibid. (Also "I, Maximus of Gloucester, to You," *MAX,* pp. 5–8.)

pp. 167–68 *"the thing . . . dance"*: ibid.

p. 168 *"long . . . sexual"*: Olson to Edward Dahlberg, June 7, 1950, *O / D* 2, p. 139.

pp. 168–69 *"lead soldiers . . . selva oscura"*: "In Cold Hell, in Thicket," *CP,* pp. 155–58.

p. 169 *"rest . . . may"*: Olson to Frances Boldereff, May 15, 1950. CtU.

p. 169 *"I prefer . . . others"*: Olson to Frances Boldereff, June 26, 1950. CtU.

p. 169 *"knivings . . . open"*: "In Cold Hell, in Thicket," *CP,* pp. 156–57.

p. 169 *"was . . . to you"*: Olson to Frances Boldereff, May 24, 1950. CtU.

p. 169 *"the sister . . . under her"*: Olson to Frances Boldereff, May 31, 1950. CtU. (Also "In Cold Hell, in Thicket," *CP,* pp. 155–56.)

p. 169 *"these hells . . . thru"*: Olson to Constance Olson, circa September 17, 1950. CtU.

p. 169 *"What . . . ambiguities"*: Olson to Vincent Ferrini, May 23, 1950, *Origin* 1 (Spring 1951), p. 53.

p. 169 *"he will . . . hell is"*: "In Cold Hell, in Thicket," *CP,* p. 160.

pp. 169–70 *"real dearth . . . imagery"*: Paul Blackburn to Olson, December 8, 1950, *O / RC* 9, p. 314.

p. 170 *"stop . . . concept"*: Frances Boldereff to Olson, May 20, 1950. CtU.

p. 170 *"I look . . . music"*: Frances Boldereff to Olson, May 19, 1950. CtU.

p. 170 *"cold . . . mother"*: Frances Boldereff to Olson, May 22, 1950. CtU.

p. 170 *"sibyl"*: Olson to Frances Boldereff, July 10, 1950. CtU.

p. 170 *"O Frances . . . the Cause"*: Olson to Frances Boldereff, May 31, 1950. CtU.

pp. 170–71 *"With . . . blood is"*: "For Sappho, Back," *CP,* p. 161.

p. 171 *"very accurate portrait"*: Frances Boldereff Phipps to author, February 3, 1987.

p. 171 *"That . . . obey"*: Frances Boldereff to Olson, May 27, 1950. CtU.

p. 171 *"catch . . . gold"*: Frances Boldereff to Olson, May 22, 1950. CtU.

p. 171 *"i am . . . m[otz]"*: Olson to Frances Boldereff, May 15, 1950. CtU.

p. 171 *"I have . . . else"*: Frances Boldereff to Olson, May 18, 1950. CtU.

p. 171 *"silver . . . root"*: "Heip Me, Venus, You Who Led Me On," *CP,* p. 163.

p. 171 *"hare . . . tortoise"*: Olson to Constance Olson, November 9, 1952. CtU.

p. 172 *"If on . . . uncertain"*: "Help Me, Venus, You Who Led Me On," *CP,* p. 163.

p. 172 *"He had . . . way"*: Frances Boldereff Phipps interview, December 2, 1986.

p. 172 *"King . . . Lions"*: Olson to Frances Boldereff, July 17, 1950. CtU.

p. 173 *"present . . . THINGS"*: Olson to Frances Boldereff, July 14, 1950. CtU.

p. 173 *"my boy BIGMANS"*: ibid.

p. 173 *"discharge . . . mess"*: Olson to Frances Boldereff, July 26, 1950. CtU.

p. 173 *"From . . . sufficiency"*: "The Gate and the Center," *HU,* p. 19.

p. 173 *"American . . . Whore"*: ibid., p. 17.

p. 173 *"primordial . . . methodologies"*: ibid., p. 23.

p. 173 *"archaic . . . produce"*: Olson to Frances Boldereff, July 6, 1950. CtU.

p. 173 *"archetype figures"*: "The Gate and the Center," *HU,* p. 21.

p. 173 *"participant . . . force"*: ibid., p. 23.

p. 174 *"You seem . . . right"*: Olson to Frances Boldereff, July 27, 1950. CtU.

p. 174 *"The smell . . . memora"*: Olson to Frances Boldereff, July 21, 1950. CtU.

p. 174 *"what she . . . off"*: "Of Mathilde," *CP,* p. 194.

p. 175 *"frugal . . . devoured"*: Elizabeth von Thurn Frawley to author, June 1, 1987.

p. 175 *"abatis . . . forest"*: Olson to Edward Dahlberg, July 24, 1950, *O/D* 2, p. 151.

p. 175 *"One of . . . separate"*: Elizabeth von Thurn Frawley to author, July 12, 1987.

p. 176 *"wondrous . . . Freud"*: Olson to Frances Boldereff, June 7, 1950. CtU.

p. 176 *"You . . . eyes"*: ibid.

CHAPTER 14: The Big Year Shift

p. 177 *"co-agitator"*: audio tape of Olson lecturing at Goddard College, April 12, 1962.

pp. 177–78 *"mystery . . . form"*: Olson to Frances Boldereff, June 28, 1950. CtU.

p. 178 *"You will . . . talk"*: ibid.

p. 178 *"goofed . . . understanding"*: Robert Creeley to Olson, May 31, 1950, *O/RC* 1, p. 62.

p. 179 *"enormously . . . endeavor"*: Grey Gowrie in Ian Hamilton, *Robert Lowell: A Biography* (New York: Random House, 1982), p. 354.

p. 179 *"Drop . . . perpetuating"*: William Carlos Williams to Olson, April 20, 1950, *O/RC* 1, p. 159.

p. 179 *"looking . . . language"*: Robert Creeley to Vincent Ferrini, March 29, 1950, *Boundary 2,* Vol. VI, No. 3 (Spring–Fall 1978), p. 130.

pp. 179–80 *"i says . . . same"*: Olson to Robert Creeley, April 21, 1950, *O/RC* 1, p. 19.

p. 180 *"I take . . . possesses"*: Robert Creeley to Olson, April 28, 1950, *O/RC* 1, pp. 22–23.

p. 180 *"poets . . . pedagogues"*: Olson to Robert Creeley, May 9, 1950, *O/RC* 1, p. 23.

p. 180 *"my . . . tandem"*: Olson to Robert Duncan, undated, summer 1951. CtU.

p. 180 *"I dont . . . it"*: Robert Creeley to Olson, May 11, 1950, *O/RC* 1, p. 25.

p. 180 *"Right . . . way"*: Olson to Robert Creeley, May 16, 1950, *O/RC* 1, pp. 28–29.

p. 180 *"FUNDAMENTALLY . . . wrong"*: Ezra Pound to Robert Creeley, reported in Robert Creeley to Olson, June 11, 1950, *O/RC* 1, p. 98.

p. 180 *"We will . . . beyond"*: Robert Creeley to Olson, June 21, 1950, *O/RC* 1, p. 119.

pp. 180–81 *"Let's . . . 'em"*: Olson to Robert Creeley, July 3, 1950, *O/RC* 2, p. 43.

p. 181 *"getting . . . push"*: Olson to Frances Boldereff, June 26, 1950. CtU.

p. 182 *"the first . . . words with"*: "The Death of Europe," *CP*, p. 309.

p. 182 *"The New . . . 'open field' "*: Robert Creeley, "Introduction to Charles Olson: *Selected Writings II,*" *The Collected Essays of Robert Creeley* (Berkeley: University of California Press, 1989), p. 126.

pp. 182–83 *"simplicities . . . aware"*: "Projective Verse," *HU*, p. 52.

p. 183 *"form . . . content"*: Robert Creeley to Olson, June 5, 1950, *O / RC* 1, p. 79.

p. 183 *"the principle . . . PERCEPTION"*: "Projective Verse," *HU*, pp. 52–53.

P. 184 *"wily intimidation"*: Olson to Frances Boldereff, August 28, 1950. CtU.

p. 184 *"dismal . . . book"*: Robert Creeley to Olson, September 11, 1950, *O / RC* 2, pp. 137–38.

p. 184 *"just . . . it"*: Olson to Edward Dahlberg, September 29, 1950, *O / D* 3, p. 150.

p. 184 *"I guess . . . Father-image"*: Edward Dahlberg to Olson, November 12, 1950, *O / D* 3, p. 175.

p. 184 *"this big . . . by"*: Olson to Robert Creeley, March 31, 1951, *O / RC* 5, pp. 113–14.

p. 185 *"could . . . life"*: Olson to Frances Boldereff, September 1, 1950. CtU.

p. 185 *"He got . . . women"*: Frances Boldereff Phipps interview, December 2, 1986.

p. 185 *"stunned, astonied"*: Olson to Frances Boldereff, September 12, 1950. CtU.

p. 185 *"depth . . . forward"*: Olson to Constance Olson, circa September 17, 1950. CtU.

p. 185 *"pejoracracy"*: "Maximus, to Gloucester: Letter 2," *MAX*, p. 10.

p. 185 *"deathly mu-sick"*: ibid., p. 12.

pp. 185–86 *"tell you . . . likewise"*: ibid., p. 9.

p. 186 *"we never . . . 20"*: Olson notes from circa 1939–1940. CtU.

p. 186 *"one . . . you"*: Olson to Edward Dahlberg, October 6, 1949, *Guide*, p. 16.

p. 186 *"they did . . . acts"*: Olson to Frances Boldereff, September 18, 1950. CtU.

p. 186 *"a question . . . love"*: Olson to Frances Boldereff, October 5, 1950. CtU.

pp. 186–87 *"contesting . . . actuality"*: "The Escaped Cock: Notes on Lawrence & the Real," *HU*, pp. 123–24.

p. 187 *"stay . . . intimate"*: ibid., p. 125.

p. 187 *"keystone . . . encountered"*: William Carlos Williams to Olson, December 16, 1950, *Boundary 2*, Vol. VI, No. 3 (Spring–Fall 1978), p. 179.

p. 187 *"looking . . . field"*: *The Autobiography of William Carlos Williams* (New York: New Directions, 1951), p. 329.

p. 187 *"along . . . TRAIL"*: Cid Corman to Olson, November 12, 1950, *O / CC*, p. 61.

p. 187 *"well-made" . . . publishing"*: Olson to Cid Corman, October 21, 1950, *O / CC*, p. 38.

pp. 187–88 *"weary . . . culture-wise"*: ibid., pp. 39, 43–44.

p. 188 *"O my son . . . wise"*: frontispiece of *Origin* 1 (Spring 1951).

p. 188 *"gone to my sources"*: Olson to Robert Creeley, March 31, 1951, *O / RC* 5, p. 114.

p. 188 *"If you . . . YET"*: Olson to Cid Corman, October 21, 1950, *O / CC*, pp. 36, 45.

p. 188 *"guarantors"*: Olson to Cid Corman, January 12, 1951, *O / CC*, p. 91.

p. 188 *"a fantastic . . . etc:"*: Cid Corman to George Evans, *O / CC*, p. 92.

p. 189 *"People . . . heads"*: Cid Corman to Olson, November 5, 1952, *O / CC*, p. 294.

p. 189 *"He would . . . snow"*: "The Moon Is the Number 18," *CP*, p. 282.

p. 189 *"to the minute . . . hour"*: "Poetry and Truth," *MUTH* II, p. 41.

p. 189 *"mother freeze"*: Olson to Constance Olson, November 4, 1952. CtU.

p. 189 *"free . . . of you"*: "Moonset, Gloucester, December 1, 1957, 1:58 AM," *CP*, p. 430.

CHAPTER 15: A Human Universe

p. 190 *"worn-out frame"*: Olson to Frances Boldereff, December 1950. CtU.

p. 190 *"the great . . . Gloucester"*: Olson to Robert Creeley, January 23, 1951, *O / RC* 4, p. 116.

p. 191 *"22 years in the Pen"*: Olson to Robert Creeley, February 18, 1951, *O / RC* 5, p. 29.

p. 191 *"shit town"*: Olson to Robert Creeley, February 13, 1951, *O / RC* 5, p. 14.

p. 191 *"documentarian"*: Olson to Cid Corman, February 9, 1951, *O / CC*, p. 93.

p. 192 *"We are . . . Maya"*: ibid., p. 95.

p. 192 *"griing-GO . . . mass"*: Olson to Robert Creeley, February 13, 1951, *O / RC* 5, p. 14.

p. 192 *"maya-espanol"*: Olson to Robert Creeley, February 9, 1951, *O / RC* 4, p. 130.

p. 192 *"clue . . . Maya were"*: Olson to Robert Creeley, February 13, 1951, *O / RC* 5, p. 13.

p. 192 *"a live . . . all"*: Olson to Robert Creeley, February 24, 1951, *O / RC* 5, p. 35.

p. 192 *"pitiful . . . inertia"*: Olson to Robert Creeley, February 18, 1951, *O / RC* 5, p. 29.

p. 192 *"I am . . . wild"*: Olson to Robert Creeley, February 19, 1951, *O / RC* 5, p. 31.

p. 192 *"better . . . been"*: "Human Universe," *HU,* p. 12.

p. 193 *"little . . . strength"*: Olson to Robert Creeley, February 18, 1951, *O / RC* 5, pp. 22–23.

p. 193 *"nits in Eden"*: Olson to Robert Creeley, February 13, 1951, *O / RC* 5, p. 13.

p. 193 *"pockets . . . apples"*: Olson to Robert Creeley, March 9, 1951, *O / RC* 5, p. 63.

p. 193 *"secret ruin"*: ibid., p. 61.

pp. 193–94 *"in the wilds . . . arse"*: Olson to Robert Creeley, March 17, 1951, *O / RC* 5, p. 78.

p. 194 *"perfect . . . Maya"*: Olson to Robert Creeley, February 28, 1953. WUSL.

p. 194 *"Quetzalcoatl's own knee-to-hip"*: Olson to Robert Creeley, March 2, 1953. WUSL.

p. 194 *"the Rosetta . . . studies"*: Kate Olson interview, February 19, 1987.

p. 194 *"total reconaissance . . . Metropolises"*: Olson to Robert Creeley, February 18, 1951, *O / RC* 5, pp. 25–26.

p. 194 *"Peabody-Carnegie . . . laziness"*: ibid., p. 25.

p. 195 *"SEA-HORSE"*: Olson to Robert Creeley, March 8, 1951, *O / RC* 5, p. 55.

p. 195 *"THE SEA . . . ART"*: Olson to Cid Corman, March 12, 1951, *O / CC*, p. 106.

p. 195 *"My only . . . outfits"*: Olson to Robert Creeley, March 22, 1951, *O / RC* 5, p. 88.

p. 195 *"the real . . . stuff"*: Olson to Robert Creeley, March 15, 1951, *O / RC* 5, p. 73.

p. 196 *"clear . . . professionals"*: Olson to Cid Corman, March 28, 1951, *O / CC*, p. 116.

p. 196 *"pushing . . . maneuvering"*: Olson to Cid Corman, April 19, 1951, *O / CC*, p. 121.

p. 196 *"golden egg"*: Olson to Cid Corman, March 28, 1951, *O / CC*, p. 118.

p. 196 *"I can't . . . entrancing"*: Cid Corman to Olson, May 3, 1951, *O / CC*, p. 137.

p. 196 *"the force of ORIGINS"*: Olson Fulbright application, *Alcheringa* #5 (Spring-Summer 1973), p. 12.

pp. 196–97 *"the fullest . . . on land"*: Olson to Cid Corman, April 27, 1951, *O / CC*, pp. 126–27.

p. 197 *"huge disappointment"*: Olson to Robert Creeley, April 28, 1951, *O / RC* 6, p. 20.

p. 197 *"highpoint"*: Olson to Cid Corman, April 27, 1951, *O / CC*, p. 127.

p. 197 *"we have . . . reality"*: Olson to Vincent Ferrini, November 7, 1950, *Origin* 1 (Spring 1951), pp. 5–6.

p. 197 *"ancient tub"*: Olson to Vincent Ferrini, July 2, 1950, *Origin* 1 (Spring 1951), p. 61.

p. 197 *"down back . . . dreams are"*: Olson to Vincent Ferrini, April 22, 1950, *Origin* 1 (Spring 1951), p. 42.

p. 197 *"The problem . . . human"*: Robert Creeley, Preface to *Mayan Letters* (London: Grossman Cape Editions, 1968), pp. 5–6.

p. 197 *"possessed . . . power"*: Olson to Robert Creeley, March 27, 1951, *O / RC* 5, p. 100.

p. 197 *"Heat Equator"*: "To Gerhardt, There, Among Europe's Things of Which He Has Written Us in His 'Brief an Creeley und Olson,'" CP, p. 212.

p. 198 *"set . . . faith"*: Olson to Cid Corman, July 31, 1951, *O / CC*, p. 183.

p. 198 *"turned . . . air"*: Olson to Robert Creeley, March 8, 1951, *O / RC* 5, p. 49.

p. 198 *"to fill . . . necessities"*: Olson to Robert Creeley, June 24, 1951, *O / RC* 6, pp. 70–71.

p. 198 *"the given . . . creation"*: ibid., p. 70.

p. 198 *"me"*: Olson to Robert Creeley, March 20, 1951, *O / RC* 5, p. 84.

pp. 198–99 *"I have . . . exaggerated"*: "Human Universe," *HU,* pp. 6–7.

p. 199 *"Men . . . images"*: ibid., p. 7

pp. 199–200 *"We have . . . discovery"*: ibid., pp. 3–5.

p. 200 *"only two . . . thing"*: ibid., p. 4.

p. 200 *"These are . . . particularity"*: ibid., pp. 5–6.

p. 200 *"There must . . . discovering"*: ibid., p. 6.

p. 201 *"words . . . seeming"*: "Review of Eric A. Havelock's *Preface to Plato*," *AP*, pp. 52–53.

p. 201 *"collectivists . . . homosexuals"*: first draft of "Human Universe," in Albert Glover, *Charles Olson: Letters for "Origin"* (Ann Arbor: U.M.I. Dissertation Information Service, 1987), pp. 258–59.

p. 201 *"Greekism"*: ibid., p. 271.

p. 201 *"a piece . . . stone"*: Olson to Cid Corman, August 12, 1951, *O / CC*, p. 187.

p. 201 *"a metric . . . Indian"*: Olson to Robert Creeley, June 26, 1951, *O / RC* 6, pp. 77–78.

p. 202 *"not know . . . meadow-sweet"*: "To Gerhardt, There, Among Europe's Things . . ." *CP*, p. 222.

p. 202 *"pissed off, jumpy"*: Olson to Robert Creeley, June 22, 1951, *O / RC* 6, p. 61.

p. 202 *"weeping . . . evenings"*: Olson to Robert Creeley, June 28, 1951, *O / RC* 6, p. 90.

p. 202 *"brilliant . . . energy"*: Olson to Robert Creeley, July 18, 1951, *O / RC* 6, p. 156.

CHAPTER 16: Lawgiver

p. 203 *"paradise . . . cross"*: Olson to Robert Creeley, July 15, 1951, *O / RC* 6, pp. 135–36.

p. 203 *"There are laws"*: "Human Universe," *HU*, p. 3.

p. 203 *"These 'laws' . . . importance"*: Olson to Robert Creeley, July 15, 1951, *O / RC* 6, p. 142.

p. 204 *"BOX . . . wisdom"*: "The Law," in Olson to Robert Creeley, October 3, 1951, *O / RC* 7, p. 234.

p. 204 *"my tribe"*: Olson to Robert Creeley, May 20, 1952. WUSL.

p. 204 *"I go . . . monologue"*: Olson to Robert Creeley, July 19, 1951, *O / RC* 6, p. 160.

p. 204 *"a man . . . fire"*: Fielding Dawson, *The Black Mountain Book*, pp. 86–87.

p. 204 *"I shall . . . them all"*: Olson to Robert Creeley, July 19, 1951, *O / RC* 6, p. 163.

p. 204 *"three-ring circus"*: Wes Huss interview, November 4, 1986.

p. 205 *"a sort of combustion"*: Olson to W. H. Ferry, August 7, 1951, *OJ* 2, p. 8.

p. 205 *"someone's . . . edge"*: Harrison score reproduced in Harris, p. 225.

p. 205 *"Katy Litz . . . bag"*: Edward Dorn interview, December 2, 1986.

p. 205 *"the best . . . forward"*: Olson to Robert Creeley, July 19, 1951, *O / RC* 6, pp. 162–63.

p. 205 *"African shadow-play"*: Olson to Robert Creeley, July 27, 1951, *O / RC* 6, p. 211.

p. 205 *"cold . . . sun"*: "Applause," *CP*, p. 225.

p. 206 *"the whole . . . Century"*: Olson to Robert Creeley, July 27, 1951, *O / RC* 6, p. 211.

p. 206 *"A sudden . . . live"*: Apollonius of Tyana, *HU*, pp. 26, 31.

p. 206 *"long go . . . EATING"*: Olson to Robert Creeley, February 9, 1952. WUSL.

p. 206 *"historic"*: Olson to Robert Creeley, July 22, 1951, *O / RC* 6, p. 177.

p. 206 *"fetish . . . hand"*: Olson to Robert Creeley, July 17, 1951, *O / RC* 6, p. 149.

p. 206 *"hidden . . . dream"*: Olson to Robert Creeley, July 18, 1951, *O / RC* 6, p. 159.

pp. 206–7 *"that goddamned . . . animals"*: Olson to Robert Creeley, July 15, 1951, *O / RC* 6, pp. 139, 144.

p. 207 *"I have . . . cannibalism"*: "Stage Fort Park," *MAX*, p. 321.

p. 207 *"The oral . . . phallic"*: Olson to Robert Creeley, February 19, 1952. WUSL.

p. 207 *"such collapsings . . . sexuality"*: Olson to Robert Creeley, July 15, 1951, *O / RC* 6, pp. 142–43.

p. 207 *"false . . . them"*: "Letter for Melville 1951," *CP*, pp. 233, 237.

p. 207 *"megalomaniac"*: Paul Metcalf interview, May 10, 1987.

p. 208 *"viral input"*: Edward Dorn to author, November 8, 1986.

p. 208 *"post-modern"*: postscript to Olson to Louis Martz (readdressed to Robert Creeley), August 8, 1951, *O / RC* 7, p. 75.

p. 208 *"pulled . . . terms"*: William Carlos Williams to Cid Corman, August 2, 1951, *O / RC* 7, p. 260.

p. 208 *"the most . . . time"*: Olson to Robert Creeley, August 10, 1951, *O / RC* 7, p. 83.

p. 208 *"too easy recognition"*: Robert Creeley to Olson, August 16, 1951, *O / RC* 7, p. 103.

p. 209 *"I honestly . . . out"*: Olson to Robert Creeley, August 22, 1951, *O / RC* 7, pp. 121–22.

p. 209 *"His great . . . elite"*: Edward Dorn to author, April 22, 1988.

p. 209 *"the dogmatism . . . discourse"*: Olson to Robert Creeley, July 30, 1951, *O / RC* 7, pp. 26–27.

p. 209 *"the Index"*: Robert Duncan interview, November 12, 1986.

p. 209 *"the first . . . Bach"*: Olson to Robert Creeley, August 20, 1951, *O / RC* 7, p. 111.

p. 209 *"destined . . . great"*: Mildred Harding, "My Black Mountain," p. 83.

p. 209 *"Resisters"*: Mary Fiore to author, February 10, 1987.

pp. 209–10 *"iconoclastic . . . ball"*: Francine Du Plessix Gray, "Charles Olson and an American Place," *Yale Review,* Spring 1987, pp. 342, 345.

p. 210 *"Me . . . mysteries"*: Mary Fiore to author, January 5, 1987.

p. 210 *"a father . . . class"*: Mary Fiore to author, February 3, 1987.

p. 210 *"handled . . . me"*: Joel Oppenheimer in Duberman, p. 400.

p. 210 *"my other father"*: Fielding Dawson, *An Emotional Memoir of Franz Kline* (New York: Pantheon, 1967), p. 18.

p. 210 *"to bear . . . major"*: "pitcher, how . . ." *CP,* p. 242.

p. 210 *"gave . . . had"*: Fielding Dawson, *The Black Mountain Book,* p. 87.

p. 210 *"I am . . . it"*: Olson to Robert Creeley, September 18, 1951, *O / RC* 7, p. 168.

p. 211 *"profound . . . talk"*: Olson to Robert Creeley, July 19, 1951, *O / RC* 6, p. 161.

p. 211 *"just . . . students"*: Olson to W. H. Ferry, August 7, 1951, *OJ* 2, p. 9.

p. 211 *"Olson's University"*: Olson to Robert Creeley, May 22, 1952. WUSL.

p. 211 *"sell . . . energies"*: Olson to W. H. Ferry, August 7, 1951, *OJ* 2, p. 9.

pp. 211–12 *"I actually . . . connective"*: Wes Huss interview, November 4, 1986.

p. 212 *"stiff things"*: Olson to Robert Creeley, July 30, 1951, *O / RC* 7, p. 25.

p. 212 *"tyranny"*: Olson to Robert Creeley, circa July 1952. WUSL.

p. 212 *"I'm not . . . many"*: Olson to Robert Creeley, December 1, 1951, *O / RC* 8, p. 215.

p. 212 *"Olson's . . . symposia"*: Mildred Harding, "My Black Mountain," p. 82.

p. 212 *"doubted . . . talking about"*: minutes of the faculty, November 21, 1951, Raleigh Archives. Reproduced in *OJ* 2, pp. 18, 21.

p. 212 *"to go . . . chaos"*: minutes of the faculty, November 9, 1951, Raleigh Archives. Cited in Duberman, p. 359.

p. 213 *"Medici . . . dough"*: Olson to Robert Creeley, October 1, 1951, *O / RC* 7, p. 222.

p. 213 *"the live . . . gives"*: Proposal for a Fulbright Lectureship in American Civilization at the University of Teheran, *Alcheringa* #5 (Spring-Summer 1973), pp. 11–12.

p. 213 *"Son of Olson"*: Olson to Robert Creeley, September 3, 1951, *O / RC* 7, p. 34.

p. 213 *"a girl . . . terrible"*: Olson to Robert Creeley, October 23, 1951, *O / RC* 8, p. 84.

p. 213 *"a boy . . . us"*: Ibby von Thurn Frawley to author, July 12, 1987.

p. 213 *"very beautiful"*: Olson to Robert Creeley, October 23, 1951, *O / RC* 8, p. 85.

p. 213 *"this lovely . . . made"*: Olson to Constance Olson, October 31, 1952. CtU.

p. 213 *"So alert . . . company"*: Olson to Robert Creeley, November 11, 1951, *O / RC* 8, p. 124.

p. 213 *"somewhat . . . name"*: Olson to Merton Sealts, March 5, 1952, *PM,* p. 114.

pp. 213–14 *"let down . . . belief"*: Olson to Robert Creeley, November 7, 1951, *O / RC* 8, pp. 100–1.

p. 214 *"sun & sex":* Olson to Robert Creeley, November 28, 1951, *O / RC* 8, p. 192.

p. 214 *"to get . . . Con":* Olson to Robert Creeley, November 29, 1951, *O / RC* 8, p. 198.

p. 214 *"Can't . . . lived":* Olson to Robert Creeley, November 28, 1951, *O / RC* 8, p. 192.

p. 214 *"root metaphors":* Olson to Robert Creeley, November 29, 1951, *O / RC* 8, p. 200.

p. 214 *"moon . . . arise":* "An Ode on Nativity," *CP,* pp. 245, 247, 249.

CHAPTER 17: In the Dark Stall

p. 215 *"obscene thing":* Jane Atherton, "Memories of Charles Olson," p. 46.

p. 215 *"If I . . . into him":* Olson to Robert Creeley, January 17, 1952, *O / RC* 9, p. 44.

p. 216 *"dragged":* Olson to Robert Creeley, January 23, 1952, *O / RC* 9, p. 55.

p. 217 *"thought . . . homosexuality":* Olson to Robert Creeley, January 29, 1952, *OJ* 8, pp. 7–9.

p. 217 *"white world men":* Fielding Dawson, *The Black Mountain Book,* p. 22.

p. 218 *"most 'Red' . . . police":* Olson to Robert Creeley, February 1, 1952, *O / RC* 9, pp. 70–71, 72.

p. 218 *"fucked . . . FBI":* Olson to Robert Creeley, February 4, 1952. WUSL.

p. 219 *"the first . . . state":* Olson to Robert Creeley, February 1, 1952, *O / RC* 9, pp. 69, 72.

p. 219 *"forever . . . time":* Olson to Robert Creeley, January 23, 1952, *O / RC* 9, p. 53.

p. 219 *"presentation . . . thrust":* Olson to Cid Corman, February 26, 1952, *O / CC,* p. 240.

pp. 219–20 *"A Stab . . . LAWS":* "Culture," in Olson to Robert Creeley, February 20, 1952, *O / RC* 9, pp. 145, 146, 147, 149.

pp. 220–21 *"twin . . . fact":* "History," in Olson to Robert Creeley, February 14, 1952, *O / RC* 9, pp. 102, 121.

p. 221 *"unsung . . . strangered":* Edward Dahlberg, "Laurels for Borrowers," *Samuel Beckett's Wake and Other Uncollected Prose,* ed. Steven Moore (Elmwood Park, Ill.: Dalkey Archive Press, 1989), pp. 77, 83.

pp. 221–22 *"physicality . . . Hero":* "The Materials and Weights of Herman Melville," *HU,* pp. 113, 114, 116.

p. 222 *"I would . . . much":* Olson to Merton Sealts, March 17, 1952, *PM,* p. 121.

p. 222 *"damned . . . wood":* Olson to Cid Corman, February 26, 1952, *O / CC,* p. 242.

p. 222 *"men . . . twin":* "A Letter to the Faculty of Black Mountain College" [March 21, 1952], *OJ* 8, pp. 26, 27.

p. 222 *"worth . . . millions":* Olson to Frances Boldereff, October 27, 1953. CtU.

p. 222 *"Great Man":* "Letter to Paul Williams" [undated], *OJ* 8, p. 34.

p. 222 *"fucking fatigued":* Olson to Robert Creeley, April 8, 1952. WUSL.

p. 223 *"tremendously beautiful":* Olson to Frances Boldereff, May 17, 1952. CtU.

p. 223 *"real . . . being":* Olson to Frances Boldereff, April 1952, CtU.

p. 223 *"stay[ing] . . . possible":* Olson to Frances Boldereff, May 17, 1952. CtU.

p. 223 *"God's . . . back":* Mary Fiore to author, January 5, 1987.

p. 223 *"limited consciousness":* Hilda Morley, quoted in Harris, p. 204.

p. 223 *"a matter . . . day":* Olson to Frances Boldereff, May 17, 1952. CtU.

p. 223 *"perfect response":* Frances Boldereff to Olson, May 4, 1952. CtU.

p. 223 *"God . . . goddess":* Fielding Dawson, *The Black Mountain Book,* p. 99.

p. 224 *"randy . . . men":* "He / in the dark stall," *CP,* p. 266.

p. 224 *"real . . . cigarette":* Mary Fiore to author, January 5, 1987.

p. 224 *"passion . . . engage":* Fielding Dawson to author, January 6, 1987, and February 29, 1988.

p. 224 *"troubles of Androgyne":* Olson to Constance Olson, November 10, 1952. CtU.

p. 224 *"corrupt an army":* "Black Mt. College Has a Few Words for a Visitor," *CP,* p. 269.

p. 224 *"never . . . recognized":* Olson to Constance Olson (recalling her remark), October 27, 1952. CtU.

p. 224 *"unbearable . . . bug"*: Olson to Frances Boldereff, July 1952 and July 3, 1952. CtU.

pp. 224–25 *"By touch . . . Flesh"*: Olson to Frances Boldereff, June 17, 1952. CtU.

p. 225 *"illumination"*: Olson to Frances Boldereff, July 5, 1952. CtU.

p. 225 *"The moment . . . yourself"*: "Interview in Gloucester," *MUTH* II, p. 102.

p. 225 *"mass-man"*: "The Carpenter Poem (Letter #33)," *OJ* 6, p. 54.

p. 225 *"O tansy . . . is"*: "Letter 3," *MAX,* p. 15.

p. 225 *"Big Boy . . . us"*: "The Methodology Is the Form," *Intent,* Vol. 1, No. 1 (Spring 1989), pp. 1, 4, 5.

p. 225 *"Polis . . . few"*: "Letter 3," *MAX,* p. 15.

p. 225 *"King of the Mountain"*: Mildred Harding, "My Black Mountain," p. 82.

p. 225 *"I am . . . you are"*: Fielding Dawson, *The Black Mountain Book,* p. 106.

p. 226 *"didn't . . . plan"*: Fielding Dawson to author, March 6, 1987.

p. 226 *"space cadets"*: Olson to Cid Corman, December 14, 1953, Glover, p. 231.

p. 226 *"A man . . . man"*: Fielding Dawson to author, March 6, 1987.

p. 226 *"softness"*: John Cage, in Duberman, p. 367.

p. 226 *"anecdote . . . tricks"*: "A Toss," *CP,* p. 273.

p. 227 *"deep . . . Ages"*: David Weinrib, in Duberman, p. 375.

p. 227 *"light walrus"*: Merce Cunningham, in Duberman, p. 380.

p. 227 *"therapy . . . himself"*: Fielding Dawson to author, January 26, 1986.

Chapter 18: Inland Waters

p. 228 *"oral . . . out"*: Olson to Cid Corman, August 24, 1955, Glover, p. 247.

p. 228 *"a part . . . with"*: "Olson in Gloucester, 1966," *MUTH* I, p. 173.

p. 229 *"REST"*: "The Charles Olson Papers at Raleigh, N.C.," compiled by Leverett T. Smith and Ralph Maud, *Credences,* vol. 2, No. 1 (Summer 1982), pp. 83, 88.

p. 229 *"STILL . . . EDUCATOR"*: Olson to the Black Mountain College, October 1952, in Harris, p. 172.

p. 229 *"rest . . . relationship"*: Olson to Constance Olson (recalling her remark), November 17, 1952. CtU.

p. 229 *"high . . . disorder"*: Robert N. Wilson, "The American Poet: A Role Investigation" (Ph.D. dissertation, Harvard, 1952), cited in George F. Butterick, "Charles Olson and the Postmodern Advance," *Iowa Review,* Vol. 11, No. 4 (Fall 1980), p. 4.

p. 230 *"whole . . . itself"*: Olson to Cid Corman, November 25, 1952, *O / CC,* p. 300.

p. 230 *"crucial privacies"*: Olson to Robert Creeley, May 31, 1953. WUSL.

p. 230 *"UNC . . . sleeps"*: Olson to Constance Olson, October 31, 1952. CtU.

p. 230 *" 'bossy . . . reality"*: Fenichel, pp. 481–82.

p. 230 *"Stage . . . hard"*: Olson to Constance Olson, November 10, 1952. CtU.

p. 230 *"President . . . fact"*: Olson to Constance Olson, November 4, 1952. CtU

p. 231 *"founders . . . buried"*: "The Present Is Prologue," *AP,* p. 39.

p. 231 *"complete . . . betrayers"*: Olson to Constance Olson, November 9, 1952. CtU.

p. 231 *"will to power"*: Olson to Constance Olson, November 13, 1952. CtU.

p. 231 *"damned . . . hill"*: Olson to Robert Creeley, November 17, 1952. WUSL.

p. 232 *"biological and evolutionary"*: Olson to Constance Olson, November 13, 1952. CtU.

p. 232 *"soft . . . fraud"*: Olson to Frances Boldereff, July 6, 1950. CtU.

p. 232 *"great . . . now"*: Olson to Constance Olson, December 1, 1952. CtU.

p. 232 *"true . . . soul"*: Olson to Carl Jung, circa November 1952, in Charles Stein, *The Secret of the Black Chrysanthemum: The Poetic Cosmology of Charles Olson and His Use of the Writings of C. G. Jung* (Barrytown, N.Y.: Station Hill Press, 1987), p. xxii.

p. 232 *"hidden myths"*: Olson to Constance Olson, December 1, 1952. CtU.

p. 232 *"buried . . . 'used' "*: Olson to Constance Olson, November 29, 1952. CtU.

p. 232 *"doppelganger"*: "Olson in Gloucester 1966," *MUTH* I, p. 172.

p. 232 *"Who . . . Moore"*: "The Librarian," *CP*, p. 414.

p. 232 *"inward . . . soul"*: C. G. Jung, *Psychological Types* (Princeton, N.J.: Bollingen Series / Princeton, 1974), p. 467.

p. 233 *"She was . . . too"*: Olson to Constance Olson, November 10, 1952. CtU.

p. 233 *"a very . . . lady"*: Olson to Robert Creeley, January 9, 1953. WUSL.

p. 233 *"the blessing . . . it"*: "The Songs of Maximus," *MAX*, pp. 18, 19.

p. 233 *"Man . . . present"*: "The Chiasma, or Lectures in the New Sciences of Man," *OJ* 10, pp. 19, 97.

p. 233 *"a chance . . . years"*: Olson to Robert Creeley, January 9, 1953. WUSL.

p. 233 *"the totality . . . man"*: "The Chiasma, or Lectures in the New Sciences of Man," *OJ* 10, p. 19.

p. 234 *"cleaner . . . with"*: Olson to Robert Creeley, March 16, 1953. WUSL.

p. 234 *"hopped up . . . deep"*: Olson to Robert Creeley, March 24, 1953. WUSL.

p. 234 *"stand-in"*: Olson to Cid Corman, November 25, 1952, *O / CC*, p. 301.

p. 234 *"I was . . . lost"*: William Carlos Williams to Olson, August 6, 1953, von Halberg, p. 233.

p. 234 *"utterly Indical"*: "Reading at Berkeley," *MUTH* I, p. 107.

p. 234 *"pushed . . . button"*: Olson to Jonathan Williams, June 24, 1953, *Guide*, p. xxxv.

pp. 234–35 *"run . . . line"*: Olson to Robert Creeley, April 24, 1953. WUSL.

p. 235 *"damned . . . dizzy"*: Olson to Robert Creeley, May 3, 1953. WUSL.

p. 235 *"islands . . . girls"*: "Letter 3," *MAX*, p. 16.

p. 235 *all those . . . fingertips*: Fielding Dawson to author, February 29, 1988.

p. 236 *"nascent capitalism"*: "Letter 23," *MAX*, p. 105.

p. 236 *"pejorocracy"*: "Maximus, to Gloucester," *MAX*, p. 10.

p. 236 *"a turning . . . attitude"*: Edward Dorn, "What I See in *The Maximus Poems*," *Views* (San Francisco: Four Seasons Foundation, 1980), p. 43.

p. 236 *"Trolley-cars . . . over"*: "The Twist," *MAX*, pp. 86, 89.

p. 236 *"The nouns . . . Gloucester"*: Edward Dorn, "What I See in *The Maximus Poems*," pp. 43–44.

pp. 236–37 *"song . . . place"*: Olson to Robert Creeley, June 19, 1953. WUSL.

p. 237 *"aware . . . ffield"*: "Letter 23," *MAX*, pp. 104, 105.

p. 237 *"the hump . . . solid"*: Olson to Frances Boldereff, October 27, 1953. CtU.

p. 237 *"an unlived . . . shut on"*: Olson's notes in his copy of *The Maximus Poems 11–22* (Stuttgart: Jonathan Williams, 1956).

CHAPTER 19: Chinese Monastery or Hill-fort

p. 238 *"The last . . . nation"*: "Obit," *CP*, p. 426.

p. 238 *"Chinese . . . hill-fort"*: Olson to Robert Creeley, May 22, 1952. WUSL.

p. 238 *"What . . . down"*: "Obit," *CP*, p. 427.

p. 238 *"company convent"*: John Schram in Duberman, p. 386

p. 239 *"Williams . . . under me"*: Olson to Robert Creeley, November 9, 1953. WUSL.

p. 240 *"phoney . . . house"*: ibid.

p. 240 *"I . . . practical"*: Olson to Robert Creeley, March 1, 1954. WUSL.

p. 240 *"I'll be rector"*: Wes Huss interview, November 4, 1986.

p. 240 *"monarch . . . Kulikowski's"*: Olson to Frances Boldereff, July 7, 1954. CtU.

p. 240 *"Olson . . . singlehandedly"*: "The Black Mountain Review," *The Collected Essays of Robert Creeley*, p. 511.

p. 240 *"mappemunde . . . Monsters"*: "On first Looking out through Juan de la Cosa's Eyes," *MAX*, pp. 81, 82.

p. 240 *"We felt . . . time"*: "The Black Mountain Review," *The Collected Essays of Robert Creeley*, p. 507.

p. 241 *"hole . . . pavement"*: Olson to Robert Creeley, November 28, 1953. WUSL.

p. 241 *"snooping . . . something"*: Olson to Robert Creeley, February 21, 1954. WUSL.

p. 241 *"oil . . . Houston"*: Olson to Robert Creeley, March 1954. WUSL.

p. 241 *"guerrilla war"*: Olson to Frances Boldereff, February 10, 1950. CtU.

p. 242 *"heat of ferreting"*: Olson to Constance Olson, July 5, 1954. CtU.

p. 242 *"changes made"*: Fielding Dawson to author, February 29, 1988.

p. 242 *"shocked"*: Robert Creeley interview, November 13, 1986.

p. 243 *"Figure of Outward"*: dedication, *MAX*, p. 3.

p. 243 *"volubleness . . . sense"*: Olson to Cid Corman, June 6, 1954, Glover, p. 240.

p. 243 *"the reasons . . . present"*: Olson to Robert Creeley, February 12, 1954. WUSL.

p. 244 *"storming . . . place"*: Michael Rumaker, quoted in footnote, *MUTH* I, p. 215.

p. 244 *"that I . . . fear"*: Olson to Frances Boldereff, June 7, 1950. CtU.

p. 244 *"got . . . steps"*: Robert Creeley interview, December 13, 1986.

p. 244 *"housemother"*: Robert Creeley interview, August 21, 1987.

p. 245 *"helplessness . . . knees"*: "Da Boyg," *CP*, p. 298.

p. 245 *"There is . . . situation"*: "Love," *CP*, p. 300.

p. 246 *"Big Charles . . . priest"*: John Wieners, "Youth," *Selected Poems 1958–1984* (Santa Barbara: Black Sparrow Press, 1986), p. 229.

p. 246 *"Love . . . ever gave"*: "Quantity in Verse, and Shakespeare's Late Plays," *HU*, pp. 82, 87, 93.

p. 246 *"stick it out"*: Jane Atherton interview, March 28, 1987.

pp. 246–47 *"I am . . . to me"*: Olson to Frances Boldereff, October 1, 1954. CtU.

p. 247 *"Isn't it . . . her in"*: Olson notebook, "1952–1955 Dream Journal." CtU.

p. 247 *"the poet . . . are"*: Robert Duncan, *From the Day Book*, quoted in George F. Butterick and Albert Glover, *A Bibliography of Works by Charles Olson* (New York: Phoenix Book Shop, 1967), p. 11.

p. 247 *"Don't . . . made"*: "O'Ryan 9," *CP*, p. 328.

p. 247 *"bare . . . window"*: Robert Duncan, *From the Day Book*, quoted in *A Bibliography of Works by Charles Olson*, p. 11.

p. 248 *"a caricature . . . shrew"*: Robert Duncan interview, November 6, 1986.

p. 248 *"close husbandish marriage"*: Olson notebook, "June 19, 1969." CtU.

p. 249 *"inchoate . . . decide"*: Robert Creeley interview, August 21, 1987.

p. 249 *"late . . . breakfast"*: Edward Dorn, "An Interview with Roy K. Okada," *Interviews* (Bolinas, Calif.: Four Seasons Foundation, 1980), p. 38.

p. 249 *"underlying . . . malevolences"*: Michael Rumaker, "Robert Creeley at Black Mountain," *Boundary 2*, Vol. VI, No. 3 (Spring–Fall 1978), p. 168.

p. 250 *"enfant . . . crutches"*: Ephraim Doner interview, February 9, 1987.

p. 250 *"drunk . . . face"*: "A Newly Discovered 'Homeric' Hymn," *CP*, pp. 363–64.

p. 250 *"offices . . . off"*: Olson to Robert Creeley, circa December 1955. WUSL.

p. 251 *"Baby . . . to go"*: Jane Atherton interview, March 28, 1987.

Chapter 20: The Last Man

pp. 252–53 *"24 hour . . . start"*: Olson to Frances Boldereff, February 24, 1956. CtU.

p. 253 *"goes . . . heart"*: "Long Distance," *CP*, p. 410.

p. 253 *"puts . . . universe"*: "Obit, *CP*, p. 427.

p. 253 *"park . . . events"*: "MAXIMUS, FROM DOGTOWN—I," *MAX*, p. 175.

p. 254 *"cleared . . . in"*: "A Later Note on Letter #15, *MAX*, p. 249.

p. 254 *"great . . . poem[s]"*: "Olson in Gloucester, 1966," *MUTH* I, p. 186.

p. 254 *"known . . . about it"*: Olson to Robert Duncan, December 23, 1959. CtU.

p. 254 *"great . . . literature"*: Edward Dorn to author, September 21, 1986.

p. 254 *"proposition . . . TIME"*: *SVH*, pp. 17, 18, 33.

p. 254 *"to produce . . . attack":* Robert Duncan in *SVH*, p. 11.

p. 255 *"spy . . . himself":* Robert Duncan interview, November 12, 1986.

p. 255 *"nary a word":* Mary Fiore to author, December 19, 1986.

p. 255 *"You're our dramatist":* Robert Duncan interview, November 12, 1986.

p. 255 *"primary images":* "The Writ," *CP,* p. 416.

p. 255 *"magic view":* Robert Duncan in *SVH*, p. 11.

p. 256 *"making . . . earnestly":* Robert Duncan interview, November 12, 1986.

p. 256 *"double-axe . . . le bonheur":* Olson to Frances Boldereff, April 13, 1956. CtU.

p. 256 *"the powers . . . poison":* "The chain of memory is resurrection," *CP,* pp. 376, 377.

p. 256 *"poison/of desire":* "The Perfume," *CP,* p. 400.

pp. 256–57 *"elixir . . . transmutations":* "Variations Done for Gerald Van De Wiele," *CP,* pp. 397–99.

p. 257 *"secret of correspondences":* "The Writ," *CP,* p. 415.

pp. 257–58 *"rise . . . my soul":* "The chain of memory is resurrection," *CP,* pp. 373–74, 378, 379.

p. 258 *"The Androgynes . . . love":* "The Lordly and Isolate Satyrs," *CP,* pp. 384, 387.

p. 258 *"the poverty . . . peace":* "As the Dead Prey Upon Us," *CP,* pp. 391, 393, 394.

p. 258 *"the garbage . . . world":* Robert Creeley recalling Stefan Wolpe's remark in *SVH*, p. 2.

p. 259 *"Why . . . blowup":* Robert Duncan interview, November 12, 1986.

p. 259 *"three . . . summer":* Robert Hawley interview, October 30, 1986.

p. 259 *"a dread . . . gerontology":* "DRAFT OF A PLAN FOR THE COLLEGE, September 1, 1956 on," *OJ* 2, pp. 51, 54.

p. 259 *"the final . . . Mt.":* Olson to Robert Duncan, September 23, 1956. CtU.

p. 259 *"Neither . . . change":* Wes Huss interview, November 4, 1986.

p. 260 *"cheerful . . . Grandma":* Robert Hawley interview, October 30, 1986.

p. 260 *"last man . . . mountains":* "Obit," *CP,* pp. 426–28.

p. 260 *"Maxies":* Olson to Robert Duncan, September 23, 1956. CtU.

p. 261 *"high . . . Gloucester":* Olson's notes in his copy of *The Maximus Poems 11–22.*

p. 261 *"so far . . . damning":* Olson to Edward Dorn, January 14, 1957. CtU.

p. 261 *"American . . . Pound":* William Carlos Williams, "Review of *The Maximus Poems / 11–22,*" *Maps #4: Charles Olson,* pp. 61–62, 64.

p. 261 *"not modest":* ibid., p. 62.

p. 261 *"the language . . . again":* Edward Dorn to Olson, January 10, 1957. CtU.

p. 261 *"the noun . . . else":* Olson to Edward Dorn, January 14, 1957. CtU.

p. 262 *"middle voice":* "Reading at Berkeley," *MUTH* I, p. 136.

p. 262 *"materials . . . space":* "The Librarian," *CP,* pp. 412–13.

p. 262 *"the best . . . wrote":* "Olson in Gloucester, 1966," *MUTH* I, p. 169.

p. 262 *"The places . . . Moore?":* "The Librarian," *CP,* p. 414.

p. 263 *"Institute . . . Literature":* Olson to Edward Dorn, January 14, 1957. CtU.

p. 263 *"anchor man":* "On Black Mountain," *MUTH* II, p. 56.

p. 263 *"or anywhere . . . wants it":* Olson to Edward Dorn, January 14, 1957. CtU.

p. 263 *"caravan . . . country":* Robert Duncan interview, November 13, 1986.

p. 263 *"flatly . . . out":* Olson to Edward Dorn, January 14, 1957. CtU.

p. 263 *"fishtailed . . . speed":* Paul Metcalf, "Charles Olson: A Gesture Towards Reconstitution," p. 26.

p. 263 *"He was . . . days' ":* Robert Duncan interview, November 13, 1986.

p. 264 *"a tone of adoration":* Thomas Parkinson interview, January 28, 1987.

p. 264 *"historiography":* Philip Whalen to author, March 26, 1987.

p. 264 *"sold . . . library":* Robert Duncan interview, November 13, 1986.

p. 264 *"three . . . cows":* "On Black Mountain II," *OJ* 8, p. 90.

p. 265 *"At this . . . sad":* Olson to Robert Creeley, July 2, 1957. WUSL.

p. 265 *"For me . . . you":* Olson to Frances Boldereff, June 1957. CtU.

p. 265 *"insulted . . . him"*: Frances Boldereff Phipps to author, May 3, 1987.
p. 265 *"gutting"*: Olson to Frances Boldereff, June 1957. CtU.
p. 265 *"handsome . . . KnockMany"*: "All My Life I've Heard About Many," *MAX*, p. 177.
p. 265 *"atavistic . . . practice"*: audio tape of Olson lecturing at Goddard College, April 12, 1962.
p. 266 *"a speck . . . eternity"*: "On Black Mountain II," *OJ* 8, p. 74.

CHAPTER 21: Isolato

p. 267 *"dirtiest . . . America"*: Olson to Elizabeth Olson, October 5–6, 1957. CtU.
p. 268 *"golden . . . light"*: "Sunday, January 16, 1966," *MAX*, p. 485.
p. 268 *"a floating . . . water"*: "December 22nd," *MAX*, p. 482.
p. 268 *"dusky old Light"*: "February 3rd 1966," *MAX*, p. 490.
p. 268 *"made . . . poet"*: "I Know Men . . ." *MUTH* II, p. 165.
p. 268 *"Stage . . .-sansui"*: "The Intended Angle of Vision is from My Kitchen," *OJ* 9, p. 26.
p. 268 *"the whole . . . lesson"*: "December 22nd," *MAX*, p. 482.
p. 268 *[Fitzhugh] . . . view"*: Olson's annotation in Sylvanus Smith, *Fisheries of Cape Ann* (Gloucester, Mass.: Press of Gloucester Times Co., 1915), p. 112.
p. 268 *"my fair window"*: "white ships all covered with ice," *MAX*, p. 511.
p. 268 *"much scorned"*: Olson to Ruth Witt Diamant, December 3, 1957. Bancroft Library, University of California at Berkeley.
p. 268 *"Algonquin-Sicilian"*: Gavin Seleri, *To Let Words Swim into the Soul: An Anniversary Tribute to the Art of Charles Olson* (London: Binnacle Press, 1980), p. 28.
p. 268 *"The Jolly . . . Giant"*: John Clarke to author, March 2, 1987.
p. 268 *"The Professor"*: Robert Creeley interview, November 13, 1986.
p. 268 *"fish . . . fish-houses"*: "Reading at Berkeley," *MUTH* I, p. 137.
p. 269 *"the fishermen . . . off"*: Paul Metcalf, "Charles Olson: A Gesture Towards Reconstitution," p. 25.
p. 269 *"petroglyphic"*: John Clarke to author, March 30, 1987.
p. 269 *"winter . . . face"*: "a Plantation, a beginning," *MAX*, p. 106.
p. 269 *"two heats"*: Olson to Ruth Witt-Diamant, December 3, 1957. Bancroft Library, University of California at Berkeley.
p. 269 *"suffocating"*: Kate Olson interview, February 21, 1987.
p. 269 *"Night . . . constriction"*: Olson to Elizabeth Olson, undated (circa 1957). CtU.
p. 270 *"my dearest . . . grave"*: "Just Inside the Vigil of Christmas," *CP*, p. 432.
p. 270 *"we grow . . . mother"*: "What's Wrong with Pindar," *CP*, p. 431.
p. 270 *"Goodbye . . . Mother"*: "Moonset, Gloucester, December 1, 1957, 1:58 AM," *CP*, p. 430.
pp. 270–71 *"to thicken . . . small"*: Olson notebook, "I . . . Sept. 15, 1957," *OJ* 5, p. 61.
p. 271 *"fourteen . . . Beach"*: "a Plantation a beginning," *MAX*, p. 106.
p. 271 *"the impetus . . . coming"*: Olson to Robert Duncan, November 2, 1957. CtU.
p. 272 *"Off . . . magnificent"*: Olson to Robert Duncan, March 6, 1958, CtU.
p. 272 *"beautiful . . . parts"*: Olson to Robert Duncan, November 2, 1957. CtU.
p. 272 *"exact . . . include"*: "Equal, That Is, to the Real Itself," *HU*, pp. 118–19.
p. 273 *"I am . . . again"*: Olson to Robert Duncan, November 2, 1957. CtU.
p. 273 *"to make . . . ourself"*: "Poetry and Truth," *MUTH* II, p. 27.
p. 273 *"It is . . . man"*: "Maximus of Gloucester," *MAX*, p. 473.
p. 273 *"You can . . . both"*: Olson in conversation, as recalled in John Clarke to author, January 31, 1987.
p. 273 *"captive . . . footnotes"*: Robert Duncan interview, November 6, 1986.
p. 273 *"getting . . . life-level"*: Olson to Elizabeth Olson, undated (circa 1957). CtU.

p. 273 *"Charles . . . that"*: Jean Radoslovich interview, February 10, 1987.

p. 273 *"stuff"*: "It isn't my word but my mother's," *CP*, p. 433.

pp. 273–74 *"What . . . hammer"*: Olson to Elizabeth Olson, undated (circa 1957). CtU.

p. 274 *"constant . . . stand"*: Olson to Kate Olson, undated. Letter in possession of Kate Olson.

p. 274 *"not . . . record"*: Olson to Constance Olson, May 28, 1958. CtU.

p. 275 *"one . . . story"*: Kate Olson interview, February 21, 1987.

p. 275 *"Kate . . . dismay"*: Olson to Edward Dorn, November 29, 1959. CtU.

p. 275 *"didn't . . . autocrat"*: John Clarke to author, March 2, 1987.

p. 275 *"trying . . . guilty"*: Fielding Dawson to author, November 10, 1986.

p. 275 *"a luminescent . . . Olson"*: Vincent Ferrini, *Hermit of the Clouds* (Gloucester, Mass.: Ten Pound Island Book Co., 1988), p. 103.

p. 275 *"I'm . . . here"*: "All Havens Astern," *CP*, p. 436.

p. 275 *"Don't . . . again"*: Olson to Elizabeth Olson, undated (circa 1959). CtU.

p. 276 *"an old . . . Gloucester"*: "Reading at Berkeley," *MUTH* I, p. 129.

p. 276 *"Jack . . . Rowser"*: Olson to Robert Creeley, December 11, 1959. WUSL.

p. 276 *"hip . . . gangster"*: Gregory Corso in Lawrence Lipton, *The Holy Barbarians* (New York: Julian Messner, 1959), pp. 132–33.

p. 276 *"bugged . . . days"*: Robin Blaser, as quoted in John Clarke to author, March 30, 1987.

p. 277 *"moral university"*: "Charles Olson, Notes for a University at Venice, California," *OJ* 2, p. 65.

p. 277 *"I sat . . . Burroughs"*: "Reading at Berkeley," *MUTH* I, p. 133.

p. 277 *"the school . . . visit"*: Olson to Edward Dorn, April 4, 1959. CtU.

p. 277 *"holyrollers . . . Burroughs"*: Olson to Robert Creeley, December 1, 1959. WUSL.

p. 278 *"popular . . . speech"*: "LeRoi Jones in the East Village," *The Beat Vision*, ed. Arthur Knight and Kit Knight (New York: Paragon House, 1987), p. 136.

p. 278 *"awe"*: *The Autobiography of LeRoi Jones / Amiri Baraka* (New York: Freundlich Books, 1984), p. 155.

p. 278 *"Jones . . . Petersburg"*: "Paris Review Inverview," *MUTH* II, p. 133.

p. 278 *"I go . . . Review"*: Olson to Robert Creeley, December 1, 1959. WUSL.

p. 278 *"my 2nd 'town' "*: "for Robert Duncan, who understands what's going on—written because of him March 17, 1961," *MAX* p. 207.

p. 279 *"pretty gone on"*: "Olson in Gloucester, 1966," *MUTH* I, p. 177.

p. 279 *"holy doctor"*: Olson to Robert Creeley, December 1, 1959. WUSL.

p. 279 *"I didn't . . . way"*: Philip Whalen to author, March 25, 1987.

p. 279 *"Around . . . was"*: Michael McClure, in *Guide*, p. 239.

pp. 279–80 *"The sea . . . sleeping"*: "MAXIMUS, FROM DOGTOWN—I," *MAX*, p. 172.

p. 280 *"When Maximus . . . whirl"*: Jeremy Prynne, "On *Maximus IV-V-VI*," lecture given at Simon Fraser University on July 27, 1971, transcribed by Tom McGauley, n.p.

p. 280 *"a strange . . . truth"*: "Charles Olson: Experience and Measurement," *OJ* 3, pp. 59–60.

p. 281 *"The Black . . . Flower"*: "MAXIMUS, FROM DOGTOWN—II," *MAX*, p. 180.

p. 281 *"twin . . . other"*: *Charles Olson Reads from* Maximus Poems IV, V, VI (London: Folkways Records, 1975).

p. 281 *"protogonic . . . LOVE"*: "MAXIMUS, FROM DOGTOWN—II," *MAX*, p. 180.

p. 281 *"mappemunde . . . being"*: "Peloria . . ." *MAX*, p. 257.

pp. 281–82 *"What . . . plays"*: Olson to Edward Dorn, February 1, 1960. CtU.

p. 282 *"Life . . . itself"*: "Introduction to Robert Creeley," *HU*, p. 127.

p. 282 *"to bring . . . presided"*: "Poetry and Truth," *MUTH* II, p. 27.

p. 282 *"straight . . . behind"*: Fielding Dawson, *The Black Mountain Book*, p. 90.

p. 282 *"the ANCIENTS . . . 1200 A.D."*: Olson to Robert Duncan, December 23, 1959. CtU.

p. 282 *"write . . . forever"*: "Paris Review Interview," *MUTH* II, p. 132.

p. 282 *"All . . . fit"*: "All night long," *MAX*, p. 327.

p. 282 *"voice . . . religion"*: Fielding Dawson, *The Black Mountain Book*, p. 20.

p. 282 *"secret . . . mysteries"*: Olson note on an envelope from Philip Whalen dated 26 January 1959. CtU.

p. 282 *"that question . . . cosmology"*: "Poetry and Truth," *MUTH II*, pp. 26–27.

pp. 282–83 *"total . . . voice"*: Henry Corbin, "Cyclical Time in Mazdaism and Ismailism," in *Man and Time: Papers from the Eranos Yearbooks*, Bollingen Series XXX.3, edited by Joseph Campbell (New York: Pantheon, 1957), pp. 166, 163.

p. 283 *"WOW . . . history"*: Olson's annotation in Corbin, p. 150.

p. 283 *"obdurate . . . condition"*: "Poetry and Truth," *MUTH* II, p. 27.

p. 283 *"as a 'fate' "*: *SVH*, p. 17.

p. 283 *"to break . . . power"*: Carl Jung, *Symbols of Transformation: An Analysis of the Prelude to a Case of Schizophrenia*, translated by R.F.C. Hull. The Collected Works of C. G. Jung, Bollingen Series XX.5 (New York: Pantheon, 1956), p. 67n.

p. 283 *"progressive . . . ocean"*: "Maximus, at the Harbor," *MAX*, p. 240.

p. 283 *"land skope view"*: "out over the land skope view," *MAX*, p. 296.

p. 283 *"overlooking . . . Creation"*: "at the boundary of the mighty world," *MAX*, pp. 330, 331.

CHAPTER 22: *In Tenebris*

p. 284 *"Writing . . . initiation"*: "Causal Mythology," *MUTH* I, p. 75.

p. 284 *"What . . . pulled"*: Theodor Adorno, *Aesthetic Theory*, translated by C. Lenhardt (London: Routledge & Kegan Paul, 1984), p. 168.

p. 284 *"Dark . . . go"*: Olson to Robert Creeley, January 9, 1960. WUSL.

p. 284 *"birthtime"*: Olson to Robert Duncan, December 23, 1959. CtU.

p. 284 *"impossible . . . money"*: Olson to Robert Creeley, April 1, 1960. WUSL.

p. 285 *"What's . . . Robert"*: Olson in conversation, recalled in Stan Brakhage, "Metaphors on Vision," *Film Culture* #30 (Fall 1963), n.p.

p. 285 *"grubby . . . it was"*: Paul Metcalf, "Charles Olson: A Gesture Towards Reconstitution," pp. 28–29.

p. 285 *"Pseudo-Vault . . . smell right"*: "not a rat-hole, a cat-hole," *CP*, pp. 501–2.

p. 286 *"hop . . . balcony"*: John Clarke to author, January 24, 1987.

p. 286 *"red . . . cloth"*: "not a rat-hole, a cat-hole," *CP*, p. 502.

p. 286 *"High Mass"*: Vincent Ferrini, *Hermit of the Clouds*, p. 93.

p. 286 *"like . . . Indian"*: Edward Dorn interview, December 2, 1986.

p. 286 *"the faeries . . . aid"*: John Clarke to author, January 24, 1987.

p. 286 *"lay . . . level"*: Olson anecdote, related in "Clark Coolidge, Notes Taken in Classes Conducted by Charles Olson at the University of British Columbia, Vancouver, August 1963," *OJ* 4, pp. 56–57.

p. 286 *"My Milliardaire . . . greaseball"*: Olson to Robert Duncan, undated (circa 1963). CtU.

pp. 286–87 *"John . . . AVOIDANCE"*: Olson to John Clarke, letter printed in Charles Olson, *Pleistocene Man* (Buffalo, N.Y.: Institute of Further Studies, 1968), p. 18.

p. 287 *"too . . . rhetorical"*: Olson to Robert Creeley, December 11, 1959. WUSL.

p. 287 *"interim . . . generation"*: Don Allen, Preface to *The New American Poetry* (New York: Grove Press, 1960), p. xi.

p. 288 *"I have . . . last"*: Maximus, to himself," *MAX*, p. 56.

p. 288 *"an Ideologue . . . Poetry"*: Harvey Shapiro, "Rebellious Mythmakers," *New York Times Book Review*, August 28, 1960, p. 6.

pp. 288–89 *"Mr. Olson . . . tuber"*: Marianne Moore, "The Ways Our Poets Have Taken in Fifteen Years Since the War," *New York Herald Tribune Book Review*, June 26, 1960, p. 1.

p. 289 *"a Babbit . . . year"*: Robert Bly, "Books of Poetry Published in 1960," *The Sixties* 5 (Fall 1961), p. 88.

p. 289 *"redskins":* Anthony Thwaite, "Good, Bad and Chaos," *Spectator,* September 1, 1961, p. 298.

p. 289 *"daily . . . completely":* Olson to Robert Creeley, November 11, 1960. WUSL.

p. 289 *"to go . . . myself":* Olson to Vincent Ferrini, recalled in Ferrini, "A Frame," *Maps # 4: Charles Olson* (1971), p. 56.

pp. 289–90 *"pro-Olson . . . Snow":* Richard Wilbur to author, July 30, 1987.

p. 290 *"intellectual . . . Bunyan":* Robert Fulford, "A Poet of Substance," *Toronto Daily Star,* May 2, 1960, p. 34.

p. 291 *"the damndest . . . Ginsberg":* Olson to Edward Dorn, November 26, 1960. CtU.

pp. 291–92 *"Democracy . . . beings":* "The Hustings," *CP,* pp. 534–35.

p. 292 *"We drink . . . know":* "MAXIMUS, FROM DOGTOWN—I," *MAX,* p. 175.

p. 292 *"peanuts":* "Under the Mushroom: The Gratwick Highlands Tape," *MUTH* I, p. 39.

p. 292 *"literally . . . creation":* "Charles Olson, Experience and Measurement," *OJ* 3, p. 61.

p. 292 *"peace . . . set":* "Under the Mushroom: The Gratwick Highlands Tape," *MUTH* I, pp. 39, 41.

p. 292 *"The startling . . . answer":* "Charles Olson, Experience and Measurement," *OJ* 3, p. 60.

p. 292 *"God . . . Him":* "Under the Mushroom: The Gratwick Highlands Tape," *MUTH* I, pp. 36–37.

p. 293 *"the father . . . possibilities":* Timothy Leary, *High Priest* (New York: World, 1968), p. 147.

p. 293 *"it was . . . confident":* "Under the Mushroom: The Gratwick HIghlands Tape," *MUTH* I, pp. 24–25.

p. 293 *"the giant . . . chiefness":* Timothy Leary, *High Priest,* pp. 147, p. 149.

p. 293 *"because . . . lost":* "Under the Mushroom: The Gratwick Highlands Tape," *MUTH* I, p. 42.

p. 294 *"now . . . plenty":* Olson to Robert Creeley, February 13, 1961. WUSL.

p. 294 *"pressure . . . profanation":* Arthur Koestler, "Return Trip to Nirvana," reprinted in Timothy Leary, *High Priest,* p. 151.

p. 294 *"a horrible . . . gunman":* "Under the Mushroom: The Gratwick Highlands Tape," *MUTH* I, p. 42.

p. 294 *"in the common . . . food":* ibid., p. 23.

p. 294 *"He never . . . like":* Edward Dorn interview, December 2, 1986.

p. 294 *"the whole . . . country":* "Olson in Gloucester, 1966," *MUTH* I, p. 192.

p. 294 *"as dark . . . work":* Olson to Robert Creeley, February 13, 1961. WUSL.

p. 295 *"like John . . . funerals":* Olson to Robert Creeley, March 25, 1961. WUSL.

p. 295 *"goyim . . . phyloSemitism":* Olson to Robert Duncan, March 10, 1961. CtU.

p. 295 *"PHYLO-JUDAISM . . . Church":* Olson to Robert Creeley, March 25, 1961. WUSL.

p. 295 *"What's . . . anthropology":* Robert Creeley interview, November 13, 1986.

p. 296 *"carrying . . . ball":* "Telepinus," *FH,* pp. 92, 95.

pp. 296–97 *"Harry . . . rousing":* Harry Levin to author, May 18, 1987.

p. 297 *"under duress":* Olson to Harry Levin, February 15, 1962. Letter in possession of Harry Levin.

p. 297 *"just . . . it":* Olson to Elizabeth Olson, undated (on back of envelope postmarked February 16, 1962). CtU.

p. 297 *"desperate glance":* Frances Boldereff to Olson, recalling the visit, March 8, 1962. CtU.

p. 297 *a real . . . tenderness":* Olson to Robert Duncan, March 11, 1963. CtU.

p. 297 *"more rambunctious":* John Finch interview, May 28, 1988.

p. 298 *"the man . . . words":* audio tape of Olson lecturing at Goddard College, April 12, 1962.

p. 298 *"told . . . there":* Olson to Robert Creeley, March 25, 1962. WUSL.

p. 298 *"He went . . . for":* Edward Dorn interview, December 2, 1986.

p. 298　*"so bold . . . company"*: Edward Dorn, "From Gloucester Out," *Selected Poems* (Bolinas, Calif.: Grey Fox Press, 1978), pp. 29, 33.

p. 298　*"make a buck"*: Olson to Edward Dorn, undated (circa 1962). CtU.

p. 299　*"wandered off"*: Edward Dorn interview, December 2, 1986.

p. 299　*"terrible time"*: "Reading at Berkeley," *MUTH* I, p. 108.

p. 299　*"all . . . Harbor"*: "Charles Olson and Edward Dorn," *MUTH* I, p. 158.

p. 299　*"those . . . mosaics"*: audio tape of Olson lecturing at Goddard College, April 12, 1962.

p. 300　*"Here . . . there"*: "Olson in Gloucester, 1966," *MUTH* I, p. 181.

p. 300　*"loss . . . control"*: Olson notebook, "July 19, 1966." CtU.

CHAPTER 23: Instructing the Angels

p. 301　*"We . . . Instruction"*: Stan Brakhage, "Metaphors on Vision," *Film Culture* #30 (Fall 1963), n.p.

p. 301　*"a Festschrift—for me"*: Olson to Elizabeth Olson, August 1963. CtU.

p. 302　*"ordering . . . Charles"*: Warren Tallman interview, February 28, 1987.

p. 302　*"We must . . . want"*: "As the Dead Prey Upon Us," *CP*, p. 394.

p. 302　*"That . . . things"*: Warren Tallman interview, February 28, 1987.

p. 302　*"like . . . house"*: Olson to Elizabeth Olson, August 1963. CtU.

p. 302　*"pious smart aleck"*: Olson to Elizabeth Olson, July 30, 1963. CtU.

p. 302　*"Get . . . dreams"*: John Clarke to author, March 30, 1987.

p. 302　*"late . . . style"*: Philip Whalen to author, March 25, 1987.

p. 302　*"hip . . . Delphi"*: Carol Bergé, "The Vancouver Report," *OJ* 4, p. 40.

pp. 302–3　*"forward . . . slowed"*: Philip Whalen to author, March 25, 1987.

p. 303　*"bacchanal"*: Pauline Wah to author, May 3, 1987.

p. 303　*"giggling . . . other"*: Clark Coolidge to author, January 12, 1987.

p. 303　*"the best . . . done"*: "Reading at Berkeley," *MUTH* I, p. 116.

p. 303　*"An American . . . skin"*: "Maximus, to Gloucester, Letter 27," *MAX*, p. 185.

p. 303　*"like . . . Independence"*: Robert Duncan interview, November 13, 1986.

p. 303　*"solitary animal"*: Bergé, p. 40.

p. 303　*"#1"*: Olson to Elizabeth Olson, July 30, 1963. CtU.

pp. 303–4　*"I am . . . admiration"*: Olson to Elizabeth Olson, August 1963. CtU.

p. 304　*"getting a vacation"*: Olson to Elizabeth Olson, July 30, 1963. CtU.

p. 304　*"shy . . . polite"*: Carol Cook to author, May 31, 1987.

p. 305　*"facilitator"*: Albert Cook to author, November 14, 1986.

p. 305　*"the cosmic . . . it"*: Albert Cook, "I Remember Olson," *Boundary 2*, Volume II, Nos. 1 & 2 (Fall 1973 / Winter 1974), p. 13.

p. 305　*"furious"*: John Clarke to author, February 18, 1987.

p. 305　*"lordly. . . gentry"*: Carol Cook to author, May 31, 1987.

p. 305　*"Papa . . . house"*: Kate Olson interview, February 27, 1987.

p. 306　*"mistake . . . alone"*: Olson loose notes, June 1964. CtU.

p. 306　*"hated . . . it"*: Jean Radoslovich interview, February 10, 1987.

p. 306　*"to get . . . struggle"*: Olson to Vincent Ferrini, circa November 1963, quoted in Ferrini, *Hermit of the Clouds*, p. 102.

p. 306　*"fascinating . . . once"*: Stephen Rodefer interview, May 13, 1987.

p. 306　*"weed. . . couldn't"*: John Clarke to author, February 13, 1987.

p. 307　*"angeloi"*: Stephen Rodefer interview, May 13, 1987.

p. 307　*"enraptured . . . oblivious"*: Albert Cook, "I Remember Olson," p. 14.

p. 307　*"being . . . retinue"*: Edward Dorn to author, December 31, 1986.

p. 307　*"simply . . . engage"*: John Clarke to author, November 29, 1986.

p. 307　*"I'll . . . again"*: Jean Radoslovich interview, February 10, 1987.

p. 308　*"midnight . . . mope"*: Kate Olson interview, February 27, 1987.

p. 308 *"incredulous . . . somehow"*: Carol Cook to author, May 31, 1987.

p. 308 *"His demands . . . kill"*: Jean Radoslovich interview, February 10, 1987.

pp. 308–9 *"Well . . . grief"*: Laurence Michel to author, December 3, 1986.

p. 309 *"deep freeze"*: John Clarke interview, January 13, 1990.

p. 309 *"Gloomy . . . change"*: Carol Cook to author, May 31, 1987.

p. 309 *"I don't . . . sixty"*: Robert Duncan interview, November 6, 1986.

p. 309 *"You're . . . botulism"*: Robert Creeley interview, November 13, 1986.

p. 309 *"utterly . . . staff"*: Olson to Robert Creeley, June 1, 1964. WUSL.

p. 309 *"I can't . . . further"*: Jean Radoslovich interview, February 10, 1987.

p. 310 *"I felt . . . too"*: Gladys Hindmarch to author, June 29 and 30, 1987.

p. 310 *"daughters . . . Sun"*: "There is a goddess / of earth . . ." *Nation*, pp. 155, 158.

p. 311 *"slammed . . . slicing"*: "Grinning monster out side the system . . ." *CP*, p. 613.

p. 311 *"King . . . keep"*: "barley or rye . . ." *CP*, pp. 611–612.

p. 311 *"no more . . . wonder"*: "Maximus to himself June 1964," *MAX*, p. 420.

p. 312 *"happy . . . sky"*: "O Quadriga," *MAX*, p. 451.

CHAPTER 24: Life Solely to Be Lived

p. 313 *"driven . . . lived"*: "O Quadriga," *MAX*, p. 451.

p. 313 *"Her skin . . . free"*: "her skin / covered me . . ." *CP*, p. 614.

p. 313 *"The World . . . wife"*: "Shenandoah," *CP*, p. 615.

pp. 313–14 *"he refused . . . work"*: Frances Boldereff Phipps interviews, December 2, 1986, and February 24, 1987; and Frances Boldereff Phipps to author, January 20, 1987.

p. 314 *"someone . . . yourself"*: Frances Boldereff to Olson, September 9, 1964. CtU.

p. 314 *"of my . . . man"*: Olson to Frances Boldereff, September 12, 1964. CtU.

p. 314 *"the times . . . universe"*: Frances Boldereff to Olson, December 7, 1967. CtU.

p. 314 *"I have . . . it"*: Olson to Frances Boldereff, September 12, 1964. CtU.

p. 314 *"Like . . . hibernate"*: John Clarke to author, March 2, 1987.

p. 315 *"We're . . . transmission"*: John Clarke interview, January 13, 1990.

p. 316 *"I went . . . life"*: Olson ms., October 9, 1964. CtU.

p. 316 *"increase the mysterium"*: Robert Creeley interview, November 14, 1986.

p. 316 *"on sleeping . . . around"*: Olson to Edward Dorn, March 19, 1965. CtU.

p. 317 *"Anyone . . . YOU"*: John Clarke to author, January 19, 1987.

p. 318 *"mind-bending . . . Gurdjieff"*: Albert Glover to author, December 17, 1986.

p. 318 *"a comfort . . . grief"*: Olson to Edward Dorn, March 19, 1965. CtU.

p. 318 *"affect"*: "Talk at Cortland," *MUTH* II, p. 1.

p. 318 *"elemental"*: Robert Creeley, Preface to John Wieners, *Cultural Affairs in Boston* (Santa Rosa: Black Sparrow, 1988), p. 1.

pp. 318–19 *"Captain . . . disappointment"*: John Clarke to author, January 28, 1987.

p. 319 *"in . . . finally"*: Olson to Robert Creeley, January 5, 1965. WUSL.

p. 320 *"This . . . piled up"*: Olson to Frances Boldereff, March 20, 1965. Letter in possession of Frances Boldereff Phipps.

p. 320 *"You're . . . right up"*: Albert Glover to author, March 11, 1987.

p. 320 *"changed my life"*: audio tape of Edward Sanders' Olson Memorial Lecture at SUNY Buffalo, March 9, 1963.

p. 320 *"new metric"*: "Ed Sanders' Language," *AP*, p. 59.

pp. 320–21 *"new public . . . Duncan"*: "Talk at Cortland," *MUTH* II, p. 2.

p. 321 *"close . . . light"*: Olson to Frances Boldereff, June 1965. CtU.

p. 321 *"with . . . delight"*: John Wieners, "To Charles," *Niagara Frontier Review*, Spring-Summer 1965, n.p.

p. 322 *"Umbrian angel"*: "Causal Mythology," *MUTH* I, p. 64.

p. 322 *"eyes of stone"*: John Wieners, "Ezra Pound at the Spoleto Festival 1965," *Cultural Affairs in Boston*, p. 63.

p. 322 *"summit conference":* Bill Berkson interview, November 23, 1986.

p. 322 *"Tremendous":* John Wieners, "Ezra Pound at the Spoleto Festival 1965," p. 64.

p. 322 *"and five . . . das":* "The Song of Ullikummi," *CP,* p. 602.

p. 322 *"fell dead":* "Causal Mythology," *MUTH* I, p. 74.

p. 322 *"Roman . . . sweaters":* Bill Berkson interview, November 23, 1986.

p. 322 *"a revival . . . humor":* "Causal Mythology," *MUTH* I, p. 74.

pp. 322–23 *"Humanist . . . war":* Caresse Crosby to Olson, August 25, 1959, Conover, p. 182.

p. 323 *"more . . . Russians":* "Reading at Berkeley," *MUTH* I, p. 131.

p. 323 *"arrived . . . myself":* "Causal Mythology," *MUTH* I, p. 66.

p. 323 *"working . . . weeks":* Robert Creeley interview, November 13, 1986.

p. 323 *"Olson . . . Speech":* Kirby Doyle to author, January 25, 1987.

p. 324 *"anchor man":* "Interview in Gloucester," *MUTH* II, p. 98.

p. 324 *"the whole . . . vision":* "Reading at Berkeley," *MUTH* I, p. 112.

p. 324 *"bombshell . . . conference":* Stephen Rodefer interview, May 13, 1987.

p. 324 *"most important person":* "West 6," *CP,* p. 599.

p. 324 *"all . . . me":* "Four Items Related to the Summer of 1965," *Documents in American Civilization,* Series II, No. 1, n.p.

pp. 324–25 *"where . . . come":* "Reading at Berkeley," *MUTH* I, pp. 110, 112.

p. 325 *"nonreading . . . War":* Thomas Parkinson interview, January 28, 1987.

p. 325 *"Is this . . . love":* Bobbie Louise Hawkins interview, March 29, 1987.

p. 325 *"cheering section":* "Reading at Berkeley," *MUTH* I, p. 126.

p. 325 *"I have . . . leave":* "Four Items Related to the Summer of 1965," n.p.

p. 325 *"Fly . . . Cart-Wheel":* Olson to Suzanne Mowatt, June 1966. CtU.

p. 325 *"loving spoonfuls":* Olson to Suzanne Mowatt, October 1965. CtU.

p. 325 *"ailing . . . herd":* John Clarke to author, January 15, 1987.

p. 326 *"gum . . . them":* John Clarke to author, January 20, 1987.

CHAPTER 25: The Conventual

p. 327 *"Only . . . either":* "Maximus of Gloucester," *MAX,* p. 473.

p. 327 *"I . . . applies":* Olson to Edward Dorn, September 1965. CtU.

p. 327 *"Captain Over-Soul":* Olson to Lawrence Ferlinghetti, March 10, 1966. Bancroft Library, University of California at Berkeley.

p. 327 *"Follow . . . God":* "Follow Bet," George F. Butterick, *Editing "The Maximus Poems"* (Storrs: The University of Connecticut Library, 1983), "Appendix 2: Rejected Poems," p. 8.

p. 327 *"the end . . . God":* "The winter the Gen. Starks was stuck," *MAX,* pp. 480–481.

p. 328 *"Pray . . . work":* Olson notebook, "Monday January 18th 1966." CtU.

p. 328 *"Modus . . . Prayer":* "The Mountain of no difference," *MAX,* p. 502.

p. 328 *"Bottled . . . Truth":* "Bottled up for days . . ." *MAX,* p. 503.

p. 328 *"never . . . fool":* Olson notebook, "Monday January 18th 1966." CtU.

pp. 328–29 *"olive . . . people":* Jean Radoslovich interview, March 12, 1987.

p. 329 *"stumbling . . . once":* Philip Green interview, May 27, 1987.

p. 329 *"unrelieved . . . fair":* Olson to Robert Creeley, May 11, 1966. WUSL.

p. 329 *"Find . . . life":* Robert Creeley interview, March 14, 1987.

p. 330 *"Yr . . . lover":* Olson to Joyce Benson, June 26, 1966, in Joyce Benson, "First Round of Letters," *Boundary 2,* Vol. II, Nos. 1 and 2 (Fall 1973 / Winter 1974), p. 363.

p. 330 *"up . . . love":* "[to get the rituals straight . . ." *MAX,* pp. 556, 557.

p. 330 *"the center . . . web":* Olson to Edward Dorn, September 27, 1966. CtU.

pp. 330–31 *"disastrous . . . monkey":* Robert Duncan interview, November 6, 1986.

p. 331 *"Gloucester . . . Conference":* Olson to Edward Dorn, September 27, 1966. CtU.

p. 331 *"that . . . dry up":* Robert Creeley interview, May 12, 1990.

p. 331 *"troupe"*: Olson to Edward Dorn, September 27, 1966. CtU.

p. 331 *"in some . . . least"*: "[to get the rituals straight . . ." *MAX,* p. 558.

p. 331 *"did . . . good"*: Olson to Edward Dorn, September 27, 1966. CtU.

p. 331 *"hot . . . table"*: audio tape of Edward Sanders' Olson Memorial Lecture at SUNY Buffalo, March 15, 1983.

p. 331 *"spontaneous . . . poet"*: "Talk at Cortland," *MUTH* II, p. 2.

pp. 331–32 *"Everybody's . . . regalia"*: audio tape of Edward Sanders' Olson Memorial Lecture at SUNY Buffalo, March 15, 1983.

p. 332 *"mad 24 hours"*: Olson to Edward Dorn, September 27, 1966. CtU.

p. 332 *"good blood"*: Joanne Kyger interview, March 12, 1987.

p. 333 *"massive"*: Tom Raworth to author, April 28, 1987.

p. 333 *"was . . . drags"*: Edward Dorn interview, December 13, 1986.

p. 333 *"too . . . heart"*: Olson to Edward Dorn, December 22, 1966. CtU.

p. 333 *"You . . . Olson"*: Olson to Robert Duncan, December 30, 1966. CtU.

p. 333 *"protectionless"*: Olson notebook, "Monday January 18th 1966." CtU.

pp. 333–34 *"my bed . . . forlorn"*: Olson to Frances Boldereff, December 30, 1966. CtU.

p. 334 *"hungry . . . boughs"*: "Hotel Steinplatz, Berlin, December 25 (1966)," *MAX,* p. 569.

p. 334 *"Truth . . . mouth"*: Olson to Robert Duncan, December 30, 1966. CtU.

p. 334 *"thought . . . kind"*: audio tape of Robert Duncan's lecture at New College of California, February 17, 1982.

p. 334 *"He was . . . maintained"*: Edward Dorn interview, March 17, 1987.

p. 334 *"Life's . . . alas"*: Olson to Robert Duncan, December 30, 1966. CtU.

pp. 334–35 *"nonstop"*: Tom Raworth to author, April 28, 1987.

p. 335 *"swirling . . . head"*: Anselm Hollo to author, November 25, 1986.

p. 335 *"bored"*: Tom Raworth to author, April 28, 1987.

p. 335 *"I'm . . . her"*: Kate Olson interview, October 3, 1987.

p. 335 *"it was over"*: Harvey Brown interview, November 12, 1986.

p. 335 *"always . . . crossroad"*: Olson to Suzanne Mowatt, May 23, 1987. CtU.

pp. 335–36 *"the event . . . word"*: Joyce Benson interview, January 24, 1987, and Joyce Benson to author, November 18, 1986.

p. 336 *"a kind . . . show"*: Boer, p. 84.

p. 336 *"angel of aid"*: Olson to Joyce Benson, November 17, 1967. CtU.

p. 336 *"WHITE guerrilla"*: Olson notebook, "July 15, 1966," October 5 entry. CtU.

p. 336 *"I believe . . . themselves"*: " 'I know men for whom everything matters': Charles Olson in conversation with Herbert A. Kenny," *OJ* 1, p. 11.

p. 336 *"I don't . . . all"*: Olson notebook, "July 15, 1966," August 25 entry. CtU.

p. 337 *"There was . . . Con"*: Kate Olson interview, May 24, 1987.

p. 337 *"message"*: "Sun / right in my eye . . ." *MAX,* p. 577.

p. 337 *"I shall . . . here"*: "Great Washing Rock . . ." *MAX,* p. 579.

p. 337 *"Gather . . . steel"*: "The Telesphere," *MAX,* p. 576.

p. 337 *"impossible . . . alone"*: Olson to Frances Boldereff, January 9, 1968. CtU.

p. 337 *"Count . . . Cristo"*: Olson to Edward Dorn, November 11, 1967.

CHAPTER 26: The Subterranean Lake

p. 338 *"HOURS . . . realisms"*: Olson annotation on Robert Duncan's "Passages 32." CtU.

p. 339 *"Time's . . . devouring"*: "And melancholy," *MAX,* p. 588.

p. 339 *"To internalize . . . one"*: Olson note, in *Guide,* p. 628.

p. 339 *"the poem . . . inside"*: "Interview in Gloucester," *MUTH* II, pp. 91–92.

p. 339 *"Wholly . . . clear"*: "Wholly absorbed . . ." *MAX,* p. 585.

pp. 339–40 *"He was . . . visit"*: Chad Walsh, "A Retrospect," in Charles Olson, *Poetry and Truth: The Beloit Lectures and Poems* (San Francisco: Four Seasons Foundation, 1971), pp. 4–5.

p. 340 *"writing . . .* Heliotrope": "Poetry and Truth," *MUTH* II, pp. 34, 35, 42, 47.

p. 340 *"keep . . . beat":* Joanne Kyger interview, March 12, 1987.

pp. 340–41 *"to stay . . . trip":* Olson to Frances Boldereff, July 1, 1968. CtU.

p. 341 *"He loved . . . him":* Jean Radoslovich interview, March 12, 1987.

p. 342 *"in Icelandic":* "*Paris Review* Interview," *MUTH* II, p. 135.

p. 342 *"Hairy . . . too":* "I'm going to hate to leave this Earthly Paradise," *MAX,* p. 592.

p. 342 *"legendary . . . calls":* Ed Sanders, "A Tribute to Harvey Brown," *Intent,* Vol. 1, No. 4 (Winter 1990), p. 12.

p. 342 *"Despite . . . life":* Olson to Constance Bunker, September 1, 1968. CtU.

p. 342 *"I knew . . . too":* Jean Radoslovich interview, February 10, 1987.

pp. 342–43 *"Gold-making . . . waves":* "I'm going to hate to leave this Earthly Paradise," *MAX,* pp. 594–95.

p. 343 *"How . . . dying":* Barry Miles, liner notes for *Charles Olson Reads from* Maximus Poems IV, V, VI (Folkways Records, 1975).

p. 343 *"not having . . .* all": Olson notebook, "June 19th 1969." CtU.

p. 343 *"shamanistic shimmer":* audio tape of Edward Sanders' Olson Memorial Lecture at SUNY Buffalo, March 9, 1963.

pp. 343–44 *"Full . . . thing":* "*Full moon . . .*" *MAX,* p. 604.

p. 344 *"Fussy . . . exasperated":* Olson notebook, "June 19th 1969." CtU.

p. 344 *"Charles . . . stayed":* Robert Creeley interview, November 13, 1986.

pp. 344–45 *"occupied . . . time":* Olson to Kate Olson, undated. Letter in possession of Kate Olson.

p. 345 *"enormous . . . forth":* Olson ms., July 15, 1969. CtU.

p. 345 *"Oedipean . . . Piper":* Olson notebook, "June 19th 1969." CtU.

p. 345 *"Frightful . . . further":* ibid.

p. 346 *"the invasion":* Edward Dorn interview, December 3, 1986.

p. 346 *"My life . . . passages":* "I live underneath / the light of day," *MAX,* p. 633.

p. 347 *"Like . . . Brea":* O. J. Ford, "Regaining the Primordial (Charles Olson as Teacher)," *Athanor,* Vol. 1, No. 1 (Winter / Spring 1971), p. 50.

p. 347 *"electric":* ibid.

p. 347 *"to register . . . space":* Charles Olson, *Last Lectures* (as heard by John Cech, Oliver Ford, Peter Rittner), Poets at Northeastern #9 (Boston: Northeastern University Press, n. d.), pp. 3, 21.

p. 348 *"the inside . . . exists":* Olson notes, December 8, 1969, in Boer, p. 129.

p. 348 *"Hepatoma-Grade 1":* Boer, p. 132.

p. 348 *"It's curtains":* ibid., p. 131.

p. 348 *"more . . . poem":* Kate Olson interview, February 21, 1987.

p. 348 *"foster . . . work":* Olson's will, dated "night of December 15th over to dawn December 16th 1969 / Manchester Memorial Hospital / Manchester, Connecticut." Copy supplied by Kate Olson.

p. 348 *" 'Secret' notes":* "The Secret of the Black Chrysanthemum," *OJ* 3, p. 71.

p. 348 *"Are . . . yet":* Boer, p. 141.

p. 349 *"everybody . . . manna":* Edward Dorn interview, December 3, 1986.

p. 349 *"ten more years":* Kate Olson interview, February 21, 1987.

p. 349 *"my wife . . . myself":* *MAX,* p. 635.

pp. 349–50 *"female . . . Okeanos":* Robert Duncan interview, November 6, 1986, and "Robert Duncan, letter to Jess after his last visit to Olson in New York Hospital, 1970," *OJ* 1, p. 5.

p. 350 *"royal pair":* Vincent Ferrini, *Hermit of the Clouds,* p. 225.

p. 350 *"Charlie . . . Charlie":* Jane Atherton, "Memories of Charles Olson," p. 72.

Index